Schirmer Encyclopedia of Film

Schirmer Encyclopedia of Film

VOLUME 2
CRITICISM–IDEOLOGY

Barry Keith Grant
EDITOR IN CHIEF

SCHIRMER REFERENCE
An imprint of Thomson Gale, a part of The Thomson Corporation

THOMSON
GALE

Detroit • New York • San Francisco • New Haven, Conn. • Waterville, Maine • London

Schirmer Encyclopedia of Film
Barry Keith Grant

Project Editor
Michael J. Tyrkus

Editorial
Tom Burns, Jim Craddock, Elizabeth Cranston, Kristen A. Dorsch, Dana Ferguson, Allison Marion, Kathleen D. Meek, Kathleen Lopez Nolan, Kevin Nothnagel, Marie Toft, Yolanda Williams

Editorial Support Services
Luann Brennan, Paul Lewon

Research
Sue Rudolph

Rights and Acquisitions
Ron Montgomery, Jessica Stitt

Imaging and Multimedia
Dean Dauphinais, Mary Grimes, Lezlie Light, Michael Logusz, Christine O'Bryan

Product Design
Jennifer Wahi-Bradley

Manufacturing
Wendy Blurton, Evi Seoud

3 1540 00298 5008

LIBRARY OF CONGRESS CATALOGING-IN-PUBLICATION DATA

Grant, Barry Keith, 1947-
  Schirmer encyclopedia of film / Barry Keith Grant.
    p. cm.
  Includes bibliographical references and index.
  ISBN-13: 978-0-02-865791-2 (set hardcover : alk. paper)
  ISBN-10: 0-02-865791-8
  ISBN-13: 978-0-02-865793-6 (vol. 2 : alk. paper)
  ISBN-10: 0-02-865793-4
  [etc.]
  1. Motion pictures–Encyclopedias. I. Title.

  PN1993.45.G65 2007
  791.4303–dc22   2006013419

ISBN-13:
978-0-02-865791-2 (set)
978-0-02-865792-9 (vol. 1)
978-0-02-865793-6 (vol. 2)
978-0-02-865794-3 (vol. 3)
978-0-02-865795-0 (vol. 4)

ISBN-10:
0-02-865791-8 (set)
0-02-865792-6 (vol. 1)
0-02-865793-4 (vol. 2)
0-02-865794-2 (vol. 3)
0-02-865795-0 (vol. 4)

British Library Cataloguing-in-Publication Data A catalogue record for this book is available from the British Library.

This title is also available as an e-book
ISBN-13: 978-0-02-866100-1 (set), ISBN-10: 0-02-866100-1 (set)
Contact your Thomson Gale sales representative for ordering information.

Printed in China
10 9 8 7 6 5 4 3 2 1

Editorial Board

Contents

List of Articles

CRITICISM

The term "critic" is often applied very loosely, signifying little more than "a person who writes about the arts." It can be defined more precisely by distinguishing it from related terms with which it is often fused (and confused): reviewer, scholar, theorist. The distinction can never be complete, as the critic exists in overlapping relationships with all three, but it is nonetheless important that it be made.

WHAT IS A CRITIC?

Reviewers are journalists writing columns on the latest releases in daily or weekly papers. They criticize films, and often call themselves critics, but for the most part the criticism they practice is severely limited in its aims and ambitions. They write their reviews to a deadline after (in most cases) only one viewing, and their job is primarily to entertain (their livelihood depends on it), which determines the quality and style of their writing. Some (a minority) have a genuine interest in the quality of the films they review; most are concerned with recommending them (or not) to a readership assumed to be primarily interested in being entertained. In other words, reviewers are an integral (and necessarily *uncritical*) part of our "fast-food culture"—a culture of the instantly disposable, in which movies are swallowed like hamburgers, forgotten by the next day; a culture that depends for its very continuance on discouraging serious thought; a culture of the newest, the latest, in which we have to be "with it," and in which "trendy" has actually become a positive descriptive adjective. Many reviewers like to present themselves as superior to all this (if you write for a newspaper you should be an "educated" person), while carefully titillating us: how disgusting are the gross-out

moments, how spectacular the battles, chases, and explosions, how sexy the comedy. There have been (and still are) responsible and intelligent reviewer-critics, such as James Agee, Manny Farber, Robert Warshow, Jonathan Rosenbaum, and J. Hoberman, but they are rare.

To be fair, a major liability is the requirement of speed: how do you write seriously about a film you have seen only once, with half a dozen more to review and a two- or three-day deadline to meet? One may wonder, innocently, how these reviewers even recall the plot or the cast in such detail, but the answer to that is simple: the distributors supply handouts for press screenings, containing full plot synopses and a full cast list. In theory, it should be possible to write about a film without even having seen it, and one wonders how many reviewers avail themselves of such an option, given the number of tedious, stupid movies they are obliged to write something about every week. What one might call today's standard product (the junk food of cinema) can be of only negative interest to the critic, who is concerned with questions of value. The scholar, who must catalogue everything, takes a different sort of interest in such fare, and the theorist will theorize from it about the state of cinema and the state of our culture. Both will be useful to the critic, who may in various ways depend on them.

Reviewers are tied to the present. When, occasionally, they are permitted to step outside their socially prescribed role and write a column on films they know intimately, they become critics, though not necessarily good ones, bad habits being hard to break. (Pauline Kael is a case in point, with her hit-or-miss insights.) This is not of course to imply that critics are tied exclusively to the distant past; indeed, it is essential that they retain a

ANDREW BRITTON
b. 1952, d. 1994

Although his period of creativity (he was the most creative of critics) covered only fifteen years, Andrew Britton was a critic in the fullest sense. He had the kind of intellect that can encompass and assimilate the most diverse sources, sifting, making connections, drawing on whatever he needed and transforming it into his own. Perennial reference points were Marxism (but especially Trotsky), Freud, and F. R. Leavis, seemingly incompatible but always held in balance. A critic interested in value and in standards of achievement will achieve greatness only if he commands a perspective ranging intellectually and culturally far beyond his actual field of work. Britton's perspective encompassed (beyond film) literature and music, of which he had an impressively wide range of intimate knowledge, as well as cultural and political theory.

His work was firmly and pervasively grounded in sociopolitical thinking, including radical feminism, racial issues, and the gay rights movement. But his critical judgments were never merely political; the politics were integrated with an intelligent aesthetic awareness, never confusing political statement with the focused concrete realization essential to any authentic work of art. His intellectual grasp enabled him to assimilate with ease all the phases and vicissitudes of critical theory. He took the onset of semiotics in stride, assimilating it without the least difficulty, immediately perceiving its loopholes and points of weakness, using what he needed and attacking the rest mercilessly, as in his essay on "The Ideology of *Screen*."

His central commitment, within a very wide range of sympathies that encompassed film history and world cinema, was to the achievements of classical Hollywood. His meticulously detailed readings of films, such as

Mandingo, Now, Voyager, and *Meet Me in St. Louis,* informed by sexual and racial politics, psychoanalytic theory, and the vast treasury of literature at his command, deserve classical status as critical models. His book-length study of Katharine Hepburn deserves far wider recognition and circulation than it has received so far: it is not only the most intelligent study of a star's complex persona and career, it also covers all the major issues of studio production, genre, the star system, cinematic conventions, thematic patterns, and the interaction of all of these aspects.

His work has not been popular within academia because it attacked, often with devastating effect, many of the positions academia has so recklessly and uncritically embraced: first semiotics, and subsequently the account of classical Hollywood as conceived by the critic David Bordwell. These attacks have never been answered but rather merely ignored, the implication being that they are unanswerable. Today, when many academics are beginning to challenge the supremacy of theory over critical discourse, Britton's work should come into its own. His death from AIDS in 1994 was a major loss to film criticism.

FURTHER READING

Britton, Andrew. "Blissing Out: The Politics of Reaganite Entertainment." *Movie*, nos. 31/32 (Winter 1986): 1–42.

———. *Katharine Hepburn: Star as Feminist.* London: Studio Vista, 1995.

———. "*Meet Me in St. Louis*: Smith, or the Ambiguities." *CineAction*, no. 35 (1994): 29–40.

———. "A New Servitude: Bette Davis, *Now, Voyager,* and the Radicalism of the Women's Film." *CineAction*, nos. 26/27 (1992): 32–59.

Robin Wood

close contact with what is happening in cinema today, at every level of achievement. But one needs to "live" with a film for some time, and with repeated viewings, in order to write responsibly about it—if, that is, it is a film of real importance and lasting value.

The difference between critic and reviewer is, then, relatively clear-cut and primarily a matter of quality, seriousness, and commitment. The distinction between

critic and scholar or critic and theorist is more complicated. Indeed, the critic may be said to be parasitic on both, needing the scholar's scholarship and the theorist's theories as frequent and indispensable reference points. (It is also true that the scholar and theorist are prone to dabble in criticism, sometimes with disastrous results.) But the critic has not the time to be a scholar, beyond a certain point: the massive research (often into unrewarding and undistinguished material) necessary to scholarship would soon become a distraction from the intensive examination of the works the critic finds of particular significance. And woe to the critic who becomes too much a theorist: he or she will very soon be in danger of neglecting the specificity and particularity of detail in individual films to make them fit the theory, misled by its partial or tangential relevance. Critics should be familiar with the available theories, should be able to refer to any that have not been disproved (for theories notoriously come and go) whenever such theories are relevant to their work, but should never allow themselves to become committed to any one. A critic would do well always to keep in mind Jean Renoir's remarks on theories:

> You know, I can't believe in the general ideas, really I can't believe in them at all. I try too hard to respect human personality not to feel that, at bottom, there must be a grain of truth in every idea. I can even believe that all the ideas are true in themselves, and that it's the application of them which gives them value or not in particular circumstances...No, I don't believe there are such things as absolute truths, but I do believe in absolute human qualities—generosity, for instance, which is one of the basic ones. (Quoted in Sarris, *Interviews with Film Directors*, p. 424)

F. R. LEAVIS AND QUESTIONS OF VALUE

One cannot discuss criticism, its function within society, its essential aims and nature, without reference to the work of F. R. Leavis (1895–1978), perhaps the most important critic in the English language in any medium since the mid-twentieth century. Although his work today is extremely unpopular (insofar as it is even read), and despite the fact that he showed no interest in the cinema whatever, anyone who aspires to be a critic of any of the arts should be familiar with his work, which entails also being familiar with the major figures of English literature.

Leavis belonged to a somewhat different world from ours, which the "standards" he continued to the end to maintain would certainly reject. Leavis grew up in Victorian and Edwardian England and was fully formed as a critic and lecturer by the 1930s. He would have responded with horror to the "sexual revolution," though he was able to celebrate, somewhat obsessively, D. H. Lawrence, whose novels were once so shocking as to be banned (and who today is beginning to appear quaintly old-fashioned).

Leavis was repeatedly rebuked for what was in fact his greatest strength: his consistent refusal to define a clear theoretical basis for his work. What he meant by "critical standards" could not, by their very nature, be

tied to some specific theory of literature or art. The critic must above all be open to new experiences and new perceptions, and critical standards were not and could not be some cut-and-dried set of rules that one applied to all manifestations of genius. The critic must be free and flexible, the standards arising naturally out of constant comparison, setting this work beside that. If an ultimate value exists, to which appeal can be made, it is also indefinable beyond a certain point: "life," the quality of life, intelligence about life, about human society, human intercourse. A value judgment cannot, by its very nature, be proved scientifically. Hence Leavis's famous definition of the ideal critical debate, an ongoing process with no final answer: "This is so, isn't it?" "Yes, but . . ." It is this very strength of Leavis's discourse that has resulted, today, in his neglect, even within academia. Everything now must be supported by a firm theoretical basis, even though that basis (largely a matter of fashion) changes every few years. Criticism, as Leavis understood it (in T. S. Eliot's famous definition, "the common pursuit of true judgment"), is rarely practiced in universities today. Instead, it has been replaced by the apparent security of "theory," the latest theory applied across the board, supplying one with a means of pigeonholing each new work one encounters.

It is not possible, today, to be a faithful "Leavisian" critic (certainly not of film, the demands of which are in many ways quite different from those of literature). Crucial to Leavis's work was his vision of the university as a "creative center of civilization." The modern university has been allowed to degenerate, under the auspices of "advanced" capitalism, into a career training institution. There *is* no "creative center of civilization" anymore. Only small, struggling, dispersed groups, each with its own agenda, attempt to battle the seemingly irreversible degeneration of Western culture. From the perspective of our position amid this decline, and with film in mind, Leavis's principles reveal three important weaknesses or gaps:

1. *The wholesale rejection of popular culture.* Leavis held, quite correctly, that popular culture was thoroughly contaminated by capitalism, its productions primarily concerned with making money, and then more money. However, film criticism and theory have been firmly rooted in classical Hollywood, which today one can perceive as a period of extraordinary richness but which to Leavis was a total blank. He was able to appreciate the popular culture of the past, in periods when major artists worked in complete harmony with their public (the Elizabethan drama centered on Shakespeare, the Victorian novel on Dickens) but was quite unable to see that the pre-1960s Hollywood cinema represented, however compromised, a communal art, comparable in many ways to Renaissance Italy, the Elizabethan drama,

the Vienna of Mozart and Haydn. It was a period in which artists worked together, influencing each other, borrowing from each other, evolving a whole rich complex of conventions and genres, with no sense whatever of alienation from the general public: the kind of art (the richest kind) that today barely exists. Vestiges of it can perhaps be found in rock music, compromised by its relatively limited range of expression and human emotion, the restriction of its pleasures to the "youth" audience, and its tendency to expendability.

Hollywood cinema was also compromised from the outset by the simple fact that the production of a film requires vastly more money than the writing of a novel or play, the composing of a symphony, or the painting of a picture. Yet—as with Shakespeare, Haydn, or Leonardo da Vinci—filmmakers like Howard Hawks (1896–1977), John Ford (1894–1973), Leo McCarey (1898–1969), and Alfred Hitchcock (1899–1980) were able to remain in touch with their audiences, to "give them what they wanted," without seriously compromising themselves. They could make the films they wanted to make, and enjoyed making, while retaining their popular following. Today, intelligent critical interest in films that goes beyond the "diagnostic" has had to shift to "art-house" cinema or move outside Western cinema altogether, to Taiwan, Hong Kong, Iran, Africa, and Thailand.

2. Political engagement. Although he acknowledged the urgent need for drastic social change, Leavis never analyzed literature from an explicitly political viewpoint. In his earlier days he showed an interest in Marxism yet recognized that the development of a strong and vital culture centered on the arts (and especially literature) was not high on its agenda. He saw great literature as concerned with "life," a term he never defined precisely but which clearly included self-realization, psychic health, the development of positive and vital relationships, fulfillment, generosity, humanity. "Intelligence about life" is a recurring phrase in his analyses.

He was fully aware of the degeneration of modern Western culture. His later works show an increasing desperation, resulting in an obsessive repetitiveness that can be wearying. One has the feeling that he was reduced to forcing himself to believe, against all the evidence, that his ideals were still realizable. Although it seems essential to keep in mind, in our dealings with art, "life" in the full Leavisian sense, the responsible critic (of film or anything else) is also committed to fighting for our mere survival, by defending or attacking films from a political viewpoint. Anything else is fiddling while Rome burns.

3. The problem of intentionality. Leavis showed no interest whatever in Freud or the development of psychoanalytical theory. When he analyzes a poem or a novel, the underlying assumption is always that the author knew

exactly what he or she was doing. Today we seem to have swung, somewhat dangerously, to the other extreme: we analyze films in terms of "subtexts" that may (in some cases must) have emerged from the unconscious, well below the level of intention.

This is fascinating and seductive, but also dangerous, territory. Where does one draw the line? The question arises predominantly in the discussion of minor works within the "entertainment" syndrome, where the filmmakers are working within generic conventions. It would be largely a waste of time searching for "unconscious" subtexts in the films of, say, Michael Haneke (b. 1942), Hou Hsiao-Hsien (b. 1947), or Abbas Kiarostami (b. 1940), major artists in full consciousness of their subject matter. But in any case critics should exercise a certain caution: they may be finding meanings that they are planting there themselves. The discovery of an arguably unconscious meaning is justified if it uncovers a coherent subtext that can be traced throughout the work. Even Freud, after all, admitted that "sometimes a cigar is just a cigar"—the validity of reading one as a phallic symbol will depend on its context (the character smoking it, the situation within which it is smoked, its connection to imagery elsewhere in the film). The director George Romero expressed surprise at the suggestion that *Night of the Living Dead* (the original 1968 version) is about tensions, frustrations, and repression within the patriarchal nuclear family; but the entire film, from the opening scene on, with its entire cast of characters, seems to demand this reading.

Why, then, should Leavis still concern us? We need, in general, his example and the qualities that form and vivify it: his deep seriousness, commitment, intransigence, the profundity of his concerns, his sense of value in a world where all values seem rapidly becoming debased into the values of the marketplace. Leavis's detractors have parodied his notion that great art is "intelligent about life," but the force of this assumption becomes clear from its practical application to film as to literature, as a few examples, negative and positive, illustrate. Take a film honored with Academy Awards®, including one for Best Picture. Rob Marshall's *Chicago* (2002) is essentially a celebration of duplicity, cynicism, one-upmanship, and mean-spiritedness: intelligent about life? The honors bestowed on it tell us a great deal about the current state of civilization and its standards. At the other extreme one might also use Leavis's dictum to raise certain doubts about a film long and widely regarded by many as the greatest ever made, *Citizen Kane* (1941), directed by Orson Welles (1915–1985). No one, I think, will deny the film its brilliance, its power, its status as a landmark in the evolution of cinema. But is that very brilliance slightly suspect? Is Welles's undeniable intelligence, his astonishing grasp of his chosen medium, too much employed as a celebration of himself and his own genius, the dazzling magician of cinema? To raise such questions, to challenge the accepted wisdom, is a way to open debate, and essentially a debate about human values. Certain other films, far less insistent on their own greatness, might be adduced as exemplifying "intelligence about life": examples that spring to mind (remaining within the bounds of classical Hollywood) include *Tabu* (F. W. Murnau, 1931), *Rio Bravo* (Hawks, 1959), *Make Way for Tomorrow* (McCarey, 1937), *Letter from an Unknown Woman* (Max Ophüls, 1948), and *Vertigo* (Hitchcock, 1958)—all films in which the filmmaker seems totally dedicated to the realization of the thematic material rather than to self-aggrandizement.

There are of course whole areas of valid critical practice that Leavis's approach leaves untouched: the evolution of a Hollywood genre or cycle (western, musical, horror film, screwball comedy), and its social implications. But the question of standards, of value, and the critical judgments that result should remain and be of ultimate importance. One might discuss at length (with numerous examples) how and why *film noir* flourished during and in the years immediately following World War II, its dark and pessimistic view of America developing side by side, like its dark shadow, with the patriotic and idealistic war movie. But the true critic will also want to debate the different inflections and relative value of, say, *The Maltese Falcon* (John Huston, 1941), *Double Indemnity* (Billy Wilder, 1944), *The Big Sleep* (Hawks, 1946), and *Out of the Past* (Jacques Tourneur, 1947). Or, to move outside Hollywood and forward in time, how one reads and values the films of, for example, the German director Michael Haneke should be a matter of intense critical debate and of great importance to the individual. A value judgment, one must remember, by its very nature cannot be proven—it can only be argued. The debate will be ongoing, and agreement may never be reached; even where there is a consensus, it may be overturned in the next generation. But this is the strength of true critical debate, not its weakness; it is what sets criticism above theory, which should be its servant. A work of any importance and complexity is not a *fact* that can be proven and pigeon-holed. The purpose of critical debate is the development and refinement of personal judgment, the evolution of the individual sensibility. Such debates go beyond the valuation of a given film, forcing one to question, modify, develop, refine one's own value system. It is a sign of the degeneration of our culture that they seem rarely to take place.

THE EVOLUTION OF CRITICISM AND THEORY

Surprisingly, given its prominence in world cinema since the silent days, none of the major movements and developments in film theory and criticism has originated in the United States, though American academics have been quick to adopt the advances made in Europe (especially France) and Britain.

A brief overview might begin with the British magazines *Sight and Sound* (founded in 1934) and *Sequence* (a decade later). The two became intimately connected, with contributors moving from one to the other. The dominant figures were Gavin Lambert, Karel Reisz (1926–2002), Tony Richardson (1928–1991), and Lindsay Anderson (1923–1994), the last three of whom developed into filmmakers of varying degrees of distinction and who were regarded for a time as "the British New Wave" (though without the scope or staying power of the French *Nouvelle Vague*). The historic importance of these magazines lies in the communal effort to bring to criticism (and subsequently to British cinema) an overtly political dimension, their chief editors and critics having a strong commitment to the Left and consequently to the development of a cinema that would deal explicitly with social problems from a progressive viewpoint. British films were preferred and Hollywood films generally denigrated or treated with intellectual condescension as mere escapist entertainment, with the partial exceptions of Ford and Hitchcock; Anderson especially championed Ford, and Hitchcock was seen as a distinguished popular entertainer. As its more eminent and distinctive critics moved into filmmaking, *Sight and Sound* lost most of its political drive (under the editorship of Penelope Houston) but retained its patronizing attitude toward Hollywood.

Developments in France during the 1950s, through the 1960s and beyond, initially less political, have been both more influential and more durable. André Bazin remains one of the key figures in the evolution of film criticism, his work still alive and relevant today. Already active in the 1940s, he was co-founder of *Cahiers du Cinéma* in 1951, and acted as a kind of benevolent father figure to the New Wave filmmakers (and almost literally to François Truffaut [1932–1984]), as well as himself producing a number of highly distinguished "key" texts that continue to be reprinted in critical anthologies. Bazin's essays "The Evolution of Film Language" (1968) and "The Evolution of the Western" (1972) led, among other things, to the radical reappraisal of Hollywood, reopening its "popular entertainment" movies to a serious revaluation that still has repercussions. Even the most astringent deconstructionists of semiotics have not rendered obsolete his defense (indeed, celebration) of realism, which never falls into the trap of naively seeing it as the unmediated reproduction of reality. His work is a model of criticism firmly grounded in theory.

Bazin encouraged the "Young Turks" of French cinema throughout the 1950s and 1960s, first as critics on *Cahiers* (to which Claude Chabrol, Jean-Luc Godard, Jacques Rivette, Eric Rohmer, and Truffaut were all contributors, with Rohmer as subsequent editor), then as filmmakers. Would the New Wave have existed without him as its modest and reticent centrifugal force? Possibly. But it would certainly have been quite different, more dispersed.

The *Cahiers* critics (already looking to their cinematic futures) set about revaluating the whole of cinema. Their first task was to downgrade most of the established, venerated "classics" of the older generation of French directors, partly to clear the ground for their very different, in some respects revolutionary, style and subject matter: such filmmakers as Marcel Carné, Julien Duvivier, René Clément, Henri-Georges Clouzot, and Jean Delannoy found themselves grouped together as the "tradition de qualité" or the "cinéma de papa," their previously lauded films now seen largely as expensive studio-bound productions in which the screenwriter was more important than the director, whose job was to "realize" a screenplay rather than make his own personal movie. Some were spared: Robert Bresson, Abel Gance, Jacques Becker, Jacques Tati, Jean Cocteau, and above all Jean Renoir (1894–1979), another New Wave father figure, all highly personal and idiosyncratic directors, were seen more as creators than "realizers."

It was a relatively minor figure, Alexandre Astruc, who invented the term *camera-stylo*, published in 1949 in *L'Ecran Français* (no. 144; reprinted in Peter Graham, *The New Wave*), suggesting that a personal film is written with a camera rather than a pen. Most of the major New Wave directors improvised a great deal, especially Godard (who typically worked from a mere script outline that could be developed or jettisoned as filming progressed) and Rivette, who always collaborated on his screenplays, often with the actors. Partly inspired by Italian neorealism, and especially the highly idiosyncratic development of it by one of their idols, Roberto Rossellini (1906–1977), the New Wave directors moved out of the studio and into the streets—or buildings, or cities, or countryside.

As critics, their interests were international. Would Kenji Mizoguchi (1898–1956) be as (justly) famous in the West without their eulogies? Would Rossellini's films with Ingrid Bergman—*Stromboli* (1950), *Europa 51* (1952), *Viaggio in Italia* [Voyage to Italy, 1953]—rejected with contempt by the Anglo-Saxon critical fraternity, ever have earned their reputations as masterpieces? Yet our greatest debt to the New Wave director-critics surely lies in their transformation of critical attitudes to classical Hollywood and the accompanying formulation of the by turns abhorred and celebrated "*auteur* theory."

Anyone with eyes can see that films by Carl Dreyer (1889–1968), Renoir, Rossellini, Mizoguchi, and Welles are "personal" films that could never have been made by anyone else. On the other hand, one might view *Red River* (1948), *The Thing from Another World* (1951), *Monkey Business* (1952), and *Gentlemen Prefer Blondes* (1953) without ever noticing that they were all directed by the same person, Howard Hawks. Before *Cahiers*, few people bothered to read the name of the director on the credits of Hollywood films, let alone connect the films' divergent yet compatible and mutually resonant thematics. Without *Cahiers*, would we today be seeing retrospectives in our Cinémathèques of films not only of Hitchcock and Ford, but also of Hawks, Anthony Mann, Leo McCarey, Vincente Minnelli, Nicholas Ray, Billy Wilder, Otto Preminger, Sam Fuller, and Budd Boetticher?

For some time the *Cahiers* excesses laid it open to Anglo-Saxon ridicule. What is one to make today of a (polemical) statement such as that of Godard: "The cinema is Nicholas Ray"? Why not "The cinema is Mizoguchi" or "The cinema is Carl Dreyer" or even, today, "The cinema is Jean-Luc Godard"? Many of the reviews are open to the objection that the readings of the films are too abstract, too philosophical or metaphysical, to do proper justice to such concrete and accessible works, and that the *auteur* theory (roughly granting the director complete control over every aspect of his films) could be applied without extreme modification to only a handful of directors (Hawks, McCarey, Preminger) who achieved the status of producers of their own works. And even they worked within the restrictions of the studio system, with its box-office concerns, the Production Code, and the availability of "stars." Nevertheless, *Cahiers* has had a lasting and positive effect on the degree of seriousness with which we view what used to be regarded as standard fare and transient entertainment.

Outside France, the *Cahiers* rediscovery of classical Hollywood provoked two opposite responses. In England, *Sight and Sound* predictably found it all slightly ridiculous; on the other hand, it was clearly the inspiration for the very existence of *Movie*, founded in 1962 by a group of young men in their final years at Oxford University. Ian Cameron, V. F. Perkins, and Mark Shivas initially attracted attention with a film column printed in *Oxford Opinion*. With Paul Mayersberg, they formed the editorial board of *Movie*; they were subsequently joined, as contributors, by Robin Wood, Michael Walker, Richard Dyer, Charles Barr, Jim Hillier, Douglas Pye, and eventually Andrew Britton. Of the original group, Perkins has had the greatest longevity as

Howard Hawks, producer of* The Thing from Another World *(Christian Nyby, 1951) was a favorite of auteur critics.
EVERETT COLLECTION. REPRODUCED BY PERMISSION.

a critic, his *Film as Film* (deliberately contradicting the usual "Film as Art") remaining an important text. *Movie* (its very title deliberately invoking Hollywood) must be seen as a direct descendant of *Cahiers*. Its tone, however, was very different, its analyses more concrete, tied closely to the texts, rarely taking off (unlike *Cahiers*) into headier areas of metaphysical speculation. The opposition between *Sight and Sound* and *Movie* was repeated in the United States, with Pauline Kael launching attacks on *Movie*'s alleged excesses and Andrew Sarris (Kael's primary target since his 1962 "Notes on the Auteur Theory") producing *The American Cinema* in 1968, with its ambitious and groundbreaking categorization of all the Hollywood directors of any consequence. It remains a useful reference text.

The British scene was complicated by developments within the more academic journal *Screen*, which, in its development of structural analysis by (among others) Alan Lovell and the introduction of concepts of iconography by Colin McArthur, in some ways anticipated the events to come. But all this was about to be blown apart by the events in France of May 1968 and the repercussions throughout the intellectual world.

MAY 1968 AND THE REVOLUTION IN FILM CRITICISM

The student and worker riots in France in May 1968, hailed somewhat optimistically as the "Second French Revolution," transformed *Cahiers* almost overnight, inspiring a similar revolution in Godard's films. The massive swing to the Left, the fervent commitment to Marx and Mao, demanded not only new attitudes but also a whole new way of thinking and a new vocabulary to express it, and a semiotics of cinema was born and flourished. Roland

ANDREW SARRIS
b. New York, New York, 31 October 1928

Eminently sensible and perennially graceful in the articulation of his views, Andrew Sarris has been one of the most important of American film critics. His influence upon the shaping of the late-twentieth-century critical landscape is inestimable—both for his hand in developing an intellectually rigorous academic film culture and for bringing the proselytizing *auteur* theory to popular attention. The acumen and resolve of his writing set a benchmark for the scrupulous and cogent close analysis of cinematic style.

Among the pioneering voices of a new generation of self-proclaimed cinephiles—or "cultists," in his own terms—Sarris began his professional career in 1955, reviewing for Jonas Mekas's seminal journal, *Film Culture*, where he helped develop one of the first American serial publications dedicated to the serious critical investigation of film. After a brief sojourn in Paris in 1960, he began writing reviews for the fledgling alternative newspaper, the *Village Voice*, in New York City. His polemical reviews generated considerable debate and helped secure Sarris a position as senior critic for the *Voice* from 1962 to 1989.

As an intellectual American film culture exploded during the 1960s, Sarris was able to provide a newly professionalized critical establishment with two enormously influential (and controversial) concepts imported from the *Cahiers* critics in France: the *auteur* theory and *mise-en-scène*. His development of a director-centered critical framework grew out of a dissatisfaction with the "sociological critic"—leftist-oriented writers seemingly more interested in politics than film—whose reviews tended simplistically to synchronize film history and social history. While his attempt to establish auteurism as a theory may not have been entirely persuasive, it generated considerable debate regarding the creative and interpretive relationships between a director,

her collaborators, and the audience itself. Further, in his own critical analyses, Sarris was one of the first critics to focus on style rather than content. This reversal was not an apolitical embracing of empty formalism, but rather a unified consideration of a film's stylistic and mimetic elements in the interests of discerning an artist's personal worldview. For him, a film's success does not hinge on individual contributions by various creative personnel, but on the coherence of the *auteur*'s "distinguishable personality," made manifest in the subtext—or "interior meanings"—of the work.

Along with his sometime rivals, Pauline Kael at *The New Yorker* and Stanley Kauffmann at *The New Republic*, Sarris was among the first of a new generation of critics dedicated to elevating the cultural status of film, particularly American cinema. In his efforts to promote film as an expressive art rather than a mere commercial product, he co-founded the prestigious National Society of Film Critics in 1966 and offered a new *auteur*-driven history of Hollywood in the canonical *American Cinema* (1968), in which he mapped and ranked the work of all the important directors ever to work in Hollywood.

FURTHER READING

Levy, Emmanuel, ed. *Citizen Sarris, American Film Critic*. Lanham, MD: Scarecrow Press, 2001.

Sarris, Andrew. *The American Cinema, Directors and Directions, 1929–1968*. Revised ed. Cambridge, MA: Da Capo Press, 1996.

———. *Confessions of a Cultist: On the Cinema, 1955–1969*. New York: Simon & Schuster, 1970.

———. *The Primal Screen: Essays on Film and Related Subjects*. New York: Simon & Schuster, 1973.

———, comp. *Interviews with Film Directors*. Indianapolis, IN: Bobbs-Merrill, 1967.

Aaron E. N. Taylor

Barthes, Christian Metz, and Jacques Lacan became seminal influences, and traditional criticism was (somewhat prematurely) pronounced dead or at least obsolete. A distinguished and widely influential instance was the meticulously detailed Marxist-Lacanian analysis of Ford's *Young Mr. Lincoln* (1939) produced collaboratively by the new *Cahiers* collective; it deserves its place in film history as one

of the essential texts. British critical work swiftly followed suit, with Peter Wollen's seminal *Signs and Meaning in the Cinema* (1969, revised 1972), which remains an essential text. Whereas *Movie* had adopted many of the aims and positions of the original *Cahiers*, it was now *Screen* that took up the challenge of the new, instantly converted to semiotics. The magazine published the *Young Mr. Lincoln*

Andrew Sarris with his wife, the critic Molly Haskell.
ROBIN PLATZER/TIME LIFE PICTURES/GETTY IMAGES.

article in translation, and it was followed by much work in the same tradition. In terms of sheer ambition, one must single out Stephen Heath's two-part analysis and deconstruction of Welles's *Touch of Evil* (1958).

Semiotics was expected by its adherents to transform not only criticism but also the world. Its failure to do so resides largely in the fact that it has remained a dauntingly esoteric language. Its disciples failed to bridge the gulf between themselves and a general readership; perhaps the gulf is in fact unbridgeable. Its influence outside academia has been negligible, though within academia it continues, if not to flourish, at least to remain a presence, developing new phases, striking up a relationship with that buzzword du jour, postmodernism. Its effect on traditional critical discourse has however been devastating (which is not to deny its validity or the value of its contribution). "Humanism" became a dirty word. But what is humanism but a belief in the importance for us all of human emotions, human responses, human desires, human fears, hence of the actions, drives, and behavior appropriate to the achievement of a sense of fulfillment, understanding, reciprocation, caring? Are these no longer important, obsolete like the modes of discourse in which they expressed themselves? Semiotics is a tool, and a

valuable one, but it was mistaken for a while for the ultimate goal. Criticism, loosely defined here as being built on the sense of value, was replaced by "deconstruction," debate by alleged "proof." It seemed the ultimate triumph of what Leavis called (after Jeremy Bentham) the "technologico-Benthamite world," the world of Utilitarianism that grew out of the Industrial Revolution and was so brilliantly satirized by Charles Dickens in *Hard Times* (1845), which in turn was brilliantly analyzed by Leavis in *Dickens the Novelist*. During the reign of semiotics Leavis was, of course, expelled from the curriculum, and it is high time for his restoration.

The massive claims made for semiotics have died down, and the excitement has faded. In addition to the articles mentioned above, it produced, in those heady days, texts that deserve permanent status: the seminal works of Barthes (always the most accessible of the semioticians), *Mythologies* (1957, translated into English in 1972) and *S/Z* (1970, translated into English in 1974), with its loving, almost sentence-by-sentence analysis of Honoré de Balzac's *Sarrasine*; Raymond Bellour's Hitchcock analyses (though it took most readers quite a time to realize that Bellour and Heath actually loved the films they deconstructed). And, more generally, semiotics has taught us (even those who doubt its claims to supply all the answers) to be more precise and rigorous in our examination of films.

Out of the radicalism of the 1970s there developed not only semiotics but also a new awareness of race and racism and the advent of radical feminism. Laura Mulvey's pioneering article "Visual Pleasure and Narrative Cinema" (1975) rapidly became, in its concise few pages, enormously influential, opening a veritable floodgate of feminist analysis, much of it concerned with the exposure of the inherent and structural sexism of the Hollywood cinema. It was impossible to predict, from Mulvey's dangerous oversimplification of Hawks and Hitchcock, that she would go on to produce admirable and loving analyses of *Gentlemen Prefer Blondes* and *Notorious* (1946); but it was the very extremeness of the original article that gave it its force. Mulvey's work opened up possibilities for a proliferation of women's voices within a field that had traditionally been dominated by men—work (as with semiotics itself) of extremely diverse quality but often of great distinction, as, for example, Tania Modleski's splendid book on Hitchcock, *The Women Who Knew Too Much* (1988, with a new expanded edition in 2004).

THE CRITICAL SCENE TODAY … AND TOMORROW?

At the beginning of the twenty-first century, the world is beset with problems ranging from the destruction of the environment to terrorism and the ever-present threat of nuclear war. The Hollywood product reflects a culture beset by endless "noise," the commodification of sex, and the constant distractions of junk culture. In such a scenario, the modest and marginalized discipline of film criticism might yet again play an active role.

What would one ask, today, within an increasingly desperate cultural situation, of that mythical figure the Ideal Critic? First, a firm grasp of the critical landmarks merely outlined above, with the ability to draw on all or any according to need. To the critics mentioned must be added, today, the names of Stanley Cavell and William Rothman, intelligent representatives of a new conservatism. As Pier Paolo Pasolini told us at the beginning of his *Arabian Nights*, "the truth lies, not in one dream, but in many": Bazin and Barthes are not incompatible, one does not negate the other, so why should one have to choose? We must feel free to draw on anything that we find helpful, rather then assuming that one new theory negates all previous ones. And in the background we should restore relations with Leavis and "questions of value," but accompanied by a politicization that Leavis would never have accepted (or would he, perhaps, today?). The value of a given film for us, be it classical Hollywood, avant-garde, documentary, silent or sound, black-and-white or color, will reside not only in its aesthetic qualities, its skills, its incidental pleasures, but also in what use we can make of it within the present world situation.

SEE ALSO *Auteur Theory and Authorship; Genre; Ideology; Journals and Magazines; Postmodernism; Psychoanalysis; Publicity and Promotion; Queer Theory; Reception Theory; Semiotics; Spectatorship and Audiences; Structuralism and Poststructuralism*

FURTHER READING

Barthes, Roland. *Mythologies.* Edited and translated by Annette Lavers. New York: Hill and Wang, 1972.

————. *S/Z: An Essay.* Translated by Richard Miller. New York: Hill and Wang, 1974.

Bazin, André. *What Is Cinema?* Edited and translated by Hugh Gray. 2 vols. Berkeley: University of California Press, 1967–1971.

Graham, Peter, ed. *The New Wave.* Garden City, NY: Doubleday, and London: Secker and Warburg, 1968.

Heath, Stephen. "Film and System: Terms of Analysis." *Screen* 16, nos. 1–2 (Spring/Summer 1975): 91–113.

Leavis, F. R. *The Great Tradition: George Eliot, Henry James, Joseph Conrad.* New York: New York University Press, 1963.

Leavis, F. R., and Q. D. Leavis. *Dickens, the Novelist.* London: Chatto and Windus, 1970.

Metz, Christian. *Film Language: A Semiotics of the Cinema.* Translated by Michael Taylor. New York: Oxford University Press, 1974.

Modleski, Tania. *The Women Who Knew Too Much: Hitchcock and Feminist Theory.* New York and London: Methuen, 1988.

Mulvey, Laura. "Visual Pleasure and Narrative Cinema." *Screen* 16, no. 3 (1975): 6–8. Reprinted in *Visual and Other Pleasures.* Bloomington: Indiana University Press, 1989.

Perkins, Victor. *Film as Film: Understanding and Judging Movies.* Baltimore: Penguin, 1972.

Sarris, Andrew. *The American Cinema: Directors and Directions, 1929–1968.* New York: Dutton, 1968. Revised ed., Chicago: University of Chicago Press, 1985.

————, ed. *Interviews with Film Directors.* New York: Discus, 1969.

Wollen, Peter. *Signs and Meaning in the Cinema*, revised ed. Bloomington: Indiana University Press, and London: British Film Institute, 1972.

Wood, Robin. *Hitchcock's Films Revisited.* New York: Columbia University Press, 1989.

Robin Wood

CUBA

Cuba is an anomaly in the history of Latin American cinema. Cuban film history is the story of a formerly quiet and docile little film industry that experienced a sudden and explosive acceleration of production after the revolution in 1959. Cuban cinema has had an unusual role in shaping a national dialogue about art, identity, consciousness, and social change and has emerged as one of the most distinct and influential national cinemas in the region. While all of the film industries in Latin America contend with Hollywood's monopoly over the industry, Cuba also faces the effects of an ongoing economic embargo—the result of a complex and defiant relationship with the United States. These factors influence both the conditions of production and the content of the films themselves.

BEFORE THE REVOLUTION

Cinema first arrived in Cuba in 1897 when an agent for the Lumière brothers came to display the newly invented cinematographe and also shoot footage of local scenes on the island. The country developed a tremendous and enduring appetite for moving pictures during the first half of the century, with cinemas springing up in great numbers. By 1920 there were 50 cinemas in Havana and more than 300 in the rest of the country. There were a number of notable and popular achievements during this prerevolutionary period, including *La Virgen de la Caridad* (*The Virgin of Charity*, 1930) and *El Romance del Palmar* (*Romance Under the Palm Trees*, 1935) both by Ramón Peón, and other early filmmakers all of which conformed with the established genres and styles that characterized Latin American cinema at the time. In spite of these these and other efforts, a national cinema failed to develop as fully in Cuba as in some other Latin American countries, largely due to economic factors and the dominant position of North American distributors in controlling the local industry.

In the 1940s and 1950s amateur filmmakers in different parts of the island grouped together to form a number of cine-clubs, organized around the screening and production of films. They established amateur film competitions and festivals, which continue to form an important aspect of Cuban cultural life today. One amateur group of particular importance, Nuestro Tiempo, fronted a radical leftist cultural organization that supported efforts to overthrow the regime of Fulgencio Batista, which had been in power since 1952. Nuestro Tiempo counted among its young members many of the figures who later became seminal to modern Cuban cinema, including Alfredo Guevara (b. 1925), Santiago Álvarez (1919–1998), Tomás Gutiérrez Alea (1928–1996), and Julio García Espinosa (b. 1926). The group strongly supported the revolution that came to power on 1 January 1959, establishing Fidel Castro as the commander in chief. It was only after the revolution that a national film industry was set in motion and national cinema developed in earnest.

A NEW INDUSTRY

Three months later, in what was to be its first cultural act, the revolutionary government created a national film industry, called the Instituto Cubano del Arte e Industria Cinematográficos (ICAIC). At its inception ICAIC dedicated itself to producing and promoting cinema as a vehicle for communicating the ideas of the revolution,

TOMÁS GUTIÉRREZ ALEA
b. Havana, Cuba, 11 December 1928, d. 16 April 1996

Cuba's most widely known and beloved director, Tomás Gutiérrez Alea (known in Cuba as "Titón"), earned a law degree at the University of Havana while concurrently making his first films. He went on to study at the Centro Sperimentale di Cinematografia in Rome, and the influence of Italian neorealism is evident in *El Mégano* (The charcoal worker), a film he made in collaboration with Julio García Espinosa in 1955 after returning to Cuba. *El Mégano* had a seminal role in the beginning of the politicized movement known as New Latin American Cinema, taking its place at the forefront of attempts by Latin American filmmakers to explore the potential political impact of the medium on social issues close to home.

A fervent supporter of the 1959 revolution, Alea was one of the founders of the Instituto Cubano del Arte e (la) Industria Cinematográficos (ICAIC). His substantial body of work describes the nuances and contradictions of everyday life in socialist Cuba. Alea spoke frankly about the reality of the Cuban revolution with all of its idiosyncrasies, citing the importance of intellectual critique in ongoing social change. His films address complex political realities, an absurdly convoluted bureaucratic process, and the persistence of reactionary mentalities in a society that had rededicated itself to the fulfillment of progressive ideals.

The warmth, vitality, and complexity of Alea's films challenge the stereotype of communist cinema as rote propaganda. Alea called for a "dialectical cinema" that would engage the viewer in an active, ongoing conversation about Cuban life.

He explored a wide range of genres and styles throughout his long career, making documentaries, comedies, and historical and contemporary dramas. His historical pieces *Una Pelea cubana contra los demonios* (*A Cuban Fight Against Demons*, 1972) and *La Última cena* (*The Last Supper*, 1976) are among the finest examples of

Cuba's many notable films in the genre. Alea's comedies *Las Doce sillas* (*The Twelve Chairs*, 1960), *La Muerte de un burócrata* (*Death of a Bureaucrat*, 1966), *Los Sobrevivientes* (*The Survivors*, 1979), and *Guantanamera* (1995) affectionately poke fun at the bureaucratic lunacy of the Cuban political system and the resilience of bourgeois values, making full use of the strategies of social satire and farce in doing so.

Alea is best known for his films *Memorias del subdesarrollo* (*Memories of Underdevelopment*, 1968) and *Fresa y chocolate* (*Strawberry and Chocolate*, 1994), which share the distinction of being the most acclaimed Cuban films to date. *Memories of Underdevelopment* chronicles the ruminations of a politically unaffiliated middle-class intellectual who becomes increasingly alienated from his surroundings after the triumph of the revolution, but lacks the conviction to leave Cuba. *Strawberry and Chocolate* was the first Cuban film to receive an Academy Award® nomination for Best Foreign Film. Set in the 1970s during a period of ideological conformity, the film concerns the friendship between a flamboyantly gay older man and a politically militant university student. In Alea's treatment of the historical period, it is the militant student who undergoes a profound emotional transformation and comes to understand that the eccentric iconoclast is in fact the real hero.

RECOMMENDED VIEWING
Las Doce sillas (*The Twelve Chairs*, 1960), *La Muerte de un burócrata* (*Death of a Bureaucrat*, 1966), *Memorias del subdesarrollo* (*Memories of Underdevelopment*, 1968), *La Última cena* (*The Last Supper*, 1976), *Fresa y chocolate* (*Strawberry and Chocolate*, 1994)

FURTHER READING
Schroeder, Paul A. *Tomas Gutierrez Alea: The Dialectics of a Filmmaker.* New York: Routledge, 2002.

Ruth Goldberg

recognizing film as a medium for education and seeking to provide an ideological alternative to the powerful media machine of Hollywood.

In 1960 the magazine *Cine Cubano* was founded, sponsored by ICAIC, and it remains one of the primary sources of film criticism and analysis by Cuban authors,

chronicling the emerging history as it unfolds. Initially, great emphasis was placed on developing a visual record of the revolutionary project, and ICAIC focused on producing newsreels and documentary films in the early years. These films were used to disseminate information about new initiatives such as agrarian reform and Cuba's

Tomás Gutiérrez Alea. © UNIFILM/COURTESY EVERETT COLLECTION. REPRODUCED BY PERMISSION.

massive literacy campaign. *Por primera vez* (*For the First Time*, Octavio Cortázar, 1967), which chronicles the beginnings of Cuba's mobile cinema movement—in which cinema was introduced into rural areas that had previously been without electricity—is one of many examples of the high quality and emotional resonance of early Cuban documentary filmmaking from the first decade of production after the revolution.

In a country known for its innovative documentary films, Santiago Álvarez distinguished himself as Cuba's best-known documentary filmmaker during his long and prolific career. Using only minimal equipment and concentrating the bulk of his efforts toward adapting the strategies of Soviet montage to his own agenda, Álvarez created an enduringly powerful, unsettling, and innovative body of work, including the films *Ciclón* (*Hurricane*, 1963), *Now* (1965), *Hanoi, martes 13* (*Hanoi, Tuesday 13th*, 1967), *LBJ* (1968), and *79 primaveras* (*79 Springs*, 1969), among others. Álvarez explored themes of anti-imperialist struggle in many of his finest works, leaving behind a polemical and hard-hitting filmic legacy that has influenced subsequent generations of Third World filmmakers.

Lesser known but of critical importance, the lyrical and haunting documentaries of Nicolás Guillén Landrián

(1938–2003) show evidence of an original cinematic voice. The thirteen films he made for ICAIC, including *Ociel de Toa*, *Reportaje* (Reportage, 1966), and *Coffea Arábiga* (Arabica Coffee, 1968), have rarely been seen, although there was a revival of critical interest in his work shortly before he died in 2003.

NATIONAL IDENTITY AND DIALECTICAL CINEMA

Many notable fiction films, too, were completed during the exciting first decade under the ICAIC, forming the basis for a "Nuevo Cine Cubano," or "New Cuban Cinema." Among these were Alea's *La Muerte de un burócrata* (*Death of a Bureaucrat*, 1966) and *Memorias del subdesarrollo* (*Memories of Underdevelopment*, 1968). *Death of a Bureaucrat* firmly established the Cuban audience's penchant for social satire. Outsiders are often surprised to see the extent to which state-sponsored films such as *Death of a Bureaucrat* openly address the idiosyncrasies of the system, but in fact this tendency, exemplified by Alea's often imitated films, defines one central tendency of Cuba's national cinema. *Memories of Underdevelopment*, on the other hand, shows an entirely different aspect of Alea's range, being an example of dialectical cinema at its finest. Stylistically and thematically rich, *Memories* creates the opportunity for elevating political consciousness within the artistic experience, and urges the spectator toward an active, open-ended exchange with the film.

Alea's early films and the others made by ICAIC largely explored issues of Cuban national identity, the colonial legacy, and the new revolutionary agenda, using different formats and genres to do so. During this same period, Humberto Solás (b. 1941) made the classic films *Manuela* (1966) and *Lucía* (1968), initiating the trend of using a female protagonist as an allegorical representation of the complex, evolving national identity, and establishing Solás as one of Cuba's original artistic voices. Both films were masterfully edited by Nelson Rodríguez (b. 1938), one of Cuba's great editing talents. Rodríguez's filmography demonstrates the extent to which he has been an integral part of Cuban cinema since the revolution, working on many if not most of the outstanding films produced to date. Solás's strategy of using a marginalized character to represent the progressive national agenda was later taken up by other Cuban directors, including *Retrato de Teresa* (*Portrait of Teresa*, 1979) by Pastor Vega (1940–2005), *Hasta cierta punto* (*Up to a Certain Point*, 1983) by Alea, and *De cierta manera* (*One Way or Another*, 1974) by Sara Gómez (1943–1974).

Also within this extraordinary first decade, both *La Primera carga al machete* (*The First Charge of the Machete*, 1969), by Manuel Octavio Gómez (1934–1988), and García Espinosa's *Las Aventuras de Juan Quin Quin* (*The Adventures of Juan Quin Quin*, 1967) dealt with issues of history and identity, using innovative stylistic formats in an overt refusal to conform to established genres or traditional means of narration. Such nonlinear narratives require a different kind of attention and participation on the part of the audience, demonstrating the ethos of experimentation that was integral to postrevolutionary Cuban cinema from the very beginning.

The period that followed the euphoric 1960s has become known as the "five gray years," during which time Cuban art was produced in an atmosphere of ideological conformity. In spite of the climate of the times, many exceptional historical dramas appeared during this period, including *Una Pelea cubana contra los demonios* (*A Cuban Fight Against Demons*, 1972) and *La Última cena* (*The Last Supper*, 1976) by Alea; *Los Días de agua* (*Days of Water*, 1971) by Gómez; *Páginas del diario de José Martí* by José Massip; and *El Otro Francisco* (*The Other Francisco*, 1975) and *Maluala* (1979), both by Sergio Giral (b. 1937).

During the same period, Julio García Espinosa wrote the essay "Por Un Cine imperfecto" ("For an Imperfect Cinema"), which called the technical perfection of Hollywood cinema a false goal and urged Third World filmmakers to focus instead on making films that actively require the engagement of the audience in constructing and shaping social reality. The essay had considerable influence, and remains one of the most important theoretical tracts written by a Latin American filmmaker. In 1974 one of the ICAIC's few female directors, Sara Gómez, made the film that is most emblematic of this period. *De cierta manera* (*One Way or Another*) is a radically innovative film that merges fiction and documentary strategies in addressing a wide range of pressing social issues (machismo, the revolution, marginality, social change) with sensitivity and depth. The film is a polemical dialogue between the two main characters that reflects tensions in the larger society. *One Way or Another*, which was completed by collaborators Alea and García Espinosa after Gómez's untimely death during production, has earned a well-deserved place in the canon of feminist film and has been the subject of international scholarship.

Two years after the Family Code sought to address the ingrained issue of machismo in Cuban society by urging a new level of male participation in child rearing, and during a period in which Cuban women were being encouraged to enter the workforce, Pastor Vega made the controversial film *Retrato de Teresa* (*Portrait of Teresa*, 1979). The film tackles the issues of women working outside the home and the double standards for men and women, among other highly sensitive topics, and it sparked widespread local debate, demonstrating that feminist ideals were far from fully integrated into Cuban society and ensuring that the reactionary legacy of machismo would continue to occupy the revolutionary agenda. Later the same year the annual Festival of New Latin American Cinema was inaugurated in Havana. The festival remains of one Cuba's defining annual cultural events and one of Latin America's major film festivals, providing a venue for exchange and dialogue and allowing many outsiders to see Cuba and Cuban cinema for themselves.

The 1980s marked a shift away from the complex films García Espinosa had envisioned in his essay on "imperfect cinema" and a general movement toward using more accessible and popular film forms. ICAIC's production was diverse, featuring a wide range of contemporary dramas, social satires, historical dramas, and genre films. A new and talented group of Cuban filmmakers emerged during this time, but for many, the explosive creativity and artistic merit of the first decade of production under ICAIC was lacking in Cuban film in the 1980s. One of several obvious exceptions, the full-length animated film *¡Vampiros en la Habana!* (*Vampires in Havana*, 1985), directed by Juan Padrón (b. 1947), was a celebrated success. Padrón had captured the popular imagination in 1979 with the animated feature *Elpidio Valdés*, a vehicle for his

Mirta Ibarra in Tomás Gutiérrez Alea's **Fresa y chocolate** *(Strawberry and Chocolate, 1994), Cuba's biggest international success.* © MIRAMAX/COURTESY EVERETT COLLECTION. REPRODUCED BY PERMISSION.

original visual style and strong narrative sensibility. Cuba has produced many talented animators—Tulio Raggi, Mario Rivas, and others—and the 1980s saw an unusually high level of productivity in the form.

In 1985 the Escuela Internacional de Cine y Televisión (EICTV, International School of Film and Television) was founded with support from the Fundación del Nuevo Cine Latinoamericano, and the Argentine director Fernando Birri (b. 1925), a pioneer in the New Latin American Cinema, was installed as its first director. The school, under the direction of Julio García Espinosa, features a distinguished international faculty and students who come to Cuba from all over the world to participate in workshops and diploma programs with such luminaries as the Colombian writer Gabriel García Marquez (b. 1928) and the US filmmaker Francis Ford Coppola (b. 1939), among many others.

THE SPECIAL PERIOD AND AFTER

With the collapse of the Soviet Union, Cuba entered what was termed the "Special Period," characterized by economic hardship, shortages, and a crisis of identity as Cuba's economic and political future was called into question. One of the outstanding films of 1991, the highly controversial black comedy *Alicia en el Pueblo de Maravillas* (Alice in Wondertown) by Daniel Díaz Torres (b. 1948), explored the tensions of the period using a surrealistic fantasy world as a backdrop, and taking the Cuban tradition of social satire to a new level.

Several years later *Fresa y chocolate* (*Strawberry and Chocolate*, 1994), directed by Tomás Gutiérrez Alea and Juan Carlos Tabio and written by Senal Paz, quickly became the most successful film in Cuban film history. It was nominated for an Oscar® for Best Foreign Film and introduced Cuban film to a wider audience than it had ever had before. Foreign audiences were surprised to learn that the Cuban government funds films such as *Strawberry and Chocolate* that are critical of political dogmatism. *Strawberry and Chocolate* was followed by what would be Alea's last film, *Guantanamera* (1995). *Guantanamera* is essentially a remake of his earlier *Death of a Bureaucrat*, set this time against the contradictions of the Special Period. The film is a loving farewell to Cuba and the Cuban people. Alea was already dying when he made it, and the film unfolds as a personal meditation on death, even as it works as both farce and national allegory.

Fernando Pérez (b. 1944), who began his career working as an assistant director under both Alea and Santiago Álvarez, has emerged as one of Cuba's most important and original directors. *Madagascar* (1994) and *La Vida es silbar* (*Life Is to Whistle*, 1998) are metaphorical, contemplative, and dreamlike films that address familiar issues—Cuban identity chief among them—in entirely new ways. His films manage to affectionately and disarmingly address the internal tensions that confront the Cuban public, including a complex inner dialogue about leaving or remaining on the island. His award-winning documentary *Suite Habana* (*Havana Suite*, 2003), a subtly moving and candid account of a day in the life of a number of residents of Havana, met with wide acclaim and a number of international awards.

Increasingly, Cuban films deal with the ideas of leaving or returning to Cuba, and the fragmentation or reunion of families, including such disparate filmic efforts as *Nada* (Juan Carlos Cremata Malberti, 2001), *Miel para Oshún* (*Honey for Oshun*, Humberto Solá, 2001), and *Video de familia* (Family video, Humberto Padrón, 2001). This heightened consciousness of Cuba's relation to the outside world is reflected in the economic realities of filmmaking as well. Increasingly, Cuba relies on co-productions with other countries to get films made, as the economic conditions of the industry continue to be unstable.

Many fine films, both documentary and fiction, are also made independently of the ICAIC. Recent efforts, including *En Vena* (In the vein, 2002) by Terence Piard Somohano, *Raíces de mi corazón* (*Roots of My Heart*, 2001) by Gloria Rolando, *Un día después* (The Day After, 2001) by Ismael Perdomo and Bladamir Zamora, and *Utopia* (2004) by Arturo Infante reflect the range of controversial topics that independent Cuban filmmakers are drawn to explore. Independent production in Cuba faces the same obstacles as independent production anywhere else: it is inherently difficult for independent filmmakers to find distribution and financing, let alone make a living as artists outside of the industry. However, with the proliferation of digital video technology, and initiatives such as Humberto Solás's Festival de Cine Pobre (International Low-Budget Film Festival), which began in 2003, all signs indicate that new possibilities of cinematic expression will continue to evolve on the island, and that Cuba will continue to make a valuable contribution to Latin American cinema.

SEE ALSO *National Cinema; Third Cinema*

FURTHER READING

Chanan, Michael. *Cuban Cinema*. Minneapolis: University of Minnesota Press, 2004.

King, John. *Magical Reels: A History of Cinema in Latin America*. London: Verso, 1990.

Martin, Michael T., ed. *New Latin American Cinema, Volumes I and II*. Detroit, MI: Wayne State University Press, 1997.

Pick, Zuzana M., and Thomas G. Schatz. *The New Latin American Cinema: A Continental Project*. Austin: University of Texas Press, 1993.

Ruth Goldberg

CULT FILMS

The phrase "cult movie" is now used so often and so broadly that the concept to which it refers has become rather difficult to delimit, especially given the sheer diversity of films that have been brought together under the term. Though cult movies are often referred to as if they were a very specific and particular genre, this is not the case; such films fall into an enormous variety of different formal and stylistic categories. Indeed, many cult movies are categorized as such precisely because of their cross- or multigenre narratives, or other offbeat qualities that take them outside the realm of genre completely.

Films can develop cult followings in various ways: on the basis of their modes of production or exhibition, their internal textual features, or through acts of appropriation by specific audiences. The usual definition of the cult movie generally relies on a sense of its distinction from mainstream cinema. This definition, of course, raises issues about the role of the cult movie as an oppositional form, and its strained relationship with processes of institutionalization and classification. Fans of cult movies often describe them as quite distinct from the commercial film industries and the mainstream media, but many such films are actually far more dependent on these forms than their fans may be willing to admit.

Most cult movies are low-budget productions, and most are undeniably flawed in some way, even if this means just poor acting or cheap special effects. Though many deal with subject matter that is generally considered repulsive or distasteful, most of the movies that have garnered cult followings have done so not because they are necessarily shocking or taboo, but rather because they are made from highly individual viewpoints and involve strange narratives, eccentric characters, garish sets, or other quirky elements, which can be as apparently insignificant as a single unique image or cameo appearance by a particular bit-part actor or actress. Many cult movies lack mass appeal, and many would have disappeared from film history completely were it not for their devoted fans, whose dedication often takes the form of a fiery passion.

Cult movies cross all boundaries of taste, form, style, and genre. There are cult Westerns, like *Johnny Guitar* (1954); cult musicals, like *The Sound of Music* (1965); cult romances, like *Gone with the Wind* (1939); cult documentaries, like *Gates of Heaven* (1978); cult drug movies, like *Easy Rider* (1969); and cult teen movies, like *American Graffiti* (1973), *Animal House* (1978), and Richard Linklater's *Dazed and Confused* (1993). There are cult exploitation films, like *Reefer Madness* (1936); cult blaxploitation films, like *Shaft* (1971); and cult porn movies, like *Deep Throat* and *Behind the Green Door* (both 1972). Many cult films are music-based and have developed a lasting following on the basis of their soundtrack alone. These include *Tommy* (1975), *Rock and Roll High School* (1979), *The Blues Brothers* (1980), and *Pink Floyd: The Wall* (1982).

There are other movies that have developed cult reputations simply because they convey a certain mood, evoke a certain atmosphere or time period, or are irrefutably strange. Examples include films as diverse as *Harold and Maude* (1971), *D.O.A.* (1980), *Diva* (1981), *Blade Runner* (1982), *Scarface* (1983), *Repo Man* (1984), *Pee-Wee's Big Adventure* (1985), *The Toxic Avenger* (1985), *Hard Boiled* (1992), and *The Big Lebowski* (1998). And while most of these movies seem to attract predominantly male cults, female followings have grown up around fashion-conscious "chick flicks" like *Valley of the Dolls* (1967), the teen movie *Clueless* (1995), and the "anti-teen" movie *Heathers* (1989).

B MOVIES AND TRASH

Perhaps the first movies to develop cult followings were B movies—those quickly made, cheaply produced films that had their heyday in Hollywood's "Golden Age." B movies began to proliferate in the mid-1930s, when distributors felt that "double features" might stand a chance of luring increasingly frugal Depression audiences back to the theaters. Their strategy worked—audiences of devoted moviegoers thrilled to cheap B movie fare like *The Mummy's Hand* (1940), *The Face Behind the Mask* (1941), *Cobra Woman* (1944), and *White Savage* (1943). Often (but not always) horror or science-fiction films, these movies were inexpensively produced and usually unheralded—except by their fans, who often found more to enjoy in these bottom-rung "guilty pleasures" than in the high-profile epics their profits supported.

B movies were cheaply made, but were not necessarily poor in quality. Throughout the 1950s and 1960s, however, a number of rather inept films were made that have subsequently developed substantial cult followings. The "trash" movie aesthetic was founded on an appreciation for these low-budget movies. Struggling with severe budgetary limitations, directors were regularly forced to come up with makeshift costuming and set design solutions that produced truly strange and sometimes unintentionally comic results. The trash aesthetic was later borrowed by underground filmmakers like Andy Warhol (1928–1987), Jack Smith (1932–1989), and the Kuchar Brothers (George [b. 1942] and Mike [b. 1942]), who also made their films in the cheapest possible way.

Most of the original trash cinema failed miserably at the box office, and has developed a cult reputation only in retrospect, after being reappropriated by a later audience with an eye for nostalgic irony. For the most part, the films were not products of the big Hollywood studios; most of them were made independently, often targeted at the drive-in theater market, and some were made outside the United States. Such films include the Japanese monster epic *Godzilla* (1954) and its low-budget Danish imitation *Reptilicus* (1962), as well as shabby Boris Karloff vehicles like *Die Monster Die* (1965), and bizarre sexploitation films like *The Wild Women of Wongo* (1958). Today, many movie buffs are drawn to the camp, kitschy qualities of these movies—their minimal budgets, low production values, and appalling acting. Many such films were made by Roger Corman (b. 1926), who originally specialized in quickie

productions with low-budget resources and little commercial marketing, including *Attack of the Crab Monsters* (1957) and *Creature from the Haunted Sea* (1961). Corman's place in cult film history is also assured by his unrivaled eye for talent; among the many notables who were employed by him at a very early stage in their careers are Jack Nicholson, Francis Ford Coppola, Martin Scorsese, Jonathan Demme, James Cameron, and Peter Bogdanovich.

The unrivaled king of trash cinema was undoubtedly Edward D. Wood, Jr. (1924–1978), whose output—films like *Bride of the Monster* (1955) and *Plan 9 from Outer Space* (1959)—are considered the nadir of naive charm. These movies have been much celebrated in retrospect because of their unique and endearing ineptitude and for the implausibility of their premises. Like most other "bad" cult movies, Wood's films lack finesse and wit, but are loved by their fans for precisely this reason. Significantly, cults have also recently grown up around more contemporary "bad" movies. For example, almost immediately after the theatrical release of *Showgirls* (Paul Verhoeven, 1995), which recouped only half its $40 million cost, the film opened in Los Angeles and then in New York as a midnight cult movie. This phenomenon suggests that the cult movie aesthetic is not necessarily antithetical to the big-budget, mass-market mode of production nourished by the major Hollywood studios.

This crossover also raises the question of the distinction between "cult" and "camp." Generally speaking, camp began in the New York underground theater and film communities, and is a quality of the way movies are received, rather than a deliberate quality of the films themselves. Indeed, camp, according to critic Susan Sontag, is always the product of pure passion—on however grand or pathetic a scale—somehow gone strangely awry. To be considered camp, it is not enough for a film to fail, or to seem dated, extreme, or freakish; there must be a genuine passion and sincerity about its creation. Camp is based on a faith and emotion in the film that is shared by director and audience, often across the passage of time, contradicting the popular assumption that camp is concerned only with surfaces and the superficial.

The two concepts—camp and cult—clearly overlap in a number of ways, and many films develop cult followings because of their camp qualities. For example, many studio films have attracted a retrospective devotion through a process of reappropriation on the part of gay audiences. This is especially true of films that feature gay icons, like Joan Crawford, Judy Garland, Liza Minelli, or Barbra Streisand, in particularly melodramatic or pathetic roles. Such films include *Mildred Pierce* (1945), *The Best of*

EDWARD D. WOOD, JR.
b. Poughskeepie, New York, 10 October 1924,
d. Hollywood, California, 10 December 1978

Often described as the "worst director in history," Wood's following has exploded since his death. For years, a small group of Ed Wood cultists treasured the two films that were commercially available—*Glen or Glenda?* (1953) and *Plan 9 From Outer Space* (1959)—without knowing much about the man himself. This all changed with the publication in 1992 of Rudolph Grey's reverent biography *Nightmare of Ecstasy: The Life and Art of Edward D. Wood, Jr.* and the release of Tim Burton's runaway success *Ed Wood* (1994), a dark comedy based on the life, times, and movies of the infamous director.

Wood's cult status is due in part to his endearingly unorthodox personality and unusual openness about his sexual fetishes. A twice-married transvestite, Wood fought in World War II and claimed to have been wearing a bra and panties under his uniform during a military landing. His ventures into Hollywood moviemaking were ill-fated until, in 1953, he landed the chance to direct a film based on the Christine Jorgensen sex-change story. The result, *Glen or Glenda?*, gave a fascinating insight into Wood's own obsessive personality, and shed light on his fascination with women's clothing (an almost unthinkable subject for an early 1950s feature) by including the director's own plea for tolerance toward cross-dressers like himself. This surreal, cheap (though well over budget), and virtually incomprehensible film is notable for Bela Lugosi's role as a scientist delivering cryptic messages about gender directly to the audience. Neither *Glen or Glenda?* nor any of Wood's subsequent movies were commercially successful, but he continued to make films until failing health and financial need sent him into a physical and emotional decline. Grey's biography presents Wood in his later years as a moody alcoholic; sadly, the last period of his career, before his premature death at age 54, was spent directing undistinguished soft, and later hardcore, pornography.

Wood's films have been canonized by cultists as high camp, and continue to be adored for their charming ineptitude, startling continuity gaps, bad acting, and irrelevant stock footage. His best-known film is the infamous *Plan 9 from Outer Space*, which features aliens arriving on earth and attempting to conquer the planet by raising the dead. The film is notorious for its pathetic, illogical script, cardboard masonry, ridiculous "special effects," and the use of kitchen utensils as space helmets. It stars the heavily accented Swedish wrestler Tor Jonson and a drug-addled, terminally ill Bela Lugosi, who died during production and is sporadically replaced by a stand-in who, even with his cape drawn over his face, looks nothing at all like the decrepit Lugosi. The film also features the glamorous Finnish actress Maila Nurmi, better known as Vampira, generally believed to be the first late-night television horror hostess (and followed by many imitators, including the more successful Elvira, Mistress of the Dark). *Plan 9 from Outer Space* contains the only surviving footage of Vampira, although she has no dialogue in the film.

RECOMMENDED VIEWING
Glen or Glenda? (1953), *Bride of the* Monster (1955), *Night of the Ghouls* (1959), *Plan 9 from Outer Space* (1959), *Ed Wood* (1994), *Ed Wood: Look Back in Angora* (1994)

FURTHER READING
Grey, Rudolph. *Nightmare of Ecstasy: The Life and Art of Edward D. Wood, Jr.* Los Angeles: Feral House, 1992.

Mikita Brottman

Everything (1959), *A Star is Born* (both the 1954 and 1976 versions), *Whatever Happened to Baby Jane?* (1962), and similar pictures that are considered by their fans to be especially mawkish, sentimental, overly serious, or too straight-faced. For example, the 1981 Joan Crawford biopic *Mommie Dearest* was almost immediately proclaimed a camp masterpiece by Crawford's gay followers and hit the midnight circuit immediately after its first run.

Other films have developed cult followings because of their unique presentation of new gimmicks or special effects. For example, Herschell Gordon Lewis's drive-in blockbuster *Blood Feast* (1963) has attained cult status partly because it was the first film to feature human entrails and dismembered bodies "in blood color." The films of William Castle (1914–1977) have attracted a cult following mainly because of their pioneering use of

Edward D. Wood, Jr. (left) directing Jail Bait *(1954) starring Dolores Fuller.* EVERETT COLLECTION. REPRODUCED BY PERMISSION.

low-budget publicity schemes and special effects, including "Percepto" (specially wired-up seats) for *The Tingler* (1959); "Emergo" (a cardboard skeleton on a wire hanging over the audience) for *The House on Haunted Hill* (1958); and "Illusion-O" (a 3–D viewer) for *13 Ghosts* (1960)—although there are those who claim that Castle's most successful gimmick was his use of the hammy, smooth-voiced actor Vincent Price (1911–1993). In a similar way, John Waters's *Polyester* (1981) is a cult film partly because of its use of "Odorama" (audience scratch-and-sniff cards), and Roger Vadim's *Barbarella* (1968) has achieved cult status mainly due to the extravagance of its costumes and sets, including Jane Fonda's thigh-high boots and fur-lined spaceship.

There are also a number of iconic directors whose every movie has attained cult status, mainly because their films tend to replicate the same individual fascinations or pathologies. A good example is Russ Meyer (1922–2004), whose films are especially popular among those fans, both male and female, who share his obsession with buxom actresses engaged in theatrical violence. Most

typical of the Meyer oeuvre is perhaps *Faster, Pussycat! Kill! Kill!* (1966), which features three leather-clad, voluptuous, thrill-seeking women in go-go boots.

A different kind of cult movie is the film that has attracted curiosity because of the particular circumstances surrounding its release. Such films may have been banned in certain states, for example; they may have had controversial lawsuits brought against them, or they may have been associated with particularly violent crimes, like *A Clockwork Orange* (1971) or *Taxi Driver* (1976). Or they may be notoriously difficult to find, like Todd Haynes's *Superstar: The Karen Carpenter Story* (1987), a study in celebrity and anorexia in the guise of a biopic performed by Barbie dolls. The movie was quickly taken off the market for copyright reasons, but has still managed to attract a substantial cult following.

In other cases, films attain retrospective cult status because of the circumstances surrounding their production. For example, *The Terror* (1963) is a cult film partly because of Jack Nicholson's early appearance in a starring role, and *Donovan's Brain* (1953) gains cult status because of the presence of the actress Nancy Davis, later to become better known as First Lady Nancy Reagan. Moreover, scandalous public disclosures that accumulate around actors or actresses inevitably give their films a certain amount of morbid cult interest. For example, in his *Hollywood Babylon* books (1975 and 1984), underground filmmaker Kenneth Anger (b. 1927) keeps a toll of films involving one or more celebrities who eventually took their own lives, all of which have since come to attain an odd kind of cult status of their own. Anger also discusses "cursed" films that feature stars who died soon after production was completed—films like *Rebel without a Cause* (1955), starring James Dean, and *The Misfits* (1961), starring Marilyn Monroe. In cases like these, fans often enjoy subjecting the film to microscopic scrutiny in a search for telltale betrayals of bad health, signals of some emotional meltdown, portents of future tragedy, or innocently spoken words of irony, regardless of what else might be happening on screen. For example, parallels are often drawn between the death of James Dean in an automobile accident and the "chicken run" scene in *Rebel without a Cause*, in which Jim Stark (Dean) and his friend are driving two stolen cars toward the edge of a cliff; the first one to jump out is a "chicken." Jim rolls out at the last second, but his friend's coat sleeve is caught in the door handle, and he hurtles over the cliff to his death. In the aftermath, we hear Dean's anguished cry: "A boy was killed!"

MIDNIGHT MOVIES

Many films now considered "cult movies" came to achieve this status through repeat screenings at independent repertory cinemas, usually very late at night. Such films were cheaper for theaters to hire than current releases, often since their ownership had fallen into public domain. It became traditional, during the 1950s and 60s, to begin showing these films at midnight, when audience attendance was lower, and sensibilities often less discriminating. However, the first movie to be "officially" shown at a midnight screening was odd drama *El Topo* (*The Mole*, Alexandro Jodorosky, 1970), which was discovered by Ben Barenholtz, booker for the Elgin theater in New York, at a Museum of Modern Art screening. Barenholtz allegedly persuaded the film's distributor to allow him to play it at midnight at the Elgin, because—as the poster announced—the film was "too heavy to be shown any other way." The disturbing film was a runaway success, and midnight premieres of offbeat movies eventually became (with varying degrees of success) a regular aspect of distribution, initially in New York and later elsewhere. The aim of the concept was to provide a forum for unusual, eccentric, or otherwise bizarre movies. The audience for these films generally

tended to be those who were not averse to going out to see a film in the middle of the night—usually a younger group of urban movie fans not easily put off by unconventional themes or scenes of drug use, nudity, or violence. Indeed, many of the midnight movies that attained cult success did so because they transgressed various social taboos. For example, when its run had come to an end, *El Topo* was followed at the Elgin by *Pink Flamingos* (John Waters, 1972), which had late-night audiences lined up around the block. In fact, all of the films of John Waters eventually became staples of the midnight movie circuit, especially *Polyester* (1981) and *Hairspray* (1988), with their grotesque vignettes held together by the loosest of narratives and a bizarre cast of garish grandmothers and oddballs, generally led by the overweight transvestite Divine.

One of the most significant midnight movies was *Eraserhead* (1977), the nightmarish first film made by cult director David Lynch (b. 1946), which contained a series of disturbing images in a postapocalyptic setting. Lynch went on to make other movies that soon developed cult followings, including *Blue Velvet* (1986) and *Wild at Heart* (1990), both filled with dark, odd, ambiguous characters. Other important movies that gradually developed cult followings after years on the midnight circuit include *Freaks* (1932), *Night of the Living Dead* (1968), *The Evil Dead* (1981), and *Re-Animator* (1985).

Essentially, the real key to the success of a midnight movie was the film's relationship with its audience and the slavish devotion of its fans. Perhaps the most successful midnight movie of all time was *Rocky Horror Picture Show* (1975), a low-budget film adaptation of Richard O'Brien's glam stage hit about two square lovebirds who enter the realm of an outrageous Gothic transsexual. A failure when it was first released, midnight screenings at the Waverly Theater in New York City quickly established *Rocky Horror* as an aberrant smash, starting a trend in audiences for interactive entertainment. As the film garnered a significant cult following over the late 1970s and early 1980s, audiences began to arrive at the theater dressed in costume, carrying various props to wave and throw in the aisles as they yelled responses to characters' lines and joined in singing and dancing to the musical numbers onscreen.

VCR and DVD viewing, network and cable television, and pay-per-view stations have significantly changed the nature of cult film viewing. Many movies that failed to find an audience upon original theatrical release now often gain cult followings through video rentals and sales. Today, word-of-mouth popularity can lead a formerly obscure film to gain a whole new audience on its video release, allowing it to earn considerably more in DVD sales than it did at the theater.

(From left) Tim Curry, Barry Bostwick, and Susan Sarandon in the midnight cult film The Rocky Horror Picture Show *(Jim Sharman, 1975).* ® ™ AND COPYRIGHT © 20TH CENTURY FOX FILM CORP./COURTESY EVERETT COLLECTION. REPRODUCED BY PERMISSION.

CULT CLASSICS

A film need not be offbeat, obscure, or low-budget to attain a cult following. On the contrary, a number of critically acclaimed movies have attained cult status precisely because their high quality and skillful performances, as well as their emotional power, have given them enduring appeal. These kinds of films are often described as "cult classics" because, while attracting a fiercely devoted band of followers, they are films that most mainstream audiences and critics have also praised and admired. Unlike ordinary cult movies, cult classics are often products of the big Hollywood studios, and most of them are made in the United States. Moreover, unlike many cult movies, cult classics are not weird, offbeat, or strange, but are often sentimental and heartwarming. They include such films as *It's a Wonderful Life* (1946), *Miracle on 34th Street* (1947), and *The Wizard of Oz* (1939). One of the most deeply loved of such films is *Casablanca* (1942), whose cult—or so legend has it—began in the early 1950s, when the Brattle Theater, adjoining Harvard University in Cambridge, Massachusetts, held a

regular "Bogart week," purportedly because the theater's student clientele so closely identified with Bogart's sense of style. The series was shown around final exam time, to bring the students some needed late-night relief from the stress of their studies, and it culminated with a screening of *Casablanca*.

SEE ALSO *B Movies; Camp; Fans and Fandom*

FURTHER READING

Anger, Kenneth. *Hollywood Babylon*. San Francisco: Straight Arrow, 1975.

———. *Hollywood Babylon II*. New York: Dutton, 1984.

Brottman, Mikita. *Hollywood Hex*. London: Creation Books, 1999.

Everman, Welch. *Cult Horror Films*. New York: Carol Publishing Group, 1993.

Hoberman, J., and Jonathan Rosenbaum. *Midnight Movies*. New York: Harper and Row, 1983.

Jancovich, Mark, Antonio Lázarro Rebolli, and Andy Willis, eds. *Defining Cult Movies: The Cultural Politics of Oppositional*

Taste. Manchester and New York: Manchester University Press, 2003.

Mendik, Xavier, and Graeme Harper, eds. *Unruly Pleasures: The Cult Film and Its Critics.* Surrey, UK: Fab Press, 2000.

Peary, Danny. *Cult Movies: The Classics, the Sleepers, the Weird, and the Wonderful.* New York: Gramercy Books, 1998.

Sontag, Susan. "Notes on Camp." In *Against Interpretation and Other Essays*, 275–292. New York: Delta, 1966.

Stevenson, Jack. *Land of a Thousand Balconies.* Manchester, UK: Critical Vision, 2003.

Telotte, J. P., ed. *The Cult Film Experience: Beyond All Reason.* Austin: University of Texas Press, 1991.

Vale, V., and Andrea Juno, eds. *Incredibly Strange Films.* San Francisco: RE/Search Books, 1986.

Mikita Brottman

CZECHOSLOVAKIA

Czechoslovakia was formed in 1918 following the break-up of the Austro-Hungarian Empire after World War I. The Czech lands of Bohemia and Moravia had been ruled from Vienna while Slovakia had formed part of Hungary. Despite close linguistic ties, this was the first time that the two nations had been linked for over a thousand years. Following the Munich conference of 1938, when the country was forced to cede its German-speaking areas to Germany, Hitler encouraged the secession of Slovakia, and Bohemia and Moravia were established as a Nazi protectorate following the German invasion of March 1939.

The country was reunited in 1945, and became part of the Eastern bloc after the Communist coup of 1948. In the 1960s, there was an attempt to move beyond the dogmatic Stalinism of the 1950s, culminating in the Prague Spring of 1968. This attempt to combine socialism and democracy was perceived as a threat to Soviet hegemony and resulted in the invasion of fellow Warsaw Pact countries in August of that year. This led to a repressive regime that was to last until the fall of Communism during the so-called "Velvet Revolution" of November 1989. The country split into the Czech and Slovak republics in 1993 after decisions taken within the political leaderships. It did not reflect popular opinion, which favored maintaining the union.

Despite these political turmoils, the Czech cinema became an established part of the European mainstream in the 1920s and 1930s and has maintained a significant level of feature production throughout its subsequent development. Its history pre-dates the formation of the independent state of Czechoslovakia and there were also important precursors to the cinema. J. E. Purkyně

(1787–1869) wrote on persistence of vision as early as 1818 and, together with Ferdinand Durst, created the Kinesiscope in 1850. The first film producer in Austria-Hungary was the Czech photographer Jan Kříženecký (1868–1921), who made his first films in 1898. His film *Smích a pláč* (*Laughter and Tears*, 1898), with the actor Josef Šváb-Malostranský miming the two emotions, could almost summarize international perceptions of the defining characteristics of Czech cinema (based on such films as the 1966 *Ostře sledované vlaky* [*Closely Watched Trains*]).

BEGINNINGS

A permanent film theater was opened in Prague in 1907 by the conjuror Ponrepo and regular film production began in 1910. By the beginning of World War I, over a third of the cinemas in Austria-Hungary were based in the Czech lands of Bohemia and Moravia. Lucernafilm was established in Prague in 1915 by Václav Havel, grandfather of the future president Václav Havel; while other companies, including Weteb, Excelsior, Praga, and Poja, followed at the end of the war. Czech cinema's first international success was Karel Degl's *Stavitel chrámu* (*The Builder of the Cathedral*, 1919) while the first Slovak feature, Jaroslav Siakel's *Jánošík*, was made in 1921 with US financing.

The first important studio was founded by the American and Biografia company (the A-B Company) in 1921, and the actor-director Karel Lamač established the Kavalírka studios in 1926, where some of the most important films were made before 1929, when they were destroyed by fire. Despite strong competition from the

German and US cinemas, feature production in the silent period averaged over twenty-six (Czech) features and was marked by both artistic and commercial success. Lamač directed a successful adaptation of Jaroslav Hašek's comic anti-war novel *Dobrý voják Švejk* (*The Good Soldier Švejk*) in 1926, which was followed by three silent sequels: *Švejk na frontě* (*Švejk at the Front*, 1926), directed by Lamač, *Švejk v ruském zajetí* (*Švejk in Russian Captivity*, 1926), directed by Svatopluk Innemann; and *Švejk v civilu* (*Švejk in Civilian Life*, 1927), directed by Gustav Machatý. In partnership with his then-wife Anny Ondra (1902–1987), who appeared in Alfred Hitchcock's *The Manxman* and *Blackmail* (both 1929), Lamač formed a successful team that achieved international success in the French, Austrian, and German cinema, although they transferred their production base to Berlin in 1930.

THE SOUND FILM

Gustav Machatý (1901–1963) was the most ambitious "art" director of the period, and attracted attention with his Expressionist-influenced adaptation of Tolstoy's *Kreutzerova sonáta* (*The Kreutzer Sonata*, 1926). He enjoyed a big success with *Erotikon* (1929), which was consolidated by his first two sound films, *Ze soboty na neděli* (*From Saturday to Sunday*, 1931) and, especially, *Extase* (*Ecstasy*, 1932), winner of the Best Direction Prize at the Venice Film Festival in 1934, which introduced Hedy Kiesler (Lamarr) (1913–2000) to world audiences and was sold to over twenty-six countries. The success of *Ecstasy* was followed by an MGM contract and film work in Italy and Austria. However, he was able to complete only one Hollywood A-feature (*Jealousy*, 1945), which was scripted by Dalton Trumbo, and was primarily employed on second unit work. The poetic lyricism of Machatý's style did much to establish the tradition of lyrical cinematography that continued through to the post–World War II period. One of his key collaborators was the photographer and avant-garde director Alexandr Hackenschmied (Alexander Hammid) (1907–2004), who directed the experimental *Bezúčelná procházka* (*Aimless Walk*, 1930), and later, in the United States, made documentaries, and co-directed films with Herbert Kline and Maya Deren.

The introduction of sound raised the question of the viability of Czech language production for a population of only 15 million. But while only eight features were produced in 1930, the average had risen to over forty by the end of the decade. The Barrandov film studios were built in 1932–1933 with the intention of attracting international production (which finally happened in the 1990s), but developed in the 1930s mainly as a center for national production, following growth in the domestic audience.

Martin (Mac) Frič, whose career extended from the 1920s to the 1960s, made some of his most important films in the 1930s, including work with such leading comic actors as Vlasta Burian (1891–1962), Hugo Haas (1901–1968), and Oldřich Nový. Perhaps most notable was his collaboration with the theatrical team of Jiří Voskovec and Jan Werich (1905–1980), whose Osvobozené divadlo (The Liberated Theatre) was a cultural phenomenon. Their musical satires and parodies, described by the eminent linguist Roman Jakobson as "pure humour and semantic clowning," took a political turn in the face of economic depression and the rise of Nazism. After appearing in Paramount's all-star revue *Paramount on Parade* (1930), they made four feature films, including two by Frič—*Hej-Rup!* (*Heave Ho!*, 1934) and *Svět patří nám* (*The World Belongs to Us*, 1937). The former deals with the destruction of a corrupt capitalist at the hands of a workers collective while in the latter, Voskovec and Werich (V+W) defeat a Hitler-like demagogue and his big-business supporters with the help of the workers.

Both *The World Belongs to Us* and the film version of Karel Čapek's anti-Fascist play *Bílá nemoc* (*The White Sickness*, 1937), directed by Haas, were the subject of Nazi protests and were suppressed following the German invasion of March 1939. Voskovec and Werich spent the war years in the United States, where Voskovec eventually settled and, as George Voskovec, became a successful Broadway actor as well as appearing in a number of Hollywood films. Hugo Haas also left for Hollywood, where he played cameo roles and directed a sequence of B features, three of them based on Czech sources.

Other Czech directors to attract attention during the 1930s included Josef Rovenský (1894–1937) (*Řeka* [*The River*, 1933]) and Otakar Vávra, who moved from experimental shorts to features in 1937. His 1938 film *Cech panen kutnohorských* (*The Guild of Kutna Hora Maidens*) won an award at Venice but was banned during the Occupation. Slovak feature film production was not to develop further until after the war, but Karel Plicka's *Zem spieva* (*The Earth Sings*, 1933), a feature-length record of Slovak folk culture edited by Alexandr Hackenschmied, attracted international attention when it was screened at Venice in 1934.

Following the Western allies' capitulation to Hitler at the Munich conference over the Sudetenland (Czechoslovakia's German-speaking areas), the Germans invaded in March 1939 and the Czech lands became the Protectorate of Bohemia and Moravia. Under "clerico-Fascist" leadership, Slovakia declared independence immediately. The Germans took a controlling stake in the Barrandov studios and issued a list of prohibited subjects, eventually extending the studios as an alternative center for German production. Although Czech production declined from forty features in 1938 to nine in 1944, a number of leading directors, including Vávra and Martin Fric, continued to make films.

The Czech star Lída Baarová, who had been signed up by the German film studio Ufa (Universum Film Aktiengesellschaft) in 1934 and had a well-known affair with Nazi Minister of Propaganda Joseph Goebbels, saw all of her films banned in Germany due to Hitler's anger at the scandal, but continued to work in Czech films. She finally returned to Czechoslovakia in 1938, making some of her best films in the late 1930s, including four for Vávra, who directed her in *Panenství* (*Virginity*, 1937) and *Dívka v modrém* (*The Girl in Blue*, 1939). The Nazis expelled her from the Czech studios in 1941 and she continued her career in Italy. A group including Vávra planned the nationalization of the film industry after the war, a goal achieved in 1945, along with the establishment of the Koliba studios in Bratislava (Slovakia), and the foundation of the Prague Film School (FAMU) in 1946. Czech films again attracted international attention when Karel Steklý's (1903–1987) *Siréna* (*The Strike*, 1947) and Jiří Trnka's feature-length puppet film *Špalíček* (*The Czech Year*, 1947) won awards at Venice.

Following the Communist takeover in 1948, there was a fairly swift adherence to the moribund formulae of Stalinist cinema, particularly in the period 1951–1955, combined with another decline in production. However, as the novelist Josef Škvorecký (b. 1924) once put it, artistic common sense always gnawed at the formulae of Socialist Realism, and filmmakers sought ways of expanding beyond official limitations. It was at this time that the Czech cinema achieved international reputation in the field of animation. Jiří Trnka, Karel Zeman (1910–1989), Hermina Týrlová, Břetislav Pojar, Jiří Brdečka, and many others led the way, with features from Trnka (*Staré pověsti české* [*Old Czech Legends*, 1953], *Sen noci svatojánske* [*A Midsummer Night's Dream*, 1959]) and from Zeman (*Cesta do pravěku /A Journey to Primeval Times*, 1955, *Vynález zkázy/,An Invention for Destruction*, 1958), who eventually made nine feature animation films. Many early films with an explicit Left orientation were clearly honest and committed, particularly before 1948. *The Strike*, a collective statement by the pre-war Left avant-garde, was one example and Vávra's *Němá barikáda* (*Silent Barricade*, 1949) about the Prague uprising, although simplified, was another. *Vstanou noví bojovníci* (*New Heroes Will Arise*, 1950), by Jiří Weiss, gave a committed account of the early years of the labor movement.

Weiss had started to make documentaries before the war and had spent the war years in Britain where, besides working with the British documentary school, he made his first fiction films. On his return, he made an impressive film about the Munich crisis, *Uloupená hranice* (*The Stolen Frontier*, 1947) and won international awards with *Vlčí jáma* (*The Wolf Trap*, 1957) and *Romeo, Julie a tma* (*Romeo, Juliet, and Darkness*, 1960), notable for their psychological depth and dramatic visual style. Another director who began in pre-war documentary was Elmar Klos (1910–1993), who began a long-term collaboration with the Slovak Ján Kadár in 1952. A sequence of challenging films culminated in the first Czech (and Slovak) Oscar®-winner, *Obchod na korze* (*The Shop on Main Street*, 1965). After the Soviet invasion of 1968, Kadár emigrated to the United States, where his films included an adaptation of Bernard Malamud's *The Angel Levine* (1970) and the award-winning Canadian film *Lies My Father Told Me* (1975). Weiss also emigrated to the United States but made no films until the German-produced *Martha und Ich* (*Martha and I*, 1990).

TOWARD THE PRAGUE SPRING

In the late 1950s, a number of new feature directors made their debuts, including František Vláčil, and early FAMU graduates such as Vojtěch Jasný, Karel Kachyňa, and the Slovak, Štefan Uher. In a world in which criticism of Stalinism was forbidden, they found their inspiration in the visual traditions of Czech lyricism and in broad humanist subject matter. Although little known to international audiences, they were to make some of the most significant films of the 1960s. In the 1990s, Czech critics voted Vláčil's historical epic *Marketa Lazarová* (1967) the best Czech film ever made and Jasný's *Všichni dobří rodáci* (*All My Good Countrymen*, 1968), which dealt with the collectivization of agriculture, was to prove one of the most politically controversial films of the Prague Spring. In 1990, Kachyňa's *Ucho* (*The Ear*, 1970) still impressed at the Cannes Film Festival when it premiered after a twenty-year ban.

Slovak cinema, which enjoyed a separate—if interactive—existence after 1945, saw the development of a number of significant talents after the production of Palo Bielik's film *Vlčie diery* (*Wolves' Lairs*, 1948), about the Slovak National Uprising of 1944. The most notable were probably Peter Solan (b. 1929) and Stanislav Barabáš. Uher, who began his career in 1961, paved the way for the innovative developments of the 1960s with his *Slnko v sieti* (*Sunshine in a Net*, (1962), which combined lyricism with significant narrative innovation.

It was against the lyrical humanist background of the late 1950s–early 1960s that the Czech New Wave made its debut in 1963 with Miloš Forman's *Černý Petr* (*Black*

MILOŠ FORMAN
b. Čáslav, Czechoslovakia, 2 February 1932

Miloš Forman is one of the major directors of the Czech New Wave. He studied screenwriting at the Prague Film School (FAMU), and made his debut as writer/director with *Konkurs* (*Talent Competition*) and *Černý Petr* (*Black Peter*) in 1963. In collaboration with his colleagues Ivan Passer and Jaroslav Papoušek, who subsequently became directors themselves, he developed a style of semi-improvised film making that used non-professional actors and focused on everyday life. This apparently accidental discovery of reality—a world of dance halls, canteens, and run-down flats—was, he argued, a reaction against the false and idealized images promoted by the official cinema.

His next two films, *Lásky jedné plavovlásky* (*Loves of a Blonde*, 1965) and *Hoří, má panenko* (*The Firemen's Ball*, 1967), were both Oscar®-nominated. *The Firemen's Ball*, the comic story of how a local fire brigade fails in its attempts to organize both a raffle and a beauty competition, was interpreted, even at script stage, as a satire on the Communist Party. In 1973, following the Soviet invasion of 1968, it was listed as one of the four Czech films to be banned "forever."

It was his last Czech film, and Forman was working on the script of his first American film in Paris in 1968 when the Soviet invasion took place. He remained abroad and became a US citizen in 1977. *Taking Off* (1971) continued the improvised, group-centered approach of his Czech films but, despite festival success, did not succeed with American audiences. He subsequently chose to work with preexisting themes from his adopted culture and not to write his own original screenplays.

His subsequent American films—frequently compared adversely with his Czech ones, although they won him two Best Director Oscars®—reveal, in fact, a decidedly off-center portrait of American life. They include adaptations of Ken Kesey (*One Flew Over the Cuckoo's Nest*, 1975); E. L. Doctorow (*Ragtime*, 1981); the James Rado–Gerome Ragni–Galt McDermott musical *Hair* (1979); and, more recently, collaborations with screenwriters Scott Alexander and Larry Karaszewski in their continuing gallery of American eccentrics (*The People vs. Larry Flynt*, 1996; *Man on the Moon*, 1999). Forman based himself in New York rather than Hollywood and his subjects always have had an intrinsic interest and have been treated in sophisticated ways. His two "European" projects, the multiple Academy Award®-winner *Amadeus* (1984), from the play by Peter Schaffer, which was made in Prague, and *Valmont* (1989), an adaptation of Choderlos de Laclos's *Les Liaisons Dangereuses*, made in France, were also his most elaborate. In both, he treated his heroes—Mozart and his wife and the sexual predators of *Valmont*—pretty much like the young innocents of his early Czech films.

RECOMMENDED VIEWING
Black Peter (1963), *Loves of a Blonde* (1965), *The Firemen's Ball* (1967), *One Flew Over the Cuckoo's Nest* (1975), *Amadeus* (1984), *Valmont* (1989)

FURTHER READING
Forman, Miloš, and Jan Novák. *Turnaround: A Memoir.* New York: Villard Books, 1994.

Hames, Peter. "Forman." In *Five Filmmakers: Tarkovsky, Forman, Polanski, Szabó, Makavejev*, edited by Daniel J. Goulding. Bloomington: Indiana University Press, 1994.

Liehm, Antonín J. *The Miloš Forman Stories.* White Plains, NY: International Arts and Sciences Press, 1975.

———. "Miloš Forman: the Style and the Man." In *Politics, Art, and Commitment in the East European Cinema*, edited by David W. Paul. London: Macmillan, and New York, St. Martin's, 1983.

Peter Hames

Peter), Věra Chytilová's *O něčem jiném* (*Something Different*), and Jaromil Jireš's *Křik* (*The Cry*). All three films addressed the problems of everyday life, with cinéma-vérité a key influence on Forman and Chytilová. While the emphasis on the look of everyday life heralded movement in a new direction, the New Wave rapidly escaped any particular stylistic form in favor of a diversity of output that also comprised lyricism, critical realism, and the avant-garde. Other directors who emerged in the mid- to late-1960s have been seen as "New Wave," including Jan Němec (*Démanty noci* [*Diamonds of the Night*, 1964], *O slavnosti a hostech* [*Report on the Party and the Guests*, 1966]); Pavel Juráček and Jan Schmidt (b. 1934) (*Postava k podpírání* [*Josef Kilián*, 1963]); Evald Schorm (*Každý den odvahu* [*Everyday Courage*, 1964], *Návrat ztraceného syna* [*Return of the Prodigal Son*,

Miloš Forman during production of **One Flew Over the Cuckoo's Nest** *(1975).* EVERETT COLLECTION. REPRODUCED BY PERMISSION.

1966]); Ivan Passer (b. 1933) (*Intimní osvětlení* [*Intimate Lighting*, 1965]); Hynek Bočan (*Nikdo se nebude smát* [*No Laughing Matter*, 1965], *Soukromá vichřice* [*Private Hurricane*, 1967]); and Jiří Menzel (*Closely Watched Trains*, 1966], *Rozmarné léto* [*Capricious Summer*, 1967], *Skřivánci na niti* [*Skylarks on a String*, 1969]). *Closely Watched Trains* was to prove the second Czech Oscar®-winner in 1967.

Criticism of the system tended to be oblique prior to 1968, when the reform Communism of the Prague Spring effectively abolished censorship but continued to fund its filmmakers. Nonetheless, there were some powerful works even before this. A director of the older generation, Ladislav Helge (b. 1927), made some strong internal criticisms with his film *Škola otců* (*School for Fathers*, 1957), about a teacher fighting a battle against hypocrisy masked by ideological correctness. Evald Schorm's (1931–1988) debut feature *Everyday Courage* focused on a Party activist who sees his image of certainty collapsing around him, while in *Return of the Prodigal Son* he examined the case of an attempted suicide, linking it explicitly to issues of conscience and compromise.

The realist and humorous approach of directors like Forman and Passer was supplemented by Juráček's and Schmidt's Kafkaesque analysis of bureaucracy in *Josef Kilián*, Němec's absurdist portrait of power in *Report on the Party and the Guests*, and Forman's farce, *Hoří, má panenko* (*The Firemen's Ball*, 1967), in which his aging firemen's inability to organize anything was inevitably interpreted as a somewhat broader parable. Avant-garde and experimental traditions began to emerge in the late 1960s with the influence of Poetism (Němec's *Mučedníci lásky* [*Martyrs of Love*, 1966]); Dadaism (Chytilová's *Sedmikrásky* [*Daisies*, 1966]); and Surrealism (Jireš's *Valerie a týden divů* [*Valerie and her Week of Wonders*, 1970]).

The Slovak Wave of the late 1960s shared a similarly radical approach to form. Dušan Hanák's *322* (1969) was a bleak and powerful allegory of contemporary life while directors such as Juraj Jakubisko (b. 1938) (*Zbehovia a pútnici* [*The Deserter and the Nomads*, 1968]) and Elo Havetta (1938–1975) (*Slávnosť v botanickej záhrade* [*The Party in the Botanical Garden*, 1969]) used folk inspiration in a way that looked forward to the work of Emir Kusturica, who graduated from FAMU ten years later.

The Czech and Slovak New Waves undoubtedly contributed to the political reform movement of the 1960s, and formed part of the Prague Spring attempts to combine democracy and Socialism—in effect, *glasnost* twenty years before Soviet leader Mikhail Gorbachev initiated the reforms that led to the end of the Cold War. The Warsaw Pact invasion and suppression of these earlier reforms led, perhaps inevitably, to the banning of writers, artists, and filmmakers. Over 100 films were banned, and Forman, Passer, Kadár, Weiss, Jasný, Němec, and Barabáš went into exile. Helge, Schorm, and Juráček found their film careers at an end while others were forced into compromises with the regime.

NORMALIZATION AND AFTER

The period between 1970 and 1989, that of so-called "normalization," was, despite substantial production, a relative lowpoint in the history of Czech and Slovak film, as it was in cultural life in general. Following the invasion, it has been estimated that over 170,000 people left the country and that 70,000 were expelled from the Communist Party. The heads of the Barrandov and Koliba studios were sacked and the films of the "wave" were condemned as expressions of petty bourgeois egoism.

The new films of the 1970s were almost devoid of substantive content. Simplified moral tales and teenage love stories were the order of the day. Nonetheless, directors such as Kachyňa, Jireš, Vláčil, and Uher walked

Miloš Forman's parodic **Firemen's Ball** *(1967)*. EVERETT COLLECTION. REPRODUCED BY PERMISSION.

the tightrope with a certain measure of success. Menzel, who returned to filmmaking in 1975, and Chytilová, who returned in 1976, kept alive some of the qualities of the New Wave—Menzel with his adaptations from Hrabal, which included *Postřižiny* (*Cutting it Short*, 1980), and Chytilová with a number of critically abrasive films such as *Hra o jablko* (*The Apple Game*, 1976) and *Panelstory* (*Prefab Story*, 1979). Menzel even gained an Oscar® nomination for *Vesničko má středisková* (*My Sweet Little Village*, 1985). But the regime was not interested in promoting its more interesting projects, preferring to champion propagandistic epics to an uninterested world film community.

It was against this background that the striking animated films of the surrealist Jan Švankmajer made their appearance (although he had been making films since the early 1960s). Largely suppressed by the authorities, his work finally emerged at the Annecy Animation Festival in 1983 and he was subsequently to make his first feature, *Něco z Alenky* (*Alice*, 1987), as a Swiss-British-German co-production. By the end of the

1980s, it was often alleged that the problems for cinema were less those of censorship than an absence of good scripts, the talent needed for their creation having been lost through years of both enforced and semi-voluntary compromise. Nonetheless, prior to the Velvet Revolution of November 1989 and the fall of Communism, it had been decided to release the banned films (although only a few, including *The Shop on Main Street* and *The Firemen's Ball*, had appeared before November) and more challenging work had began to appear from directors such as Zdeněk Tyc (b. 1956) (*Vojtěch, řečený sirotek* [*Vojtěch, Called Orphan*, 1989]) and Irena Pavlásková (b. 1960) (*Čas sluhů* [*The Time of the Servants*, 1989]).

The fall of Communism did not lead to a sudden cinematic rebirth. The nationalized industry was dismantled in 1993 (although the process had begun earlier) and the Barrandov studios have been largely given over to American and other foreign producers, with domestic producers excluded by cost. Government subsidy was virtually removed (unlike the subsidies in Poland and Hungary) and, until 2004, the burden of production fell mainly upon the public service Česká televize (Czech Television), with a consequent emphasis on low budget production. The New Wave did not bounce back, although Němec returned from exile and has made some interesting low budget films (notably *Noční hovory s matkou* [*Late Night Talks with Mother*, 2001]) and Drahomíra Vihanová made her second feature film, *Pevnost* (*The Fortress*, 1994), after a twenty-year hiatus. Menzel withdrew to theater for ten years rather than face the problems of production in an underfunded industry.

But, despite everything, the Czech industry survived and, in the mid- to late-1990s, a number of younger directors again attracted international attention. They included Jan Svěrák, who won an Oscar® with his *Kolya* (*Kolja*, 1996), Petr Zelenka (*Knoflíkáři* [*Buttoners*, 1997]), Saša Gedeon (*Návrat idiota* [*Return of the Idiot*, 1999]), David Ondříček (*Samotáři* [*Loners*, 2000]), and Alice Nellis (*Ene bene* [*Eeny meeny*, 2000]). Jan Hřebejk's *Musíme si pomáhat* (*Divided We Fall*, 2000) and Ondřej Trojan's *Želary* (2004) were also Oscar®-nominated, and Švankmajer produced a sequence of four features, including *Lekce Faust* (*Faust*, 1994) and *Otesánek* (*Little Otik*, 2001). *Kolya*'s bittersweet story of an unemployed musician and his relationship with a 5-year-old Russian enjoyed an international box office success and many of the films, echoing the "new wave," focussed on the "small" events of everyday life. Švankmajer pursued his course of "militant surrealism" while Zelenka exhibited an original line in black humor. Both *Divided We Fall and Želary* were set during World War II. Hřebejk's film told the ironic story of a Czech man who hides a Jewish refugee during the war. He arranges for the Jewish man to make his wife pregnant in order to avoid sharing his flat with a Nazi bureaucrat. The existence of a strong film culture and tradition seemed to have transcended the government's post-Communist view of film culture-as-commodity.

The breakup of Czechoslovakia into the Czech and Slovak republics in 1992–1993 has favored Slovakia somewhat less. Compared with Czech production of fifteen to twenty films a year (thirty-two in 1990), Slovak production dropped to an average of two films a year in the late 1990s (compared with twelve in 1990). A number of directors made their debuts, but only one, Martin Šulík, was able to establish a body of work, with a sequence of five films including *Záhrada* (*The Garden*, 1995) and *Krajinka* (*Landscape*, 2000). Like those of other Slovak directors, they showed a folk inspiration, but their mood is reflective and exhibits a subdued melancholy. He is arguably the sole "auteur" to have established himself in the Czech and Slovak cinemas since 1989.

SEE ALSO *National Cinema*

FURTHER READING

Hames, Peter. "Czechoslovakia: After the Spring." *Post New Wave Cinema in the Soviet Union and Eastern Europe*, edited by Daniel J. Goulding. Bloomington: Indiana University Press, 1989.

———. *The Czechoslovak New Wave.* 2nd ed. London, Wallflower Press, 2005.

———, ed. *The Cinema of Central Europe.* London: Wallflower Press, 2004.

———, ed. *Dark Alchemy: The Films of Jan Švankmajer.* Westport, CT: Greenwood Press/Praeger, 1995.

Iordanova, Dina. *Cinema of the Other Europe: The Industry and Artistry of East Central European Film.* London: Wallflower Press, 2003.

Liehm, Antonín J. *Closely Watched Films: The Czechoslovak Experience.* White Plains, NY: International Arts and Sciences Press, 1974.

Liehm, Mira, and Antonín J. Liehm, *The Most Important Art: East European Film After 1945.* Berkeley: University of California Press, 1977.

Škvorecký, Josef. *All the Bright Young Men and Women: A Personal History of the Czech Cinema.* Toronto: Peter Martin Associates, 1971.

Peter Hames

DANCE

The arts of movement and of the moving image have co-existed since the late 19th century. They fill each other's most important needs. Film documents movement. For early forms of pre-cinema and film, dance provided proof of movement. Dancers and choreographers saw film as a solution to the ephemeral nature of movement. The art forms were disappointed by the other for various reasons—both technological and artistic—so they have had to negotiate ways to coexist and collaborate over the century. Concert, ballet, and vaudeville dancers appeared in dozens of early films. But, as narrative became the principle focus on film, dance took a subsidiary role, providing entertainment and an occasional dream sequence.

Some concert (early modern) dancers experimented with cuing music simultaneous to filmed performance, but, for the most part, silent film did not meet their needs for either documentation or creative collaboration. Sound technology appeared at the period in which the early modern dance vocabularies and structure were developing in America and Germany. But the new dancers' emphasis on weighted movements and philosophical leanings to the left saw little in common with Hollywood and they couldn't afford their own equipment. The avant garde of American dance waited until the 1940s to discover the artistic possibilities of film. Since the 1950s, all forms of dance have used film to document the rehearsal process and choreography. As dance became more and more abstract and non-narrative, it found colleagues in experimental film. Filmmakers and choreographers have worked together to create experimental projects. For the most part, the dance world ignored film as an artistic partner until the 1940s.

Although dance as film has never been as popular in the United States as in Europe, there are now annual dance film festivals and screening series in urban centers and university programs.

DANCE IN SILENT FILM

Dance was featured in late pre-cinema and early film because it showed movement in human scale. Among the earliest films—nickelodeons, Mutoscopes, and other mechanical projections—are dozens of studio films produced by Thomas Edison showing social or musical-comedy dance performances, ranging from Annabelle (Moore) (1878–1961) twirling her skirts, in imitation of another dancer of the period, Loie Fuller (1862–1928), in *Annabelle Butterfly Dance* (1894) to the *Cake Walk* series (1897–1903). Edison also filmed well-known vaudeville stars, such as Dave Montgomery and Fred Stone (who played the Tin Man and the Scarecrow in the 1903 Broadway musical version of *The Wizard of Oz*), as examples of eccentric dance. Early narrative films set the pattern for using social dance to indicate period or social class. The first full-length extant films to feature dancers were both made in 1915: *The Whirl of Life*, starring and based on the lives of the ballroom dancers Irene (1893–1964) and Vernon Castle (1887–1918), integrated their specialty, the Castle walk, into the plot. *The Dumb Girl of Portici*, Lois Weber's version of the opera *Maisannello*, or *La Muette di Portici*, starring the great Russian ballerina Anna Pavlova (1881–1931), did the same with ballet.

In the 1920s feature films frequently used social dance to depict chronology. Present tense or contemporary

Fayard and Harold Nicholas in* Sun Valley Serenade *(H. Bruce Humberstone, 1941). ® ™ AND COPYRIGHT © 20TH CENTURY FOX FILM CORP./COURTESY EVERETT COLLECTION. REPRODUCED BY PERMISSION.

scenes were signaled by fast couple dances such as the Charleston or black bottom performed by dissolute youths. Films starring "It" girl Clara Bow (1905–1965) were enormously popular, and *Our Dancing Daughters* (1928) was the film that made Joan Crawford (1904–1977) a star. Slower contemporary social dances were used to show romantic situations. Dance as *mise-en-scène* was expanded to accommodate experiments with narrative structure. The past was signaled with historical movement, from the Denishawn troupe performing on the Babylon steps in *Intolerance*, to social dances from the minuet to the waltz. Directors relied on dance to signal shifts caused by their use of flashbacks, flash-forwards, and dream sequences. The contemporary, Amazon, and classical sequences in *Man, Woman, Marriage* (1921), staged by Marion Morgan, are memorable examples of period dance as atmosphere. A famous scene is the dance in a dirigible, developed by Theodore Kosloff (1882–

1956), LeRoy Prinz (1895–1983), and Cecil B. DeMille (1881–1959), in DeMille's *Madam Satan* (1930).

FROM MUSICALS TO MUSIC VIDEOS

Studios' early experiments with sound tended to imitate Broadway or Prologs, vaudeville shows at motion picture palaces. Among the featured dance acts were precision tap lines, ethnic (called "character") dances, adagio or exhibition ballroom work, and such eccentric work as rag doll dances. Examples of all four can be seen in *The King of Jazz* (1930), the finale of which features successive episodes of ethnic dancers representing immigrants as they march into an onscreen melting pot.

As Hollywood relaxed into sound technology, dance directors developed a new structure for dance-based routines. As exemplified by Busby Berkeley's films for Warner Bros., the routines opened on a traditional stage

NICHOLAS BROTHERS

Fayard Nicholas, b. Mobile, Alabama, 20 October 1914, d. 24 January 2006
Harold Nicholas, b. Winston-Salem, North Carolina, 27 March 1921, d. 3 July 2000

The extraordinary acrobatic dancing of the Nicholas Brothers enlivened musical films in the 1940s, and offscreen they were also considered one of the best tandem tap teams of the century with major careers in musical theater. The children of pit orchestra musicians, they were influenced by the up-tempo early jazz of Louis Armstrong and Fletcher Henderson. Both were coached by performers on the black vaudeville circuit who appeared at their parents' theater in Philadelphia. They adopted the tandem tap style, then epitomized by Buck and Bubbles, emphasizing synchronization of movements in complicated rhythms. They ended with "flash" sequences, including their signature leaps over each other in full, stretched-out side splits. They moved to New York and appeared in revues at Harlem's hottest nightclub, the Cotton Club, through the 1930s, where they were influenced by both the music and the personal style of Cotton Club orchestra leaders Cab Calloway and Duke Ellington.

Like Calloway and Ellington, they were featured in shorts, soundies, and early sound films, including Vitaphone shorts such as *Pie, Pie Blackbird* (1932), featuring the composer Eubie Blake, and the Eddie Cantor comedy *Kid Millions* (1934). Their Hollywood roles were sequences in feature films that could be cut for the segregated markets in the South. They worked with Cotton Club dance directors Nick Castle and Geneva Sawyer, who had relocated to Twentieth Century Fox for a series of seven backstage musicals featuring jazz. In each film the brothers added spatial elements to the tandem and flash dances. They enlivened their splits sequence in

Orchestra Wives (with the Glen Miller Orchestra, 1942) by adding runs up walls and flipping over themselves and each other. Their best-remembered variation is in the black all-star revue *Stormy Weather* (1943): in tribute to co-star Bill Robinson, whose specialty was tapping up and down staircases, the Nicholas Brothers restaged their signature moves down successive stairs.

They continued to tour with jazz ensembles, moving from the big band sound to bebop, and to appear on stage, notably in the musical *St. Louis Woman* in 1946. Harold Nicholas appeared as an actor in *Uptown Saturday Night* (1974) and other movie comedies. They received Kennedy Center honors in 1981 and are recognized as a major influence on later tap dancers such as Gregory Hines, Maurice Hines, and Savion Glover. The Nicholas Brothers, with the Copasetics and other greats of their generation, were featured in the documentary short *Tapdancin'* (1981) and the feature film *Tap* (1989), and are the subjects of the documentary *The Nicholas Brothers: We Sing and We Dance* (1992).

RECOMMENDED VIEWING
Pie, Pie Blackbird (1932), *Kid Millions* (1934), *The Big Broadcast of 1936* (1935), *Down Argentine Way* (1940), *Sun Valley Serenade* (1941), *Stormy Weather* (1943), *The Pirate* (1948)

FURTHER READING
Hill, Constance Valis. *Brotherhood in Rhythm: The Jazz Tap Dancing of the Nicholas Brothers.* New York: Oxford University Press, 2000.

Barbara Cohen-Stratyner

but expanded into 360-degree effects possible only on a soundstage. Berkeley's first feature films were Samuel Goldwyn vehicles for the comedian Eddie Cantor (1892–1964), such as *Roman Scandals* (1933). In 1933 he began his association with Warner Bros./First National with *42nd Street.* Based on a popular melodramatic novel about a dying director staging a musical during the Depression, the film switched the focus to Ruby Keeler (1909–1993) as a spunky understudy and

became a popular icon of the early sound era. Warner Bros. produced a cycle of comedies, featuring its contract character actors, singers, and dancers, about staging musicals during the Depression, including *Gold Diggers of 1933* (1933), with its Pig Latin "We're in the Money" opening, and *Footlight Parade* (1933). Apart from solos for Keeler, most of Berkeley's choreography is based on simple movements made by a large number of synchronized dancers, sometimes magnified by mirrors and cameras.

Most are based on social dances or on tap dancing but are done on staircases. Mirrors and reflective floor surfaces expanded black and white design schemes. All of Berkeley's work features his signature techniques—animation, stage scenes that open up to huge sets, and prismatic overhead camera shots.

Many of the Hollywood dance films of the 1930s and 1940s were film versions of popular modern-dress musicals, with dance sequences expanded rather than reimagined. The studios assigned their staff choreographers and arrangers to the task, and the prevailing Hollywood style determined what reached the screen. Operettas, made popular by the singing film stars Jeanette MacDonald (1903–1965) and Nelson Eddy (1901–1967), used social dance to set place and time.

Vestiges of vaudeville and Broadway dance remained in the large number of films with backstage settings or with visits to the theater or nightclub built into the plot. The most prevalent style derived from live theater performance was the retention of the proscenium orientation, with the action taking place as if on a stage and the camera standing in for the audience. Gene Kelly (1912–1996) never broke free of frontal performance but developed many experiments to vary the form, such as his duet with Hanna-Barbera's animated mouse Jerry in *Anchors Aweigh* (1945), choreographed by Kelly and Stanley Donen (b. 1924). In "The King Who Couldn't Dance," Kelly teaches the cartoon mouse to tap. The setting is curtained like a stage set, with the throne in dead center. Following the pattern of a tap duet, he demonstrates steps, and the mouse repeats the movements, gradually dancing alongside and finally with him, bouncing off Kelly's biceps.

A defining aspect of dance in films of the 1930s through 1950s was movement inspired by or growing out of walking. Many of Hermes Pan's (1909–1990) solos and duets for Fred Astaire (1899–1987) convey a naturalness by beginning with walking. Classic examples include the "Walking the Dog" and roller skating sequences in *Shall We Dance* (1937), and the stroll through Central Park with Cyd Charisse (b. 1921) that begins and ends "Dancing in the Dark" in *The Band Wagon* (1953). The most famous walking dance in film is performed by Gene Kelly to the title song in *Singin' in the Rain* (1952).

Royal Wedding (1951) includes a classic pedestrian prop dance and two dances possible only on a soundstage. In the first of two sequences danced onboard a ship, Astaire, one-half of a sister-brother dancing team, partners with a coat stand when his sister (Jane Powell) fails to show up for rehearsal. Their social dance number a few scenes later begins conventionally, but the performance is converted into acrobatics when the ship encounters a storm. They attempt to dance, but when the floor begins to tip their steps are turned into slides. Later in the film, choreographed by Nick Castle, Astaire is dancing alone in his hotel room when he begins to push off against the wall. This movement usually signals flips off the wall (as in Donald O'Connor's "Be a Clown" number in *Singin' in the Rain*), but instead, he taps his way up the wall and on to the ceiling. The magical effect was produced on a soundstage equipped with hydraulic lifts.

Other memorable examples of pedestrian dances in film include the "garbage can" found percussion trio in *It's Always Fair Weather* (1955), choreographed by Gene Kelly; the Olympic team exercisers who ignore Jane Russell singing "Isn't Anyone Here for Love?" in *Gentlemen Prefer Blondes* (1953), choreographed by Jack Cole (1911–1974); and the rhythmic sawing and log splitting performed by the frustrated brothers in *Seven Brides for Seven Brothers* (1954), choreographed by Michael Kidd (b. 1919).

Surrealism was a second strong influence on choreographers for films of the 1940s and 1950s, with Jack Cole and Eugene Loring (1911–1982) at the forefront. Many dances featured moves for separated parts of the body, such as Loring's orchestra dance for *The 5,000 Fingers of Dr. T.* (1953), written by Dr. Seuss. In Charles Walters's *Easter Parade* (1948), Ann Miller's (1923–2004) "Shaking the Blues Away" is famously accompanied by instrument-playing arms.

Broadway choreographers were only occasionally hired to reproduce their work. Agnes de Mille (1905–1993) did the stage and film versions of *Oklahoma!* (on Broadway from 1943, but not filmed until 1955), but not *Brigadoon* (1954), although both had dance sequences that were integral to the plot. *Oklahoma*'s dream ballet, "Laurey Makes Up Her Mind," had already influenced many film choreographers by 1955. The French postcards that the villain Jud keeps in his shack come to life in her imagination as symbols of sexual depravity. The blank faces and angular movements of the "Post Card Girls" inspired Bob Fosse (1927–1987). Many directors and choreographers have copied or adapted empty soundstage with abstract clouds painted on the cyclorama for their dream sequences, most notably the "Gotta Dance" scene in *Singin' in the Rain*. Michael Kidd reproduced on film his movements for two highly stylized shows—the Damon Runyon gamblers in *Guys and Dolls* (1955), and the comic strip come-to-life, *Li'l Abner* (1959). *The King and I* (1956) was filmed with Jerome Robbins's (1918–1998) "Siamese" dances intact, including the "Small House of Uncle Thomas" sequence. Robbins choreographed and co-directed *West Side Story* (1961), which scuttled the musical's dream ballets but kept the famous opening dance sequence.

The Nicholas Brothers and Gene Kelly perform "Be a Clown" in **The Pirate** *(Vincente Minnelli, 1948).* EVERETT COLLECTION. REPRODUCED BY PERMISSION.

Dance reemerged in Hollywood with the disco era, through popular films such as *Saturday Night Fever* (1977) and its many imitators, and the 1950s-era musical *Grease* (1978), choreographed by Patricia Birch. *The Wiz* (1978), choreographed by Louis Johnson (b. 1930), employed modern, tap, and jazz techniques, as well as club and break dancing around New York City locations. Dance was featured as atmosphere and plot material in *La Bohème* (1990), an Australian television production on which Baz Luhrmann (b. 1962) served as opera director, and *Strictly Ballroom* (1992) and *Moulin Rouge* (2001), directed by Luhrmann. The popular and critical successes of *Moulin Rouge* and Rob Marshall's (b. 1960) version of the Bob Fosse musical *Chicago* suggest that the musical is still a viable genre.

There have been feature films about dance as a profession since the silent era. Most, like Rouben Mamoulian's *Applause* (1929), include performance as well as backstage scenes. Ballet films tend to be highly melodramatic, among them Michael Powell and Emeric Pressburger's influential *The Red Shoes* (1948), in which a ballerina torn between love and art commits suicide. Ben Hecht's forgotten *Specter of the Rose* (1946), and *The Turning Point* (1977), directed by Herbert Ross (1927–2001), a former ballet dancer and choreographer, are equally obsessed with the emotional life of dancers. All three inspired their viewers to experience live performance. Similarly, art cinemas and university film societies made Soviet and French ballet films available in the 1960s and enlarged the audiences for touring ballet companies. Carlos Saura's Spanish collaborations with the flamenco choreographer Antonio Gades (1936–2004)—*Bodas de sangre* (1981), *Carmen* (1984), and *El Amor brujo* (1986)—achieved great popularity in the United States.

Fame (1980), based on New York City's High School of the Performing Arts, featured adolescents in

FRED ASTAIRE and GINGER ROGERS

Fred Astaire, b. Frederick Austerlitz, Omaha, Nebraska, 10 May 1899, d. 22 June 1987
Ginger Rogers, b. Independence, Missouri, 16 July 1911, d. 25 April 1995

Fred Astaire and Ginger Rogers epitomized exhibition ballroom dance in film and beyond. Both dancers had stage careers before their first film pairing. Astaire and his sister Adele began in vaudeville as children, reaching Broadway as specialty dancers in *Over the Top* (1917). Their reputations grew in New York and London with roles in the Gerhswins' *Lady, Be Good* (1925) and *Funny Face* (1927), *The Bandwagon* (1931), and many other musicals and revues. Adele retired in 1932. Rogers reached Broadway via Charleston competitions, vaudeville, and stints as a band singer. In Hollywood, she had roles that combined comedy and tap dancing in Busby Berkeley's *42nd Street* and *Gold Diggers of 1933*.

They were playing secondary comic roles when they were paired by Dave Gould for "The Carioca" number in the RKO musical *Flying Down to Rio* (1933). Their subsequent collaborations, staged by Hermes Pan, who had been Gould's assistant, were all starring roles. The classic Astaire and Rogers films were plotted musicals with songs by Broadway's greatest songwriters—*The Gay Divorcee*, with songs by Cole Porter (1934); *Top Hat* (1935), *Follow the Fleet* (1936), and *Carefree* (1938), by Irving Berlin; *Roberta* (1935) and *Swing Time* (1936), by Jerome Kern; and *Shall We Dance* (1937), by George and Ira Gershwin. Each accommodated at least one newly invented social dance, one competitive tap routine, and one love duet, as well as a tap solo for Astaire. Pan's romantic duets began simply, often with rhythmic walking, and progressed through flowing movements to lifts and dips, before returning to a quiet ending. Astaire and Rogers were cast in the title roles in *The Story of Vernon and Irene Castle* (1939), RKO's tribute to the pre–World War I ballroom dancers. The RKO publicity machine promoted them, the films, the songs, and ballroom dances extracted from the musicals.

Although they reunited for the backstage musical *The Barkleys of Broadway* (1949), their dance partnership ended in 1939. Rogers went on to star in comedy roles for MGM and Twentieth Century Fox; Astaire kept dancing in film and on television, primarily to Pan's choreography. He was able to adapt his expertise to each partner—in tap with Eleanor Powell, languorous ballroom with Rita Hayworth and Cyd Charisse, and musical comedy with Judy Garland, Jane Powell, and Leslie Caron. For many, his tap solos with props were the highlight of the films. They began with objects setting a rhythm, such as the ship's engine in "Slap That Bass" in *Shall We Dance*. Although Astaire is recognized as one of the greatest of American dancers, as a popular quip has it, "Ginger Rogers did everything that Fred Astaire did, but backwards and in high heels."

RECOMMENDED VIEWING

Flying Down to Rio (1933), *The Gay Divorcee* (1934), *Top Hat* (1935), *Roberta* (1935), *Follow the Fleet* (1936), *Swing Time* (1936), *Shall We Dance* (1937), *Carefree* (1938), *The Story of Vernon and Irene Castle* (1939), *The Barkleys of Broadway* (1949)

FURTHER READING

Astaire, Fred. *Steps in Time*. New York: Perennial Library, 1987.

Croce, Arlene. *The Fred Astaire and Ginger Rogers Book*. New York: Vintage Books, 1977.

Gallafent, Edward. *Astaire & Rogers*. New York: Columbia University Press, 2002.

Barbara Cohen-Stratyner

ballet, modern, and jazz dance training. The modern dancer Louis Falco (1942–1993) staged the famous "improvised" sequences, in which the characters groove at lunchtime and spill onto the street. Dance (social and modern) has frequently been used as a language of self-expression in such popular films as *Flashdance* (1983) about a welder who wants to dance; *Voices* (1979), about a deaf woman who wants to dance; and *Footloose* (1984), about a teen who wants his town to dance.

In the 1980s Music Television (MTV), and following it, VH1 and Black Entertainment Television (BET), popularized music videos as an integral part of promoting recorded popular music. Many were filmed and spliced performances, relying heavily on editing, but

Fred Astaire and Ginger Rogers in* Swing Time *(George Stevens, 1936). EVERETT COLLECTION. REPRODUCED BY PERMISSION.

some were staged and choreographed. Some refer clearly to film choreography, such as Madonna's "Material Girl" (1984) music video, an adaptation of Cole's staging of "Diamonds Are a Girl's Best Friend" from *Gentlemen Prefer Blondes*, complete with human chandelier. Memorable music videos as dance include the robotic, stylized "Video Killed the Radio Star," and Michael Jackson's (b. 1958) take on a *West Side Story*–like gang war in "Beat It" (1982). Jackson's "moon walk" excited his teen fans and reminded their elders of the African American tap greats who developed such eccentric steps. Other directors worked with seemingly spontaneous dance steps, adapted from break dancing, voguing, and hip-hop, including Prince's "Purple Rain" (1984). The recognizable editing style associated with music videos, fast cross-cutting between the performance and dance scenes, has spread to influence feature films as well as television.

DANCE AS FILM

The few extant examples of collaborations between film and dance from the early twentieth century come from the French avant-garde and include films made in Paris by Loie Fuller, considered a forerunner of modern dance and who was also a pioneer in the use of lighting design. French experimental filmmakers considered ballet to be a partner of animation, as in Fernand Léger's *Ballet mécanique* (1924). The Dadaist work for Les Ballets Suedois, *Relâche* (1924), included René Clair's film *Entr'acte* in the live performance. Serge Diaghilev's Ballets Russes commissioned *Ode* (1928), with choreography by Leonide Massine, designs by Pavel Tchelitchev, and projections by Pierre Charbonneau. It is likely that Soviet Constructivist filmmakers also worked with dance, but if so no such work has been found. Among several instances of photographers, filmmakers, and dancers working together, Mura Dehn and Roger Pryor Dodge filmed concerts of jazz dance in the late 1930s. Gjon Mili, best known as a *LIFE* magazine still photographer, filmed concerts in the early 1940s, releasing *Jammin' the Blues* in 1944.

Maya Deren (1917–1961) and Alexander Hammid (1907–2004) are generally considered the first major proponents of "cinedance," or dance as film. Deren's first film, *Meshes of the Afternoon* (1943), shows her walking on a new surface with each step. Her *A Study in Choreography for Camera* (1945), a four-minute film of Talley Beatty dancing, contains one effect still cited as influential for generations of filmmakers: Deren edited Beatty's side leap, which had been filmed in a variety of backgrounds, so that it seemed to stretch from exterior to interior settings. Later, Shirley Clarke (1919–1997) worked with modern dancers, cross-cutting between their

movements and evocative nature images. Contemporary figures include Doris Chase and Amy Greenfield, best known for her *Antigone/Rites of Passion* (1991).

The experimental generation of modern dance, led by the choreographer Merce Cunningham (b. 1919) and the composer John Cage (1912–1992), combined film and choreography in performance. Pioneering work in early video was done by Nam June Paik (1932–2006). The choreographers Trisha Brown, Carolee Schneeman, and Joan Jonas combined the genres, and Yvonne Rainer worked separately in each. Many events combined live task dances in environments that included video or film projection, such as Elaine Summers's *Walking Dance for Any Number* (1965). The Nine Evenings of Theater and Engineering, organized by RCA engineer Billy Kluver, were collaborations among choreographers, composers, and filmmakers with technology to enable live creation and viewing of performance on film. Cunningham himself made scores of films and videos beginning in the 1950s, collaborating with Paik, Stan VanDerBeek, Elliot Caplan, and Charles Atlas. The abstract expressionist painter Ed Emshwiller (1926–1990) made stop-motion films with Alwin Nikolais (1910–1993), a painter as well as a choreographer who manipulated shapes and color. Their *Fusion* (1967) was both a dance work performed in front of film and a separate film.

Ballet as film has never developed in the United States but is a respected medium in Canada and Europe. The integration of film into ballet was popularly known only in the late 1960s, when it was also used by experimental opera directors such as Frank Carsaro. The best-known American work is Robert Joffrey's psychedelic *Astarte*, which was featured on the cover of *Newsweek* on 15 March 1968. The Canadian filmmaker Norman McLaren (1914–1987) has made a number of important cinedance films, including *Pas de deux* (1968), *Ballet Adagio* (1972), and *Narcissus* (1983).

The postmodern generation has worked in both film and video but views the latter as a more flexible medium. Performances often use projections or screens as part of the environment for dance, as in Trisha Brown's *Set and Reset* (1983), with films and screens by Robert Rauschenberg. The choreographer Bill T. Jones's controversial *Still/Here* (1994) combined dancers with personal narratives of disease viewed on movable monitors. The composer/choreographer Meredith Monk (b. 1942) has included film in her cantatas, such as *Quarry*, and has made films that stand on their own, most prominently *Book of Days* (1988) and several documentaries about her choreography. Eiko & Koma, Kai Takei, and other butoh-influenced choreographers use film to emphasize the slow pace of movement in their work. At the other extreme, Elizabeth Streb's collaborations with Michael

Schwartz made visual sense of her impossibly fast dynamics. Many of the experiments were commissioned by and shown on *Alive from Off Center* (PBS, 1985–1994).

FILM AS DOCUMENTATION OF DANCE

The frustratingly ephemeral nature of dance has remained a problem despite the development of choreographic notation systems. Film, and later videotape, has provided a form of visual documentation and preservation for dance. In the 1910s and 1920s, the mechanical piano firm Ampico developed instructional films for "name" dancers and choreographers, such as Anna Pavlova, the Broadway dance director Ned Wayburn (1874–1942), and the concert dancers Ruth St. Denis (1878–1968) and Ted Shawn (as Denishawn).

Most early filming was done by ethnographers or individual choreographers for their own use. Early attempts by institutions to document dance include Carol Lynn's 8mm films, made at Ted Shawn's summer workshop, Jacob's Pillow, in Becket, Massachusetts, and Helen Priest Rogers's films, made at the American Dance Festival. These silent films have been restored by the Jerome Robbins Dance Division of the New York Public Library for the Performing Arts, whose projects endeavor to match music exactly to the movements. Ethnographers have used film to document nonchoreographed traditional, indigenous, and popular dance forms. Major figures have connected the worlds of film and ethnography, including the anthropologists/choreographers Katherine Dunham and Pearl Primus and the filmmaker Maya Deren. Rhoda Grauer, a pioneering producer of dance on television, has recently focused on films documenting the traditional arts of Indonesia. Her *Libraries on Fire: When an Elder Dies, a Book Burns* series includes the portrait of an elderly Topeng performer in *Rasinah: The Enchanted Mask* (2005).

Mura Dehn (1902–1987) pioneered documentation of African American social dance in her *The Spirit Moves* films. Collaborating with dancers and historians, she has created films about the Savoy Ballroom swing dancers, rock and roll moves, and break dancing. Documentaries on underground genres within African American social dance have received wide distribution and praise, including Jennie Livingston's *Paris Is Burning* (1990), on voguing; Sally Sommer and Michael Schwartz's project *Goin' ta Work* (released as *Check Your Body at the Door*, 1994), on club dancing; Jon Reiss's *Better Living through Circuitry* (1999), on raves; and David LaChapelle's *Krumped* (short, 2004) and *Rize* (2005), on the Los Angeles dance movement called krump.

With the development of video technology, documentation has become common. Character Generators, Inc. (Michael Schwartz and Mark Robison) and Studio D (Dennis Diamond) use single- and multiple-camera shoots to document dance and performance art for choreographers and historians. The Jerome Robbins Dance Division of the New York Public Library for the Performing Arts is the depository of record for most dance documentation. Its own projects and those of the Dance Heritage Coalition have identified collections throughout North America and developed standards for cataloging and preservation.

SEE ALSO *Choreography; Musicals*

FURTHER READING

Arnheim, Rudolf. *Film as Art.* Berkeley: University of California Press, 1957.

Dance Perspectives. "Cine Dance" issue, no. 30 (Summer 1967).

Dodds, Sherill. *Dance on Screen: Genres and Media from Hollywood to Experimental Art.* New York: Palgrave, 2001.

Heider, Karl G. *Ethnographic Film.* Austin: University of Texas Press, 1976.

Johnson, Catherine, and Allegra Fuller Snyder. *Securing Our Dance Heritage.* Washington, DC: Council for Library and Information Resources, 1999.

Snyder, Allegra Fuller. *Dance Films: A Study of Choreo-Cinema.* Albany: State University of New York Press, 1973.

Barbara Cohen-Stratyner

DENMARK

For a thousand years, Denmark has been an independent kingdom. Since 1849 it has been ruled with a democratic constitution and for over a century has enjoyed a generally peaceful history. Perhaps this history explains why Danish cinema in general is characterized by an atmosphere of jovial, often self-ironic humor and provincial calm. Denmark has been a film nation since the beginning of film history in the 1890s, and for some years around 1910, the Danish film industry was among the leading in Europe. This position, however, did not last long and after World War I, the impact of Danish cinema declined.

With the arrival of sound in Denmark in 1931, Danish film, soon dominated by popular comedies, became a profitable national business. However, with the arrival of television in the 1950s, cinema attendance declined, and in the 1960s the state began supporting the production of artistic films, since 1972 through The Danish Film Institute. Since the mid-1990s, Denmark has won a new position in world cinema, rather surprising for a nation with a population of 5.4 million and a yearly output of around twenty-five feature films (in all, about 1,000 Danish feature films have been produced since 1930). In particular, a groundbreaking filmmaker like Lars von Trier and his initiative, Dogma 95, have received international attention.

THE GOLDEN AGE AND AFTER

Film came to Denmark in 1896 when the first short films (probably British) were presented in a pavilion on the City Square of Copenhagen. Since December 1897 Danish productions, made by photographer Peter Elfelt

(1866–1931), were also shown. The first film pioneer in Denmark, he made more than one hundred short films between 1897–1907—on sport, royalty, city life, and public events in the style of Auguste and Louis Lumière.

The first important Danish film production company was Nordisk Films Kompagni (now: Nordisk Film), established in 1906 by Ole Olsen. Nordisk, which has been a major player in Danish media for a century, took the lead with short, dramatic films, such as *Løvejagten* (*Lion Hunt*, 1907), directed by house director Viggo Larsen (1880–1957), a former army sergeant. Beginning in 1910 the longer feature films appeared. The first, Alfred Cohn's *Den hvide Slavehandel* (*The White Slave Traffic*, 1910) for Fotorama, was immediately plagiarized by Nordisk under the same title, with August Blom (1869–1947) as director. The small company Kosmorama made Urban Gad's (1879–1947) *Afgrunden* (*The Abyss*, 1910), in which Asta Nielsen (1881–1972) plays a young woman who leaves her sensible fiancé for a reckless circus artist, whom she murders when he betrays her. Nielsen and husband Gad soon left for Germany where Nielsen, in a diversity of roles, became one of the greatest European stars because of her psychological acting style.

During the silent years Denmark produced about 1,600 fictional films (features and shorts) and over 1,000 nonfiction films, although only about 250 are extant. In the Golden Age of Danish Cinema (circa 1908–1913) Danish films benefited from the internationalism of the silent era and were seen all over Europe, especially melodramas with a social and erotic theme, such as *The Abyss* and in Blom's *Ved Fængslets Port* (*At the Prison Gates*, 1911), starring Valdemar Psilander

(1884–1917), the leading male star, and sensational films like the circus drama *De fire Djævle* (*The Four Devils*, 1911). A major artist and the most innovative figure in early Danish silent cinema was Benjamin Christensen (1879–1959). His spy story *Det hemmelighedsfulde X* (*The Mysterious X*, 1914) and the social crime story *Hævnens Nat* (*Night of Revenge*, 1916) explored new visual styles. Although the cinematic essay *Häxan* (*Witchcraft Through the Ages*, 1922), financed in Sweden, was a commercial failure, it is one of the most original and daring silent films in world cinema.

Nordisk's biggest production was Blom's costly and impressive *Atlantis* (1913), inspired by the Titanic disaster, which was a commercial disappointment. During World War I when Denmark was neutral, Nordisk made pacifist dramas, for example, the science fiction film *Himmelskibet* (*A Ship to Heaven*, 1917). Although Nordisk had a strong position in Germany, the Berlin branch was swallowed up in 1917 when the German military decided to nationalize the film industry with the Ufa (Universum Film Aktiengesellschaft). This restructuring contributed to the decline of Nordisk, which then concentrated on such costly productions as Carl Dreyer's (1889–1968) first films and A. W. Sandberg's literary adaptations of novels by Charles Dickens, including *Store Forventninger* (*Great Expectations*) and *David Copperfield* (both 1922), but without the expected international success. Only the new company, Palladium, established in Denmark in 1922, enjoyed international success with the comic team Fyrtaarnet og Bivognen (literally, the Lighthouse and the Sidecar), known abroad as Pat and Patachon (their actual names were Carl Schenstrøm [1881–1942] and Harald Madsen [1890–1949]).

POPULAR CINEMA FOR A SMALL NATION

Already in 1923 the Danish engineers Axel Petersen and Arnold Poulsen had presented their sound system. Nordisk went into liquidation in 1928 but was re-established in 1929 with the new sound system. The first feature film with Danish dialogue was *Præsten i Vejlby* (*The Vicar of Vejlby*, 1931), based on a literary classic and directed by George Schnéevoigt. In the 1930s, Denmark, too, was marked by depression and unemployment, but perhaps for that reason the dominating film genre was the jovial "folk comedy"—a light comedy with songs, and marked by an unfailing optimism—whose leading stars were Marguerite Viby (1909–2001) and Ib Schønberg. Outside the mainstream, Poul Henningsen (1894–1967) created *Danmark* (*Denmark*, 1935), the seminal and controversial work of the new Danish documentary film, a description of Denmark in a lyrical style

that anticipated that of the British documentary *Night Mail* (1936).

The Nazi German occupation of Denmark from 1940 to 1945 meant restrictions for Danish film as well as for the society in general. There was soon a ban on showing American and British films in Danish movie theaters, and censorship did not allow the realities of the Occupation to be shown in Danish films. Instead, there was a demonstrative change to other darker genres, such as Danish noir films influenced by French poetic realism. In addition to sophisticated entertainment, there existed heritage films that presented nostalgic visions of a lost Denmark. After a long hiatus, Dreyer returned with the witch hunt drama, *Vredens Dag* (*Day of Wrath*, 1943), set in Denmark in the 1600s. With its story of torture and persecution, it was generally understood as an implicit commentary on the German Occupation. In addition, a short documentary by Hagen Hasselbalch (1915–1997), *Kornet er i Fare* (*The Harvest Is in Danger*, 1945), became famous because it appeared to be an informational film about agricultural pest control but clearly was a witty allegory about the Nazi invaders.

A few months after the end of the Occupation, the first films about the Danish Resistance appeared, and soon thereafter, a realistic breakthrough in Danish cinema came about with films about everyday life and social problems that somewhat resembled Italian neorealistic films. Most important were Bjarne Henning-Jensen's *Ditte Menneskebarn* (*Ditte, Child of Man*, 1946) and Johan Jacobsen's *Soldaten og Jenny* (*Jenny and the Soldier*, 1947). In the 1950s, a number of didactic films warning the nation about alcoholism and juvenile crime appeared, but generally the 1950s meant a return to the popular, cosy style of prewar Denmark. *Die røde heste* (*The Red Horses*, 1950), based on a novel dealing with an idyllic rural Denmark that probably never existed, by Morten Korch, a popular kitsch writer, was seen by over 60 percent of the population. The production company, ASA, made a whole series of successful Korch films (1950–1967) and also a series of more modern comedies about suburban life, *Far til fire* (*Father of Four*, 1953–1961), based on a comic strip about a widowed father with four children. Most of ASA's films were directed by Alice O'Fredericks (1900–1968), who had started at Palladium in the 1930s and probably is the only woman director in world cinema who for several decades was a major force in mainstream cinema. Her example may have been the inspiration for the relatively large number of female directors in Danish cinema, among them Astrid Henning-Jensen (1914–2002), who made *Palle alene i verden* (*Palle Alone in the World*, 1949), the seminal work of the Danish children's film tradition, and later Susanne Bier (b. 1960) and Lone Scherfig (b. 1959). Nordisk released the first Danish feature film in color, Erik

CARL THEODOR DREYER
b. Copenhagen, Denmark, 3 February 1889, d. 20 March 1968

Carl Dreyer is the great Danish auteur, one of the masters of the cinema who created his own dark vision of human suffering and sacrifice. However, his increasingly formalistic style and austere universe placed him very far from mainstream Danish cinema. Dreyer's work is characterized by an intense formalism with carefully planned shots and by an uncompromising search for the inner life behind the surface of reality.

He started as a balloonist and journalist and came by coincidence into films in 1912. He wrote a number of manuscripts for Nordisk Film and also worked as editor. After his first film, the melodrama *Præsidenten* (*The President*, 1919), he made the ambitious *Blade af Satans Bog* (*Leaves Out of the Book of Satan*, 1920), four episodes about Satan's work in four different ages inspired by D. W. Griffith's *Intolerance* (1918). During the next decade he worked in several countries. In Norway he shot a Swedish film, *Prästänkan* (*The Witch Woman*, 1920), a bittersweet comedy about a young man who has to marry the old widow in order to get the job as parson. In Germany he made *Die Gezeichneten* (*Love One Another*, 1922), a love story set in Czarist Russia against the background of pogroms, and *Mikaël* (*Chained*, 1924) about a master painter (played by Benjamin Christensen) who becomes jealous when his young protégé falls in love with a countess.

In Denmark he made the realistic comedy *Du skal ære din Hustru* (*Master of the House*, 1925), about a father and husband whose tyrannical attitude is changed when his old nanny arrives. Its success led to an invitation to visit France, where he made *La Passion de Jeanne d'Arc* (*The Passion of Joan of Arc*, 1928), one of the uncontested classics of world cinema. For this gripping presentation of the trial and execution of Joan of Arc, he developed a new ascetic style of closeups of an almost transcendental intensity. After directing the poetic horror story *Vampyr: Der Traum des Allan Grey* (*The Vampire*, 1932), he returned to Denmark. Several international projects were aborted and it was not until 1943, during the German Occupation, that he again made a feature film, the witch-hunt drama *Vredens Dag* (*Day of Wrath*, 1943).

After World War II, he wrote the manuscript for a film about Jesus and, for the rest of his life, tried untiringly but unsuccessfully to secure financing for it. He made two more films, *Ordet* (*The Word*, 1955), based on a play by Kaj Munk about a young woman who dies giving birth but miraculously is called back to life by her disturbed brother-in-law, and the spare and slow-moving melodrama *Gertrud* (1964), the story of a woman doomed to solitude because the men in her life are unwilling to sacrifice work and career for love.

Dreyer's personal background is a strange drama. His Swedish mother, probably made pregnant by her Danish master at an estate in southern Sweden, put him up for adoption in Denmark and died soon after. In his work, Dreyer, born Nilsson, constantly circles around the women suppressed in a man's world.

RECOMMENDED VIEWING
Prästänkan (*The Witch Woman*, 1920), *Blade af Satans Bog* (*Leaves Out of the Book of Satan*, 1921), *Mikaël* (*Chained*, 1924), *La Passion de Jeanne d'Arc* (*The Passion of Joan of Arc*, 1928), *Vampyr: Der Traum des Allan Grey* (*The Vampire*, 1932), *Vreden Dag* (*Day of Wrath*, 1943), *Ordet* (*The Word*, 1955), *Gertrud* (1964)

FURTHER READING
Bordwell, David. *The Films of Carl-Theodor Dreyer*. Berkeley: University of California Press, 1981.

Dreyer, Carl. *Dreyer in Double Reflection*. Translated by Donald Skoller. New York: Dutton, 1973.

Drum, Jean, and Dale D. Drum. *My Only Great Passion: The Life and Films of Carl Th. Dreyer*. Lanhan, MD: Scarecrow, 2000.

Milne, Tom. *The Cinema of Carl Dreyer*. New York: A. S. Barnes and London: Zwemmer, 1971.

Schrader, Paul. *Transcendental Style in Film: Ozu, Bresson, Dreyer*. Berkeley: University of California Press, 1972.

Peter Schepelern

Balling's (1924–2005) *Kispus* (1956), a romantic comedy set in the fashion world. Outside all the typical trends and traditions is Dreyer's religious drama *Ordet* (*The Word*, 1955), the only one of his films to enjoy general popularity with both Danish and international audiences (it earned a Golden Lion at the Venice Film Festival).

Carl Theodore Dreyer. EVERETT COLLECTION. REPRODUCED BY PERMISSION.

The 1960s was marked by the drastic decline in cinema attendance—from 1950 through 1970 admissions fell from 52 million to 23 million people—due to the arrival of TV (Danmarks Radio started regular TV broadcasting in 1951, and was a monopoly until 1988). This decrease led to new film legislation in 1965 in which state support for the production of artistic films was introduced. In the long period when movie theaters were a very lucrative business, Denmark had a licensing system by which having a license was a precondition to running a movie theater and was given as a special reward to well-merited artists (such as Christensen and Dreyer) or to production companies that produced culturally valuable films. However, the decrease in cinema attendance led to the deregulation of cinema exhibition in 1972.

Overall, European cinema gained cultural respectability during the 1960s. New artistic movements flourished—most importantly, the French New Wave and modernist films by Fellini and Antonioni. In Denmark the 1960s became a transitional period: groundbreaking New Wave films, such as Palle Kjærulff-Schmidt's *Weekend* (1962), about disillusion among couples in their thirties, written by the versatile writer Klaus Rifbjerg, and

modernist works, such as Henning Carlsen's *Sult* (*Hunger*, 1966), based on Knut Hamsun's novel about a starving writer in Kristiania (now Oslo) of the 1890s, appeared alongside the ever-popular folk comedy. Of particular note is Balling's *Olsen-banden* (*The Olsen Gang*, 1968–1981) series of thirteen films, in which the population recognized itself in the unsuccessful trio of petit bourgeois criminals who, guided by their leader Egon, are always involved in fantastic heists that inevitably go wrong. As had been his practice throughout his career, Dreyer produced a film that went completely against the grain of contemporary taste, the melodrama *Gertrud* (1964), his last work.

EROTICISM AND HUMANISTIC REALISM

In 1967 Denmark probably was the first country in the world to legalize literary pornography and in 1969 pictorial pornography for adults. The result was a short but profitable wave of erotic films that made Denmark famous as a liberal country. Palladium, the producer of *Gertrud*, started a series of erotic comedies. These so-called bedside comedies can hardly be described as pornographic, but rather as a combination of popular comedy and sex. Hugely profitable for some years, they vanished when, after *Deep Throat* (1972) and other hardcore films, the United States became the world's leading producer of pornographic material.

The 1970s became a period of diversity. The erotic films and the popular *Olsen Gang* comedies flourished and with the establishment in 1972 of The Danish Film Institute, art films gained support. A Danish Film School had been established in 1966 and a new generation appeared, the most original of whom was the documentarist Jørgen Leth. The state favored films for children and young adults (25% of the subsidy must be used on this category), resulting in a special trend. Such films as Nils Malmros's (b. 1944) *Drenge* (*Boys*, 1977), Søren Kragh-Jacobsen's (b. 1947) *Vil du se min smukke navle?* (*Wanna See My Beautiful Navel?*, 1978), Bille August's (b. 1948) *Honning Måne* (*Honeymoon*, 1978), and Morten Arnfred's (b. 1945) *Johnny Larsen* (1979) describe the vulnerable, marginalized young people, presented in undramatic, low-key stories with a melancholy atmosphere. This humanistic realism could be seen as related to the Danish literary tradition for focusing on the weak dreamer and reluctant antihero.

The tendency continued in the 1980s with masterpieces like Malmros's *Kundskabens Træ* (*Tree of Knowledge*, 1981), about desire and disillusion among school children, and Kragh-Jacobsen's children's fable *Gummi-Tarzan* (*Rubber Tarzan*, 1981). The most famous films of the period, however, were the two Academy Award® winners, Gabriel Axel's *Babettes*

Thorkild Roose (left), Preben Lerdoff, and Lisbeth Movin in Carl Dreyer's **Vredens Dag** *(*Day of Wrath, *1946).* EVERETT COLLECTION. REPRODUCED BY PERMISSION.

gæstebud (*Babette's Feast*, 1987), a conventional adaptation of an Isak Dinesen (Karen Blixen) story about an exiled French cook in the late 1800s who wins a fortune and spends all the money making a dinner so she can once again show provincial Denmark her art, and August's moving *Pelle erobreren* (*Pelle the Conqueror*, 1987), based on Martin Andersen Nexø's classical novel about a boy's childhood among poor farm workers in the late 1800s.

State support for film production had started as support for film art, but during the 1970s and 1980s it became increasingly clear that all types of film needed state support if Danish film production were to survive. Danish movie theaters, which numbered 462 in 1960, 180 (with 347 screens) in 1990, and 166 theatres (379 screens) in 2003, depended on Danish films with popular appeal. In 1989 a new support system—the so-called 50/50 system, now the 60/40 system—was established, which, with some restrictions, gave 50 percent of the funding

(yet only up to 3.4 million Danish kroner), later 60 percent and up to 5 million Danish kroner, if the company could provide the rest, on the condition that the film could be expected to have broad appeal (approximately 175,000 admissions). This support created a new wave of popular comedies, and especially successful in the domestic market were films that imitated the style of popular family films from the 1950s and 1960s, such as *Krummerne* (*The Crumbs*, 1991) and sequels.

A new tendency appeared with Ole Bornedal's *Nattevagten* (1994, remade in the United States as *Nightwatch*, 1997). Breaking with humanistic realism, it presented an effective horror plot with splatter and suspense totally foreign to Danish traditions. Where the unwritten rule of artistic Danish cinema was always to keep a distance from Hollywood mainstream genres, *Nattevagten* faced the challenge. The film was a refreshing landmark in new Danish cinema and was followed by such other mainstream films as Bier's comedy *Den eneste* ene (*The One and Only*, 1999), which was hugely successful with the Danish audience. It was not the traditional "folk comedy" or family entertainment, but a romantic comedy in the style of Mike Newell's *Four Weddings and a Funeral* (1994).

LARS VON TRIER'S KINGDOM

Outside of all these trends stood the young Lars von Trier (b. 1956), who introduced his own personal style and original universe with the trilogy *The Element of Crime* (1984), *Epidemic* (1987), and *Europa* (*Zentropa*, 1991), which presented a flamboyant look in a postmodern style, influenced by Dreyer and Andrei Tarkovsky, of an apocalyptic Europe in the past, present, and future. Trier is also the main reason, though not the only one, that Denmark won a new position in world cinema since the mid-1990s.

It was also Trier who was behind the other important trend, Dogma 95. It started with a manifesto published by Lars von Trier with young Thomas Vinterberg (b. 1969) as co-signatory in March 1995. During the shooting of the TV serial *Riget* (*The Kingdom*, 1994; part two, 1997), Trier realized that it was possible to ignore the normal technical standards and cinematic rules when working with a strong story and fascinating characters. He had always believed in creative development through obstructions. On this basis he came up with a set of rules that prescribe that the films should take place "here and now," that all shooting should take place on location with no added props, that there should always be direct sound, that the camera should always be hand-held, and that there should be no artificial lighting, no optical work or superficial action, and no crediting of the director! Dogma was meant as a "rescue operation," an anti-illusion and anti-Hollywood initiative, in which the director swears "to force the truth out of my characters and settings."

When all cosmetics and effects are banished, story and character are left. This method allows for the actors to develop their characters. The first Dogma 95 films—Vinterberg's *Festen* (*The Celebration*) and Trier's *The Idiots*—came out in 1998, followed by Kragh-Jacobsen's *Mifunes sidste sang* (*Mifune's Last Song*, 1999) and Scherfig's *Italiensk for begyndere* (*Italian for Beginners*, 2000). The first Dogma films received prizes and much international attention, especially *The Celebration*, an incest drama, and *Idioterne* (*The Idiots* 1998), about a group of young people who pretend to be retarded in order to "reach their inner idiot." The Dogma films have continued to add new energy to Danish cinema, although twenty or so foreign Dogma films generally have been less interesting.

Before *The Idiots* Trier made his international breakthrough with *Breaking the Waves* (1996), a bizarre religious melodrama about a young Scottish woman who believes that her sexual martyrdom and death will make God cure her disabled husband. The miracle ending has reminiscences of Dreyer's *Ordet*. The film, internationally co-financed like most of his later work, was dominated by a hand-held camera style and Emily Watson's intense acting. Trier continued with the theme of the self-sacrificing woman in *Dancer in the Dark* (2000), in which Icelandic singer Björk, who also wrote the music, plays a Czech woman who must go to the gallows to save her son from blindness. It, too, is a simple and highly emotional fable, but also a groundbreaking experiment with the musical genre. In *Dogville* (2003), the first part of a projected American trilogy, Trier continued his fearless attempts to find different approaches. In this film, Grace (Nicole Kidman), who has run away from pursuers, finds shelter in a small American mountain village in 1933; first she is kindly received, but gradually there is a change of attitude and she is suppressed and abused. Contrary to the earlier Trier heroines, she fights back. A didactic and ironic fable about power and morality, the film is perhaps most striking for its Brechtian formalism, taking place on an almost bare stage with sets only outlined and dominated by a narrator's voice-over. The story about Grace continued with *Manderlay* (2005), in which Grace takes over an estate in the Deep South where slavery has been maintained. For Trier, an important intention behind the Dogma concept was to force himself out of routines and habits, and he continued this general method in the highly original *De fem benspænd* (*The Five Obstructions*, 2003). Here he challenges senior colleague Jørgern Leth to remake one of his early experimental films according to Trier's whimsical instructions.

In more mainstream Danish cinema, there has been considerable national success with realistic stories about everyday life, typically about couples and infidelity, parents and children, as in Bier's Dogma film *Elsker dig for evigt* (*Open Hearts*, 2002). Also popular have been bittersweet buddy movies that continue the typical Danish taste for stories about jovial, small-time crooks, such as *Blinkende lygter* (*Flickering Lights*, 2000), directed by Anders Thomas Jensen (b. 1972), who won an Academy Award® for the short *Valgaften* (*Election Night*, 1998). In the new generation the most promising art film talent is Christoffer Boe (b. 1974), who directed the subtle drama of the eternal triangle, *Reconstruction* (2003), about the illusions of love and reality.

FAR FROM HOME

Since the 1920s American films have dominated Danish movie theaters. In the last fifteen years of the twentieth century, there has been a tendency in most European countries for Hollywood blockbusters to dominate the movie theaters (55–60%), but the national films make up a relatively large percentage of the box office as well. In Denmark in the 1990s, 10 or 15 Danish films represented 30 percent of the box office. The losers are clearly films from other European countries, which accounted for only 10 percent. Of the 25 most often seen films in Danish cinemas between 1976 and 2004, 13 were from the United States, 11 from Denmark, and only one (a James Bond film) from another country.

For a small country, it is especially important to preserve the national culture and language, but it is also tempting to try one's luck in the international film world. Nielsen, Dreyer, and Christensen all went abroad to international careers during the silent years. Other Danes who went away to international careers are actors Jean Hersholt (1886–1956), who was seen in early Hollywood films, including Erik von Stroheim's *Greed* (1924); Torben Meyer, who is most remembered for *Judgment at Nuremberg* (1961); Brigitte Nielsen for *Red Sonya* (1985); and Connie Nielsen for *Gladiator* (2000).

In addition, August has produced international films, among them *The House of the Spirits* (1993), based on Isabel Allende's novel of the same title. In the twenty-first century, many Danish directors have made Danish films in English, for example, nearly all of Trier's films, as well as Vinterberg's *It's All About Love* (2002) and *Dear Wendy* (2005), Bornedal's *I Am Dina* (2002), and

Scherfig's *Wilbur Wants to Kill Himself* (2003). However, often the result is that the filmmakers lose the Danish public without attracting a large international audience, for while the Danes go to the cinema to find entertainment and excitement, they also desire to see themselves and their own world portrayed on the screen.

SEE ALSO *National Cinema*

FURTHER READING

Cowie, Peter. *Scandinavian Cinema: A Survey of Films and Filmmakers of Denmark, Finland, Iceland, Norway, and Sweden.* London: Tantivy, 1992.

Hjort, Mette. *Small Nation, Global Cinema: The New Danish Cinema.* Minneapolis: University of Minnesota Press, 2005.

Hjort, Mette, and Ib Bondebjerg, eds. *The Danish Directors: Dialogues on a Contemporary National Cinema.* Translated by Metle Hjort. Bristol, UK: Intellect, 2001.

Hjort, Mette, and Scott MacKenzie, eds. *Purity and Provocation: Dogma 95.* London: British Film Institute, 2003.

Lumholdt, Jan, ed. *Lars von Trier: Interviews.* Jackson: University Press of Mississippi, 2003.

Mottram, Ron. *The Danish Cinema before Dreyer.* Metuchen, NJ: Scarecrow, 1988.

Nestingen, Andrew, and Trevor G. Elkington, eds. *Transnational Cinema in a Global North: Nordic Cinema in Transition.* Detroit, MI: Wayne State University Press, 2005.

Peter Schepelern

DIALOGUE

Cinematic dialogue is oral speech between fictional characters. This distinguishes dialogue from other types of cinematic language such as voice-over narration, internal monologue, or documentary interviews, which have different characteristics.

Since the birth of the cinema, it has been said that "film is a visual medium." Supposedly, films must tell their stories visually—editing, deep focus, lighting, camera movement, and nifty special effects are what really count. Dialogue, on the other hand, is just something we have to put up with. Even the term "film viewing" does not take into account the role of dialogue. We are accustomed to the analogy of the filmgoer as voyeur, surreptitiously spying on the actions of the on-screen characters. Yet what is overlooked is that viewers are also auditors. In fact, they are eavesdroppers, listening in on conversations purportedly addressed to others, but conversations that—in reality—are designed to communicate vital information to the listeners in the dark.

Dialogue, by its very nature, is deceptive. The characters on the screen speak not from their hearts but from a script; they whisper secrets to a vast public; they speak to inform the audience, not each other. Watching a film, on one level we are conscious of this duplicity, but on another we willingly suspend disbelief. Dialogue that betrays its true address to the moviegoer or sounds implausible is often condemned as clumsy because it fractures this fictional compact. But sometimes screenwriters intentionally use dialogue to wink at the audience, as in *Scream* (1996), when one of the characters says: "Oh, please don't kill me, Mr. Ghostface, I wanna be in the sequel!" Moreover, who is to say what is "out of character" for a fictional character? In *Hollywood Shuffle*

(1987) Robert Townsend asks us to reconsider our expectations about what is "true to life" when he presents an African American actor speaking in a stereotypical black dialect and then reveals the actor's actual speaking voice to be British and very cultured. Thus, all of the rules about dialogue usage offered by screenwriting handbooks should be viewed skeptically, as any rule may be violated for calculated effect.

FUNCTIONS OF DIALOGUE IN NARRATIVE FILM

Often, incidental dialogue works in movies to create a realistic flavor, to represent the everyday exchanges people have while ordering food or buying a newspaper. But dialogue also serves important functions within a film's story. Those who seek to minimize the value of dialogue have underestimated how much it contributes to every aspect of narrative film. Prescriptive rules might be better replaced by careful description and analysis of dialogue's typical functions.

1) The identification of the fictional location and characters. As an example of dialogue's ability to anchor a narrative, consider the following exchange from an early scene in John Ford's *Stagecoach* (1939). The stagecoach driver has just directed a well-dressed lady passenger toward the hotel for a cup of coffee. As she starts walking to the hotel porch, another young woman addresses her:

GIRL: Why, Lucy Mallory!

LUCY: Nancy! How are you, Captain Whitney?

CAPTAIN WHITNEY: Fine, thanks, Mrs. Mallory.

NANCY: Why, whatever are you doing in Arizona?

LUCY: I'm joining Richard in Lordsburg. He's there with his troops.

CAPTAIN WHITNEY (*offscreen*): He's a lot nearer than that, Mrs. Mallory. He's been ordered to Dry Fork.

NANCY: Why, that's the next stop for the stage-coach. You'll be with your husband in a few hours.

This interchange tells us who Lucy is, where she is, where she is going, why she is going there, what her husband does, where her husband is, where the stage stops next, and how long it should take until the couple is reunited.

2) The communication of narrative causality. The ulterior motive of much of film dialogue is to communicate "why?" and "how?" and "what next?" to the viewer. The "what next" may be a simple anticipation of a plot development, such as takes place during one of Devlin's meetings with Alicia in Alfred Hitchcock's *Notorious* (1946):

DEVLIN: Look. Why don't you persuade your husband to throw a large shindig so that he can introduce his bride to Rio society, say sometime next week?

ALICIA: Why?

DEVLIN: Consider me invited. Then I'll try and find out about that wine cellar business.

The dialogue has set up the party scene, Devlin's appearance there, and his and Alicia's surreptitious canvassing of the cellar, where they find that the wine bottles really contain uranium ore.

3) The enactment of plot-turning events. Sometimes a verbal statement, a speech act, can itself be a major turning point in the plot. A soldier may be given a mission, characters may break down on the witness stand, someone in disguise may reveal his true identity. James Cameron's *The Terminator* (1984) is undeniably an action-oriented film with exciting chase scenes, explosions, and shootings. Yet even in this case, many of the key events are verbal, such as Sarah Connor's inadvertent betrayal of her location when the Terminator impersonates her mother on the phone, or Reese's declaration of a lifetime of devotion to a woman he had not yet met: "I came across time for you, Sarah. I love you. I always have." Verbal events—such as declarations of love or jury verdicts—can be the most thrilling moments of a narrative film.

4) Character revelation. In our real lives we get to know acquaintances better by listening to them; obviously, dialogue helps audiences understand the characters' per-

sonalities and motivations. At one point in *Casablanca* (1942), Rick (Humphrey Bogart) is invited over to the table of Major Strasser (Conrad Veidt), where he learns that the Gestapo officer has been keeping a dossier on him. Rick borrows the notebook, glances at it, and quips, "Are my eyes really brown?" Such a statement shows his refusal to be intimidated and his satirical view of Germanic efficiency. This is important in the context of a conversation in which the major is warning Rick not to involve himself in the pursuit of resistance leader Victor Lazlo, and Rick seems to be agreeing not to interfere. Only Rick's verbal irreverence shows that he is not cowed.

5) Providing "realistic" verbal wallpaper. Screenplays often insert lines that seem appropriate to the setting and situation: photographers yell out for one more picture, flight attendants offer something to drink, or children shout while at play. Sometimes, the wallpaper is so rococo that it has significant aesthetic appeal of its own, as in John Frankenheimer's *The Manchurian Candidate* (1962), where we are treated to a wonderfully bizarre rendition of a ladies' garden club meeting about "hydrangeas' horticultural importance."

6) Guiding the viewer. Filmmakers accomplish this by using dialogue to control pacing or atmosphere. "That plane's dustin' crops where there ain't no crops" turns the audience's attention from the vacant highway to the airplane in *North by Northwest* (1959). In Ridley Scott's *Alien* (1979), Captain Dallas (Tom Skerritt) is trying to chase the loathsome creature through the space ship's air ducts with a flamethrower. A female crewmember, Lambert, is coaching Dallas over a walkie-talkie as she watches a motion detector. She screams: "Oh God, it's moving right towards you!...Move! Get out of there! [Inaudible] Move, Dallas! Move, Dallas! Move, Dallas! Get out!" Such lines are not particularly informative. Their main function is to frighten the viewer, to increase the scene's tension. In this case, dialogue is accomplishing the task often taken by evocative background music—it is working straight on the viewer's emotions.

7) The insertion of thematic messages. Putting thematic or moral messages in the mouths of their characters allows filmmakers to talk to the audience. For example, at the end of Hitchcock's *Foreign Correspondent*, filmed and released in 1940, the hero, a radio reporter, warns of the Nazi threat and urges Americans to join in the fight:

All that noise you hear isn't static; it's death coming to London. Yes, they're coming here now; you can hear the bombs falling on the streets and the homes....It's as if the lights were all out everywhere, except in America. Keep those lights burning. Cover them with steel, ring them with guns. Build a canopy of battleships and bombing planes around them. Hello America!

Hang on to your lights. They're the only lights left in the world.

Such explicit messages are not confined to wartime persuasion. Peter Jackson's *The Lord of the Rings: The Fellowship of the Ring* (2001) includes an effective passage from J. R. R. Tolkien's novel in which Gandalf instructs Frodo on the merits of pity and the danger of passing judgment.

8) Exploitation of the resources of language. Dialogue opens up vistas unreachable by silent film. With the addition of verbal language, cinema was offered infinite possibilities in terms of puns, jokes, misunderstandings, witticisms, metaphors, curses, whispers, screams, songs, poetry, or storytelling. In *The Wizard of Oz* (1939), when the Wizard challenges his supplicants, he does so with relish:

> WIZARD: Step forward, Tin Man. You dare to come to me for a heart, do you? You clinking clanking, clattering collection of caliginous junk?... And you, Scarecrow, have the effrontery to ask for a brain, you billowing bale of bovine fodder?

Viewers commonly adopt a film's most memorable lines—such as Bette Davis's "Fasten your seatbelts—it's going to be a bumpy night" in *All About Eve* (1950)—much the same way that earlier generations used to learn and quote maxims and proverbs. Cinematic dialogue has had an immense influence on how we speak and, consequently, on how we understand our culture and ourselves.

HISTORY OF DIALOGUE IN AMERICAN FILM

The history of film dialogue starts with the silent era. Speech sometimes literally accompanied silent films—some exhibitors hired lecturers to narrate silent films and local actors to speak lines for the characters. As the industry moved toward standardization, film producers found it desirable to include printed dialogue and expository intertitles. Silent film historian Barry Salt has found dialogue intertitles as early as 1904; Eileen Bowser has recorded that from 1907 to 1915 producers experimented with finding the exactly right placement and format for such titles. After 1915, with feature-length films, title writing became a specialty, and dialogue intertitles were used for humor, to convey important information, and to individualize characters. The critical reverence of the few films that torturously managed to avoid intertitles, such as F. W. Murnau's *The Last Laugh* (1924), should not be taken as indicative of the typical practices of the silent era. After all, in silent movies the characters were not supposed to be mutes. The characters spoke to one another; the incapacity was on the side of the filmgoers— we were the ones who were deaf.

The transition to sound in the late 1920s was complicated for American studios and theater owners, demanding great outlays of capital and entailing negotiation between competing technologies and corporate strategies. Equally upsetting for some in the film community was the wrenching shift in their approach to their craft caused by the possibilities of sound. The apprehension that sound would be the death of the visual artistry of silent film was initially abetted by the limitations of early microphones and recording apparatus, which restricted camera movement. From a historical perspective, what is remarkable about the conversion to sound is not that it was bumpy, but that the technical and aesthetic problems were solved so quickly and successfully, so that by the early 1930s the use of dialogue, sound effects, and music betrays none of the restrictions, tinniness, or fumbling of the transition films.

Immediately after the incorporation of sound, Hollywood began a wholesale importation of East Coast writers. The newspapermen, playwrights, and vaudevillians who went West in the early 1930s brought with them new sensibilities, novel stories, and a fresh approach to language.

In addition, sound instantly altered the balance of genres. Film musicals burst forth, as did literal adaptations of stage plays, which now could retain not just plot points, but much of the original stage dialogue. Verbally based comedies, featuring performers such as the Marx Brothers or W. C. Fields, expanded the contours of film comedy. Moreover, genres that had been established during the silent era underwent sea changes because of the new aesthetic capabilities. Each genre developed its own dialogue conventions, such as the street argot in gangster films or the dialect in westerns, conventions that turned out to be just as important to genre dynamics as their visual iconography.

A third event of the 1930s was the adoption of the Motion Picture Production Code, written in 1930 and more stringently enforced by the Hays Office after 1934. One of the reasons why this formal practice of industry self-censorship was put in place at this time is that verbal transgressions of prevailing standards were now possible. Although much of the Code deals with overall plot development, moral attitudes, and what viewers might learn about illicit behavior, several of the tenets deal specifically with language. For example:

- *Oaths* should never be used as a comedy element. Where required by the plot, the less offensive oaths may be permitted.

- *Vulgar expressions* come under the same treatment as vulgarity in general. Where women and children are to see the film, vulgar expressions (and oaths) should be cut to the absolute essentials required by the situation.

- The name of *Jesus Christ* should never be used except in reverence.

PRESTON STURGES
b. Chicago, Illinois, 29 August 1898, d. 6 August 1959

No one quite had such a way with dialogue as Preston Sturges. As a screenwriter, he constructed plots that were far-fetched and sometimes incoherent; as a director, his visuals were competent but uninspired. But as a dialogue writer, Sturges was unparalleled.

Preston Sturges had an eccentric upbringing; his mother divorced his father and married a Chicago socialite, only to leave him for a free-spirited life in Europe, following dancer Isadora Duncan. He lived in Europe off and on from 1901 to 1914. Sturges studied in a series of private schools in the United States and Europe and began writing plays in the late 1920s—some of which were acclaimed, others spectacular flops. He was hired as a writer by Universal in 1932.

Sturges worked as a screenwriter for numerous studios, and several of his scripts—such as *The Good Fairy* (1935), *Easy Living* (1937), and *Remember the Night* (1940)—were turned into successful movies. In 1940 Paramount agreed to let him direct his own scripts. The Paramount years were his most productive, with Sturges turning out a series of sparkling comedies in quick succession. Then Sturges's career fell off dramatically in the late 1940s when he left Paramount for a disastrous venture with Howard Hughes; he could not regain his footing during his short contract with Fox, and developed a reputation for being overpriced, arrogant, and unable to bring a film in on budget.

Sturges's dialogue is never "realistic"; no real person ever talked like his characters. He created a made-up, nonsense language for his vaguely European gigolo, Toto, in *The Palm Beach Story* (1942), but the rest of his people—from rich socialites, to Texas millionaires, to constables, to card sharks, to film producers—speak with equal disregard of verisimilitude. Sturges moved back and forth between long, eloquent phrasemaking to abrupt, staccato interchanges, and he mixed in noises such as hiccups or barking dogs. He imagined characters from every social sphere and cast actors with a wide range of voices, from mellifluous to gravelly.

The words flying out of these characters' mouths are improbable, unpredictable, and funny. For instance, in *Easy Living*, J. B. Ball throws his wife's fur coat off the roof. It lands on Mary Smith (Jean Arthur) as she is riding on the top level of a New York bus. Surprised, angry, she turns around to the innocent passenger sitting behind her, asking, "Say, what's the big idea, anyway?" He calmly replies: "Kismet." In *Sullivan's Travels* (1941), studio head Mr. LeBrand recalls Sullivan's previous hit films: "So Long, Sarong," "Hey Hey in the Hayloft," and "Ants in Your Plants of 1939." LeBrand and his associate suggest that Sully's new project should be "Ants in Your Plants of 1941," and they offer him Bob Hope, Mary Martin, and, maybe, Bing Crosby. And in *The Lady Eve* (1941), when Jean hatches her plan to impersonate a British Lady and get her revenge on Charles, she remarks, "I need him [Charles] like the ax needs the turkey." Hollywood romantic comedies needed Sturges's wit to the same degree.

RECOMMENDED VIEWING
Christmas in July (1940), *The Great McGinty* (1940), *The Lady Eve* (1941), *Sullivan's Travels* (1941), *The Palm Beach Story* (1942), *Hail the Conquering Hero* (1944), *Miracle of Morgan's Creek* (1944)

FURTHER READING
Curtis, James. *Between Flops: A Biography of Preston Sturges*. New York: Harcourt Brace Jovanovich, 1982.

Harvey, James. *Romantic Comedy in Hollywood: From Lubitsch to Sturges*. New York: Knopf, 1987.

Sturges, Preston. *Five Screenplays by Preston Sturges*, edited by Brian Henderson. Berkeley: University of California Press, 1985.

————. *Four More Screenplays by Preston Sturges*. Berkeley: University of California Press, 1985.

Ursini, James. *The Fabulous Life and Times of Preston Sturges: An American Dreamer*. New York: Curtis Books, 1973.

Sarah Kozloff

Along with the Production Code, another key pressure on dialogue throughout the studio years was the star system. The famous advertising slogan for *Anna Christie* (1930)— "Garbo Talks!"—is representative of the public's interest in hearing its favorite movie stars. Scripts have always been specifically tailored for their stars' personae and verbal abilities.

Preston Sturges. EVERETT COLLECTION. REPRODUCED
BY PERMISSION.

Studio-era directors and screenwriters developed distinctive dialogue styles. Especially in screwball comedies, such as *Bringing Up Baby* (1938) and *His Girl Friday* (1940), director Howard Hawks (1896–1977) would have his actors speak quickly and jump on each others' lines; his overlapping dialogue became a central element of his films' breakneck pacing. Billy Wilder (1906–2002), who had emigrated from Germany and taught himself English by listening to baseball games, often foregrounded his fascination with American slang. Orson Welles (1915–1985) put his experience with radio into the soundtracks of his movies, so that each character's voice is inflected by his or her spatial surroundings. Joseph Mankiewicz's (1909–1993) forte was depicting literate, urbane characters, such as Addison DeWitt (George Sanders) in *All About Eve* (1950), while Preston Sturges excelled at snappy comic dialogue.

The dissolution of the Production Code in the late 1950s, along with the gradual loosening of cultural restrictions throughout the 1960s, prompted a seismic upheaval in scriptwriting, allowing the frank treatment of taboo subject matter, the incorporation of street language, and the inclusion of obscenity. Changes in social expectations were also matched by technological developments, such as improvements in mixing and the invention of radio mikes, which led to more flexibility in sound recording.

During the late 1960s and early 1970s American movies, influenced by the breezy French New Wave, featured dialogue that was noticeably more colloquial, less careful about rhythm, less polished, more risqué, and marked by an improvisational air. The accompanying acting style was less declamatory, faster, and more throwaway; the recording of lines allowed much more overlapping and a higher degree of inaudibility. This more realistic, informal style of dialogue appears in John Cassavetes's (1929–1989) *Faces* (1968), which relies on improvisation; in the films of Robert Altman (b. 1925), who pioneered the use of radio mikes to allow multiple actors to speak at once in *M*A*S*H* (1970), *McCabe and Mrs. Miller* (1971), and *Nashville* (1975); and in Martin Scorsese's (b. 1942) *Mean Streets* (1973) and *Alice Doesn't Live Here Anymore* (1974).

Since the mid-1980s, low-budget and independent productions have continued an adventuresome approach to dialogue. This stems partially from independent filmmakers' genuine desire to break new ground, but novel manipulations of dialogue have also moved to the fore because they are cheaper and more easily accomplished than extensive special effects or lush production values. Clear examples can be found in Louis Malle's *My Dinner with André* (1981), which confines the film to a dinnertime conversation between two friends; David Mamet's *House of Games* (1987), in which the characters speak in carefully polished cadences approaching blank verse; Gus Van Sant's *My Own Private Idaho* (1991), which literally mixes Shakespeare with prosaic speech; and Julie Dash's *Daughters of the Dust* (1992), in which characters speak in a Gullah dialect. Finally, Spike Lee and Quentin Tarantino have made verbal dexterity downright fashionable.

Yet big-budget blockbusters, which depend so heavily on earning back their investments with overseas distribution, are less likely to prioritize their dialogue or to exploit the resources of language. An expensive release, such as Wolfgang Petersen's *Troy* (2004), incorporates speech only as necessary for narrative clarity, has the actors articulate each sentence pointedly (woodenly), and focuses audience attention instead on action sequences and special effects.

The issue of international distribution brings up the one aspect of dialogue that opponents were right to fear—the fact that inclusion of national languages restricts audience comprehension. Advocates of silent film felt that the cinema had discovered a universal language that would enhance international community. From one perspective, sound cinema has managed to continue that ideal: the international dominance of American cinema has been a tool of global English language dispersal. Audiences around the world have learned English, or accepted dubbing, or coped with subtitles. The isolating effects of national

Eddie Bracken (front center) and William Demarest (far right) in Preston Sturges's** **Hail the Conquering Hero** **(1944).
EVERETT COLLECTION. REPRODUCED BY PERMISSION.

language have primarily injured American viewers, who with less incentive to work through language difference, have cut themselves off from most international cinema. The solutions to this drawback are educational and social: to embrace linguistic variety, not to bring narrative complexity back down to the level of pantomime.

SEE ALSO *Film History; Silent Cinema; Sound*

FURTHER READING

Altman, Rick, ed. *Sound Theory/Sound Practice.* New York: Routledge, 1992.

Chion, Michel. *Audio-Vision: Sound on Screen.* Edited and translated by Claudia Gorbman. New York: Columbia University Press, 1994.

Chothia, Jean. *Forging a Language: A Study of the Plays of Eugene O'Neill.* Cambridge, UK and New York: Cambridge University Press, 1979.

Devereaux, Mary. "'Of Talk and Brown Furniture': The Aesthetics of Film Dialogue." *Post Script* 6 (1986): 32–52.

Faulkner, Christopher. "René Clair, Marcel Pagnol, and the Social Dimension of Speech." *Screen* 35 (1994): 157–170.

Kozloff, Sarah. *Overhearing Film Dialogue.* Berkeley: University of California Press, 2000.

Motion Picture Producers and Distributors of America. "The Motion Picture Production Code of 1930. In *The Movies in Our Midst: Documents in the Cultural History of Film in America*, edited by Gerald Mast. Chicago: University of Chicago Press, 1982: 321–333.

Page, Norman. *Speech in the English Novel.* London: Longman, 1973.

Sarah Kozloff

DIASPORIC CINEMA

The word "diaspora" is derived from the Greek word *diasperien*. It denotes the dispersion of a population group or community of people from their country of birth or origin. Overseas diasporas or transnational communities are created by international migration, forced or voluntary, and are motivated by economic, political, and colonial factors. During classical antiquity, "diaspora" referred to the exodus and exile of the Jews from Palestine. Later historical references to "diaspora" are associated with the slave trade and forced migration of West Africans to the "New World" in the sixteenth century. Twentieth-century formations include the Palestinian and Armenian diasporas. More recent diasporas originate from the Caribbean, Latin America, South and East Asia, and Central Europe. As a subject area and critical category of study, diaspora has become a theoretical tool in film studies, ethnic studies, and cultural studies, among other fields, and resonates in debates and critiques of migration, identity, nationalism, transnationality, and exile.

The second half of the twentieth century, referred to by some demographers as "the century of migration," is distinguished by the magnitude, direction, and composition of international migration, with women now constituting nearly 50 percent of international migrants. Several factors have accelerated the movement of people across borders: globalizing economic processes linked to the internationalization of capital and the labor market, the cumulative effects of political instability caused by ethnic strife and civil wars, population pressures, environmental degradation, human rights violations, and the decline of transportation costs. Taken together, these factors, along with worsening poverty that compounds the already vast inequalities among the world's 6.4 billion population, account for the "global migration crisis" at the beginning of the twenty-first century. It has affected an estimated 175 million people, who now reside outside their country of origin and whose destination increasingly is North America, Asia, and Western Europe. Globalization and geopolitics, along with the rise of transnational media, accelerate diasporic formations. Constituting "new" and hybrid ethnicities, diasporas disrupt the cultural and social practices of the societies they inhabit. They also contest accepted ideas about Western modernity and nationhood, especially racialized constructions related to citizenship.

DIASPORIC FORMATIONS IN CINEMA

The dislocating effects of globalization, migrating cultures, and postcoloniality form the subtext of diasporic cinema. Thus this category of film is neither linguistically nor culturally monolithic. A number of scholars have discussed diasporic and exilic films as an international genre or movement consistent with the world today. Hamid Naficy outlines vital and nuanced distinctions between "diasporic," "exilic," and "postcolonial ethnic and identity" filmmakers, who collectively comprise "accented cinema" and, as he suggests, are in conversation with dominant and alternative cinemas.

However differentiated, though, diasporic films and other types of "accented" films share similar concerns, characteristics, and production practices. In culturally diverse and often compelling narratives and styles, they address the paradoxes of exile and the negotiation of difference and belonging in indifferent and frequently

MERZAK ALLOUACHE
b. Algiers, Algeria, 6 October 1944

The Algerian director and writer Merzak Allouache consistently explores the displacement of exile and marginality of North Africans living in France and its former colony, Algeria. After studying at France's renowned film school, École Nationale Supérieure des Métiers de L'image et du Son, as well as graduating from Algeria's short-lived film school, Allouache worked in French television. His first feature film, *Omar Gatlato* (1976), presents in documentary style an exposé of Algerian males who fear intimacy with women as much as alienation from male peers. The title is derived from the phrase *gatlato al-rujula*, roughly "a machismo that kills," and refers to the social practices that exacerbate male insecurity. The focus on a dynamic urban milieu and its youth—its street slang, rituals, and passion for popular culture—is a theme that runs through many of Allouache's films.

Bab El-Oued City (1994) earned him international acclaim and put him in peril in Algeria. Its title refers to a working-class district of Algiers where Allouache grew up and which is a site of intense unrest. Allouache updates his focus on urban youth who, once struggling with a nation in the making, are now experiencing an increasing spiral of violence. It tells the story of an ordinary baker who flees for his life after impulsively ripping out a rooftop loudspeaker that incessantly broadcasts propaganda by religious activists. A warning about the dangers of replacing colonial despotism with theocratic authoritarianism, the film won the International Film Critics prize in the *Un Certain Regard* category at the 1994 Cannes Film Festival and that year's grand prize at the Arab Film Festival. In Algeria, Allouache faced enough political pressure to prompt his departure.

Once in exile, Allouache used a comedic frame for *Salut cousin!* (1996), a diasporic and exilic film that features the related ordeals of two cousins from Algeria who navigate French society in different ways. Allouache laces the cousins' stories with enough empathy and sense of whimsy to temper what some call his customary fatalism. Allouache expanded his take on gender and diaspora in *L'Autre Monde* (*The Other World*, 2001), which traces the arduous journey of a woman and her fiancé, both born in France to Algerian immigrants, who travel to Algeria to experience a country they only previously "imagined." After her fiancé—torn between his birthplace and his ancestral homeland—leaves for Algeria to join the military, the young woman dons a veil and follows, facing danger and further disorientation related to her own conflicting loyalties.

This film, by a director who humanizes characters ordinarily understood through the lens of prejudice, highlights the contradictory sources of their vulnerability and survivability. Allouache has repeated this message in films that span nearly two decades, and which similarly forced him to straddle two nations with a shared, violent history as the colonizer and the colonized. His commitment to give voice to the disempowered is what gives his films their greatest weight.

RECOMMENDED VIEWING

Omar Gatlato (1976), *Un amour à Paris* (A love in Paris, 1987), *L'Après-Octobre* (Following October, 1989), *Bab El-Oued City* (1994), *Salut cousin!* (*Hey Cousin!*, 1996), *L'Amour est à Réinventer* (*Love Reinvented*, segment "Dans la décapotable," 1996), *Alger-Beyrouth: Pour mémoire* (*Algiers-Beirut: A Souvenir*, 1998), *L'Autre Monde* (*The Other World*, 2001), *Chouchou* (2003)

FURTHER READING

Allouache, Merzak. *Bab El-Oued: A Novel*. Boulder, CO: L. Rienner, 1997.

Malkmus, Lizbeth, and Roy Armes. *Arab and African Film Making*. London: Zed Books, 1991.

Shafik, Viola. *Arab Cinema: History and Cultural Identity*. Cairo: American University in Cairo Press, 1998.

Michael T. Martin
Marilyn Yaquinto

xenophobic communities and nation-states. Moreover, diasporic films, such as *Vivre au paradis* (*Living in Paradise*, 1998), set in France during the last years of the Algerian war of independence (1954–62), and *Hop* (2002), in which an innocent boy finds himself in trouble and separated from his father, foreground the struggle for recognition, community, and citizenship. As is evident in *Salut cousin!* (*Hey Cousin!*, 1996), about two

Merzak Allouache. © PELLETIER MICHELINE/CORBIS SYGMA.

cinema, like diasporas, problematizes national identity and the nation as an imagined and bounded territorial space. For example, in *Sammy and Rosie Get Laid* (1987), the characters' identities are framed by London's cosmopolitanism, whereas in *Pièces d'identités* (*Pieces of Identity*, 1998), they are informed by a monolithic African (or continental) affiliation along with tribal distinctions.

Diaspora cinema, paradoxically, comprises the global as a distinctive transnational style, as well as the local to reflect some manner of specificity. Diasporic cinema's political project expresses a transcendent realism, in which "home truths" about the social experience of postcoloniality are rendered transparent. An apt example is *Drachenfutter* (*Dragon Chow*, 1987), in which two displaced refugees—one Pakistani, the other Chinese—start a restaurant, whose viability is eventually thwarted by the insensitive immigration policies of their host country of West Germany. This feature also corresponds to and resonates with a growing corpus of films that address the *fracture sociale*, especially in First World societies, in which the gendered and marginalized lives of the underclass and growing economic disparities between social classes are explored. Examples include *La Vie rêvée des anges* (*The Dreamlife of Angels*, 1998) and *Rosetta* (1999). Diasporic cinema, however, is less schematic, theorized, and committed to being oppositional as a collective project than its precursor, the 1960s cinema of political engagement. Nevertheless, it heralds a renewed preoccupation with the global and historical affairs of the contemporary period.

BEUR CINEMA

As South and East Asian, African, and Caribbean diasporas disrupt the prevailing Christian and racialized delineation of Europe, nation-states in the European Union are undergoing economic and political integration and dramatic demographic changes. Since the 1980s filmmakers, especially diasporic and exilic ones, have explored the émigré experience with increasing frequency and in greater depth. Accented cinema formations have developed in Britain (black and Asian film and video collectives), in the United States (Iranian, African American, and Asian American), and, to a lesser extent, in Canada (South Asian).

Among filmmakers who reside in France, a *cine beur*, or *beur* cinemas, has evolved, exploring the preoccupations and concerns of transnational migrant communities that have settled there. The word *beur* is French slang for "Arab" and signifies the ambivalence associated with bicultural identity despite French nationality. It also signifies the distinction and tension between French of Maghreb ancestry and their North African immigrant parents. *Les beurs* constitute a distinctive bicultural

Algerian cousins in racially tense Paris, and *Gegen die Wand* (*Head-On*, 2004), which centers on a marriage of convenience between two German Turks, they also explore the ambivalence and contingency of diasporic identities. These films, and others such as *Heremakono* (*Waiting for Happiness*, 2002) and *Le Grand voyage* (2004), suggest a counterpoint to the dislocating experience of global migrations, using journey narratives to interrogate the "homeless subject."

Since the 1980s, alongside the emergence of postcolonial diasporic filmmaking, new and more complex accounts of the "national" and "national cinema" have evolved largely in response to the ascendance of transnational media and other supranational entities (multinational corporations) under global capitalism. As a critical category, national cinema presents problems: one can no longer define national cinema in terms of where films are produced and by whom, or by a comparative approach that differentiates between national cinemas. Diasporic group. As the children of North African immigrants from Algeria, Tunisia, and Morocco (the Maghreb), concentrated particularly in the *banlieues* (housing projects on the peripheries of French cities), *la génération beur* attained prominence during the late 1970s amid racial tension, the rise of extreme right-wing movements (such as the Front National), and national debates about immigration, integration, and assimilation in France.

Beur cinema, which has a kinship with *banlieue* and "hip hop" cinemas, is part of a larger *beur* artistic tradition and social movement in music, art, photography, theater, and literature. *Beur* films are for the most part narratives told in a realist mode that have popular appeal; they are shaped by a shared colonial experience and language (French) and, with few exceptions, are by men about male-centered narratives in which women are largely marginalized. Recurrent themes are the urban multiethnic realities of unemployment, street crime, poverty, and state surveillance and regulation; the institutional, social, and personal consequences of racism; the conflicts and tensions between North African and French cultures; the intergenerational conflicts between North African émigrés and their *beur* children, especially with regard to patriarchal authority; and the tensions caused by uprootedness, exile, deterritorialization, nostalgia, escape, and repatriation.

The more recent evolution of *beur* cinema, however, suggests that its composition and concerns are provisional, as some filmmakers make the transition to other areas of filmmaking in France and address non-*beur* subjects. Addressing themes related to *beur* (and *banlieue*) cinema, the film *Bye-Bye* (1995) examines contemporary French society, which is becoming increasingly multiethnic, multiracial, hybridized, and fractured along class lines. Directed by Karim Dridi (b. 1961), a Franco-Tunisian filmmaker, *Bye-Bye* chronicles the anguished, violent, and indeterminate odyssey of Ismaël, a Franco-Maghrebi who escorts his younger brother, Mouloud, south from Paris via Marseilles to their parents' "homeland" in Tunisia. By framing the narrative in the context of a journey, the film emphasizes two features of postcoloniality: the territorial divide between France and its former colonies and their diasporic settlement, and the cultural paradoxes of postcoloniality. These paradoxes are signified in an effective counterpoint, in which the imperatives of capitalism and pluralism contest Islamic traditions and practices, along with parental fealty. Neither side of this deterritorialized and dislocating space offers Ismaël solace.

Ismaël's ambivalence, and Mouloud's unequivocal rejection of the "home country," underscores their generation's displacement and break with tradition and familial, especially paternal, authority. At ease neither in French nor in Maghreb cultures, Ismaël longs for another home (land), which attests to his marginality as a diasporic subject. Thus, in *Bye-Bye* the émigré experience forsakes the collective for the personal and exemplifies the existential characteristic of *beur* cinema.

SEE ALSO *National Cinema; Race and Ethnicity*

FURTHER READING

Bloom, Peter. "*Beur* Cinema and the Politics of Location: French Immigration Politics and the Naming of a Film Movement." In *The Historical Film: History and Memory in Media*, edited by Marcia Landy, 44–62. New Brunswick, NJ: Rutgers University Press, 2001.

Bluher, Dominique. "Hip-Hop Cinema in France." *Camera Obscura* 17, no. 4 (2001).

Braziel, Jana Evans, and Anita Mannur, eds. *Theorizing Diaspora: A Reader*. Boston: Blackwell, 2003.

Desai, Jigna. *Beyond Bollywood: The Cultural Politics of South Asian Diasporic Film*. New York: Routledge, 2004.

Fielder, Adrian. "Poaching on Public Space: Urban Autonomous Zones in French *Banlieue* Films." In *Cinema and the City: Film and Urban Societies in a Global Context*, edited by Mark Shield and Tony Fitzmaurice. Boston: Blackwell, 2001.

Higson, Andrew. "The Concept of National Cinema." *Screen* 30, no. 4 (1989): 36–46.

Martin, Michael T., ed. *Cinemas of the Black Diaspora*. Detroit, MI: Wayne State University Press, 1995.

———, ed. *New Latin American Cinema: Studies of National Cinemas*. Vol. 2. Detroit, MI: Wayne State University Press, 1997.

Naficy, Hamid. *An Accented Cinema: Exilic and Diasporic Filmmaking*. Princeton, NJ: Princeton University Press, 2001.

Papastergiadis, Nikos. *The Turbulence of Migration*. Cambridge: Polity Press, 2000.

Rueschmann, Eva, ed. *Moving Pictures, Migrating Identities*. Jackson: University Press of Mississippi, 2003.

Shohat, Ella, and Robert Stam. *Unthinking Eurocentrism: Multiculturalism and the Media*. New York: Routledge, 1994.

Tarr, Carrie. "Questions of Identity in Beur Cinema: From *Tea in the Harem* to *Cheb*." *Screen* 34, no. 4 (1993): 321–342.

Williams, Alan. *Film and Nationalism*. New Brunswick, NJ: Rutgers University Press, 2002.

Michael T. Martin
Marilyn Yaquinto

DIRECTION

———————■———————

The opening credit sequence of contemporary American films typically proclaim that the ensuing work is "a film by" a particular director. This assertive title is both an acknowledgment of professional responsibility (that the creative process is led by a central administrative figure) and an authorial intention (that the work in question is the product of a single, creative individual). However, within such a deceptively simple credit lies an implicit array of controversial assumptions about the position of the director. The significance of such a credit is historically contingent: it depends on the film's given production context, as well as the changing professional status of the director from decade to decade. Indeed, the ubiquity of such a credit is a fairly recent phenomenon; in most cases during the classical era, movies were credited as being "authored" by the studio that produced them. Moreover, it is not simply that a credit such as "a Jay Roach Film" is potentially misleading; it also gives very little indication as to the precise nature of the director's creative enterprise.

What, then, are the technical duties and professional responsibilities of the director? How do they differ according to a director's cultural, historical, and industrial situation? Why have certain professional and critical discourses encouraged us to regard the director as the prominent "authorial" voice among a hierarchy of film artists? Finally, what is the use-value of promoting the director as a "celebrity"—a creative personality whose name comes to signify quality, exclusivity, and/or fashionability? Answering these questions requires a consideration of the director's position within a hierarchy of film production given to structural fluctuation, as well as an analysis

of the power dynamics involved in both authorial and star politics.

RESPONSIBILITIES

In the business of film production, the designation of "director" is a somewhat enigmatic title. Comparatively speaking, most of the other principal creative personnel involved in filmmaking hold titles that give a fairly clear indication of their professional responsibilities. Generally, one individual is responsible for overseeing the labor that is relevant to a single facet of production, whether it be cinematography, writing, editing, music, sound, production design, or costumes. With the notable exception of the producer, however, the range of the director's tasks is quite broad, and involves coordinating innumerable creative activities throughout the course of developing, shooting, completing, and marketing a film.

It shall be assumed here that the director is the individual who actively oversees the realization of a film from shooting script to finished product, harmoniously coordinating the creative activities of the key personnel involved in the production processes. He or she will liaise with each of these artists, deliberate over various expressive and/or technical options to be implemented, and arrive at a decision that is commensurate with the requirements of the developing work. Correspondingly, the director will also be answerable to the executive body that finances and/or distributes the work and therefore must ensure that production runs smoothly and within an allotted budget. The director's job, then, is twofold: to maintain a consistency of style and quality throughout production and ensure that the production itself proceeds efficiently and economically.

In other words, before one considers the director's position in evaluative terms (as a potential author), one must come to a more objective understanding of the director's position in descriptive terms (as an effective delegate). Serving as the funnel through which all of the decisions affecting a film's form and style are exercised, a director's primary task is to cultivate and coordinate the creative contributions of a production company's principal artists. In the interests of specificity and demystification, it is worth enumerating the various duties assigned to the director during all three stages of filmmaking: preproduction, production, and postproduction.

During the preproduction stage, the director's responsibilities can be divided into four principle tasks: (1) collaborating with the writer(s) on the development of the script; (2) assisting the casting director in hiring appropriate actors, and conducting rehearsals; (3) cooperating with the producer(s) in developing a practical shooting schedule; and (4) planning the overall visual "look" of the film with the production designers and the director of photography (DOP). The extent of a director's involvement in each of these phases varies according to production context and the director's personal working habits. A director may insist on meticulously preplanning a film before beginning to shoot, which is the method preferred by Satyajit Ray (1921–1992), or, the director may treat the film organically, allowing it to develop spontaneously during the process of shooting. Wong Kar-wai (b. 1958), for example, frequently devises and shoots several different versions of a loosely scripted scenario before settling on one that will become the "official" film.

Throughout the actual shooting of the work, the director must multitask efficiently, ensuring that all tasks are executed effectively, solving any unforeseen complications that may arise during production. First, the director and the DOP will supervise the electricians and grips in the lighting of a set—ensuring the correct placement of lights, cutters, and nets. Second, all camerawork—including framing and composition, lens selection, and tracking shots—must be reviewed and potentially rehearsed with the DOP, camera operator, and focus puller. Third, he or she will consult the head carpenter, set dresser, and assistant director (AD) to ensure that there are no logistical problems with the staging of a scene. The director and the AD must also properly block and coach any extras appearing in the scene. Fourth, the director confers with the sound crew regarding the proper placement of microphones and any additional sound equipment. Finally, the director will provide the actors with instructions and suggestions, guiding them through the playing of a scene based on decisions agreed upon during rehearsals. Practical directions will be given to ensure that the actors stay in frame and compensate for any camera movement, but less concretely, the director will also coach actors through improvisations, modulating the "tone" of their performances.

It is at the completion of a take that the director's most crucial decision emerges: whether or not the photographed action will be printed. If all of the above elements have been fulfilled to his or her satisfaction, the director will order the shot to be taken to the lab for processing. The processed shot will most likely appear in the final cut of the film after being carefully scrutinized at the daily rushes by the principal crewmembers. Given the enormous amount of work required during the production stages, the average amount of time needed to shoot a modestly budgeted, 120-minute film is about forty days. Independent directors working with a small crew on a shoestring budget will usually take considerably less time. For example, while working for AIP Productions, Roger Corman (b. 1926) was able to shoot eighty-minute exploitation films, such as *Little Shop of Horrors* (1960), in three days. By contrast, Frances Ford Coppola (b. 1939) required over sixteen months to shoot the problem-laden art-house blockbuster, *Apocalypse Now* (1979).

Once actual filming has finished, the director must preside over the completion of the work during postproduction. Again, the degree of a director's involvement in these stages varies according to historically determined production contexts and individual practice. Before 1940, for example, a Hollywood director often had literally no input in the cutting of a film; the footage was sent directly to the editing department, and the director might not even see it again until a rough cut was completed for previewing. By contrast, the contemporary digital manipulation of images has increased to such a degree that the director's close involvement in postproduction stages is often a necessity. Indeed, digital filmmaking has significantly blurred the distinction between filmic creation and modification, and has therefore expanded the director's postproduction role dramatically.

As in preproduction, there are four principal postproduction areas in which a director's input is necessary: (1) editing, (2) visual effects, (3) music, and (4) sound. In most cases, an editor and director will develop the film's pace and rhythm, reinforce continuity between shots, trim moments of unwanted excess, and ensure that the montage generally serves to reinforce the work's intent. The visual effects category encompasses the manipulation of the raw footage by color timers, processing technicians, special effects designers, and an array of digital artists, compositors, and animators. Broadly speaking, a director will convey instructions to supervisors in each of these groups, indicating the specific "look" the director wishes to convey. Such post-filmic "treatment" affecting the overall appearance of a work can range from Robert Altman's (b. 1925) decision to "preflash" the negative of *The Long Goodbye* (1973) in order to amplify the washed-out pastels of its hazy Los Angeles milieu, to Robert Rodriguez's (b. 1968) development of the entirely digital, black-and-white cityscape of *Sin City* (2005). The director will oversee a film's aural elements as well. In working with the composer, he might intimate how the score reinforces the affective intent of key sequences, accentuates notable action, or even organizes the structure of the montage. The director may also specify to the sound designer how various audio cues will function, indicate the expressive intent of ambient noise, and/or explain the interplay between aural effects and edits. A favorite composer might be relied upon—as in Danny Elfman's recurring scores for Tim Burton (b. 1958)—or in some rare cases, a director might personally compose the film's music (as Charlie Chaplin [1889–1977] did for his features), or co-design the sound (as David Lynch [b. 1946] often does).

COLLABORATIONS

In describing the various responsibilities of the director, it would seem that he or she occupies a central position within the cinema's creative division of labor. Despite this apparent centrality, however, it must be established that the title of "director" is not necessarily synonymous with the designation "author." Understanding the role of the director is an objective concern and does not require the subsequent appreciative assertion that he or she is the most important individual in this process. Nor should it be assumed that a director's supervisory status is ipso facto proof of his or her status as the center of the work's significance. Rather, the director's centrality should refer to his or her position within a system of creative labor. Again, a director is first and foremost a delegate—one whose primary duties are to coordinate numerous creative endeavors in the interest of maintaining a consistent style and quality across an efficient production process. Given the collaborative nature of this process, it is important to understand the basic ways in which a director can work with key personnel within a filmmaking collective.

Since the screenplay serves as the primary source material in the director's process of adaptation, the screenwriter and director ideally will collaborate closely during the preparation of a film's shooting script. While the writer(s) and director will have their own opinions about the work's nascent significance, they will strive to reach an objective understanding of the script's intent—one that represents an unforeseen synthesis of their respective attitudes toward the material. In practical terms, this partnership may include identifying the work's central ideas, resolving any potentially disruptive ambiguities in the story, tightening narrative structure, and rewriting dialogue or adjusting characterization if necessary. Their work may continue through the shooting process itself should circumstances require further adjustments to be made.

Again, the actual proactive involvement of the director will vary. Alain Resnais (b. 1922), for example, allows his screenwriters to have virtual autonomy in preparing their screenplay. Milos Forman (b. 1932), by contrast, will labor over a script with a writer, line by line. Directors may prefer to work on the script personally with a favored collaborator (as evidenced by the long-time partnership between Billy Wilder [1906–2002] and I. A. L. Diamond [1920–1988]), or film his or her own screenplay (Ousmane Sembene [b. 1923], Pier Paolo Pasolini [1922–1975], and Preston Sturges [1898–1959] are all prominent examples of director-screenwriters). Alternatively, a film's working script may emerge through improvisations overseen by the director during rehearsals: John Cassavetes (1924–1989) and Mike Leigh (b. 1943) are celebrated exemplars of this tendency. It is important to note, however, that if there is a substantial degree of financial investment in the film, investors may insist on approving every draft of the work in progress. Hollywood screenplays, for example, have been subject to the whims of producers, executives, censorial boards, and even stars—all of whom have wielded creative authority over the majority of screenwriters and directors.

Just as the shooting script is frequently outside of the director's complete control, the casting of a film's principal roles is often dictated by the economic logic of the star system, especially in mainstream Hollywood cinema. Orson Welles (1915–1985), for example, may have despaired at Universal's insistence on casting Charlton Heston as a Mexican in *Touch of Evil* (1958), but the casting of the film's principal players was not his decision to make. In the studio era, a contracted star might be assigned to a particular film, while contemporary stars may be "packaged" along with a screenplay by a talent agency as part of a non-negotiable deal. However, the director typically has much more independence in the casting of secondary and minor roles. The director will oversee the work of the casting director, who will organize auditions for these roles and/or present the director and producer(s) with a selection of actors to handpick for smaller parts.

For certain directors, their influence in the casting of the film is of paramount importance. Sergei Eisenstein's (1898–1948) reliance on *typage* in the casting of his early

Soviet films is a good example, with the director often personally selecting the ideal faces needed to personify particular ideological positions. John Waters's (b. 1946) entire filmography is founded upon casting director Pat Moran's selection of the perfect assortment of lumpen freaks. Andy Warhol (1928–1987) and Paul Morrissey (b. 1938) transformed casting into a quasi-political act, by selecting whoever happened to be hanging around the Factory and proclaiming them to be instant "movie stars." Other directors may choose to work with favorite actors or cultivate a stock company. Such reliance on familiar faces not only potentially simplifies communication between actor and director, but it may also serve as a kind of expressive shorthand within the film itself. John Wayne (1907–1979), for example, is John Ford's (1894–1973) idealized emblem of the frontier's potential for self-determination, while Liv Ullman (b. 1938), Bibi Andersson (b. 1935), and Max von Sydow (b. 1929) are not so much part of Ingmar Bergman's (b. 1918) "troupe" as they are his recurring muses and creative partners.

For certain directors, performance is the very heart of cinematic art. Jean Renoir (1894–1979) provides the most prestigious example of a humanist aesthetic: his famed deep-focus photography, elaborate tracking shots, and long takes represent a concerted, empathetic effort to preserve the integrity of his actors' performances within a fully realized social world. Other directors frequently showcase the technical ingenuity of gifted actors. Elia Kazan's (1909–2003) close involvement with Lee Strasberg and Stella Adler in the cultivation of American "method" acting often resulted in films that foregrounded the intense psychodynamics of their principal characters. Occasionally, the better part of a director's career might be dedicated to exploring a single actor's persona. Examples include Zhang Yimou's (b. 1951) early feature-length "tributes" to Gong Li and Josef von Sternberg's (1894–1969) obsession with Marlene Dietrich—the radiant focal point of his films' *mise-en-scène.* In all of these cases, the director's function is to facilitate the actor's cultivation of a performance that will satisfy a shared aesthetic ambition. Actual working methods might range from encouraging improvisation (Shirley Clarke [1919–1997]), the use of provocation and multiple takes (Stanley Kubrick [1928–1999]), or blatant manipulation and intimidation (Roman Polanski [b. 1933]).

Often at complete variance with the "actor's director" is the filmmaker who aspires to a rigorous aestheticism, treating the artistic process as an opportunity to explore the parameters of the medium itself. Such a director's fellow artists might be encouraged to consider the filmic image as a graphic design, rather than an indexical referent to a profilmic reality. In such cases, the production designer and director of photography are frequently the formalist director's chief collaborators. In *The Cook, the Thief, His Wife and Her Lover* (1989) and *Prospero's Books* (1991), for example, production designers Jan Roelfs and Ben van Os and director Peter Greenaway (b. 1942) treat the screen like a canvas, creating an intricately layered onscreen space and occasionally "writing" on the surface of the screen itself. For Alfred Hitchcock's (1899–1980) color films of the 1950s, Hal Pereira (1905–1983) helped the director devise some of his most superbly crafted set pieces: the multi-windowed courtyard that provides voyeuristic glimpses of multiple levels of action in *Rear Window* (1954) is a triumph of design. Another example is the sumptuous formalism of Sally Potter's (b. 1949) work since *The Tango Lesson* (1997), which can largely be attributed to her recurring collaboration with designer Carlos Conti.

Congruently, the DOP is equipped with the technical knowledge to help a director visually realize his or her conception of the significance, mood, and/or affective intent. Bernardo Bertolucci's (b. 1940) most stylized efforts—particularly *Il Conformista* (*The Conformist,* 1970)—are a result of Vittorio Storaro's (b. 1940) mastery of expressive lighting and color. The invariable steely iciness of David Cronenberg's (b. 1943) films since *Dead Ringers* (1988) is largely cultivated by Peter Suschitzky (b. 1941), just as the warm romanticism and nostalgia that pervades Woody Allen's (b. 1935) work in the late 1970s and early 1980s can primarily be attributed to Gordon Willis's (b. 1931) photography. Or, we might reference the lyricism of F. W. Murnau's (1888–1931) "unchained," moving camera in *Der Letzte Mann* (*The Last Laugh*, 1924)—an innovation developed by master cinematographer Karl Freund (1890–1969). Despite Andrew Sarris's assertion that an *auteur* must be "technically proficient," the majority of directors in his catalog of great filmmakers rely heavily on the technological ingenuity of the DOP to develop and realize their visual ideas.

On a similar note, a skilled editor effectively shapes a film's structure, pace, and intended significance. Again, directors may formulate an outline of their intent, but most often the creative onus is on the editor to bring this objective to fruition. Even a director as heralded as Martin Scorsese (b. 1942) is reliant on the precision and innate sense of timing of his long-time editor, Thelma Schoonmaker. Certain directors believe montage to be the essence of their medium and develop an aesthetic that foregrounds the expressive potential of the various relations between shots. Eisenstein, Vsevolod Pudovkin (1893–1953), and Aleksandr Dovzhenko (1894–1956)—the chief exponents of Soviet montage— are the obvious examples here. As equally inventive are prominent figures from the various international "new waves" of the 1960s, whose editing styles are informed by an irreverent admixture of radical politics, anti-classicism,

***Provocation embodied by the drill sergeant (R. Lee Ermey) in Stanley Kubrick's* Full Metal Jacket *(1987).* EVERETT COLLECTION. REPRODUCED BY PERMISSION.**

and blistering energy. Notable exemplars of such politicized dynamism include Glauber Rocha (1938–1981), Věra Chytilová (b. 1929), and Jean-Luc Godard (b. 1930).

While the pyrotechnic editing evident in much contemporary commercial filmmaking is frequently reviled for its perceived pandering to decreasing audience attention spans, several directors have turned this tendency to their creative advantage. Taking their cue from the use of sampling in hip-hop music, director Darren Aronofsky (b. 1969) and editor Jay Rabinowitz devised a montage for *Requiem for a Dream* (2000) that is a lightning-fast form of crosscutting synched with exaggerated sound effects. Harmony Korine (b. 1973) and Valdís Óskarsdóttir developed an editing style for *Julien Donkey-Boy* (1999) that emulates the elliptical and erratic perception of the schizophrenic protagonist. Also noteworthy are John Woo's (b. 1946) dynamic alterations between expertly choreographed, slow-motion action and almost subliminally fast cutting in *Hard Boiled* (1992) and *Face/Off* (1997)—

a contemporary update of a style devised by Sam Peckinpah (1925–1984) for the bloody climax of *The Wild Bunch* (1969). Conversely, a director's signature style may be founded upon a preference for minimal edits and a long-take aesthetic. Kenji Mizoguchi's (1898–1956) delicate exploration of an intricately crafted *mise-en-scène*, Andrei Tarkovsky's (1932–1986) attempts to evoke the felt duration of time, and Chantal Akerman's (b. 1950) minimalist emphasis on the domestic labor of her female characters are notable examples. Contemporary artists such as Tsai Mingliang (b. 1957), Abbas Kiarostami (b. 1940), Michael Haneke (b. 1942), and Béla Tarr (b. 1955) continue this tradition, collaborating with their various editors to produce slowly paced films that reward patient, studied attention.

The most potentially contentious of the director's various working relationships is with the producer. Since the producer's chief tasks are to secure finances and ensure that filming adheres to schedule and budget, the

A scene from Erich von Stroheim's **Greed** *(1924), which was drastically cut by producer Irving Thalberg.* EVERETT COLLECTION. REPRODUCED BY PERMISSION.

partnership between producer and director is frequently an anxious one. During preproduction, they will select shooting sites found by location scouts based on availability, affordability, and practicality. Script changes will be discussed and approved, and casting choices finalized. A shooting schedule will be devised by a production manager in order to maximize the availability of the principal actors, local crew, and locations. The schedule is of vital importance, as it represents the culmination of all approved, pre-planned aesthetic decisions that will affect the completed film. The more expensive the production, the more inflexible is a director's commitment to the schedule and the shooting script. Producers are almost always present during a shoot, keeping a close eye on the proceedings, and they will often make suggestions regarding the director's rough cut of a film before it is delivered to the studio for testing and/or distribution.

On the one hand, a positive working relationship can lead to an extremely creative partnership, as evidenced by the work of producer Val Lewton (1904–1951) and director Jacques Tourneur (1904–1977) collaborative RKO.

On the other, certain directors perceive the producer's close involvement as interference with his or her creative autonomy, and their relationship to producers is typically hostile. Indeed, Erich von Stroheim (1885–1957), Orson Welles, and Nicholas Ray (1911–1979) are often characterized as artist-martyrs whose Hollywood careers were destroyed by gross materialists. During the late 1930s, the emerging Directors Guild made a concentrated effort to secure the director's right to supervise the first rough cut, participate in casting and script development, and wield more authority during the actual production stages. However, it is also worth noting that the creative tensions that arise between producers and directors during the most tempestuous production circumstances can sometimes yield riches. For example, *Gone with the Wind* (1939) was produced amidst stormy relationships between producer David O. Selznick and the various directors hired and fired from work on the film, including Victor Fleming (1889–1949), George Cukor (1899–1983), and Sam Wood (1883–1949), yet it went on to become the most widely seen American movie in history.

AUTHORITY AND CELEBRITY

The history of the producer/director relationship is quite complex, especially throughout the changing infrastructure of the studio system in the United States. In fact, the director's role, responsibilities, and level of authority can shift quite dramatically depending upon the larger industrial organization of filmmaking. As a brief case study, it is useful to summarize the historical transformation of the Hollywood director from cameraman to contemporary celebrity.

Prior to the standardization of multi-shot narrative films around 1905, cameramen such as William K.L. Dickson, Billy Bitzer, and Edwin S. Porter selected the subject matter, arranged, shot, and edited a scenario. Exhibitors' demand for a higher output necessitated a more detailed division of labor among manufacturers. Therefore, between 1907 and 1909, a second individual—the director—was contracted to stage the action while the cameraman was relegated to the purely technical role of filming. During this brief period, in which filmmaking labor began its centralization within studio conditions, the role of the director and producer was synonymous, with individuals such as D.W. Griffith (1875–1948) and Alice Guy (1873–1968) occupying the dual position of both artist and manager. With the introduction of the multiple-reel feature and a more efficient distribution system between 1909 and 1914, a single director could no longer keep up with the technical demands or rapidity of production. Labor became even more departmentalized, with a director heading a small unit working from a detailed continuity script—a procedure developed in 1913 by the first producer-director proper, Thomas Ince (1882–1924), during his tenure at Mutual.

As the classically structured, multiple-reel feature became the norm, the director's technical responsibilities and managerial decisions actually decreased. Encroaching upon the director's administrative capacities, the "central producer" came to ascendancy as the Hollywood system achieved consolidation between 1914 and the late 1920s. These "efficiency experts" assumed managerial control of planning and controlling a continuity script, with the director relegated to the task of its execution. Creative decisions once wielded by the director were now coordinated by a central producer in advance of the director's involvement in the filmmaking process. Such figures as Allan Dwan (1885–1981), Cecil B. De Mille (1881–1959), and Lois Weber (1881–1939) became studio functionaries who no longer legally controlled the product on which they labored; instead, they worked under the direct orders of a studio's central producer (such as MGM's production chief, Irving Thalberg).

By 1931, production was relegated to a number of generically specific units under the supervision of a production chief responsible for overseeing six to eight films a year. If there were author-figures in classical Hollywood, then it is these producers who best occupy the role, as they held the ultimate authority over a film at every level of production from script development to final editing. Contract directors were often quite literally reduced to a glorified stage director, chiefly responsible for supervising the dramatic action of the performers and largely adhering to predefined "house" styles. Assigned by studio executives to six different pre-planned projects a year, a director might have only one to two weeks to prepare for shooting.

The director's creative fortunes changed only after the Directors Guild's first president, Frank Capra (1897–1991), threatened to call a general directors' strike in 1939. An executive decision was made to create the "hyphenate" category of "producer-director" in order to placate the guild. From then on, those elite filmmakers who could select their own writer, cast, and cameraman and were allowed to supervise production at all levels held the designation of producer-director. Preparation time and salaries were increased, and A-list directors were responsible for making only two to three films a year—either as freelance directors, or as the head of their own in-house independent units. Capra, Hitchcock, Fritz Lang (1890–1976), and Leo McCarey (1898–1969) all held this quasi-independent status in the late 1940s.

With the development of the package-unit system in the mid-1940s, directors were granted even more creative autonomy. As the studios sought to cut their overhead expenses, especially following the court-ordered divestiture of their theater chains in 1948 and declining box-office receipts, the shift from in-house units to a more decentralized system was accelerated. As the majors now had to distribute their films on a film-by-film basis, directors became important means of pre-selling and differentiating their product. Films were "packaged" by producers, and increasingly by talent agencies, both of whom could draw on an industry-wide pool of talent to produce a film. A director would lead a production company that was assembled on a short-term basis and dissolved after their work was completed. Interestingly, many of the major Hollywood stylists beloved by French and American auteur critics emerge during this period, including Max Ophüls (1902–1957), Vincente Minnelli (1903–1986), Otto Preminger (1906–1986), and Douglas Sirk (1897–1987). In other words, the authorial "signatures" of so-called Hollywood *auteurs* emerged and were subsumed within the economic logic of disaggregated (rather than centralized) film production.

Since the absorption of the studios by major media conglomerates in the late 1980s and early 1990s, the director has become an even more valuable commodity in a production horizon dominated by blockbusters and franchises designed to generate profits in multiple ancillary

ERICH VON STROHEIM
b. Vienna, Austria, 22 September 1885, d. 12 May 1957

Probably the most iconic image of the working director is conjured up in the person of Erich "von" Stroheim: a monocled European despot stalking the set and barking orders through a bullhorn. Indeed, von Stroheim's persona of an actor—"the man you love to hate"—was equal parts tyrannical egoist and unappreciated genius. Fittingly, in most critical retrospectives of his career, von Stroheim is typically represented as either a megalomaniac of monstrous proportions or the victim of studio philistinism.

Erich Oswald Stroheim emigrated to the United States from his native Vienna, Austria, in 1909. The son of a Jewish hat manufacturer, he left the country penniless and disgraced after the family business failed, and the Austrian army discharged him as an invalid after five months of service. Little is known about his early years in America, but by the time he arrived in Los Angeles in 1915 to work as an extra, he had created an elaborate biography for himself, claiming to be a German aristocrat with a distinguished record in the imperial army. Simultaneously cultivating experience as both an actor and assistant director, von Stroheim directed his first feature, *Blind Husbands* (1919), to considerable commercial and critical success.

All of his films are concerned with characters who degrade themselves in the pursuit of money, sex, and/or status. What is remarkable about von Stroheim's representations of these endeavors, however, is the density of sociocultural detail against which they are enacted. His two masterpieces, *Greed* (1924) and *The Wedding March* (1928), recreate prewar San Francisco and Vienna in obsessive detail. Not simply exercises in slavish verisimilitude, the films are informed by the naturalism of Émile Zola, so the degeneracy of the films' characters is always determined by circumstances and environment. *Greed*'s shambling protagonist fumbles his way from the filth of Polk Street to the blistering hell of Death Valley, and the decline of the debauched aristocrats in *The Wedding March* is a microcosm of the general collapse of the Hapsburg empire.

The exactitude of Von Stroheim's vision and struggles against the emerging studio system make him a *cause célèbre* for *auteur* theorists. Conversely, studio apologists reference his career as a cautionary tale for egomaniacal filmmakers. Most of von Stroheim's work is incomplete, truncated, or has been lost entirely. His excesses on *Merry-Go-Round* (1923) prompted Universal's head of production, Irving Thalberg, to fire him after shooting only one-fourth of the film. Thalberg also ordered *Greed* to be reduced from forty-seven reels to a mere ten, and *The Wedding March* was similarly eviscerated under the order of Pat Powers at Paramount. Similarly, his final two projects—*Queen Kelly* and *Walking Down Broadway*—are severely truncated as well. Whatever one's opinions of his ambitions, von Stroheim remains one of the most controversial and uncompromising filmmakers in Hollywood history.

RECOMMENDED VIEWING

As Director: *Blind Husbands* (1919), *Foolish Wives* (1922), *Greed* (1924), *The Wedding March* (1928), *Queen Kelly* (1929); As Actor: *Hearts of the World* (1918), *Blind Husbands* (1919), *The Great Gabbo* (1929), *As You Desire Me* (1932), *La Grand illusion* (*Grand Illusion*, 1937), *Five Graves to Cairo* (1943), *The Great Flamarion* (1945), *Sunset Boulevard* (1950)

FURTHER READING

Curtiss, Thomas Quinn. *Von Stroheim*. New York: Farrar, Straus and Giroux, 1971.

Koszarkski, Richard. *The Man You Loved to Hate: Erich von Stroheim and Hollywood*. Oxford and New York: Oxford University Press, 1983.

Lennig, Arthur. *Stroheim*. Lexington: University Press of Kentucky, 2000.

Rosenbaum, Jonathan. *Greed*. London: British Film Institute, 1993.

Thomson, David. "Stroheim and Seeing Money." In *The Whole Equation: A History of Hollywood*, 202–216. New York: Knopf, 2005.

Aaron E. N. Taylor

markets. As labor is now almost exclusively outsourced, a director frequently acts as a lynchpin within a temporary, electronically maintained network of technicians, pro-grammers, and artisans—many of whom he will not even meet in person. In order to remain visible within a highly differentiated and hit-driven market, a commercially savvy,

Erich von Stroheim in **Foolish Wives** *(1922).* EVERETT COLLECTION. REPRODUCED BY PERMISSION.

freelance director is encouraged to develop an ostentatious style that will attract a younger and lucrative demographic. Examples include the flamboyant, but ultimately superficial post-classical aesthetics of such "shooters" as McG (b. Joseph McGinty Nichol in 1970), Brett Ratner (b. 1969), David Fincher (b. 1962), Michael Bay (b. 1965), and Gore Verbinski (b. 1964). For these music video alumni, "style" is no longer regarded romantically as an indication of personal expressivity; instead, it is motivated by a commercial logic (the acquisition and retention of work) and its value is purely fiscal.

The current prominence of the director's position is underlined by the substantial financial compensation awarded in the United States. In 2004, for example, the minimum salary of a director working on a film whose budget exceeded $1.5 million was $13,423 per week. Of course, salaries can climb much higher depending upon the profitability of the director's past films. Warner Bros., for example, paid Peter Jackson over $20 million against twenty percent of the grosses to write, direct, and produce the 2005 remake of *King Kong*. Other commercially successful Hollywood directors whose fee runs into eight fig-

ures include Robert Zemeckis (b. 1952), M. Night Shyamalan (b. 1970), and Steven Spielberg (b. 1946). However, as an indication of the rising star power of the director, it has become a frequent practice for such commercially successful filmmakers to negotiate deals that consist of low upfront fees compensated with higher percentage points from their film's gross profits. As the "hyphenates" continue to gain power and influence, their business acumen has become as important as their creative powers.

Moreover, as Warren Buckland argues, contemporary Hollywood directors achieve the status of *auteur* not simply because a recurring personal style is manifested in the treatment of his or her material; rather, they wield control over the production, distribution, and exhibition of their work. By "vertically integrating" all three stages of filmmaking, they exert considerable influence over the external conditions of their authorship: finances, talent, and distribution. Spielberg and George Lucas (b. 1944)—the premier twenty-first century filmmaker-moguls—are notable as directors, producers, owners of filmmaking facilities, and holders of lucrative franchises because their integrated labor is personally, rather than externally, controlled.

Thus, the contemporary celebrity director has become a brand image based on singularity, familiarity, and reliability. Hollywood has found the myth of the auteur highly congenial to contemporary business practices in that it promotes a sense of product continuity. Yet to invoke the director's name is not necessarily to invoke an author; a manufactured authorial signature merely evokes a series of pleasurable expectations on behalf of the viewer. Attributing a film to a single creative individual is a strategy designed to remind viewers of a previously enjoyed product in the hopes that they will pay to repeat a similar experience. Major studios care little about ascribing creative authority to the director's name. Indeed, studios are quick to stress multiple authorial sources if they believe such emphasis will contribute to a film's marketability—hence the contemporary proliferation of promotional taglines that link a film to the past commercial successes of unspecified "creators," producers, and even writers.

While the conception of "style" and its relation to "personal expression" retains residual romantic connotations in the international art cinema tradition, the "author-value" of the director has become increasingly commodified in a global marketplace. With exhibitors in most countries importing over 85 percent of their films from Hollywood, international festival circuits are emerging as the primary means for art films to secure distribution. In North America, art cinema has been perceived as a "director's cinema" since the 1950s, when films directed by Luis Buñuel (1900–1983), Federico Fellini

STANLEY KUBRICK
b. New York, New York, 26 July 1928, d. 7 March 1999

Renowned for the icy, near-clinical elegance with which he represents human folly, obsession, and perversion, Stanley Kubrick produced thirteen feature films spanning most of the major genres, many of which are regarded as canonical. His work exhibits a near-metaphysical preoccupation with geometrical design that often finds expression within narrative situations featuring passionate characters who flail and crash against the boundaries of a rigorously formal(ized) world.

With little patience for formal education, Kubrick spent most of his adolescence in the Bronx, New York, frequenting chess clubs and taking photographs for *Look* magazine. Using his savings from a *Look* photo-essay on boxing, Kubrick made his film debut, *Day of the Fight* (1951), a sixteen-minute documentary on boxer Walter Cartier. This early short demonstrates two of Kubrick's stylistic trademarks: elaborately choreographed hand-held camera work and the use of available light. Kubrick's first independent features were *Fear and Desire* (1953), a psychosexual war thriller that he subsequently disowned, and the hard-boiled, occasionally surreal *Killer's Kiss* (1955).

During this period of apprenticeship, Kubrick's technical fastidiousness and insistence on complete creative control brought him to the attention of United Artists, which distributed his heist thriller, *The Killing* (1956). Yet they also drew the ire of producer-star Kirk Douglas during filming of *Paths of Glory* (1957) and *Spartacus* (1960). Resolving not to be compromised again by the restrictions of studio filmmaking, Kubrick relocated to MGM British Studios, at Borehamwood, England, where he directed his remaining work with near-complete autonomy.

His remaining eight films are uncompromising studies of violence, sexual pathology, and the limitations of rationality. *Lolita* (1962) and *Eyes Wide Shut* (1999) examine the sexual frustrations that drive their ostensibly cultivated male protagonists to ruin. *Dr. Strangelove* (1964) and *Full Metal Jacket* (1987) offer devastating portraits of an American military ethos hell-bent for an apocalypse. *A Clockwork Orange* (1971) and *The Shining* (1980) explore the confluence of culture and murder, with a Beethoven-loving sadist in the former and a novelist whose failures lead to psychosis in the latter. While *2001: A Space Odyssey* (1968) depicts a near-mystical cycle of humanity's discovery of and transcendence over technology, *Barry Lyndon* (1975) charts the social ascent and decline of an eighteenth-century Irish rogue; both are technically astounding critical essays on the cultural imperative of progress.

Throughout his independent work, Kubrick continually pushed technical boundaries, using "Slitscan photography" in *2001*, candlelight in *Barry Lyndon*, and extensive Steadicam tracking shots in *The Shining*. Careful cultivation of his actors' performances has resulted in some of the most memorable characterizations in cinematic history (Peter Sellers in *Dr. Strangelove*, Malcolm McDowell in *A Clockwork Orange*, and Jack Nicholson in *The Shining*). Above all, Kubrick's films are structured with mathematical intricacy, and their ambiguous emotional address is nearly unprecedented in commercial cinema.

RECOMMENDED VIEWING

The Killing (1956), *Paths of Glory* (1957), *Lolita* (1962), *Dr. Strangelove, or How I Learned to Stop Worrying and Love the Bomb* (1964), *2001: A Space Odyssey* (1968), *A Clockwork Orange* (1971), *Barry Lyndon* (1975), *The Shining* (1980), *Full Metal Jacket* (1987), *Eyes Wide Shut* (1999)

FURTHER READING

Baxter, John. *Stanley Kubrick: A Biography*. New York: Carroll & Graf Publishers, 1997.

Chion, Michel. *Kubrick's Cinema Odyssey*. Translated by Claudia Gorbman. London: British Film Institute, 2002.

Falsetto, Mario. *Stanley Kubrick: A Narrative and Stylistic Analysis*. 2nd ed. Westport, CT: Praeger, 2001.

Nelson, Thomas Allen. *Kubrick: Inside a Film Artist's Maze*. Expanded ed. Bloomington: Indiana University Press, 2000.

Walker, Alexander, Sybil Taylor, and Ulrich Ruchti. *Stanley Kubrick, Director*. Revised and expanded ed. New York: Norton, 1999.

Aaron E. N. Taylor

Stanley Kubrick on the set of* Barry Lyndon *(1975).
EVERETT COLLECTION. REPRODUCED BY PERMISSION.

(1920–1993), Akira Kurosawa (1910–1998), François Truffaut (1932–1984), and others achieved substantial box-office success in the emerging art house scene. However, the cultural cachet of the "name" director has assumed even greater prominence, as the star status of the director is now the imperative that largely drives the economics of the art house market. Certainly, to promote such names as Pedro Almodóvar (b. 1949), Catherine Breillat (b. 1948), Jane Campion (b. 1954), Hou Hsiao-Hsien (b. 1947), Mohsen Makhmalbaf (b. 1957), Mira Nair (b. 1957), Idrissa Ouedraogo (b. 1954), Walter Salles (b. 1956), or Lars von Trier (b. 1956) is to portend a unique cinematic experience, attributed to the artistry of a singular filmmaker. Yet one must also recognize that this authorial status is both a political and economic strategy maintained within the high-stakes business of a global culture market. Now more than ever, the director is a conflicted figure, owing a divided allegiance to the demands of both art and commerce.

SEE ALSO *Auteur Theory and Authorship; Mise-en-scène; Production Process*

FURTHER READING

"Basic Agreement of 2005." *Directors Guild of America Inc.* http://www.dga.org/index2.php3.

Bogdanovich, Peter. *Who the Devil Made It: Conversations with Legendary Film Directors.* New York: Knopf, 1997.

Bordwell, David, Staiger, Janet, and Kristin Thompson. *The Classical Hollywood Cinema: Film Style and Mode of Production to 1960.* New York: Columbia University Press, 1985.

Buckland, Warren. "The Role of the Auteur in the Age of the Blockbuster: Steven Spielberg and DreamWorks." In *Movie Blockbusters,* edited by Julian Stringer, 84–98. London and New York: Routledge, 2003.

Lumet, Sidney. *Making Movies.* New York: Knopf, 1995.

Nichols, Bill. "Discovering Form, Inferring Meaning: New Cinemas and the Festival Circuit." *Film Quarterly* 41, no. 3 (1994): 16–30.

Perez, Gilberto. *The Material Ghost: Films and Their Medium.* Baltimore: John Hopkins University Press, 1998.

Perkins, V. F. *Film as Film.* London and New York: Penguin, 1972.

Rothman, Jack. *Hollywood in Wide Angle: How Directors View Filmmaking.* Lanham, MD: Scarecrow Press, 2004.

Sarris, Andrew. *The American Cinema: Directors and Directions, 1929–1968.* New York: Dutton, 1968.

———. "Notes on the Auteur Theory." In *Film Theory and Criticism: Introductory Readings.* 6th ed., edited by Leo Braudy and Marshall Cohen, 561–565. Oxford and New York: Oxford University Press, 2004.

Tirard, Laurent. *Moviemakers' Master Class: Private Lessons from the World's Foremost Directors.* New York: Faber and Faber, 2002.

Wilkinson, Charles. *The Working Director.* Studio City, CA: Michael Wiese Productions, 2005.

Aaron E. N. Taylor

DISASTER FILMS

———◼———

Naturally, the disaster film began by accident. When Georges Méliès (1861–1938) jammed his camera and a bus inexplicably turned into a hearse, the accidental merging of two documentary images created the spectacle of disaster. That begat films such as *Collision and Shipwreck at Sea* (1898). Ever since, audiences have relished the vicarious terror and awesome spectacle of films where comfort turns into catastrophe.

The disaster film is defined less by conventions and imagery than by its plot situation: a community confronts natural or supernatural annihilation. As a result, the disaster tends to overlap several more formal genres. Nonetheless, it is possible to define ten basic types—four by the nature of the threat, five by the situation, and the last by tone.

THE TYPES

One group of disaster films features attack by creatures, from ants normal (*The Naked Jungle,* 1954) or abnormal (*Them!*, 1954) to elephants (*Elephant Walk*, 1954). Monsters created by nature run amok include *The Giant Gila Monster* (1959) and the mutants Godzilla, Mothra, Reptilicus, Gappa, and Rodan, which relived Japan's atomic nightmare. The United States's 1950s nuclear anxieties spawned more modest monsters, from the Black Lagoon, from 20,000 fathoms, and from beneath the sea. Smaller threats undercut mankind's higher link on the Great Chain of Being, most notably in Alfred Hitchcock's *The Birds* (1961), but also in the second threatening group, "bully bacteria."

Seen killers—such as David Cronenberg's phallic little bleeders in *Shivers* (or *The Parasite Murders*,

1975)—are terrifying, but those unseen are worse. *Anthrax* (2001) anticipated North America's post-9/11 fear of chemical attack, and Wolfgang Petersen's *Outbreak* (1995) unleashed an ebola crisis. The television film *Plague Fighters* (1996) reminds us that a disaster film can also be a documentary.

Worse than terrestrial creatures, aliens frighten whether they are peaceful (*The Day the Earth Stood Still*, 1951), malevolent (*Invasion of the Body Snatchers*, 1956; 1978), or even vegetable (*The Thing*, 1951). Man creates his own monsters from mud (*Der Golem*, 1920), body parts (*Frankenstein*, 1931), or computer (*Westworld*, 1974). The monster is a primeval shapeless evil in *The Quatermass Experiment* (or *The Creeping Unknown*, 1955) and *The Green Slime* (1969). Ang Lee's *Hulk* (2003) provides a green personification of rage—a monster for our post-psychoanalytic age. These first three types overlap with the horror and science-fiction film, with their threats of dehumanization and our suppressed dark energies.

The unleashed elements can be even crueller than nature's creatures. Volcanoes have lavished lava from *The Last Days of Pompeii* (1908) to *Deep Core* (2000). Whether working with wind (*The Hurricane*, 1937), water (*The Rains Came*, 1939), both wind and water (*The Perfect Storm*, 2000), or quaking earth (*Earthquake*, 1974), these films draw moral weight from the renewal stories of Noah and Sodom and Gomorrah. Natural-disaster films remind us that our technology shrinks before the forces of nature. The communal confrontation with nature distinguishes the disaster film from the action-adventure genre that centers on individual hero and human villainy.

Urban disaster in **The Towering Inferno** *(Irwin Allen, 1974).* © 20TH CENTURY FOX FILM CORP./COURTESY EVERETT COLLECTION. REPRODUCED BY PERMISSION.

Disasters based on situations begin with cities destroyed (the "edifice wrecks" cycle), which shatter our urban security. From Pompeii to the terrorist attack on New York on September 11, 2001, films have imagined the destruction of our cities, which are emblems of both community and comfort. *The Towering Inferno* (1974) gave a modern Babel a fire on the eighty-fifth floor. In *The Neptune Factor* (1973) giant fish threaten an underwater living experiment. *Invasion USA* (1952) and *Red Planet Mars* (1952) annihilate America and Russia, respectively. Anti-materialist destruction is celebrated in the endings of two 1970 films, Michelangelo Antonioni's *Zabriskie Point* and John Boorman's *Leo the Last,* examples of explosive flower power. As the United States grew more city-centered, instances of urban destruction outnumbered the rural; few disaster films are set in Kansas anymore.

An alternative community is the ship of fools, where a cross-section of humanity on a micro–journey of life face disaster. Sometimes the folks are all at sea, as in the various *Titanic* films (1915, 1943, 1953, 1997) and *A Night to Remember* (1958)—or under it, as in *The Abyss* (1985). Or they're up in the air, as in *The High and the Mighty* (1954) and *Airport* (1969). Nor are we safe in the earth, as shown in *The Core* (2003). As in the nature disasters, mankind is punished for the hubris of complacency.

Survival films detail the aftermath of a disaster, as in *Lifeboat* (1944) and *Marooned* (1970). Some films begin after a war is over: *Soylent Green* (1973), *The War Game* (1967), *Teenage Caveman* (1958), and George Miller's *Mad Max* series (1979, 1981, 1985). The edifice, ship, and survival disaster types share the melodrama's focus on societal conflicts.

Similarly, the war genre edges into disaster when the film emphasizes carnage and the human conflict tends to be internecine, as in *Slaughterhouse Five* (1972) and the post-battle scenes in *Gone with the Wind* (1939). Some space war films such as *The Day the Sky Exploded* (1958) and *The Day the World Ended* (1956) visualize the disaster as Day of Judgment.

In the more general, history disaster, a doom is set in the distant past—most notably in the tradition of biblical epics, as well as films such as *San Francisco* (1936) and *Cabiria* (1914). A variation on the period disaster projects into the future, as in the *Planet of the Apes* series (1968–1973), *When Worlds Collide* (1951), *Things to Come* (1936, 1979), and *War of the Worlds* (1953, 2003, 2005). Arguably the best historical disaster film is Ingmar Bergman's *The Seventh Seal* (1957), which used the period angst of the Black Plague in the Middle Ages for an art-house meditation upon the life of honor and the dance of death.

The disaster includes—and perhaps is apotheosized as a genre by—the *comic* treatment. Much slapstick comedy exults in massive destruction, from Mack Sennett to Buster Keaton. *The Bed-Sitting Room* (1968) and *A Boy and His Dog* (1976) provide comic takes on nuclear apocalypse. Jim Abrahams and David Zucker sent up *Airport* with their *Airplane!* larks (1980, 1982). Woody Allen parodied the monster film in *Everything You Always Wanted to Know About Sex, But Were Afraid to Ask* (1972) when a giant breast threatens an isolated countryside, and in *New York Stories* (1989), when the hero's dead mother fills the sky, nagging. In *The Big Bus* (1976), the detailed parody virtually defines the conventions of the journey disaster film, in the preposterous context of a nuclear-powered bus.

THE CONVENTIONS

Film conventions are recurring elements that distinguish works in a particular genre. They are tendencies and cross-referents, not rules. Thus, for example, notwithstanding the

IRWIN ALLEN
b. New York, New York, 12 June 1916, d. 2 November 1991

The "master of disaster" started from science. Irwin Allen wrote, produced, and directed an adaptation of Rachel Carson's *The Sea around Us* (1952), which won an Oscar® for best documentary feature. His documentary *The Animal World* (1956) featured prehistoric effects by master animator Ray Harryhausen. Oddly, Allen's *The Story of Mankind* (1957) marked the last collective appearance of the Marx Brothers (Groucho, Harpo, and Chico respectively played Peter Minuit, Isaac Newton, and a monk). Allen switched to fiction to direct *The Lost World* (1960), based on the Arthur Conan Doyle novel, which was a precursor to Steven Spielberg's *Jurassic Park* (1997).

Allen also had a prolific career in TV. His *Voyage to the Bottom of the Sea* ran from 1964 to 1968 (110 episodes). Although his favorite of his TV series, *The Time Tunnel* (1966), folded after only thirty episodes, Allen returned with *Lost in Space* (83 episodes, 1965–1968), about an outer-spaced Family Robinson; *Land of the Giants* (51 episodes, 1967–1970); *Swiss Family Robinson* (20 episodes, 1975–1976); and *Code Red* (13 episodes, 1981–1982).

Allen is best known as the producer of the two key 1970s disaster-film prototypes. *The Poseidon Adventure* (1972) set the pattern: a large, famous cast, a dramatic crisis, clear moral lines, and spectacular special effects. When a luxury cruise ship capsizes in a tidal wave, the survivors struggle to reach the top (i.e., the bottom) of the vessel. Inverting the formula, in *The Towering Inferno* (1974), the all-star cameos struggle to get down safely from a burning skyscraper. Though it lost the Oscar® for best picture (to *Godfather II*, not unjustly), *The Towering*

Inferno won Oscars® for cinematography, editing, and song ("We May Never Love Like This Again"). Allen directed the action scenes in *Poseidon* and *Inferno*, and all the scenes of *Voyage to the Bottom of the Sea* (1961), *Five Weeks in a Balloon* (1962), *The Swarm* (1978), and the *Poseidon* sequel *Beyond the Poseidon Adventure* (1979), which was symptomatically about attempts to loot the earlier success.

Addressing the inevitable tragedy in human life, Allen used expensive disaster effects to lure viewers away from TV, for which he later produced three smaller disaster films: *Hanging by a Thread* (1979), and *Cave-In* and *The Night the Bridge Fell Down* (both 1983). He was reportedly planning another *Lost in Space* movie when he died of a heart attack in 1991.

RECOMMENDED VIEWING
The Sea around Us (1952), *The Story of Mankind* (1957), *The Lost World* (1960), *Voyage to the Bottom of the Sea* (1961), *Five Weeks in a Balloon* (1962), *The Poseidon Adventure* (1972), *The Towering Inferno* (1974), *The Swarm* (1978), *Beyond the Poseidon Adventure* (1979)

FURTHER READING
Doyle, Arthur Conan. *The Lost World*. New York: Doran, 1912.

Fox, Gardner. *Jules Verne's Five Weeks in a Balloon*. New York: Pyramid Books, 1962.

Leinster, Murray, and Irwin Allen. *Land of the Giants*. New York: Pyramid Books, 1968.

Sturgeon, Theodore. *Voyage to the Bottom of the Sea*. New York: Pyramid Books, 1961.

Maurice Yacowar

period disasters, dramatic immediacy prefers that films be set in the here and now. The first US film version of H.G. Wells's *The War of the Worlds* (1952) shifted the setting from Victorian London to contemporary Los Angeles. Cornel Wilde set his survival film *No Blade of Grass* (1970) in London to emphasize the culture threatened by anarchy ("Keep up your Latin, David; it will stand you in good stead"). *Volcano* (1997) pours Pompeiian lava through the streets of modern Los Angeles. In the Sensurround *Earthquake*, our first tremor comes when the

film shows people at a movie. In *Night of the Living Dead* (1968) and *Cujo* (1983), the attacks on women in cars played most effectively at drive-in screenings.

To reflect the makeup audience, disaster films usually feature a social cross-section. The disaster challenges humanity rather than the individual. The group fractures variously: the businessman will clash with the ethicist, the character who knows from experience with the theoretician, the rich with the poor, the black with the white. In *Jaws* (1975) the mayor in the sharkskin suit sells out safety for

Irwin Allen. © WARNER BROS./COURTESY EVERETT COLLECTION.

business, while the noble savage Quint (Robert Shaw) spars with college man Hooper (Richard Dreyfuss) until they bond over beer and wounds. In *Lifeboat* the key tensions are between the working-class guy (John Hodiak) and the rich bitch (Tallulah Bankhead), and between the American "family" and the outsider Germans (both the Nazi and the assimilated Schmidt/Smith). In this respect, John Ford's classic western *Stagecoach* (1939) is exemplary, as it afflicts various social antitheses with savage nature, as problematically embodied by the Indians, and with the dubious "blessings of civilization," represented by the puritan bigots and the crooked banker. The genre dissolves internal squabbles before a common enemy.

Often society is imaged as a besieged family. In Hitchcock's *The Birds*, Mitch's cold, tight family stretches to admit Melanie. In the last shot the caged lovebirds seem a tentative talisman against the feathered force poised around the retreating characters. In *Twister* (1996) the family/crew are threatened not just by flying tanker trucks and cows but by unscrupulous corporate rivals. In the isolated setting the besieged are left to their own resources, with no help from the outside.

Confirming the characters' need for self-sufficiency, the disaster film plays with ideas of religion in an irreligious age. Religious figures question their faith rather

than assert it. Crackpots such as the drunken seer in *The Birds* recall Old Testament prophets, calling down punishment for our godless pride and corruption. The *San Francisco* earthquake seems prompted, at least in part, by Clark Gable's knocking down a priest played by Spencer Tracy. Rene Auberjonois's priest in *The Big Bus*, a doubter who gloats over God's giving him the window seat but who wants to date, is a parody of Gene Hackman's pragmatic priest in *The Poseidon Adventure* (1972). The disaster film's happy ending derives from the hero's intuition/experience/courage—but it is often preceded by a prayer. Absent a presiding god, the disaster characters often gamble, flipping a coin or drawing straws or cards for guidance. *The Seventh Seal* typically privileges the individual quest for salvation over the corrupted church.

In the disaster film the law and the learned prove as impotent as the church, as the genre reminds us of the fragility of our social institutions. A rare policeman hero in a disaster film is James Whitmore in *Them!*. The heroism of the cop (George Kennedy) in *Earthquake* is tempered by his disillusionment with the force and his suspension from it. Disaster usually includes a specialist—a scientist, professor, or an amateur such as the ornithologist in *The Birds*—but even their factual framework can't handle nature. Mystery dwarfs science, even when impressive new science enables the adventure, as in outer-space disasters and the underground burrowing in *Deep Core*. Specialists start out smug, but as the disaster's complacent characters slip from security into terror, the genre teaches old-fashioned humility.

Against all this fragmentation, the obligatory romantic subplot serves more than box-office appeal. It confronts chaos, dehumanizing antisocial individualism, and the opposite dangers of emotional excess and suppression, with the positive value of love. It signifies community renewal and generosity.

Older than the Old Testament, the disaster genre can speak pointedly to its particular time. During the Red Scare in the 1950s the favorite disaster threats were inhuman, cold monsters from outer space (representing Communists from Russia) and atomic science backfiring. With the United States divided over the Vietnam War, Hollywood generally steered clear of making war films and featured amoral cops and spies, projecting the war's moral dilemmas onto civilian genres. The disaster cycle of the 1970s made the United States the battleground that TV news depicted as elsewhere.

Armageddon (1998), in which a Texas-size asteroid threatens to wipe out Earth, demonstrates how the disaster film's conventions work in practice. Oil-driller Harry Stamper (Bruce Willis) and his maverick crew are despatched to nuke the asteroid from within.

Implicitly evoking *Planet of the Apes*, Charlton Heston's opening narration evokes cataclysm: "It happened before. It will happen again. It's just a question of time." We see digital destructions in New York City, Paris, Shanghai, then on the asteroid itself. As if Earth's annihilation wasn't a sufficient enough cause for concern, Stamper's crew clash with the more conventional NASA staff and Harry has to deal with the love affair between his daughter Grace (Liv Tyler) and his best worker, A. J. Frost (Ben Affleck). On both the personal and global levels, explosive dangers require explosive solutions, a strategy that gained momentum after 9/11. As the despairing Stamper asks God for "a little help here," A. J. rises from the presumed dead to save mankind. Stamper accepts him as his son and—despite the straw draw—sacrifices himself to restore A. J. to his Grace. Extending the allegory, of the team's two rockets, the Independence is destroyed and the Freedom survives. Religion here is subordinated to (a not unrelated) American patriotism. Apart from the asteroid, our heroes' biggest danger comes from the dilapidated Russian technology and the lunatic Red astronaut (Peter Stormare). Post–Cold War, the Russian threat is just a vodka-addled fool rather than the malevolent foe of the Cold War. In the American populist tradition, the maverick Willis, Affleck, and Steve Buscemi characters prove more humane and effective than the textbook officers. After fighting all film long, our two heroes express their mutual love at the end. The film's emotional conclusion provides a catharsis, even for the viewer not seduced by special effects.

The disaster film's commercial appeal has been strengthened by new technology's ever more special effects and surprising imagery. Yet the deeper pleasure derives from the familiarity of its human material—the characters, their challenges, their resolutions. In virtually every particular, *Armageddon*, this representative film draws upon the viewer's familiarity with the earlier films and legends of its type. The genre continuity facilitates the viewer's identification with the characters, intensifying both the vicarious chill at their peril and their heartening survival.

SEE ALSO *Action and Adventure Films; Genre; Science Fiction*

FURTHER READING

Annan, David. *Catastrophe: The End in the Cinema*. New York: Bounty, 1975.

Broderick, Mick. *Nuclear Movies*. Jefferson, NC: McFarland, 1988, 1991.

Dixon, Wheeler Winston. *Disaster and Memory: Celebrity Culture and the Crisis of Hollywood Cinema*. New York: Columbia University Press, 1999.

Forshey, Gerald E. *American Religious and Biblical Spectaculars*. Westport, CT and London: Praeger, 1992.

Keane, Stephen. *Disaster Movies: The Cinema of Catastrophe*. London and New York: Wallflower Press, 2001.

Neale, Steven. *Genre and Hollywood*. London and New York: Routledge, 2000.

———, ed. *Genre and Contemporary Hollywood*. London: British Film Institute, 2002.

Newman, Kim. *Millennium Voices: End of the World Cinema*. London: Titan, 1999.

Maurice Yacowar

DISTRIBUTION

———■———

In the film industry, distribution is the intermediary between production and exhibition and involves the following functions: sales, that is, the securing of rental contracts for specific play dates; advertising directed to theaters through trade publications and to filmgoers through the print and electronic media; the physical delivery of prints to theaters; and the method of release. New York City, the media and communications capital of the country, has served as the distributing center of the industry throughout most of its history. Distribution originally serviced motion picture theaters exclusively in the domestic and foreign markets, but as new electronic technologies were developed, distribution subsumed ancillary markets such as network television, cable television, home video, and the Internet. Nontheatrical distribution involved similar functions, but serviced educational, social, and religious organizations outside commercial exhibition.

Distributing a feature film, a company charges the producer a fee based on the gross receipts (i.e., rentals) taken in by the film. In Hollywood, the schedule of fees ranges from 30 to 45 percent of the gross, depending on the market. The fees remain in effect for the duration of the distribution contract and are levied each time a film is released to a new "window," for example, home video, cable television, or network television. The revenue from these fees is designed to offset the distributor's overhead expenses in maintaining a permanent sales organization, to recoup advertising and promotion costs, and to generate profits. When the distributor puts up financing for a feature film, the fee also serves to reward the company for taking the risk of production financing.

Hollywood has operated on a global basis since the 1920s. Overseas, American film companies dominated the screen just as they did at home. They distributed the biggest box office attractions and captured the lion's share of ticket sales. Before World War II, about a third of Hollywood's revenues came from abroad; by the 1960s, the proportion rose to about one-half. As demand for film entertainment increased worldwide, especially in western Europe, the Pacific Rim, and Latin America during the 1980s, Hollywood entered the age of globalization. In practice, globalization meant that film companies upgraded international operations to a privileged position by expanding "horizontally" to tap emerging markets worldwide, by expanding "vertically" to form alliances with independent producers to enlarge their rosters, and by "partnering" with foreign investors to secure new sources of financing. Achieving these goals has led to a merger movement in Hollywood that has yet to run its course. The history of these mergers would reveal how today's media giants, such as Time Warner, News Corp., Disney, and Viacom, protected their entrenched positions by strengthening their distribution capabilities.

EARLY PRACTICES

Considered visual novelties, the first films reached audiences by way of vaudeville. Pioneering companies assembled packages, consisting of projector, projectionist, and films, which traveled the vaudeville circuit as an act that lasted from ten to twenty minutes. In playing a circuit, a new act would typically open in the flagship theater in New York and then move to the other houses in sequence. This so-called peripatetic form of distribution ideally suited the infant film business, with its limited number of film subjects, equipment, and trained personnel.

While films were finding a ready place in metropolitan vaudeville houses, distributors also took to the road. Once projectors became available for purchase on the open market, traveling showmen brought the movies to small-town America by exhibiting their films in amusement parks, lodge halls, and vacant storefronts. Showmen originally had to purchase their films outright from producers, which was expensive, but the creation of film exchanges beginning around 1903 solved the problem by enabling showmen to rent films at a fraction of the purchase price. The availability of films for rental, in turn, stimulated the rise of the nickelodeon theater beginning in 1905.

To capitalize on this growing demand for motion picture entertainment, the pioneering film companies formed the Motion Picture Patents Company in 1909 and attempted to take control of the industry. The Trust, as the MPPC was called, standardized the playing times of films to around fifteen minutes—the playing time of a single thousand-foot reel—and created a national distribution system by licensing the requisite number of existing exchanges. The goal was to supply nickelodeons with a steady supply of shorts for programs that might change daily. In 1910 the MPPC took over the distribution function by forming a subsidiary, General Film. Although the courts eventually ruled that the MPPC setup was illegal, the Trust brought stability to the industry. General Film, for example, improved the chaotic conditions in the marketplace by inaugurating a system of "zoning" so that theaters in a particular locale would not show the same pictures simultaneously, by classifying theaters by size and location, and by regularizing pricing, among other measures.

With the arrival of feature films—defined by the trade as multiple-reel narratives with unusual content that merited special billing and advertising—a new distribution system was needed to generate more revenue to recoup higher production costs. At first, producers and importers used the "states' rights" method, which involved selling the marketing rights of an individual feature territory by territory to local distributors, who would then rent out the picture for a flat fee or on a percentage basis to theaters. Producers and importers also used road showing to market their pictures. The technique got rid of the middleman and enabled a showman to book a theater on a percentage-of-the-gross basis and then take over the actual operations for the run. Such a strategy enabled the producer or importer, rather than the subdistributor, to capture most of the box office revenue should the picture prove to be a hit. From 1912 to 1914, nearly three hundred features were distributed using these methods. States' rights distribution and road showing were satisfactory techniques to exploit one picture at a time, but if producers ever hoped to expand and regularize their output, a better method had to be found.

W. W. Hodkinson (1881–1971), a former General Film exchange man, created such a system in 1914 by convincing a group of regional states' rights exchanges to join forces and form Paramount Pictures Corporation, the first national distributor of feature films. Hodkinson's plan guaranteed exhibitors a steady supply of features because Paramount would help producers finance and advertise their pictures with advance rentals collected by the exchanges. In return, the company would charge producers a distribution fee of 35 percent of the gross to cover operating costs and a built-in profit margin. This innovative scheme attracted the country's best producers—Adolph Zukor's Famous Players, the Jesse L. Lasky Feature Play Company, among others—who signed long-term franchise agreements granting Paramount exclusive rights to their pictures.

Paramount was geared to release 104 pictures a year, enough to fill the playing time of a theater that changed bills twice a week. Exhibitors contracted for the entire Paramount program, a practice known as block booking. Though block booking would later be much abused, selling poor films on the strength of the good, the practice at its inception worked to everyone's satisfaction. Hodkinson also codified prevailing practices into a system that graded houses playing features from first-run to fifth, depending on size, condition, and location (from downtown in large cities to village). As the "feature craze" spread, other national distributors entered the market, among them Metro Pictures, Universal, and the Fox Film Corporation.

This tremendous expansion of the movie business convinced Adolph Zukor (1873–1976) that Paramount and its producers should merge, not only to effect economies of scale in production, but also to capture a greater share of the market. Hodkinson vetoed the idea, arguing that the three branches of motion pictures—production, distribution, and exhibition—should be kept separate. In his view, better pictures, better distribution, and better theater management would result if a lively independence existed among them. But Zukor was not to be denied. In a series of intricate maneuvers, Zukor had Hodkinson deposed in June 1916. Then he merged Famous Players with the studio owned by Jesse Lasky (1880–1958). Separately they might be the first- and second-ranked producers in the country; together, as the Famous Players–Lasky Corporation, they were in a class by themselves. Paramount became the distribution subsidiary of the new company. (Paramount later became the name of the parent company.) When Zukor completed his consolidations and acquisitions in December 1917, he had created the largest motion picture company in the world.

Implementing the next stage of his thinking, Zukor increased film rentals and expanded his production program, so that by 1918, Paramount distributed 220 features, more in one year than any one company before or since.

STUDIO SYSTEM PRACTICES

Zukor's tactics led to a backlash by resistant exhibitors and ultimately to a merger movement that created a vertically integrated industry controlled by a handful of companies at the end of the 1920s—Paramount; Warner Bros.; Loew's, Inc. (MGM); Twentieth Century Fox; and RKO. During the golden age of Hollywood, distribution adhered to the run-clearance-zone system. The country was divided into thirty markets, each of which was subdivided into zones that designated theatrical runs. Theaters first showing newly released pictures were designated first-run. Located in the large metropolitan areas and owned mainly by the circuits affiliated with the majors, these theaters seated thousands, commanded the highest ticket prices, and accounted for nearly 50 percent of all admissions. Second-run houses were typically located in the neighborhoods and charged lower ticket prices. Later-run houses were located in outlying communities and charged still less. Over a course of time, a feature played every area of the country from metropolis to village. This merchandising pattern for movies was similar to that of other consumer goods: first, the exclusive shops; next, the general department store; and finally, the close-out sales.

Spawned during the Great Depression as a two-for-one form of price cutting to attract customers, double features required the majors to produce two types of features, class A and class B. Class A films contained stars, had high production values, and were based on best-selling novels and plays; class B movies were, at best, inexpensive genre films that were considered filler by the companies. To recoup the higher costs of its quality product, companies rented such films on a percentage-of-the-gross basis, while the cheapies were sold at a flat fee. The former practice enabled the majors to benefit from surges at the box office, while the latter allowed them to cover their costs and operate their studios at full capacity.

The trade practices of the industry—run-clearance-zoning, block booking, admission price discrimination—were used by the majors to wrest the greatest possible profits from the market and to keep independent exhibitors in a subordinate position. The US Justice Department, as a result, instituted an antitrust case against the majors in 1938. Ten years later, the *Paramount* case, as it was called, reached the Supreme Court. In a landmark decision, the court held that the Big Five (Loew's Inc. [MGM], Paramount, RKO, Twentieth Century Fox, and Warner Bros.) conspired to monopolize exhibition. Trade practices such as block booking, whereby the majors rented their pictures to independent exhibitors in groups on an all-or-nothing basis, unfair clearances and runs that prolonged the time subsequent-run theaters had to wait to receive new films, and preferential arrangements among members of the Big Five were declared illegal restraints of trade. To break the monopoly in exhibition, the Supreme Court mandated that the Big Five divorce their theater chains from their production and distribution branches.

Although the majors concentrated their production efforts on the big picture, demand for low-budget films remained strong until the advent of television in the 1950s, especially in small towns. During the 1930s and 1940s, the industry defined exploitation films as those films that dealt with social problems in a sensational way, such as Warner Bros'. *I Am a Fugitive from a Chain Gang* (1932), which exposed the sordid conditions in a Georgia prison and the same studio's *Black Fury* (1935), which dramatized labor and industrial unrest in the coal mines of Pennsylvania. After television came in, exploitation films became associated with low-budget science fiction, horror, rock 'n' roll, and drag racing films designed to appeal to teenagers and the drive-in trade. The distribution of these films was handled by independent producers and small studios outside mainstream Hollywood, such as Edward Small (1891–1977), Columbia's "Jungle Sam" Katzman (1901–1973), Allied Artists (formerly Monogram), and American International Pictures.

Although the *Paramount* decision restructured the industry, it by no means reduced the importance of the big companies. By allowing the majors to retain their distribution arms, the court, wittingly or not, gave them the means to retain control of the market. The reason, simply stated, is that decreasing demand for motion picture entertainment during the 1950s foreclosed the distribution market to newcomers. Distribution presents high barriers to entry. To operate efficiently, a distributor requires a worldwide sales force and capital to finance twenty to thirty pictures a year. Since the market absorbed fewer and fewer films during this period, it could support only a limited number of distributors—about the same as existed at the time of the *Paramount* case.

MARKETING THE BIG PICTURE

After World War II, things were never the same for the motion picture industry. Beginning in 1947, the winds of ill fortune blew incessantly for ten years, during which movie attendance dropped by one-half. Television, the main culprit, replaced the movies as the dominant

STEVEN J. ROSS
b. Steven Jay Rechnitz, Brooklyn, New York, 19 September 1927, d. 20 December 1992

Regarded in the industry as a consummate deal maker, Steven J. Ross's greatest coup was orchestrating the merger of his company Warner Communications with Time, Inc., in 1989 to create Time Warner, the world's largest media and entertainment company. Anticipating the need to strengthen Warner Communications' distribution capabilities as Hollywood entered an era of globalization, Ross brokered a $14 billion deal that combined his company's record labels, book division, cable television systems, and Hollywood studio with the magazines of Time's publishing empire. Ross became chairman and co–chief operating officer of the new Time Warner, and he received as compensation nearly $80 million in 1990, more than any other executive of a public company.

Ross started out during the Great Depression selling trousers in New York's garment district. Marrying well to Carol Rosenthal in 1954, he joined his father-in-law's funeral business in Manhattan as a trainee. A plan Ross devised to rent out the company's limousines in off hours ultimately led to the creation of Kinney National Services—a conglomerate, which Ross headed, that operated funeral homes, a car rental agency, parking lots and garages, and a building maintenance service. Ross expanded into entertainment by purchasing the Ashley Famous talent agency in 1967 and then, in 1969, the ailing Warner Brothers-Seven Arts, a Toronto-based television syndicator that had recently acquired the venerable Warner Bros. studio in Hollywood, along with its post-1948 film library and record labels. He then branched out into cable television by launching Warner-Amex Cable Communications in partnership with American Express (which he later bought out), and he eventually added toys, cosmetics, video games, and other businesses to his

company, which he renamed Warner Communications in 1972 after selling off the old Kinney business.

Following the collapse of Warner's video game business in 1982, Ross downsized the company, selling off Warner's peripheral operations to become a vertically integrated entertainment conglomerate engaged in film and television programming, recorded music, and mass market book publishing. The restructuring allowed for diversification while enabling the company to meet increased demand worldwide for feature films and television shows, videos and compact discs, and cable TV.

During Ross's stewardship, Warner's film division consistently captured top shares of the box office, producing blockbusters such as the *Superman*, *Batman*, and *Lethal Weapon* series, Steven Spielberg's *The Color Purple* (1985), and numerous Clint Eastwood action films, including *The Unforgiven* (1992), which won Academy Awards® for best picture and best director. Ross came under criticism for saddling the company with enormous debt to pay the cost of the merger with Time, for his pay package, and for his lavish treatment of Warner's stars. Nonetheless, Ross is remembered as a creative entrepreneur who was willing to take great risks to realize his vision of a global media complex.

FURTHER READING

Bruck, Connie. *Master of the Game: Steve Ross and the Creation of Time Warner.* New York: Simon & Schuster, 1994.

Klein, Alec. *Stealing Time: Steve Case, Jerry Levin, and the Collapse of AOL Time Warner.* New York: Simon & Schuster, 2003.

Tino Balio

leisure-time activity of the American people. Studios cut back on production, and audiences became selective and more discerning in their moviegoing tastes. Motion pictures, therefore, were produced and marketed individually. During the 1960s, Hollywood adopted a blockbuster formula to reach the masses. The new formula to "make them big, show them big, and sell them big" succeeded; it resulted in family-oriented hits like *Around the World in Eighty Days* (1956), *Ben-Hur*

(1959), *Exodus* (1960), *The Sound of Music* (1965), and *Fiddler on the Roof* (1971).

The big picture transformed the three-tier playoff of the run-clearance-zone pattern to a two-tiered playoff. Typically, a blockbuster was released in each market, first to selected houses for extended runs as road shows or exclusive engagements, and subsequently to large numbers of theaters to capture the leavings. Another way of characterizing this distribution pattern is "slow and fast."

Kurosawa, 1951). Foreign films paled in significance to Hollywood fare at the box office, but their influence on American film culture was enormous. Foreign films became regular subjects of feature stories and reviews in the *New York Times*, mass-circulation magazines, highbrow periodicals, and the trade press. They were also promoted by museums, film festivals, and college film and literature departments around the country.

Foreign film distribution was handled originally by small independent companies operating out of New York, such as Joseph Burstyn, Janus Films, and Lopert Films, but by the 1960s the art film market had been taken over by Hollywood. The commercial potential of the art film market became apparent when films like *Et Dieu... créa la femme* (*And God Created Woman*, Roger Vadim, 1956), starring Brigitte Bardot, and *Pote tin Kyriaka* (*Never On Sunday*, Jules Dassin, 1960), starring Melina Mercouri, broke box office records. Since foreign films might have difficulty securing a seal of approval from the Production Code Administration because of their sexual content, the majors got around the problem simply by forming art film distribution subsidiaries. The new subsidiaries either acquired the distribution rights to completed films or formed alliances with new talent by offering young directors production financing. Soon, the majors had absorbed nearly the entire pantheon of European auteurs, including Michelangelo Antonioni (b. 1912), Luchino Visconti (1906–1976), and Federico Fellini (1920–1993) of Italy; Tony Richardson (1928–1991), Joseph Losey (1909–1984), and Karel Reisz (1926–2002) of Britain; François Truffaut (1932–1984), Jean-Luc Godard (b. 1930), Louis Malle (1932–1995), and Eric Rohmer (b. 1920) of France; and Ingmar Bergman (b. 1918) of Sweden.

The core audience for foreign films consisted mostly of America's "cinephile" generation, university students in their twenties and thirties. In response to this student interest, colleges and universities began offering courses in film history, theory, and criticism. Colleges and universities also supported an estimated four thousand film societies, which were attracting 2.5 million persons annually by 1968. Foreign films were a mainstay of these societies, which also showed Hollywood classics, documentaries, and experimental films. To cultivate this audience in the so-called 16 mm nontheatrical market, independent foreign film distributors such as Janus Films and New Yorker Films abandoned regular art film distribution and concentrated on the university scene. They were soon joined by the Hollywood majors, who also wanted a share of the bonanza. Since the art films in distribution had already made names for themselves in the theatrical market and in the national media, companies catering to the 16mm market promoted their rosters mainly through catalogs, which simply described the

Steven J. Ross. KEITH MEYERS/NEW YORK TIMES CO./HUTTON ARCHIVE/GETTY IMAGES.

The blockbuster changed release schedules as well. Instead of releasing pictures throughout the year at regular intervals, companies brought out their important pictures during the Christmas and Easter holidays and at the beginning of summer.

ART FILM MARKET

Largely shut out of the American market since the 1920s, foreign films did not really reach US theaters until after World War II. Before the war, foreign films played only in New York and in a few other major cities. After the war, they played in a growing number of art film theaters around the country and created a subindustry known as the art film market, which was devoted to the acquisition, distribution, and exhibition of foreign-language and English-language films produced abroad. Waves of imported feature films from Italy, France, Sweden, Britain, and Japan entered the country, represented by such classics as *Roma, città aperta* (*Open City*, Roberto Rossellini, 1945), *Les vacances de Monsieur Hulot* (*Mr. Hulot's Holiday*, Jacques Tati, 1953), *Det Sjunde inseglet* (*The Seventh Seal*, Ingmar Bergman, 1957), *Hamlet* (Laurence Olivier, 1948), and *Rashomon* (Akira content of the films and listed the rental terms. This market had existed since the 1930s and had done most of its business renting instructional films to colleges and schools until foreign films came along.

The art film market declined after 1969, as American films with adult themes targeted at the youth market, such as *In the Heat of the Night* (1967), *The Graduate* (1967), and *Bonnie and Clyde* (1967), captured the spotlight. The demise of the Production Code in 1968 and a cultural revolution in the United States ushered in a period of unprecedented frankness in the American cinema that rivaled most anything on the art film circuit. Although university film societies replaced the art film theater during the 1970s, they too declined when home video made huge numbers of old films—foreign and domestic—available for rent. Since 1970, the art film market has functioned as a niche business that depended on foreign-language films and English-language films produced abroad without any US backing. Although the majors reentered the art film market during the 1990s either by forming classics divisions or by acquiring successful independent distributors, such as Miramax and New Line Films, the market continued to generate only a few hits each year.

ANCILLARY MARKETS

Before television, feature films played in motion picture theater almost exclusively; after television, the new medium extended the commercial life of films by creating ancillary markets. During the 1950s, studios in desperate need of money sold off their pre-1948 film libraries to television syndicators, who, in turn, leased the films to local television stations to fill out their programming schedules. The studios were free to dispose of the pre-1948 films since they controlled television performance rights and all ancillary rights to their pictures. The sale of recent vintage Hollywood films to television had to wait until 1960, when Hollywood reached a settlement with the talent guilds regarding residual compensation. NBC became the first network to use post-1948 Hollywood films for prime-time programming in the fall of 1961 by launching *NBC Saturday Night at the Movies*. ABC followed suit in 1962 and CBS in 1965.

Thus, by the 1960s, network television had become a regular secondary market for theatrical films. The development of home video and "pay TV" created additional ancillary markets for feature films. Today, after a feature film completes its theatrical run, it is released to the following "windows" at specific intervals: first to home video and pay-per-view, then to cable television, and finally to network and syndicated television. Going through the distribution pipeline, a motion picture is exploited in one market at a time, with the exception of home video, which has a window that remains open almost indefinitely. At each point, the price of the picture to the consumer drops. Economists call the process "price tiering," which can be explained as follows: movies are first released to theaters at top prices to "high value" consumers, that is, those who are most eager to see them and are thus willing to pay the most for a ticket; movies are then released to "lower value" consumers at prices that decline with time. Thus a consumer willing to wait long enough will eventually get to see a favorite film for "free" over network television. Distributing pictures in this manner allows a distributor to tap every segment of the market in an orderly way and at a price commensurate with its demand. Home video became the most lucrative of the ancillary markets, and by 1989 had surpassed revenue from the domestic theatrical box office by a factor of two.

PORNOGRAPHY MARKET

The same electronic distribution systems that created new ancillary markets for feature films also created new distribution channels for pornography. Once a clandestine industry operating on the fringes of society, the pornography market has now gone mainstream. The VCR enabled adult entertainment to enter the home during the 1980s. Today, adult films can be purchased or rented from local video and music stores and major chains, they can be ordered at home and in the finest hotels on cable TV with video-on-demand, and they can be accessed on the Internet. The widespread acceptance of pornography has created an industry that rivals that of Hollywood in both revenues and size. Located in the nearby San Fernando Valley, the porn industry consists of 75 or 85 major production companies that churn out literally thousands of titles a year, generating billions of dollars in revenues.

THE NEW HOLLYWOOD

After undergoing a period of conglomerization in the late 1960s and 1970s, the "New Hollywood" that emerged targeted the youth audience almost exclusively. To hit this target—the "teen and preteen bubble" demographic, consisting of avid filmgoers ages ten to twenty-four—studios developed high-concept blockbusters and star vehicles for the mainstream theatrical market. High-concept blockbusters went hand in hand with saturation booking, particularly during the fourteen weeks in the summer between Memorial Day and Labor Day when school is out. A standard marketing practice since *Jaws* in 1975, saturation booking was designed to recoup production costs quickly by opening a new film simultaneously at over two thousand screens, backed by an

Jaws *(Steven Spielberg, 1975) was given saturation release and a strong advertising campaign.* © UNIVERSAL PICTURES/
COURTESY EVERETT COLLECTION. REPRODUCED BY PERMISSION.

intensive national advertising campaign. Saturation booking took advantage of changing demographics by servicing shopping-center theaters in the suburbs, far away from the decaying central cities and their fading motion picture palaces.

Although television had already become a potent advertising medium, Hollywood publicity campaigns continued to rely on the print medium almost exclusively until the 1970s, when television became the principal medium to advertise most pictures. Studios relied more and more on massive media advertising to sell their films; today, the cost of selling a picture might equal its actual production cost. Simultaneously, studios relied more and more on merchandising tie-ins. At one time, merchandising was a form of free advertising, but during the 1970s the sale of all manner of consumer goods, such

as T-shirts and toys, became a profit center. Following the Walt Disney Company's lead in the licensing of rights to use film characters, all the studios got on the bandwagon, and in the case of Twentieth Century Fox's *Star Wars* (1977) and *The Empire Strikes Back* (1980), Columbia's *Close Encounters of the Third Kind* (1977), Universal's *E.T. the Extra Terrestrial* (1982), and Warner's *Superman* (1978), merchandising revenues could sometimes even rival the box office.

Hollywood also relied more and more on market research in devising their advertising campaigns. During the studio system era, companies sometimes relied on sneak previews to pretest new films by simply asking audiences for their written comments as they went out. In the New Hollywood, companies used more sophisticated means. Columbia Pictures became the most research minded of the major film companies after Coca-Cola acquired it in 1982 and tested the proposition that it could sell movies like soft drinks. Marketing research was used at first to evaluate newspaper ads, television commercials, and radio spots in an attempt to get a reaction from the public before a distributor committed massive amounts of money to the advertising campaign. Tests were devised to discover how to categorize a picture as to genre, create a viable competitive position in the market, determine a target audience, and choose the best media to reach the target audience.

Such tests were conducted after a film was finished but before it was released. Later, companies used marketing in advance of production in an attempt to discover what the public might want in the way of entertainment. Pretesting, for example, was designed to obtain moviegoer feedback to concepts for films or to key elements while a picture was in preproduction or being evaluated for pickup. Fortunately, the studio executives never discovered what motivates an audience to see a movie or determined in advance all the ingredients of a hit picture. The unpredictability of audiences has remained a significant factor in making motion pictures such a viable art form.

SEE ALSO *Exhibition; Independent Film; Publicity and Promotion; Studio System; Television; Theaters*

FURTHER READING

Balio, Tino. *United Artists: The Company That Changed the Film Industry.* Madison: University of Wisconsin Press, 1987.

Conant, Michael. *Antitrust in the Motion Picture Industry.* Berkeley: University of California Press, 1960.

Dale, Martin. *The Movie Game: The Film Business in Britain, Europe, and America.* London: Cassell, 1997.

Daly, David A. *A Comparison of Exhibition and Distribution in Three Recent Motion Pictures.* New York: Arno, 1980.

Goldberg, Fred. *Motion Picture Marketing and Distribution.* Boston: Focal Press, 1991.

Guback, Thomas H. *The International Film Industry.* Bloomington: Indiana University Press, 1969.

Lewis, Howard T. *The Motion Picture Industry.* New York: Van Nostrand, 1933.

Mayer, Michael. *Foreign Films on American Screens.* New York: Arco, 1965.

Squire, Jason E., ed. *The Movie Business Book.* Englewood Cliffs, NJ: Prentice Hall, 1983.

Wilinsky, Barbara. *Sure Seaters: The Emergence of Art House Cinema.* Minneapolis: University of Minnesota Press, 2001.

Wyatt, Justin. *High Concept: Movies and Marketing in Hollywood.* Austin: University of Texas Press, 1994.

Tino Balio

DOCUMENTARY

Documentary exploits the camera's affinity for recording the surface of things, what the realist film theorist Siegfried Kracauer called the "affinity" of film as a photographic medium for capturing "life in the raw." Even before the invention of motion pictures, photographers of the nineteenth century, such as Eadweard Muybridge (1830–1904), with his "animal locomotion" series, demonstrated the extent to which the camera might reveal facts and details of the world to us that we could not perceive with the naked eye.

Documentary images are different from fiction precisely because they possess an indexical bond, a referent, to the historical real. Thus documentaries are unique in engaging what the documentary theorist Bill Nichols calls our epistephilia, a pleasure in knowing about the real world. At the same time, however, no matter how marvelous the special effects in a fiction film, a death scene will never produce the same kind of horror as that generated by, say, the Zapruder footage of President John F. Kennedy being assassinated or the explosion of the space shuttle Challenger as caught by television news cameras. Therefore, documentary film has the power to bring about change in the audience, whether to influence attitudes, increase understanding, or persuade to action, and for this reason documentary film has frequently been used for propaganda purposes, both overtly and subtly.

John Grierson (1898–1972), the filmmaker, producer, and advocate who spearheaded the British documentary movement in the 1920s, coined the term "documentary" in a review of Robert Flaherty's *Moana* (1926). The film, he wrote, "being a visual account of events in the daily life of a Polynesian youth and his family, has documentary value" because the camera cap-

tured and revealed truths about Polynesian culture (Hardy, p. 11). Although later on such assertions would be challenged as First World privilege and presumption, for filmmakers of Grierson's generation the relation of the camera to the profilmic event was for the most part unproblematic.

Because of the wide stylistic diversity of films commonly categorized as nonfiction, documentary has been notoriously difficult to define. In seeking to be inclusive, inevitably most definitions have been vague, clumsy, and prescriptive. As Nichols observes, "Documentary as a concept or practice occupies no fixed territory. It mobilizes no finite inventory of techniques, addresses no set number of issues, and adopts no completely known taxonomy of forms, styles, or modes" (p. 12). Clearly documentary cannot be understood as a genre in any sense equivalent to the genres of commercial fiction cinema; yet whatever the style of individual documentary films, all documentaries make truth claims about the real world. Perhaps the most useful definition, then, is the one offered by Grierson: the "creative treatment of actuality." It not only has the virtue of brevity, but also incorporates both documentary's connection to the real world ("actuality") and the filmmaker's inevitable shaping influence ("creative treatment"). Of course, the perennial problem, for documentary filmmakers as well as critics and audiences, has been to negotiate a proper balance between the two.

BEGINNINGS

Documentary was crucial to the early development of the cinema. Film history conventionally begins in 1895, when Louis and Auguste Lumière publicly exhibited their first program of short films in the basement of the Grand Café in Paris. With titles such as *Workers Leaving the Lumière Factory* (1895), *Arrival of a Train* (1895), and *Le Repas de Bébé* (*Feeding the Baby*, 1895), the Lumières' films, or "actualités," were brief slices of life captured by the camera. According to the media historian Erik Barnouw, the Lumière programs were so popular that within two years they had approximately one hundred operators at work around the world, both showing their films and photographing new ones to add to a steadily increasing catalogue (p. 13). Many of the new enterprising film companies that sprang up at the turn of the century featured nonfiction titles, particularly travelogues. In an era before world travel was common and every tourist had a camera, scenes of foreign lands and life had considerable exotic appeal for film patrons, most of whom at this time were working class and could not afford travel.

As filmmakers such as Edwin S. Porter (1870–1941) and D. W. Griffith (1875–1948) perfected editing techniques for the purposes of advancing a story, nonfiction films were quickly eclipsed in popularity by narrative films, which exploited editing and other cinematic techniques such as framing and camera movement to involve spectators emotionally. As a result, nonfiction film assumed a subsidiary position, ultimately institutionalized in movie theaters as the newsreels or travelogues, one of a series of shorts shown before the feature attraction. Thus documentary has remained on the margins of mainstream cinema, only periodically producing a feature-length work that has managed to find distribution in commercial theaters.

In commercial motion pictures programming, documentary found a niche in the form of newsreels, which became a regular part of commercial film exhibition, along with previews and cartoons, all in support of the narrative feature films. Even though newsreels could only report on news after the fact, when the stories covered were already known, they appealed to audiences because they provided an experiential immediacy that surpassed the temporal immediacy of the daily newspaper. Each newsreel contained coverage of several stories and, after the introduction of sound, authoritative voice-over narration. Pathé News, which was begun in the United States by the Frenchman Charles Pathé (1863–1957) in 1910, proved so popular that by 1912 several other companies and studios, including Hearst, Universal, Paramount, and Fox, entered the newsreel field. Orson Welles's renowned first film, *Citizen Kane* (1941), assumes that newsreel conventions were familiar enough to movie audiences to begin with a mock newsreel ("News on the March"), which is at once a clever expository device and a parody of such newsreels, specifically

of Louis de Rochemont's *The March of Time*. Newsreels lasted through the 1950s, until the disappearance of the double bill and the rise of television, with its nightly news broadcasts providing an even greater sense of immediacy and intimacy than did newsreels.

In 1922 Robert Flaherty (1884–1951), a former explorer and prospector with little prior training in cinematography, made *Nanook of the North*, a film about Inuit life in the Canadian far north, which demonstrated that documentary could be both art and entertainment. Flaherty deftly employed fictional techniques such as the use of close-ups and parallel editing to involve viewers in Nanook's world. The film moved beyond the picturesque detachment of the conventional travelogue to offer a poetic vision of human endurance against the natural elements. The film shows the hardships Nanook faces in finding food for his family in the icy Arctic, while at the same time creating an intimate sense of them as individuals about whom viewers might care (even if on occasion it might lapse into condescension, such as when Nanook is described in one of the insert titles as a "happy-go-lucky Eskimo"). A commercial success, *Nanook of the North* had a lengthy run on Broadway (as the second feature with a Harold Lloyd comedy, *Grandma's Boy* [1922]), and its distributor, Paramount Studios, commissioned Flaherty to go to the South Pacific to "make another *Nanook*" (Barnouw, p. 43). The film that resulted was the aforementioned *Moana*.

Despite the artistry of *Nanook*, Flaherty did take liberties with his subjects. Some were necessary because of technological limitations: the scenes of Nanook and his family in igloos, for example, actually were shot in cutaway igloos constructed for the purpose of filming, since the camera was too big to get inside a real igloo and they did not provide sufficient light for filming. Other manipulations are more troubling. The Inuit were already acquainted with modern weapons and tools, but Flaherty chose to film Nanook without them, falsifying their actual lifestyle in order to present a more traditional view of their culture. When Nanook was being filmed seal hunting, he was unable to catch one, so a dead one was tied onto the end of his fishing line and he enacted his "struggle" with it. In response to criticism that he manipulated his subjects, Flaherty replied, "One often has to distort a thing in order to catch its true spirit." The comment has significant implications for documentary practice, for it opens up the possibility that documentary films may legitimately seek to document more spiritual or intangible aspects of life beneath the physical and visible world.

Grierson's approach to documentary is often seen as antithetical to Flaherty's more romantic vision. For Grierson, the documentary was first and foremost a tool

ROBERT J. FLAHERTY
b. Iron Mountain, Michigan, 16 February 1884, d. 23 July 1951

The only documentary filmmaker to be included in Andrew Sarris's notorious auteurist "pantheon," Robert Flaherty brought to the documentary form his personal vision of humankind's ceaseless struggle against nature, finding this theme in a variety of cultures. A mineralogist and explorer by profession, with only rudimentary training in filmmaking, Flaherty was interested in using film as a means to capture the passing existence of traditional societies, which he saw as both noble and untainted by modern values.

Flaherty's first film, the landmark *Nanook of the North* (1922), for which he obtained funding from Revillon Frères fur company, was a travelogue about Inuit life in the Canadian Arctic that made use of cinematic techniques until then associated more with fiction films than documentary. By frequently weaving together close-ups of Nanook and his family with artfully composed long shots of them in the vast frozen landscape, Flaherty encourages the viewer both to identify with the hunter and his family and to understand the awesome natural power of their environment. In the brutal snowstorm that constitutes *Nanook*'s dramatic climax, Flaherty used crosscutting between the Inuit family huddling inside their igloo and their dogs outside in the fierce wind to suggest the difference between humans and other animals and to emphasize his theme of romantic survival against the crucible of nature.

Moving beyond the picturesque detachment of the conventional travelogue, *Nanook* was a surprising commercial hit. Flaherty went on to make *Moana* (1926) in the South Pacific, where he also worked uncredited on fiction films with W. S. Van Dyke and with F. W. Murnau. In 1931 Flaherty moved to England, where he influenced the British documentary school led by John Grierson. *Man of Aran* (1934), set on the rugged island off the western coast of Ireland, contains thrilling scenes of the islanders hunting basking sharks—a skill that had been largely forgotten and had to be retaught to the islanders so that the sequences could be filmed. His final film, *Louisiana Story* (1948), photographed by Richard Leacock, shows almost no sign of modern technology except for a glimpse of a derrick belonging to Standard Oil (the company that sponsored the film) in the background, apparently functioning in harmony with the environment.

At one time Flaherty's films received much critical praise, although anthropologists complained that they were inaccurate because of the director's manipulation of his subjects. Where once Flaherty was celebrated for his sensuous imagery and compelling footage, today his documentaries are more often considered a prime example of the exoticized, colonial gaze.

RECOMMENDED VIEWING
Nanook of the North (1922), *Moana* (1926), *Tabu* (1931), *Man of Aran* (1934), *The Land* (1942), *Louisiana Story* (1948)

FURTHER READING
Barsam, Richard. *The Vision of Robert Flaherty: The Artist as Myth and Filmmaker*. Bloomington and Indianapolis: Indiana University Press, 1988.

Calder-Marshall, Arthur. *The Innocent Eye: The Life of Robert J. Flaherty*. New York: Harcourt, Brace, 1966.

Danzker, Jo-Anne Birnie, ed. *Robert Flaherty: Photographer/Filmmaker, the Inuit, 1910–1922*. Vancouver, BC: Vancouver Art Gallery, 1980.

Rotha, Paul. *Robert J. Flaherty: A Biography*, edited by Jay Ruby. Philadelphia: University of Pennsylvania Press, 1983.

Rothman, William. "The Filmmaker as Hunter: Robert Flaherty's *Nanook of the North*." In *Documenting the Documentary: Close Readings of Documentary Film and Video*, edited by Barry Keith Grant and Jeannette Sloniowski, 23–39. Detroit, MI: Wayne State University Press, 1998.

Barry Keith Grant

of social propaganda, in the sense of the medium's potential to reach and educate the masses. Thus he attacked Flaherty's lyricism and preference for documenting isolated, pre-industrial cultures rather than to grapple with specific and immediate social issues of modern industrial society—in other words, the problems and issues facing audiences who would be seeing the films. Grierson emphasized the social utility of documentary, proclaiming the desire "to make drama from the ordinary" in films that emphasized social rather than

Robert Flaherty at the time of **Louisiana Story** ***(1948).***
EVERETT COLLECTION. REPRODUCED BY PERMISSION.

aesthetic issues. Influenced by the ideas of his contemporary, the social philosopher Walter Lippmann (1889–1974), Grierson felt that the individual citizen was becoming less informed and consequently less able to participate responsibly in the democratic process; the cinema, however, had the potential to solve the problem through mass education.

Grierson's only film as director, *Drifters* (1929), about the British herring fishing industry, reveals the influence of the Soviet filmmaker Sergei Eisenstein, not only in its editing but also in its comprehensive coverage of its subject, from the stalwart fishermen who bring the fish to port to the packaged goods ready for distribution across the nation. Although Grierson is credited with directing only this one film, more important was his contribution as producer and advocate for state-sponsored documentary. He became the shaping influence of the British documentary movement in the late 1920s through the 1930s, building a film unit under the aegis of the government's Empire Marketing Board, with its mandate of marketing the British Empire, from 1928 to 1933; he brought together such talented filmmakers as Basil Wright (1907–1987), Arthur Elton (1906–1973),

Harry Watt (1906–1987), Paul Rotha (1907–1984), and Edgar Anstey (1907–1987). The EMB Film Unit produced almost one hundred films in the five years of its existence, including *Drifters* and Flaherty's *Industrial Britain* (1932). When the EMB was shut down in 1933, its public relations chief, Sir Stephen Tallents, moved to the General Post Office, taking with him the Board's film unit. Among the most well known of the documentaries to come out of Grierson's unit were *Night Mail* (Harry Wright and Basil Wright, 1934), *Song of Ceylon* (Wright, 1934), and *Coal Face* (Alberto Cavalcanti, 1935), about coal mining in northern England.

Despite Grierson's insistence on the social utility of documentary, the documentary films made under his leadership, both in Great Britain and later in Canada, display a considerable degree of formal experimentation. Leading figures in the arts such as the composer Benjamin Britten and the poet W. H. Auden contributed to EMB documentaries. By the early 1930s the approach to montage included not just images but also sound, especially after Brazilian Alberto Cavalcanti joined the Unit in 1934, as evidenced in his film *Coal Face*. *Night Mail* attempts to synchronize the poetic rhythms of Auden's voice-over verse with the film's pace of the editing to suggest the rhythm of the mail train that climbs steadily upward from London to Scotland. Despite such formal adventurousness, however, the Griersonian style was typically exhortatory, often including an omniscient patriarchal narrator and sharing implicit ideological assumptions about the benefits of capitalism, industrial progress, and colonial paternalism.

DEPRESSION AND THE WAR YEARS

Grierson understood the potential of documentary cinema to affect the political views of the nation and its people, a view shared by other film-producing nations such as Germany and post-Revolutionary Russia. During World War II many governments relied on the propaganda value of documentary film. Already by the late 1930s, filmmaking in both Japan and Germany had come under government control. In Great Britain, where Grierson's Film Unit had evolved into the Crown Film Unit, documentaries helped boost morale on the home front, particularly with the poetic approach of Humphrey Jennings (1907–1950) in such films as *Fires Were Started* (1943) and *A Diary for Timothy* (1945), which presented rich humanist tapestries of the British people during wartime.

In the Soviet Union, Communist Party leader Vladimir Lenin famously proclaimed that for the new Communist state cinema was the most important of the arts. Traveling trains that made and screened newsreels were a means of connecting the many republics of the

Allakariallak as Nanook hunting in Nanook of the North *(Robert Flaherty, 1922).* EVERETT COLLECTION. REPRODUCED BY PERMISSION.

vast Soviet Union, and even feature films such as Sergei Eisenstein's *Bronenosets Potyomkin* (*Battleship Potemkin*, 1925), based on an actual historical event, incorporated elements of documentary. Dziga Vertov (1896–1954) brought a more formalist, experimental approach to the newsreel, and with the feature-length *Chelovek s kino-apparatom* (*The Man with a Movie Camera*, 1929), which presents a "day-in-the-life" of a modern Soviet city, created a reflexive documentary masterpiece that, along with Walter Ruttmann's *Berlin: Die Sinfonie der Großstadt* (*Berlin: Symphony of a Great City*, 1927), established the "city-symphony" form.

Later in Germany, after Hitler's rise to power, his National Socialist Party quickly nationalized the film industry under the leadership of Dr. Joseph Goebbels, Minister of Propaganda, which produced films promulgating Nazi ideology. The most prominent documentary filmmaker of the Nazi era was Leni Riefenstahl, a former star actress, who made *Triumph des Willens* (*Triumph of*

the Will, 1935), about the 1934 Party rally in Nuremberg, and the two-part *Olympia* (1938), about the 1936 Berlin Olympics. *Triumph of the Will* is widely considered a powerful expression of fascist ideology and aesthetics. Although sources vary on the exact number, Riefenstahl clearly had many cameras at her disposal (on occasion in the film camera operators may be glimpsed on tall elevators constructed on site). *Triumph of the Will* celebrates the rally's mass spectacle of fascist unity, which was staged in part precisely to be filmed, successfully turning history into theater and overwhelming viewers just as party rallies were intended to do to participants.

In the United States in the 1930s, documentary emerged as a dominant form of cultural expression in America, informing the aesthetics of all the arts, including painting, theater, literature, and the popular media. The documentary impulse also animated many Works Progress Administration (WPA) arts projects and important books of the period, like *Let Us Now Praise Famous*

DZIGA VERTOV

b. Denis Abramovich Kaufman, Bialystok, Poland, 2 January 1896, d. 12 February 1954

Dziga Vertov was instrumental in using the cinema for the purposes of social education after the Russian Revolution. He not only chronicled the revolution as it happened, but approached the production of newsreels in terms of interaction with the proletariat. His brother Mikhail also became an important documentary filmmaker, while a third brother, Boris, became an important cinematographer for Jean Vigo and others.

At the outbreak of World War I, the Kaufmans, an educated Jewish family, moved to Moscow. In 1916 Vertov enrolled in the Petrograd Psychoneurological Institute, where he studied human perception, particularly sound, editing bits of recorded sound in novel ways in his "Laboratory of Hearing." These experiments would influence Vertov's experiments with sound film over a decade later in *Entuziazm: Simfoniya Donbassa* (*Enthusiasm: The Donbass Symphony*, 1931) and *Tri pesni o Lenine* (*Three Songs of Lenin*, 1934). Changing his name to Dziga Vertov, which loosely translates as "spinning top," he began editing newsreel footage after the revolution, exploring the possibilities of montage in the context of documentary film.

In 1919 Vertov, along with his future wife, the film editor Elisaveta Svilova, and later his brother Mikhail and several other young filmmakers, established the *Kinoks* (from *kinoki*, or cinema-eyes), a group that argued for the value and superiority of documentary filmmaking. They issued an artistic manifestos and published journal articles in which they rejected fiction filmmaking, with its stars, studio shooting, and predetermined scripts, in favor of what Vertov celebrated as "life caught unawares." The camera lens (or *kino* eye), Vertov proclaimed, had the power to penetrate and record visible reality better than could the human eye, making documentary the preferred practice for a Marxist society based on rational and scientific principles of organization. From 1922 to 1925 Vertov directed a series of twenty-three newsreels entitled *Kino-Pravda*; *pravda*, meaning truth, was also the name of the official Soviet party newspaper.

Vertov's masterpiece, *Chelovek s kino-apparatom* (*The Man with a Movie Camera*, 1929), was a visionary "city symphony" documentary that reflected on its own status as both document and illusion. It presented a lyrical view of an idealized Soviet city (a combination of Moscow, Odessa, and Kiev), utilizing virtually every special effect and cinematic technique available to show life in Soviet society while encouraging viewers to consider the nature of cinematic construction and the relation between film and reality. Vertov's reflexive practice was later continued in Jean Rouch's *cinéma verité* (the French term deriving from Vertov's *kino-pravda*) and Jean-Luc Godard's experiments in collective political filmmaking with the Dziga Vertov Group in the early 1970s. Vertov's avant-garde style challenged the constraints of official doctrine, and by the end of the 1930s Vertov found himself unable to secure funding for further projects. He spent the last two decades of his life editing newsreels, as he had begun.

RECOMMENDED VIEWING

Chelovek s kino-apparatom (*The Man with a Movie Camera*, 1929), *Entuziazm: Symfonia Donbassa* (*Enthusiasm: The Donbass Symphony*, 1931), *Tri pesni o Lenine* (*Three Songs of Lenin*, 1934)

FURTHER READING

Feldman, Seth. *Dziga Vertov: A Guide to References and Resources.* Boston: G. K. Hall, 1979.

———. "'Peace Between Man and Machine': Dziga Vertov's *The Man with a Movie Camera*." In *Documenting the Documentary: Close Readings of Documentary Film and Video*, edited by Barry Keith Grant and Jeannette Sloniowski, 40–54. Detroit, MI: Wayne State University Press, 1998.

Petrić, Vlada. *Constructivism in Film: The Man with the Movie Camera, A Cinematic Analysis.* Cambridge, UK and New York: Cambridge University Press, 1987.

Vertov, Dziga. *Kino-Eye: The Writings of Dziga Vertov.* Edited by Annette Michelson, translated by Kevin O'Brien. Berkeley: University of California Press, 1984.

Barry Keith Grant

Men (begun in 1936 but not published until 1941), by James Agee (1909–1955) with photographs by Walker Evans (1903–1975). In film, beginning in 1930 a network of local Film and Photo Leagues developed in major American cities as a response to the avoidance of controversial material by mainstream theatrical newsreels.

Dziga Vertov. THE KOBAL COLLECTION. REPRODUCED BY PERMISSION.

Together the leagues produced a Worker's Newsreel that concentrated on documenting the intense labor activities of the early Depression period. Many important documentary filmmakers of the time were associated with the particularly active New York Film and Photo League, and later with Frontier Films, a socially committed production company that produced a series of important films about international politics beginning in 1936.

Under Franklin Roosevelt's presidency (1933–1945), the Resettlement Administration (RA) sponsored a photographic unit that included Evans, Dorothea Lange, and others. It moved into documentary film with *The Plow That Broke the Plains* (1936) and *The River* (1938), both by Pare Lorentz (1905–1992), about the dust bowl and the Tennessee Valley Authority, respectively. Both films effectively endorsed government policy by combining Griersonian authority with American colloquialism, reinforced by fine scores by the American composer Virgil Thomson that wove folk themes throughout. Although various government agencies had previously sponsored documentaries, Lorentz's films were the first to garner serious attention and considerable

theatrical distribution. Roosevelt established the US Film Service in 1938, but it died by 1940 because Congress refused to appropriate the necessary funds, largely as a result of pressure from Hollywood studios that viewed the initiative as unfair competition and not in the spirit of free enterprise.

The popular Hollywood director Frank Capra (1897–1991) oversaw for the military the production of *Why We Fight* (1942–1944), a series of seven documentaries designed to provide background information about the global conflict so as to help shake Americans from their strong isolationist position. These films were widely screened at home and as part of military training for troops sent overseas. Many Hollywood professionals were involved in the various aspects of their production. The films effectively simplified the political complexities leading to the war by cleverly employing patriotic mythology and national iconography. Other important Hollywood directors who accepted military commissions and lent their filmmaking talents to documenting the war effort included John Ford (1894–1973), who made *The Battle of Midway* (1942), William Wyler (1902–1981), maker of *The Memphis Belle* (1944), and John Huston (1906–1987), who produced *The Battle of San Pietro* (1945) and the controversial *Let There Be Light* (1946), initially banned by the Armed Forces because of its candid footage of soldiers who had been traumatized by combat.

With the domestic prosperity of the postwar years, government sponsorship of documentary in the United States disappeared. In this period documentary production was sponsored largely by industry, often with pronounced ties to government interests, and so the films tended to be conventional in both style and content. Cold War paranoia also served as a strong disincentive to originality. Through the 1950s the various newsreel series ceased production, as their function was increasingly taken over by television.

The most notable exception to the new conservatism in documentary was the CBS-TV series *See It Now*, started in 1951 by the journalist Edward R. Murrow (1908–1965) and the producer Fred Friendly (1915–1998). Murrow's stature as a war correspondent and his high administrative position at CBS enabled him to produce the show with relative freedom. In 1953–1954 he successfully exposed the demagoguery of Senator Joseph McCarthy, a prime mover behind the Cold War blacklists and witch hunts (a historical moment vividly captured in George Clooney's feature film *Good Night and Good Luck* [2005]). Nevertheless, as a result of continued political pressure, by 1959 network policy declared that documentaries were the responsibility of network news departments; "independents" no longer were to be employed because their authenticity might not be verifiable. Even today, there are very few documentary filmmakers whose work is broadcast on network television; documentaries are more likely to be found on specialty cable channels such as the Documentary Channel or *Biography* on A&E. However, some regard so-called "reality TV" as a form of televisual documentary; and although shows such as *Survivor* (beginning in 2000), *Fear Factor* (beginning in 2001), and *Trading Spaces* (beginning in 2000) are highly structured and carefully edited, they do use nonprofessional actors and observe profilmic events as they unfold.

OBSERVATIONAL DOCUMENTARY

Inspired by the powerful immediacy of actual combat footage and the emergence of Italian neorealism toward the end of the war, Hollywood feature films began absorbing the influence of documentary. Both *The Naked City* (Jules Dassin, 1948) and *On the Waterfront* (Elia Kazan, 1954), for example, used actual locations in New York City to enhance their dramatic realism, and independent filmmakers such as Morris Engel (1918–2005) with *Little Fugitive* (1953) and *Weddings and Babies* (1958), and John Cassavetes, (1929–1989) with *Shadows* (1959) and *Faces* (1968), made feature films with portable 35 mm equipment.

The development of portable 16mm cameras and synch-sound equipment brought significant changes to documentary film practice. Filmmakers now gained the ability to shoot with relative ease on location. The new light weight and portability of cameras that before had been bulky and heavy meant that they no longer had to be the center of profilmic events, but could follow events as they happened. Filmmakers could enter a situation directly, without having to alter events because of technological limitations, as had been the case with, for example, Flaherty's camera in igloos. The tripod was abandoned, and the camera gained a new mobility carried on the shoulder of the operator as filmmakers began to work in a mode Stephen Mamber has called an "uncontrolled cinema." As further improvements were perfected, the tape recorder and the camera, which before had been connected by a limiting cable, were able to operate entirely independently. The crew required to make a documentary was reduced to only two people—one to operate the camera, the other to record sound. In the case of Ross McElwee (b. 1947), whose films such as *Sherman's March* (1986) and *Bright Leaves* (2003) are documentaries of his own life, the crew is just himself, shooting with a video camera and attached microphone. With these technological advances, documentary filmmaking acquired a freshness and immediacy, both visually and aurally; by contrast, the Griersonian tradition, which the new style supplanted, typically used omniscient voice-over narration displaying ideological biases. As a result, documentary experienced a revitalization internationally, particularly in North America and Europe.

An entire generation of documentarians embraced the new observational style and valorized the technology. Most advocated an unproblematic view of cinematic realism whereby the camera could apprehend the world directly, penetrating even surface reality to reveal deeper truths. *An American Family*, a twelve-part series by Craig Gilbert broadcast on public television in 1973, sought to capture the unadorned life of one particular family and thus reveal the ordinary realities of middle-class American existence. In these observational documentaries, the presence of the camera was not thought to affect the profilmic event to any significant degree, and if it did, filmmakers could search for "privileged moments" that would reveal the real person hiding behind the social facade. Perhaps the most extreme example of this approach was *Portrait of Jason* (Shirley Clarke, 1967), a film consisting entirely of a series of talking-head close-ups of an unsuccessful actor who, fueled by alcohol, marijuana, and prodding questions from behind the camera, lets down his smug intellectual persona and wallows in self-pity.

In Great Britain in the 1950s, filmmakers such as Tony Richardson (1928–1991), Lindsay Anderson (1923–1994), and Karel Reisz (1926–2002) began making observational films of everyday life as part of the movement known as Free Cinema, often focusing on common aspects of popular culture. The Free Cinema movement consisted of six programs of films shown at the National Film Theater in London from 1956 to 1959, including Anderson's *O Dreamland* (1953), about the Margate amusement park, and *Every Day Except Christmas* (1957), about activity in Covent Garden, and Reisz and Richardson's *Momma Don't Allow* (1955), a portrait of a jazz club. In France, anthropologist-filmmaker Jean Rouch (1917–2004) made a series of films about people and life in western Africa, often including their own voices on the soundtrack, as in *Les Maîtres fous* (*The Mad Masters*, 1955), which records devotees of a religious cult speaking in tongues, and *Jaguar* (1967). Turning his camera closer to home, Rouch filmed a cross-section of Parisians in *Chronique d'un été* (*Chronicle of a Summer*, 1961), co-directed with the sociologist Edgar Morin. Rather than being observant flies on the wall, the filmmakers appeared onscreen, functioning as catalysts by asking their subjects provocative questions and freely interacting with them. The film was subtitled "une experience de cinéma vérité," and Rouch's assertive approach developed into the cinema verité style of observational documentary. And in Canada in the early 1960s, both English- and French-speaking Canadian filmmakers working for the National Film Board, founded by Grierson in 1939, concentrated on making films about ordinary people and events in order to "interpret Canada to Canadians and the rest of the world." The Board's initial focus was the production of wartime propaganda films, but in the early 1960s it was a pioneer of observational documentary, both in its more passive direct cinema form in English Canada, with the films of Terence Macartney-Filgate, Roman Kriotor, and Wolf Koenig, and, in Quebec, of cinéma vérité. Michel Brault, who had photographed *Chronique d'un été*, co-directed with Gilles Groulx *Les Raquetteurs* (*The Snowshoers*, 1958), a film about an annual snowshoe race that was a breakthrough in the representation of Quebecois life on the screen.

In New York in the 1960s, a group of young filmmakers organized by Robert Drew (b. 1924) began making films for Time, Inc., in an attempt to do a more truthful "pictorial journalism," as Louis de Rochemont had said of *The March of Time*. Known as the Drew Associates, the group included many of the pioneering figures of American observational cinema, including D. A. Pennebaker (b. 1925), Albert Maysles (b. 1926),

and Richard Leacock, who had been the cameraman on Flaherty's last film, *Louisiana Story*, in 1949. The Drew Associates sought to be invisible observers of events transpiring before the camera—ideally, in Leacock's famous phrase, like a "fly on the wall." *Primary* (1960), about the Wisconsin presidential campaigns of John F. Kennedy and Hubert Humphrey, showed the candidates both in public appearances and behind the scenes; and although it shows Kennedy as the more adept media personality, it avoids explicit political comment. A famous shot in the film follows Kennedy as he emerges from a car and enters a hall where he is about to speak, moving through a tightly packed crowd to the stage—all despite changing conditions of light, sound, and depth of field. Impressed by *Primary*, ABC contracted with Time, Inc., so that the Drew group became in effect a network unit. The Drew filmmakers made a series of nineteen pioneering films for television, beginning with *Primary* and ending with *Crisis: Behind a Presidential Commitment* in 1963.

Their films tended to favor famous and exciting figures as their subjects: a race car driver in *Eddie* (Leacock and Pennebaker, 1960), film producer Joseph E. Levine in *Showman* (Albert and David Maysles, 1963), and pop stars in *What's Happening! The Beatles in the U.S.A.* (Maysles brothers, 1964). The documentaries of their contemporary Frederick Wiseman (b. 1930) focus on institutions rather than individuals, but his films were exceptions. Because celebrities, particularly pop-music stars, possess inherent commercial appeal, when these and other filmmakers sought to make feature-length documentaries they gravitated toward them as subjects; thus was created the "rockumentary" genre, with such films as *Woodstock* (Michael Wadleigh, 1970) and *The Last Waltz* (Martin Scorsese, 1978). Perhaps the most notorious of these is *Gimme Shelter* (1970), by Albert and David Maysles (1931–1987) and Charlotte Zwerin, which focuses on the Rolling Stones' American tour. At the last concert of the tour, in Altamont, California, a man in the audience was stabbed to death by the Hell's Angels—a sensational event caught on camera. Because rockumentaries often purport to show the person behind the persona, they remain popular with audiences, as the publicity surrounding *Living with Michael Jackson: A Tonight Special* (2003), which aired on network television, demonstrates.

The documentary aesthetic also informed the New American Cinema movement of the 1950s and 1960s, much of it representing the seemingly antithetical traditions of experimental or avant-garde film, as in the "diary" style of Stan Brakhage (1933–2003) and the structural films of Michael Snow (b. 1929). A film such as Brakhage's *The Act of Seeing with One's Own Eyes* (1971) is at once an experimental film, employing a

FREDERICK WISEMAN
b. Boston, Massachusetts, 1 January 1930

A major figure in American documentary, Frederick Wiseman began making his extraordinary series of award-winning films during the direct cinema movement in the 1960s. Over the course of three decades he produced more than thirty feature-length documentaries and garnered numerous awards. Unlike the rich and famous individuals chronicled in the films of his contemporaries Richard Leacock, D. A. Pennebaker, and the Maysles brothers, Wiseman's films focus less on particular individuals than on institutions of various kinds, ranging from those concentrated within individual buildings (*High School*, 1968) to those of international scope (*Sinai Field Mission*, 1978), and from institutions established and maintained by government (*Juvenile Court*, 1973) to those less tangible ones organized by principles of ideology and culture (*Model*, 1980). A former lawyer, Wiseman captures American life more fully than any other documentary filmmaker, and, taken together, his documentaries are a magnum opus about life in contemporary America.

Wiseman began his career in film producing Shirley Clarke's *The Cool World* (1964), a fiction film about teenage gangs shot on location in Harlem. In 1967 he began his institutional series with *Titicut Follies* (1967), about life in a prison for the criminally insane in Bridgewater, Massachusetts. The film quickly became mired in lengthy litigation with state authorities, and the ensuing controversy established Wiseman's somewhat inaccurate reputation as an uncompromising muckraker. Although the earlier films do seem to be exposés, Wiseman's later films are less didactic and more complex aesthetically. *Meat* (1976), for example, is composed of many short shots, the duration of the cutting analogous to the repetitive slicing by the butchers; *Model* is a reflexive examination of modeling as the manufacturing of advertising images—a process not very different from some forms of filmmaking—and relies more on long takes.

During shooting, Wiseman operates the tape recorder rather than the camera. He determines where the camera goes through a series of hand signals worked out in advance with his camera operator or by leading him with the microphone. This method gives him greater freedom to see what is around him than if he were looking at profilmic events through the viewfinder of the camera.

Wiseman encourages a reading of each institution as a metaphor of American society at large. Thus, though at first glance Wiseman's films may seem to be fly-on-the-wall observation, they often rely on elements of cinematic style, particularly editing, to express his subjective vision of how institutions operate and what their significance is culturally. If Wiseman's documentaries are news, they are also editorials, subjective accounts about the institutions on which he is reporting. More dialectical than didactic, Wiseman's films refuse to condescend to the viewer by assuming a position of authorial superiority.

RECOMMENDED VIEWING

Titicut Follies (1967), *High School* (1968), *Essene* (1972), *Primate* (1974), *Meat* (1976), *Model* (1980), *Near Death* (1989), *Public Housing* (1997), *Belfast, Maine* (1999), *Domestic Violence* (2001)

FURTHER READING

Anderson, Carolyn, and Thomas W. Benson. *Documentary Dilemmas: Frederick Wiseman's Titicut Follies.* Carbondale and Edwardsville: Southern Illinois University Press, 1991.

Atkins, Thomas R., ed. *Frederick Wiseman.* New York: Simon & Schuster, 1976.

Benson, Thomas W., and Carolyn Anderson. *Reality Fictions: The Films of Frederick Wiseman.* Carbondale and Edwardsville: Southern Illinois University Press, 1989.

Grant, Barry Keith. *Voyages of Discovery: The Cinema of Frederick Wiseman.* Urbana: University of Illinois Press, 1992.

———, ed. *Five Films by Frederick Wiseman: Titicut Follies, High School, Welfare, High School II, Public Housing.* Berkeley: University of California Press, 2006.

Barry Keith Grant

Frederick Wiseman. EVERETT COLLECTION. REPRODUCED BY PERMISSION.

variety of expressive cinematic techniques, and a documentary, showing the different steps in the autopsy process. In many experimental films the otherwise diverse documentary and avant-garde impulses come together in the shared aim of allowing the viewer to look at something in a new or different way.

TRUTH OR DARE: THEORETICAL AND ETHICAL CONSIDERATIONS

Observational films seemed more truthful in large part because they were not constrained by earlier technological limitations that often required more overt manipulation. "Dramatic reconstruction" was conventional in documentaries concerning people and events before the invention of the camera. Early documentaries, like Biograph's *Eruption of Mt. Vesuvius* (1905), often used scale-model replicas in place of actuality footage in films. *The March of Time*, which began in 1935, freely combined actuality footage with dramatized sequences in a style that Henry Luce, head of Time, called "fakery in allegiance to the truth" (Barnouw, p. 121). The ideology of observational documentary has become so standard that its stylistic conventions, such as the jerky movements of the handheld camera, noticeable changes in focus, and the graininess of fast film

stock, have become the common techniques for representing a "reality effect" in fiction film and on commercial television in both dramatic shows and commercials.

Nevertheless, questions concerning the camera's physical presence, along with the issue of whether and to what extent the camera *exploits* or *documents* its social actors, have been hotly debated issues concerning both Griersonian-style and observational documentary. Films such as *Portrait of Jason* and the Maysles brothers' *Grey Gardens* (1975), about an eccentric mother and daughter who live as recluses in a decaying mansion, foreground these ethical issues because of the filmmakers' apparent encouragement of their social actors to display themselves for the camera. But in fact ethical questions have surrounded the making of documentaries since the genre's beginnings.

Although the immediacy of observational cinema made the stylistic conventions associated with the Griersonian tradition seem outmoded and ideologically suspect, manipulation in documentary inevitably is a matter of degree. For although documentaries are factual, they are never objective or ideologically neutral. Aesthetic choices such as the selection of camera position, angles, and movement; lighting; and editing make the expression of point of view or perspective unavoidable, even if unintentional. Just as the "fly on the wall" aesthetic of the Drew filmmakers was compromised to some extent by the commercial imperatives of television, so the nature of the film medium ensures that the hand of the maker must always work over the raw material on the editing table. *Dead Birds* (Robert Gardner, 1965), which aimed at being an ethnographic study of the Dugum Dani culture in New Guinea, is almost embarrassing today for the degree to which it presumes to attribute values and thoughts to the people it presents as characters in a narrative.

The debate around documentary film's moral obligation to be objective, or at least fair, has been rekindled by the recent and commercially successful films of Michael Moore, who makes no secret of his political views but rather speaks out on political issues. His first film, *Roger & Me* (1989), the most commercially successful documentary to date, established Moore's trademark approach, a combination of an unabashedly personal tone, his own provocative verité presence, and a strong sense of humor. He has been attacked for manipulating facts and for violating ethical proprieties, as when in *Bowling for Columbine* (2002) he ambushes the actor Charlton Heston, then president of the National Rifle Association, questioning him about his culpability in the accidental death of a child by gunfire.

Although for many viewers documentary still means objectivity, today it is much more commonly accepted that documentaries are inevitably biased. This is probably less a postmodern crisis in signification than the result of

Filmmaker Michael Moore receives a rifle for opening a bank account in Bowling for Columbine *(2002).* © UNITED ARTISTS/ COURTESY EVERETT COLLECTION. REPRODUCED BY PERMISSION.

the proliferation of camcorders and a greater increase in basic visual literacy. Yet it is symptomatic that many documentaries of the late twentieth and early twenty-first centuries, such as *The Thin Blue Line* (1988), seek to uncover ambiguities of truth rather than a unified, singular Truth. Stylistically, nonfiction films are now employing a more pronounced mixing of modes, combining elements of fiction and documentary, or creating an ambiguity concerning their documentary status, as in *Madonna: Truth or Dare* (1991). British documentary filmmaker Nick Broomfield places himself squarely within his films as a character seeking the truth about his subject, whether about the murder of grunge rock icon Kurt Cobain in *Kurt & Courtney* (1998) or the female serial killer Aileen Wournos in *Aileen: Life and Death of a Serial Killer* (2003), but never quite finding it. Broomfield's quandary as a documentary filmmaker bespeaks contemporary viewers' loss of faith in the ability of documentary film to provide unequivocal truths.

Documentary film also has been critiqued from postcolonial and feminist perspectives. Robert Flaherty's films have come to be seen as examples of a white Eurocentric perspective imposed on other cultures. This colonizing gaze informs much of the history of travelogues and other documentary filmmaking; it is partic-

ularly egregious in the films of Martin E. Johnson (1884–1937) and Osa Johnson (1894–1953), such as *Simba: The King of the Beasts* (1928) and *Congorilla* (1932), which paraded "primitive" natives in front of the camera for comic relief along with local fauna. Luis Buñuel's *Las Hurdes* (*Land Without Bread*, 1933), an audacious documentary about an impoverished region of Spain and its inhabitants, is regarded as one of the first films to be aware of the imbalance of power between First World filmmakers and their less wealthy subjects. T. Minh-ha Trinh, a teacher and theorist as well as a practicing filmmaker, has employed a variety of expressive techniques in documentaries such as *Naked Spaces: Living Is Round* (1985) and *Surname Viet Given Name Nam* (1989) to give voice to women in other cultures.

Documentary filmmakers have sought to use documentary politically to help create a sense of shared purpose, to offer the legitimation of subcultures through the presentation of recognizable images that have been marginalized by mainstream or dominant culture. In the 1950s Quebecois filmmakers discovered that training the camera on themselves facilitated the Quiet Revolution, the province's discovery of itself as a new and distinct culture within Canada. The heightened political polarization of the Vietnam era influenced the pronounced partisanship of many documentaries, as in the work of Peter Davis (*The Selling of the Pentagon*, 1971; *Hearts and Minds*, 1974). The introduction in the 1960s of video porta-paks and public access of local cable TV allowed for grassroots concerns to be heard. Some filmmakers, such as Emile de Antonio (1920–1989), established themselves as counter-culture heroes by making documentaries that exposed government corruption (*Point of Order*, 1964, about the 1954 Army-McCarthy Senate hearings) or challenged official policies (*Rush to Judgment*, 1967, about the report of the Warren Commission).

Much contemporary documentary practice continues to be politically engaged, and some films—*Harlan County, U.S.A.* (Barbara Kopple, 1976), *The Panama Deception* (Barbara Trent, 1992), *The Fog of War* (Errol Morris, 2003)—are able to find limited commercial distribution. Documentary film's appeal has filtered down to mainstream popular culture in the television exposé form, in such shows as *60 Minutes*, the most successful nonfiction series in television history, and on reality-TV. Subcultures and various interest groups have used the documentary successfully to help develop a sense of identity and solidarity. In the 1970s feminist documentary filmmakers developed a distinctively intimate, "talking-head" style that promoted the shared rediscovery of mutual experience with the viewer, as in *With Babies and Banners* (Lorraine Gray, 1978) and *The Life and Times of Rosie the Riveter* (Connie Field, 1980). Documentaries about gay sexuality, such as *Word Is Out* (Rob Epstein, 1978) and *The Times of Harvey Milk* (Epstein, 1984), appeared with the emergence of the gay movement in the 1980s. In *Tongues Untied* (1990) Marlon Riggs (1957–1994) explored issues of gay black identity. Since the 1980s many documentaries have addressed AIDS, chronicling the struggles of its victims and promoting awareness.

SEE ALSO *Camera; Ideology; Propaganda; Russia and Soviet Union; Technology; World War II*

FURTHER READING

Barnouw, Erik. *Documentary: A History of the Nonfiction Film.* New York: Oxford University Press, 1974.

Barsam, Richard Meran. *Nonfiction Film: A Critical History.* New York: Dutton, 1973.

———, ed. *Nonfiction Film: Theory and Criticism.* New York: Dutton, 1976.

Ellis, Jack C. *The Documentary Idea: A Critical History of English-Language Documentary Film and Video.* Englewood Cliffs, NJ: Prentice-Hall, 1989.

Grant, Barry Keith, and Jeannette Sloniowski. *Documenting the Documentary: Close Readings of Documentary Film and Video.* Detroit, MI: Wayne State University Press, 1998.

Hardy, Forsyth. *Grierson on Documentary.* London and Boston: Faber and Faber, 1979.

Jacobs, Lewis, ed. *The Documentary Tradition,* 2nd ed. New York: Norton, 1979.

Kracauer, Siegfried. *Theory of Film: The Redemption of Physical Reality.* New York: Oxford University Press, 1965.

Mamber, Stephen. *Cinema Verite in America: Studies in Uncontrolled Documentary.* Cambridge, MA: MIT Press, 1974.

Nichols, Bill. *Representing Reality: Issues and Concepts in Documentary.* Bloomington: Indiana University Press, 1991.

Renov, Michael. *Theorizing Documentary.* New York and London: Routledge, 1993.

Rothman, William. *Documentary Film Classics.* Cambridge, UK and New York: Cambridge University Press, 1997.

Stott, William. *Documentary Expression and Thirties America.* New York: Oxford University Press, 1973.

Trinh, T. Minh-ha. *Framer Framed.* New York and London: Routledge, 1992.

Waugh, Thomas, ed. *"Show Us Life": Toward a History and Aesthetics of the Committed Documentary.* Metuchen, NJ, and London: Scarecrow Press, 1984.

Barry Keith Grant

DUBBING AND SUBTITLING

Dubbing and subtitling are two major types of screen translation, the two most used in the global distribution and consumption of filmic media. Since their arrival with the introduction of sound to cinema, both have been seen as compromised methods of translating dialogue because they interfere in different ways with the original text, sound track, or image. Since the early 1930s, most countries have tended to favor either one mode or the other. While there are many forms of language versioning or transfer in current use in the global audiovisual industries, and any one of these might be used in some cases on its own or in combination with others, dubbing and subtitling have remained the most recognizable, as well as the most debated, methods for cinema.

DEFINITIONS

Dubbing is a form of post-synchronized revoicing that involves recording voices that do not belong to the on-screen actors, speaking in a language different from that of the source text and ideally in synch with the film image. But dubbing can also refer more generally to adding or replacing sound effects or spoken lines by the source actors themselves in the language of the film's production, often because of poor sound quality in the original recording or for the deletion of expletives from the theatrical version for release on television. While this latter form of post-synchronized revoicing is present in virtually all modern films, it is often called "looping" to distinguish it from dubbing as language translation. Another form of revoicing is the "voice-over," in which a nonsynchronous voice that does not replace the source text and language is added to the sound track but does not replace the

source text and language. Popular in Russia and Poland and used more in television than in film translation, voice-over is a relatively minor mode compared to dubbing and subtitling.

Subtitling, like voice-over, presents the translated and source languages simultaneously, but it transforms speech into writing without altering the source sound track. Subtitling may be either intralingual or interlingual. In the former, the written text that appears over the image is that of the source language. This kind of subtitling, for viewers who are deaf and hard-of-hearing, is often called "captioning," and it is in prevalent use in television broadcasting. Interlingual subtitling translates the source language into the target language (or languages) in the form of one or more lines of synchronized written text. These verbal messages may include not only speech, such as dialogue, commentary, and song lyrics, but also displays, such as written signs and newspaper headlines. Subtitles usually appear at the bottom of the screen, though their placement may vary among language groups. In bilingual subtitling countries such as Belgium, Finland, and Israel, film subtitles are often present in both languages.

The national preferences for subtitled or dubbed films stem from several factors, including historical and political circumstances, traditions and industries, costs, the form to which audiences are accustomed, and the generic and artistic standing of the films themselves. Before these can be considered, it is necessary to address the historical circumstances that gave rise to dubbing and subtitling and to their emergence as the preferred forms of verbal translation in film.

EARLY SOUND FILM AND MULTIPLE LANGUAGE VERSIONS

Silent films presented few problems for language transfer, though they still entailed translation for international audiences. While silent films were well suited to consumption in a variety of cultural contexts, this was due less to their status as a universal language of images than to their intertitles and the flexibility they provided. Intertitles were not simply translated from source to target languages but creatively adapted to cater to diverse national and language groups: the names of characters, settings and plot developments, and other cultural references were altered as necessary in order to make the films internationally understandable for different national audiences. By 1927, the intertitles of Hollywood films were routinely translated into as many as thirty-six languages.

With the sound film, it was no longer possible simply to replace intertitles. Subtitling and dubbing have been in use since 1929, but when the first American sound films reached Europe they did not immediately become the preferred solutions to the new problem of sound film translation. Instead, multilingual productions or multiple language versions (MLVs) experienced a period of ascendency and decline from 1929 to 1933. During this time, American film studios either brought foreign directors, scriptwriters, and actors to Hollywood or set up film production studios in Europe. Warner Bros. was the first American producer to engage in MLV production, with some European producers and all of the major Hollywood studios following suit. Paramount invested the most, building a huge studio in early 1930, at Joinville in the suburbs of Paris, that was soon producing films in as many as fourteen different languages. Films that were shot simultaneously in two or three languages usually had just one director, but for a higher number of MLVs each could have a different director. Polyglot actors might perform in more than one language version, but the norm was different casts for different versions. Sets and costumes were reused, which meant shooting versions in shifts according to a twenty-four-hour schedule. Production time was short, often less than two weeks per feature. At its peak, between March 1930 and March 1931, Joinville turned out an astonishing one hundred features and fifty shorts.

Despite such rationing of production time, MLVs meant an enormous increase in costs, and their standardized plots worked against satisfying the cultural diversity of their target audiences. Their lack of profitability, inability to meet generic requirements across cultures, and the perception that they were purely commercial products led to a precipitous decline in MLVs, with Hollywood ceasing multilingual production entirely in 1933 and Germany and France soon thereafter. Although many established and promising young directors made MLVs, few of their works are considered to be of lasting artistic value. An exception is Josef von Sternberg's *Der Blaue Engel* (*The Blue Angel*, 1930), shot in English and German versions for Ufa (Universum Film Aktiengesellschaft) and Paramount. *The Blue Angel* was a substantial international hit and features the same actors (Emil Jannings and Marlene Dietrich) voicing their lines in both versions.

While the MLVs are generally considered to be a failed experiment of the early sound period, multilingual versions continued to be made sporadically in Europe. Jean Renoir's *Le carrosse d'or* (*The Golden Coach*, 1953), for example, was shot at Cinecittà with a largely Italian cast, most of whom, including the star, Anna Magnani (1908–1973), played and spoke all three languages in separately shot English, Italian, and French versions. Werner Herzog's *Nosferatu: Phantom der Nacht* (*Nosferatu the Vampyre*, 1979) was double shot, with the same cast performing separate German and English versions.

THE DUBBING AND SUBTITLING INDUSTRIES

The most common explanation for the divide between dubbing and subtitling countries derives from cost: dubbing, the more expensive translation mode, is adopted by the larger, wealthier countries with significant single-language communities, subtitling by the smaller countries whose audiences comprise more restricted markets. While there is some truth to this rationale, cost alone does not dictate national choice: small Central European countries such as Bulgaria, the Czech Republic, Hungary, and Slovakia prefer dubbing, despite its high cost. Historical and political developments, along with tradition, are equally important factors.

In Western Europe, dubbing emerged in the early 1930s as the standard method of language transfer in France, Italy, Germany, and Spain (sometimes referred to as the FIGS group). In France, where the Joinville studio was converted into a dubbing center, the supremacy of dubbing derives from the nation's cultural mission to preserve and protect the French language in the face of foreign (especially American) influence, and the prevalence of French as the lingua franca for a populace accustomed to hearing it in its own films. For the other countries of the FIGS group, culture and political ideology were determining causes. Italy, Germany, and Spain, all of which faced cultural boycotts in the mid-1930s and were ruled by fascist governments, only allowed dubbed versions of foreign films. The dictators of these countries understood how hearing one's own language served to confirm its importance and reinforce a sense of national identity and autonomy. In Italy especially—where most people, including the filmmakers themselves, spoke dialect rather than the official Tuscan—dubbing forged the synthetic unity of a shared national language. As early as 1929, Benito

Mussolini's government decreed that all films projected on Italian screens must have an Italian-language sound track regardless of where it was produced. Both Francisco Franco's Spain and Adolf Hitler's Germany established strict quotas regarding imports, almost all of which were dubbed. Through the quickly established and standardized dubbing industries that were built up in these nations, dubbed movies came to be seen as local productions. The highly developed and still active dubbing industries in these countries are thus remnants of their political contexts of the early 1930s, when sound film emerged.

Dubbing is a labor-intensive process. In a sound booth, dubbing actors view film segments repeatedly while voicing their lines from a prepared script. Several recording attempts may be necessary to achieve, as near as possible, the synchronization of translated lines of dialogue or other vocalizations with the lip movements of the original on-screen actors. Films are dubbed well or badly depending on the time and care taken and the resources devoted to the process. Until the 1960s, lip synchrony was held by the dubbing industry as the most important factor for sustaining the illusion of watching and hearing a homogeneous whole. Now, lip synch is considered to be of secondary importance, since research has shown that the viewer cannot discern minor slips and discrepancies in lip movements, and asynchrony is not bothersome to audiences in dubbing countries. Audio synchrony, or using voices that fit the characters on the screen, is important to the overall effect, and studios tend to employ the same dubbing actors for well-known foreign stars. This has led in some cases to voice actors achieving star power within the industry, or even becoming film actors in their own right: for example, Monica Vitti (b. 1931), the star of several Michelangelo Antonioni films in the 1960s, came to the director's notice through a dubbing assignment for his film *Il Grido* (*The Cry*, 1957). In the postwar Indian film industry (now commonly referred to as "Bollywood"), the ubiquitous song sequences are sung not by the actors but by professional singers who can become as famous as the screen stars who lip-synch their recordings during shooting.

Even in the dubbing countries there are sectors of the audience who prefer to watch subtitled films. In France these are advertised as "version originale sous-titrée" ("original version with subtitles"); in Spain, cinemas increasingly offer both subtitled and dubbed versions of foreign films. Source-language countries—which means English-speaking countries, especially the United States and the United Kingdom—import few films that are not in English and so use these language transfer modes as needed and in a mixed manner. But several non-English-speaking nations, many of which import a high proportion of films, prefer subtitling, including Belgium, Croatia, Cyprus, Greece, Japan, the Netherlands, Portugal, and the Scandinavian countries.

Subtitling, more cost-effective than dubbing because it dispenses with sound recording and voice actors, is nonetheless complex work. The subtitling industry is not nationalized to the same degree as the dubbing one, since the translators are the key personnel and need not reside in the target country. But a primary issue for subtitling lies in the translation, which entails enormous cuts to the source dialogue—as much as half. While the ideal in subtitling is to translate each utterance in full, the limitation of screen space is a major obstacle. The average viewer's reading speed is 150–180 words per minute, with necessary intervals, which severely limits the duration and hence completeness of the subtitles. The final part of the process involves striking a duplicate photographic print of the master print, while simultaneously exposing it with titles to produce a new print with the titles "burned in." Companies hired to affix the subtitles to film prints face a myriad of possibilities concerning type size and typeface, background and placement, indications for extended sentences and multiple speakers, and the like. As with dubbing, films can be subtitled well or badly.

SUBTITLING VERSUS DUBBING

Many introductory film textbooks discuss a debate regarding subtitled versus dubbed prints of foreign films viewed by Anglo-American film studies students, and all state a preference for subtitling. The case against dubbing includes imperfect synchronicity between lip and audio or voice and body, flatness of performances and acoustics, and alteration or elimination of the original film's sound track and design. The quality of the acting is frequently noted as suffering in dubbed films, as the vocal qualities, tones, and rhythms of specific languages, combined with the gestures and facial expressions that mark national characters and acting styles, become literally lost in translation. While subtitling is acknowledged to have drawbacks as well—it is distracting and impedes concentration on the visuals and often leaves portions of the dialogue untranslated—it is seen to alter the source text the least and to enable the target audience to experience the authentic "foreignness" of the film.

But this position often does not acknowledge the selected acceptance of dubbing in subtitling countries or cases where dubbing makes more sense than subtitling. Foreign films and television programs aimed at children are dubbed in target countries that tend otherwise to subtitle because their viewers have not yet learned to read or cannot read quickly enough for subtitles to be effective. While serious moviegoers demand that art films be subtitled, they rarely complain that foreign films in lower, more commercial genres such as the "spaghetti western," *giallo*, martial arts, comedies, and anime are usually released in dubbed versions. For Italian cinema, popular or art, the authenticity argument does not hold: almost all Italian films are shot silent and then dubbed after filming has been completed, so there is no original sound track to speak of. The postwar era saw increased levels of co-production among nations, with the casts of co-produced films often coming from different countries and not speaking the same languages; their parts were thus dubbed by voice actors of the country in which the film was shot, and the international nature of what is in fact a polyglot film was erased. Federico Fellini's *La strada* (*The Road*, 1954) features two lead performers from the United States speaking English (Anthony Quinn and Richard Basehart) and one from Italy speaking Italian (Giulietta Masina). In terms of screen time and verbal utterances, the two American actors predominate; the Italian lead's lines are negligible. In spite of this, Anglo-American purists invariably judge the dubbed-in-Italian, subtitled-in-English version to be the more authentic even though the lips of two of the three main characters are clearly out of synch with their voices and the film was shot without sound.

The claim that subtitling involves the least interference with the original film is also arguable. Subtitles obstruct the integrity of composition and *mise-en-scène* by leading the viewers' eyes to the bottom of the frame. They focus audience attention on the translated words and the actors speaking them to the exclusion of peripheral or background dialogue, sound, or characters. They do not provide as full a translation as dubbing, and audiences of subtitled films do not experience the words and the expressions of the performers simultaneously. Subtitling may thus be regarded as undoing the synergy of performance and script, elevating selectively translated dialogue and downgrading the impact and importance of visual expression.

Although neither subtitling nor dubbing is an ideal form of audiovisual translation, recent technological developments have widened their application and reception. The number of individual sound tracks used in feature film sound design has increased (twenty-four tracks or more are now commonplace), as has the number of sound tracks used in the dubbing process. When each speaking character has a separate voice track in the film's original recording, dubbing only for language is possible, leaving the rest of the original aural expression of the film intact. For subtitling, laser processing has enabled the introduction of larger letters, outlined words, broader color ranges, and translucent background bands to increase legibility. But it is digitalization that has brought the most dramatic changes. Analyzing and resynthesizing the voices of dubbing actors make it possible

for intonation, tone, and timbre to be adjusted to match those of the source actors almost identically. Asynchrony between lip movements and translated revoicings can also be corrected digitally to achieve lip synchrony, which is especially important in close-ups. The introduction of "soft titles," which are similar to the simultaneous translation one may experience with opera, has been enabled by CD-ROM technology and has allowed for high-quality subtitling for films that have no existing subtitled prints, providing a cheaper and more easily transportable solution than the expensive process of burning subtitles onto a newly struck print.

Finally, the introduction of Digital Video Broadcasting (DVB) and the Digital Versatile Disc (DVD) has produced increasing user choice and demand for television and film in other languages. Digital TV (DVB) enables transmission of a number of signals and thus live or simultaneous subtitling—a particularly important development for those countries accustomed to reading subtitles, as it means new access to foreign satellite channels. DVDs have become a crucial mode of film consumption. Their viewers can choose between dubbed or subtitled streams in a range of languages— up to four dubbing tracks and thirty-two subtitled tracks. Translations or subtitles are also required for the extra features frequently found on DVDs, such as trailers, behind-the-scenes documentaries, and biographical information on key cast members. While the subtitling versus dubbing debate is unlikely to ever be resolved, digital technologies have provided new opportunities for both modes of audiovisual translation.

SEE ALSO *Dialogue; Sound; Technology*

FURTHER READING

Betz, Mark. "The Name above the (Sub)Title: Internationalism, Coproduction, and Polyglot European Art Cinema." *Camera Obscura* 46 (2001): 1–44.

Danan, Martine. "Dubbing as an Expression of Nationalism." *Meta: Journal des Traducteurs/Translator's Journal* 36, no. 4 (1991): 606–614.

Egoyan, Atom, and Ian Balfour, eds. *Subtitles: On the Foreignness of Film.* Cambridge, MA: The MIT Press, 2004.

Ivarsson, Jan, and Mary Carroll. *Subtitling.* Simrishamn, Sweden: TransEdit, 1998.

Vincendeau, Ginette. "Hollywood Babel: The Coming of Sound and the Multiple-Language Version." *Screen* 29, no. 2 (Spring 1988): 24–39.

Whitman-Linsen, Candance. *Through the Dubbing Glass: The Synchronization of American Motion Pictures into German, French, and Spanish.* New York: Peter Lang, 1992.

Mark Betz

EARLY CINEMA

Emerging at the tail end of the nineteenth century, cinema owed its existence as a technological invention to key developments in motion study and optics, and, as a visual novelty to traditions of screened entertainment. The medium would soon shed its affiliation with science when its potential for widespread commercial success became more apparent, facilitating its entry into the mainstream of twentieth-century popular culture. Even so, cinema's earliest years were marked by a variety of representational tendencies and viewing contexts whose diversity would diminish once commercial imperatives imposed themselves more fully. Had cinema proved less successful, it might have enjoyed freedom from borrowed aesthetic conventions somewhat longer than it did. But by the first years of the new century, as films became longer and their content incorporated story material with greater regularity, the potential for the cinema to rival stage-based forms and generate greater profit attracted numerous entrepreneurs, leading to sustained growth throughout the early 1900s.

Within ten years of the medium's debut, motion pictures had established themselves as a staple within the cultural landscape of most countries, and the uncertainty of the medium's novelty phase had been replaced by more concerted efforts to standardize the production of films for a growing audience. The increasing popularity of motion pictures meant that for the final ten years of the early cinema period, the medium would enter into a process of institutionalization. With movies readily available in most urban areas and narrative the dominant form that most films assumed, the commercial future of cinema pointed progressively toward industrial models favoring rationalized modes of production and predict-able systems of distribution and exhibition. To some degree, the history of cinema's first years is a steady (if uneven) reduction of options, leading to the enshrinement of the feature-length fiction film, shown in theaters designed for movie projection.

EARLY TECHNOLOGY AND FIRST FILMS

Building on the advancements made in series photography by such figures as Étienne-Jules Marey (1830–1904) and Eadweard Muybridge (1830–1904) in the 1870s and 1880s, coupled with the animation principles at the center of motion toys like the zoetrope, numerous inventors in the late nineteenth century attempted to devise an instrument that could produce the illusion of movement through the recording and playback of many photographic images in rapid succession. The process required a flexible base medium, made available with the patenting of celluloid stock by George Eastman (1854–1932) in 1889, and an intermittent mechanism that would allow the film to pass through the camera, pause for recording, and then proceed without tearing. Parallel experimentation resulted in workable motion picture cameras in many countries at virtually the same time: William Kennedy Laurie Dickson (1860–1935), working for Thomas Alva Edison (1847–1931), developed the kinetograph in the United States, while Louis and Auguste Lumière perfected the *cinématographe* in France, and Robert W. Paul (1869–1943), in collaboration with Birt Acres (1854–1918), and William Friese-Greene (1855–1921), working separately, devised cameras in England.

The kinetograph and the *cinématographe* proved the most successful of these inventions, the former propelled by the business acumen of Edison and the latter spurred by its incorporation of three functions (camera, printer, and projector) into one machine. In fact, the portability and flexibility of the *cinématographe* led the Lumière brothers to send camera operators around the globe, and screenings of their films became the inaugural experience of motion picture projection in many countries in 1896, including Russia, India, Brazil, Mexico, and Egypt. The most famous of the Lumière screenings took place in the Grand Café of Paris on 28 December 1895, often singled out as the first public exhibition of motion pictures for a paying audience, and thus the inauguration of cinema as a commercial enterprise. Though Edison had already been filming subjects with the kinetograph since 1893, these films could only be viewed for the first few years on a private viewing machine called a kinetoscope; projection of Edison films on a screen before an audience did not occur in the United States until 23 April 1896 with the debut of the Vitascope, a projecting device developed by Thomas Armat (1866–1948) but marketed as Edison's own.

The earliest films tended to be brief, often lasting no longer than a minute. Because the first audiences appeared to respond to the visual appeal of oversized, moving images projected before them, subjects were deliberately varied, ranging from the observation of intimate actions (*Baby's Breakfast*, 1895) to larger-scaled events (*Train Arriving at the Station*, 1895). The Lumières quickly became known for their recordings of seemingly unstaged events, often labeled *actualités*, while Edison's first films tended to be brief records of vaudeville performances. Initially restricted to the confines of the Edison studio, called the Black Maria, kinetoscope subjects played up the performative value of their act, be it the flexing of Sandow the Strongman's muscles or the swirling skirts of Annabelle. Though relatively static, these films emphasized cinema's appeal as a permanent record of a moment's movement in time, the camera capturing whatever was placed before it for posterity, in much the same way that still photography had done in previous decades.

The *cinématographe* had the added advantage of increased mobility, thereby allowing the Lumière camera operators to pursue a wider range of actions in their natural settings. This meant that the Lumière films could trade on the recognition that familiar places possessed for local audiences as well as exploiting the exoticism of faraway locales. Equally important to the success of these early *actualités* was the way they functioned as visual newspapers, giving imagistic weight to events of the day, such as natural disasters or visits by royal dignitaries.

For the first few years, the vast majority of films were single shots, and it was left to exhibitors to combine these shots into longer works if they so desired. The elaboration of films into multi-shot entities occurred with greater regularity after 1900, and with this shift came a concomitant increase in filmed narratives. Nonetheless, early films offered a surprisingly diverse array of formal strategies: while many films employed a fixed camera position that kept filmed subjects at a considerable distance, others exploited the camera's capacity for magnification by employing a series of closely scaled shots (for example, *Grandma's Reading Glass*, 1900) or featuring a constantly moving camera, either as a panorama or mounted on a mobile vehicle, particularly locomotives, for a cycle of films often labeled "kinesthetic films" or "phantom rides."

One notable feature of many early films is their self-conscious use of features that created visual pleasure: the mobile camera in the kinesthetic films and the masked close-ups in various peephole films stress the capacity of the medium to provide a technologically enhanced view that allows the spectator to see differently. This approach operated in contradistinction to later, more narratively oriented cinema in which style often functioned to underscore the story. The overt nature of aspects of early cinema style has led some commentators, most notably Tom Gunning, to label the first ten years or so of film as constituting a cinema of attractions. The cinema of attractions is not defined so much by its unique attributes as by the distinct relationship it creates between the spectator and the film. In the cinema of attractions, film addresses itself directly to the viewer, often quite literally when vaudeville actors solicit the spectator's attention by looking directly toward the camera. More generally, it is the modus operandi of the films themselves that qualifies them for this designation, as they are designed to provoke an immediate reaction, predicated on shock or surprise, rather than on the cumulative pleasures that narrative films provide. One might think that the move to multi-shot films would have diluted the intensity of attractions, but at least initially, editing became another form of attraction. According to Gunning, in many of the early multi-shot films, editing becomes a kind of surprise in itself, as in the fanciful transitions one observes in films such as *Let Me Dream Again* (1900) or *What Happened in the Tunnel* (1903) or the accelerated sensation of displacement and mobility editing helps to promote in chase films, in which large groups of people run from one locale to the next, the cut introducing a new setting while sustaining the sense of frantic movement.

One feature of editing in early multi-shot films in particular that has invited scholarly attention is the propensity toward noncontinuity in such films. Unlike later films, in which editing strives to promote a sense of continuity by disguising the potential disruptiveness of the cut, the editing in many early films draws attention to

EDWIN S. PORTER
b. Connellsville, Pennsylvania, 21 April 1870, d. New York, 30 April 1941

Often credited with popularizing the story film in the United States, Edwin S. Porter is most notable for embodying the diverse tendencies of early cinema. Commentators have referred to Porter as "Janus-faced," a figure who pointed toward the medium's future at the same time that he epitomized its period-bound qualities. In particular, Porter pioneered certain aspects of narrative filmmaking, such as linear editing and intertitles, while also adhering to many of early cinema's unique traits, such as temporal overlap and direct address of the camera by performers.

Porter entered the motion picture business as a traveling exhibitor, and that experience probably influenced his early experiments as a filmmaker. Hired by Edison to work on the company's projector in 1900, he soon became the firm's chief cameraman and head of production. From the outset, his interest in the types of transitions possible when moving from one shot to another is evident. Yet, for every film that features a fluid set of linked actions, such as *The Great Train Robbery* (1903), another one depends upon tableau—the story held together only by the audience's knowledge of the source material, as in Porter's adaptation of *Uncle Tom's Cabin* (1903). Porter's achievements crystallized that year, which also saw the release of *Life of an American Fireman* and *The Gay Shoe Clerk*, two of his best-known works, that demonstrate how point of view functions at this time. In *Life of an American Fireman*, his insistence on showing the event in its entirety from one perspective and then again from another highlights the importance of retaining an established viewpoint, even at the expense of intimating simultaneity. In *The Gay Show Clerk*, the famous close-up of a stocking-clad ankle demonstrates how magnification of detail can

satisfy the viewer's voyeuristic desire for illicit visual pleasures.

Though Porter continued to find success with such nickelodeon-era shorts as *The Kleptomaniac* and the Winsor McCay–inspired *Dream of a Rarebit Fiend* (both 1906), his style of filmmaking did not survive the changes wrought by increased narrational self-sufficiency during the transitional period. By 1908, his approach already seemed antiquated, and he was let go by Edison the following year. He continued to work in the industry, lasting into the feature era to become production head at Famous Players in 1912. But his interests focused on the development of cinematic technology from 1915 onward. Fittingly, given his beginnings in the industry, his final lasting contribution was the shepherding of the Simplex projector to a position of supremacy.

RECOMMENDED VIEWING
The Finish of Bridget McKeen (1901), *Uncle Josh at the Moving Picture Show* (1902), *Life of an American Fireman* (1903), *Uncle Tom's Cabin* (1903), *The Great Train Robbery* (1903), *European Rest Cure* (1904), *The Seven Ages* (1905), *The Dream of a Rarebit Fiend* (1906), *Kathleen Mavourneen* (1906), *The "Teddy" Bears* (1907)

FURTHER READING
Burch, Noël. "Porter, or Ambivalence." *Screen* 14, no. 4 (1978/79): 91–105.

Gaudreault, André. "Detours in Film Narrative: The Development of Cross-Cutting." *Cinema Journal* 19, no. 1 (1979): 39–59.

Musser, Charles. *Before the Nickelodeon: Edwin S. Porter and the Edison Manufacturing Company.* Berkeley: University of California Press, 1991.

Charlie Keil

itself. Moreover, the logic of editing in multi-shot films follows a principle whereby, as André Gaudreault has noted, autonomy of space overrides temporal unity. The clearest demonstration of his observation can be seen in instances of temporal overlap, in which a portion of the time frame from a previous shot is repeated in a subsequent shot, the action in the latter occurring in a different locale or viewed from a changed perspective. The most celebrated case of temporal overlap occurs in

Edwin S. Porter's (1870–1941) *Life of an American Fireman* (1903), when the rescue of the mother and child from the burning building is shown twice, both from within the building and from the outside. Though later practice (and a subsequently re-edited version of the film) would rely on crosscutting to portray the same action from two vantage points, at this stage in early cinema's stylistic development, it apparently made more sense to show the action in its entirety from one perspective before shifting to another. Rather than a mistake, temporal overlap should be understood as evidence that the logic underwriting early cinema style traded on distinctive viewing procedures and the influence of other, visually based storytelling forms prevalent at the time.

EXHIBITION AND EARLY VIEWING CONTEXTS

One of those influential forms was the magic lantern show, which depended on projected images to tell stories visually. Charles Musser, among others, has suggested that film exhibition practice developed within traditions of screen entertainment aligned with such media as magic lanterns and stereopticons. Highly dependent on lecturers, elaborate transitional effects, and a multitude of still images, magic lantern shows may have affected the way early film exhibition developed in a variety of ways. For one, they provided a model for exhibitors to construct programs of single-shot films that had the potential to transform the material into something entirely different. Depending on the will and the creativity of the exhibitor, various short films could be combined into multi-shot assemblages, whose meaning might be further transformed by an accompanying text read by a lecturer. This allowed the exhibitor to function as a proto-editor in the years before multi-shot films became the industry norm. As Musser has also argued, the power of the exhibitor to supply additional narrational force to the films he projected complicates the applicability of the cinema of attractions model, insofar as the films might have been understood quite differently, depending on how they were presented.

Nonetheless, Gunning has found further confirmation of the pervasiveness of attractions by considering the effect of exhibition on early films. Because films often functioned as one act among many on a vaudeville bill, their status as attractions was reinforced by the modular presentational format of vaudeville itself. Much like the variety acts it was sandwiched among, the short film traded on making an immediate impact on its audience before being replaced by some other, disparate piece of entertainment. In other words, the vaudeville program fostered early cinema's tendency toward surprise and novelty by virtue of the interchangeability of elements on any given bill. Even when cinema came to be shown in theaters designed primarily for film exhibition, this variety format persisted, placing film among a host of appealing entertainments, including illustrated songs, lecturers, and vaudeville acts, only now these elements supported the films.

Before films found themselves featured as the main attraction in venues specifically built or reconfigured for the purpose of screening them (these were typically termed nickelodeons in the United States), cinema

appeared in a variety of exhibition sites. The diversity of places films were screened points to the broad potential envisioned for film from the outset. Everywhere from outdoor fairs to department stores, opera houses to dime museums, offered films. The venue and context determined the role films would play: films documenting war-related activities might be screened in a community hall to boost morale during wartime, while a church might show a filmed Passion Play to coincide with a religious service. In certain countries, particularly in Europe, itinerant exhibitors played a crucial role in spreading cinema across the countryside, often screening films in the fairground circuit. For this reason, films tended to be sold outright, since exhibitors would move from site to site, ideally finding new audiences for their programs at each locale.

Such strategies failed to build a permanent base for cinema's growth, however, and risked alienating audiences who might be exposed to either worn-out prints or collections of titles already viewed. In the United States, the solution to such problems arose in the form of the film exchange, an early type of film distribution in which a middleman bought prints and then rented them out to exhibitors at a fraction of the purchase price. The inauguration of the exchange system facilitated the establishment of permanent movie theaters in America, providing exhibitors with a steady supply of reliable prints at a reduced cost.

How is it that motion pictures had achieved a sufficient level of popularity by 1903–1905 to entice enterprising business people to risk investing in the exchange system and then in permanent exhibition sites? Scholars differ in their explanations, but the increased production of longer story films, most obviously *Le voyage dans la lune* (*A Trip to the Moon* [1902]) and *The Great Train Robbery* (1903), must have played a significant role, as both these films proved to be successes with the moviegoing public.

Still more questions arise concerning just who that moviegoing public might have been. It has frequently been assumed that the audience for early cinema was composed primarily of working-class, immigrant men (at least in the United States), that conclusion reached on the basis of contemporaneous reports and the locations of theaters. Though such a portrait of the American moviegoer might have been accurate in the initial years of the nickelodeon boom, it scarcely does justice to the diversity of audiences viewing cinema during the entirety of the early cinema period and in regions and countries beyond that of the United States' industrialized northeast. Accounts of well-heeled patrons frequenting motion picture programs at private salons in turn-of-the-century France, fairground visitors of all ages and social backgrounds taking in films as part of the presentations by

Edwin S. Porter's* The Great Train Robbery *(1903) marked a number of advances in the story film. EVERETT COLLECTION. REPRODUCED BY PERMISSION.

traveling showmen in Great Britain, and rural, middle-class churchgoers viewing films at a Chautauqua in the rural Midwest of the United States indicate that motion pictures attracted different types of audiences, depending on the venue and the mode of presentation.

Nonetheless, much has been made of the anxiety that cinema engendered among those who felt compelled to protect citizens from society's evils. Reformers feared the potentially negative effects of cinema from the outset, and as permanent homes for film exhibition became established, efforts at regulation found an easy target. Nickelodeons were criticized for being dark, dirty sites of social mixing. Ironically, the National Board of Censorship (NBC) came into being in the United States as a defensive strategy on the part of exhibitors reacting to the citywide closing of nickelodeons by New York's mayor in 1908. One can see the establishment of the NBC as the

first in a series of self-regulatory moves made by the American film industry to circumvent state-controlled censorship. At the same time, it demonstrates how early—and how closely—exhibition and regulation are tied together, and how principles of regulation are formulated with an eye to "protecting vulnerable" audience members from the excesses of motion picture content, thereby controlling their behavior by shaping the films those audience members will see. In the years after 1908, the film industry would exercise progressively greater control over every aspect of the film experience, from production through to exhibition, in attempts to standardize the product and its entry into a growing marketplace.

CHANGES IN PRODUCTION

Early production in the preeminent film-producing nations of France, Great Britain, and the United States

The travellers arrive at their destination in Georges Méliès's **Un Voyage dans la lune *(A Trip to the Moon, 1902).*** EVERETT COLLECTION. REPRODUCED BY PERMISSION.

has often been likened to a cottage industry. Firms tended to be fairly small and typically operated in an artisanal fashion, which restricted their ability to respond to increased demand with expanded output. When the equipment permitted it, *actualités* could be filmed by a single cameraperson, but a collaborative model of film-making usually prevailed for fictional works, indicating that a division of labor was deemed appropriate from the outset in the production of story films. France proved most forward-thinking in this regard, particularly the firms of Gaumont and Pathé: the latter moved to a director-unit system of production by 1906, in which numerous directors (overseen by supervising producer Ferdinand Zecca [1864–1947]) worked with their own small crews to put out a film on a weekly basis, while prints were mass-produced, courtesy of a workforce over 1,000 strong. The growth of these companies allowed

them to produce films at a prodigious rate and to move beyond the relatively small market of France to become dominant internationally. Diversification of product further differentiated Pathé and Gaumont from their chief French competitor, Georges Méliès (1861–1938). Whereas Méliès tended to concentrate on trick films and *féeries* (elaborate story films employing fantasy), the other two companies produced a range of films, eventually incorporating melodramas and chase films into the mix. Pathé, always the most enterprising of the French firms, capitalized on the limited capacity of the major American producers of the mid-1900s (Edison, Biograph, Vitagraph, Selig, and Lubin) and easily dominated the US market once it started distributing its films there in 1904.

England's companies proved far less stable than those of France but still enjoyed periods of prominence, especially in the early years of the twentieth century. There were several notable firms, most of which operated on an artisanal model. These included the company headed by early pioneer Robert W. Paul, whose success in manufacturing equipment led him to film production; those producers belonging to the so-called "Brighton School," chief among them G. A. Smith (1864–1959) and James Williamson (1855–1933), as well as the most successful and durable of the British filmmakers, Cecil Hepworth (1873–1953). The stylistic range of British films was particularly impressive, incorporating the self-consciously inventive trick comedy of two films from 1900, Williamson's *The Big Swallow* and Hepworth's *How It Feels to Be Run Over* (both convincing examples of how attractions-era filmmaking could render acknowledgment of the camera's presence a source of uniquely cinematic humor, Hepworth's involving reformulation of the chase film), the enterprising use of cut-ins in Smith's *Sick Kitten* and transitional devices in his *Mary Jane's Mishap* (both from 1903), and the multi-shot *Rescued by Rover* (1905). The latter proved one of England's most popular productions, so much so that Hepworth had to shoot the film several times as each of the negatives wore out. In its fusing of proven plot situations (stolen child saved by heroic dog) with propulsive linear editing, *Rescued by Rover* points toward the last-minute rescue scenario perfected by D. W. Griffith (1875–1948) a few years later at Biograph.

In the United States, the relatively stagnant production levels before 1908 can be attributed in part to Edison's continued threats of legal reprisals for patent violation. While two firms, Kalem and Essanay, entered into production in 1907, the output of American companies lagged far behind the nickelodeon-fueled demand, allowing Pathé's films and other imports to command 75 percent of the American market. The solution to the patent infringement impasse came in the form of a patent pooling agreement reached in late 1908; after it, productivity by American firms increased significantly.

The company established to implement the conditions of this agreement was known as the Motion Picture Patents Company (MPPC). All the major American producers became members and complied with its policies. The MPPC aimed to control every aspect of the industry by implementing a system of royalties to be paid for use of equipment and, more importantly, by working to bring distribution practices into line with producers' desires. The MPPC aimed to curb the excesses of distribution that had contributed to industrial instability, primarily the circulation of aging prints and the reliance on duped copies. Moreover, the MPPC exerted control over exchange schedules, introducing regularly timed releases. Exchanges had to be licensed by the MPPC, ensuring that distributors would abide by schedules dictated by producers. (The MPPC extended its control over the distribution sector by taking over the licensed exchanges altogether with the formation of the General Film Company in 1910, bringing it one step closer to becoming an oligopoly.)

Though clearly working for its own monetary gain, the MPPC did effect substantial and positive changes in the American production landscape. Productivity soared from 1909 onward, in part because the MPPC limited the number of imports allowed into the domestic market, but also because its distribution reforms provided security to producers, who could now depend upon predictable delivery schedules. Even so, the MPPC-related firms failed to address all exhibitor needs. In part, these needs arose because certain exhibitors chafed against the royalties imposed upon them; further dissension appeared in the form of exchanges left out of the MPPC fold at the time of the General Film Company's formation. These disenfranchised elements within the distribution and exhibition sector constituted a sufficient percentage of the market to support the emergence of a competing faction of producers, known as the Independents, the first of which appeared in 1909. Their ranks grew over the next few years, leading to a clogged production field of more than twenty manufacturers by 1911, whose production levels were far in excess of pre-MPPC rates. The combined force of MPPC and Independent producers led to the release of over 5,000 films in 1913, the vast majority of them still single reelers.

THE SINGLE-REEL FILM AND CHANGES TO FILM FORM

One of the most important changes to occur at the same time that the MPPC was formed was the adoption of the single reel (a 1,000-foot length) as the industry standard. This move to a standardized format had repercussions not only for industry practice but also for the formal properties defining story films during the next five years. Reliance on a single, interchangeable film length rendered print delivery and rental charges to distributors much more straightforward. Exhibition programs became more predictable, as audiences came to expect films to last a prescribed amount of time. In many ways, the move to a single-reel standard helped push films toward the status of a mass consumer good, insofar as they became a commodity whose value was now regularized.

The changes wrought by the adoption of the single-reel format also registered themselves at the level of production methods and formal features. Now that producers knew exactly how long a film narrative should run, they could fashion stories designed to fit within the specified 1,000 feet. Film narratives began to assume a structural sameness from 1908 onward, hastened in part

GEORGES MÉLIÈS
b. Paris, France, 8 December 1861, d. 21 January 1938

Famed for his elaborately staged fantasy films and whimsical trick films, Georges Méliès has often been described as the antithesis of the Lumière brothers, his fictional flights of fancy viewed as the inverse of their slice-of-life *actualités*. Nonetheless, one can overstate Méliès's contribution to the development of film narrative: for example, his famed "substitution splice" operates according to the logic of trickery rather than continuity and demonstrates how his early career as a magician clearly influenced his subsequent filmmaking practice.

First and foremost, Méliès's films are the work of a showman, the tricks proudly displayed while the wizardry is kept under wraps. Usually prized for their intricate *mise-en-scène,* his films are also feats of editing-as-illusion, a fact easily missed by those accustomed to associating cuts with spatial transitions. Instead, many of Méliès's disguised cuts operate to facilitate a transformation; accordingly, all elements of the *mise-en-scène* must remain in the same place while a single object is removed or repositioned to enable the visual trick to work effectively. Through these substitution splices, Méliès engaged in a form of invisible editing, though not the type associated with later classical storytelling methods.

Equally exacting was Méliès's approach to *mise-en-scène,* and his films are a cornucopia of visual effects, whether they be the reflexive displays of projection and technological reproduction in films such as *La Lanterne magique* (*The Magic Lantern*, 1903) and *Photographie électrique à distance* (*Long Distance Wireless Photography*, 1908) or the creation of fantasy worlds in longer works like *Le Voyage dans la lune* (*A Trip to the Moon*, 1902) and *Le Voyage à travers l'impossible* (*The Impossible Voyage,* 1904). It is these multi-shot story films that have contributed to Méliès's reputation as an early master of film narrative, but in truth, they are a collection of intricate and distinct tableaux. Méliès's primary interest was the visual capacity of the individual shot, and he excelled at devising ever more elaborate sets, populated by

sprites who disappear in a puff of smoke, mermaids surrounded by varieties of exotic sea life, and improbably conceived traveling machines capable of propelling their inhabitants beyond the earth's surface.

Exercising total control over all aspects of the filmmaking process, Méliès created perfectly self-contained worlds, most of them shot within the confines of his glass-walled studio in Montreuil. Yet his artisanal approach to filmmaking would prove his financial undoing as he was dwarfed by the industrially advanced Pathé Frères in his home country and cheated by American competitors who duped his most popular films without asking permission (or providing compensation). Though still making films as late as 1913, Méliès found himself outpaced by an industry increasingly dependent on production methods foreign to his preferred approach and gravitating toward subject matter rooted in a more prosaic realism.

RECOMMENDED VIEWING

Cendrillon (*Cinderella*, 1899), *Barbe-bleue* (*Bluebeard*, 1901), *L'Homme à la tête de caoutchouc* (*The Man with the India-Rubber Head*, 1902), *Le Voyage dans la lune* (*A Trip to the Moon*, 1902), *La Royaume des fées* (*Kingdom of the Fairies*, 1903), *La Lanterne magique* (*The Magic Lantern*, 1903), *La Sirène* (*The Mermaid*, 1904), *Le Voyage à travers l'impossible* (*The Impossible Voyage*, 1904), *La Photographie électrique à distance* (*Long Distance Wireless Photography*, 1908), *À la Conquête du Pôle* (*The Conquest of the Pole*, 1912)

FURTHER READING

Ezra, Elizabeth. *Georges Méliès.* Manchester, UK: Manchester University Press, 2000.

Gaudreault, André. "Theatricality, Narrativity, and 'Trickality': Reevaluating the Cinema of Georges Méliès." *Journal of Popular Film and Television* 15, no. 3 (1987): 110–119.

Hammond, Paul. *Marvelous Méliès.* New York: St. Martin's, 1975.

Charlie Keil

Georges Méliès. EVERETT COLLECTION. REPRODUCED BY
PERMISSION.

by the adoption of the scenario script. These scripts
served as skeletons for finished films and provided producers with blueprints for production schedules. The
increased rationalization of production practices followed
directly from the introduction of scenario scripts, allowing producers to organize sets, locations, and personnel
according to shooting demands. Departmental organization of personnel provided further streamlining of the
production process, resulting in writing departments,
which further refined the crafting of scenario scripts.

The emerging trade press in the United States also
contributed to the standardization of the script writing
process from 1907 onward. Existing publications such as
New York Daily Mirror and *Variety* began to devote space
to the film industry, and new journals aimed specifically
at exhibitors also appeared, most notably *Moving Picture
World* and *Nickelodeon*. Along with advice to exhibitors
on how to enhance the moviegoing experience, film
reviews and columns outlined the ideal ways to structure
film scenarios. The trade press coached aspiring writers in
the nascent craft of screenwriting while pointing out the
clichés and overused devices that would mark their scripts

as derivative. Though one cannot be certain how seriously such advice was taken by those responsible for the
scripts, these primers on crafting film narratives nonetheless indicate which principles of narrative construction
were prized at this time.

With films now longer, the stories that filmmakers
could tell inevitably grew in complexity as well. While an
involving narrative might well produce a satisfied viewer,
a muddled set of events would only result in frustration
and bafflement. Filmmakers had to ensure that as narratives increased in intricacy, they did not tax viewers'
powers of comprehension. As Charles Musser has
argued, this resulted in a crisis of representation for
the industry around 1907, as filmmakers struggled to
find ways to guarantee that audiences would understand
the stories presented. Various extratextual aides to comprehension were tested, including the reintroduction of
the lecturer and the employment of actors behind the
screen to utter dialogue explaining silent scenes. But
solutions unique to a single exhibition situation did
not address the problem in a systematic way; instead,
audience comprehension had to be ensured by internally
generated means, and these needed to function the
same way for every spectator, regardless of viewing
circumstances.

This led to a period of protracted experimentation
during which filmmakers devised a series of text-based
strategies to provide narratives that would ideally "tell
themselves": aspects of the medium were enlisted to
ensure comprehension of plot points, provide the look
of a believable fictional world, and promote a sense of
viewer engagement. The methods filmmakers developed
emerged over time and through trial and error. What
they came up with was one of the most striking transformations in film style ever undergone within such a
short timeframe. In effect, this involved a wholesale
change to the narrative approach already entrenched in
early cinema. What Kristin Thompson has identified as a
"neutral and unobtrusive" manner of providing information in the earliest years shifted gradually to a more
directive guiding of the viewer's attention.

Numerous scholars have coined the term "transitional era" to identify the years following 1907 and
extending to the introduction of features. What distinguishes this period on a formal level is the ongoing
experimentation in storytelling methods and the shifting
functions of various stylistic devices, as those devices
were enlisted in the service of a developing narrative
system. Comparisons to the earlier, pre-1907 mode can
help make the distinctions clearer: during the cinema
of attractions period, one finds a bias favoring the
autonomy of the shot: shots operate as individual units
rather than as pieces fitting together to make a whole.

Even when editing stitches together numerous shots, it is more like beads on a string rather than integrally interrelated component pieces. This emphasis on discrete shots translates into filmmakers exhausting the narrative potential of a single space before replacing it with another. Even in chase films, defined by the principle of advancing action, all the characters must exit the frame before a shot is deemed complete.

In many films made prior to 1907, style existed as a system only loosely connected to narrative concerns; what the next five or so years witnessed was the gradual but increased bending of style to narrative prerogatives. Conveying temporal continuity offers one striking example of this narrational shift: whereas in the earlier period, depictions of events occurring at the same time had occasioned instances of temporal overlap (even in films that employed sustained versions of linear editing, such as *The Great Train Robbery* and *Rescued by Rover*), now actions would be interrupted—literally cut into by edits—to produce the sensation of simultaneity for the viewer.

Nowhere is this more evident than in D. W. Griffith's celebrated last-minute rescues, perfected during his tenure at Biograph (which more or less coincides with the period under examination here, 1908–1913). In numerous films during the transitional period, crosscutting clarified spatial relationships between two physically separated locales while incorporating temporal pressure into the representation of space. Such an approach generates suspense, because of its constant reliance on delay in showing the outcome of one line of action while switching to another. Suspense works to involve the viewer in the narrative, in much the same way other stylistic strategies developed during this period pull the viewer into the narrative world on view: changing approaches to set decoration and arrangement of actors enhance the depth and volume of the spaces depicted; performance style moves toward greater restraint, with fewer grand gestures and a more internalized approach to expressing emotion; shifts in performance style are reinforced by moving the camera closer to the actors, making their faces more legible. Many of these changes make the fictional world on display both more believable and more engaging, placing the characters and their motivations at the center of the drama. For this reason, flashbacks, dreams, visions, and cut-ins to inserts (especially those revealing extracts from letters) become much more prevalent during this period, helping to convey characters' internal states. Overall, the individual elements of style become subordinated to a narrational program that fosters interdependency and integration, as when editing allows for shifts in shot scale, which in turn helps to register changes in performance style.

CINEMA AS AN INSTITUTION

The significant changes occurring to film form during this period operated in concert with other forces of transformation so that by 1915, numerous developments pointed toward the institutionalization of cinema. By 1915, the MPPC had been dissolved by court order. The move toward increased consolidation inaugurated by the struggle between the Independents and the MPPC (the latter dissolved by court order in 1915) continued apace: corporate entities that would become pivotal in the studio era, such as Universal and Paramount, were founded during this period. The move of the American film industry to Hollywood was already underway, as was the establishment of a star system, with figures such as Mary Pickford (1892–1979) and Charlie Chaplin (1889–1977) acquiring the substantial fame and the power that came with it. Feature-length films had begun to dislodge the primacy of the single reeler, while large-scale picture palaces usurped the role of nickelodeons within the exhibition landscape. Movies had moved noticeably closer to the status of mass entertainment, and the increased social responsibility that attends such a shift produced a new phase in the medium's development, a clear departure from the hallmarks of the period that we label retrospectively the era of early cinema.

SEE ALSO *Film History; Narrative; Pre-Cinema; Silent Cinema*

FURTHER READING

Abel, Richard. *The Ciné Goes to Town: French Cinema, 1896–1914.* Berkeley: University of California Press, 1994.

———, ed. *Silent Film.* New Brunswick, NJ: Rutgers University Press, 1996.

Bordwell, David, Janet Staiger, and Kristin Thompson. *The Classical Hollywood Cinema: Film Style and Mode of Production to 1960.* New York: Columbia University Press, 1985.

Bowser, Eileen. *The Transformation of Cinema, 1907–1915.* New York: Scribner, 1990.

Burch, Noël. *Life to Those Shadows.* Berkeley: University of California Press, 1990.

Elsaesser, Thomas, ed. *Early Cinema: Space, Frame, Narrative.* London: British Film Institute, 1990.

Fell, John L., ed. *Film Before Griffith.* Berkeley: University of California Press, 1983.

Gaudreault, André. "Temporality and Narrativity in Early Cinema." In *Film Before Griffith*, edited by John L. Fell. Berkeley: University of California Press, 1983: 311–329.

Grieveson, Lee, and Peter Krämer. *The Silent Cinema Reader.* New York: Routledge, 2004.

Gunning, Tom. *D. W. Griffith and the Origins of American Narrative Film: The Early Years at Biograph.* Urbana: University of Illinois Press, 1991.

Keil, Charlie. *Early American Cinema in Transition: Story, Style, and Filmmaking, 1907–1913*. Madison: University of Wisconsin Press, 2001.

Keil, Charlie, and Shelley Stamp, eds. *American Cinema's Transitional Era: Audiences, Institutions, Practices*. Berkeley: University of California Press, 2004.

Musser, Charles. *The Emergence of Cinema: The American Screen to 1907*. New York: Scribner, 1990.

Popple, Simon, and Joe Kember. *Early Cinema: From Factory Gate to Dream Factory*. London: Wallflower Press, 2004.

Salt, Barry. *Film Style and Technology: History and Analysis*. 2nd ed. London: Starword, 1992.

Charlie Keil

EDITING

Editing is a postproduction phase of filmmaking that begins following the completion of principal cinematography. An editor (and his or her team of assistant editors) works in close collaboration with the film's director and producer. This means that, as with all areas of filmmaking, editing is a collaborative enterprise, even though, in practice, the film editor is typically responsible for the overall ordering and design of the shots in sequence.

Many editing decisions, however, may originate from the film's director or producer. The famous and unconventional series of dissolves in *Taxi Driver* (1976) that join shots of Robert DeNiro walking down the same street originated from director Martin Scorsese (b. 1942) rather than editor Tom Rolf (b. 1931). The editing design that opens *The Wild Bunch* (1969), first establishing the band of outlaws riding into town and then cutting to close-ups of a pair of scorpions struggling in a nest of fire ants, was the idea of producer Phil Feldman (1922–1991). Anne V. Coates (b. 1925) was hired to edit *Lawrence of Arabia* (1962) after first cutting a trial sequence, prompting director David Lean (1908–1991) to proclaim that for the first time in his career he'd found an editor who cut a sequence exactly the way he would have. Many directors, in fact, are known for having excellent editing skills, including Akira Kurosawa (1910–1998) (*Shichinin no samurai* [*Seven Samurai*, 1954]), Nicolas Roeg (b. 1928) (*Don't Look Now* [1973]), Frederick Wiseman (b. 1930) (*Hospital* [1970]), and Sam Peckinpah (1925–1984) (*The Wild Bunch*). Even many of these directors, though, employ first-rate editors on their productions.

THE WORK OF EDITING

What is true about editing, therefore, is common to all phases of film production—the creative decisions involved typically have numerous authors. What, then, as a key collaborator on the production, does the editor do? The film editor reviews all of the footage shot on a production, selects the best takes of individual shots, and then orders these to produce an edited sequence that will convey the narrative action and emotion of the film's scenes. To accomplish this, editors must continually view and re-view the footage, trying different combinations of shots and gradually shaping the correct ones. Doing so moves their edit from a rough cut to a fine cut of the material. To maximize their ability to see all of the creative possibilities for combining the shots, most editors will not go on location while the film is being shot or watch the director at work. Seeing the actual layout of a set or other physical locale will tend to inhibit their perceptions about the ways that the shots may be joined, causing them to think in terms of the physical realities of place rather than the spatial realities they can create through editing.

Indeed, in earlier decades throughout most of the medium's history, editors worked on celluloid, physically cutting and splicing film using large bulky machines that ran footage in a linear and sequential fashion, from the beginning of a take to its end. The Moviola was an upright editor with a single screen that was used throughout much of Hollywood's history. Of European derivation, the Steenbeck, or KEM, was a horizontal, flatbed machine equipped with two screens and two soundtracks. It, too, was a linear editor because the footage could advance only in a sequential fashion, from head to tail

Complex editing appears in **Don't Look Now** *(1973) by director-editor Nicolas Roeg.* EVERETT COLLECTION. REPRODUCED BY PERMISSION.

of a clip or vice versa. Since the 1990s editors have been working on digital, nonlinear machines, such as Avid or Lightworks. These machines do not work on celluloid film; they provide computerized access to footage on digital video and enable an editor to go instantly to any point in this footage without having to scroll manually through every frame, the way a Moviola or Steenbeck requires. Rather than physically cutting and splicing film, the editor using a nonlinear system works at a keyboard, manipulating via computer the footage that has been digitized as video. Once the fine cut is finished, the camera negative is conformed to the final cut. Nonlinear editing has become the industry norm today, and it has had some important consequences for the stylistics of editing in contemporary film.

The foregoing description of editing makes it seem to be a very straightforward and relatively simple process. It is not. Many editors have a background in music or have musical affinities, and they speak of *feeling* where the cut needs to go, of responding kinesthetically to the emerging rhythms of the sequence. Edit points, therefore, often owe more to an editor's intuitive response to the emerging flow of the sequence than to coolly intellectual decisions. Indeed, there is no single right way to cut a sequence. There are many possible cuts, all of which will inflect the material in different ways. As this suggests, while editing plays a variety of narrative functions, presenting basic story information that advances the story, it also helps set the emotional tone and coloration of a sequence, the rhythm and pace of scenes; helps create performances by the actors; and solves the innumerable continuity problems that arise when trying to connect the footage shot during production.

These are very powerful interventions into the material of the film, and they suggest why so many directors have found editing to be a supremely decisive phase of filmmaking. It is commonly said that a director makes his or her film three times—first, as the screenplay is written; second, as the screenplay is altered at the point of filming; and third, as the material that has been directed and photographed is changed again in the editing process. For this reason, directors frequently partner with a favorite editor across many film productions, finding that this collaboration is a key means of achieving the results they want. Martin Scorsese regularly teamed with editor Thelma Schoonmaker (b. 1940) (*Raging Bull* [1980],

GoodFellas [1990], *Gangs of New York* [2002]). Susan E. Morse has edited most of the films that Woody Allen (b. 1935) has directed (*Manhattan* [1979], *Crimes and Misdemeanors* [1989], *Celebrity* [1998]). Clint Eastwood (b. 1930) likes to work with Joel Cox (*Every Which Way But Loose* [1978], *Unforgiven* [1992], *Mystic River* [2003]). Blake Edwards (b. 1922) used Ralph E. Winters (1909–2004) (*The Pink Panther* [1964], *10* [1979], *Victor/Victoria* [1982]).

THE DEVELOPMENT OF EDITING

Although the earliest films in cinema were done in one shot without any editing, cutting is so fundamental to the medium that it began to emerge relatively quickly. There was a basic disparity between the amount of film that a camera's magazine could hold and the evolving desire of filmmakers and audiences for longer and more elaborate story films. Only by editing shots together could longer narrative forms be achieved. *A Trip to the Moon* (1914), directed by Georges Méliès (1861–1938), for example, creates a narrative by assembling a series of scenes, with each scene filmed in a single shot. The edit points occur between the scenes, in order to link them together.

Life of an American Fireman (1903), directed by Edwin S. Porter (1870–1941), presents the same narrative events—a fireman rescuing a woman from a burning building—as seen first from inside the building and then from camera setups outside the building, repeating the same narrative action. From the standpoint of continuity as it would develop in cinema, this duplication of event was a deviant use of editing, although other early films feature this kind of overlapping action. It demonstrated, however, the manner in which cutting could impose its own laws of time and space on narrative.

Porter's *The Great Train Robbery* (1903) follows a band of Western outlaws robbing a train and interrupts the chronology of the action with a cutaway showing the rescue of a telegraph operator whom the outlaws earlier had tied up. Following the cutaway, Porter introduces a second line of action, showing the roundup of a posse and the pursuit of the outlaws. Film historians commonly cite this as an early example of parallel editing, showing two lines of narrative action happening at the same time, although Porter's use of this device here is ambiguous. It is not clear that he means for the parallel editing to establish that the two lines of action are in fact happening simultaneously. In other respects, editing in *The Great Train Robbery* remains very primitive, with cuts used only to join scenes and with no intercutting inside a scene.

In contrast with Porter, D. W. Griffith (1875–1948) freed the camera from the conventions of stage perspective by breaking the action of scenes into many different shots and editing these according to the emotional and narrative rhythms of the action. Griffith explored the capabilities of editing in the films he made at Biograph studio from 1908 to 1913, primarily the use of continuity matches to link shots smoothly and according to their dramatic and kinesthetic properties. Cutting from full-figure shots to a close-up accentuated the drama, and matching the action on a cut as a character walks from an exterior into a doorway and, in the next shot, enters an interior set enabled Griffith to join filming locations that were physically separated but adjacent in terms of the time and place of the story.

Griffith became famous for his use of crosscutting in the many "rides to the rescue" that climax his films. In *The Girl and Her Trust* (1912), for example, Griffith cuts back and forth from a pair of robbers, who have abducted the heroine and are escaping on a railroad pump car, to the hero, who is attempting to overtake them by train. By intercutting these lines of action, Griffith creates suspense, and by shortening the lengths of the shots, he accelerates the pace. Crosscutting furnished a foundation for narrative in cinema, and there is little structural difference between what Griffith did here and what a later filmmaker such as Steven Spielberg (b. 1946) does in *Jaws* (1975). Griffith extended his fluid use of continuity editing and crosscutting in his epics *The Birth of a Nation* (1915) and *Intolerance* (1916). The latter film is a supreme example of crosscutting, which is here used to tell four stories set in different time periods in simultaneous fashion.

The Soviet filmmaker Sergei Eisenstein (1898–1948) wrote that Griffith's crosscutting embodied the essential class disparity of a capitalist society. He meant that the lines of action in Griffith's editing remained separated, like the classes under capitalism. Inspired by the October Revolution, Eisenstein and other Soviet filmmakers developed in the 1910s and 1920s a more radical approach to editing than Griffith had countenanced. Griffith had championed facial expression and used close-ups to showcase it, but Lev Kuleshov (1899–1970), teaching at the Moscow Film School, proclaimed that editing itself could essentially create facial expression and the impression of an acting performance. The "Kuleshov effect" has become part of the basic folklore of cinema. Kuleshov allegedly took a strip of film showing an actor's emotionless face and intercut it with shots of other objects—a bowl of soup, a woman grieving at a gravestone, a child playing with a toy—and the edited sequence (according to Kuleshov) led audiences to remark on the skill of the actor, who looked hungry when he saw the soup, sad at the sight of the woman, and happy when he saw the child. Because the face remained unchanged, Kuleshov announced that his

SERGEI EISENSTEIN
b. Riga, Russian Empire (now Latvia), 23 January 1898, d. 11 February 1948

Sergei Eisenstein is a wholly unique figure in cinema history. He was a filmmaker *and* a theoretician of cinema who made films and wrote voluminously about their structure and the nature of cinema. Both his filmmaking and his writing (which fills several volumes) have been tremendously influential.

Frustrated by the creative limitations of his work in the theater, Eisenstein turned to cinema and in 1925 completed his first feature, *Stachka* (*Strike*), which depicted the plight of oppressed workers. Eisenstein's next two films are the ones by which he remains best known, *Bronenosets Potyomkin* (*Battleship Potemkin*, 1925) and *Oktyabr* (*Ten Days That Shook the World* and *October*, 1927), each depicting political rebellion against czarist rule.

Eisenstein believed that editing was the foundation of film art. For Eisenstein, meaning in cinema lay not in the individual shot but only in the relationships among shots established by editing. Translating a Marxist political perspective into the language of cinema, Eisenstein referred to his editing as "dialectical montage" because it aimed to expose the essential contradictions of existence and the political order. Because conflict was essential to the political praxis of Marxism, the idea of conflict furnished the logic of Eisenstein's shot changes, which gives his silent films a rough, jagged quality. His shots do not combine smoothly, as in the continuity editing of D. W. Griffith and Hollywood cinema, but clash and bang together. Thus, his montages were eminently suited to depictions of violence, as in *Strike*, *Potemkin*, and *Ten Days*. In his essays Eisenstein enumerated the numerous types of conflict that he found essential to cinema. These included conflicts among graphic elements in a composition and between shots, and conflict of time and space created in the editing process and by filming with different camera speeds.

As a political filmmaker, Eisenstein was interested in guiding the viewer's emotions and thought processes. Thus, his metric and rhythmic montages were supplemented with what he called "tonal" and "intellectual" montage, in which he aimed for subtle emotional effects and to convey more abstract ideas. *Ten Days* represents Eisenstein's most extensive explorations of intellectual montage, as he creates a series of visual metaphors to characterize the political figures involved in the October Revolution, such as shots that compare Alexander Kerensky with a peacock.

Stalin's consolidation of power in the 1930s accompanied cultural and artistic repression, which forced Eisenstein, now criticized as a formalist, to recant the radical montage style of his silent films. Thus his last films, *Aleksandr Nevskiy* (*Alexander Nevsky*, 1938) and *Ivan Groznyy I* and *II* (*Ivan the Terrible Part One* [1944] and *Two* [1958]) lack the aggressive, visionary editing of his work in the silent period. Although he completed only seven features, these contain some of the most famous sequences ever committed to film, such as the massacre on the Odessa steps in *Potemkin*. Together, Eisenstein's films and essays represent the supreme expression of the capabilities and power of montage in the cinema.

RECOMMENDED VIEWING

Stachka (*Strike*, 1925), *Bronenosets Potyomkin* (*Battleship Potemkin*, 1925), *Oktyabr* (*Ten Days That Shook the World* and *October*, 1927), *Ivan Groznyy I* (*Ivan the Terrible Part One*, 1944), *Ivan Groznyy II* (*Ivan the Terrible Part Two*, 1958)

FURTHER READING

Bordwell, David. *The Cinema of Eisenstein*. Cambridge, MA: Harvard University Press, 1993.

Eisenstein, Sergei. *Film Form*. Translated by Jay Leyda. New York: Harvest, 1969.

———. *The Film Sense*. Translated by Jay Leyda. New York: Harvest, 1969.

Leyda, Jay, ed. *Film Essays and a Lecture*. New York and Washington: Praeger, 1970.

Taylor, Richard. *October*. London: British Film Institute, 2002.

Stephen Prince

Sergei Eisenstein. EVERETT COLLECTION. REPRODUCED BY PERMISSION.

experiment proved that editing had created the meanings viewers attributed to the sequence.

While it is extremely doubtful that Kuleshov's experiment worked exactly as he claimed (for one thing, it is likely that the actor's face actually contained an ambiguous expression since Kuleshov had taken the footage from an existing film), the Soviet filmmakers of the 1920s followed Kuleshov's lead in fashioning a much more aggressive method of editing than what they had found in the films of Griffith. Eisenstein believed that editing or montage was the essence of cinema, and beginning with his first film, *Stachka* (*Strike*, 1925), and continuing most famously with *Bronenosets Potyomkin* (*Battleship Potemkin*, 1925), he created an editing style that he called "dialectical montage" that was abrupt and jagged and did not aim for the smooth continuity of Griffith-style cutting. The massacre of townspeople on the Odessa Steps in *Potemkin* exemplifies the principles of dialectical montage and is possibly the most famous montage in the history of cinema. The jaggedness of Eisenstein's editing in this sequence captures the emotional and physical violence of the massacre, but he also aimed to use editing to suggest ideas, a style he termed "intellectual montage." The massacre sequence concludes with three shots of statues of stone lions edited to look like a single lion rising up and roaring, embodying the idea of the wrath of the people and the voice of the revolution.

Although Eisenstein's sound films, *Aleksandr Nevskiy* (*Alexander Nevsky*, 1938) and *Ivan Groznyy I* and *II* (*Ivan the Terrible Part One* [1944] and *Two* [1958]), do not exhibit the radical editing of his silent films, Eisenstein's approach to montage—the extreme way he would fracture the action into tiny, brief shots—proved to be tremendously influential. The gun battles in Peckinpah's *The Wild Bunch*, edited by Lou Lombardo (1932–2002), was quite consciously based on Eisenstein, and the hyperactive editing of much contemporary film, with edit points only a few frames apart, is part of Eisenstein's legacy.

The dominant style of editing practiced during the classical Hollywood period, from the 1930s to the 1950s, was quite different from Soviet-style montage. It is sometimes called "invisible editing" because the edit points are so recessive and so determined by the imperative of seamless continuity. Hollywood-style editing carefully matches inserts and close-ups to the physical relations of characters and objects as seen in a scene's master shot, and follows the 180-degree rule (keeping camera setups on one side of the line of action) so that the right–left coordinates of screen geography remain consistent across shot changes. Cut points typically follow the flow of dialogue, and shot–reverse shot editing uses the eyeline match to connect characters who are otherwise shown separately in close-ups. This style of editing assured the utmost clarity about the geography of the screen world and the communication of essential story information. For these reasons, it is sometimes called "point-of-view" editing or "continuity editing." That it became the standard editing style of the Hollywood system is evident in the fact that it can be found in films across genres, directors, and studios.

In the late 1950s and early 1960s, films of the French New Wave introduced a more aggressive editing style than was typical of the Hollywood studios. *À bout de souffle* (*Breathless*, 1960), directed by Jean-Luc Godard (b. 1930), used jump cuts that left out parts of the action to produce discontinuities between shots, and American directors a decade later assimilated this approach in pictures such as *Bonnie and Clyde* (1967) and *Easy Rider* (1969). As a result, by the 1970s the highly regulated point-of-view editing used in classical Hollywood began to break down as an industry standard, and the cutting style of American films became more eclectic, exhibiting a mixture of classical continuity and more abrupt, collage-like editing styles.

A forceful style of montage characterizes Sergei Eisenstein's **Battleship Potemkin *(1925).*** EVERETT COLLECTION.
REPRODUCED BY PERMISSION.

NONLINEAR EDITING

Along with the breakdown of classical continuity as the industry's sole standard cutting style, the other major stylistic development in recent films has been due to the switch from linear to nonlinear editing systems. This changeover has helped produce an increase in the cutting rate of contemporary film and a bias in favor of close-ups. Edit points occur more rapidly than in films of previous decades, with a much greater profusion of shot changes. *Moulin Rouge* (2001) exemplifies the hyperactive editing style found in many films today.

Several features of nonlinear systems have motivated this shift. For one, they give editors much greater control over the available footage, with greatly increased abilities to access individual shots and manipulate them more easily in complex editing constructions. But there is a paradox. Editor Walter Murch (b. 1943) (*Apocalypse Now* [1979], *The English Patient* [1996]) points out that an editor working on a linear system may actually come to know the footage better as a result of having to search it sequentially looking for a particular piece of film.

Editors on nonlinear systems are more dependent on their notes about the footage and may overlook valuable material because their notes have excluded it.

In addition, the image as viewed on the editor's monitor tends to be of relatively low resolution because of the necessary trade-off between resolution and the computer storage space needed for the digitized video of the film footage. The higher the resolution, the greater the storage space that is needed. The low-res image will tend to bias editors toward close-ups rather than long shots and toward frequent shot changes as a means of maintaining visual interest. As a result, many contemporary films have come to look more and more like television, with quick editing and a tendency to play the story as a montage of close-ups.

What this approach loses is not so much the aesthetic tradition in cinema that developed in opposition to montage, such as the long shot–long take style celebrated by French critic André Bazin and found in such films as *La Grande illusion* (*The Grand Illusion*, Jean Renoir, 1937), *Csillagosok, katonák* (*The Red and the White*,

Miklós Jancsó, 1967), *Playtime* (Jacques Tati, 1967), and *Citizen Kane* (Orson Welles, 1941). This style never had much presence in American cinema. Rather, what is vanishing from American film are all of the ways that an individual shot can function as a unit of meaning, through composition, production design, lighting, and the actor's performance as it unfolds in the real time of a shot that is held. An essential component of editing is knowing when not to edit, when to hold the shot. Films of earlier decades routinely exhibit this quality. Many contemporary films do not, and in this respect it can be said that their hyperactive editing style is cannibalizing other essential elements of cinema. When every shot is only a few frames long, the art of the cinematographer, of the production designer, and of the actor necessarily suffers. Sergei Eisenstein always maintained that the point of montage was to overcome the characteristics of the single shot taken in isolation. Ironically, his objective is being realized in the montage style that has emerged with the advent of nonlinear editing.

THE EXPRESSIVE FUNCTIONS OF EDITING

Editors join shots using a variety of optical transitions. These serve narrative, dramatic, and emotionally expressive functions. The most common transitions are the cut (which creates an instantaneous change from one shot to the next), the fade (during which one shot fades completely to black before the next shot fades in from black), and the dissolve (which overlaps the outgoing and incoming shots). Cuts are the most frequent transitions, and typically indicate an uninterrupted flow of narrative information, with no breaks of time or space. Dissolves and fades, on the other hand, may be used to indicate transitions in time and space.

Other optical transitions are available but are used infrequently, and some have become archaic in that they were more common in earlier periods of cinema. The iris was used throughout silent cinema, and the wipe in early sound film. George Lucas (b. 1944) regularly uses irises and wipes in his *Star Wars* films in order to evoke the visual qualities of early cinema (one source for the films being the old cliff-hanging serials that moviegoers saw in the first half of the twentieth century). Editors may also create split screen effects, putting several shots on screen at once by splitting the image into small windows. This technique enjoyed a brief vogue in the late 1960s and 1970s (*The Thomas Crown Affair* [1968], *Junior Bonner* [1973], *Twilight's Last Gleaming* [1977]). It has been revived in recent years (*Timecode* [2000]) and can be found in the films of Brian De Palma (b. 1940).

As noted, parallel editing and crosscutting are building blocks of narrative, and they enable editors to control time and space. Indeed, this control of time and space is one of the key functions of editing. Editors may use continuity cutting to create a stable and reliable spatial geography onscreen, or they may break continuity to undermine spatial coherence, as in films such as *Straw Dogs* (1971) and *Gladiator* (2000).

With respect to time (i.e., the duration of an event onscreen), editors may expand it by using devices such as slow motion, or by increasing the number of cutaways from a main line of action or increasing the number of shots that are used to cover the action. In either case, the screen time of the event stretches out. During the Odessa massacre scene in *Potemkin* a mother with a baby carriage is shot in the stomach, and Eisenstein prolongs the moment of her agony by covering the action with numerous shots and then editing among them. The result is that it takes her a very long time to collapse to the ground, and this duration is a function of editing rather than the actor's performance. Conversely, editors may shrink or contract time by leaving out portions of the action. Jump cuts are an obvious and aestheticized way of doing this. The more common method, however, is to employ a "cheat." In *Vertigo* (1958), James Stewart has to walk down a very long chapel corridor in order to reach the bell tower, where an important scene will occur. It would be tedious to show him walking the length of the corridor. A judicious cut telescopes the action in a way that is imperceptible to the viewer.

Editors employ cheats all the time, and they routinely do many other things that viewers never notice. They may flip shots to get a proper eyeline match or screen direction, make the action move backwards (when Jack Palance mounts his horse in *Shane* [1953], it's the dismount shot played in reverse), or solve problems in the continuity or blocking of a scene's action by using cutaways to move things around.

Editors also help shape the actors' performances, and in doing so they help create the dramatic focus of a scene. An editor's decision to play a line of dialogue with the camera on the speaker will inflect the scene in one direction, whereas the decision to use a reaction shot of another character while the line is spoken will give the moment a different tone and emphasis. Film viewers are typically quite unaware of the extent to which editing intersects with film acting. Viewers may attribute to the actor much that results, in fact, from editing. If the editor elects to respect the performance, he or she may work with the master shot, allowing the performances to unfold in the relatively unbroken time of unedited shots. On the other hand, if the editor goes to coverage, building a scene with cutaways, inserts, and switches in camera position, then the editing is subtly reworking the performance. Examples include trimming the ends of shots to tighten an actor's apparent psychological reflex or to

LOU LOMBARDO
b. 15 February 1932, d. 8 May 2002

Lou Lombardo's seminal contribution to the history of editing is his work on *The Wild Bunch* (1969), directed by Sam Peckinpah. The complex montages of violence that Lombardo created for that film influenced generations of filmmakers and established the modern cinematic textbook for editing violent gun battles. Lombardo didn't originate the essentials of this design. Dede Allen's editing of *Bonnie and Clyde* (1967) furnished an immediate inspiration, and Allen's work in turn was modeled on Akira Kurosawa's *Seven Samurai* (1954) and Sergei Eisenstein's general approach to montage. But it was Lombardo, working under Peckinpah's guidance, who created the most elaborate and extended design and set the style for other filmmakers.

Peckinpah shot the film's violent gun battles using multiple cameras, and Lombardo took this footage and wove it into complex collages of action, meshing multiple lines of action by intercutting them and mixing normal speed action with varying degrees of slow motion. The editing is audacious and visionary, as the montages bend space and elongate time in a manner whose scope and ferocity was unprecedented in American cinema. Working without benefit of today's nonlinear editing systems that facilitate the control of huge amounts of footage, Lombardo created a final cut that contained more edit points than any American film in history to that time. Making this achievement more impressive yet is the fact that *The Wild Bunch* was Lombardo's first substantive feature film. Prior to this he had worked on television (editing *Felony Squad*, where he tried integrating slow-motion and normal-speed footage) and had edited the feature *The Name of the Game Is Kill* (1968).

Lombardo continued his partnership with Peckinpah on *The Ballad of Cable Hogue* (1970), where they experimented less successfully with edits combining normal speed and accelerated action. Peckinpah wanted to use Lombardo again on *Straw Dogs* (1971), but Lombardo was by then busy editing Robert Altman's *McCabe and Mrs. Miller* (1971), one of five Altman pictures that he cut (the others were *Brewster McCloud* [1970], *The Long Goodbye* [1973], *Thieves Like Us* [1974], and *California Split*, 1974). Though his work for Altman was less trendsetting than that for Peckinpah, the partnership with Altman lasted much longer, and Lombardo found the perfect visual rhythms for Altman's wandering and diffuse audio style.

Lombardo was also a very effective editor of comedy (*Uncle Buck* [1989], *Other People's Money* [1991]), with *Moonstruck* (1987) being a particular standout. The superb comic timing of that film is due to Lombardo's editing as much as to the fine direction by Norman Jewison and the sparkling performances.

Lombardo's career was cut short by a stroke in 1991, and he spent the last decade of his life in a coma. But he had left an indelible mark on modern cinema with *The Wild Bunch*.

RECOMMENDED VIEWING
The Wild Bunch (1969), *McCabe and Mrs. Miller* (1971), *The Long Goodbye* (1973), *Moonstruck* (1987)

FURTHER READING
Lobrutto, Vincent, ed. *Selected Takes: Film Editors on Editing.* New York: Praeger, 1991.

Weddle, David. *If They Move ... Kill 'Em!: The Life and Times of Sam Peckinpah.* New York: Grove Press, 1994.

Stephen Prince

make him or her seem to jump on another character's line, or dropping inserts into the action to draw out the length of an actor's pause.

More extreme examples include using close-ups that have been lifted from other action but that seem to work best in the new context. In *One Flew Over the Cuckoo's Nest* (1975), editor Sheldon Kahn (b. 1940) took some footage of actress Louise Fletcher (b. 1934) in con-

versation with the film's director, Milos Forman (b. 1932), lifted a piece of her expression from this footage, and used it in a scene where her character looks archly at the film's hero (Jack Nicholson). It worked in the scene but, in reality, it was not a moment in which the actress was acting. The surrounding material of the scene, organized by the editing, effectively recontextualized her expression. George Lucas used editing to completely rework his actors' performances in the recent *Star Wars* film, *Attack of the Clones* (2002), to the point of cutting and pasting eye blinks and lip movements from one scene to the next.

These considerations suggest that the term "invisible editing," as critics have selectively used it to describe the cutting style of classical Hollywood cinema, is a naïve description. In fact, nearly *all* editing is invisible editing because the vast bulk of what the editor does, the myriad ways that editing transforms the raw footage of a shoot, remains subliminal and imperceptible to viewers. Some films call attention to their editing style by virtue of aggressive montage or jagged, discontinuous cut points (*Easy Rider, Don't Look Now, Moulin Rouge*), and it is this kind of filmmaking that scholars and critics commonly posit as the alternative to the "invisible" style of classical Hollywood. But such a dichotomy of Hollywood and anti-Hollywood editing styles is too simplistic. It minimizes the numerous ways that editors on every production work "below the radar," creating effects, emphasis, and continuity in ways that do not advertise themselves as editing.

Shooting on digital video now makes it possible to create a feature film in one shot, without any traditional editing (as in *Russian Ark* [2003]). Alfred Hitchcock (1899–1980) once tried to do without editing by making *Rope* (1948) as if there were no edits between shots. But these superlatively designed films are aberrations from cinema's essential nature, which is, and has always been, an edited construction transforming the realities of what has existed before the cameras.

SEE ALSO *Direction; Narrative; Production Process; Technology*

FURTHER READING

Dmytryk, Edward. *On Film Editing*. Woburn, MA: Focal Press, 1984.

Murch, Walter. *In the Blink of an Eye: A Perspective on Film Editing*. Los Angeles: Sliman-James Press, 1995.

Oldham, Gabriella. *First Cut: Conversations with Film Editors*. Berkeley: University of California Press, 1992.

Ondaatje, Michael. *The Conversations: Walter Murch and the Art of Editing Film*. New York: Knopf, 2002.

Prince, Stephen, and Wayne Hensley. "The Kuleshov Effect: Recreating the Classic Experiment." *Cinema Journal* 31, no. 2 (Winter 1992): 59–75.

Reisz, Karel, and Gavin Millar. *The Technique of Film Editing*. Boston: Focal Press, 1983.

Stephen Prince

EGYPT

The history of Egyptian cinema is long and varied. From modest beginnings with the projection of Lumière shorts in the Tousson Pasha hall of Alexandria and the Hammam Schneider baths of Cairo in 1896, film was transformed from an exclusively foreign import for the foreign elite into a national industry by the 1940s. This "Hollywood on the Nile," established in its initial phase in the mid-1930s by nationalist financier Talaat Harb, was equipped with studios, a star system, the production of syncretic genres, and mastery of the three-tiered system of production, distribution, and exhibition. Its subsequent domination over the cinema of other Arab and North African countries was uniquely binding at the cultural level, working in conjunction with the radio (established in 1926) and music recording industries. Together these media familiarized the inhabitants of other countries with the Egyptian dialect and culture; drew upon the preexisting cultural diversity of Egypt to further the aims and sense of pan-Arabism and Arab nationalism, from the cosmopolitanism of Alexandria to the work of Lebanese and Syrian artists in Cairo's theater and recording industries; entertained the masses through generic forms copied from Hollywood but customized to fit the cultural context and issues specific to Egyptian culture; and proved that while the technology of cinema was a Western invention, it could be used to serve the needs and contexts of the non-Western world—in this case, cultures that were predominantly Islamic in religion but tolerant and culturally diverse.

ECONOMICS AND POLITICS

The evolution of Egyptian film history reflects the economic and political changes that have swept the country since the beginnings of a national film industry. These changes have been distinguished by widely divergent economic directions and opaque ideological systems that became more pronounced following the 1952 Free Officer's Coup—a revolution led by a group of young military officers. This group effectively unseated from power the former British mandate puppet, King Farouk, descendent of the Ottoman Turkish dynasty, in a bloodless coup that served as a model revolution to other Arab countries seeking independence from colonial European rule. The subsequent rise of Gamal Abdel Nasser (1918–1970) to power in 1954 extended to his leadership of the Pan-Arab movement, which forged ties between Egypt, Syria, and Iraq after Egypt's successful resolution of the 1956 Suez crisis, when French and British air forces were overpowered by the Egyptians after Nasser announced the nationalization of the Suez Canal.

Nasser's social reforms included nationalizing the cinema in the 1960s, and this had a great and negative impact on the film industry. Soon after the establishment of the General Organization of Egyptian Cinema in 1961 and the nationalization of the theatres in 1963, directors, producers, and talent fled to Lebanon, where they worked in the Lebanese film industry until the outbreak of civil war in 1975. In spite of these problems, Egypt's nationalized cinema organization made most of the films of the 1960s. One positive contribution from this period was the opening of the Higher Institute of Cinema in 1959, by the Ministry of Culture, where students received training in different aspects of production. Since then, this institute has produced much of Egypt's film and television talent. After Egypt's demoralizing 1967 defeat in the Six-Day War with Israel, Nasser's death in 1970, and the rise of Anwar Sadat (1918–1981), who promoted normalization of economic ties with Israel and the United States, the country underwent a general shift back to privatization. Nationalization was over by 1972, but relations with neighboring Arab countries were strained by Egypt's open-door policy with Israel, and the country's economic and political ties with Syria were broken.

As soon as Nasser nationalized the radio and television industries in the early 1960s, attendance at movie theatres dropped drastically. In the period from 1955 to 1975, the number of film theatres declined from 350 to fewer than 250. Meanwhile, imported foreign films continued to flood the Egyptian market. Tickets to films were heavily taxed, and the state film organization lost about 7 million Egyptian pounds, slowly bringing state film production to a halt by the early 1970s. The pendulum effect in funding between private and public sectors was also damaged by the increasingly predominant investment from the oil-rich Gulf countries, which financed films for television in the 1980s and later for satellite distribution in the 1990s. In addition to their more stringent censorship requirements of the usual subjects (sex, politics, and religion), the Gulf producers generally lacked awareness of the aesthetics of cinema. After the 1981 assassination of Sadat by a member of the Islamic Brotherhood, Hosni Mubarek's (b. 1928) regime was installed and with it emergency law, eventually diffusing the student movement that had erupted in the 1970s in reaction to Sadat's economic and political moves.

The Gulf petrodollars of the 1980s caused an outpouring of funded television shows, which led to further decline in the film industry. By 1994, Egyptian cinema was considered to be in a state of crisis: the annual production of films had fallen to single digits, a far cry from the annual output of fifty narrative features in 1944. More recently, independent directors have concentrated their efforts on serial television shows for Ramadan, the holy month in which Muslims fast during the day, then relax in the evening, creating large popular audiences. Meanwhile, the reconstruction of post-war Beirut was fueling the media explosion of the second half of the 1990s, which led to such satellite channels as Rotana and Good Day from Beirut and the Gulf states, which now produce many films for the Egyptian market.

Another challenge to independent Egyptian film is the power of censors to stifle artistic work and freedom of expression at the slightest hint of perceived criticism of religion or of taboo subjects presented in anything other than a denunciatory way. Between 1971 and 1973, during Sadat's early years, any films that dealt with the 1967 defeat were banned, including *Il Usfur* (*The Sparrow*,

Youssef Chahine, 1973), but since the early 1990s, censorship has been more acutely attentive to religious issues.

FROM SILENT CINEMA TO GOLDEN AGE

In the early years of the twentieth century, only foreign studios (German, Italian, and French) operated in Egypt, most of them in Alexandria because of its optimal lighting conditions. It was not until the 1920s that Egyptians made their own films. The first long feature to be financed by Egyptian money was *Leila* (1927), produced by a woman, Aziza Amir (1901–1952), who also acted in the film, and directed by Estephan Rosti (1891–1964; not a native Egyptian). Mohamad Bayoumi (1894–1963) and Mohamad Karim (first Egyptian film actor), who studied filmmaking in Germany, were early pioneers. Bayoumi was the first Egyptian to produce and shoot a newsreel, *Amun*, about the return of nationalist Saad Zaghloul Pasha from exile in 1923, and the first Egyptian to shoot and direct a short fiction film, *al-Bashkateb* (*The Head Clerk* [1924]). Mohamad Karim, who claimed to have learned filmmaking at "the university of *Metropolis*," where he spent a year assisting and observing in the production of Fritz Lang's 1927 expressionist classic on the sets of Ufa (Universum Film Aktiengesellschaft), directed his first film, *Zaynab*, based on the novel by Mohamad Husayn Haykal, in 1930. In 1932, he directed the first Egyptian talking film *Awlad al-dhawat* (*The Children of the Aristocrats*), starring theater actors Yussef Wahbi and Amina Rizq; in 1933, he directed his first musical, *al-Warda al-bayda'* (*The White Rose*), which showcased the talents of musician and composer Mohamad Abdel Wahab (1901–1991). This was also the first film to solve the problem of compressing long classical Arabic songs (usually 15 to 20 minutes in duration) into sixminute sequences. From then on, Karim was known as Mohamad Abdel Wahab's director, and they made several other films together.

Talaat Harb, the savvy businessman and nationalist financier, founded Bank Misr in the 1920s as well as Studio Misr in 1935, which produced its first talking feature in 1936, *Widad*, directed by Fritz Kramp after a dispute broke out between original Egyptian director Ahmed Badrakhan and the studio manager, Ahmed Salem. After this, Studio Misr dominated productions in the film industry for the next thirty years. To ensure technical and aesthetic quality, Talaat Harb sent young filmmakers abroad to acquire professional training and recruited European technicians as consultants in Cairo. With the preexisting industries of radio and music recording and with Cairo's position since the nineteenth century as a refuge for artists and musicians fleeing the more constraining conditions of Greater Syria, this unique confluence of talent and technology led to the

YOUSSEF CHAHINE
b. Alexandria, Egypt, 25 January 1926

Born in 1926 to a middle-class Catholic family of Lebanese and Greek origins, Youssef Chahine's formative years were spent in the cultural melting pot of Alexandria, living under British occupation. There he was exposed to a polyphonic culture of Eastern and Western flavors, surrounded by English, Italian, French, Greek, and Arabic languages, and living in a religiously tolerant environment where Muslim, Christian, and Jew coexisted. These elements, along with Egypt's changing politics since 1950, have strongly influenced his body of work.

Adept at mixing genres and styles, Chahine has made films for over fifty years, during which time he has revealed a commitment to social and political critique. His early tendency toward social realism is hallmarked by *Bab al Hadid* (*Cairo Station*, 1958) and *Al Ard* (*The Land*, 1969). In the former, he played a disturbed and crippled newspaper vendor in the Cairo train station who murders a voluptuous drink vendor out of unrequited desire; in the latter, based on a novel by Marxist Abdel Rahman Sharkawi, he shows the bonds of kinship and rivalry that destroy the solidarity of the peasants under the new land reforms of the Nasser period. His historical epic, *Nasr Salah el Din* (*Saladin*, 1963), depicts the twelfth-century uniter of the Arabs, Salah el Din, as a merciful and religiously tolerant leader who is an obvious allegory for Gamal Abdel Nasser, Egypt's leader from 1954 to 1971. In his 1973 film *Il Usfur* (*The Sparrow*), he attempts to reconcile the ideals of Nasserism with the disappointing results of Egypt's 1967 defeat in its war with Israel and the aftermath. His 1997 *Le Destin* (*Destiny*) about the twelfth-century Andalusian philosopher Averroes (Ibn Sinna), is an allegory for the contemporary struggles in Arab countries between Islamic fundamentalism and political despots,

on the one hand, and free thinkers, on the other, mirroring his own battles with censorship on religious grounds in his film *Al Muhajir* (*The Immigrant*, 1994), banned for representing a character who is somewhat similar to the Biblical and Quranic Joseph. His autobiographical films were the first in the Arab world to treat non-normative sexuality as something human, seen in his quartet *Alexandria ... Why?* (1978), *Egyptian Story* (1982), *Alexandria, Again and Forever* (1989,) and *Alexandria ... New York* (2004).

Chahine has offered a new model for the Arab filmmaker as an independent auteur of a personal cinema. While his films attempt to cater to popular Egyptian tastes with their musical numbers and well-known film stars, the majority of Egyptians relate best to his realist films, finding the others too obscure. Those he has mentored include established film auteurs Yousry Nasrallah and Atef Hetata, who face similar problems of censorship and lack of local markets for their films.

RECOMMENDED VIEWING
Bab al Hadid (*Cairo Station*, 1958), *Nasr Salah el Din* (*Saladin*, 1963), *Al Ard* (*The Land*, 1969), *Il Usfur* (*The Sparrow*, 1973), *Return of the Prodigal Son* (1974), *Alexandria ... Why?* (1978), *Egyptian Story* (1982), *Adieu Bonaparte* (1984), *Alexandria Again and Forever* (1989), *Cairo as Illuminated by Her People* (1991), *Al Muhajir* (*The Immigrant*, 1994), *Le Destin* (*Destiny*, 1997), *Alexandria ... New York* (2004)

FURTHER READING
Fawal, Ibrahim. *Youssef Chahine.* London: British Film Institute, 2001.

Stollery, Martin. *Al-Muhajir, L'émigré.* Wiltshire, UK: Flicks Books, 2005.

Samirah Alkassim

hegemony of Egyptian cinema over the Arab and North African region.

Once the talking feature had been established in 1936, films were made in the genres of farce, melodrama, and the musical. These were collaborations by established musicians, star singers, and actors, including Yussef Wahbi (1897–1982, actor and theatre director), come-

dian Naguib Al Rihani (1891–1949), and musicians Umm Kulthoum (1904–1975), Mohamed Abdel Wahab, Farid al Attrach (1915–1974), Layla Murad (1918–1995), and Mohamed Abdel Wahhab. The period from the early 1940s until the early 1950s is considered the golden age of Egyptian cinema, with annual output averaging forty-eight films a year between 1945 and

Youssef Chahine. © ATTAR MAHER/CORBIS SYGMA.

1952. In the immediate post–World War II years, the film industry was more profitable than the textile industry, and by 1948, there were seven operating film studios, and 345 feature films had been produced. But the dominance of Western cinema in the market impeded national film production, even during the post-independence period after 1952, when Egyptian productions did not exceed 20 percent of all distributed films.

REALISM

Realism has been a tendency in Egyptian cinema since the 1939 classic, *Determination* (Kamal Selim, al-Azma), but this tendency became particularly strong in the 1950s when serious realist writers like Naguib Mahfouz (b. 1911) and Abdel Rahman Sharkawi (1920–1987) involved themselves in the cinema, penning screenplays or lending their novels to filmic adaptations. Of all the directors, Salah Abu Seif (1915–1996) is hailed as the father of Egyptian film realism, especially after his 1951 film *Lak yawm ya Zalim* (*Your Day Will Come*), adapted from Zola's novel *Therese Raquin* by Naguib Mahfouz.

Seif's adaptation of the Mahfouz novel into *al futuwa* (*The Tough Guy* [1957]) is joined by Tawfik Saleh's (b. 1927) notable 1955 adaptation from Mahfouz's novel *Darb al mahabil* (*Street of Fools*). Abu Seif made twenty-four features between 1946 and 1966; between 1963 and 1965, he was head of the General Organization of Egyptian Cinema. Many of his films are social melodramas about the city of Cairo, its neighborhoods and working-class inhabitants. Due to the problems related to the nationalized cinema, he had difficulties making films during the late 1960s and 1970s; his only film of the 1980s was his feature *Al-Qadisiya* (1981), made in Iraq. Saleh, a younger director, also had difficulties and made only four films in Egypt, including *Al Mutamarridun* (*The Rebels* [1966]), before leaving for Syria, where he directed his best-known film, *al Makhdu'un* (*The Duped* [1972]), based on the novel *Men under the Sun* by Palestinian writer Ghassan Khanafani. Saleh later moved to Iraq to become head of the film institute in Baghdad.

Among Saleh's peers, each of whom suffered from the decline in state funding, Shadi Abdel Salam (d. 1986), originally a set and costume designer on numerous Egyptian films, heralded a new kind of art cinema with his sole feature, *Al Mumiya* (*Night of the Counting Years* [1969]). This film was hailed as a "renaissance" in Egyptian cinema, but Salam has since left Egypt because he was unable to secure funding for other projects; he died in 1986. The demands of the market have dominated the type and level of artistry in Egyptian cinema, with few exceptions, one of whom is Youssef Chahine (b. 1926). The most prolific independent film director of the post-war period, a master of different genres, and the instigator of an auteurist and critical cinema in the Arab world, Chahine is probably the best known Egyptian figure abroad. This is due to his cultural blend of East and West, idiosyncratic style, international acclaim at Cannes and major film institutes, and critical feelings about the West, which are evident in his films. Notable among his films are *Bab al hadid* (*Cairo Station* [1958]), *Al Ard* (*The Land* [1969]), *il Usfur* (*The Sparrow* [1973]), *Alexandria . . . Why?* (1978), and *Le Destin* (*Destiny* [1997]).

The New Realist directors of the 1980s are arguably the most interesting development in recent Egyptian cinema. Belonging to the post-1967 generation, they participated in the student movement that questioned the corruption of new businessmen and the economic policies of Anwar Sadat. While taking advantage of funding from the Gulf states, they have played with conventions of realism and melodrama and addressed serious social issues. Significant directors from this movement include Atef El Tayeb (d. 1995), *Sawwaq al-utubis* (*Busdriver* [1982]), Mohamed Khan (b. 1942), *Zauga ragil muhim* (*Wife of an Important Man* [1987]); Khairy

Beshara (b. 1947), *Yawm hulw, yaum murr* (*Bitter Day, Sweet Day* [1988]), and Daoud Abd El-Sayyed (b. 1946), *KitKat* (1991).

SEE ALSO *Arab Cinema; National Cinema*

FURTHER READING

Armes, Roy. *Third World Film Making and the West*. Berkeley: University of California Press, 1987.

Armes, Roy, and Lizbeth Malkmus. *Arab and African Filmmaking*. London: Zed Books, 1991.

Darwish, Mustafa. *Dream Makers on the Nile: A Portrait of Egyptian Cinema*. Cairo: American University in Cairo Press, 1998.

Shafik, Viola. *Arab Cinema: History and Cultural Identity*. Cairo: American University in Cairo Press, 1998.

Samirah Alkassim

EPIC FILMS

———■———

Like "musical," "comedy," "war film," and "Western," "epic" is a term used by Hollywood and its publicists, by reviewers, and by academic writers to identify a particular type of film. It was first used extensively in the 1910s and the 1920s: *Variety*'s review of *Ben-Hur* (1925) noted that "the word epic has been applied to pictures time and again" (6 January 1926: 38). It was particularly prevalent in the 1950s and 1960s, when epics of all kinds were produced to counter a decline in cinema attendance. And it has been recently revived with films such as *Gladiator* (2000), *Troy* (2004), and *The Alamo* (2004). As a term, "epic" is associated with historical films of all kinds, particularly those dealing with events of national or global import or scale. As a genre it thus encompasses a number of war films and westerns as well as films set in earlier periods. But because of its links with ancient classical literature, it is associated above all with films set in biblical times or the ancient world. However, the term "epic" has also been used to identify—and to sell— films of all types that have used expensive technologies, high production values, and special modes of distribution and exhibition to differentiate themselves from routine productions and from rival forms of contemporary entertainment. There are therefore at least two aspects to epics, two sets of distinguishing characteristics: those associated with historical, biblical, and ancient-world films and those associated with large-scale, high-cost productions.

These aspects have often coincided, as is true not only of films such as *The Ten Commandments* (1923 and 1956), *El Cid* (1961), *55 Days at Peking* (1963), *How the West Was Won* (1962), and *Troy*, but of films with more recent historical settings such as *The Big Parade* (1925), *Exodus* (1960), *The Longest Day* (1962), *Schindler's List*

(1993), and *Pearl Harbor* (2001). However, the production of large-scale, high-cost comedies, musicals, and dramas such as *It's a Mad, Mad, Mad, Mad World* (1963), *The Sound of Music* (1965), and *Gone with the Wind* (1939)—some of them with historical settings, some without—and the production of more routinely scaled historical and biblical films such as *Salome* (1953), *Hannibal* (1960), and, indeed, most war films, Westerns, and swashbucklers tend to make hard-and-fast definitions more difficult. Generalizations can be made about the scale of the films and the events they depict, the prominence of visual and aural spectacle, and a recurrent preoccupation with political, military, divine, or religious power, but, as is often the case with Hollywood's genres, anomalies and exceptions of one kind or another can nearly always be found. It is easier to be more precise about specific periods, cycles, and trends.

THE SILENT ERA

The generic and industrial traditions of the epic film date back to the 1890s, when several Passion plays (plays representing the life of Christ) were filmed and exhibited in unusually lengthy, multi-reel formats. In the period between 1905 and 1914, a number of relatively large-scale, high-cost historical, biblical, and ancient-world films—among them *La vie du Christ* (1906), *The Fall of Troy* (1910), *La siège de Calais* (1911), *Quo Vadis?* (1913), and *Cabiria* (1914)—were made in Italy, France, and elsewhere in Europe and helped to establish the multi-reel feature. Multi-reel films of a similar kind were produced in the United States as well. But at a time when production, distribution, and exhibition in the United

States were geared to the rapid turnover of programs of single-reel films, films like this were often distributed on a "road show" basis. Road show films were shown at movie theaters as well as alternative local settings such as town halls for as long as they were financially viable.

Many of these films drew on nineteenth-century traditions of historical and religious representation, particularly paintings and engravings, toga plays, Passion plays, pageants, and popular novels such *The Last Days of Pompeii* and *Ben-Hur* and their subsequent theatrical adaptations. They also drew on nineteenth- and early twentieth-century preoccupations with Imperial Rome and early Christianity, and on an association between religious and historical representation and nationhood and empire. These traditions and preoccupations were particularly prominent among the middle and upper classes, to whom many of the earliest multi-reel films and features were directed and to whom the aura of respectability associated with religious and historical topics and the legitimate theater was important. Augmented by films such as *The Coming of Columbus* (1912) and *The Birth of a Nation* (1915), which dealt with aspects of US history, productions like this helped found a tradition of large-scale, high-cost spectacles, "superspecial" productions that would be road shown not just in legitimate theaters but in the large-scale picture palaces that were being built in increasing numbers in major cities. Ticket prices were high. The films were shown, usually twice a day, at fixed times and with at least one intermission. They were usually accompanied by an orchestra playing a specially commissioned score. Only after a lengthy run in venues like this, a practice essential to the recouping of costs and the making of profits, would superspecials be shown in more ordinary cinemas at regular prices.

The production of road shown superspecials reached a peak in the United States in the 1920s with films like *Orphans of the Storm* (1922), *Robin Hood* (1922), *The Covered Wagon* (1923), *The Ten Commandments* (1923), *The Thief of Bagdad* (1924), *The Big Parade* (1925), *The Iron Horse* (1924), *Ben-Hur* (1925), *Wings* (1927), *The King of Kings* (1927), and *Noah's Ark* (1928). Although these films are diverse in setting and type (*Robin Hood* is a swashbuckler, *The Thief of Bagdad* an exotic costume adventure film, *The Ten Commandments* a biblical epic, *The Iron Horse* a western, and *Wings* a World War I film), there are aesthetic, structural, and thematic links among them. Like the epics and spectacles of the 1910s, they exhibit what Vivian Sobchack has called "historical eventfulness" (p. 32)—that is to say, they mark themselves and the events they depict as historically significant. In addition, nearly all these films narrate stories that interweave the destinies of individual characters with the destinies of nations, empires, dynasties, religions, politi-

cal regimes, and ethnic groups. While some focus on powerful characters (generals, pharaohs, princes, and leaders), many focus on more ordinary characters who either become caught up in events over which they have little control (as in *The Big Parade*, *Wings*, and *Orphans of the Storm*) or are unsung agents of significant historical or epochal change (as in *The Iron Horse*). *Robin Hood* and *The Thief of Bagdad* are variants in which, as vehicles for star and producer Douglas Fairbanks (1883–1939), the power of the central character to effect change is, however fancifully, bound up with his physical prowess.

Following the precedent established by *Intolerance* (1916), the contemporary relevance of the events depicted in *The Ten Commandments*, *The King of Kings*, and *Noah's Ark* is underscored by including story lines and scenes from the present as well as the past. However, it is the story lines and scenes from the past that provide the most obvious occasions for spectacle. Difficult to define, spectacle is clearly not restricted to epics and to spectacle films as such; however, films of this kind played an important role in exploring, organizing, and legitimizing cinema's spectacular appeal and potential, in maintaining the involvement of contemporary audiences in much longer films than they had initially been used to, in mediating between competing contemporary demands for realism and spectacle, narrative and display. This was evident not just in their expansive battle scenes, crowd scenes, and settings, their expensive costumes and sets, or their use of new technologies. Epic films were regularly used to showcase new special effects, new camera techniques, and new color processes such as two-color Technicolor. It was evident, too, in their capacity to encompass incidental details, intimate scenes, and individualized story lines and to make sequences of spectacle such as the exodus from Egypt and the parting of the Red Sea in *The Ten Commandments* clearly serve dramatic and narrative ends.

FROM THE DEPRESSION TO THE POSTWAR ERA

With the advent of the Great Depression in 1929, Hollywood companies cut back on expensive productions and road shows. These practices were revived in the early 1930s, establishing a cross-generic trend toward what Tino Balio calls "prestige pictures" (pp. 179–211). However, although many prestige pictures were top-of-the-range costume films of one kind or another (adaptations of classic literature, biopics, swashbucklers, and the like), very few were made and road shown on the scale of the silent superspecial. Fewer still were biblical films and films with ancient-world settings. Cecil B. DeMille (1881–1959), who had produced and directed *The Ten Commandments* and *The King of Kings* in the silent era,

CECIL B. DeMILLE
b. Cecil Blount de Mille, Ashfield, Massachussetts, 12 August 1881, d. 21 January 1959

Cecil Blount DeMille was a major figure in Hollywood from the mid-1910s to the late 1950s. Remembered now mainly as a showman and as the producer/director of a number of biblical epics, he was in fact a versatile innovator who made important films of all kinds throughout his career.

DeMille's parents were involved in the theater. When his father died, he worked as actor and general manager for his mother's theatrical company and also produced and wrote plays with his brother, William. In 1913, he left the theater to work in motion pictures as cofounder of the Jesse L. Lasky Feature Play Company. In 1914, he coproduced, cowrote, and codirected its first film, *The Squaw Man*, a six-reel adaptation of Edwin Royle's play, which was a success. When the Lasky company became part of Paramount later that year, DeMille supervised its production program. He also wrote, produced, directed, and edited many of its films.

By the mid-1920s, DeMille had been at the forefront of a number of key developments: the use of plays as a template for feature-length films; the production of feature-length westerns; the dramatic use of low-key lighting effects, most notably in *The Cheat* (1915) and *The Heart of Nora Flynn* (1916); the production of Jazz Age marital comedies such as *Don't Change Your Husband* (1919) and *Why Change Your Wife?* (1920) (both of them written, as many of DeMille's films were, by or with Jeannie Macpherson); and the production of "superspecials" such as *The Ten Commandments* (1923).

The Ten Commandments, a Paramount film, was the first of DeMille's biblical epics. His second, *The King of*

Kings (1927), was released through Producers Distributing Corporation, a company for whom he began making films in 1925. Following a period with MGM, DeMille returned to Paramount to make *The Sign of the Cross* in 1932. He remained with Paramount for the remainder of his career, making social problem dramas, westerns, and spectacles like *Samson and Delilah* (1949), *The Greatest Show on Earth* (1952), and the 1956 remake of *The Ten Commandments*. From 1936 to 1945, he also hosted and directed adaptations of Hollywood films and Broadway plays for Lux Radio Theater.

DeMille's films are usually said to be marked by a formula in which seductive presentations of sin are countered by verbal appeals to a Christian ethic inherent in scenes of redemption and in the providential outcome of events. However, it is worth stressing the extent to which, as the actions of characters like Moses, Samson, and John Trimble (in *The Whispering Chorus*) all illustrate, acts of virtue as well of sin in these films entail unusually perverse or destructive behavior.

RECOMMENDED VIEWING
The Cheat (1915), *The Whispering Chorus* (1918), *Why Change Your Wife?* (1922), *The Ten Commandments* (1923 and 1956), *This Day and Age* (1933), *Union Pacific* (1939)

FURTHER READING
Birchard, Robert S. *Cecil B. DeMille's Hollywood*. Lexington: University of Kentucky Press, 2004.

DeMille, Cecil B. *The Autobiography of Cecil B. DeMille*. Englewood Cliffs, NJ: Prentice-Hall, 1959.

Higashi, Sumiko. *Cecil B. DeMille and American Culture: The Silent Era*. Berkeley: University of California Press, 1994.

Steve Neale

produced and directed *The Sign of the Cross* (1932) and *Cleopatra* (1934). But along with *The Last Days of Pompeii* (1935), which was produced by Merian C. Cooper (1893–1973) and directed by Ernest B. Schoedsack (1893–1979), these productions were the only biblical and ancient-world productions made between 1928 and 1949. All three may be interpreted as films that engage the Depression and its moral impli-

cations in various ways. Toward the end of the 1930s, David O. Selznick (1902–1965) explicitly appealed to the traditions of the silent road shown superspecial when producing and planning the distribution of *Gone with the Wind*. He went on to produce *Since You Went Away* (1944), an epic home-front drama, and *Duel in the Sun* (1946), an epic western. DeMille, meanwhile, sought to revive the biblical epic by re-releasing *The Sign of the*

Cecil B. DeMille. EVERETT COLLECTION. REPRODUCED BY PERMISSION.

Cross in 1944 and producing and directing *Samson and Delilah* in 1949.

By 1949, Hollywood was undergoing a long-term process of change. Audiences, ticket sales, and profits were in decline; the ownership of theater chains by major studios was declared illegal; competition from television, domestic leisure pursuits, and other forms of entertainment were on the rise; and at a time when income from overseas markets was more important to Hollywood companies, a number of European countries were taking steps to protect their domestic economies, to stimulate domestic film production, and hence to limit the earnings Hollywood companies could take out of these countries each year. At the same time, the Cold War, nationalist and anti-imperial struggles, the superpower status of the United States, the marked increase in church-going, and the prevalence of religious discourse in the US itself provided a set of contexts and reference points for many of the films, in particular the big-budget road shown epics Hollywood was to produce, co-fund, or distribute during the course of the next two decades.

The postwar growth in epic production was the result of a decision to spend more money on enhancing the cinema's capacity for spectacle through the use of stereophonic sound and new widescreen, large-screen, and large-gauge technologies and on an increasing number of what were beginning to be called "blockbuster" productions—productions that, in road show form in particular, could be used to justify higher prices and generate high profits in a shrinking market. MGM led the way in road showing remakes of silent spectacles and in using income held abroad to fund the use of overseas facilities, locations, and production personnel with *Quo Vadis* in 1951. Two years later, Twentieth Century Fox pioneered the use of CinemaScope and stereophonic sound with its adaptation of Lloyd C. Douglas's best-selling novel *The Robe*. In 1956, DeMille released a four-hour remake of *The Ten Commandments*, which used Paramount's new VistaVision process, was shot in Egypt, Sinai, and Hollywood, and cost over $13 million. The film made more than $30 million on its initial release in the US and Canada alone. The following year, Columbia released *The Bridge on the River Kwai*, one of the first in a series of road shown epic war films. And in 1960, the road show release of *Cimarron* and *The Alamo*, the latter filmed in Todd-AO, helped cement a trend toward epic Westerns.

The Bridge on the River Kwai was produced by Sam Spiegel (1901–1985), an internationally based independent producer. Along with *Lawrence of Arabia* (1962), it was one of a series of epics he made with British director David Lean (1908–1991). *The Bridge on the River Kwai* was filmed in Ceylon using a mix of British, American, Japanese, and Ceylonese actors, stars, and production personnel. Ceylon was a British colony, and *The Bridge on the River Kwai* was registered as a British film in order to take advantage of British subsidies. Although credited to the French writer Pierre Boulle (who wrote the novel on which it was based), its script actually was written by Carl Foreman and extensively revised by Michael Wilson, both of them blacklisted US Communists.

The national identity of a film like *The Bridge on the River Kwai* is thus hard to pin down. This was an era of increasing independent production, in which funding for films was increasingly obtained on a one-off basis from a variety of international sources and international settings, locations, and casts were becoming the norm for big-budget productions. Blacklisted writers, whether officially credited or not, were hired to write or co-write scripts for epic productions such as *Exodus*, *Spartacus* (1960), *El Cid*, *The Guns of Navarone* (1961), *Lawrence of Arabia*, *Sodom and Gomorrah* (1962), *55 Days at Peking*, and *The Fall of the Roman Empire* (1964), and cut-price Italian "peplums" (toga films) such as *Hercules* (1958) and *Hercules Unchained*

Charlton Heston as Moses in Cecil B. DeMille's remake of his own **The Ten Commandments** ***(1956).*** EVERETT COLLECTION. REPRODUCED BY PERMISSION.

(1959) proved popular at the box office in the US as well as in Europe.

Hence the ideological characteristics of postwar epics are difficult to categorize. While the prologue to *The Ten Commandments* explicitly declares its anti-Communist agenda, *Quo Vadis, The Robe, Spartacus,* and *The Fall of the Roman Empire* are anti-fascist. Most of the remainder, even some of the westerns, are hostile to imperialism and to the brutal, cynical, and dictatorial exercise of political and military power. But they are often compromised by their focus on white ethnic characters. And their displays of male heroism, sometimes in stark contradiction to an apparent concern with the ethics of war, add a further layer of ideological complication. Only in films like *The Egyptian* (1954), *King of Kings* (1961), and *The Greatest Story Ever Told* (1965) are male heroism, male ambition, and the options of political and

military engagement explicitly qualified, eschewed, or rejected.

THE NEW HOLLYWOOD ERA

Although epic war films and big-budget musicals continued to be made in the 1970s and early 1980s, the road shown superspecial and the prestige epic were increasingly displaced by what has come to be known as the New Hollywood blockbuster. As exemplified by *Jaws* (1975), *Star Wars* (1977), *Superman* (1978), and *Raiders of the Lost Ark* (1981), New Hollywood blockbusters drew their inspiration from the B film, the serial, comic books, and action-adventure pulps rather than from the culturally prestigious traditions of the Hollywood epic. Wide-released rather than road shown, they were designed to appeal to teenagers and families with young children and to garner profits as rapidly as possible. However, productions in the prestige epic tradition such as *Dances with Wolves* (1990), *The English Patient* (1996), and *Schindler's List* were still occasionally made. Some of them received a relatively exclusive "platform" release. And the New Hollywood blockbuster, like the old Hollywood epic, functioned as a special vehicle for spectacle, large-scale stories and new technologies. Indeed, the advent of CGI (computer-generated imagery) seems to have been a major factor in the recent revival of the epic not just in its traditional forms, as exemplified by *Gladiator*, *Troy*, *King Arthur* (2004), and *Alexander*, but in the guise of the *Lord of the Rings* trilogy as well. In all these films the themes of heroism, justice and the uses and abuses of power, representational prowess, large-scale spectacle, and large-scale stories and settings remain among the epic's principal ingredients.

SEE ALSO *Action and Adventure Films; Genre; Historical Films; Religion*

FURTHER READING

Babington, Bruce, and Peter William Evans. *Biblical Epics: Sacred Narrative in the Hollywood Cinema.* Manchester: Manchester University Press, 1993.

Balio, Tino. *Grand Design: Hollywood as a Modern Business Enterprise, 1930–1939.* New York: Scribner, 1993.

Bowser, Eileen. *The Transformation of Cinema: 1907–1915.* New York: Scribner, 1990.

Cohan, Steve, and Ina Rae Hark, eds. *Screening the Male: Exploring Masculinities in Hollywood Cinema.* London: Routledge, 1993.

Elley, Derek. *The Epic Film: Myth and History.* London: Routledge and Kegan Paul, 1984.

Forshey, Gerald E. *American Religious and Biblical Spectaculars.* London: Praeger, 1992.

Hall, Sheldon. "Tall Revenue Features: The Genealogy of the Modern Blockbuster." In *Genre and Contemporary Hollywood*, edited by Steve Neale, 11–26. London: British Film Institute, 2002.

King, Geoff. *Spectacular Narratives: Hollywood in the Age of the Blockbuster.* London: I. B. Tauris, 2000.

Sobchack, Vivian. "'Surge and Splendor': A Phenomenology of the Hollywood Epic." *Representations* 29 (Winter 1990): 24–49. Reprinted in *Film Genre Reader III*, edited by Brian Keith Grant, 296–323. Austin: University of Texas Press, 2003.

Wyke, Maria. *Projecting the Past: Ancient Rome, Cinema, and History.* New York: Routledge, 1997.

Steve Neale

EXHIBITION

———————◼———————

Exhibition is the retail branch of the film industry. It involves not the production or the distribution of motion pictures, but their public screening, usually for paying customers in a site devoted to such screenings, the movie theater. What the exhibitor sells is the experience of a film (and, frequently, concessions like soft drinks and popcorn). Because exhibitors to some extent control how films are programmed, promoted, and presented to the public, they have considerable influence over the box-office success and, more importantly, the reception of films.

Though films have always been shown in non-theatrical as well as theatrical venues, the business of film exhibition primarily entails the ownership, management, and operation of theaters. Historically, film exhibitors have been faced with a number of situations common to other sectors of the commercial entertainment industry: shifting market conditions, strong competition, efforts to achieve monopolization of the field, government regulatory actions, and costly investment in new technologies.

FILM EXHIBITION AND THEATER OWNERSHIP

The first moving picture exhibitors were itinerant show-men who exploited the novelty of projected moving pictures by using the same film program for a series of brief engagements in different locations. They typically purchased outright the short films they screened at theaters, churches, and public halls. As early as 1903, film exchanges that owned and rented moving pictures emerged in Boston, Chicago, and New York City, creating a separation between exhibition and distribution and helping to standardize the emerging film industry. Exhibitors rented films by the reel from an exchange, allowing for more frequently changed programs at one specific location and therefore the establishment of nickelodeons, which were inexpensive storefront movie theaters.

One important early variant of the exchange system was the "states rights" model, in which the distribution rights for a film were sold by territory, often by individual state. Exhibitors then contracted with the rights owner. Within the constraints of price and print availability, the early exhibitor had considerable latitude in booking films of special interest to the local audience.

With the advent of the multi-reel feature film in the early 1910s, certain high profile films, like *The Birth of a Nation* (1915), were circulated through the country as "road shows." Much like touring stage productions, road show films were promoted as special events that were booked into individual venues (often legitimate theaters or small-town "opera houses") for multi-day runs. This strategy remained in place through the 1920s, then re-emerged in the 1950s and 1960s, when the most expensive, spectacular, star-laden productions (usually in color and widescreen) like *Ben-Hur* (1959) were first exhibited on a road show basis with patrons paying notably higher admission prices for reserved seats at these heavily promoted motion picture events.

Somewhat akin to the road show was a practice called "four-walling," where a theater was rented for a special screening that in some fashion was quite distinct from standard motion picture fare. Four-walling was used, for instance, during the 1930s to present foreign-language films to immigrant audiences in the United States. But it was most commonly employed from the 1920s through the 1950s as an exhibition strategy for sensationalistic "exploitation" films about childbirth, drug addiction, prostitution, and sexually transmitted diseases. At the other end of the spectrum, Sun Classic Pictures and other firms specializing in family-oriented product had considerable success during the 1970s with four-wall exhibition of films like *The Life and Times of Grizzly Adams* (1974).

As lucrative as road shows and four-walling proved to be in the selling of individual films, the crux of the film exhibition business has remained the ownership and daily operation of movie theaters, which requires a steady stream of product booked through film distributors. Given the low start-up costs, the first theaters dedicated to offering moving pictures as their primary, regular drawing card were usually independently owned and operated. From early on, however, exhibitors realized that it made economic sense to adopt a strategy then used for vaudeville theaters and penny arcades and operate more than one theater under the auspices of a single amusement company. Thus a key exhibition strategy that emerged during the nickelodeon era was the theater chain. A chain (or circuit of theaters) might encompass more than 100 venues or might be as small as a string of picture shows in adjacent neighborhoods or towns. Regional theater chains became especially prominent in the 1910s. The Stanley Company based in Philadelphia, for example, had by the mid-1920s grown to 250 theaters across the entire East Coast. Regional chains based in, among other places, Milwaukee (the Saxe Brothers), Detroit (John Kunsky), and St. Louis (the Skouras Brothers) became dominant forces in the industry even before these companies combined in 1917 to form the First National Exhibitors' Circuit. First National was one of several attempts in the 1920s to create a national network of theaters, including Publix Theaters, the exhibition branch of Paramount studios. For its national chain, Publix borrowed managerial strategies based on the principles of successful grocery and department store chains.

Perhaps most successful among this first generation of exhibition entrepreneurs who would later shape the Hollywood studio system was Marcus Loew (1870–1927), who began his career running arcades and nickelodeons in New York City. To guarantee the regular supply of films for his theaters, Loew acquired production and distribution companies and in 1924 formed Metro-Goldwyn-Mayer (MGM), a vertically integrated company that produced and distributed films as well as owning and operating a chain of first-run theaters in major metropolitan areas. Controlling a significant part of the exhibition market was an essential strategy not only for MGM, but for all of the major Hollywood studios. Paramount, for example, followed a similar logic when it merged with the Balaban & Katz chain of theaters (based in Chicago), and so did Warner Bros. when it acquired the Stanley theaters in the same period.

While weekly attendance in the United States reached 22 million by 1922 and rose to approximately 80 million by the end of the decade, the construction of opulent picture palaces during the 1920s further solidified the prominence of the major studio-owned theater chains, most of which expanded by acquiring more theaters as the industry completed its transformation to sound during the late 1920s. Independent exhibitors had few options: sell out to a chain, invest in the costly equipment required for sound films, or close. The Great Depression exacerbated the dilemma of the independent exhibitor, as movie attendance dropped precipitously after the novelty of sound had worn off, dropping off to 50 million per week. New theater construction stopped almost completely, and even the largest chains felt the strain: Paramount-Publix went into receivership, as did Fox; Loew's reduced its holdings to 150 big-city theaters; and Warner Bros. sold 300 of its 700 theaters.

EXHIBITION AND THE CLASSIC HOLLYWOOD SYSTEM

One reason that the major studios could attain virtually monopolistic control over the film industry is that they developed several business strategies during the 1910s and 1920s that all in some way constrained the independent exhibitor's freedom in booking films. These strategies continued to play a central role in film exhibition until the end of the 1940s. Perhaps most important was the run-zone-clearance system, which enabled the "Big Five" major studios (MGM, Paramount, RKO, Warner Bros., and Twentieth Century Fox) to control the distribution of the films they produced. This system was designed to guarantee that films were circulated so as to ensure broad exhibition and to bring in maximum profits to the parent company. The national exhibition market (especially the urban market) in the United States was divided into geographical zones. In each zone, films moved consecutively from first-run through several intermediate steps (second-run, third-run, and so on) to final-run venues. Ticket prices tended to drop with each run. There was, in addition, a "clearance" time between runs, which meant that moviegoers could expect to wait months or up to a year after a film premiered at a downtown picture palace before it reached a neighborhood theater or a small-town venue. By privileging their own theaters and organizing distribution according to the run-zone-clearance system, the Big Five assured their dominance of the American motion picture industry.

MARCUS LOEW
b. New York, New York, 7 May 1870, d. 5 September 1927

Marcus Loew, the creator of MGM and one of the most successful figures in the motion picture industry during the silent era, was, first and foremost, an exhibitor. "I don't sell tickets to movies," he is said to have declared, "I sell tickets to theaters."

Born to immigrant parents on New York's Lower East Side, Loew moved into commercial entertainment after working in the garment industry. In 1904, he co-founded the People's Vaudeville Company, which soon expanded its holdings to include several penny arcades in New York City and one in Cincinnati, Ohio, where he built a 110-seat theater on the second floor to screen motion pictures.

Loew ran nickelodeons, but he made his mark with what was called "small-time vaudeville," a show that combined live vaudeville performance with motion pictures—all for a relatively inexpensive ticket price. In the first of many acquisitions, in 1908 he purchased and refurbished the Royal Theater in Brooklyn. His chain of New York theaters grew to forty small-time vaudeville venues, including impressive new theaters, like the 2,400-seat Loew's National. By the end of the 1910s, Loew owned or leased more than fifty large theaters from Canada to New Orleans, with an especially prominent presence in the major Northeast cities.

Like other moguls, Loew became committed to developing a vertically integrated motion picture company, which controlled production and distribution as well as exhibition. He formed Loew's, Incorporated in 1919, purchased the Metro film studio and then Goldwyn

Pictures. Loew's theater holdings increased to more than 100 first-class venues, topped by the 3,500-seat Loew's State Theater in Times Square. In 1924, Loew acquired Louis B. Mayer's Los Angeles studio and Metro-Goldwyn-Mayer was formed, with Loew's Inc. as its parent company. Until his death in 1927, Marcus Loew served as president of Loew's/MGM, continuing to expand his theater holdings, including newly built picture palaces.

Loew's legacy lasted long after his death, beyond the success of MGM in the 1930s. Following the Paramount decision in 1948, which ordered studios to divest themselves of their theater holdings, Loew's became by the late 1950s a separate entity from MGM, with fewer than 100 theaters. Over the next twenty years, Loew's diversified its holdings but maintained a relatively small number of theaters. However, through ensuing expansion and corporate mergers, Loew's by the 1990s had become an 885-screen chain owned by Sony Pictures Entertainment. Merged with Cineplex Odeon, Loew's Cineplex Entertainment eventually controlled almost 3,000 screens in 450 North American and European locations. With much hoopla, Loew's Cineplex in 2004 celebrated its 100 years of being in the exhibition business.

FURTHER READING

Crowther, Bosley. *The Lion's Share: The Story of an Entertainment Empire*. New York: E. P. Dutton, 1957.

Gomery, Douglas. *The Hollywood Studio System*. New York: St. Martin's Press, 1986.

Gregory A. Waller

Exhibition at independently owned and operated theaters was also constrained by procedures that governed how major studio films were booked by exhibitors. "Blind booking" meant that exhibitors had to schedule the films for the coming season based only on descriptions provided by the studio, with no actual preview prints available. Furthermore, exhibitors had little choice but to agree to "block booking," which required that they take a full season or at least a significant number of films (shorts as well as features) from the same studio. Exhibitors were thus less able

than in the past to pick and choose titles and thus tailor their programming, week-by-week, to a particular clientele.

Exhibitors had always been constrained in other ways as well. For instance, from the nickelodeon era onward, they had faced considerable pressure from religious and reform groups and actual policing from municipal and state authorities, especially in the form of building and safety codes, Sunday closing laws, and license fees. However, exhibitors stood to benefit from government intervention when the Federal Trade

Marcus Loew. EVERETT COLLECTION. REPRODUCED BY PERMISSION.

Commission in 1921 accused Paramount of unfair business practices and illegal restraint of trade, beginning a legal process that continued on and off for more than twenty years. In 1938, the Justice Department initiated anti-trust proceedings against the major Hollywood studios, leading to a temporary consent decree in 1940 that prohibited blind booking and limited block booking to groups of no more than five films. Finally, in 1948, the United States Supreme Court delivered its decision in what was called the "Paramount case," a sweeping ruling that eliminated block booking, challenged monopolistic practices, and significantly altered the relationship between film distribution and exhibition.

The major decision in *United States v. Paramount, et al.* was to restrict Hollywood studios from owning and operating movie theaters. This divestiture took place over the next six years and to some degree it opened up the American market for independent theaters and newly formed theater chains. The 1948 court ruling also prohibited block booking, meaning that films were henceforth to be rented to a theater not as a package or a season, but individually. In addition, the ruling put an

end to the frequently long clearance time between when a film was shown at a first-run theater and when it reached subsequent run theaters. In sum, the Paramount case dramatically opened up the marketplace and altered how exhibitors selected and scheduled movies. But since the production companies were by the 1950s no longer directly in the film exhibition business, they did not have their previous incentive to deliver many new films year round. Furthermore, blind booking was not explicitly banned as part of the Paramount decision, and this practice re-emerged, especially in the 1970s, as production costs rose and wider distribution patterns became the norm for first-run films.

FILM EXHIBITION AFTER TELEVISION

The World War II years, with a fully employed workforce, marked a high point in the film exhibition business in the United States. Weekly attendance topped 80 million annually from 1943 to 1946. Exhibitors not only sold a record number of tickets, but reinforced their civic role through public service gestures: selling government war bonds and staging drives to collect rubber, scrap metal, and other material needed for the war effort. Yet between 1946 and 1953, ticket sales in the United States dropped by almost 50 percent. By 1960, weekly attendance at the movies was only 30 million, dipping further, to 18 million, by 1970.

If the Paramount case seemed to assure greater latitude for theater owners, Hollywood's mid-1950s commitment to color and wide-screen processes (like Cinemascope) meant that exhibitors were strongly encouraged to invest in another costly technological upgrading of projectors, screens, and sound equipment. At the same time, the film audience through the 1950s and 1960s became progressively younger and more male than had previously been the case. Drive-ins came to form a key part of the larger exhibition market, even as the industry suffered continuing effects from the rise of commercial television as a readily available source of entertainment in the home.

Television, however, quickly became another outlet, or exhibition window, for Hollywood films, as studio film libraries were sold or rented to TV stations, with RKO leading the way in 1954. By the mid-1960s it was commonplace for new films to move relatively quickly to prime time television after they had completed their theatrical runs. Even with poor quality sound, panned-and-scanned images (that is, wide-screen films cropped to fit the dimensions of the TV screen), and commercial interruptions, movies drew large audiences on American network television. By the end of the 1960s the precedent had been firmly set for later developments of the television set as "home [movie] theater." With the emergence and widespread diffusion of cable and satellite networks, videocassettes, and DVDs, watching movies no longer necessarily meant going to the movies. One result was that the second- and third-run theaters that had been so important during the first half of the twentieth century disappeared, leaving the theatrical exhibition business overwhelmingly dependent on first-run venues.

As theatrical exhibition shrank, the movie theater changed as well, partly in response to the Paramount decision. Multiplex cinemas, first situated in shopping centers, then in shopping malls, became the core of the business by the 1970s. New theater chains emerged, like General Cinema, which began with a handful of drive-ins and ultimately grew to more than 200 venues, mostly shopping mall multiplexes. American Multi-Cinema, which pioneered the multiplex concept in Kansas City in 1963, refined this particular exhibition model as the company opened increasingly larger multiplexes. By 1980 American Multi-Cinema's 130 theaters across the United States contained some 700 screens. That year attendance stood at 20 million weekly. (It would rise to 25 million by 1995 and to 30 million by 2002.) The spread of the multiplex meant that film exhibition increasingly became a matter of scheduling nationally advertised, widely available, first-run films with little regard for the particularities of locality or audience.

The exhibition business went through another round of significant changes during the mid-1980s, when the Reagan administration encouraged a return to the pre-1948 era by allowing a much greater corporate consolidation of production, distribution, and exhibition. Entertainment companies quickly sought to create vertical monopolies that included the ownership of theaters, as well as new exhibition windows like satellite television. At the same time, corporate mergers and takeovers meant that fewer companies came to control a greater number of screens, with much investment in free-standing megaplex theaters, not only in suburbs but also in metropolitan areas.

From the late 1970s on, exhibition also changed because wider release patterns for first-run films—called "saturation booking"—increasingly became the norm after the success of films like *Jaws* (1975). This move was prompted by the high cost of film production, the drop in the number of major studio releases, the need for distributors to pre-sell as-yet-uncompleted films to exhibitors (a form of blind booking), and the reliance on television as the prime advertising medium for new films. Not only did distributors aim toward saturating the market by making new films simultaneously available on a thousand or more screens, but they also insisted that new releases be given extended theatrical runs, moving from larger to smaller auditoria inside the same multi-screen theater. Thus while newly designed, high-

quality theater complexes with eight or more screens held out the possibility that moviegoers might choose among a more diverse array of films, this was, in practice, rarely the case.

THE FILM PROGRAM

What the exhibitor delivers to paying customers is more than a film, it is the experience of a film program, which has varied significantly since the first public screening of moving pictures in 1896. Three key variables are involved here: (1) the exhibitor's degree of control over the program; (2) the range of films available; and (3) the actual composition of the program, including the variety of screened material (slides as well as motion pictures) and the role, if any, of live performance.

The exhibitors who introduced moving pictures in 1896–1898 had considerable creative control over the programs they offered to a curious public. While they very rarely shot the footage they screened, these traveling exhibitors did acquire and arrange a series of short films, which meant that they could juxtapose *actualités* (such as the Lumière films of everyday life that were shot outdoors on location) with filmed vaudeville acts or staged scenes. Depending on the venue and the intended audience, the array of short films was, in turn, combined in different ways with a wide range of other entertainment options: magic lantern slides or phonograph recordings, vocal or instrumental performances, novelty acts or educational lectures. In such cases, the program was typically designed to offer a variety of distinct attractions, though it soon became possible for exhibitors to create more unified shows in which the screened material and the live performances were arranged around a particular theme, such as the Spanish American War.

By 1900, moving pictures had become a regular feature on certain vaudeville circuits, where they served as one self-enclosed part of a program that might include six or more separate attractions, each occupying the stage for ten to twenty minutes. In this type of program, film was merely another interchangeable component, comparable to an acrobatic act or an ethnic comedy routine. In a similar fashion, moving pictures also served as novelty entertainment screened between the acts of touring melodramas and as part of the midway attractions offered by traveling carnivals and circuses.

When permanent movie theaters emerged during the nickelodeon era, the program changed significantly. Nickelodeons typically ran a continuous show in which a forty-five- or sixty-minute program was repeated throughout the day, then changed daily or at least several times each week. Using films rented from film exchanges, the nickelodeon operator offered several split or full reel films, each running from approximately five to fifteen minutes, combined in almost all cases with live entertainment: musical accompaniment for the screenings (on piano or some sort of mechanical musical device) as well as illustrated songs. Illustrated songs featured a singer whose vocal rendition of a popular song accompanied the projection of a series of colorful slides indicating the lyrics and, more ingeniously, "illustrating" the song with staged tableaux and sometimes extraordinary visual effects. Other slides offered information about the show or instructions on movie-theater etiquette (for example, "Don't Spit on the Floor").

Within the standard programming format of short films and illustrated songs, the nickelodeon operator in fact had a great deal of latitude in tailoring the show for a specific audience. Exhibitors might hire performers to add sound effects to the silent films or even have off-stage actors voice the on-screen dialogue. A speaker, called a "lecturer," sometimes provided a continuous spoken plot synopsis and description, especially for films based on Biblical, literary, or high cultural sources.

Magicians, vocal trios, and other vaudeville-style acts might appear on the same bill as moving pictures.

With the consolidation of the American film industry in the 1910s and the growing prominence of the serial and the multi-reel "feature" film, one common programming strategy was the "balanced" program offering a full evening's worth of entertainment. Until the end of the silent film era in the late 1920s, the feature film was usually accompanied, if not always preceded, by two or more shorts: a one or two-reel comedy or western, newsreel installment, serial episode, "scenic" (a travelogue or other nonfiction short), or animated cartoon. Advertising slides, too, continued to figure as part of the program—pitching nationally available products, local stores and services, and coming attractions.

As larger and more grandiose picture palaces began to appear, as well as more modest neighborhood and small-town theaters, programming could be quite varied, not only in terms of the quality and length of the feature film, but also in the number of shorts and, more importantly,

Crowds outside the Strand Theater in New York City. EVERETT COLLECTION. REPRODUCED BY PERMISSION.

in the live components of the program. For instance, in 1918, a major big-city theater, like the Strand in New York City, presented its program four times daily, beginning with an overture from the house orchestra, followed by a newsreel and scenic, two numbers from a female singer, a feature film, two numbers from a male singer, a comic short, and an organ solo. Organists like Paul Ash and Jesse Crawford became major drawing cards in their own right. During the 1920s, picture palaces added even more spectacular live performances to the show, including elaborate Broadway-styled production numbers, which sometimes took the form of a "prologue" that was connected thematically to that day's featured film.

Smaller venues continued to provide some form of musical performance, if only by a pianist or a mechanical music machine. But such theaters might also add, on occasion, a special attraction: a pared-down prologue, a band performing Hawaiian music, or, by the mid-1920s, jazz; traveling musical comedy troupes, minstrel shows, and magic acts; or participants in a local talent contest. Indeed, film exhibitors' widespread reliance on all manner of live music meant that by the end of the silent era, more musicians worked in movie theaters than in concert halls, hotels, and nightclubs combined.

The coming of sound fundamentally altered the film program, at least in terms of its live component. Short sound films of vaudeville acts and famous orchestras were intended to replace certain live performers on the bill. More significantly, Hollywood's rapid transformation to sound put countless musicians and theater organists out of work, leading the Musicians Union to undertake a futile public relations campaign against "canned" music. Live performance did, however, remain a special attraction for a great many movie theaters well into the 1940s, which booked touring variety shows, radio performers, amateur contests, magicians and midnight "spook" shows, and, by the late 1930s, the film industry's own singing cowboys, like Gene Autry (1907–1998).

Newsreels, cartoons, serial episodes, and a range of other shorts continued to accompany the feature film in programming during the 1930s (and, indeed, into the 1960s). But the Depression also saw the widespread use of another exhibition strategy, the double feature, which paired selected shorts with two feature films, sometimes each of less than an hour in length. This popular programming strategy went hand-in-hand with the increased production of low-budget, sixty-minute, series films (frequently westerns) and other B movies, which were designed to fit the requirements of the double feature. About 300 different films were needed annually by a theater that offered three changes of double-feature programs each week. For the independent theater owner, the

demand for more feature films allowed for somewhat more control over the program. Highly vocal opposition to the double feature came especially from concerned parents and teachers, who worried about the effect on children. Yet by the end of the 1930s, more than half of the theaters in the United States were regularly offering double features, with some even resorting to triple features or to continuous programs of low-budget "action" films. The double feature also allowed for a regularly scheduled intermission, which boosted concession sales.

The double (or triple) feature with intermission breaks also became the standard program at drive-in theaters during the 1950s, while some form of the balanced program (combining shorts with a feature film) survived well into the 1960s. Overall, from 1950 on, there was increased attention given to coming attraction trailers as part of the show and less to comic and dramatic short films. But even as the industry focused increasingly during the 1980s on the high-budget blockbuster designed to be the sole drawing card in a multiplex or megaplex cinema, the program continued to involve more than simply or solely a feature film. Trivia games, innocuous recorded music, advertising slides, filmed commercials, public service announcements, instructions on correct audience behavior, and, most notably, flashy trailers for coming attractions—all these elements served as components of the film program in the late twentieth century, though there was little opportunity for the individual theater to customize its offerings.

SPECIALIZED PROGRAMMING

While the exhibition business has always depended on attracting a core of regular or habitual moviegoers, exhibitors have also been quick to exploit specialized screening and programming occasions, often directed toward a more niche audience. For example, Saturday matinee screenings specifically designed to attract children were initially promoted by progressive civic organizations in the 1910s, but soon evolved into a profitable staple for many film exhibitors. The 1930s saw an increased interest in the Saturday matinee, which favored cartoons, comic shorts, and serial episodes, sometimes coupled with live performances, giveaway contests, and talent shows.

Independent exhibitors in the pre-television era also took advantage of other specialized programming possibilities by scheduling commercially sponsored shows designed to display new appliances and other consumer goods to female audiences. Especially in areas where there were no theaters catering specifically to an African American clientele, exhibitors might also offer special "colored" screenings, usually late in the evening. Sometimes called "midnight rambles," these shows reinforced prevailing

Publicity outside a movie theater screening **Show Boat** (*James Whale, 1936*). EVERETT COLLECTION. REPRODUCED BY PERMISSION.

codes of racial segregation, while also suggesting that even a small-town theater owner could profit by attracting a number of different audiences.

As early as the 1920s but especially in the 1950s and 1960s, art house cinemas in major urban areas and college towns offered a self-consciously high cultural alternative to mainstream moviegoing. Specializing principally in non-American films and independent productions, these venues promised a more intimate, adult, and "refined" experience both in terms of their programming and also their ambience and décor, which often included an art gallery and low-key concession area. In many cases, the art house eventually was transformed into the repertory theater, which thrived until the late 1980s, offering an array of feature films (sometimes programmed into mini-festivals centering on a particular director or genre): foreign art cinema, revivals of Hollywood classics, cult movies, rockumentaries, and new independent films.

Among the most notable features of the repertory theater was the midnight movie. Midnight screenings, which were once principally "colored" shows or special premiere screenings, took on a much different flavor from the late 1960s through the mid-1980s. The midnight movie in these years was likely to be *The Rocky Horror Picture Show* (1975) or some other cult film, screened to a highly participatory audience of teenagers and college students. From its origins in New York City, the midnight movie spread nationwide, becoming a lucrative programming option, even for multiplexes housed in shopping malls.

PROMOTION

Early promotional efforts included colorful posters and banners that added to the already striking effect of what by the mid-1910s had become a standard feature of the movie theater, the electrically illuminated marquee, which announced the current show. To complement newspaper advertising, exhibitors relied on a range of "ballyhoo," all designed to attract attention to the program and, more generally, to the theater itself: trucks with promotional displays, billboards, signs on streetcars, poster displays in store windows, sidewalk stunts, and—perhaps most memorable—extraordinarily elaborate facades constructed to match the film then being screened. In such instances, the front of the theater might be decorated to promote a jungle adventure one day and a prison melodrama the next.

In addition to the promotion of individual films, exhibitors were frequently engaged in the ongoing promotion of their theaters, which often meant establishing and maintaining strong ties both to other local businesses and, more generally, to the home community. Thus a theater might put appliances and other products on display in the lobby, arrange tie-ins with local merchants involving free movie tickets or product giveaways, or even offer free screenings sponsored by the Chamber of Commerce or the retail merchants' association. From the 1910s through the 1940s theaters also developed community relations by opening their doors for benefits, public interest programming, school events, patriotic drives, amateur shows, and even church services. Handbooks like Harold B. Franklin's *Motion Picture Theater Management* (1928) provided practical guidance about promotion and a range of other topics of concern to the theater manager.

In an attempt to counter falling attendance during the early 1930s, exhibitors relied not only on advertising, but also on sometimes elaborate promotional contests designed to lure customers. These included the giving away of free "premiums," like glassware, fans, and cooking utensils, and contests that encouraged audience participation. Bingo-styled games like SCREEN-O games were common, as were "Bank Nights," perhaps the most widespread of these contests. Bank Night featured a drawing for a cash prize, which required that entrants register at the theater and that the winner be present at (though not necessarily inside) the theater when the winner was announced.

Increasingly after the 1940s, theatrical promotion became less spectacular and more restricted to on-site posters and displays, which were part of national marketing campaigns for individual films. By the 1970s, given the prominence of theater chains and the role of media advertising (eventually including the Internet as well as television and radio), there was no longer neither the incentive nor the need for individual exhibitors to come up with unique promotional schemes.

NON-THEATRICAL EXHIBITION

From the late nineteenth century's traveling moving picture shows to the late twentieth century's home theaters, films have been screened outside of movie theaters in a host of non-theatrical sites. Highly visible traveling exhibitors like Lyman H. Howe (1856–1923) had great success in this market between 1900 and 1915, offering ambitious film programs that involved elaborate sound effects. (In Europe, traveling moving picture shows were extremely common at fairgrounds.) As automobiles and expanded highway systems allowed for greater mobility, a host of other itinerant exhibitors brought moving pictures to rural audiences throughout the silent period and well into the 1940s. Traveling exhibition thrived in the Depression and World War II years, especially with the increased availability of highly portable 16mm sound projection equipment. At the same time, the non-theatrical market also included individuals and companies (including government agencies like the United States Department of Agriculture) that sought to tap the vast interest in regularly exhibiting motion pictures at schools, churches, military bases, YMCAs, and retail stores. These non-theatrical exhibitors offered a variety of programs, some very similar to what was being screened in contemporary theaters, others highly idiosyncratic and tailored to a particular audience.

One other form of non-theatrical exhibition that has figured prominently in film history, particularly in terms of the creation of what might be called a cinema culture, is the non-profit film society. The film society, very much dedicated to promoting an appreciation of cinema, typically sold tickets by subscription and featured precisely the sort of films that were not likely to be screened in mainstream commercial theaters: innovative alternative cinema, foreign-language film, and older classics. (There was some significant overlap in this regard between the non-commercial film society and the commercial repertory cinema.) One model for the more than 250 film societies that had emerged by 1960 was Amos Vogel's Cinema 16, which began in New York City in 1947 screening a mix of experimental cinema, socially conscious documentaries, and international films. Film societies were often affiliated with a university, college, museum, or community arts center, where their actual screenings were held.

The most significant development in non-theatrical film exhibition has been the shift to home viewing made possible by a host of different technologies: satellite and cable television, videocassettes, DVDs, and projection and sound equipment specifically designed for the domestic consumer. The home exhibition of film has been a viable option since the introduction of portable 16mm equipment in the 1920s. However, it was not until the late 1980s that the home became the major site for film exhibition in the United States, a trend that was only reinforced by the subsequent introduction of digital cinema, available on DVD and the Internet. Given the ease and relatively low cost of watching movies at home, perhaps the most surprising fact about film exhibition in the 1990s is that theatrical attendance in the United States increased by one-third from 1985 to 2002, even as the total number of movie screens grew from a little over 20,000 in 1985 to more than 37,000 in 2000.

SEE ALSO *Distribution; Publicity and Promotion; Studio System; Television; Theaters*

FURTHER READING

Acland, Charles A. *Screen Traffic: Movies, Multiplexes, and Global Culture*. Durham, NC: Duke University Press, 2003.

Franklin, Harold B. *Motion Picture Theater Management*. New York: Doran, 1927.

Gomery, Douglas. *Shared Pleasures: A History of Movie Presentation in the United States*. Madison: University of Wisconsin Press, 1992.

Huettig, Mae D. *Economic Control of the Motion Picture Industry*. Philadelphia: University of Pennsylvania Press, 1944.

Hulfish, David S. *Motion Picture Work: A General Treatise on Picture Taking, Picture Making, Photo-Plays, and Theater Management and Operation*. Chicago: American School of Correspondence, 1913.

Klinger, Barbara. *Beyond the Multiplex: Cinema, New Technologies, and the Home*. Berkeley: University of California Press, 2006.

Musser, Charles with Carol Nelson. *High-Class Moving Pictures: Lyman H. Howe and the Forgotten Era of Traveling Exhibition, 1880–1920*. Princeton, NJ: Princeton University Press, 1991.

Ricketson, Frank H., Jr. *The Management of Motion Picture Theatres*. New York and London: McGraw-Hill, 1938.

Schaefer, Eric. *Bold! Daring! Shocking! True!: A History of Exploitation Film, 1919–1959*. Durham, NC: Duke University Press, 1999.

Stones, Barbara. *America Goes to the Movies: 100 Years of Motion Picture Exhibition*. North Hollywood, CA: National Association of Theatre Owners, 1993.

Waller, Gregory A., ed. *Moviegoing in America: A Sourcebook in the History of Film Exhibition*. Malden, MA: Blackwell, 2002.

Wilinsky, Barbara. *Sure Seaters: The Emergence of Art House Cinema*. Minneapolis: University of Minnesota Press, 2000.

Gregory A. Waller

EXPERIMENTAL FILM

Experimental films are very different from feature-length Hollywood fiction films. In *Mothlight* (1963), Stan Brakhage (1933–2003) completely avoids "normal" filmmaking (he doesn't even use a camera) by sprinkling seeds, grass, dead moths, and bee parts directly onto the film stock; the result is a three-minute rhythmic "dance" between nature and the projector mechanism.

There are many types of experimental film, but despite their diversity, it is possible to pin down tendencies that help make experimental film a discrete genre. Edward Small identifies eight traits of experimental films and in the process defines important differences between the avant-garde and Hollywood.

Most obviously, production is a collaborative enterprise, but most experimental filmmakers conceive, shoot, and edit their films alone or with a minimal crew. Often they even assume the responsibility for the distribution of the finished film. It follows that experimental films are made outside of industry economics, with the filmmakers themselves often paying for production (sometimes with money from small grants or the rentals on previous films). This low-budget approach buys independence: Maya Deren (1917–1961) bought an inexpensive 16mm Bolex camera with money she inherited after her father's death, and used this camera to make all of her films, forging a career completely apart from the Hollywood mode of production.

Unlike mainstream feature films, experimental works are usually short, often under thirty minutes in length. This is in part because of their small budgets, though most filmmakers make short films for aesthetic reasons too: to capture a fleeting moment, perhaps, or to create new visuals with the camera. *Ten Second Film* (Bruce Conner, 1965) was originally shown at the 1965 New York Film Festival, and all ten seconds were reproduced in their entirety, as strips of film, on the festival's poster. Experimental filmmakers are usually the first to try out new ways of making movies, after which these technologies are adopted by Hollywood. Scott Bartlett's (1943–1990) films, such as *OFFON* (1967, with Tom DeWitt), were the first to mix computer and film imagery, and influenced Douglas Trumbull's (b. 1942) light show in *2001: A Space Odyssey* (1968). The reverse is also true: avant-garde filmmakers continue to use formats such as Pixelvision or 8mm long after the height of their popularity. Also like *OFFON*, experimental production often focuses on abstract imagery. The quintessential example is Stan Brakhage's notion of "closed-eye vision," the attempt to duplicate on film the shimmers of light we see on our eyelids when our eyes are closed.

As Brakhage's films suggest, most experimental films avoid verbal communication, giving primacy to the visual. Unlike "talkie" Hollywood movies, experimental films are typically silent, or use sound in nonnaturalistic ways. As well, experimental films typically ignore, subvert, or fragment the storytelling rules of Hollywood cinema. Some films—such as Harry Smith's (1923–1991) *Early Abstractions* (1939–1956)—abandon narrative altogether and focus instead on creating a colorful, ever-changing picture plane. When experimental films do settle down into a story, it's often one that shocks or disturbs conventional sensibilities. Sometimes their subject is themselves and the medium of cinema.

Many experimental films violate one or more of the above traits. Andy Warhol's (1928–1987) *Empire* (1964) is over eight hours long, and Peter Hutton's

MAYA DEREN
b. Eleanora Derenkowsky, Kiev, Russia, 29 April 1917, d. 13 October 1961

One of the most important women in American experimental cinema, Maya Deren emigrated with her parents in 1922 to the United States, where Eleanora developed a keen interest in the arts that launched her into a varied early career, including a stint touring with Katherine Dunham's dance company. In 1941, while with the company in Los Angeles, she met and married filmmaker Alexander Hammid. In 1943 Deren adopted the first name *Maya* (Hindu for "illusion") and made *Meshes of the Afternoon*, a psychodrama rife with symbolic, fascinating repetition that rejuvenated the American avant-garde.

Deren's love of dance manifests itself in the films following *Meshes*. *At Land* (1944) is a dream of female empowerment that foregrounds Deren's own graceful movements, while *A Study in Choreography for Camera* (1945) is a portrait of dancer Talley Beatty as he moves from repose to a vigorous, ballet-like jump. *Meshes, At Land*, and *A Study* are unified by Deren's signature editing strategy: flowing motions that bridge abrupt cuts between different locales. In *A Study*, for instance, Beatty's single leap travels through a room, an art museum, against a backdrop of sky, and then ends in the woods, as he falls into a crouch and stops moving.

The combination of real-life incident and artistic manipulation is, for Deren, the essence of cinema. In her essay "Cinematography: The Creative Use of Reality" she argues that photography and cinema is the art of the "controlled accident," the "delicate balance" between spontaneity and deliberate design in art. Deren further extends the notion of the controlled accident to include those formal properties—slow-motion, negative images, disjunctive editing—that shape and alter the images of real life provided by the film camera.

Deren's other films are the *Meshes*-like *Ritual in Transfigured Time* (1946), the dance film *Meditation on Violence* (1948), and *The Very Eye of Night* (1958). In 1946 Deren divorced Alexander Hammid. In the late 1940s she became passionately interested in Haitian religion and dance, and traveled three times to Haiti to do research that resulted in the book *Divine Horsemen: The Voodoo Gods of Haiti* (1953) and hours of footage of Haitian rituals (some of which was edited into the video release *Divine Horsemen*). Deren became a legend in New York City's Greenwich Village, both for her practice of voodoo and for the assistance she provided to younger experimental filmmakers. The Creative Film Foundation (CFF) was founded by Deren to provide financial help to struggling filmmakers; Stan Brakhage, Stan Vanderbeek, Robert Breer, Shirley Clarke, and Carmen D'Avino received CFF grants.

RECOMMENDED VIEWING
Meshes of the Afternoon (1943), *At Land* (1944), *A Study in Choreography for Camera* (1945), *Ritual in Transfigured Time* (1946), *Meditation on Violence* (1948)

FURTHER READING
Clark, VeVe, Millicent Hodson, and Catrina Neiman. *The Legend of Maya Deren: A Documentary Biography and Collected Works*, vol. 1, part 1: *Signatures (1917–42)*. New York: Anthology Film Archives/Film Culture, 1984.

Clark, VeVe, Millicent Hodson, and Catrina Neiman. *The Legend of Maya Deren: A Documentary Biography and Collected Works*, vol. 1, part 2: *Chambers (1942–47)*. New York: Anthology Film Archives/Film Culture, 1988.

Deren, Maya. "Cinematography: The Creative Use of Reality." *Film Theory and Criticism*, edited by Leo Braudy and Marshall Cohen, 187–198. New York: Oxford University Press, 2004.

Nichols, Bill, ed. *Maya Deren and the American Avant-Garde*. Berkeley: University of California Press, 2001.

Craig Fischer

movies photograph nature in objective terms, avoiding the avant-garde tendency toward subjective psychology. The traits, though, provide a rough guide to the ways that experimental films differ from feature-length narratives, and provide an entrance into the history of the avant-garde.

EARLY HISTORY
Many of the seminal texts of US experimental film history, such as P. Adams Sitney's *Visionary Film*, begin with a discussion of the production of Maya Deren's *Meshes of the Afternoon* (1943). More recent scholarly work, however, has unearthed a vibrant post–World

Maya Deren. EVERETT COLLECTION. REPRODUCED BY PERMISSION.

War I avant-garde American film movement with roots in European art and culture. American artists such as Man Ray (1890–1976) and Dudley Murphy (1897–1968) lived in France and took inspiration from dadaism and surrealism in the 1920s; Ray made his first film, *Le Retour à la raison* (*Return to Reason*, 1923), for a famous dada soirée, and Murphy collaborated with Fernand Léger (1881–1955) on the surrealist *Ballet mécanique* (Mechanical ballet, 1924). Technological innovation,

specifically Kodak's 1924 introduction of 16mm film and the user-friendly Cine-Kodak 16mm camera, helped to jump-start the 1920s avant-garde (*Lovers of Cinema*, p. 18).

The creators in this first wave of experimental film-making came from different careers and interests. Elia Kazan (1909–2003), Orson Welles (1915–1985), and Gregg Toland (1904–1948) dabbled in the avant-garde, but achieved true success in mainstream film. Douglass

Crockwell was a magazine illustrator of the Norman Rockwell school, but his *Glens Falls Sequence* (1934–1946) is an abstract dance of mutating shapes. Several film teachers and scholars (Theodore Huff, Lewis Jacobs, Jay Leyda) made avant-garde films too. Yet, despite these different backgrounds and motivations, most experimental film practitioners thought of themselves as amateurs rather than professional filmmakers, but the term "amateur" was praise rather than a pejorative, implying a commitment to art over commerce. The types of films by these "amateur" avant-gardists fall into distinct genres. Many made offbeat stories inspired by literary sources and cutting-edge art movements. James Sibley Watson, Jr. (1894–1982) and Melville Webber (1871–1947) invoke such sources as Edgar Allan Poe, German expressionism, and Old Testament narratives in *The Fall of the House of Usher* (1928) and *Lot in Sodom* (1933). Other films told stories that parodied film genres, such as Theodore Huff's first movie, *Hearts of the West* (1931), which features an all-children cast in a spoof of silent westerns. Filmmaker and artist Joseph Cornell (1903–1972) made collage films that turned Hollywood narratives into studies in surrealism. In *Rose Hobart* (1936), Cornell took footage from a Universal B movie that featured the contract player Rose Hobart, scored all of Hobart's actions to an old samba record, and projected the reedited footage through red-tinted lenses.

Other filmmakers abandoned narrative. Paul Strand (1890–1976) and Charles Sheeler's (1883–1965) *Manhatta* (1921), the first avant-garde film produced in the United States, was the first "city symphony" film, a genre of associative documentaries that celebrate urban life and the machines of modernity. Other American examples of the genre include *A Bronx Morning* (Jay Leyda, 1931) and *The Pursuit of Happiness* (Rudy Burkhardt, 1940), but the most famous city symphony of all, *The Man with the Movie Camera* (Dziga Vertov, 1929), was made in Soviet Russia. Another common type of nonnarrative documentary was the dance film; *Hands* (Stella Simon, 1926) and *Introspection* (Sara Arledge, 1941–1946) use innovative form to capture bodies reacting to music, and are clear inspirations for Maya Deren's work. Rhythms are at the center of both dance films and abstract films, those works that focus on unfamiliar objects and patterns. *H2O* (1929) by Ralph Steiner catalogs how water reflects light in raindrops and rivers; the films of Oskar Fischinger (1900–1967), Mary Ann Bute, and Dwinell Grant are paintings in motion, dances of colors and shapes instead of the human body.

There were four venues for the exhibition of early experimental film. In the United States, for example, the "little cinemas," the art theaters that emerged during the 1920s and 1930s to program repertory classics and European fare, sometimes showed experimental shorts before their features. *The Life and Death of 9413—A*

Hollywood Extra (1928) was paired with a German/Indian coproduction, *Light of Asia* (1926), at the Philadelphia Motion Picture Guild, and Roman Freulich's *Prisoners* (1934) was followed by *Sweden, Land of the Vikings* (1934) at the Little Theatre in Baltimore (*Lovers of Cinema*, p. 24). On occasion, avant-garde shorts were even on the same program as Hollywood features. Art galleries were another venue for experimental films, as were the screenings of the Workers Film and Photo League, a branch of the Communist Party that regularly exhibited nonmainstream films of all types. The most important exhibition space for the avant-garde during this period was provided by the Amateur Cinema League (ACL), founded in New York City in 1926. The ACL nationally distributed key avant-garde films, organized "ten best" contests for amateur filmmakers, and published extravagant praise for experimental work in the ACL magazine, *Amateur Movie Makers*. As Patricia Zimmerman points out, the activities of the ACL were just a small part of the amateur film phenomenon: "The *New York Times* speculated that that there were over one hundred thousand home moviemakers in 1937 and five hundred services for rental of films for home viewing" (Zimmerman in Horak, p. 143). No wonder experimental filmmakers from this period embraced the "amateur" label so readily. However, most of these activities vanished as the Depression ground on. Though several important experimental filmmakers—Arledge, Burkhardt, Cornell—began to make work in the second half of the 1930s, it would be another ten years before a new avant-garde generation would build systems of production, distribution, and exhibition that rivaled those of the amateur film movement.

POSTWAR POETICS

In the immediate postwar period, the most important exhibition space for experimental films were the ciné clubs, organizations of film fans who would rent and discuss offbeat films. The first flowering of ciné clubs occurred in France in the 1920s, as venues for the impressionist work of such avant-gardists as Germaine Dulac (1882–1942) and Jean Epstein (1897–1953). Luis Buñuel made *Un Chien Andalou* (1929) in collaboration with the painter Salvador Dali. Hans Richter, Viking Eggeling, Oskar Fischinger, Jon Jost, and Jean Cocteau are among the many other avant-garde filmmakers to work in Europe.

In the United States, the first such club, Art in Cinema, whose screenings were helmed by Frank Stauffacher at the San Francisco Museum of Art, was established in 1947. Stauffacher helped Amos and Marcia Vogel start a club, Cinema 16, in New York City, and for sixteen years (1947–1963) the Vogels sponsored programs that included experimental shorts such as Kenneth

***Gay iconography in Kenneth Anger's* Fireworks *(1947)*.**
FANTOMA FILMS/THE KOBAL COLLECTION.

Anger's (b. 1927) *Fireworks* (1947) and Bruce Conner's *A Movie* (1957) with documentaries, educational shorts, art films, and special events featuring speakers such as playwright Arthur Miller and Alfred Hitchcock. In 1950 the Vogels also began to distribute experimental films around the country (primarily to colleges and other ciné clubs) through Cinema 16. Although financial troubles forced the Vogels to shut down Cinema 16 in 1963, its effect was lasting and profound.

Other exhibition spaces besides ciné clubs included college classes, art galleries and museums, and bars. Occasionally, an entrepreneurial filmmaker might even screen in a mainstream theater. Between 1946 and 1949, for instance, Maya Deren rented the two-hundred-seat Provincetown Playhouse eight times for programs of her films. As opportunities for the exhibition of avant-garde films grew, trends began to form. Following Deren's example, several filmmakers in the immediate postwar period made surrealist, dream-inflected narratives. Sidney Peterson (1905–2000) and James Broughton (1913–1999) collaborated on *The Potted Psalm* (1946), a loose-limbed tale featuring gravestones, mannequins, and other irrational symbols. Peterson's subsequent films, such as *The Cage* (1947) and *The Lead Shoes* (1948),

combine disturbing images with recursive narratives and compulsive repetition. Broughton made his first film, *Mother's Day*, in 1948, and across four decades of film-making his works shifted in emphasis from offbeat, erotic comedy to an unabashed celebration of gay sexuality. Willard Maas (1911–1971) was another practitioner of the postwar experimental narrative; his *Geography of the Body* (1946) turns close-ups of human anatomy into a travelogue of a surreal continent. For his first film, Stan Brakhage made *Interim* (1952), a romantic Derenesque narrative, but afterwards he quickly took off in new directions.

Animation was also a vibrant part of the postwar avant-garde. The most prolific avant-garde animator was Robert Breer (b. 1926), who between 1952 and 1970 produced at least one film a year. James (1921–1982) and John Whitney (1917–1995) pioneered computer-generated films, and their success gave them the opportunity to make cartoons for the mainstream UPA studio and to produce animated effects for Alfred Hitchcock's *Vertigo* (1958). Australian artist Len Lye (1901–1980) painted directly on the surface of the film strip in such films as *A Colour Box* (1935) and *Free Radicals* (1958). And Jordan Belson's (b. 1926) San Francisco light shows evolved into symmetrically patterned, Buddhist-influenced films such as *Mandala* (1953) and *Allures* (1961).

Several postwar filmmakers explored film form in ways different from animation. Bruce Conner began his career in the arts as a sculptor, but became famous as the conceptualizer-editor of a series of "found footage" films that edited previously shot footage into new and bizarre combinations. In *A Movie*, Conner subverts our cause-effect expectations (and makes us laugh) by juxtaposing, for example, a shot of a German soldier staring into a periscope with a picture of a girl wearing a bikini and staring into the camera. Other Conner films subject newly shot footage to unorthodox cutting: in *Vivian* (1963), Conner filmed his friend Vivian Kurz in various environments—in an art gallery, in her bedroom—and then edited the rolls into a kinetic flow of images that comments on the nature of photographic representation. *Vivian* has a pop music soundtrack—as do other Conner films, such as *Cosmic Ray* (1961) and *Mongoloid* (1978)—and Conner's synchronization of editing and musical rhythm is the origin of the music video.

Marie Menken (1909–1970) used time-lapse photography as the formal center of many of her films. A team player in the New York Underground—she worked on films by Warhol, Deren, and her husband, Willard Maas—Menken also crafted miniature movies that condense time. *Moonplay* (1962) is a collection of full moons photographed over the course of several years,

ANDY WARHOL
b. Andrew Warhola, Forest City, Pennsylvania, 6 August 1928, d. 22 February 1987

Probably the best-known American artist of the twentieth century, Andy Warhol studied commercial art at Carnegie Mellon University. In 1949 he moved to New York City and carved out a career as an advertising artist. In the early 1960s Warhol became a pioneer of pop art by creating paintings that showcased the most ubiquitous icons of American popular culture: Campbell's Soup cans, Brillo boxes, celebrities such as Elvis Presley and Marilyn Monroe. With his paintings and silkscreens in high demand, Warhol established the Factory, a workshop and hangout where he supervised "art workers" in the making of Warhol "originals." The subjects of his art were the mass media and mass production, and the art was created on the Factory's improvisational assembly line.

A neglected aspect of Warhol's 1960s artistic production was his work in experimental film. Just as his graphic art used simplicity to challenge notions of "art," Warhol's avant-garde films embraced the realist aesthetic strategies of the putative fathers of cinema, Louis and Auguste Lumière. Warhol returned to cinema's zero point by setting up a 16mm camera and encouraging the artsy types who inhabited the Factory to perform for the lens. Sometimes Warhol commissioned writers (most notably off-off-Broadway playwright Ronald Tavel) to provide screenplays, but usually the Factory crew filmed with just a central conceit—open to extended improvisation—as a rough guide. In *Kiss* (1963), Warhol showcased various couples (hetero- and homosexual) kissing, each for the three-minute length of the camera magazine; *Sleep* (1963) uses a few camera angles to photograph poet John Giorno's body as he slumbers. Warhol's films had a profound effect on avant-garde film practice of the 1960s, especially the decade's structural filmmakers.

Warhol's movies of the mid-1960s built on the simple structures of his earlier work. *Inner and Outer Space*

(1965) juxtaposes ghostly video images of Warhol "superstar" Edie Sedgwick with film footage of her commenting on her own video reflection, while *Chelsea Girls* (1966), which played commercially in New York City, uses two screens to depict the inhabitants of the Chelsea Hotel in Manhattan. Warhol's epic was perhaps **** (*Four Stars*, 1966–1967), a twenty-five-hour explosion of superimpositions (two projectors fired footage simultaneously on the same screen) that was shown only once and then disassembled.

After Warhol was shot and almost killed by Valerie Solanas in June 1968, he stopped making films. Instead, he farmed out the Factory's filmmaking activities to his protégé, Paul Morrissey, who went on to direct several Warhol-influenced but more mainstream features, including *Flesh* (1968), *Trash* (1970), *Heat* (1972), *Flesh for Frankenstein* (1973), and *Blood for Dracula* (1974).

RECOMMENDED VIEWING

Kiss (1963), *Sleep* (1963), *Empire* (1964), *Poor Little Rich Girl* (1965), *My Hustler* (1965), *Chelsea Girls* (1966), *The Nude Restaurant* (1967), *Blue Movie* (1969)

FURTHER READING

Gidal, Peter. *Andy Warhol: Films and Paintings*. New York: Dutton, 1971.

Koch, Stephen. *Stargazer: Andy Warhol's World and His Films*. 2nd ed. New York: M. Boyars, 1985.

Koestenbaum, Wayne. *Andy Warhol*. New York: Penguin, 2001.

O'Pray, Michael, ed. *Andy Warhol: Film Factory*. London: British Film Institute, 1989.

Warhol, Andy. *The Philosophy of Andy Warhol (From A to B & Back Again)*. New York: Harcourt Brace Jovanovich, 1975.

Craig Fischer

while Menken herself described *Go! Go! Go!* (1962–1964) as "a time-lapse record of a day in the life of a city."

Radical content as well as form was common in the postwar avant-garde, particularly films that addressed homosexual desire. Probably the most famous "queer" experimental filmmaker of this period is Kenneth Anger,

who made the trailblazing *Fireworks* at the age of seventeen. *Fireworks* is a mélange of same-sex flirtation, sadomasochism, and sailors; the film's finale features a sailor lighting a Roman candle (firework) in his crotch. (*Fireworks* was shown several times at Cinema 16, often as part of a "Forbidden Films" program, and Amos

Andy Warhol. PHOTO BY REX FEATURES/EVERETT COLLECTION. REPRODUCED BY PERMISSION.

Vogel also distributed Anger's work.) Anger's epic *Scorpio Rising* (1963) connects gay desire and satanism—for Anger (as for Jean Genet), being gay means repudiating traditional norms and embracing the subversive and decadent—and the film juxtaposes a chronicle of California biker culture with a pop-rock soundtrack in ways that, like Conner's works, anticipate music videos. Anger's films treat homosexuality as inherently transgressive; in contrast, many of Gregory Markopoulos's (1928–1992) works place same-sex desire in a classical context. *The Iliac Passion* (1967), for example, features several members of the 1960s New York gay demimonde—Andy Warhol, Jack Smith, Taylor Mead—cast as mythic characters such as Poseidon and Orpheus. Markopoulos also pioneered a single-frame, scattershot approach to editing that made his films tightly wound, dense fabrics of allusions, classical and otherwise.

As Markopoulos explored the deep connections between sexuality and myth, Jack Smith turned popular culture into his own queer playground. Soon after meeting experimental filmmakers Ken Jacobs (b. 1933) and Bob Fleischner in a film class at the City College of New York in 1956, Smith collaborated with Jacobs on a series

of films—including *Star Spangled to Death* (1958/2004) and *Little Stabs at Happiness* (1959)—that ditch plot and instead allow Smith to improvise personas for the camera. Both the charm and narcissism of this approach finds its perfect expression in Jacobs, Fleischner, and Smith's *Blonde Cobra* (1963), where Smith delivers a monologue to his image in a mirror. After a falling out with Jacobs, Smith directed several films himself, the most notorious being *Flaming Creatures* (1963), a mad chronicle of a pansexual orgy, complete with simulated rape and *faux*-earthquake, that was declared obscene in New York Criminal Court. Even while Smith worked on such films as the unfinished *Normal Love* (begun 1964) and *No President* (1968), he increasingly shifted his energies to performance art, letting his love of Z-grade Hollywood stars (especially the beloved Maria Montez) and radical politics run rampant in theater pieces, slide shows, and "expanded cinema" experiences such as *I Was a Male Yvonne de Carlo for the Lucky Landlord Underground* (1982).

THE 1960s

The 1960s deserves its own subsection primarily because of Andy Warhol, who began making 16mm long-take, quotidian extravaganzas in 1963, and whose popularity throughout the decade brought visibility to experimental films as a whole. In addition, the rise of a leftist counterculture during the decade and the increased distribution of nonmainstream movies led to an exponential increase in the number of artists who made avant-garde films during this time. Among the most important filmmakers of the era were Bruce Baillie (b. 1931), Ken Jacobs, the Kuchar brothers (George, b. 1942, and Mike, b. 1942), Robert Nelson, Stan Vanderbeek (1927–1984), Michael Snow (b. 1929), and Joyce Wieland (1931–1998). However, much of the credit for the explosion of creativity in the 1960s in the United States belongs to Jonas Mekas (b. 1922).

Born in Lithuania, Mekas published several books of poetry and literary sketches—and spent time in forced-labor and displaced-persons camps during World War II—before he and his brother Adolfas emigrated to the United States in 1949. He quickly became a fixture at Cinema 16, where he shot footage that would later appear in his diary film *Lost Lost Lost* (1975). In January 1955 he began *Film Culture*, "America's Independent Motion Picture Magazine," whose early topics included classical Hollywood filmmaking (the journal published Andrew Sarris's first articles on auteurism), the international art cinema, and Mekas's own criticism. Within a few years, *Film Culture*'s focus zeroed in on the avant-garde and Mekas became experimental film's hardest working promoter.

Viva and Taylor Mead in Andy Warhol's **Lonesome Cowboys** *(1969).* EVERETT COLLECTION. REPRODUCED BY PERMISSION.

In the 1960s his weekly "Movie Journal" column in the *Village Voice* publicized experimental filmmakers and the events where their films could be seen, and Mekas himself was one of these filmmakers: his feature *Guns of the Trees* (codirected by Adolfas) was released in 1961, his film document of the play *The Brig* in 1964, and his first ambitious diaristic film, *Walden*, in 1969. In 1964 he organized the Film-Makers' Cinematheque, a venue for US avant-garde film that provocatively overlapped with vanguard artists in other fields as well. With Shirley Clarke (1919–1997) and Lionel Rogosin (1924–2000), Mekas started the Film-Makers' Distribution Center, a distribution exchange that he hoped would supply an ever-expanding circuit of theaters with experimental work. Although both the Cinematheque and Distribution Center failed, Mekas established Anthology Film Archives in 1970, a museum/theater/preservation complex devoted to experimental films. Although various controversies have erupted throughout its history—most notably, perhaps, around its attempt to establish a list of canonical "essential" films that would be in permanent repertory—Anthology endures to this day, a tribute to Mekas's commitment to the avant-garde.

Perhaps Mekas's most unusual contribution to experimental film exhibition was the midnight movie. Mekas's midnight screenings at Manhattan's Charles Theatre between 1961 and 1963 followed an open-mic structure: audience members either paid admission or brought a reel of film to show, and Mekas supplemented these submissions with works by Markopoulos, Menken, Jacobs, and others. Later in the decade, entrepreneur Mike Getz resurrected the midnight movie model when he used family connections to begin Underground Cinema 12. Getz's uncle, Louis Sher, was the owner of a chain of Midwest art cinemas, and Getz persuaded Sher to exhibit midnight programs of avant-garde shorts at many of these theaters. Underground Cinema 12 brought experimental film out of its centers in New York City and San Francisco and gave it exposure elsewhere in the country. In 1967, for instance, in the college town of Champaign, Illinois, viewers had the opportunity to see Conner's *A Movie*, Vanderbeek's *Breathdeath* (1964), *Peyote Queen* (Storm De Hirsch, 1965), and *Sins of the Fleshapoids* (Mike Kuchar, 1965) at Sher's local art theater. Mekas's Charles screenings and Getz's

Underground Cinema 12 were important precursors to the 1970s midnight movie experience as it coalesced around cult films such as *The Rocky Horror Picture Show* (1975) and *Eraserhead* (1977).

Mekas's nurturing of the avant-garde led to an explosion of experimental auteurs. In such works as *Mass for the Dakota Sioux* (1963–1964) and *Quick Billy* (1967–1970), Bruce Baillie welds his love for the West with a poetic, Brakhage-inspired spontaneity. In his best-known film, *Castro Street* (1966), Baillie, who also cofounded in 1961 Canyon Cinema, an exhibition program that evolved into the biggest distributor of experimental films in the United States, uses multiple superimpositions to celebrate his beloved San Francisco neighborhood; *All My Life* (1966) consists of a single three-minute shot (a track along a picket fence that ends with a pan up to the sky) that captures the ravishing light in a California backyard. After collaborating with Jack Smith, Ken Jacobs made a number of avant-garde films, including *Tom, Tom, the Piper's Son* (1969). Subsequently, Jacobs began researching optical effects and illusions, which resulted in his "Nervous System" performances, improvisations where Jacobs "plays" two projectors in ways that display how various properties of the film medium (flicker, lenses, projection) can mold and alter images. The Kuchar brothers, George and Mike, grew up in the Bronx, and as teenagers used an 8mm camera to shoot their own tawdry versions of Hollywood melodramas. They then showed tiny epics such as *I Was a Teenage Rumpot* (1960) and *Pussy on a Hot Tin Roof* (1961) at open screenings for amateur filmmakers, where they garnered attention from the avant-garde. Later films jumped up to 16mm, but their movies remained campy, unprofessional, rude, and thoroughly hypnotic, implicit subversions of Hollywood standards of "quality." After the mid-1960s the brothers worked separately, and Mike has made few films since. George has remained astonishingly prolific, producing films and videotapes at the rate of at least two a year.

The profane jokester of the 1960s avant-garde explosion, Robert Nelson first courted controversy with *Oh Dem Watermelons* (1965), his second film, a chaotic mix of gags and images involving melons accompanied in part by a racist Stephen Foster soundtrack. Nelson's tour de force, *Bleu Shut* (1970), functions as both a ruthless parody of structural film and a perfect example of Nelson's tendency to pack his films with crazed digressions and absurd asides. Best known as a performance artist, Carolee Schneemann (b. 1939) made several influential autobiographical avant-garde movies, including *Fuses* (1967), a portrait of Schneemann's sex life with composer James Tenney, for which Brakhage inspired Schneemann to paint and scratch directly on the footage to capture the joy and energy of lovemaking. While

studying filmmaking at New York University, Warren Sonbert (1947–1995) shot a number of short diary films—including *Where Did Our Love Go?* (1966), *Hall of Mirrors* (1966), and *The Bad and the Beautiful* (1967)—that combine pop music soundtracks with candid footage of such 1960s Manhattan scenemakers as René Ricard and Gerald Malanga. With *The Carriage Trade* (1971), Sonbert shifted into a more rigorous type of filmmaking based on silence, extremely brief shots, and graphic contrasts. Sonbert's later films, such as *Divided Loyalties* (1978) and *Honor and Obey* (1988), use this rigorous form to create portraits of a world full of alienation and sorrow. Sonbert died of AIDS in 1995. Stan Vanderbeek pioneered the use of computer imagery, collage animation, and compilation filmmaking. Terry Gilliam's cutout animation for *Monty Python's Flying Circus* was inspired by Vanderbeek's *Science Friction* (1959), and many of Vanderbeek's earliest films were political satires in collage form. In the late 1960s Vanderbeek collaborated with Kenneth Knowlton of Bell Telephone Laboratories to make some of the first computer-generated films, and built an avant-garde movie theater, the Movie Drome of Stony Point, New York, that was equipped to properly present his own multiprojector works.

In Canada, painter Joyce Wieland (1931–1998) also made films with a dry wit that anticipates many structural films. *Rat Life and Diet in North America* (1968) juxtaposes footage of mice with a narrated soundtrack that defines the rodents as heroes of a narrative about political oppression and liberation. After making two avant-garde films—*La Raison avant la passion* (*Reason Over Passion*, 1968–1969) and *Pierre Vallières* (1972)—devoted to Canadian issues, Wieland reached out to a larger audience with her narrative feminist feature *The Far Shore* (1976).

During this period, many challenging experimental films were made outside the United States. From the 1930s to the 1980s, Norman McLaren (1914–1987) produced playful animated and live-action shorts for Canada's National Film Board. French philosopher Guy Debord made several films—including *Sur le passage de quelques personnes à travers une assez courte unité de temps* (*On the Passage of a Few People through a Rather Brief Period in Time*, 1959) and *Critique de la séparation* (*Critique of Separation*, 1961)—designed to vex conventional audience expectation and dissect mass media manipulation. In Japan, Takahito Iimura (b. 1937) began a series of scandalous shorts with *Ai* (*Love*, 1962).

THREE TYPES OF EXPERIMENTAL FILM

In the late 1960s experimental film headed in a new aesthetic direction. In an article published in *Film*

Culture in 1969, critic P. Adams Sitney defined the structuralist film as a "tight nexus of content, a shape designed to explore the facets of the material" (*Film Culture Reader*, p. 327), which becomes clear when these films are compared with previous avant-garde traditions. In the films of lyricists such as Brakhage and Baillie, rhythm is dependent on what is being photographed, or on the associations possible through manipulations of form. In *Window Water Baby Moving* (1962), for example, Brakhage's quick cuts fragment time and connect his wife Jane's pregnant stomach to the birth of their daughter. In contrast, structuralist films don't have "rhythms" as much as they do systems that, in Sitney's words, render content "minimal and subsidiary to the outline" (*Film Culture Reader*, p. 327). Watching a structuralist film, then, is a little like watching a chain of dominoes: after the first domino tumbles, our attention is on how the overall organization plays out rather than on the individual dominoes. Sitney considers such Andy Warhol Factory films as *Sleep* (1963) and *Eat* (1963) to be important precursors of structural film, particularly because of their reliance on improvisatory performance and fixed camera positions. Later in the decade, other avant-garde filmmakers turned to structural film. Michael Snow's influential *Wavelength* (1967) is organized around a forty-five-minute zoom that moves from a wide shot of a New York loft to a close-up of a picture of ocean waves on the loft's farthest wall. Snow continued to explore reframing with *Back and Forth* (1969), a shot of a classroom photographed by a camera that pans with ever-increasing speed, and *La Région centrale* (The Central Region, 1971), a portrait of a northern Quebec landscape photographed by a machine that runs through a series of automated circular pans.

Critic David James has isolated the origin of structural film in the "radical film reductions" of the 1960s Fluxus art movement: works such as Nam June Paik's (1932–2006) *Zen for Film* (1964)—a projection of nothing but a bright, empty surface, occasionally punctuated by scratches and dirt—points to a cinema preoccupied with its own formal properties. Fluxus films, and the structuralist movies they spawned, explore the material nature of film as a medium and the various phases of the production process. For example, Peter Kubelka's (b. 1934) *Arnulf Rainer* (1958–1960) and Tony Conrad's *The Flicker* (1966) consist solely of alternating black-and-white frames of various lengths to explore the optical effects of flicker. Paul Sharits's (1943–1993) *Ray Gun Virus* (1966) and *S:TREAM:S: S:ECTION:S:ECTION:S:S:ECTIONED* (1968–1971) add color, emulsion scratches, and even portraits of faces to rapid-fire flicker. The distortion of space through changes in lens focal length is the subject of Ernie Gehr's (b. 1943) *Serene Velocity* (1970), which juxtaposes long shots of an empty corridor with shots

of the same hallway while the camera zooms in. Larry Gottheim's *Barn Rushes* (1971) explores the nature of filmic representation and duplication by photographing a landscape under different light conditions and with different film stocks. J. J. Murphy's *Print Generation* (1973–1974) subjects a one-minute piece of film to fifty duplications, and the process renders the footage abstract and unintelligible. (Murphy also distorts sound, and one twist of *Print Generation* is that as the image distorts, the sound becomes clearer, and vice versa.) In Britain, Malcolm le Grice and Peter Gidal, and in Germany Wilhelm and Birgit Hein, also worked in this mode.

The graininess and dirtiness of the film image is considered in *Film in Which There Appear Edge Lettering, Sprocket Holes, Dirt Particles, Etc.* (Owen Land, 1966), which offers a starring role to one of cinema's most ignored performers: the "Chinagirl" that lab workers would use to check the quality of a print. Ken Jacobs's *Tom, Tom, the Piper's Son* (1969) analyzes a 1905 short of the same name by speeding up and rewinding the original footage, and by zooming in on portions of the *mise-en-scène* to such a magnified degree that details become grainy abstractions and blobs of light. The nature of projection itself is the subject of *Line Describing a Cone* (Anthony McCall, 1973), which requires an audience to stand in a gallery space and watch a projector throw a light beam that gradually (over a half-hour) changes shape into a cone.

The most important structuralist filmmaker is Hollis Frampton (1936–1984), who began his career with a series of films that explore minimalist elements. *Manual of Arms* (1966) organizes portraits of New York artists into a rigid grid structure, and *Lemon* (1969) subjects the fruit to a series of ever-shifting lighting designs. Frampton's vision expanded and deepened with *Zorns Lemma* (1970), which was strongly influenced by the animal locomotion studies of proto-filmmaker Eadweard Muybridge. The seven-film series *Hapax Legomena* (1971–1972) is Frampton's *Ulysses*, a compendium of formal innovations that, at its most accomplished—as in part 1, *Nostalgia* (1971)—is both intellectually and emotionally moving. Frampton died in 1984 at age forty-eight, having spent the last decade of his life on the unfinished epic *Magellan* (1972–1980), fragments of which (particularly *Gloria!* [1979]) function as stand-alone films.

Structuralist film was influential enough to spread to many different countries. Filmmakers such as Malcolm Le Grice and Peter Gidal congregated at the London Film Makers' Cooperative to screen their structuralist works and debate the future of the avant-garde, while in France, Rose Lowder began a series of 16mm loops

STAN BRAKHAGE
b. Kansas City, Missouri, 14 January 1933, d. 9 March 2003

The most prolific and influential experimental filmmaker in US film history, Stan Brakhage also wrote insightfully about his own films and the work of other filmmakers. The most oft-quoted passage in experimental film criticism is the opening of Brakhage's text *Metaphors on Vision* (1963): "Imagine an eye unruled by man-made laws of perspective, an eye unprejudiced by compositional logic, an eye which does not respond to the name of everything but which must know each object encountered in life through an adventure of perception." This passage explicates the major aesthetic strain in Brakhage's films: abstraction. From the beginning of his career, Brakhage combined the photographic image with marks and paint applied directly onto the filmstrip, and many of his films of the 1980s and 1990s are completely abstract, partly for financial reasons and partly because he believed in the liberating power of nonlinear, nonnarrative aesthetic experiences. Some of Brakhage's abstract "adventures in perception" are *Eye Myth* (1967), *The Text of Light* (1974), *The Dante Quartet* (1987), and *Black Ice* (1994).

Brakhage briefly attended Dartmouth College on a scholarship, but he found academia so uncongenial that he had a nervous breakdown, left school, and spent four years traveling and living in San Francisco and New York. During this period Brakhage made his earliest films, including psychodramas such as *Interim* (1952) and *Desistfilm* (1954).

While making *Anticipation of the Night* (1958), which he intended to end with footage of his suicide, he fell in love with and married Jane Collom. Stan and Jane remained married for twenty-nine years, and a major subgenre of Brakhage's work chronicles the rise and fall of this marriage, from domestic quarrels (*Wedlock House:*

An Intercourse, 1959) and the birth of children (*Window Water Baby Moving*, 1959) to Brakhage's increasing estrangement from Jane and his teenage children (*Tortured Dust*, 1984). Many critics consider Brakhage's singular achievement to be *Dog Star Man* (1962–1964), a four-part epic that uses multiple superimpositions to connect the activities of his family (then living a back-to-the-land existence in rural Colorado) to myth and the rhythms of nature.

In 1996 Brakhage was diagnosed with cancer, which might have been caused by the dyes he had used to paint on film. His last works include the live-action self-portrait *Stan's Window* (2003), and *Chinese Series* (2003), a film Brakhage made on his deathbed by using his fingernail to etch dancing white marks into black film emulsion.

RECOMMENDED VIEWING

The Wonder Ring (1955), *Reflections on Black* (1955), *Anticipation of the Night* (1958), *Window Water Baby Moving* (1959), *Mothlight* (1963), *Dog Star Man* (1962–1964), *The Act of Seeing with One's Own Eyes* (1971), *The Text of Light* (1974), *Murder Psalm* (1980), *The Loom* (1986), *Commingled Containers* (1996)

FURTHER READING

Brakhage, Stan. *Essential Brakhage: Selected Writings on Film-Making.* New York: McPherson, 2001

James, David E., ed. *Stan Brakhage: Filmmaker.* Philadelphia: Temple University Press, 2005.

Sitney, P. Adams. *Visionary Film: The American Avant-Garde, 1942–2000.* 3rd ed. New York: Oxford University Press, 2002.

"Stan Brakhage: Correspondences." *Chicago Review* 47/48, nos. 4/1 (Winter 2001–Spring 2002): 11–30.

Craig Fischer

that explored frame-by-frame transitions and their effects on audiences.

Yet the structural film movement was essentially over by the mid-1970s. Structuralist films were triumphs of formal design, but a new generation of leftist experimental artists criticized the apolitical nature of films such as *Wavelength* and *Tom, Tom, the Piper's Son*, and began to make movies with ideological content that tackled social

issues such as feminism and colonialism. Yet, reverberations of structuralist film continue into later avant-garde film. *Sink or Swim* (Su Friedrich, 1990) follows a *Zorns Lemma*–like alphabetical structure, while *Teatro Amazonas* (Sharon Lockhart, 1999) is a witty commentary on cultural colonialism and a stylish update of Standish Lawder's structuralist *Necrology* (1971), a one-shot film of people on an escalator projected backwards.

Stan Brakhage. © ZEITGEIST FILMS/COURTESY EVERETT COLLECTION. REPRODUCED BY PERMISSION.

But structuralist filmmakers realized that cinema's formal properties could do more than just tell stories, and made artworks that revealed to us that sometimes a zoom can be more than just a zoom, that it can embody nothing less than a way of seeing.

Another important wave in 1970s experimental film, roughly concurrent with structuralist film, was the rise of the "new talkies," feature-length works influenced by critical theory and the politicized art films of Jean-Luc Godard (b. 1930), Jean-Marie Straub (b. 1933), and Daniele Huillet (b. 1936). Although most experimental films are short, the feature-length experimental film has a long pedigree. During the 1950s and 1960s, as Deren and Brakhage were making their influential short films, other avant-gardists dabbled in longer, more narrative forms. Ron Rice's (1935–1964) Beat-saturated *The Flower Thief* (1960) and *The Queen of Sheba Meets the Atom Man* (1963) are feature-length showcases for actor Taylor Mead's inspired improvisations, while Warhol's 1960s films were often longer than most Hollywood films. Some, such as *Chelsea Girls* (1966), ran in first-run mainstream movie theaters.

The feature-length new talkies that emerged in the 1970s were a more specific type of avant-garde genre.

The new talkies are typified by an engagement with critical theory and a return to storytelling, albeit to deconstruct storytelling as a signifying practice. (Many new talkies are simultaneously narratives and essays on narrative.) These traits are clear in the quintessential new talkie, Laura Mulvey (b. 1941) and Peter Wollen's (b. 1938) *Riddles of the Sphinx* (1977), which tells the story of Louise, a woman who talks with coworkers about childcare and decides to move from a house to an apartment. *Sphinx*'s form owes much to Godard, but its narrative is something new: an attempt to capture the life of a woman without recourse to genre, "erotica," or the male gaze.

Other key new talkie auteurs are Yvonne Rainer (b. 1934) and Trinh T. Minh-ha (b. 1953). Rainer began her career in dance, bringing aesthetic and political radicalism to the performances she orchestrated as part of the Judson Dance Theater. Her movies such as *Film About a Woman Who . . .* (1974) and *Privilege* (1990) form a kind of spiritual autobiography, tackling various subjects as Rainer herself goes through a lifetime of experiences and observations. Shot through all these films is Rainer's belief in everyday life as a site of political struggle, showing how the personal is always political.

Trinh T. Minh-ha's own multicultural background—she has lived in France, the United States, and West Africa—informs *Reassemblage* (1982), *Naked Spaces—Living Is Round* (1985), and *Surname Viet Given Name Nam* (1989). These films renounce traditional narrative and documentary forms, and search for avant-garde ways of representing people of different societies (including Senegal, Mauritania, Burkino Faso, and Vietnam) to First World audiences. But Minh-ha's recent career reveals the difficulty of sustaining new talkie practices in today's film culture. In his seminal essay "The Two Avant-Gardes," Peter Wollen argues that the politicized Godardian art film and the formalist experimental film were the twin poles of 1960s cinematic radicalism, and that the new talkies can be understood as an attempt to bring these poles together (*Readings and Writings*, pp. 92–104). Yet, since the 1960s, art cinema has shifted decisively away from radical politics, while experimental cinema has exploded into a multiplicity of approaches, some formal in emphasis and some not.

One mutation in experimental film occurred in the late 1970s and early 1980s, when a group of New York artists made films that emulated the do-it-yourself aesthetics and catchy nihilism of early punk rock. Made in 8mm on miniscule budgets, these films rejected both Hollywood norms and the pretensions of the more formalist tendency in experimental film. Although this movement went by various names ("new cinema," "no wave cinema"), "cinema of transgression" is the most common because of its defining use in Nick Zedd's infamous "The Cinema of Transgression Manifesto" (1985), which begins with a denunciation of the "laziness known as structuralism" and the work of "profoundly undeserving non-talents like Brakhage, Snow, Frampton, Gehr, Breer, etc." and a celebration of films that directly attack "every value system known to man" (p. 40). Like most manifestoes, Zedd's "Transgression" slays the father and claims a complete break with an outmoded past. But many of the cinema of transgression films were, in essence, exhibitions of scandalous behavior, and are logical descendants of an experimental film tradition that includes Kurt Kren's (1929–1998) material action shorts of the 1960s and Vito Acconci's (b. 1940) early 1970s 8mm performance documentaries (which record Acconci plastering up his anus and crushing cockroaches on his body). One significant difference between these precursors and the cinema of transgression is venue: Kren's and Acconci's works were screened in film societies and art galleries, while the transgression films were shown mostly in New York City punk bars.

Although Zedd's manifesto was clearly an act of publicity-seeking hyperbole, the cinema of transgression delivered, throughout the 1980s, a robust wave of avant-garde filmmakers and films. In several works made between 1978 and 1981 (*Guérillère Talks* [1978], *Beauty Becomes the Beast* [1979], and *Liberty's Booty* [1980]), Vivienne Dick combined documentary interviews, melodramatic narratives, and a jittery camera style perfectly suited to low-fi 8mm. Beth and Scott B.'s *Black Box* (1978) is a stroboscopic aural assault that treats its spectators like tortured prisoners. Other important transgressors include Richard Kern, Alyce Wittenstein, Cassandra Stark, Eric Mitchell, Kembra Pfahler, James Nares, and Zedd himself, whose affinity for over-the-top parody is present in his films from *Geek Maggot Bingo* (1983), a send-up of cheesy B-movie horror, to the video spoof *The Lord of the Cockrings* (2002). Several factors, including the steady gentrification of New York City's Lower East Side and the spread of AIDS, ended the cinema of transgression. Yet the films of many contemporary avant-gardists, including Peggy Ahwesh, Jon Moritsugu, Luther Price, and Martha Colburn, bear the influence of the transgression example.

THE CONTEMPORARY SCENE

According to many critics, the experimental film world went through a period of flagging energy and diminished creativity during the 1980s. Among the reasons, according to Paul Arthur, were the skyrocketing costs of 16mm processing, cutbacks in government and private-foundation funding, and the economic and aesthetic challenges posed by video. By the 1990s, however, it was clear that the movement had undergone a resurgence. Older figures such as Brakhage, Mekas, and Jacobs remained active, and a new generation of artists, aesthetic trends, and exhibition strategies emerged.

One such trend in contemporary experimental production is the use of "outdated" formats. Sadie Benning (b. 1973), the daughter of filmmaker James Benning (b. 1942), shot ghostly autobiographical movies like *If Every Girl Had a Diary* (1990) and *It Wasn't Love* (1992) with the Pixelvision–2000, a black-and-white toy video camera that records small, blurry images on audio cassette tape. The Pixelvision camera was only available from 1987 to 1989, but the work of Sadie Benning and other filmmakers (Joe Gibbons, Michael Almereyda, Peggy Ahwesh, Eric Saks) have kept Pixelvision alive. Many avant-gardists have continued to use both regular 8mm and super-8mm, and are passionate about the aesthetic qualities of small-gauge filmmaking. Perhaps the ultimate validation of human-scale small-gauge filmmaking was the exhibition "Big as Life: An American History of 8mm Films," which exhibited small-gauge works by Conner, Brakhage, Wieland, and many others at both New York's Museum of Modern Art and the San Francisco Cinematheque from 1998 to 1999.

Museum retrospectives such as the "Big as Life" program are an important part of experimental film distribution, but the real screening innovation of the last decade were microcinemas—small theaters run by dedicated filmmakers and fans as showcases for non-mainstream work. Total Mobile Home Microcinema, the first contemporary microcinema, was established in 1993 by Rebecca Barton and David Sherman in the basement of their San Francisco apartment building, and by the late 1990s, at least a hundred had sprung up in various cities around the United States. Some of the highest-profile microcinemas include Greenwich Village's Robert Beck Memorial Cinema, begun by filmmakers Bradley Eros and Brian Frye; San Francisco's Other Cinema, curated by master collagist Craig Baldwin; and the Aurora Picture Show, Andrea Grover's microcinema, housed in a converted church in Houston. Perhaps the microcinema with the most ambitious programming was Blinding Light (1998–2003), a one-hundred-seat, six-night-a-week theater in Vancouver.

The New York Film Festival's "Views from the Avant-Garde," founded by critic Mark McEllhatten and *Film Comment* editor Gavin Smith in 1997, is an annual cross-section of the experimental film world. The continued activity of established venues such as Anthology Film Archives, Chicago Filmmakers, and the San Francisco Cinematheque, coupled with the rise of microcinemas and touring programs such as John Columbus's Black Maria Film and Video Festival and the MadCatFilm Festival, have made it somewhat easier to see experimental films, a trend pushed even further by the more recent ability to download films from Internet sites such as www.hi-beam.net.

SEE ALSO *Animation; Surrealism; Video*

FURTHER READING

Arthur, Paul. *A Line of Sight: American Avant-Garde Film Since 1965*. Minneapolis: University of Minnesota Press, 2005.

Dixon, Wheeler Winston. *The Exploding Eye: A Re-Visionary History of 1960s American Experimental Cinema*. Ithaca: State University of New York Press, 1998.

Horak, Jan-Christopher, ed. *Lovers of Cinema: The First American Film Avant-Garde, 1919–1945*. Madison: University of Wisconsin Press, 1995.

James, David E. *Allegories of Cinema: American Film in the Sixties*. Princeton, NJ: Princeton University Press, 1989.

Le Grice, Malcolm. *Abstract Film and Beyond*. Cambridge, MA: MIT Press, 1977.

MacDonald, Scott. *Cinema 16: Documents Toward a History of the Film Society*. Philadelphia: Temple University Press, 2002.

———. *A Critical Cinema: Interviews with Independent Filmmakers*. Berkeley: University of California Press, 1988.

Posner, Bruce, ed. *Unseen Cinema: Early American Avant-Garde Film, 1893–1941*. New York: Anthology Film Archives, 2001.

Rabinovitz, Lauren. *Points of Resistance: Women, Power, and Politics in the New York Avant-Garde Cinema, 1943–1971*. 2nd ed. Urbana: University of Illinois Press, 2003.

Rees, A. L. *A History of Experimental Film and Video*. London: British Film Institute, 1999.

Sitney, P. Adams, ed. *Film Culture Reader*. 2nd ed. New York: Cooper Square Publishers, 2000.

Small, Edward S. *Direct Theory: Experimental Film/Video as Major Genre*. Carbondale: Southern Illinois University Press, 1994.

Wollen, Peter. "The Two Avant-Gardes." *Readings and Writings: Semiotic Counter-Strategies*, 92–104. London: Verso, 1982.

Zedd, Nick. "The Cinema of Transgression Manifesto." *Film Threat Video Guide* 5 (1992): 40.

Craig Fischer

EXPLOITATION FILMS

Exploitation movies have been a part of the motion picture industry since its earliest days. The term "exploitation movie" initially referred to any film that required exploitation or ballyhoo over and above the usual posters, trailers, and newspaper advertising. Originally this included films on risqué topics, documentaries, and even religious films. But by the 1930s it referred specifically to low-budget movies that emphasized sex, violence, or some other form of spectacle in favor over coherent narrative.

Exploitation films grew out of a series of sex hygiene films that were made prior to and during World War I in an effort to stave the scourge of venereal diseases. Using movies as a modern educational tool to convey the dangers of the diseases and their potential treatments, movies like *Damaged Goods* (1914) drove home a moralistic message about remaining clean for family and country. Following the war several films commissioned by the government for use in training camps were released to the general public. *Fit to Win* (1919) and *The End of the Road* (1918) did not have the same level of moralizing of pre-war films, but they did include graphic clinical footage in many situations. These elements left the films open to severe cuts or outright bans by state and municipal censorship boards. In 1921 a meeting of top motion picture directors adopted a self-regulatory code, The Thirteen Points and Standards, that condemned the production of movies that were susceptible to censorship. Sex hygiene, white slavery, drug use, vice, and nudity led the list of disapproved topics. The same topics were among the list of forbidden subjects of the MPPDA's "Don'ts and Be Carefuls" when it was approved in 1927 and the Production Code when it was written in 1930.

With a collection of salacious topics off-limits to mainstream moviemakers, low-budget entrepreneurs quickly moved in to fill the gap and reap the profits. Just as the bizarre sights of the sideshow had been segregated from the big top in the circus, the subjects of exploitation films were shunted aside by the mainstream movie industry.

CLASSICAL EXPLOITATION MOVIES

From the late teens through the late 1950s classical exploitation films operated in the shadow of the classical Hollywood cinema. The men that made and distributed exploitation films were sometimes called "the Forty Thieves," and several came from carnival backgrounds. Some companies were fly-by-night outfits that produced a film or two and then disappeared. However, many individuals and companies were around for years: Samuel Cummins (1895–1967) operated as Public Welfare Pictures and Jewel Productions; Dwain Esper (1892–1982) used the Road Show Attractions name; J. D. Kendis (1886–1957) made films under the Continental and Jay Dee Kay banners; Willis Kent's (1878–1966) companies included Real Life Dramas and True Life Photoplays; and Louis Sonney's Sonney Amusement Enterprises dominated West Coast distribution.

Exploitation movies were invariably low budget—usually made for far less than the average B movie. Most exploitation films were made for under $25,000 and some for as little as $5,000. Shooting schedules were less than a week, with some films being shot in as little as two or three days. (Unlike B movies, which were used to fill out the bottom half of a double feature, exploitation films were often expected to stand on their own.) Their low budgets and accelerated shooting schedules meant that exploitation films featured stilted performances, poor photography, confusing plots, and startling gaps in continuity. On almost every level they were bad films. Many of these movies have a delirious quality, shifting between long passages of expository dialogue and confusing action. But what they lacked in narrative coherence they made up for by offering audiences moments of spectacle that could not be found in mainstream movies. That spectacle might come in the shape of scenes in a nudist camp, footage of childbirth or the effects of venereal diseases, prostitutes lounging around in their underwear, or women performing striptease dances. These scenes of spectacle often brought the creaky narrative to a grinding halt, allowing the viewers to drink in the forbidden sights. As a result of such scenes exploitation movies were always advertised for "adults only."

In addition to the forbidden sights on the screen, exhibitors were often provided with elaborate, garish lobby displays. Sex hygiene films could be accompanied by wax casts showing the process of gestation and birth or the effects of VD. Drug movies came with displays of drug paraphernalia. In many instances the films were accompanied by lectures, which were little more than excuses to pitch books on the subject of the film. For a dollar or two the audience could buy booklets with titles like "The Digest of Hygiene for Mother and Daughter." Pitchbooks provided an additional source of income to the distributor.

A small core of urban skid row grindhouses played exploitation films constantly. But the best market for these films consisted of regular theaters, in cities or small towns, that periodically took a break from Hollywood product to play a racy—and profitable—exploitation movie. The movies cloaked their suggestive stories and images in the mantle of education. Almost all exploitation films began with a square-up—a brief prefatory statement that explained the necessity of showing a particular evil in order to educate the public about it. Given the difficulty of getting information on such issues as childbirth and birth control, some of the movies did have a legitimate educational component. But they were produced primarily to make a buck. Exploitation movies were often available in "hot" and "cold" versions to accommodate local censorship or taste, and to extend the potential of pocketing that buck. And if audiences did not get the spectacle that they had been led to believe they would see from the lurid advertising, a roadshowman could always throw on a "square-up reel" of nudist camp footage or a striptease dance to sate the crowd.

Because only a handful of prints of any film circulated around the country at any one time, many classical exploitation films were in release for decades. It was a common practice to re-title a film to extend its life on the road; some movies were known by as many as five or six titles over time. Among the perennial hits on the exploitation circuit were sex hygiene movies such as *The Road to Ruin* (1934) and *Damaged Goods* (1937); drug movies like *Marihuana* (1936), *The Pace That Kills* (1935), and *She Shoulda Said No* (1949); vice films such as *Gambling with Souls* (1936) and *Slaves in Bondage* (1937); nudist movies like *Elysia, the Valley of the Nude* (1933) and *The Unashamed* (1938); and exotic movies (often featuring nearly naked natives) such as *Virgins of Bali* (1932) or *Jaws of the Jungle* (1936).

The most successful exploitation film of the classical era was *Mom and Dad* (1944). Producer Kroger Babb (1906–1980) had toured with earlier sex hygiene films and in 1944 decided to make a more up-to-date film. The story of a high school girl who discovers that she is "in trouble," *Mom and Dad* included films within it that showed childbirth, a Caesarian operation, and venereal diseases and their treatment. Babb sold the film aggressively and at one point after World War II he had more than twenty units on the road with the film, each with its own "Elliott Forbes," an "eminent hygiene commentator" who provided the lecture and book pitch. Millions of men, women, and teenagers saw *Mom and Dad* and it soon had competition from several direct imitations: *The Story of Bob and Sally* (1948), *Because of Eve* (1948), and *Street Corner* (1948). Eventually the owners of the four films joined together in a consortium to distribute the movies in a way that minimized direct conflict. *Mom and Dad* was still playing drive-in dates into the 1970s and some estimates have placed its total gross over the years at $100 million. But as the 1950s progressed, the Production Code was relaxed and many of the old topics that had been grist for exploitation movies—drug use, unwed motherhood—were folded back into the list of acceptable subjects for Hollywood films.

THE EXPLOITATION EXPLOSION

The post–World War II years saw the continued production and rerelease of classical exploitation films. But other types of exploitation movies were on the horizon. Following on the heels of the Supreme Court's *Paramount* decision (1948) and declining output from the majors, American theaters were forced into bitter competition for product during the 1950s. Hungry theater owners had to look beyond the majors for movies to light up their screens. James H. Nicholson (1916–1972) and Samuel Z. Arkoff (1918–2001) founded American Releasing Corporation in 1954, soon changed to American International Pictures (AIP). AIP specialized in making cheap genre pictures geared toward the growing youth market and often developed a colorful title and

ROGER CORMAN
b. Roger William Corman, Detroit, Michigan, 5 April 1926

Roger Corman has been a major force in exploitation filmmaking for half a century. His career spans an era from the earliest days of American International Pictures (AIP) in the mid-1950s through the exploitation golden age to the rise of home video.

While in his teens Corman moved with his family to Los Angeles, where he developed an interest in the motion picture industry. Following a stint in the Navy, he completed his engineering degree at Stanford, then broke into the film business by selling a script. He soon signed a three-picture deal with the newly formed AIP. Producing and directing all his films, Corman worked in a variety of genres, although his science fiction films are the most fondly remembered. Some of those films, such as *Attack of Crab Monsters* (1957), *Not of This Earth* (1957), and *X: The Man with X-Ray Eyes* (1963), feature genuinely chilling moments despite their low budgets. *The Little Shop of Horrors* (1960), a horror-comedy about a ravenous plant, developed a cult following because of its quirky humor and legendary status as a film shot in just two days. During that same year Corman and AIP initiated a series of bigger-budget, widescreen, color adaptations of the works of Edgar Allan Poe, many featuring Vincent Price. *House of Usher* (1960), *The Pit and the Pendulum* (1961), and *The Masque of the Red Death* (1964) established him as a director of considerable style. Some critics have ascribed an apocalyptic vision to Corman, and many of his films he directed begin or end with some sort of cataclysmic event.

Corman continued to look to hot-button issues to exploit, including integration in the South with *The Intruder* (1962), one of his few financial failures. For *The Wild Angels* (1966) he worked with members of The Hell's Angels, and prior to his film about the drug culture, *The Trip* (1967), Corman experimented with LSD. Both films initiated long-lived exploitation cycles.

In 1970 Corman broke with AIP to form New World Pictures. Its first effort, *The Student Nurses* (1970), established the company formula: R-rated nudity and sex, action, some laughs, and a slightly left-of-center political stance. New World's brand of exploitation films became drive-in staples for more than a decade, during which Corman discovered, or gave a major boost to, a number of filmmakers such as James Cameron, Joe Dante, Jonathan Demme, Ron Howard, Gale Ann Hurd, and Martin Scorsese. In an effort to diversify, New World also distributed several European art films, including works by Federico Fellini and Ingmar Bergman.

Corman sold New World in 1983 and formed Concorde-New Horizons. As theaters increasingly booked big-budget blockbusters, Corman has concentrated on making exploitation movies—many remakes of his earlier hits—for cable television and the direct-to-video market.

RECOMMENDED VIEWING

Not of This Earth (1957), *Teenage Doll* (1957), *House of Usher* (1960), *The Little Shop of Horrors* (1960), *The Intruder* (1962), *The Wild Angels* (1966), *The Trip* (1967)

FURTHER READING

Corman, Roger, with Jim Jerome. *How I Made a Hundred Movies in Hollywood and Never Lost a Dime*. New York: Random House, 1990.

Frank, Alan. *The Films of Roger Corman: "Shooting My Way Out of Trouble."* New York: Batsford, 1998.

Gray, Beverly. *Roger Corman: An Unauthorized Biography of the Godfather of Indie Filmmaking*. Los Angeles: Renaissance Books, 2000.

McGee, Mark Thomas. *Roger Corman: The Best of the Cheap Acts*. Jefferson, NC: McFarland, 1988.

Morris, Gary. *Roger Corman*. Boston: Twayne, 1985.

Will, David, and Paul Willeman, eds. *Roger Corman*. Edinburgh, UK: Edinburgh Film Festival, 1970.

Eric Schaefer

eye-catching advertising for a film long before a script was written. AIP offered favorable terms to exhibitors, and many theater owners found that the prepackaged AIP double bills brought in more money than major studio releases. Working with producers like Roger Corman (b. 1926) and Herman Cohen (1925–2002), AIP released dozens of low-budget films with titles like *Day the World Ended* (1956), *I Was a Teenage Werewolf* (1957), *Dragstrip Girl* (1957), *Reform School Girl* (1957), and *High School Hell Cats* (1958). The term exploitation

Roger Corman with machine gun on the set of **Bloody Mama** *(1970).* EVERETT COLLECTION. REPRODUCED BY PERMISSION.

film was expanded to encompass these "teenpics" and virtually any ultra-low-budget movie. Throughout the 1960s AIP was always on the cutting edge of exploitation: *The Wild Angels* (1966) initiated a long string of nihilistic biker films and movies such as *Riot on Sunset Strip* (1967), *The Trip* (1967), and *Psych-Out* (1968) that explored the blossoming counterculture.

Budget and content were not the only markers of what constituted an exploitation movie. In the late 1950s former B-movie director William Castle (1914–1977) produced a series of fairly conventional chillers that graduated to exploitation status through their use of elaborate exploitation gimmicks to secure an audience. *Macabre* (1958) promised to insure the lives of all ticket buyers for $1,000 against death by fright. *The House on Haunted Hill* (1959) featured "Emergo" (a plastic skeleton that swung out over the audience at an appointed time during the film). And in what was perhaps Castle's most auda-

cious gimmick, *The Tingler* (1959) was presented in "Percepto," with some seats in theaters wired to give select audience members a mild electric shock.

Other theaters hungry for product turned to art films—foreign films sold as a highbrow alternative to Hollywood fare. But many of these films also approached sex and nudity in a franker fashion than mainstream movies. The term "art film" became synonymous with nudity for a large segment of American audiences. One film was most responsible for cementing this equivalence in the minds of the public—*Et Dieu . . . créa la femme* (*And God Created Woman*, 1956) by Roger Vadim (1928–2000). The film, with its nude shots of French sex kitten Brigitte Bardot (b. 1934), played in both art houses and the existing exploitation theaters. Films imported by Radley Metzger's (b. 1929) Audubon in the early 1960s, such as *Les Collégiennes* (*The Twilight Girls*, 1957) and *Nuit la plus longue* (*Sexus*, 1964), capitalized on a similar dual market. While they had a patina of art films as a result of their foreign—usually French—origin, they also included racy inserts, filmed by Metzger in New York, that made them marketable as sex exploitation, or sexploitation as it came to be known, as well.

American-made films capitalized on this hunger for racy fare by continuing a tradition of adults-only movies. With the first generation of exploitation producers retiring or dying, new filmmakers moved in to take their place with movies that approached sex in a more direct fashion and without pretense to education. In 1959 cheesecake photographer Russ Meyer (1922–2004) made *The Immoral Mr. Teas*. The film, about a deliveryman who can see through women's clothes, spawned dozens of so-called nudie-cuties—a filmic equivalent to *Playboy* magazine. Although the nudity in the films was only above the waist and from the rear, films such as *The Adventures of Lucky Pierre* (1961), *Mr. Peter's Pets* (1962), and *Tonight for Sure* (1962)—directed by a young Francis Ford Coppola (b. 1939)—were extremely popular with their predominantly male clientele.

Sexploitation films were soon pushing into new territory with a series of black-and-white psychosexual dramas. Some, such as *The Defilers* (1965), were similar to the lurid paperbacks that crowded the shelves of bus stations. Others, like *Sin in the Suburbs* (1964), directed by the prolific Joe Sarno (b. 1921), made a more sincere effort to blend drama with sex. Hundreds of sexploitation movies were made or imported over the ensuing decade with companies such as AFD (American Film Distributing Corp.), International, Cambist, Distribpix, and Mitam releasing dozens of films. Several distinct subgenres developed. Among the most popular were those about bored housewives and sexually frustrated commuters, and exposés about changing morals and sexual practices, including *The Sexploiters* (1965), *Moonlighting Wives* (1966), and *The Commuter Game* (1969). Some films featured heavy doses of sadomasochism, like the series about the sadistic Olga, initiated with *White Slaves of Chinatown* (1964). Other movies operated as thrillers about the dangers of the urban environment such as *Aroused* (1966) and *To Turn a Trick* (1967). Rural or hillbilly movies such as *Country Cuzzins* (1970), *Sassy Sue* (1972), and *The Pigkeeper's Daughter* (1972) were popular, as were films set on college campuses like *Campus Swingers* (1972). By the late 1960s some exploitation movies, notably Meyer's *Vixen* (1968) and several of Metzger's films, were achieving play dates in showcase cinemas in major cities.

In 1963, successful nudie producer David F. Friedman (b. 1923) and director Herschell Gordon Lewis (b. 1926) cast about for a genre in which they

would have less competition. They settled on gore. *Blood Feast* (1963) was a grand guignol farce about a cannibalistic caterer in Florida who disembowels his victims and lops off their limbs. The Eastmancolor effects seemed remarkably realistic at the time and moviegoers challenged themselves and their stomachs to sit through the film. Although gore had occasionally been a form of spectacle in classical exploitation films, the unblinking violence of *Blood Feast* elevated the gore film to a whole new subgenre of exploitation, populated by machete-wielding maniacs, bloodthirsty butchers, and flesh-eating zombies. Around the same time the Italian-produced *Mondo Cane* (1962) was released. The "shockumentary" combined real and staged footage of bizarre, violent, and erotic behavior in the human and animal worlds. It was followed by a parade of other "mondo movies" that blurred the line between authenticity and fakery.

In the climate of auteurism of the 1960s and early 1970s several sexploitation filmmakers were singled out for their distinctive styles. Topping the list was Meyer, whose sharp cinematography and rapid-fire editing made his tales of amply proportioned yet sexually frustrated women and their square-jawed, dimwitted men instantly recognizable. Metzger's films were slick, languid exercises in European eroticism, exemplified by *Carmen, Baby* (1967) and *Camille 2000* (1969). Companies often developed distinct niches. Friedman's Entertainment Ventures turned out amusingly leering genre send-ups: *Space Thing* (1968) lampooned science fiction, *Thar She Blows* (1969) played with sea story conventions, *Trader Hornee* (1970) roasted the jungle adventure. Robert Cresse's (1936–1998) Olympic International was known for making and distributing films that focused on sadism such as *Love Camp 7* (1968) and *Hot Spur* (1968). More recently other filmmakers have received attention, including Michael and Roberta Findlay, who made a series of grim, gritty films that fetishized torture and degradation. Andy Milligan's (1929–1991) movies, such as *Vapors* (1965), *The Degenerates* (1967), and *Fleshpot on 42nd Street* (1972), became an outlet for his personal demons. And Doris Wishman (1920–2002) is recognized for her films like *Bad Girls Go to Hell* (1965) and *Double Agent 73* (1974), which feature her quirky *mise-en-scène* that concentrates as much on set décor, shoes, and pigeons strutting in the park as it does on characters.

Although sexploitation films saw some decline in business as hard-core pornographic features began to achieve public exhibition in 1970, other types of exploitation movies continued to thrive. In 1970 Corman formed New World Pictures, which produced and distributed a variety of exploitation films, often featuring the adventures, sexual and otherwise, of assertive career women, such as *Private Duty Nurses* (1971), *The Student Teachers* (1973), and *Cover Girl Models* (1975). Women in prison

Roger Corman's **The Trip** *(1967) exploited the period's drug culture.* EVERETT COLLECTION. REPRODUCED BY PERMISSION.

films became another staple at New World with *The Big Doll House* (1971), *The Big Bird Cage* (1972), and *Caged Heat* (1974), directed by Jonathan Demme (b. 1944). Crown International, Dimension, Group 1, Hemisphere Pictures, Independent International, Monarch, and a long list of other companies cranked out similar films that combined nudity, sexual situations, violence, and some laughs for drive-ins around the country.

Among the theaters most consistently in need of product were inner-city movie houses. In 1971 *Sweet Sweetback's Baad Asssss Song* by Melvin Van Peebles (b. 1932) launched the "blaxploitation" cycle. Most of the films featured black characters, usually in an urban environment, battling for independence, against injustices, or for a good score—and always with a hefty dose of violence and skin. Although the major studios contributed films like *Shaft* (1971) and *Superfly* (1972), it was AIP, New World, and other exploitation companies that milked the cycle with *Slaughter* (1972), *Blacula* (1972),

The Mack (1973), *Hell Up in Harlem* (1973), and *Black Mama, White Mama* (1972), among others. Among the most popular films were those staring the beautiful but tough Pam Grier, including *Coffy* (1973), *Foxy Brown* (1974), and *Friday Foster* (1975).

EXPLOITATION IN THE VIDEO ERA

Exploitation films had always found success in the aisles of struggling theaters. By the 1980s the marginal exhibition sites that had sustained exploitation movies were disappearing. Crumbling inner-city movie palaces gave way to urban renewal projects. Neighborhood theaters were bulldozed for parking lots and acres of suburban drive-ins were converted to shopping malls as the number of drive-ins in the US dropped from more than 3,000 in 1980 to fewer than 1,000 in 1990. Exploitation movies were less desirable in a new era of saturation bookings, national advertising campaigns, and blockbuster films. However, they have not entirely disappeared.

Lloyd Kaufman and Michael Herz's Troma, Fred Olen Ray's American Independent Productions, and Corman's Corcorde-New Horizons initially concentrated on theatrical releases. But by the late 1980s video and cable television proved to be greener pastures and theatrical releases became token efforts. Full Moon Entertainment, Tempe Entertainment, Seduction Cinema, and other companies were formed specifically to make films for the direct-to-video market. Most of these companies depended on the loyalty of the fans of low-budget genre films, whether horror, science fiction, splatter, or erotic thrillers. Fans have gotten into the act as well, picking up cameras and making their own films, hawked in the pages of fanzines, at conventions, and on the Internet. Other entrepreneurs, who scour old film depots and vaults, have released hundreds of old exploitation movies to new generations on videotape and DVD. It would appear that as long as audiences will search for a cheap thrill, there will be exploitation movies available to satisfy their demand.

SEE ALSO *Art Cinema; B Movies; Exhibition; Pornography; Publicity and Promotion*

FURTHER READING

Arkoff, Sam, with Richard Trubo. *Flying Through Hollywood by the Seat of My Pants: From the Man Who Brought You I Was a Teenage Werewolf and Muscle Beach Party*. Secaucus, NJ: Carol Publishing, 1992.

Frasier, David K. *Russ Meyer—The Life and Films: A Biography and a Comprehensive, Illustrated, and Annotated Filmography and Bibliography*. Jefferson, NC: McFarland, 1990.

Friedman, David F., with Don De Nevi. *A Youth in Babylon: Confessions of a Trash-Film King*. Buffalo, NY: Prometheus Books, 1990.

McDonough, Jimmy. *The Ghastly One: The Sex-Gore Netherworld of Filmmaker Andy Milligan*. Chicago: A Cappella Books, 2001.

Muller, Eddie, and Daniel Faris, *Grindhouse: The Forbidden World of "Adults Only" Cinema*. New York: St. Martin's Griffin, 1996.

Ray, Fred Olen. *The New Poverty Row: Independent Filmmakers as Distributors*. Jefferson, NC: McFarland, 1991.

Schaefer, Eric. *Bold! Daring! Shocking! True!: A History of Exploitation Films, 1919–1959*. Durham, NC: Duke University Press, 1999.

Turan, Kenneth, and Stephen F. Zito, *Sinema: American Pornographic Films and the People Who Make Them*. New York: Praeger, 1974.

Vale, V., and Andrea Juno, eds. *Incredibly Strange Films*. San Francisco: RE/Search Publications, 1986.

Eric Schaefer

EXPRESSIONISM

—■—

The term *expressionism* has been abused by previous generations of film scholars to such a point that the word has become virtually meaningless. Expressionism in its most narrowly defined meaning has referred to a specific group of six or seven modernist art films produced in Weimar Germany between 1920 and 1924, while in its broadest sense it has been utilized as a catchall term to define any film or style in the history of cinema opposed to realism or attempting to convey strong emotions. Between these extremes, expressionism has connoted all of German cinema in the 1920s, and has been invoked in connection with American horror films produced by Universal Studios in the 1930s and American film noir in the 1940s. Most problematically, its usage has often failed to specify whether its referent is a film movement, an ideology, a film style, or a film design (strictly speaking, art direction). Both the legitimate and some of the less credible usages of the term and their origins are examined here.

GERMAN EXPRESSIONISM

According to Rudolf Kurtz (1884–1960), one of the earliest historical commentators on the movement called expressionism, the semantic instability of *Expressionismus* was already inherent in its first usage by a group of visual artists in imperial Germany prior to World War I. Those painters, associated with the German modern art groups Der blaue Reiter ("the Blue Rider," Munich) and Die Brücke ("the Bridge," Berlin/Dresden), coined the term in opposition to French impressionism, rejecting the notion of the artist as a receptacle for impressions of the moment. The Bridge (1905–1913) included painters such as Emil Nolde (1867–1956), Ernst Kirchner (1880–

1938), and Erich Heckel (1883–1944), while the Blue Rider (1911–1914) was associated with Alexei von Jawlensky (1864–1941), Wassily Kandinsky (1866–1944), Gabrielle Münter (1877–1962), Franz Marc (1880–1916), and Paul Klee (1879–1940). They favored the concept of the artist as an active creator through will power, as a producer of visual images reflecting interior states rather than surface reality. In contrast to the pale pastels of impressionism, the expressionists favored broad brush strokes and rich, dense hues, which were applied without regard to the natural look of the object depicted. Thus, the reproduction of a photographic impression of reality was rejected, supplanted by the artist's subjective vision of the world. Kurtz allied German art expressionism with both the cubism of Pablo Picasso (1881–1973) and the Russian constructivist art of Aleksandr Archipenko (1887–1964) and Kasimir Malevich (1878–1935), while seeing the wildly saturated portraits of Vincent van Gogh (1853–1890) and the South Sea paintings of Paul Gauguin (1848–1903) as precursors. With the painter George Grosz (1893–1959), expressionism also took on an overt political, even revolutionary tone, attacking postwar social conditions and calculated to shock bourgeois sensibilities mired in "archaic" forms of realism. In other words, expressionism began more as an attitude and ideology than as a style, since strong vibrant color and an interest in painting as an artistic medium rather than as a window onto the world was perhaps the only common denominator of these artists.

This fact becomes clear when looking at German expressionist literature, where the term became a revolutionary cry for poets and dramatists such as Georg Kaiser (1878–1945), Ernst Toller (1893–1939), Georg Trakl

EMIL JANNINGS
*b. Theodor Friedrich Emil Janenz, Rorschach, Switzerland, 23 July 1884,
d. 2 January 1950*

One of the most famous German film actors, Emil Jannings is the one most closely associated with German expressionist acting, although he was never connected to expressionist theater. He became a household name in Hollywood in the late 1920s, and was a key figure in the Nazi cinema.

Jannings's breakthrough role was in Ernst Lubitsch's *Madame Dubarry* (1919), in which he played Pola Negri's doomed lover, Louis XV. Overweight and hardly an image of beauty, Jannings nevertheless conveyed a strong sexuality and *joie de vivre*, making him an international star when the film became a hit in the United States as *Passion* in 1920. In the following years Jannings appeared in such classics as *Anna Boleyn* (1920), *Danton* (1921), *Peter der Grosse* (*Peter the Great*, 1922), and Paul Leni's *Das Wachsfigurenkabinett* (*Waxworks*, 1923). In these and other films he was typecast in the role of a despotic ruler, his large girth and coarse features underlining his usually horrific actions. With a strong tendency to chew up the scenery, Jannings finest hour probably was as Mephisto in F. W. Murnau's *Faust* (1926), which, along with his signature role as the demoted hotel doorman in Murnau's *Der Letzte Mann* (*The Last Laugh*, 1924), solidified his reputation as an actor forever associated with German expressionism. And while his performances in these films displayed the expressionist tendency toward stylized gesture and facial expressions, his role as the jealous acrobat in *Varieté* (*Variety*, 1925) was much more realistic. As in *Last Laugh*, Jannings here made himself a sympathetic character verging on the tragic.

Jannings subsequently accepted an invitation by Paramount to go to Hollywood, where he played similarly tragic characters in *The Way of All Flesh* (1927) and *The Last Command* (1928), winning the first Oscar® for best actor in both roles. Jannings then returned to Berlin, where he starred in *Der Blaue Engel* (*The Blue Angel*, 1930), but Marlene Dietrich stole the show, sending his career into eclipse.

He made his comeback in the Nazified German film industry after 1933 with the role of Wilhelm the Elector (Frederick the Great's father) in *Alte und der junge König* (*The Making of a King*, 1935). Thereafter, he regularly played great men as paradigmatic *führer* figures in a series of biopics with strong propagandistic content: *Der Herrscher* (The Ruler, 1937), *Robert Koch* (1939), *Ohm Krüger* (1941), and especially as Bismark in *Die Entlassung* (*The Dismissal*, 1942). He also repeated a role he had performed countless times onstage, that of the village judge in *Der zerbrochene Krug* (*The Broken Jug*, 1937). His last film remained uncompleted in January 1945.

RECOMMENDED VIEWING
Madame Dubarry (*Passion*, 1920), *Der Letzte Mann* (*The Last Laugh*, 1924), *Faust* (1926), *Der Blaue Engel* (*The Blue Angel*, 1930), *Der zerbrochene Krug* (*The Broken Jug*, 1937)

FURTHER READING
Dreyer, Carl. "Sur un film de Jannings," and "Du jeu de l'acteur." *Cahiers du Cinéma* (January 1962).

Truscott, Harold. "Emil Jannings—A Personal View." *Silent Picture* 8 (1970): 5–26.

Jan-Christopher Horak

(1887–1914), and Gottfried Benn (1886–1956). Produced as a reaction to the insanity of World War I and the realist aesthetic of nineteenth-century naturalism, the poetry of August Stramm (1874–1915), for example, was considered by traditionalists to be the stammering of an insane person, while Kaiser's dramas were perceived to be part and parcel to a generational revolt against the old order. Kasimir Edschmid may have best summarized the attitude of the expressionist artist when he wrote: "He doesn't see, he looks. He doesn't describe, he experiences. He doesn't reproduce, he shapes. He doesn't take, he searches. No more chains of facts: factories, houses, illnesses, whores, screaming and hunger. Now we have visions of those things" (quoted in Kurtz, p. 17).

German expressionist writers and painters found common ground in the theater, creating dramatic spaces through abstract set designs that attempted neither to reproduce the real world nor to function as mirrors of psychological states; the plays themselves were filled with angry young men and vitriolic attacks on middle-class sensibilities. It was not, as some have argued, German theatrical impresario Max Reinhardt (1873–1943) who

Emil Jannings in* The Patriot *(Ernst Lubitsch, 1928).
EVERETT COLLECTION. REPRODUCED BY PERMISSION.

Aktiengesellschaft [Ufa], Germany's largest film combine), *Caligari* featured painted sets by Hermann Warm and Walter Röhrig that opposed the general trend toward film realism by highlighting their artificiality, becoming visual equivalents of the twisted and tortured interior states of the mad Dr. Caligari (Emil Jannings) and his puppet, the somnambulist Cesare (Conrad Veidt). While lighting is a key formal element in most definitions of expressionism, *Caligari*, like subsequent expressionist films, relied on flat lighting to capture the highlights and shadows *painted* directly on the sets. Carl Mayer (1894–1944) and Hans Janowitz (1890–1954), the film's scriptwriters, later claimed that the film's revolutionary message was diluted by the film's producers, who decided to present the frame story in a realistic set, thus transforming the narrative vision of a society in chaos to the solitary ranting of a madman. In fact, though, the film's use of expressionist elements is consistent, down to the intertitles and even the advertising campaign, while the film's production history remains as convoluted as the various participants taking credit for its success. In any case, the film was an immediate box-office hit, both in Germany, where it opened in February 1920, and internationally. The French even coined the term *caligarisme* to denote expressionism, while American filmmakers and critics who saw the film after it opened in the United States in March 1921 enthusiastically embraced the notion that cinema could indeed be a high art and not just a base form of entertainment for the masses.

While no one associated with German expressionist art or theater had been directly involved in the making of *Caligari,* the artists who produced another film, *Von morgens bis Mitternacht* (*From Morn to Midnight*, 1920), were conscious of bringing an expressionist aesthetic to the cinema. The film's director, Karl Heinz Martin (1886–1948), the set designer, Robert Neppach (b. 1890), and the writer, Georg Kaiser, whose play was adapted, all had worked at Die Tribüne, and many critics consider their film to be the most consistently expressionist of the films of the period. In the film, a lowly bank teller embezzles funds after seeing a beautiful woman, his flight from bourgeois existence ending in suicide. But *Von morgens bis Mitternacht* apparently never opened in Germany, despite the efforts of a distributor to sell it through trade advertisements; it only became widely known after a print was discovered in Tokyo in the 1960s. Like *Caligari,* Martin's film featured highly stylized, hand-painted sets that seemingly collapsed space; light painted on the props and costumes; and expressionistic acting that bordered on the seemingly catatonic.

led the way, but rather theatre director Karlheinz Martin (1886–1948) at Die Tribüne, whose stagings of Ernst Toller's "Transfiguration" (1919) and Walter Hasenclever's "The Decision" (1919) scandalized and revolutionized Weimar theater. Not only were abstract sets utilized, created out of painted murals and light, but also the acting was highly stylized, with actors' bodies contorted to complement the wild diagonals of the stage and their voices eschewing normal patterns of speech. These stagings were also a product of material shortages due to the war and its aftermath, and audiences experienced color, light, and sound in new ways that mirrored the alienation of the postwar generation. Bertolt Brecht's (1898–1956) early play *Baal* (1918), whose *Sturm and Drang* hero is fiercely antibourgeois, is typical of how Weimar theater mirrored the political chaos in the streets of Berlin, where revolutions and counterrevolutions passed with amazing rapidity.

Das Kabinett des Dr. Caligari (*The Cabinet of Dr. Caligari*, 1920) remains the signature work of German film expressionism. Produced at the Decla Studios in Berlin by Erich Pommer (1889–1966) (who soon after became production head at Universum Film

Meanwhile, Pommer, Carl Mayer, and Robert Wiene followed up *Caligari* with another film in the expressionist style, *Genuine* (1920), featuring fancifully painted sets and outrageous costumes by the well-known

Das Kabinett des Dr. Caligari (The Cabinet of Dr. Caligari, *1920) is the signature work of German expressionism.*
EVERETT COLLECTION. REPRODUCED BY PERMISSION.

expressionist artist Cesar Klein (1876–1954). While *Caligari*'s narrative was relatively linear, *Genuine* focused on the machinations of a man-eating, blood-drinking vamp (Fern Andra) who is held captive by a mysterious lord. While Andra's hysterical acting style mirrored the impenetrable narrative, the film's emotional core was the depiction of unbridled sexual desire.

Karl Heinz Martin also directed *Das Haus zum Mond* (The House at the Moon, 1921), with a script by the expressionist writer Rudolf Leonhardt (1889–1953) and sets by Neppach. Unfortunately, the film is now lost, making any visual analysis impossible. *Brandherd* (*Torgus*, 1921) also featured sets by Neppach and a script by Carl Mayer, but the visual design involved three-dimensional sets that only featured expressionist highlights. With its moralistic, melodramatic narrative, Robert Wiene's (1873–1938) adaptation of *Crime and Punishment*, *Raskolnikow* (1923), on the other hand, was as much a product of its all Russian-exile crew as it was a manifestation of expressionism. White Russians also financed *Das Wachsfigurenkabinett* (*Waxworks*, 1924) by Paul Leni (1885–1929), which employed stylized three-dimensional sets, and could be identified as expressionist through its acting style, some of its set pieces, and its lighting. The sets themselves hark back to *Der Golem* (*The Golem*, 1915) and other German Gothic films. In any case, except for *Caligari* and *Waxworks*, none of these films entered the canon of German expressionist cinema, and hardly influenced German national cinema in the 1920s. Expressionism became conflated with what are now considered the classics of German silent cinema largely through the writings of two seminal historians, Lotte Eisner and Siegfried Kracauer.

EXPRESSIONISM AND FILM HISTORY

As early as 1930 Paul Rotha was conflating expressionist cinema with German national cinema, but the responsibility

FRITZ LANG
b. Vienna, Austria, 5 December 1890, d. 2 August 1976

Considered one of the greatest directors of the classical German and Hollywood cinemas, Fritz Lang was equally at home in large-scale studio epics and dark, brooding melodramas. Throughout his career he was known for his intense visual style, which wed expressionist lighting techniques with highly geometric compositions to articulate a fatalistic, entrapping world.

After beginning as a scriptwriter in 1917, Lang attained a huge commercial success directing *Die Spinnen* (*The Spiders*) in 1920. That same year he married Thea von Harbou, his scriptwriter on all his subsequent German films, including *Der Müde Tod* (*Between Worlds*, 1921), *Dr. Mabuse, der Spieler* (*Dr. Mabuse, the Gambler*, 1923), *Die Nibelungen* (1924), and *Metropolis* (1927). Created at the giant Neubabelsberg Studios of Universum Film Aktiengesellschaft (Ufa), these films are characterized by German mysticism, monumental sets and costumes, and stylized compositions. With *M* (1931), Lang immediately set new standards for the sound film, in particular through his montages of sound and image. That film starred Peter Lorre as a "sympathetic" child murderer, introducing darker themes that would become more prevalent in his American work.

Lang was forced into exile by the Nazis, ending up in Hollywood in June 1934. His first American film was *Fury* (1936), which featured Spencer Tracy as a man falsely accused of murder and almost lynched by a mob. Equally downbeat, *You Only Live Once* (1937) was a reworking of the Bonnie and Clyde story. Without a studio contract, Lang worked only occasionally in the next years. With four anti-Nazi films, including *Hangmen Also Die!* (1943) and *Ministry of Fear* (1944), Lang attempted to educate the public about fascism. Both films are suffused with a film noir atmosphere, as are *Woman in the Window* (1944) and *Scarlet Street* (1945). Lang was soon forced to take on a variety of low-budget projects, and was temporarily blacklisted during the McCarthy era due to his association with writer Bertolt Brecht, a known Communist sympathizer. In 1957 Lang returned to Germany to direct the two-part *Das indische Grabmal* (*Indian Tomb*, 1958), and *Die tausend Augen des Dr. Mabuse* (*The Thousand Eyes of Dr. Mabuse*, 1960). In 1963 he appeared as a disenchanted Hollywood film director in Jean-Luc Godard's *Le Mépris* (*Contempt*, 1963).

While for decades critics considered Lang to have gone into decline after his great German films, auteurist and more recent feminist readings have recuperated his American work. Reevaluating his contributions to both the anti-Nazi film cycle and to film noir, critics see Lang's Hollywood films in terms of his dark vision of the American bourgeoisie: Edward G. Robinson's characters in *Window* and *Scarlet Street*, for example, are middle-class citizens who commit or cover up murder for a femme fatale. Stylistically, Lang's films wed German expressionism to American genre cinema, finding film noir a congenial form for the expression of his dark, determinist vision.

RECOMMENDED VIEWING
Der Müde Tod (*Between Worlds*, 1921), *Die Nibelungen* (1924), *Metropolis* (1927), *M* (1931), *Fury* (1936), *Hangmen Also Die!* (1943), *Woman in the Window* (1944), *Scarlet Street* (1945), *The Big Heat* (1953)

FURTHER READING
Bogdanovich, Peter. *Fritz Lang in America*. New York: Praeger, 1969.

Grant, Barry Keith, ed. *Fritz Lang Interviews*. Jackson: University Press of Mississippi, 2003.

Gunning, Tom. *The Films of Fritz Lang: Allegories of Vision and Modernity*. London: British Film Institute, 2000.

Jenkins, Stephen, ed. *Fritz Lang: The Image and the Look*. London: British Film Institute, 1981.

McGilligan, Patrick. *Fritz Lang: The Nature of the Beast*. New York: St. Martin's, 1997.

Jan-Christopher Horak

for the semantic expansion of the term rests primarily with the influential German film historians Kracauer and Eisner. Both writers discuss only a handful of films while ignoring the thousands of comedies and other genre films produced in Berlin in the 1920s. Ironically, what for Kurtz had still been a revolutionary and liberating aesthetic form is inverted in their histories, turning expressionism into a prescient manifestation of German fascism and romantic doom—visual evidence for the German predilection toward Nazism and mass murder.

Fritz Lang during production of* Metropolis *(1927).
EVERETT COLLECTION. REPRODUCED BY PERMISSION.

Kracauer, a former film critic in Weimar Germany, wrote his book *From Caligari to Hitler* (1947) while in exile in New York during and immediately after World War II, primarily to explain to Americans why the German nation sank into barbarism. Kracauer almost completely ignores German expressionism's stylistic features, focusing instead on narrative threads and typologies that buttress his case that the cinema of the Weimar Republic gave evidence of the deluge to come by visualizing German psychology, specifically a supposed national character trait that embraced authoritarian figures. Critics have noted that Kracauer's analyses are highly selective and teleological, and the book leaves the impression that the expressionism of *Caligari* was inherent in all subsequent German cinema.

Eisner's *The Haunted Screen*, first published in France in 1952, was likewise the work of a German Jewish film critic in exile, although, unlike Kracauer, Eisner's purpose was less ideological than art historical. Attempting to analyze the stylistic uniqueness of German art cinema in the 1920s while acknowledging its precedents in German romanticism, Eisner discusses two essentially unrelated phenomena: the influence of theater impresario Max Reinhardt and film expressionism. In fact, Reinhardt's utilization of chiaroscuro (interplay of

light and shadow) and *Kammerspiel* (an intimate stage, involving only a few characters and sparse sets) *mise-en-scène* had little to do with German expressionism, as Eisner herself admitted in a series of articles published in the wake of her book's reception. Yet her description of formal lighting techniques and *mise-en-scène* in the films of Fritz Lang (1890–1976) and F. W. Murnau (1888–1931) have been associated with German expressionism ever since, as have the stylized acting common to much German silent cinema.

By the dawn of Anglo-American film studies, then, expressionism and German Weimar cinema had become so conceptually intertwined that the terms were virtually interchangeable. Lang's *Der Müde Tod* (*Between Worlds*, 1921) and *Metropolis* (1927), G.W. Pabst's (1885–1967) *Die Freudlose Gasse* (*The Joyless Street*, 1925) and *Die 3groschenoper* (*The Threepenny Opera*, 1931), Ernst Lubitsch's (1892–1947) *Die Bergkatze* (*The Wildcat*, 1921), E.A. Dupont's (1891–1956) *Varieté* (*Variety*, 1925), and numerous other German films were subsumed under the term *German expressionist cinema*, which itself became a stylistic signpost in the film historical canon, situated somewhere between D.W. Griffith's American cinema of the 1910s and Soviet revolutionary cinema of the 1920s. If expressionism did enter into idiom of silent German art cinema, it was probably the highly stylized, somewhat static acting style of German expressionist thespians. This is particularly obvious in a film such as *Hintertreppe* (*Backstairs*, Leopold Jessner, 1921), which is a Kammerspiel without any expressionist trappings in its visual design, but features pure expressionist performances by Fritz Kortner (1892–1970), William Dieterle (1893–1972), and the usually nonexpressionist actress Henny Porten (1890–1960). Expressionist actors, including Werner Krauss (1884–1959), Conrad Veidt (1893–1943), Reinhold Schünzel (1886–1954), and Kortner, became among the most sought-after in German films of that period.

In the past, traditional and formalist film critics differentiated films, filmmakers, and epochs through a series of binary oppositions whereby "realism" signified all attempts at depicting the world in terms of the conventions of a unified space and time, as had been passed down from the Renaissance (according to André Bazin), while expressionism defined attempts to visualize the universe from the strictly subjective point of view of the artist. According to this view, the push and pull of film forms began with the Lumière brothers (realism) and Georges Méliès (expressionism) at the very dawn of cinema. However, more recent early cinema studies have demonstrated that no such polarity existed at the time. Furthermore, film semiotics and postmodern theory have taken the field well beyond such simple, binary oppositions so that it is questionable whether

Fritz Lang's costly **Metropolis** *(1927) was one of the last silent German expressionist films.* EVERETT COLLECTION. REPRODUCED BY PERMISSION.

the continued use of the term *expressionism* in its broadest sense remains useful.

What, then, should *expressionism* mean? Given its origins in modernist art, expressionism should be seen as a particular form of film design that privileges the subjective over the objective, the fantastic and the uncanny over the mundane and everyday, packaging both trivial and high art into film works that address cinema audiences within the context of commercial film culture. Contrary to Edschmid's pronouncements, subjectivity in expressionist film is not seen merely as the "expression" of an individual artist, but rather as a subjectivity shared by an audience willing to enter into an alien world in order to partake of the visual pleasures such a design affords. Unlike classical Hollywood narrative, expressionist cinema tends toward self-reflexivity, toward making audiences aware of the image's artifice and their own subject position as consumers of images,

whether through the undisguised use of painted sets, through the nonnaturalistic use of color film stock and lenses, or by distancing the audience from the actors' performances through stylized poses. In any case, it seems clear that such a definition no longer carries with it any specific ideological connotations, other than a style in opposition to classical Hollywood narrative.

Expressionism, properly speaking, refers exclusively to the artistic movement in the specific historical period in Germany in the early 1920s. The term also refers to German art films in the 1920s that were strongly influenced by expressionism. These films include such stylistic qualities as high key lighting, canted camera angles, subjective camera movement, stylized sets, nonnaturalistic acting, nonlinear narratives, a tendency toward dreamlike images, and Gothic content that often privileges narratives of sexual excess, like *Genuine*. More broadly defined, expressionism may refer to Universal's horror films of the 1930s and films noir (many made by exiled German filmmakers) of the 1940s and 1950s, as well as contemporary films that quote German expressionist cinema, such as the films of Guy Maddin (b. 1956).

SEE ALSO *Acting; Germany; Production Design; Realism; Silent Cinema; Theater; Ufa (Universum Film Aktiengesellschaft); Universal*

FURTHER READING

Bazin, André. *What Is Cinema?*, vol. 1, edited and translated by Hugh Gray. Berkeley: University of California Press, 1967.

Barlow, John D. *German Expressionist Film.* Boston: Twayne, 1982.

Eisner, Lotte. *The Haunted Screen: Expressionism in the German Cinema and the Influence of Max Reinhardt.* Berkeley: University of California Press, 1969.

Elsaesser, Thomas. *Weimar Cinema and After: Germany's Historical Imaginary.* London: Routledge, 2000.

Gay, Peter. *Weimar Culture.* London: Penguin, 1968.

Gianetti, Louis. *Understanding Movies.* Englewood Cliffs, NJ: Prentice-Hall, 1990.

Huaco, George. *The Sociology of Film Art.* New York: Basic Books, 1965.

Kracauer, Siegfried. *From Caligari to Hitler.* Princeton, NJ: Princeton University Press, 1947.

Kurtz, Rudolf. *Expressionismus und Film.* Berlin: Verlag der Lichtbildbühne, 1926; Reprinted Zurich: Verlag Hans Rohr, 1965. All quotations translated by Jan-Christopher Horak (2006).

Salt, Barry. *Film Style and Technology: History and Analysis.* London: Star Word, 1989.

Thompson, Kristin, and David Bordwell. *Film History: An Introduction.* New York: McGraw-Hill, 1994.

Jan-Christopher Horak

FANS AND FANDOM

———■———

Film fans and film fandom do not amount to quite the same thing: one can be a fan of a particular film, genre, actor, or director, but still not participate in the social organizations, interactions, and gatherings of "fandom." Being a fan is, at least in the first instance, a matter of appreciating particular films, and being affectively or emotionally invested in them. Fans are often individuals who are not in contact with other people sharing their emotional attachments to specific films or stars. Although being a "lone" fan of specific films or genres may not necessarily involve actual face-to-face communication with other fans, film buffs frequently imagine themselves as part of an extended fan community, along with absent but like-minded fans. Commercially published magazines help with this process of community building, enabling individual fans to sustain their sense of being part of a group even when they are not directly in touch with other fans.

FANDOM AS A SOCIAL ACTIVITY

Unlike the individual fan, whose peer group or colleagues may coincidentally include like-minded film lovers, organized fandom involves fans specifically seeking out those who share their tastes, thereby becoming involved in a range of social, cultural, and media activities that take this shared fandom as their starting point. Film fandom can involve participating in online discussion and posting to sites such as the Internet Movie Database (imdb.com), joining film clubs or groups, or producing one's own fan magazine or "fanzine." Being part of organized fandom—whether for a certain film or star—is, first and foremost, linked to values of participation and production. Henry Jenkins stresses that fandom's participatory culture "is always shaped through input from other fans and motivated, at least partially, by a desire for further interaction with a larger social and cultural community" (Jenkins, 1992, p. 76). Those participating in socially organized fandom often watch their favored films in fan groups, wanting to share the experience with others who they know similarly appreciate them. And fans also tend to wait together in long lines in order to see the first showings of blockbuster releases, again knowing that the audience will be full of fans like themselves with whom they will share an emotional experience and pleasure.

These highly communal experiences, responses, and interpretations of fandom also translate into activities beyond simply viewing a highly anticipated and appreciated film. Film fans approach watching a film as just one stage within a wider process of consumption and production, with secondary texts such as promotional materials and reviews leading up to the moment of viewing, fanzine reviews and commentaries following the initial filmic encounter, and repeated viewings and the collecting of DVDs with their special features. Film fandom is never about just "going to see a movie."

Seeking to highlight the distinctiveness of fandom and its cultural practices, John Fiske has distinguished between different types of productivity, which he labels "semiotic," "enunciative," and "textual" production (Fiske, pp. 37–39). The first, semiotic, concerns producing meaning from a film text—something that all audiences necessarily do as they cognitively process and make sense of a film. "Enunciative productivity" means talking about a film. Again, this is something that most film audiences do, but that fans tend to carry out distinctively, within the community of fandom. Fiske's third type,

179

"textual productivity," is most specific to fan cultures, since it is very rarely the case that those outside fandom are motivated to write reviews, critiques, or analyses of favorite films (unless perhaps this forms a part of their professional identity as a film critic or academic). According to David Sanjek, fanzines are the clearest example of fandom's textual productivity, being "amateur publications, which by form and content distinguish themselves from 'prozines': the commercial, mainstream magazines" (p. 316). Although there is some truth to his distinction, Sanjek presents a somewhat exaggerated contrast between fanzines and professionally published "prozines," suggesting that amateur fanzine editors have far greater freedom to write what they want, as they are not directly beholden to the movie industry and to patronage; while "prozine" editors are concerned almost exclusively with commercial cinema, amateur fanzines have little interest in "the slavish devotion to accepted formulae and conventions of the mainstream Hollywood product (p. 317). If an excessively neat and tidy opposition, it does acknowledge an important aspect of film fandom: its communities often set themselves apart from what they view as "mere" film "consumers" lacking in genre, textual, and production-history knowledge.

"RESISTANT" AND CONSUMERIST FANDOM

Fandom is, in part, about acquiring and displaying forms of expertise. Rather like scholarly "readings" of films, fandom's favored mode of interpretation involves very close examination wherein films and their surrounding secondary texts are scrutinized for every detail and nuance. This interpretive practice is very much opposed to "casual" film viewing, which is assumed by fans to constitute a less knowledgeable and less discriminating type of viewing characteristic of those who operate outside of fandom.

Sanjek's depiction of fanzines also stresses the anticommercial nature of film fandom, and the manner in which it can be opposed to mechanisms of promotion and publicity. This resonates both with the "underground" and anticommercial/antimainstream value systems of many fan cultures, and with other scholarly work on film fandom that has viewed fans as "resistant" to capitalism and consumerism. For Greg Taylor, "fans are not true cultists unless they pose their fandom as a resistant activity," a position that keeps fan-cultists "one step ahead of those forces which would try to market their resistant taste back to them" in what seems to amount to an ongoing struggle between fandom and the forces of film commerce (p. 161).

However, given this confluence of fan and academic values—where both groups may seek to keep their distance from "the commercial"—it is possible that fandom's "resistant" qualities may be overstated. Many film fans are in fact dedicated fans of blockbuster films, and may fully embrace the commerciality of Hollywood "product" even while reading texts closely and analyzing them in a community of like-minded spectators. It cannot be assumed that fans are necessarily "outside" mechanisms of film promotion, publicity, and commerce, nor that their distinctive fan practices are inherently transgressive or resistant to film commerce. Indeed, fans are of great value to media conglomerates as "reliable consumers" for their product lines, and that subcultures do indeed have a place within capitalism (Meehan, pp. 85–89). This means taking a more complex approach than that of contrasting fan "culture" and the "commerce" of media conglomerates. While Sanjek is certainly right to argue that mainstream magazines are dependent on good will and supplies of material from the film industry, it does not follow that fandom is wholly "independent" of commercial forces, pressures, and interests.

If much work in film and cultural studies from Henry Jenkins's *Textual Poachers* (1992) onwards has tended to take an overly celebratory stance on the participatory and productive cultures of film fandom, some writers have been excessively negative and dismissive of fandom. For example, Barbara Klinger has suggested that a crucial part of how contemporary films work as commodities, and so are sold to audiences, is their "fragmentation into a series of specialized or 'starred' elements" (p. 126), referring to the way films are promoted by focusing on elements extracted from their overall narrative, production, and *mise-en-scène*. Publicity texts can then focus on specific saleable items such as the star, the director, state-of-the-art special effects, or controversial issues or themes raised in the narrative. This means that any given film can be sold to different audiences by stressing different elements, whether matters of romance, special effects, or directorial "art." Klinger argues that fans' expertise is therefore not at all independent of promotional and publicity mechanisms, since their behind-the-scenes knowledge, far from testifying to fans' autonomy, instead frequently indicates "the achieved strategies" of commercial, publicity material (p. 132).

However, just as the argument that film fans are wholly opposed to, or outside of, capitalist forces seems strained, so too does the alternative viewpoint representing fans wholly as the dupes or slaves of the Hollywood dream factory. This debate over the "resistant" or commercially "incorporated" nature of fandom has underpinned an entire paradigm of study, but recent approaches to fandom have begun to pose new questions. Film historian Janet Staiger has pointed out that many studies of fandom have emphasized the positive social aspects of fans' community-building activities, arguing for approaches to fandom that do not singularly celebrate or decry it (2000, p. 54).

Indeed, it also may be difficult to "balance" representations of fans as "good" (resistant) and "bad" (incorporated into the industry). Matt Hills argues that any such balanced or "multiperspectival" approach to fandom is fraught with problems insofar as it seeks to resolve what may be inherent contradictions within fandom and audience identities. Against such attempts to resolve fandoms into clearly definable binaries, a more general, dialectical model of fandom is called for, one capable of dealing with actual contradictions within cultural phenomena (see Hills, pp. 27–45). Fans may be simultaneously inside and outside market forces, resisting economic pressures in some ways and behaving as "reliable consumers" in others. In defense of media studies' work seeking to ascertain fans' resistance to commercial forces, it could be argued that such resistance can still be clearly identified, whether it is resistance to the commodification of film culture via a kind of "underground" film appreciation, or whether it is a reaction against specific types of film such as the blockbuster. But this assertion relies on a zero-sum view of power as something that fans either do or do not possess, as well as assuming that resistance can be critically isolated by scholars. Such an academic approach returns us to a type of fan studies premised on identifying "good" and "bad" objects, thereby claiming the moral authority to label fan practices as either "progressive" or "reactionary" (see *Fan Cultures*).

STEREOTYPING FANS AND FANDOM

Fans and fandom have been subjected to moral surveillance, and a powerfully moralizing gaze, throughout film history. In common-sense terms, the fan audience (whether socially organized into fandom or not) has typically been represented as a bit weird, excessively emotional in relation to favored stars, too interested in the trivia of films' production and the miniscule details of close reading, or too obsessed with the world of film to live successfully in the real world. Film fans sometimes have to defend themselves against accusations that they are losers or maladjusted geeks. Even the notion that film is an art with its own visionary auteurs has not been enough to dispel the image of the pathological movie fan, and neither has the term *cinephilia*, with its high-cultural overtones. For example, the US documentary *Cinemania* (2002) portrays a group of self-professed cinephiles as variously dysfunctional: unable to hold down jobs or have sex lives, instead they obsessively devote their time to attending art-house cinemas in New York. Movie fandom is an object of ridicule in such media portrayals, however affectionate or highbrow they are. It is against this background of negative stereotyping of fans as losers

and geeks that much scholarly work on fans and fandom has sought to positively reevaluate fandom as instead indicating participation in a like-minded community and involving healthy audience creativity.

The importance of stardom within film culture also has led to fans being morally devalued and stereotypically represented as hysterical obsessives. Analyzing the beginnings of movie fan culture from the 1910s onward, as regional variations in film exhibition were supplanted by a national popular culture through a wide range of films, books, plays, and popular songs from the early twentieth century, movie fans were depicted as celebrity-obsessed female daydreamers, the archetypal image of the fan being that of a hysterical, starstruck teenage girl (see Fuller, p. 116). This feminizing of film fans—including males—was powerfully reinforced by the film industry in the wake of the development of the star system. Once the star system began to take hold, and stars' names were promoted and publicized, it then became possible for fans to be represented as feminized, celebrity-obsessed consumers.

Academic work on movie fans has sometimes assumed that their fandom can be equated with being a fan of a specific celebrity. Jackie Stacey offers a sensitive study of female fans that challenges negative stereotypes surrounding the subject and argues that fans do not simply "identify" with film stars (that is, perceive stars as sharing qualities with themselves, or wish to "be like them") or desire them as idealized fantasy figures. Instead, the ways in which fans—and organized fandoms—relate to film stars are far more complicated, involving a range of cinematic and extracinematic practices. Again, fans and fandom are linked to activities that go beyond just watching a star's movies. Stacey analyzes fans' feelings of devotion, worship, and even transcendence: appreciating a particular film star allows them to tune out everyday worries, disappointments, and stresses (p. 145). Stacey highlights a range of fan practices that occur outside the moment of film viewing, such as self-consciously pretending to be a favorite star or otherwise imitating and copying them. These imitations do not mean that such fans have "lost touch with reality," nor that they really want to be someone else; instead, their fandom is merely expressed and displayed through specific cultural activities (p. 171).

Other work on star–fan relationships has stressed the role of organized fandom in communally shaping audiences' reactions to, and appreciations of, movie stars. For example, Richard Dyer observes how Judy Garland became an icon for gay audiences, who interpreted her career and personal struggles as "representing the situation and experience of being gay in a homophobic society" (p. 153). It can be argued that Garland's star text

CONRAD VEIDT
b. Potsdam, Germany, 22 January 1893, d. 3 April 1943

Conrad Veidt appeared in such classic German expressionist films as *Das Kabinett des Dr. Caligari* (*The Cabinet of Dr. Caligari*, 1920), in which he played somnambulist Cesare; *Orlacs Hände* (*The Hands of Orlac*, 1924); and *Der Student von Prag* (*The Student of Prague*, 1926). In *Caligari*, Veidt's androgynous sleepwalker elicits fear and dread from everyone else in the film while being both the instrument and victim of Dr. Caligari (Emil Jannings). Some have seen Veidt as a forerunner of later movie monsters that elicit some degree of sympathy, such as Boris Karloff's creature in *Frankenstein* (1933).

A star of silent film who was strongly linked to the German expressionist movement in the initial phases of his career, Veidt went on to play evil Nazi characters in later sound films such as *Escape* (1940). He was typecast in sinister, creepy, or just plain monstrous roles, often representing the "bad German" partly as a result of the historical and cultural context in which he was working, and partly because of his own looks and acting style. The role of Major Strasser in the classic cult film *Casablanca* (1942) was one of Veidt's final Hollywood roles, coming after he had taken a break from working in the United States to act in Britain from 1932 to 1940. Veidt's performances were frequently highly stylized, in line with the calculated distortions typical of German expressionism.

Being an unusual star, and given his appearances in classic and cult films such as *Casablanca* and *Caligari*, Veidt himself has been embraced as a cult icon, particularly by cinephiles who have an awareness of film history. The Conrad Veidt Society was formed in 1990 by James Rathlesberger, and its members commemorated the fiftieth anniversary of Veidt's death (and the one hundredth anniversary of his birth) in 1993. According to its Internet homepage, the society is dedicated to promoting "classic" films, working to place "Veidt in the context of his times—Germany during the fame of the Expressionist film, England after the rise of Hitler, and America gearing up to fight WWII." Its members particularly value Veidt for his anti-Nazi humanism and his career-long fight against intolerance and prejudice. Onscreen, though, Veidt ended his career playing a Nazi in the escapist *Above Suspicion* (1943), his last film.

RECOMMENDED VIEWING

Das Kabinett des Dr. Caligari (*The Cabinet of Dr. Caligari*, 1920), *Orlacs Hände* (*The Hands of Orlac*, 1924), *Der Student von Prag* (*The Student of Prague*, 1926), *The Man Who Laughs* (1928), *Jew Süss* (1934), *Under the Red Robe* (1937), *The Thief of Baghdad* (1940), *All Through the Night* (1942), *Casablanca* (1942)

FURTHER READING

Allen, Jerry C. *Conrad Veidt: From* Caligari *to* Casablanca. Revised ed. Pacific Grove, CA: Boxwood, 1993.

Brosnan, John. *The Horror People*. New York: St. Martin's Press, and London: MacDonald and Jane's, 1976.

Budd, Mike, ed. *The Cabinet of Dr. Caligari: Texts, Contexts, Histories*. New Brunswick, NJ: Rutgers University Press, 1990.

Conrad Veidt Society Official Home Page, available online at http://www.geocities.com/Hollywood/Studio/7624/Official.html.

Telotte, J. P. "Beyond All Reason: The Nature of the Cult." In *The Cult Film Experience: Beyond All Reason*, edited by J. P. Telotte, 5–17. Austin: University of Texas Press, 1991.

Matt Hills

still is widely perceived as the special province of a gay male fandom. Other types of subcultural fandom may also be linked to the revaluation of particular stars. For example, fans of classic horror may especially appreciate movie stars from the silent era, such as Conrad Veidt (1893–1943), whose appearances in films such as *Das Kabinett des Dr. Caligari* (*The Cabinet of Dr. Caligari*, 1920) and *Orlacs Hände* (*The Hands of Orlac*, 1924) linked him to stylized acting performances and representations of the sinister. Far from being a main- stream "leading man," Veidt nevertheless has become a focal point for a specific horror fan and cinephile community who can interpret his "monstrous" and marginal characters in relation to the antimainstream difference of their own fan culture. Rather than suggesting that particular types of fandom may be especially linked to certain stars, the case of gay male fandom shows that mainstream male stars such as Keanu Reeves can also be revalued or reinterpreted, especially stars whose publicity images represent their sexuality in an ambiguous manner.

Conrad Veidt. EVERETT COLLECTION. REPRODUCED BY
PERMISSION.

Organized fandom can thus sustain different readings of
ubiquitous star images as well as especially valuing certain
stars as a badge of distinction and marker of distance
from "the mainstream."

"FILM ART" AND FANDOM

In comparison with the early twentieth-century creation
of movie fandom, the figure of the movie fan is perhaps
less clearly gendered as feminine/feminized today, but
this is because of a much changed cultural context,
wherein both men and women are frequently targeted
and imaged as consumers. In addition to the star system,
with its "picture personalities," directors and those
involved in the technical craft of filmmaking are now
also increasingly publicized celebrities in their own right.
This shift means that film fans can align themselves more
clearly with notions of film as art—and partly avoid
negative stereotypes of celebrity obsession—by indicating
their fandom of film directors.

This aspect of fandom moves closer to the scholarly
appreciation of film, since treating film as art and digni-
fying certain directors with "authorial" or *auteurist* status

is a strategy that has historically characterized film studies, and that still retains more than a foothold today.
So-called "auteur theory" was initially employed solely
by intellectuals and cinephiles seeking to value film as a
medium, and although it carried cultural cachet, it was
also accessible enough for nonacademic audiences to
appreciate (Taylor, p. 87). Moving from being an exclu-
sive/elitist view of film held by French cinéastes, auteurism entered the US scene and became popularized to the
extent that Hollywood incorporated its discourse into its
own publicity. Auteurism is no longer just a critical
approach, but also a commercial strategy for organizing
how audiences may respond to film texts. Uniting filmmakers, scholars, publicists, and fans, the notion that
certain privileged directors are artists has tended to create
and sustain aesthetic personality cults around them. This
type of "personality cult" also has been significant to
certain organized fandoms, such as those surrounding
offbeat, sleeper, quirky, and classical Hollywood films
labeled "cult movies." These organized fandoms have
tended to use auteur theory as a means of claiming to
find artistic value within the terrain of independent film.

One of the most significant cultural activities under-
taken by film fans, then, is the way in which they seek to
invest the work of their preferred performers and directors with cultural capital, setting their tastes against what
they perceive and construct as mainstream cinema.
However, such an apparent detachment from "the commercial" is itself commercial, since these fans are still
placed within a specific market. Though this is related
to the debate over fandom's resistant capability, it can
also be viewed as a matter of film fans' cultural practices.
Cult-film fans seek to defend and value their favored
texts, but by doing so they also hope to reflect their
own aesthetic taste, for they can see "true" artistic worth
where general audiences cannot. Such fan audiences' bids
for distinction are especially clear in relation to genres
that are frequently devalued in "dominant" film
criticism, such as "trash" and exploitation cinema.
Mark Kermode argues that horror fans actively perceive
the genre's aesthetic value, whereas nonfans passively
consume horror as if its representations are actual rather
than aestheticized images of gore; he offers a convincing
opposition between "active" fans who read horror films
in relation to surreal genre precedents and "passive"
nonfans who are characterized as reading horror films
more naively.

In Kermode's account, horror fans are, crucially,
"genre literate." Like fans of other genres or specific
movie stars, they are expert consumers, able to trace
generic histories and interpret new films in relation to
countless preceding examples. This type of movie fan has
a keen sense of intertextuality; thus, boundaries around
"the text itself" tend to be partly dissolved by fans who,

Conrad Veidt and Annabella in Under the Red Robe *(Victor Seastrom, 1937).* EVERETT COLLECTION. REPRODUCED BY PERMISSION.

even while they carry out close readings of certain films, relate texts to others, either by generic category, in auteurist terms, or by focusing on a favored star. Organized fandoms, like those for cult movies or the horror genre, therefore challenge the idea that any film's meaning and significance are inherent. Rather, it is by reading films in relation to, and through, other texts that fans can convert "the film" into those meanings and values that characterize their fandom as a kind of interpretive community. Fans read films not only through official publicity texts such as DVD extras, but also in relation to fan-produced texts (fan fiction). Henry Jenkins proffers the example of one fan who wrote an alternative ending to the film *Thelma and Louise* (1991) in which these female characters transform themselves into bats (Jenkins, 2000, p. 177). Recontextualizing the film as a lesbian vampire tale, this creative fan interpretation (and production) of meaning indicates how generic identities and textual

boundaries can be reinscribed by film fans, sometimes working against what producers, and other audiences, may view as the obvious categories, boundaries, and identities of a film. Thus, whether it is the interpretive activities of individual fans, or the socially organized, communal practices of fandom, fans and fandom have been as important to film studies as to the film industry. They demonstrate how loyal audiences can be a part of film commerce and also set themselves apart from commercial processes.

SEE ALSO *Auteur Theory and Authorship; Cinephilia; Cult Films; Journals and Magazines; Reception Theory; Spectatorship and Audiences; Stars*

FURTHER READING

Abercrombie, Nicholas, and Brian Longhurst. *Audiences: A Sociological Theory of Performance and Imagination*. London: Sage, 1998.

Barker, Martin, and Kate Brooks. *Knowing Audiences: Judge Dredd—Its Friends, Fans, and Foes*. Luton, UK: University of Luton Press, 1998.

Dyer, Richard. *Heavenly Bodies: Film Stars and Society*. London: British Film Institute, 1986.

Fiske, John. "The Cultural Economy of Fandom." In *The Adoring Audience*, edited by Lisa A. Lewis, 30–49. New York and London: Routledge, 1992.

Fuller, Kathryn H. *At the Picture Show: Small Town Audiences and the Creation of Movie Fan Culture*. Washington, DC and London: Smithsonian Institution Press, 1996.

Hills, Matt. *Fan Cultures*. London and New York: Routledge, 2002.

Jenkins, Henry. "Reception Theory and Audience Research: The Mystery of the Vampire's Kiss." In *Reinventing Film Studies*, edited by Christine Gledhill and Linda Williams, 165–182. London: Arnold, 2000.

———. *Textual Poachers*. London and New York: Routledge, 1992.

Kermode, Mark. "I Was a Teenage Horror Fan, or, How I Learned to Stop Worrying and Love Linda Blair." In *Ill Effects: The Media/Violence Debate*, edited by Martin Barker and Julian Petley, 57–66. London and New York: Routledge, 1997.

Klinger, Barbara. "Digressions at the Cinema: Commodification and Reception in Mass Culture." In *Modernity and Mass Culture*, edited by James Naremore and Patrick Brantlinger, 117–134. Bloomington: Indiana University Press, 1991.

Meehan, Eileen R. "Leisure or Labor?: Fan Ethnography and Political Economy." In *Consuming Audiences?: Production and Reception in Media Research*, edited by Ingunn Hagen and Janet Wasko, 71–92. Cresskill, NJ: Hampton Press, 2000.

Sanjek, David. "Fans' Notes: The Horror Film Fanzine." In *The Horror Reader*, edited by Ken Gelder, 314–323. London and New York: Routledge, 2000.

Stacey, Jackie. *Star Gazing: Hollywood Cinema and Female Spectatorship*. London and New York: Routledge, 1994.

Staiger, Janet. *Perverse Spectators: The Practices of Film Reception*. New York: New York University Press, 2000.

Taylor, Greg. *Artists in the Audience: Cults, Camp, and American Film Criticism*. Princeton, NJ: Princeton University Press, 1999.

Matt Hills

FANTASY FILMS

Arguably, any film relying on fictional situations and characters might be considered fantasy. Indeed Hollywood's "dream factory" prides itself on transporting its audience to myriad fictional settings. In practice, however, fantasy is a term reserved for a specific subset of films featuring characters, events, or settings that are improbable or impossible in the world as we know it. This loose definition yields a staggering array of films that vary widely in subject matter, tone, and intended audience. The children's film *Willy Wonka and the Chocolate Factory* (1971), for example, would seem to have little in common with *Conan the Barbarian* (1982), yet both are considered fantasy because of their fantastical characters and events. While some films feature isolated moments of fantasy in otherwise realistic or dramatic contexts, the designation fantasy is usually reserved for movies whose imaginary elements pervade the entire story. For example, despite the miraculous rain of toads occurring near its end, the gut-wrenching drama *Magnolia* (1999) is not considered fantasy.

In addition to the wide variety of films that fall within the fantasy classification, confusion often arises about science fiction and horror. Although many consider these to be separate genres, their relation to fantasy cannot be overlooked since all three revolve around elaborate fantasy scenarios. Defining fantasy film as a discrete genre is problematic due to the large number of story types it encompasses, and therefore it may be more useful to consider fantasy as a "mode" rather than as a genre. Seen in this light, science fiction and horror are genres that express distinct aspects of the fantasy mode, while other story types might be considered as additional subgenres of the mode.

QUESTIONS OF GENRE

The term "speculative fiction" is sometimes used to avoid making a distinction between various strands of fantasy, science fiction, and horror or to account for the considerable overlap among the three. While both science fiction and horror films are certainly types of fantasy, many would agree that each is distinct in its purview and that each operates differently in terms of themes, conflicts, and iconography.

Whereas science fiction relies on scientific paradigms, technologies, facts, and paraphernalia to create hypothetical but scientifically credible scenarios, fantasy is subject to no such restrictions. Fantasy does not need to convince the audience that its story is realistic—rather, it invites the audience to temporarily *expand* its credulity—hence the phrase so often associated with this genre, "the willing suspension of disbelief." Rather than appeal to science, fantasy favors magical or mystical explanations. Fantasy films are usually logically consistent, but their internal logic belongs to an imagined rather than a scientific world. Although the iconography of science fiction includes spaceships, computers, and ray-guns, a fantasy film is more likely to feature flying horses, crystal balls, or magic wands. In practice, however, many films are hybrids. For example, the science fiction film *The Empire Strikes Back* (1980) invokes no scientific premise to explain Yoda's mystical powers or Luke's mastery of the "the Force," a skill that defies logic and must be accessed through a kind of intuition. Likewise, *E.T. the Extraterrestrial* (1982) features an adorable alien whose ability to heal wounds seems more miraculous than medical.

While some science fiction films are dramatic or upbeat, many attempt to frighten the audience, thus blurring the line between science fiction and horror. Typically, the divide between pure horror and science fiction depends on the presence of scientific elements. Another distinguishing factor concerns the nature and the source of the horror: science fiction is more likely to be concerned with an external threat on a grand scale (for example, aliens attacking the Earth in *War of the Worlds* [1953]), whereas horror is more likely to stem from internal, human evil on a more personal scale (for example, evil ghosts threatening a family in *Poltergeist* [1982]). While some fantasies invoke horror and some horror films are clearly fantasies, films of terror that would *not* be considered fantasy include slasher films such as *Friday the 13th* (1980) or thrillers such as *Dial M for Murder* (1954), since in each case the source of fear is rooted in a (hypothetically) realistic threat. A science fiction film such as *The Andromeda Strain* (1971) may also provoke fear, thus overlapping with horror, but it too would be excluded from a pure fantasy classification because its horrific scenario is grounded in the logical conclusions to scientific hypotheses.

Horror films most often overlap with fantasy when they feature monsters or creatures with no clear scientific explanation (the frightening but misunderstood ape in the classic 1933 film, *King Kong*), or when they enter the supernatural realm (ghosts, vampires, unexplained phenomena). What distinguishes supernatural horror from pure fantasy is the pervasive presence of a horrific and threatening scenario. Ghosts in films like *A Guy Named Joe* (1943) or *Beetlejuice* (1988) function very differently from ghosts in horror films like *The Haunting* (1963); the tone of the films differ accordingly.

Even though science fiction and horror blend with fantasy in many movies, many fantasy films fit neither of those categories and instead find their roots in fairy tales, myths and legends, comic strips, and children's stories. Excluding pure science fiction and horror, the major strands of fantasy might be grouped into the following general subcategories: sword and sorcery/medieval fantasy: *Dragonslayer* (1981), *Willow* (1988), *The Lord of the Rings* trilogy (2001–2003); children's stories: *Peter Pan* (1953), *James and the Giant Peach* (1996), the *Harry Potter* series (beginning in 2001); fairy tales and myths: *La belle et la bête* (*Beauty and the Beast*, 1946), *Jason and the Argonauts* (1963); creatures and monsters: *King Kong* (1933), *Monsters, Inc.* (2001); supernatural: *Here Comes Mr. Jordan* (1941), *Bedazzled* (1967), *Ghost* (1990); magic or miracles: *Big* (1988), *The Santa Clause* (1994); comic book or superheroes: *Dick Tracy* (1990), *Spider-Man* (2002); romantic fantasy: *Splash* (1984), *Groundhog Day* (1993); comic fantasy: *Beetlejuice* (1988), *Ghostbusters* (1984); dream fantasy: *The Wizard of Oz* (1939); action fantasy: *Raiders of the Lost Ark* (1981); martial arts fantasy: *The Matrix* (1999), *Wo hu cang long* (*Crouching Tiger, Hidden Dragon*, 2000); musical fantasy: *Brigadoon* (1954), *The Lion King* (1994); utopian fantasy: *Lost Horizon* (1937); dystopian fantasy: *Brazil* (1985); time travel: *Time Bandits* (1981), *Bill and Ted's Excellent Adventure* (1989); self-referential: *8½* (1963), *Purple Rose of Cairo* (1985), *Pleasantville* (1998); avant-garde or surreal: *Le Sang d'un poète* (*The Blood of a Poet*, 1930).

These subcategories account for some of the major strands of fantasy, but they are by no means exhaustive, nor do they include such films as the delightfully warped *Being John Malkovich* (1999). Moreover, no matter how many highly particular categories are devised for fantasy films, many films nonetheless fit into a number of categories. *The Princess Bride* (1987), for example, is a romantic comedy but also a fairy tale; *The Wizard of Oz* (1939) is a musical but also a dream fantasy with a fairy-tale bent. A further distinction might be made between fantasies that are live-action (*Edward Scissorhands*, 1990), animated (*Peter Pan*), puppet-based (*The Dark Crystal*, 1982), or entirely computer-generated (*Toy Story*, 1995). Here again, many films combine categories—for example, *Mary Poppins* (1964), which employs interludes of animation within a live-action setting, or the live-action/animated film, *Who Framed Roger Rabbit?* (1988), widely acclaimed for its innovative special effects.

HISTORY

One of the first filmmakers associated with fantasy film was the French filmmaker Georges Méliès (1861–1938), who used trick photography and elaborate sets to create fantastic stories such as *Le voyage dans la lune* (*A Trip to the Moon*, 1902). As longer feature films developed in the silent era, a smattering of science fiction and fantasy narratives appeared such as *Twenty Thousand Leagues Under The Sea* (1916), and *The Thief of Bagdad* (1924), which starred the silent film idol Douglas Fairbanks (1883–1939). In Germany, directors such as Robert Wiene (1873–1938), Fritz Lang (1890–1976), and F. W. Murnau (1888–1931) set the stage for a darker type of fantasy associated with German Expressionism. Highly influential to the horror genre, these disturbing tales of evil and supernatural forces included such classics as *Das Kabinett des Doktor Caligari* (*The Cabinet of Dr. Caligari*, 1920), *Metropolis* (1927), and the vampire movie *Nosferatu* (1922), known for its chilling visuals and trick photography. Hans Richter (b. 1919) took a more experimental approach to special effects, using stop-motion animation in *Vormittagsspuk* (*Ghosts before Breakfast*, 1928), a short avant-garde film that featured flying bowler hats and other inanimate objects brought to life.

Jean Cocteau. EVERETT COLLECTION. REPRODUCED BY
PERMISSION.

The advent of sound film in 1927 was accompanied
by innovations in special effects, creating new possibilities
for cinematic fantasy. Though not as dark or gruesome as
the German silent films, Hollywood's spate of monster
and horror films in the 1930s, such as *Dracula* (1931)
and *Frankenstein* (1931), used a similar bag of special
effects tricks, including miniatures and stop-motion photography to create fantastical creatures such as the ape
in *King Kong*, created by special-effects pioneer Willis
O'Brien (1886–1962). On a lighter note, the 1940
remake of *The Thief of Bagdad* delighted audiences with
its vibrant colors and fantastic scenarios. Fantasy also
benefited hugely from the special effects wizardry of
O'Brien's protégé Ray Harryhausen (b. 1920) and from
George Pal (1908–1980), who produced and directed
Tom Thumb (1958), *The 7th Voyage of Sinbad* (1958),
and *Jason and the Argonauts* (1963).

By the 1950s, science fiction had emerged as a major
genre in its own right. Playing on fears of nuclear holocaust and anxiety associated with space travel, most science fiction films used special effects to create frightening
aliens from outer space or monsters created by atomic

radiation. During the same period, Hollywood audiences
were treated to *The Thing From Another World* (1951),
The Blob (1958), and a host of alien invasions. Japanese
filmmakers introduced their own infamous monster in
Gojira (*Godzilla, King of the Monsters*, 1954).

The confluence of sound, special effects and
Technicolor could also yield a more light-hearted type
of fantasy, as evidenced by the perennially popular musical, *The Wizard of Oz* (1939). Combining song and
dance within a fairy-tale narrative, the film drew on the
conventions and sensibilities of the musical, a genre
known for creating its own particular versions of utopian
and romantic fantasy. Musical fantasy also became a
common element in many Indian films, such as *Awaara*
(*The Vagabond*, 1951) by Raj Kapoor.

The combination of music and fantasy has long been
a hallmark of Disney films. Perhaps best known for its
work in animation, Disney has specialized in fantasy
stories since its inception, with a heavy emphasis on
musicals and children's fare. Classics such as *Pinocchio*
(1940) and *Snow White and the Seven Dwarfs* (1937),
hailed as the first full-length animated film, were precursors to the recent trend in animated musicals like *The
Little Mermaid* (1989). While many fantasy films are
intended for youthful audiences and are derived directly
or indirectly from children's books or fairy tales, some
successfully operate on the adult level as well. The term
"family film" often denotes films like *Shrek* (2001) that
appeal to all ages by combining fantasy worlds with
clever animation and more sophisticated humor.

Children's stories, fairy tales, and myths have influenced many American fantasy films, yet other cinematic
strands of fantasy could be found in the "art" films of
Europe, which often featured innovative, complex, and
sometimes disturbing fantasies. Eschewing narrative
coherence, the Surrealists used vivid set pieces, special
effects, and montage to explore the possibilities of cinema
as an expression of subversive and subconscious impulses.
In France, the Spanish-born Salvador Dali (1904–1989)
and Luis Buñuel (1900–1983) collaborated to produce
Un chien Andalou (*An Andalusian Dog*, 1929), a short
experimental piece that has retained its ability to shock
and disorient film viewers. In 1930, the two applied their
artistic sensibility to the politically explosive feature *L'age
d'or* (*The Golden Age*).

Avant-garde and experimental filmmakers pushed
the boundaries of cinematic expression, but fantasy also
continued to flourish in more traditional forms. Drawing
on his earlier explorations of surreal effects, Jean Cocteau
(1889–1963) applied his imaginative skills to the creation of a classic fairy tale, *La belle et la bête* (*Beauty and
the Beast*, 1946). Current audiences are familiar with
Disney's animated version of the story, but for many,

JEAN COCTEAU
b. Maurice Eugène Clément Cocteau, Maisons-Lafitte, France, 5 July 1889,
d. 11 October 1963

Jean Cocteau is perhaps best known for his classic fantasy film, *La belle et la bête* (*Beauty and the Beast*, 1946), based on the fairy tale by Madame Leprince de Beaumont. The multi-talented Cocteau was a painter, poet, and dramatist who is also remembered for his experiments in surrealist and avant-garde techniques.

Founded in the early 1920s, the Surrealist movement concerned itself with the connection between reality and fantasy, rationality and the unconscious. By harnessing and combining these opposing spheres, the Surrealists attempted to create a kind of "super-reality" characterized by disturbing, irrational, and dream-like images. While many employed shocking images in order to critique the status quo, Cocteau devoted himself to the aesthetic ramifications of the movement. In *Le Sang d'un poète* (*The Blood of a Poet*, 1932), Cocteau used special effects to create a disjointed, expressionistic commentary on the angst of the artist. Inspired by the myth of Orpheus, this short experimental film used dream-like images to suggest the sacrifices that the artist makes in the service of art.

In *Beauty and the Beast*, Cocteau created a more traditional, full-length narrative. Starring Jean Marais and Josette Day, this beautiful black-and-white film tells the story of a young woman who finds herself a prisoner of a strange man/beast in atonement for her father's theft of a rose from the Beast's garden. Beauty is frightened by the growling Beast and by the enchanted manor he inhabits. Bodiless human hands usher Beauty into the castle and magically serve her dinner, while lifeless statues periodically awaken to observe her actions. Cocteau used simple but clever mechanical effects to create these and other celebrated moments of cinematic fantasy. Ultimately, Beauty and the Beast come to love one another, and when the Beast is killed at the end of the film, he turns into a prince as he and Beauty fly into the sky in a romantic embrace. Jean Marais plays three characters here: the Beast, the Prince, and Beauty's original suitor (Avenant), who simultaneously changes into the Beast just as the Beast is transformed into the Prince.

In *Orphée* (*Orpheus*, 1950), Cocteau returned to the mythological theme of his first film, updating the story and creating a full-length narrative with a surreal bent. Set in modern-day France and once again starring Jean Marais, the film tells the story of Orpheus and his lover Eurydice as he follows her into the underworld following her death. Here and in other films, Cocteau employed a mirror motif to connote either a window into a distant place or a portal into another world. Continuing his obsession with the role of the artist, Cocteau rounded out his trilogy of Orpheus films in 1960 with *Le Testament d' Orphée* (*The Testament of Orpheus*), in which he appeared as himself.

Beauty and the Beast earned Cocteau the Prix Louis Delluc as well as a number of prizes at the Cannes Film Festival. Cocteau was elected to the French Academy in 1955.

RECOMMENDED VIEWING

Le Sang d'un poète (*The Blood of a Poet*, 1932), *La belle et la bête* (*Beauty and the Beast*, 1946), *L'Aigle à deux têtes* (*The Eagle Has Two Heads*, 1947), *Orphée* (*Orpheus*, 1950), *Le Testament d' Orphée* (*The Testament of Orpheus*, 1960)

FURTHER READING

Cocteau, Jean. *Beauty and the Beast: Diary of a Film*. New York: Dover, 1972.

Evans, Arthur B. *Jean Cocteau and His Films of Orphic Identity*. Philadelphia: Arts Alliance Press, 1977.

Fraigneau, Andre. *Cocteau on the Film: Conversations with Jean Cocteau*. New York: Dover, 1972.

Katherine A. Fowkes

Cocteau's black-and-white, live-action fantasy remains the quintessential version.

Elsewhere, Sweden's Ingmar Bergman (b. 1918) was responsible for a number of surreal films, such as *Det sjunde inseglet* (*The Seventh Seal*, 1957), in which a knight returns from the Crusades and challenges Death to a chess game. In Italy, Federico Fellini (1920–1993) broke from the neorealist movement to produce his disjointed, dreamlike classics *8½* (1963) and *Giulietta degli spiriti* (*Juliet of the Spirits*, 1965). And in Japan, Kenji Mizoguchi (1898–1956) produced the ghostly *Ugetsu monogatari* (1953).

Jean Cocteau creates a charming fantasy world with minimal means in La belle et la bête *(*Beauty and the Beast, *1946).* EVERETT COLLECTION. REPRODUCED BY PERMISSION.

Beginning in the late 1970s, Hollywood experienced a renewed interest in science fiction and fantasy, stoked in part by the films of George Lucas (b. 1944) and Steven Spielberg (b. 1946). *Star Wars* (1977) and *E. T.: the Extraterrestrial* (1982) were among the many popular films to whet movie-goers' appetites for a more upbeat type of science fiction than had been popular in the 1950s and 1960s. *Star Wars* drew inspiration from *Kakushi-toride no san-akunin* (*The Hidden Fortress,* 1958), directed by the well-known Japanese filmmaker Akira Kurosawa. The 1980s also saw a spate of medieval sword and sorcery films, spurred by the popularity of the role-playing game Dungeons and Dragons. While films such as *Dragonslayer* (1981) and *Ladyhawke* (1985) were not widely popular, they paved the way for the hugely successful *Lord of the Rings* trilogy, the first of which premiered in 2001. That same year, the runaway success of the Harry Potter children's books spawned the franchise for another film series about magic and heroism with *Harry Potter and the Sorcerer's Stone* (2001).

In the 1990s, *Ghost* (1990) emerged as the most popular among a series of supernatural melodramas that eschewed horror for comic or dramatic stories. Even *The*

Sixth Sense (1999), which initially presented itself as horror/suspense, eventually revealed itself to be more of a melodrama in the tradition of *Ghost* (1990), *Always* (1989), and *Truly Madly Deeply* (1991). Many supernatural melodramas drew inspiration from earlier films. *City of Angels* (1998) was a mainstream remake of the art film *Der Himmel über Berlin* (*Wings of Desire,* 1987), directed by the German filmmaker Wim Wenders (b. 1945). *The Preacher's Wife* (1996), *Michael* (1996), and *Meet Joe Black* (1998) provided variations on a type of non-horror, supernatural film that had experienced popularity in the 1930s and 1940s—for example, *The Bishop's Wife* (1947), *Here Comes Mr. Jordan* (1941), and *Death Takes a Holiday* (1934).

In the United States and elsewhere, it was computer-generated imagery (CGI) that most affected the look and feel of cinematic fantasy in the 1980s and 1990s. The technology didn't truly come of age until the underwater fantasy *The Abyss* (1989) and later *Toy Story* (1995), an "animated" film made completely with computer imagery. Also notable for their reliance on CGI were the highly successful *Jurassic Park* (1993), *Terminator 2: Judgment Day* (1991), *Forrest Gump* (1994), and *The Mask* (1994). *The Matrix* (1999) introduced a striking new approach to the choreography of action and fight sequences. *The Matrix* was heavily influenced by martial arts specialists in Hong Kong and China, including John Woo (b. 1946) and the Vietnamese-born Tsui Hark (b. 1950), whose popular action/fantasies such as *Suk san: Sun Suk san geen hap* (*Zu: Warriors from the Magic Mountain,* 1983) have earned him comparison to Spielberg. *The Matrix* also drew inspiration from Japanese anime films such as Mamoru Oshii's (b. 1951) *Kô kaku kidôtai* (*Ghost in the Shell,* 1995). One of the first anime films to make an impact on Hollywood was Katsushiro Otomo's (b. 1954) violent techno-fantasy, *Akira* (1988). And although Hayao Miyazaki's (b. 1941) *Mononoke-hime* (*Princess Mononoke,* 1997) and *Sen to chihiro no kamikakushi* (*Spirited Away,* 2001) have not been widely viewed in the United States, their box-office success in Japan has helped make anime fantasy a major movement in international cinema.

THEORY AND IDEOLOGY

Much that has been written about fantasy focuses on it as a literary genre, but it can be equally applied to cinema. Although it is common to classify fantasy texts by themes and motifs or by the extent to which story-worlds and events deviate from realistic representations, Tzvetan Todorov concentrates on the *response* generated by the "fantastic" events in the story. In this light, fantasy must be considered not just *one* "mode," but *three,* since it creates a continuum stretching from "the marvelous" to "the uncanny," depending on the extent to which the characters and/or the reader experience feelings of awe and hesitation provoked by strange, improbable events. If the narrative's impossibility can be explained rationally or psychologically (as a dream, hallucinations), then the term "uncanny" is applied. The purely "fantastic" comes into play only during the hesitation and uncertainty experienced by the characters and/or the reader/viewer when faced with an impossible occurrence. By contrast, the term "marvelous" is applied to self-contained story worlds such as those of *The Lord of the Rings* or *The Dark Crystal* (1982), which do not ask the reader or viewer to question the reality of the story. (J. R. R. Tolkien called this "subcreation," also referred to as "High Fantasy.")

The Wizard of Oz demonstrates all three modes operating within a single fantasy. Unlike films that propose an alternate, imaginary universe as the setting for the entire tale, *The Wizard of Oz* frames its fantasy world with the real world of Kansas, suggesting that Oz is only a fantasy of the imagination. In light of Todorov's definitions, we can see that upon first encountering Oz, both Dorothy and the audience are operating in a "fantastic" capacity. But wonder and disbelief eventually give way to "marvelous" acceptance, and Dorothy and the audience participate in the quest to find the wizard and ultimately kill the wicked witch. While Dorothy and the audience may continue to "marvel" at the strangeness of creatures and events in Oz, it is never suggested that Oz is not actually "real" until the end, when the dream explanation shifts our understanding of the events into the "uncanny" mode. Our prior willing suspension of disbelief only adds to the impact of the final scene, when the audience shares Dorothy's consternation at being told it was all "only" a dream.

As a psychological phenomenon, the term "fantasy" refers to our unconscious desires (dreams, daydreams, wishes). For this reason, Rosemary Jackson notes that fantasy stories are perhaps the type of fiction most amenable to psychoanalytic interpretations. Although Jackson applies her analysis only to fantasy literature, it can be easily extrapolated to film. Drawing on Todorov's definition, Jackson argues that the fantastic is inherently subversive. By raising questions about reality and by revealing repressed dreams or wishes, fantasy makes explicit what society rejects or refuses to acknowledge. Indeed, to the extent that it includes the surreal and experimental, fantasy is often *explicitly* subversive. The original surrealists thought art should be shocking and politically progressive, and they intentionally disrupted those cinematic conventions that help create coherence and meaning for the viewer. But most mainstream fantasy films take care to adhere to the conventions of classical cinematic storytelling while constructing coherent space, time, and narrative causality. Nevertheless,

horror differs from fantasy in this respect: it is a form of mainstream fantasy whose formulaic content is often examined for its subversive potential and for symptoms of a culture's repressed desires.

While horror has received much critical attention, other types of fantasy are often rejected as being merely "escapist"—a term generally associated with works of art that one is not supposed to take seriously. Most fantasy films are considered escapist because they temporarily transport viewers to impossible worlds and provide unrealistic solutions to problems. Even Jackson concedes that most fantasy is "marvelous" instead of truly "fantastic," more a matter of wish fulfillment than of challenge. Indeed, referring to *The Lord of the Rings* trilogy from which the films were adapted, Jackson describes Tolkien's fantasy as inherently conservative and nostalgic. With its magic, fantastical beings and clear-cut delineations of good and evil, *The Lord of the Rings* presents a compelling fantasy mirrored to some extent in the *Harry Potter* films. Many would argue that *Harry Potter*, like *The Lord of the Rings*, uses imagination to uphold rather than to transcend traditional values. Both tend to reinforce a hierarchical world based in traditional notions of morality, gender, and heroism. Both rely on a sense of mystical destiny and grace that, while not explicitly religious in nature, exhibits the strong influence of a traditional Western and Christian perspective. Both series feature a reluctant and somewhat unlikely young hero, and both offer the audience an escape into a different world where difficult problems are solved through magic as well as old-fashioned courage and integrity. The *Harry Potter* films differ from *The Lord of the Rings* trilogy, however, in pitting the viewer's own sense of "reality" against the magical world of wizards and witches.

A psychoanalytic approach to fantasy must take into account not just the psychological underpinnings of the characters but the pleasure and appeal of the story for the viewer. The most successful fantasy films provide viewers with vicarious experiences that resonate with emotional, if not physical, reality. Both *Harry Potter* and *The Lord of the Rings* demonstrate the appeal of fantasy as a vehicle for wish fulfillment through their glorification of magical (hence unrealistic) solutions to serious problems. The viewer lives vicariously through the characters of Frodo and Harry, who strive to overcome the forces of evil. The psychological appeal of fantasy helps to explain the frequency of the Oedipal scenario in these types of narratives. For example, *Star Wars* features a classic Oedipal struggle between Luke and his father. Superhero movies also construct appealing fantasy scenarios, often starring unlikely or reluctant male heroes reminiscent of Frodo and Harry. *Superman* (1978), *Batman* (1989), and *Spider-Man* (2002) were popular movies that featured "ordinary" protagonists whose unremarkable talents presumably resonate on some level with most viewers. This ordinary-ness is revealed as a mere facade, however, masking the true superhuman powers of the character—another attractive problem-solving solution for consumers of fantasy.

Similarly, many recent supernatural/ghost movies also deny the reality of death by magically bringing back beloved characters as ghosts, as in *Ghost* and *Truly Madly Deeply*. A psychoanalytic interpretation of such fantasies, however, yields a more subtle interpretation. Whether or not such films are wish-fulfillment fantasies matters less than whether or not wish-fulfillment fantasies are inherently conservative. There is certainly nothing subversive about a story in which a male character wishes to become more macho (as in *Spider-Man*), for such fantasies merely reinforce traditional Western ideas about masculinity, echoed in many of the fantasy films discussed here. But just because some fantasies are conservative does not necessarily mean that escapism is a worthless denial of reality and therefore of no cultural value. For example, recent melodramatic and comedy ghost films share a tendency to challenge traditional gender roles by creating passive and "emasculated" male characters (*Ghost, Truly Madly Deeply, The Sixth Sense*) who contrast sharply with the active male protagonists found in most Hollywood movies.

Regardless of whether or not these and other fantasy films are truly subversive or politically liberating, many fantasy movies provide an interlude in which viewers are invited to entertain forbidden desires and other heretofore unimagined possibilities. Thus, to draw on Jean Laplanche and Jean-Bertrand Pontalis's definition of fantasy as a psychological phenomenon, a fantasy film is thus literally the "*mise-en-scène* of desire," the setting whereby impossible desires may play out to their logical conclusions.

SEE ALSO *Children's Films; Genre; Horror Films; Science Fiction*

FURTHER READING

Barron, Neil. *Fantasy and Horror: A Critical and Historical Guide to Literature, Illustration, Film, TV, Radio, and the Internet.* Lanham, MD: Scarecrow Press, 1999.

Brosnan, John. *Movie Magic: The Story of Special Effects in the Cinema.* New York: St. Martin's Press, 1974.

Burgin, Victor, James Donald, and Cora Kaplan, eds. *Formations of Fantasy.* New York: Methuen, and London: Routledge, 1986.

Clute, John, and John Grant, eds. *The Encyclopedia of Fantasy.* New York: St. Martin's Press, 1997.

Donald, James, ed. *Fantasy and the Cinema.* London: British Film Institute, 1989.

Fowkes, Katherine A. *Giving Up the Ghost: Spirits, Ghosts and Angels in Mainstream Comedy Films.* Detroit, MI: Wayne State University Press, 1998.

Jackson, Rosemary. *Fantasy: The Literature of Subversion.* New York: Methuen, 1981.

Laplanche, Jean, and Jean-Bertrand Pontalis. "Fantasy and the Origins of Sexuality." In *Formations of Fantasy*, edited by Victor Burgin, James Donald, and Cora Kaplan. London: Routledge, 1986.

Mathews, Richard. *Fantasy, the Liberation of the Imagination.* New York: Twayne, and London: Prentice-Hall, 1997.

Nicholls, Peter. *The World of Fantastic Films: An Illustrated Survey.* New York: Dodd, Mead, and London: Ebury Press, 1984.

Slusser, George, and Eric S. Rabkin, eds. *Shadows of the Magic Lamp: Fantasy and Science Fiction in Film.* Carbondale: Southern Illinois University Press, 1985.

Sobchack, Vivian Carol. *Screening Space: The American Science Fiction Film.* Brunswick, NJ: Rutgers University Press, 1997.

Todorov, Tzvetan. *The Fantastic: A Structural Approach to a Literary Genre.* Trans. Richard Howard. Cleveland, OH: The Press of Case Western Reserve University, 1973.

Tolkien, J. R. R. "On Fairy-Stories." In *Tree and Leaf.* Boston: Houghton Mifflin, 1989.

Weinstock, Jeffrey Andrew, ed. *Spectral America: Phantoms and the National Imagination.* Madison: University of Wisconsin Press, 2004.

Katherine A. Fowkes

FASHION

———■———

Fashion's relationship to film is characterized by two factors: how film has influenced fashion and how fashion and the work of specific fashion designers have been used in film. These are not mutually exclusive but parallel trajectories. The extrovert couturier Elsa Schiaparelli (1890–1973) once remarked that what Hollywood did today, fashion would do tomorrow, but it could be said equally that what fashion did today, cinema would do tomorrow. Hollywood, for example, instantly dropped its hemlines following the vogue for longer fashions set by Jean Patou (1887–1936) in 1929. More commonly, a monolithic institution like Hollywood has not always been swift to change; once it has found a fashion it likes, it tends to stick with it, as was the case with Patou's long, bias-cut style, which prevailed with few exceptions throughout its films of the 1930s.

CINEMA'S FASHIONABILITY

Fashion—or rather the fashionability of film, particularly Hollywood's—has always been an important element of cinema's appeal. There are many individual examples of garments having had a direct impact on off-screen fashions and sales. For example, one of the designer Adrian's (1903–1959) robes for Joan Crawford in *Letty Lynton* in 1932, the year Crawford was first named "The Most Imitated Woman of the Year," was widely copied, as was Edith Head's (1897–1981) white party dress for Elizabeth Taylor in *A Place in the Sun* (1951). Head herself once declared that she had seen more than thirty copies of the dress at a single party. Other elements of a movie star's look were mimicked by an adoring film-going public: Veronica Lake, for example, was reputedly asked to change her peek-a-boo hairstyle because as worn by her many female fans, it was causing accidents in the wartime factories of the 1940s. Later, one could point to the notable effect films such as *Bonnie and Clyde* (1967) and *Annie Hall* (1977) had on contemporary fashions. Faye Dunaway's thirties wardrobe in *Bonnie and Clyde* has been credited with re-launching the beret and the cardigan, while Diane Keaton's androgynous ensembles as Annie Hall—created by the American fashion designer Ralph Lauren (b. 1939)—were swiftly copied in both the exclusive pages of *Vogue* and on the High Street, where the wearing of masculine trousers, shirts, and waistcoats by women became the epitome of chic. Through the influence of film on fashion, one can see the true democratization of the movies and movies' relationship with spectatorship: the fans might not be able to become their favorite stars, but they can mimic and emulate them.

Similarly, in contemporary cinema one can see the same pattern of mimicry when it comes to both clothes and accessories—a crucial difference being that it is now more often the male stars who have become fashion icons, in keeping with a heightened awareness of male fashion that has been evident since the early 1990s. Retro aviator shades made a comeback after Tom Cruise wore them in *Top Gun* (1987); after the success of Quentin Tarantino's second movie, *Pulp Fiction* (1994), the black suits and monochrome outfits of French designer Agnès (b. 1941) (along with Uma Thurman's Chanel "Rouge Noir" nail varnish) became synonymous with masculinity and cool. In this millennium, one could point to the innate fashionability of *The Matrix* (1999): Keanu Reeves's long swishing coat, his mobile phone, and his glasses.

However, fashion's relationship to film extends beyond the domain of film's fashionability. In the 1920s,

Joan Crawford wearing one of Adrian's gowns for **Letty
Lynton** *(Clarence Brown, 1932).* EVERETT COLLECTION.
REPRODUCED BY PERMISSION.

[1955]). Dior himself lent his designs to a relatively small and eclectic series of films, including René Clair's *Le silence est d'or* (*Man About Town*, 1947), Jean-Pierre Melville's *Les enfants terribles* (1950), and Alfred Hitchcock's *Stage Fright* (1950).

Although historically significant overlaps have existed between the two, fashion and costume design remain separate arts. Whereas the costume designer, more often than not, serves the dominant purposes of character and narrative, the fashion designer, when used in a film, frequently is brought in to achieve virtually the opposite result (an exception here would be cinema's use of classic designers, such as the Italian Giorgio Armani [b. 1934]). In rare instances, individuals have had dual careers as fashion and costume designers, the most notable example being Jean Louis (1907–1997), who was born in Paris and trained at the Paris couture house of Drecol before going to New York to work for Hattie Carnegie. Louis then made the switch to Hollywood and became head designer at Columbia Pictures from 1944 to 1958, when he moved to Universal. Simultaneously, Louis ran his own couture business, often supplying clothes for his favorite female stars (Doris Day, for instance) for their appearances both on and off the screen. In the same vein, Edith Head (1897–1981) was fond of recounting how Grace Kelly was so enamored of her designs for *To Catch a Thief* (1955) that she wore one of her costumes on a date with future husband Prince Rainier; later Kelly commissioned MGM designer Helen Rose (1904–1985) to design her wedding dress and Head to design her going-away outfit.

FASHION DESIGNERS AND FILM

It was Hubert de Givenchy's (b. 1927) collaboration with Audrey Hepburn that fundamentally changed the relationship between film and fashion. In *Sabrina* (1954), as in *Funny Face*, the distinction between the costume designer and the *couturier* co-opted into costume design is signaled ironically within the films' Cinderella narratives. In both, Edith Head, the films' costume designer, produced the drab, ordinary clothes that Hepburn wore as the still-immature chauffeur's daughter or bookshop assistant. In both films, Head's role as designer was usurped by Givenchy who designed the show-stopping evening gowns that Hepburn wore after her character had metamorphosed into a sophisticated, glamorous woman. The joke in *Funny Face*—in which Hepburn's character models clothes on a Paris catwalk—is ultimately that, for all the appeal of high fashion, Hepburn is happiest (and most iconic) when dressing down in black leggings, polo neck, and flats.

Following these films, *couturiers* it became far more commonplace to use couturiers alongside costume

1930s, and 1940s, few fashion designers did much work for films, the notable exception being Chanel (1883–1971), who in 1931 went to MGM. Her Hollywood film work was not deemed a success; Chanel was too meticulous and precise (insisting at one point on making several copies of the same dress, one for each individual scene), and she soon elected to return to Paris, later designing costumes for such films as Louis Malle's *Les Amants* (1958) and Alain Resnais's *L'année dernière à Marienbad* (*Last Year in Marienbad*, 1961). The most important fashion designers have not always been those who have become involved in film and film costume design. While the influence of Christian Dior's "New Look," launched in 1947, endured within Hollywood far longer than it did outside it (so much so that the much more fashionable *Funny Face* [1957] looked slightly anachronistic alongside mid-1950s contemporaries, such as *Rear Window* [1954] and *All That Heaven Allows*

GIORGIO ARMANI
b. Piacenza, Italy, 11 July 1934

The Italian designer Giorgio Armani, known for his classic designs, neutral tones, and unstructured suits, has made a significant intervention into film history. Armani is arguably best known for the Hollywood stars he has dressed for the Academy Awards® (for example, Jodie Foster and Michelle Pfeiffer). However, his costumes for Richard Gere's character Julian in *American Gigolo* (1980) helped to alter the way in which mainstream cinema perceived and represented masculinity. The most cited scene in the movie shows Julian choosing an outfit to wear for an evening appointment. He lays out on his bed a selection of Armani jackets, then matches them with some shirts and finally adds an array of possible ties. While choosing what to wear, Julian shimmies sensuously to music, dressed only in his boxer shorts. Then he gets dressed and checks his appearance in the mirror. Julian's overt narcissism, coupled with his love of Armani's expensive clothes, ushered in a radical recodification of heterosexual masculinity on screen.

Since *American Gigolo*, Armani has costumed many films, particularly in Hollywood. Sometimes he has provided only items for the stars' wardrobes: for Eddie Murphy in *48 Hours* (1982), Mel Gibson and Rene Russo in *Ransom* (1996), and Samuel L. Jackson in the remake of *Shaft* (2000). By 2000, Armani's name itself had gained enough narrative significance for Shaft to be able to warn another character possessively not to touch his Armani. Dressing male characters has set Armani apart, and he has been particularly effective at dressing groups of men. He uses costumes to denote camaraderie, support, and affection between the protagonists of *The Untouchables*

(1987) and characters in the remake of *The Italian Job* (2003), deftly dressing them in the Armani capsule wardrobe of the time. In both films, the group's leader (Kevin Costner and Donald Sutherland, respectively) wears a paternal, safe, and suavely unstructured wool coat, while the young turks (Andy Garcia and Mark Wahlberg, respectively) wear slightly spiffier leather jackets and casuals. This form of typage through costume is quintessential Armani.

Armani has made himself synonymous with effortless elegance. This equation was not automatic, because his suits were used in the TV series *Miami Vice* and in *Cadillac Man* (1990) to suggest shallow tackiness. The crucial component in his innate class has been his Italianness. Most enduring has been his friendship and collaboration with Martin Scorsese. The two worked together on *Made in Milan* (1990), a twenty-minute short Scorsese directed about Armani that was notable for its extravagant and stylized filming of a catwalk show. Armani later acted as executive producer for Scorsese's reverential history of Italian cinema, *Il mio viaggio in Italia* (1999), thus cementing his integration into cinema history.

RECOMMENDED VIEWING
American Gigolo (1980), *48 Hours* (1982), *The Untouchables* (1987), *Cadillac Man* (1990), *Ransom* (1996), *Il mio viaggio in Italia* (1999), *Shaft* (2000), *The Italian Job* (2003)

FURTHER READING
Celant, Germano, and Koda, Harold, eds. *Giorgio Armani.* New York: Guggenheim Museum, 2000.

Stella Bruzzi

---

designers on movies, and certain couturiers were given virtual license to use the films on which they worked as showcases for their own fashion designs. There is little sense here of costume's traditional subservience to character and narrative. Hardy Amies (1909–2003) (the British Queen's favorite fashion designer) designed the wardrobe for films such as *The Grass Is Greener* (1960) and *2001: A Space Odyssey* (1968). His designs for the latter, though muted compared to much of the 1960s "space age" fashion, were very much of their time and quintessentially Hardy Amies: classic, refined, but never

too daring. This incorporation of classic as opposed to outrageous fashion designers into film increasingly predominated, particularly in Hollywood. In European cinema, one can point to the example of Yves Saint Laurent (b. 1936), whose muse was the French actress Catherine Deneuve. Saint Laurent's designs for Deneuve as Severine in Luis Bunuel's *Belle de Jour* (1967) epitomized his approach: her clothes are straight and muted, notable for their unsexy elegance (ironic considering Severine's day job as a prostitute), much like Saint Laurent's own classic-with-a-twist late-1960s lines. Severine is enigmatic

Giorgio Armani. PHOTO BY GREGORIO BINUYA/EVERETT COLLECTION. REPRODUCED BY PERMISSION.

and unobtainable; her wearing of an Yves Saint Laurent capsule wardrobe in *Belle de jour* (1967) confirms the use of fashion as a means of maintaining this distance and representing her exclusivity, her wealth, and her class.

Within Hollywood, the most prolific *couturier* costume designer is Giorgio Armani, whose costumes work to define character and narrative. Other designers whose work is used in films in a similar way have been Nino Cerruti (b. 1930), with whom Armani trained, Ralph Lauren (b. 1939), Donna Karan (b. 1948), and Calvin Klein (b. 1942), all quintessentially classic designers. Lauren's most important film as costume designer is *The Great Gatsby* (1974), soon followed by *Annie Hall.* These two films together defined the retrogressive and romantic trends in US fashions that would begin to predominate off as well as on the screen in the 1970s. The significance of fashion designers' contributions to film should perhaps be judged by their ability to manufacture a pervasive image and to evoke a lifestyle. Lauren achieved this with his films of the 1970s (the class aspirations encapsulated by *The Great Gatsby,* the feminist aspirations represented by Keaton's androgynous look in *Annie Hall*), although recently he is probably better known for having dressed Gwyneth Paltrow in pink for her Academy Award® Best Actress acceptance speech. Cerruti's costumes for Richard Gere in *Pretty Woman* (1990) or Karan's for Gwyneth Paltrow in Alfonso Cuaròn's modern-day *Great Expectations* (1998), like those of Lauren and Cerruti, remain stylish but unobtrusive, conjuring a look that connotes a certain class, breeding, and refinement. Cinema's most popular *couturier* costume designers, it seems, are those who follow the underpinning conventions of costume design and produce safe, middle of the road designs rather than more spectacular, outrageous costumes.

Fashion is more often considered a craft than an art, and self-consciously artistic, spectacular fashions have been reserved for self-consciously spectacular, art-house movies. Jean-Paul Gaultier (b. 1952) has been the most prolific of these designers, doing costumes for various nonmainstream films, including *The Cook, the Thief, His Wife, and Her Lover* (1989), *Kika* (1993), and *La cité des enfants perdus* (*The City of Lost Children,* 1995), as well as producing all the costumes for Luc Besson's more mainstream sci-fi extravaganza, *The Fifth Element* (1997). In all of these, Gaultier's designs are exaggerated versions of his signature fashion styles, in the way they make underwear into outerwear, juxtapose asymmetrical cutting with classic tailoring. In *Kika,* the smooth surface of classicism—exemplified by Victoria Abril's black, bias-cut dress—is ruptured by radical flourishes, such as the prosthetic breasts bursting out of the dress. Gaultier, unlike many other fashion designers turned costume designers, immerses himself in his films, designing costumes for all the characters, not just the protagonists, and reputedly checking all costumes before they go on set. Just as his designs are fantastical rather than wearable (his designs for *The Fifth Element* include Gary Oldman's asymmetrical suits and Milla Jovovich's minimal bondage gear), so Gaultier's personality is important. Unlike Armani or Lauren, who have taken their involvement in film extremely seriously, Gaultier has not been averse to sending himself—and by implication, the fashion world—up. Gaultier's personality has demystified high fashion; he has appeared as himself in Robert Altman's parody of the Paris fashion scene *Prêt-a-porter* (1994), mixing white and red wine together to make rosé, and from 1993 to 1997 he fronted the TV show *Eurotrash,* a broadcast that, as its title suggests, sought out and edited together examples of trashy, gross, and comic European television.

The accessibility of fashion in film has become a hugely significant factor in its appeal reminiscent of the prewar era of *Letty Lynton,* when women bought patterns of their favorite movie dresses to sew them for themselves. Quentin Tarantino's *Reservoir Dogs* (1992), which inspired the design of London department store windows and led to an increase in the wearing of dark suits and shades among younger men, is just such an example of film's democratization of fashion. The costume designer Betsy Heimann bought the suits seen in *Reservoir Dogs* cheaply. When the film became successful, so did the clean-silhouetted French gangster look, which Tarantino readily admitted to having borrowed from a look created by French director Jean-Pierre Melville (1917–1973) for his movie gangsters. *Reservoir Dogs* offered style on the cheap because it offered a look rather than an exclusive range of garments.

Audiences respond positively to being able to buy and emulate what they see on the screen—for example, Nicole Kidman's half-fitted, half-loose teddy in *Eyes Wide Shut* (1999). Once women found out what the garment was, it was sold out everywhere. What has emerged is a fluid, flexible interaction between fashion and film—sometimes fashion borrows from film, often the exchange is reversed.

SEE ALSO *Costume*

FURTHER READING

Bruzzi, Stella. *Undressing Cinema: Clothing and Identity in the Movies.* London and New York: Routledge, 1997.

Head, Edith, and Jane Kesner Ardmore. *The Dress Doctor.* Boston and Toronto: Little, Brown and Co., 1959.

Keenan, Brigid. *The Women We Wanted to Look Like.* London: Macmillan, 1977.

Maeder, Edward, ed. *Hollywood and History: Costume Design in Film.* Los Angeles: Los Angeles County Museum of Art, and London: Thames and Hudson, 1987.

Pritchard, Susan Perez. *Film Costume: An Annotated Bibliography.* Metuchen, NJ, and London: Scarecrow Press, 1981.

Saint Laurent, Yves. *Yves Saint Laurent: Images of Design 1958–1988.* London: Ebury Press, and New York: Knopf, 1988.

Wollen, Peter. "Strike a Pose." *Sight and Sound* 5, no. 3 (March 1995): 10–15.

Stella Bruzzi

FEMINISM

The emergence of the women's liberation movements in the late 1960s and early 1970s had a profound impact on scholarship as well as on society. Betty Friedan's *The Feminine Mystique* (1963) set the stage for liberation movements by detailing middle-class women's isolation, even oppression, within the suburban household. Women's roles in the antinuclear movements, such as the Aldermaston marches in the United Kingdom or SANE (Students Against Nuclear Energy) in the United States, further served as catalysts in the mid-1960s within diverse social sectors. For example, women within the male-dominated Students for a Democratic Society (SDS) began to resist their relegation to food preparation and child care, and to argue for women's rights to be included in the SDS agenda. In NUC (the New University Community), a faculty wing of SDS, pressure increased in regard to addressing women's issues, such as discriminatory employment practices, unfair divorce laws, and attention to medical and biological issues specific to women. Independent Marxist-feminist groups emerged along with so-called radical feminists, often linked to lesbian-centered groups. Protests and demonstrations on behalf of women's rights regarding sexual choice, day care, and equality in the workplace pushed women's liberation into the public spotlight. Gradually public awareness and involvement in debates about feminist issues increased. Meanwhile, female perspectives, long neglected in mainstream academic research, began to gain the attention of historians and literary and film scholars. Indeed, these two faces of feminism can hardly be separated: Academic women were often actively involved in working for social change on a range of women's issues, while activist women often enjoyed the support of universities in furthering their ends.

Women film scholars were among the first to reject the traditional male-centered perspectives in academia and, with Copernican force, to reverse the position from which texts were approached to engage a female-centered one. With *Sexual Politics* (1970), a forceful critique of misogyny in the male modern novel and of Freud's male-centered psychoanalytic theories, Kate Millett burst on the literary scene and was soon followed by other (less vitriolic) feminist literary critics. Women film scholars, too, eagerly took up the baton. Meanwhile, male film theory (especially in England) introduced structuralist approaches in the wake of research by scholars such as Louis Althusser, Roland Barthes, and Jacques Lacan. In this context, some feminist film theory also turned to neo-Marxism, structuralism, and psychoanalysis in ways not so common at the time in feminist literary analyses. Feminist critics began to look at the ways in which women were represented on film as well as to expose the utter neglect of female directors in male scholarship; in the wake of these initiatives, film scholarship was never again the same. Three main strands (in practice, often mixed) emerged early on in feminist film theory: "archival" and historical approaches, sociological role-focused approaches, and what has been called cine-psychoanalysis. A certain coherence within the limited frame of 1970s and 1980s feminist film research can be demonstrated, built around the concept of the gendered gaze of the camera; but in the 1990s, as a result of changing political, social, and intellectual contexts, including the waning of feminism as a widespread activist movement, several alternate perspectives developed. There was the flood of research by minority and women of the Third World (itself a problematic and much-debated term). Masculine studies, inspired by feminist theory, emerged, as well as queer studies, which severely challenged some of the concepts basic to feminist film theories. Finally, the introduction of new interdisciplinary fields like visual studies and digital media, related to film studies, had the effect of broadening the somewhat narrow gaze-related theories to consider historical, technological, and institutional contexts given short shift in cine-psychoanalysis. Second-wave feminist theorists have further revised gaze theories.

FROM ARCHIVAL RESEARCH TO CINE-PSYCHOANALYSIS

In tandem with ongoing scholarship in history and literature, women film scholars have long endeavored to identify forgotten filmmakers—forgotten because most male film critics and scholars writing before the 1960s were not interested in women directors. Because their films were in distribution, Dorothy Arzner (1897–1979) and Ida Lupino (1914–1995) were the first women directors in the sound era to be studied. Foreign directors, like Mai Zetterling (1925–1994), also gained attention at this time. Later, feminists took a great deal of interest in women directors and producers from the silent era, like Lois Weber (1881–1939) and Mary Pickford (1892–1979). Since the 1990s, the Women Film Pioneers Project has been engaged in intensive international study of early women in cinema in their many roles.

Sociological analysis of women in film soon followed. Three books on women and film emerged at nearly the same time in the early 1970s, mainly using a sociological and role-focused analysis: Molly Haskell's *From Reverence to Rape* (1973), Marjorie Rosen's *Popcorn Venus* (1972), and Joan Mellen's *Women and Their Sexuality in the New Film* (1974). Although perhaps insufficiently appreciated by academic feminists in its historical moment, Haskell's book has had the longest-lasting impact. Feminist film theorists of the time, frustrated by sociological and role analyses, were seeking to move beyond Haskell's approach. Drawing on a vast knowledge of Hollywood as an institution and of movies themselves, Haskell took a penetrating look at the shabby treatment of women on- and offscreen. She had a strong feminist understanding of how threatened American men felt by women, as well as an intense appreciation of actresses and their performances. Haskell points out the irony that both the Production Code and the Depression "brought women out of the bedroom and into the office" (p. 30). She argues that actresses of the 1930s and 1940s (such as Rosalind Russell, Katharine

Hepburn, and Joan Crawford) offered images of intelligence, forcefulness, and personal power, far surpassing roles of actresses in later films. Male directors who "integrate women into the flow of life" enjoyed the spunky, smart woman capable of challenging the hero. Haskell defines herself as a film critic first and a feminist second, hoping to address "the wholeness and complexity of film history" (p. 38).

A new generation of women film scholars turned to the melded disciplines of metaphysics, semiotics, and psychoanalysis, a shift prompted by what they saw as the limits of studies focusing on individual actresses and women's roles in cinema. To compare images of women in film with women's lived reality seemed simply to critique the current gendered organization of society or to expand it by, for instance, insisting on more male involvement in domestic matters. The new scholars hoped instead to discover the root cause of women's secondary status in Hollywood and society in the first place. Laura Mulvey's groundbreaking essay, "Visual Pleasure and Narrative Cinema" (1975), partly inspired by reaction to American sociological film analyses, seemed to fulfill the need for a new kind of analysis, and her ideas rapidly took hold. Mulvey's polemical contribution was to isolate three related "looks" in Hollywood cinema, and to argue that these were all male: the look of the camera (mainly operated by men) in the pro-filmic studio site; the look of the spectator, which of necessity followed the camera's masculine gaze; and the dominating look of male characters within the filmic narrative, depriving women of agency and subjectivity. Theorizing the cinematic gaze from a psychoanalytic perspective, Mulvey argued that in film viewing the screen paralleled Jacques Lacan's mirror phase in which the child misrecognized his perfect self. Cinema was set up so that men could identify with the idealized male hero within the symbolic order as presented by the narrative, while women were left to identify with figures relegated to inferior status and silenced. Mulvey was one of the first to appropriate psychoanalysis as a political weapon to demonstrate how the patriarchal unconscious has structured film form. The essay's significance derived in part from her vivid language: "Woman's desire is subjugated to her image as bearer of the bleeding wound: she can exist only in relation to castration and cannot transcend it." Man, she argued, can live out his fantasies by "imposing them on the silent image of woman still tied to her place as bearer, not maker, of meaning" (*Visual and Other Pleasures*, p. 14).

In the wake of Mulvey's deliberately polemical essays, certain tropes and conventions began to develop in relation to a "male" gaze and the three "looks" that Mulvey outlined. In addition, British and American television studies had an impact on psychoanalytic feminist

DOROTHY ARZNER
b. San Francisco, California, 3 January 1897, d. 1 October 1979

Dorothy Arzner and Ida Lupino were the only female directors in the classical Hollywood era (roughly 1930 to 1960). Both received scant attention until scholars began to study film from a feminist perspective. After serving her apprenticeship in Hollywood, first as typist and then as screenwriter and successful film editor, Arzner directed films for Paramount from 1927 to 1933, when she left to make films independently. She retired from filmmaking in 1943 for reasons that remain unclear but perhaps have to do with her health or the exhaustion of working in a male-dominated establishment. Despite Arzner's short Hollywood career, she made several important films, including *Christopher Strong* (1933), *Craig's Wife* (1936), and *Dance, Girl, Dance* (1940), that now belong to a canon of what have been called "resisting" Hollywood melodramas.

Although many of her films appear to conform to Hollywood's patriarchal ideology—something Arzner no doubt was careful to do to keep her job—there is often a critical undertow to her narratives. In *Christopher Strong* Katharine Hepburn plays an independent, pioneering female pilot, Lady Cynthia Darrington (loosely modeled on Amelia Earhart). In love with a married man by whom she has become pregnant, she apparently commits suicide when attempting to break an aviation record. Arzner clearly intends the viewer to identify with the courageous female aviation pioneer, and to see in her suicide her sense of responsibility both toward Strong's wife and her unborn child. *Craig's Wife* offers a contrasting type of heroine and demands other kinds of identification from the viewer. Harriet Craig (Rosalind Russell) dominates her daughter,

intervenes in her love life, and tries to prevent her from marrying the man she adores. Although it is hard to identify with Harriet, Arzner manages to show how the entire upper-middle-class family system produces women like her.

Dance, Girl, Dance offers an interesting insight into the often degrading lives of female performers. The film's perhaps dated binary opposition between "high" and "low" female performance art—presented as an opposition between a ballerina (Maureen O'Hara) and a sexy dancer (Lucille Ball)—nevertheless allows her to critique the male gaze and to reveal the crudity of male voyeurism. Women, the film suggests, are split apart because of what men want from them. Thus, in her films Arzner is able to render "strange" the patriarchal ideology pervasive in classical Hollywood cinema.

RECOMMENDED VIEWING
Christopher Strong (1933), *Craig's Wife* (1936), *Dance, Girl, Dance* (1940)

FURTHER READING
Johnston, Claire, ed. *The Work of Dorothy Arzner: Toward a Feminist Cinema*. London: British Film Institute, 1975.

Kaplan, E. Ann. *Motherhood and Representation: The Mother in Popular Culture and Melodrama*. London and New York: Routledge, 1992, 2000.

Mayne, Judith. *Directed by Dorothy Arzner*. Bloomington and Indianapolis: Indiana University Press, 1994.

Suter, Jacqueline. "Feminine Discourse in *Christopher Strong*." *Camera Obscura* 1, no. 2 (1979): 135–150.

E. Ann Kaplan

---

film theory, for the medium of TV necessitated different theories of the spectator–screen relationship. These theories were seen to have some application to film, expanding the rather restricted notion that there was just one "male" gaze.

Mulvey's essay was often misread as a depressing description of woman's fate rather than as a call to action. Mulvey in fact believed that psychoanalytic theory could advance our understanding of the position of women and thereby enable women to move forward. Her effort to challenge the pleasures of Hollywood cinema arose from Hollywood's reliance on voyeurism—the male gaze at the

woman deprived of agency. Her polemical call "to free the look of the camera into its materiality in time and space and the look of the audience into dialectics and passionate detachment" (p. 26) clearly related to her own practice (together with Peter Wollen) as an avant-garde filmmaker.

Mulvey's article prompted a good deal of research, as well as intelligent critiques of her theories. Early on, E. Ann Kaplan's *Women and Film* (1983) tried to straddle some of the debates about feminist film theory ongoing in the 1970s. Asking why some women were so strongly drawn to psychoanalysis and poststructuralism, she

Dorothy Arzner in the 1930s. EVERETT COLLECTION.
REPRODUCED BY PERMISSION.

argued that pointing to social oppression per se could not account for women's second-class status. Attention to language and the unconscious seemed to offer some hope of understanding what increasingly seemed a mystery that biology—namely, that women gave birth and were needed to care for children and that this very function limited what they could achieve—could not explain. Too many exceptions showed that women could overcome or deal with their biological roles; there had to be something deeper, something much harder to change than social policies or cultural norms.

Like other work in the field at the time, Kaplan's conception of the feminine, given its generally heterosexual and Eurocentric focus and orientation, was apparently a monolithic "woman" who was really a white, Western woman, neglecting the specificity of minority and other marginalized women. A bit later, David Rodowick pointed out that Mulvey did not attend to Freud's complex remarks about the contradictoriness of desire that calls into question strict gender binaries such as male/female and activity/passivity. Mary Ann Doane extended Mulvey's research, pursuing avenues that Mulvey only touched on. For example, Doane intro-

duced the concept of the female body in its relation to the psyche, as against the prior focus on image and psyche. She contrasted representation of the female body in Hollywood and in avant-garde cinema, influencing later research. Doane also contrasted male and female distance from the image, arguing that for the male the distance between film and spectator must be maintained, whereas the female overidentifies with the image, obliterating the space between viewer and screen, thereby producing a degree of narcissism. Turning to Joan Riviere's concept of the female masquerade, Doane explores what it might mean to "masquerade" as a spectator. She concludes that there are three possible positions for the female spectator: the masochism of overidentification with the image, the narcissism involved in becoming one's own object of desire, and the possibility of cross-gender identification, as women choose to identify with the male hero. Doane objects to theories of repression because they lack feminine power, instead taking the position that women need to develop a theory of spectatorship apart from those that male culture has constructed for them.

Gaylyn Studlar has suggested that a focus on pre-Oedipality makes more sense than the conventional attention to Oedipal scenarios for explaining how films construct gendered spectators. Substituting Gilles Deleuze's study of Sacher-Masoch's novels for Mulvey's Freudian/Lacanian framework, she argues that masochism can also ground narrative. Studlar replaces Oedipal sadism with pre-Oedipal pleasure, viewing masochism as a "subversive" desire that affirms the compelling power of the pre-Oedipal mother.

BEYOND CINE-PSYCHOANALYSIS

As these debates show, there was never any uniformity within cine-psychoanalysis about the gaze, or about what kind of psychoanalysis was most appropriate to cinematic modes. But with its binarisms, psychoanalytic film theories fitted the Cold War era in that they looked back to nineteenth-century Europe and reflected a world fixed on a framework in which communism versus capitalism was a subtext. Freud's theories enabled an understanding of the neuroses produced in the nineteenth-century bourgeois family—itself the anchoring institution for the Industrial Revolution. In this light, using psychoanalysis in a critique of capitalist ideology made sense. In the years since 1983, US culture and society have changed dramatically, as have international relations. It took the collapse of the Soviet Union to open space for rethinking imperialism and it took the increased flows of peoples across borders and into the academy to encourage new perspectives, such as postmodernism and its related postcolonialism.

Dorothy Arzner's **Dance, Girl, Dance** *(1940) examines male voyeurism.* EVERETT COLLECTION. REPRODUCED BY PERMISSION.

As cine-psychoanalytic theories began to seem rather formulaic—despite the efforts of Doane and other scholars to underscore the complexities and penetrating questions that such theory involved, and despite Mulvey's own continuing "corrections" to her polemical 1975 essay—more resistance to gaze theories arose. In the 1980s B. Ruby Rich, Gayle Arbuthnot, Sue-Ellen Case, and other gay women offered strong critiques emerging from their alternate perspectives (even if these were not so explicitly marked as "lesbian" as in later work). It was primarily the dominance of French structuralism—Lacanian theories, Saussurian semiotics, and Althusserian Marxism—in gaze theories that troubled critics, along with the obvious heterosexual foundation on which the theories were based. It was this foundation that Teresa De Lauretis so profoundly interrogated. Working with Freud's and Luce Irigaray's theories among others, De Lauretis notes the intimate relationship of sexual and social indifference in Western culture

for centuries—a link that served to bolster colonial conquest and racist violence—before turning to examine lesbian representation through diverse attempts of lesbian writers and artists to deploy their struggles in ways that engage the body as linked to language and meaning. Meanwhile, the so-called *Stella Dallas* debate, referring to the 1937 film in which Barbara Stanwyck portrays a woman who gives up her beloved daughter in hopes of giving her a better life among more "respectable" people, dramatized differences emerging in feminist film theory. Kaplan argued that filmic identification with the figure of Stella invited audiences to accept as proper her giving up her daughter and therefore forgoing motherhood through her internalization of patriarchal familial norms. By contrast, Linda Williams argued that the film invited audiences to share multiple points of view, and that Stella's actions could be seen as showing strength and agency. Responses published in *Cinema Journal* between 1984 and 1985 opened for debate and critique some of the

---

LAURA MULVEY
b. Oxford, England, 15 August 1941

Laura Mulvey could not have anticipated the widespread impact of her short polemical essay, "Visual Pleasure and Narrative Cinema," published in 1975 in the British journal *Screen*. The essay's psychoanalytic formulation of a "male gaze," and its condemnation of classical Hollywood cinema's patriarchal bias, immediately provoked interest, debate, and in some quarters dismay. Those who appreciated Mulvey's theories went on, as did Mulvey herself in her extensive writings, to deepen, adjust, and further her insights; those who responded negatively to the essay were challenged to articulate why, and in so doing to develop other theories. Much of the criticism of the essay called into question its strong psychoanalytic stance, shortchanging its political argument. Since the essay's publication, debates within film theory about the utility of psychoanalytic theories have continued.

In a subsequent essay published in 1981, "Afterthoughts on 'Visual Pleasure and Narrative Cinema' inspired by King Vidor's *Duel in the Sun*," Mulvey addressed persistent questions about her lack of attention to the material female spectator in her "Visual Pleasure" essay. She noted that she was less interested in the female spectator who resists the "masculinization" that Hollywood cinema demands than the one who secretly enjoys the freedom of action and agency that identifying with the male protagonist offers. Using Freudian theories about female sexuality as well as Vladimir Propp's analysis of narrative structure in folk tales, Mulvey examined the

difficulty of sexual difference in the western *Duel in the Sun* (1946).

Mulvey is also a filmmaker and has made several with Peter Wollen, including *Penthesilea* (1974), *Riddles of the Sphinx* (1977), and *Amy!* (1979). These films reflect Mulvey's theoretical views of Hollywood cinema, exploring the difficulty of representing the feminine in a patriarchal world. In each film the struggles of women in patriarchy are transformed by placing them within the discourses of psychoanalysis and history. Some of the films make reference to Hollywood cinema—*Amy!*, for example, refers specifically to Dorothy Arzner's *Christopher Strong*—in order to examine the ideological bases of that film.

RECOMMENDED VIEWING

Penthesilea (1974), *Riddles of the Sphinx* (1977), *Amy!* (1979)

FURTHER READING

Fischer, Lucy. *Shot/Countershot: Film Tradition and Women's Cinema*. Princeton, NJ: Princeton University Press, 1989.

Kaplan, E. Ann. *Motherhood and Representation: The Mother in Popular Culture and Melodrama*. London and New York: Routledge, 1992, 2000.

———. *Women in Film: Both Sides of the Camera*. London and New York: Routledge, 1983, 2000.

Mulvey, Laura. *Fetishism and Curiosity*. Bloomington: Indiana University Press, 1996.

———. *Visual and Other Pleasures*. Bloomington: Indiana University Press, 1989.

E. Ann Kaplan

---

assumptions in feminist film theory of the time and introduced research on images of the mother in cinema.

Objections to cine-psychoanalysis included: 1) objection to psychoanalytic film criticism's obvious heterosexism; 2) its apparent exclusion of the body; 3) its equally apparent pessimism about social change because of investment in linguistic theories; 4) its incipient "whiteness"; and 5) its a- or even antihistorical bias. Scholars critiquing psychoanalytic theories refused the inherently Cartesian mind–body split; denied that language was totally determining; attended to cinematic practices and representations of minority, Third World, and gay women; and, finally, corrected the lack of basic historical information by seeking to find out what

women had actually accomplished in Hollywood from its earliest days. If earlier gay and lesbian critiques anticipated the explosion in gay and lesbian approaches to film, as well as the related "queering" of gender images and psychoanalysis, later work was inspired by Judith Butler's theory of gender as performative rather than biological. Black and Latino studies were instituted as more minority students attended college, and debates about US and international racism raged. Inspired work in feminist film and cultural studies began to develop, led by African American critics and filmmakers, such as bell hooks, Michele Wallace, Jacqueline Bobo, and Julie Dash. In *Black Looks: Race and Representation*, for example, hooks justly criticized feminist theorists for their lack of attention to the specificity of race in film. Building on white feminists' gaze theories, hooks coined the term "the oppositional gaze" as she shifted the point of view in a series of readings to the gaze of the hitherto oppressed black subject, whose look at white culture was for so long forbidden. Carol Clover moved gaze theories forward, and feminism backward perhaps, in her groundbreaking 1992 study of the horror film, the genre in which emerges, she argues, a gender crossing that is liberating for males. Heroines in slasher films, she says, are "transformed males," and what looks like male-on-female violence stands in for male-on-male sex. Clover goes on to show, however, that this gender game, once observed, applies in other kinds of film in which, perhaps in response to feminist agendas and analyses, males appropriate the female form for their own ends and desires, a process that challenges gender-specific theories of identification.

The directions in which the field grew and changed, through its destabilization by questions raised by minority, gay, and Third World women, eroded older, seemingly secure binaries of feminist film theory. Psychoanalytic theories of the gaze no longer were central to feminist analysis. However, these ideas then informed "masculinity" studies of Steve Neale, Krin Gabbard, and Peter Lehman, which followed feminist film theory and which were part of the shift from feminist film theory to gender studies in film. Within feminist scholarship, approaches broadened to combine historical, sociological, psychological, and genre aspects in research by Miriam Hansen, Lucy Fischer, Annette Kuhn, and Janice Welsch, among others. Hansen's study of gender in early American cinema brought feminist theory to silent cinema studies, while Kuhn's cultural studies approach includes an ethnographic study of cinema viewing practices through interviews with elderly London residents.

A solid body of feminist research, including feminist film theory, has provided the foundation for much cultural work by third-wave feminists, whose interest in cross-identification, transvestism, and transgender images is taking feminist work in new directions. Psychoanalysis may not be the central focus of many studies, but, like gaze theory, it is now being revised to fit new family paradigms, digital media, and phenomena of late global capitalism. Although the pioneers of feminist film theory have moved on to new topics, feminist theory continues to be relevant to film scholarship. A great deal has been written about feminist film theory and its vicissitudes, including many edited anthologies. Significantly, in 2004 the prestigious journal *Signs* devoted an entire issue to

reevaluating feminist film theory. Almost from its origins, feminist film theory has been defined by lively debates; but important also are the strong links between the feminist movement and feminist scholarship, which have persisted as feminisms have arisen and waned and then reemerged in different environments.

SEE ALSO *Gay, Lesbian, and Queer Cinema; Gender; Marxism; Melodrama; Psychoanalysis; Queer Theory; Woman's Pictures*

FURTHER READING

Clover, Carol. *Men, Women, and Chain Saws: Gender in the Modern Horror Film.* Princeton, NJ: Princeton University Press, 1992.

De Lauretis, Teresa. *The Practice of Love: Lesbian Sexuality and Perverse Desire.* Bloomington, Indiana: Indiana University Press, 1994.

Doane, Mary Ann. "Film and the Masquerade: Theorizing the Female Spectator." *Screen* 24 (September-October 1982): 74–87.

———. "Woman's Stake: Filming the Female Body." In *Feminism and Film*, edited by E. Ann Kaplan, 86–118. Oxford: Oxford University Press, 2002.

Gledhill, Christine, ed. *Home Is Where the Heart Is: Studies in Melodrama and the Woman's Film.* London: British Film Institute, 1987.

Hansen, Miriam. *Babel and Babylon: Spectatorship in American Silent Film.* Cambridge, MA: Harvard University Press, 1994.

Haskell, Molly. *From Reverence to Rape: The Treatment of Women in the Movies.* 2nd ed. Chicago, IL: University of Chicago Press, 1987.

hooks, bell. *Black Looks: Race and Representation.* Boston: South End Press, 1992.

Kaplan, E. Ann. *Women and Film: Both Sides of the Camera.* London and New York: Routledge, 1983, 2000.

Kuhn, Annette. *Cinema, Censorship and Sexuality, 1909–1925.* London and New York: Routledge, 1988.

Mellen, Joan. *Women and Their Sexuality in the New Film.* New York: Horizon Press, 1974.

Mulvey, Laura. "Visual Pleasure and Narrative Cinema." In *Visual and Other Pleasures*, 14–26. Bloomington: Indiana University Press, 1989.

Rodowick, David. "The Difficulty of Difference." *Wide Angle* 5, no. 1 (1982): 4–15.

Rosen, Marjorie. *Popcorn Venus: Women, Movies, and the American Dream.* New York: Avon Books, 1973.

Studlar, Gaylyn. *In the Realm of Pleasure: Von Sternberg, Dietrich, and the Masochistic Aesthetic.* New York: Columbia University Press, 1988.

E. Ann Kaplan

FESTIVALS

———■———

A film festival is an event designed to exhibit, celebrate, and promote a selection of motion pictures chosen according to the particular aims and ambitions of the event's organizers and sponsors. Although the exact origin of the term "film festival" is difficult to determine, its near-universal use probably stems more from its alliterative lilt than from its precision as a descriptive tool. Most film festivals do have characteristics that can be described as festive, such as gala opening ceremonies and guest appearances by directors and celebrities. Still, the events are generally taken quite seriously by the movie buffs, film-industry insiders, and journalists who attend them. Many find festivals to be occasions for prolonged and intensive activity including long hours of screenings, press conferences, question-and-answer sessions, and networking with like-minded professionals and fans.

Beyond these aspects it is hard to generalize about film festivals, which vary widely in their purposes and goals. Some are regional, focusing on productions with limited budgets and ambitions and appealing primarily to local audiences. Others are national or international, drawing attendees from near and far by showcasing a diverse array of movies from many countries. Some have expansive programs with hundreds of titles, whereas others limit their slates to a modest number of rigorously selected entries. Some are eclectic and all-embracing in scope; others have specific interests with regard to genre or format, specializing in such areas as animation, documentary, short films, gay and lesbian films, and films for children. Some give prizes to films, filmmakers, and performers; others deliberately avoid this practice. Few rules for film-festival organizing exist beyond knowing what might currently attract cinema enthusiasts.

HISTORY OF FILM FESTIVALS

The origin of film festivals can be traced to the rise of film societies and cine-clubs, which sprang up in various countries during the 1920s, often as a reaction to what many regarded as the dominance of the newly powerful Hollywood film industry over the cinemas of less well-endowed nations and over noncommercial movements devoted to such causes as documentary and avant-garde film. Such clubs and societies flourished in countries as different as France, where they fostered the emergence of the historically important impressionist and surrealist cinemas, and Brazil, where they provided the only consistent outlet for domestically produced movies. Although most film clubs and societies were in Western Europe, some were established in Latin America and the United States as well. As such groups grew and spread, they started to arrange international conclaves where their members—many of whom were practicing or aspiring filmmakers—could share ideas and inspirations without regard to national borders. Activities like these were the predecessors and prototypes of film festivals per se.

The first true film festival came into being as a direct result of Italian dictator Benito Mussolini's (1883–1945) enthusiasm for motion pictures as a tool for political public relations and propaganda. Eager to spur the development of state-run Italian cinema in the face of competition from Hollywood and elsewhere, he spent lavishly to build up the native film industry while imposing heavy taxation on the dubbing of foreign-language movies, thus hampering their distribution and exhibition. Among the cultural projects he chose to support through his Ministry of Information was the already existing Venice Biennial Exhibition of Italian Art, which gave birth to the

International Exhibition of Cinematographic Art in August 1932 as part of an effort to make the Biennial more varied and multidisciplinary in content. The first cinema program commenced with the premiere of the horror classic *Dr. Jekyll and Mr. Hyde* (Rouben Mamoulian, 1931) and included twenty-four other entries from seven countries. The declared purpose of the exhibition was to allow "the light of art to shine over the world of commerce," but it soon became clear that power politics were a major subtext of the event. In 1935, its first year as an annually scheduled festival, it marked the ongoing rise of European fascism by instituting official prizes in place of the popularity poll and "participation diploma" of the 1932 program. This paved the way not only for a yearly Best Italian Film award but also for productions of Nazi Germany, an Italian ally at that time, to win the Best Foreign Film laurel four times between 1936 and 1942. The arrangement also allowed Leni Riefenstahl's (1902–2003) two-part *Olympia* (1938), a paean to Aryan supremacy in the 1936 Olympic Games, to share the highest prize (the Mussolini Cup) in 1938 with an Italian drama about a fascist soldier in the Ethiopian campaign. It seemed hardly coincidental that Mussolini's oldest son, Vittorio, appeared in the credits as "supervisor" of the latter film. American and British members of the festival jury resigned as soon as these awards were made public.

French participants in the festival also walked out, protesting the Mussolini Cup decisions and expressing belated anger over the 1937 veto by festival authorities of a top prize for Jean Renoir's great war drama *La grande illusion* (*The Grand Illusion*, 1937), the much-admired French entry. This proved to be an unofficial first step toward the establishment of a French film festival designed to outdo and overshadow its Italian counterpart, which was now politically and morally tainted in the eyes of much of the cultural world. The cinema authority Robert Favre le Bret and the historian Philippe Erlanger, who was chief of an organization called Action Artistique Français, headed the committee charged with creating such a festival, and pioneering filmmaker Louis Lumière (1864–1948) served as the group's president. Overcoming fears that such a move would provoke Mussolini's anger, the French government declared its willingness to provide necessary funding, and a few months later the Riviera city of Cannes—having staved off competition from sundry French, Belgian, and Swiss cities—started planning a state-of-the-art Palais des Festivals to house the new event.

Other, smaller festivals had sprung up in the wake of Venice's early success, but it was the advent of Cannes that established the film festival as a staple of the modern cultural scene. Formally dubbed the Cannes International Film Festival, it debuted in September 1939, a time of year

selected so as to extend the traditional tourist season by a couple of weeks. The program included *The Wizard of Oz* (1939) and *Only Angels Have Wings*. Gary Cooper, Mae West, Douglas Fairbanks, Norma Shearer, and Tyrone Power were on the "steamship of stars" dispatched to Cannes by Hollywood's mighty MGM studio. A cardboard model of the Cathedral de Nôtre-Dame was erected on the beach, heralding William Dieterle's (1893–1972) version of *The Hunchback of Notre Dame* (1939) as the festival's opening-night attraction. In a shocking twist, however, the opening film was the only film to be screened: Germany's invasion of Poland on the same day (1 September) led the festival's leaders to close its doors only hours after they had opened. The doors would not reopen until September 1946. (Ironically, the Venice festival also reopened in 1946 after three years of suspension due to the chaos of World War II.) Despite technical problems—projection glitches interrupted the opening-night screening, and reels of Alfred Hitchcock's (1899–1980) thriller *Notorious* (1946) were shown out of order—the Cannes program of 1946 was a great success. Still, the 1947 edition was diminished by the absence of such major countries as England and the Soviet Union, and the 1948 program was canceled. Not until 1951 did Cannes become a dependable yearly event, changing its dates to the spring, when more major movies are available. Since then it has reigned as the world's most prestigious and influential film festival, attracting thousands of journalists to its daylong press screenings and armies of industry professionals to both the festival and the Film Market held concurrently in the Palais and theaters scattered throughout the city.

Festivals proliferated at a growing rate in Europe and elsewhere during the 1950s, affirming the ongoing artistic (and commercial) importance of film at a time when global warfare was becoming a memory and world culture was energetically entering the second half of the twentieth century. Politics played a far smaller role in this phase of festival history than when the Venice and Cannes festivals were founded, but political considerations did not entirely vanish from the scene. The large and ambitious Berlin International Film Festival, for example, was established in 1951, presenting itself as a geographical and artistic meeting ground between East and West as the Cold War climbed into high gear. This was not an easy position to assume, given that socialist nations of the Eastern bloc did not participate officially until 1975, although individual films did represent such countries in the program from time to time.

The most important new festival to emerge in the 1960s was the New York Film Festival, founded in 1963 at Lincoln Center, one of the city's leading cultural venues. Modeled to some extent after the London Film Festival, the New York festival took advantage of Lincoln Center's enormous prestige in the artistic community—

as home to such various institutions as the Metropolitan Opera and the New York Philharmonic, among others—to underwrite the aesthetic pedigree of the art films, avant-garde works, and documentaries that dominated its programs. Such cinema found an enthusiastic (if limited) audience at a time when sophisticated spectators were unusually receptive to innovative foreign movies (from Europe and Japan especially) presented in their original languages with subtitles. Unlike the heavily programmed festivals at Cannes and Berlin, the New York festival showed a limited quantity of films—about two dozen features and a similar number of shorts, chosen by a five-member selection committee—and it declined to give prizes, asserting that its highly selective nature made every work shown there a "winner."

Two key events in film-festival history took place in the 1970s. The first was the 1976 debut of the Toronto International Film Festival, originally known as the Festival of Festivals, a name that underscored its commitment to importing major attractions from other festivals for Canadian audiences. Its first year was marred by the withdrawal of expected contributions from some Hollywood studios, apparently because its Toronto audience base was considered too parochial. Still, in subsequent years it has grown into one of the most all-embracing festivals in the world, with an annual slate ranging from domestic productions to international art films and (ironically) more Hollywood products than are likely to be found at any comparable event. Canada also hosts two other major festivals, the Montreal World Film Festival and the Vancouver International Film Festival.

The other major development of the 1970s was the founding of the United States Film Festival in Salt Lake City in 1978, devised by the Utah Film Commission as a means of spotlighting the state's assets as a site for film production. After concentrating its energies on retrospectives and discussion-centered events for three years, during which it also sponsored a nationwide competition for new independent films, the event moved to the smaller community of Park City in 1981 and began to seek a higher profile. It was acquired in 1985 by actor Robert Redford (b. 1936) and the four-year-old Sundance Institute, which Redford had established to foster the growth of "indie" filmmaking outside the Hollywood system. Renamed the Sundance Film Festival in 1989, it has become an eagerly covered media event as well as a wide-ranging showcase for both independent and international productions.

Alongside the attention-getting world-class festivals, over a thousand more modest events have cropped up. Some have tried to establish uniqueness by using a word other than "festival" in their names, such as the French-American Film Workshop held in New York and Avignon, France, and the Lake Placid Film Forum in upstate New York, which emphasizes relationships between cinema and the written word. Major festivals also exist outside the United States and Europe, such as the Ouagadougou Festival in the African nation of Burkina Faso and the Shanghai and Tokyo festivals in Asia.

LEADING FESTIVALS: NEW YORK, CANNES, TORONTO

Festivals vary in how they choose their films and what types they show, in the degree of geographical diversity they seek, in their willingness to give prizes, and in many other respects. The New York Film Festival presents films chosen by a five-member selection committee—two permanent members who are full-time employees of the Film Society of Lincoln Center and three rotating members (film critics or scholars) who serve terms of three to five years. The event has broadened its scope over the years, adding more special screenings and sidebar programs, including an annual weekend of avant-garde cinema that is unique among major festivals. It remains noncompetitive, however, and considers itself a "public festival" where the intended audience consists primarily of movie buffs, in contrast to the large contingents of film professionals who attend larger-scale North American and European festivals.

By common consensus, Cannes is the single most important film festival in the world. This is partly because of its age, partly because of its size, and partly because success tends to breed success—in other words, the festival traditionally thought of as the most influential is indeed the most influential for that very reason. The Cannes program is chosen by the festival director with the advice of assistant programmers assigned to specialized fields (documentary, Asian cinema, short films, and so on). Robert Favre le Bret, Gilles Jacob, and most recently Thierry Frémaux have had final say over the selection since 1972, when the festival eliminated its policy of allowing each participating country to choose its own presentations. Cannes divides its programs into several categories. The most highly visible is the Competition, usually comprising two features for each day of the twelve-day event, many of them directed by established auteurs of world cinema. Films directed by favored newcomers, including actors with Cannes credentials like Johnny Depp (*The Brave*, 1997) and Vincent Gallo (*The Brown Bunny*, 2003), also make their way into the Competition from time to time, although in the eyes of most critics the results in these two cases were disastrous. The main sidebar program, Un Certain Regard ("A Certain Look"), focuses on movies by newer

ROBERT REDFORD
b. Charles Robert Redford Jr., Santa Monica, California, 18 August 1937

Robert Redford is an internationally known actor, producer, and director who has become an influential festival impresario via the Sundance Film Festival, until 1991 known as the United States Film Festival. Redford acquired the seven-year-old festival in 1985 as an adjunct to the Sundance Institute, which he founded in 1981 to encourage filmmaking outside Hollywood by supporting new directors and screenwriters, and by facilitating the exhibition of independently made fiction and documentary features. The institute now sponsors film-development workshops, a film-music program, and theater projects as well as the festival and the television outlet (the Sundance Channel) for which it is most widely recognized. It has also established the Sundance Collection at the University of California at Los Angeles, an archive that acquires and preserves independent films.

Screening movies is still the institute's most prominent activity: in 2005 the Sundance festival showed more than 200 films for almost 47,000 spectators, three times the attendance of a decade earlier. It also serves as an important marketplace for American and international cinema, attracting distributors and exhibitors on the lookout for fresh, offbeat work. Its reputation for such fare was sparked largely by the 1989 premiere of Steven Soderbergh's debut film *sex, lies, and videotape*. The festival's openness to a wide range of fiction, nonfiction, and international movies has also helped Sundance programmers retain a commitment to "indie" filmmaking while sidestepping issues related to the increasingly blurred boundaries between mainstream (i.e., Hollywood) and independent styles and modes of production.

As a youth Redford studied painting in Europe and attended New York's prestigious American Academy of Dramatic Arts to hone his acting skills. He is also a longtime environmental activist. Such activities signal an artistic ambition and social awareness that run against the grain of Redford's commercially driven Hollywood career, perhaps explaining his decision to put so much money and muscle into organizations dedicated to independent cinema. His performance in the hugely popular western *Butch Cassidy and the Sundance Kid* (1969) made him a top-ranking celebrity. He also starred in such box-office hits as *Barefoot in the Park* (1967), *The Sting* (1973), *The Natural* (1984), and *Indecent Proposal* (1993). The more thoughtful side of his creative personality has surfaced in films such as *All the President's Men* (1976), in which he played one of the *Washington Post* reporters who exposed the Watergate political scandal, and *Ordinary People* (1980) and *Quiz Show* (1994), which he directed.

RECOMMENDED VIEWING

As Actor: *Butch Cassidy and the Sundance Kid* (1969), *The Sting* (1973), *The Way We Were* (1973), *Three Days of the Condor* (1975), *All the President's Men* (1976); As Actor and Director: *The Horse Whisperer* (1998); As Director: *Ordinary People* (1980), *The Milagro Beanfield War* (1988), *A River Runs Through It* (1992), *Quiz Show* (1994), *The Legend of Bagger Vance* (2000)

FURTHER READING

Anderson, John. *Sundancing: Hanging Out and Listening In at America's Most Important Film Festival*. New York: Avon Books, 2000.

Dyer, Richard, and Paul McDonald. *Stars*. London: British Film Institute, 1998.

Friedenberg, Richard, and Robert Redford. *A River Runs Through It: Bringing a Classic to the Screen*. Livingston: Clark City Press, 1992.

David Sterritt

or less-known talents whom the festival considers worthy of attention and support.

Two other series operate outside the formal boundaries of the festival: the International Critics Week, where selections are chosen by a panel of film critics, and the Directors' Fortnight, founded in 1969 as a competitor to the official festival, which was interrupted in the politi-cally charged year of 1968 by disruptive protests involving such major directors as François Truffaut (1932–1984) and Jean-Luc Godard (b. 1930), leading figures in France's revolutionary New Wave filmmaking movement. All of these programs coexist peacefully with the festival and with the concurrent Film Market, established in 1960 as a place where producers, distributors, exhibitors, and

Robert Redford in **All the President's Men** *(1976).* EVERETT COLLECTION. REPRODUCED BY PERMISSION.

others involved in the circulation of new movies can meet, network, and do business with one another. Features shown in the festival may have additional exposure in the market's eighteen screening rooms, although priority for entry to these showings is given to film-industry professionals who purchase market credentials in advance. The market's program for 2004 included approximately fifteen hundred screenings of more than nine hundred films, more than five hundred of them world premieres and the great majority not included in the festival itself. The market also sponsors a Short Film Corner that typically screens hundreds of shorts. In all, these programs attracted more than eight thousand participants in 2004, representing seventy-four countries. The market is thus considered a key interchange for international acquisition and distribution of movies made around the world.

Overall attendance at Cannes is skewed heavily toward film professionals, including film journalists and critics, who see the major entries in regularly scheduled press screenings beginning at 8:30 every morning and proceeding until late evening. The prizes at Cannes are awarded by a jury with a different membership of notable film-world personalities (directors, producers, performers, screenwriters, etc.) each year. At times jury decisions diverge greatly from the impression made by a given film on festival-goers in general, as when Bruno Dumont's ambitious French production *L'Humanité* (1999) won the Grand Prize of the Jury as well as best actress (shared) and best actor awards after being jeered at during its press screening. The prizes given at Cannes vary a bit from one year to another, but always include the top Palme d'Or (Golden Palm) award as well as a Grand Prize, a Jury Prize given to a technician, and prizes for best actress, actor, screenplay, and director. In addition, honors are given by a separate jury to three short films; the Cinéfondation of France bestows three awards; and the Caméra d'Or prize is given to the best Competition or Certain Regard film directed by a first-time filmmaker. The highest prizes at Cannes, especially the Golden Palm, are considered the most prestigious of all motion-picture honors with the possible exception of the Academy Awards®.

The Toronto festival awards several prizes, but the practice has a lower profile than at Cannes. The People's Choice Award is determined by audience ballots after each public screening; the Discovery Award is voted on by members of the press, representing several hundred international media outlets; and juries select the recipients of awards for best Canadian feature, best Canadian feature by a first-time director, and best Canadian short film. In addition, an independent jury administered by the International Federation of Film Critics gives an award for the best feature by an emerging filmmaker. (More commonly known by its European acronym, FIPRESCI, this organization establishes prize-giving juries, composed of film critics, at many festivals around the world.) Toronto is generally seen as the most important North American festival and a close second to Cannes in terms of global influence. Its wide-ranging program is divided into numerous categories including Galas and Special Presentations for high-profile features, Masters for works by recognized auteurs, Director's Spotlight for works by especially adventurous or under-recognized filmmakers, National Cinema for features from a particular country selected for attention that year, Wavelengths and Visions for experimental and avant-garde works, and until 2004, Perspective Canada for domestic productions. As at Cannes, film professionals make up much of the audience, but many local movie-goers can be found in the public screenings (as opposed to the press screenings) as well.

LESSER-KNOWN FESTIVALS

Festivals with lower profiles, from the interestingly specialized to the obscure, abound. One film critic has estimated that New York City alone has no fewer than thirty. Iowa has the Hardacre Film Festival, North Carolina the Hi Mom Film Festival. Other festivals signal their specialties via their unusual names. Examples include the Rendezvous with Madness Film and Video Festival in Canada, organized around works about mental illness and addiction; the Madcat Women's International Film Festival in California, featuring independent and experimental work by women; and the Tacoma Tortured Artists International Film Festival in Washington, devoted to independent filmmakers.

One of the most respected specialized festivals is Pordenone-Le Giornate del Cinema Muto, established in 1982 by the Cinemazero Film Club and La Cineteca del Friuli, a film archive. Focusing entirely on silent cinema, this event in the north of Italy draws an international audience of archivists, scholars, critics, and adventurous movie fans to a wide range of programming that has included everything from Krazy Kat cartoons and Cecil B. DeMille melodramas to century-old kinetoscopes and comedies with forgotten American entertainers. Also highly regarded is the Locarno International Film Festival, launched by its Swiss founders in 1946 and celebrated for

its attention to films by first- and second-time directors, and for its screenings of underrated movies chosen by currently well-known filmmakers. The hugely ambitious Rotterdam International Film Festival in the Netherlands has earned high marks for its commitment to avant-garde cinema as well as children's films, new features by innovative directors, and an Exploding Cinema sidebar devoted to multimedia projects. This festival also presents film-related lectures and gives monetary grants to promising directors from developing nations through the Hubert Bals Fund, which it administers. The San Francisco International Film Festival, established in 1957, helped blaze various trails for the growing American festival scene with its eclectic blend of major new productions, classics restored to mint condition, and retrospectives devoted to filmmakers better known by art-film enthusiasts than by the general public.

Among the more unusual American festivals is the Telluride Film Festival, founded in 1974 in a small Colorado town—once a mining community, now a popular skiing site—and considered by many to be one of the world's most intelligently programmed cinema events. It refuses to divulge its schedule until ticket-holders arrive at the festival gate, making attendance less a matter of access to particular premieres than of overall faith in the programmers. Telluride ensures the presence of celebrities—a diverse lot ranging from the actress Shirley MacLaine to the novelist Salman Rushdie—by holding tributes, complete with screenings of relevant films and the awarding of medals, to three film-world notables each year. Screenings are held in several venues including a community center and an intimate opera house where Sarah Bernhardt (1844–1923) and Jenny Lind (1820–1887) performed during the mining-boom era; the original marquee of the opera house, displaying the word "SHOW" in large letters, is still standing and serves as the festival's trademark. The legendary Warner Bros. animator Chuck Jones (1912–2002), a frequent attendee until his death in 2002, once paid his respects to Telluride's nine-thousand-foot elevation by saluting the festival as "the most fun you'll ever have without breathing."

THE FUTURE OF FILM FESTIVALS

Film festivals will most likely retain their popularity. However, they are also likely to change their selection standards and exhibition formats as technological developments in cinema—such as the increasing use of digital systems in cinematography and projection processes—alter the nature of cinema itself. Most festivals have already shown an increased willingness to judge films for potential selection on the basis of video copies rather than 35 mm prints, and many have opened the door (in some cases grudgingly) to public screenings using video-projection systems, especially when the movie was originally shot on video. Another question that confronts the program directors of many general-interest festivals is whether they should focus primarily on the best of cinematic art—which may include obscure, difficult, and esoteric works—or turn in more commercially oriented directions. By courting movies with trendy themes, palatable styles, and major stars who may agree to make personal appearances, festivals could potentially draw larger audiences, attract greater press attention, and satisfy financial sponsors banking on association with celebrities and their projects.

The staying power of film festivals will continue to depend, in part, on providing an alternative to the multiplex. The shrinking number of art-film theaters, owing to competition from cable television and the home-video industry, also lends increasing importance to festivals. Exhibition patterns have always influenced cinematic styles, and the festival phenomenon has given indispensable exposure to new and unconventional works that might not otherwise be seen by the producers, distributors, exhibitors, and others who largely control the financial infrastructure of theatrical film. Also invaluable is many festivals' practice of spotlighting overlooked or forgotten movies from the past that would otherwise remain unknown to—or at least unviewable by—scholars and critics as well as curious movie fans. Ever since

Venice commenced its festival activities in the 1930s, such events have amply proven their merit as what Richard Peña, the New York Film Festival program director, describes as "a refuge from the vicissitudes of the marketplace." Film festivals are indeed one of the vital signs of a thriving cinema.

SEE ALSO *Academy Awards®; Prizes and Awards*

FURTHER READING

Anderson, John. *Sundancing: Hanging Out and Listening In at America's Most Important Film Festival.* New York: Avon Books, 2000.

Beauchamp, Cari, and Henri Béhar. *Hollywood on the Riviera: The Inside Story of the Cannes Film Festival.* New York: Morrow, 1992.

Gaydos, Steven. *The Variety Guide to Film Festivals: The Ultimate Insider's Guide to Film Festivals around the World.* New York: Perigee, 1998.

Langer, Adam. *The Film Festival Guide: For Filmmakers, Film Buffs, and Industry Professionals.* Chicago: Chicago Review Press, 2000.

Stolberg, Shael, ed. *International Film Festival Guide.* Toronto: Festival Products, 2000.

Turan, Kenneth. *Sundance to Sarajevo: Film Festivals and the World They Made.* Berkeley: University of California Press, 2002.

David Sterritt

FILM HISTORY

There is no single or simple history of film. As an object of both academic and popular interest, the history of film has proven to be a fascinatingly rich and complex field of inquiry. Coffee-table books, multipart documentaries, television networks that predominantly feature movies, scholarly monographs, and textbooks have cut different paths through this field. As a result, film history can look quite different, depending on whether the focus of attention is on individual films, institutional practices, national cinemas, or global trends. Indeed, the history of film's remarkable rise in the twentieth century has been told in a variety of ways: as the story of artistic triumphs and box-office winners; of movie moguls and larger-than-life stars; of corporatization and consumption; of auteur directors and time-honored genres; of technology and systemization; and of audiences and theaters. Taken even more broadly, the history of film becomes an account of the shifting roles and multiple effects of cinema—culturally, socially, and politically.

Across this range of options, film history confronts, implicitly or explicitly, a number of provocative and knotty questions: From a larger historical perspective, what is the role of the individual film and the individual filmmaker? What are the social and cultural contexts within which the movies were produced and consumed? What does the history of film have to do with other twentieth-century histories—of technology, business, commercial entertainment, the modern nation-state, globalization?

VARIETIES OF FILM HISTORY

Given the fact that film is at once art, industry, mass media, and influential form of cultural communication, it is not surprising that the history of film can be approached from a number of quite distinct angles. A concern with technology, for example, raises questions about the invention, introduction, and diffusion of moving picture projection systems and cameras, as well as color, sound, and wide-screen processes. Technological history has been especially prominent in discussions of the pre-1900 period, the transformation to sound in the late 1920s and the 1930s, and the struggle to compete with television during the 1950s. To explore the history of home movies and amateur film also necessarily involves questions of so-called "small-gauge" technology (most notably, 8 mm and 16 mm), and any broader overview of film exhibition must take into account the technology of the movie theater, including the projection apparatus and, from the 1980s on, sophisticated sound systems.

Technology is intimately connected to the economics of the motion picture industry, another key aspect of film history that has received considerable interest from scholars. Most attention has been given to the internal workings and the ongoing transformations of the Hollywood studio system, both in terms of how individual studios have operated and also in terms of the concerted efforts by studios to maintain monopolistic control over the industry. Economic history also takes up labor relations and unionization, government attempts to regulate the film industry through antitrust actions, and the financial framework and corporate affiliation of major studios in the United States and Europe. Equally central to any historical understanding of the economics of the industry are the complex relations among production, distribution, and exhibition, including the role of Hollywood in exporting American films to the rest of the world. While exhibition has recently received considerable attention—as in, for example, Douglas Gomery's *Shared Pleasures* (1992) and Gregory A. Waller's *Moviegoing in America* (2002)—distribution remains understudied.

More than economics, technology also figures in what has been called formalist or aesthetic histories of film, which tend to focus on questions concerning narrative and audio-visual style and, more generally, the art and craft of cinema. This approach has tended to emphasize masterworks and great directors, celebrating their innovations and contributions to a tradition of cinematic art. The auteur theory, for example, has informed much popular film history. At the same time, more systematic (even statistically based) approaches to the history of film style have looked less at world-famous directors like D. W. Griffith (1875–1948), Sergei Eisenstein (1898–1948), and Jean Renoir (1894–1979) and more at the norms and opportunities available to filmmakers under specific conditions of production, in and out of Hollywood. Such approaches consider, for example, how editing practices, camera movement, and uses of the soundtrack have changed over time.

The historical study of film genres also takes up formal concerns, as well as other topics having to do with the cultural and ideological role of popular film. American film history has sometimes been understood primarily in terms of the changing fortunes of genres like the gangster film, western, film noir, and the musical. More interesting is the considerable amount of historical work that has been done on individual genres, offering a complex picture of how genres emerge, flourish, and decline both in terms of the films produced and the reception of these films by audiences at the time and by later generations of fans and critics. The history of film genres, as presented, for example, by James Naremore in *More Than Night* (1998), has also raised important questions about intermedia relations, that is, the way the course of film history has been significantly affected by contemporary practices in literature, live theater, radio, popular music, and television.

Popular genres, as might be expected, often figure prominently in social or cultural histories, which seek in a variety of different ways to situate film within a broader context or to shift focus away from individual films, directors, and studios to questions about how cinema is constructed, circulated, understood, and monitored in a particular class, region, or subculture or in society at large. One prominent concern of social history is the film audience: How has it been defined and policed? What is its makeup in terms of class, race,

and gender? What is its reception of particular movies and cinema in general? To explore what moviegoing has meant in specific historical situations has necessarily involved a greater attention to the practices and strategies of film exhibition. From nickelodeon and picture palace to drive-in and suburban megaplex, the movie theater has proven to be a key site for exploring the place of film in the everyday life of the twentieth century and for considering how a film experience intended for a national or global audience is presented and consumed at a local level.

Other major areas of social and cultural historical research are the ideological import of cinematic representations (of race, gender, and sexuality, for example); the formal and informal processes of censorship; the role of official government cultural policy (which is of particular import outside the United States); and the connections between cinema and consumer culture, through advertising, product tie-ins, and so on. Of crucial importance in this regard is the vast amount of written material surrounding and concerning the movies, from trade journals and promotional matter to reviews, fan magazines, and—more recently—Internet sites.

TRENDS IN FILM HISTORY

The earliest film histories, like Terry Ramsaye's *A Million and One Nights* (2 vols., 1926; originally published in *Photoplay* magazine, beginning in 1921), were intended for a general audience. These works offered first-person, highly anecdotal accounts written by journalists, inventors, and filmmakers who frequently were insiders to the motion picture industry. Ramsaye, for instance, had worked as a publicist. His book and others like it set a model for a sort of film history that is preoccupied with movie personalities and filled with broad claims about the step-by-step "progress" of film as art and industry. Foregrounded in such works is the role of inventors like Thomas Edison and directors like D. W. Griffith, certain landmark films, influential stylistic innovations, and major technological advances. Much popular history concerning, in particular, classic Hollywood, carries on this tradition, offering a narrative account of movie history that features individual artists, inventors, and executives rebelling against or working securely within the demands of the commercial entertainment industry. This "great man" version of history typically goes hand in hand with a belief that the historian's task is, in part, to identify and celebrate a canon of cinematic masterworks.

Writing at the end of the silent era, the British filmmaker and critic Paul Rotha (1907–1984) took a somewhat different tack in *The Film till Now* (1930), emphasizing distinctive national cinema traditions and giving special attention to films and filmmakers that challenged standard Hollywood practices. Both of these emphases have also frequently been features of film history textbooks. After Rotha there have been several significant attempts at world or global histories of film, like *Histoire du Cinema* (5 vols., 1967–1980), by Jean Mitry. Until recently, with, for example, *The Oxford History of World Cinema* (1999), attempts at international film history have generally been plagued by a decidedly Eurocentric, if not always American, bias. The lack of full attention to non-Western film has arisen from the assumption that film history is above all concerned with film production, filmmakers, and film studios (principally the domain of Hollywood, Bollywood, and a few European companies) rather than with exhibition, reception, and worldwide film audiences.

Most typically, film history has been understood in national terms. This is reflected in the number of books devoted exclusively to Hollywood and American cinema, beginning with Lewis Jacobs's *The Rise of the American Film* (1939) and culminating in Scribner's ten-volume *History of the American Cinema* (1990–2000), a towering achievement. Other national cinemas, too, have frequently been a key subject for historians, from New Zealand and Japan to Cuba and Canada. While specific details vary from country to country, this form of film history reinforces what is assumed to be a strong correlation between the cultural, economic, and social life of a particular nation and the films produced in that nation. National histories of film typically celebrate homegrown auteurs and award-winning titles, "new waves," and the sort of films that circulate on the international film festival circuit. More recently, however, the widespread interest in industry practices, government cultural policy, and popular genres has led to groundbreaking research on national cinemas that draws heavily on archival sources, as in Peter B. High's *The Imperial Screen* (2003), a study of Japanese film during the Pacific War era.

The 1970s and 1980s saw a major turn toward historical research in academic film studies, led in part by a new interest in early silent cinema (1895–1910), which completely reshaped our understanding of the origins of the American film industry, the audience that took up moviegoing during the nickelodeon era, and the introduction of narrative film. This type of revisionist history, which makes extensive use of primary documents (including the trade press and archival motion-picture holdings) and rejects simple notions of progress and celebrations of "great men," got a major boost in *Film History: Theory and Practice* (1985), Robert C. Allen and Douglas Gomery's assessment of the discipline and blueprint for future research. Equally

significant was the publication that year of David Bordwell, Janet Staiger, and Kristin Thompson's *Classical Hollywood Cinema*, an exhaustively researched study based on a randomly selected body of films and a range of industry-related print material. This influential book set out to investigate Hollywood's evolving mode of production, its incorporation of technological change, and its elaboration of a cinematic style that served as the norm for American movies between 1917 and 1960.

Since the mid-1980s the study of film history has been strongly influenced by other major scholarly trends, notably, feminist, postcolonial, and cultural studies, as well as reception studies that focus on social identities and film-related public discourses. There has also been an increasing emphasis on historical case studies in article or monograph form that rely on significant primary research to focus in detail on a relatively narrow period, topic, or institutional practice. Works like Eric Schaefer's *"Bold! Daring! Shocking! True!"* (1999), a history of exploitation films, and Lee Grieveson's *Policing Cinema* (2004), an account of early film censorship, exemplify the highly focused yet still very ambitious research that has continued to enrich and complicate our understanding of film history in and out of Hollywood, within and beyond the walls of the movie theater.

SEE ALSO *Canon and Canonicity*

FURTHER READING

Allen, Robert C., and Douglas Gomery. *Film History: Theory and Practice*. New York: Knopf, 1985.

Bordwell, David, Janet Staiger, and Kristin Thompson. *The Classical Hollywood Cinema: Film Style and Modes of Production to 1960*. New York: Columbia University Press, 1985.

Crafton, Donald. *The Talkies: American Cinema's Transition to Sound, 1926–1931*. New York: Scribner's, 1997.

Gomery, Douglas. *Shared Pleasures: A History of Movie Presentation in the United States*. Madison: University of Wisconsin Press, 1992.

Grieveson, Lee. *Policing Cinema: Movies and Censorship in Early Twentieth-Century America*. Berkeley: University of California Press, 2004.

High, Peter B. *The Imperial Screen: Japanese Film Culture in the Fifteen Years' War, 1931–1945*. Madison: University of Wisconsin Press, 2003.

Jacobs, Lewis. *The Rise of the American Film: A Critical History*. New York: Teachers College Press, 1939.

Musser, Charles. *The Emergence of Cinema: The American Screen to 1907*. New York: Scribner's, 1990.

Naremore, James. *More Than Night: Film Noir in Its Contexts*. Berkeley: University of California Press, 1998.

Nowell-Smith, Geoffrey, ed. *Oxford History of World Cinema.* New York: Oxford University Press, 1999.

Ramsaye, Terry. *A Million and One Nights: A History of the Motion Picture through 1925.* New York: Simon & Schuster, 1926.

Rotha, Paul. *The Film till Now.* London: J. Cape, 1930.

Schaefer, Eric. *"Bold! Daring! Shocking! True!": A History of Exploitation Films, 1919–1959.* Durham, NC: Duke University Press, 1999.

Waller, Gregory A. *Moviegoing in America: A Sourcebook in the History of Film Exhibition.* Malden, MA: Blackwell, 2002.

Gregory A. Waller

FILM NOIR

In 1946, French film critics coined the term *film noir*, meaning black or dark film, to describe a newly emergent quality in wartime Hollywood films. At that time, the term signified an unexpected strain of maturity in contemporary American film, marking the end of a creatively ossified era and the beginning of a bold new one. By the time the term achieved wide English language usage in the 1960s, however, it had come to mean dark Hollywood films of the past—films whose era and style were no longer current. Despite such a slippage in definition, *film noir* remains arguably the most protean and influential of American film forms. It has demonstrated a limitless capacity for reinvention, has undergone major cycles of redefinition, and has analogues not only in other national cinemas but also in radio, television, theater, fiction, graphic novels, comic books, advertising, and graphic design. The term has moved beyond the domain of film discourse and has been used to describe narratives in other media and genres. There is even a "*Film Noir*" lipstick.

OVERVIEW

Film noir indicates a darker perspective upon life than was standard in classical Hollywood films and concentrates upon human depravity, failure, and despair. The term also implies a cinematic style: a way of lighting, of positioning and moving the camera, of using retrospective voice-over narration. Its narrative often relies heavily on flashbacks and choice of setting—usually a seedy, urban landscape, a world gone wrong. *Film noir* has stylistic and thematic antecedents in American hardboiled fiction of the 1920s and 1930s, German expressionist films of the 1920s, American horror films and radio dramas of the 1930s and 1940s, and French cinema of the 1930s. Its first cycle ran from the 1940s to the late 1950s. After 1960, neo-*noir* films have included a component antithetical to the earlier films: a conflicted nostalgia for the post–World War II era evoked in references to the period's sociocultural atmosphere as well as to its filmmaking practices.

Film noir emerged during World War II with films like *Double Indemnity* (1944); *Laura* (1944); *Murder, My Sweet* (1944); *Phantom Lady* (1944); *Mildred Pierce* (1945); *Scarlet Street* (1945); and *The Woman in the Window* (1945). Its foundations had been laid in the early 1940s, in films such as *Stranger on the Third Floor*, with its sinister look, nightmare sequence, and atmosphere of perverse and unstable masculinity, *The Maltese Falcon*, with its themes of widespread evil and deviant as well as manipulative sexuality, and *Citizen Kane* (1941), with its dark, expressionist look and fragmented narration.

Although reviews at the time commented on the depravity, sexual degradation, and violence in many of these films, they linked them only insofar as they manifested a gritty "realism." Other common elements among many of the films are retrospectively apparent, such as the large number of Germanic émigré directors, including Fritz Lang (1890–1976), Otto Preminger (1906–1986), Robert Siodmak (1900–1973), and Billy Wilder (1906–2002); their dark "studio" look, often employing expressionistic "mystery" lighting; their use of retrospective, voice-over narration; their engagement with potentially censorable material; their themes of unstable identity, often involving amnesia or identity alteration, and of gender instability, concentrating in particular upon *femmes fatales* and weak men; their

***Expressionist style in Anthony Mann's* T-Men *(1947).* EVERETT COLLECTION. REPRODUCED BY PERMISSION.**

deterministic view of human behavior; their narratives of failed enterprises; the influence of psychoanalytic concepts (such as fetishism, masochism, repression, and various compulsions) upon their characters' construction; and their atmosphere of disorientation and anxiety.

Not surprisingly, neo-*noir* films display a self-consciousness alien to earlier ones. Many creative participants in the earlier films were not being disingenuous when they claimed that they never knew they were making *films noirs* when they were making *films noirs*. The films initially appeared under many guises, only to be categorized as *film noir* at a great distance, first by the French in 1946 and then by English-speaking critics after 1960. But lack of intentionality does not mean that the filmmakers did not draw on a common sensibility and gravitate toward similar filmmaking practices. Over time, those commonalities have conferred a powerful generic status on the films that is much stronger than earlier, more diverse perceptions of them.

The first *films noirs* were made as detective films, mysteries, melodramas, social problem films, crime films,

and thrillers. They were produced as A films by major studios, as products of B-movie divisions of major and minor studios, and as low-budget, independent films. Some studios, like RKO, developed divisions for the production of inexpensive genre films, many of which have subsequently been called *films noirs*. While these films were products of Hollywood's "Golden Age," they collectively deviate from popular notions of Hollywood entertainment.

INFLUENCES

Hard-boiled popular fiction gave *film noir* its narrative models, major themes, and verbal style. The genre is commonly associated with the detective fiction of writers like Dashiell Hammett (1894–1961) and Raymond Chandler (1888–1959), which first appeared in the 1920s and provided an alternative to the then-dominant British detective fiction of writers like Sir Arthur Conan Doyle, Dorothy Sayers, and Agatha Christie. The British model presumes a benign society into which crime erupts as an aberration: once a detective has solved the crime, society returns to tranquility. Hard-boiled fiction, to the contrary, presumes a corrupt world in which crime is an everyday occurrence. Its characters are often driven by destructive urges that they can neither understand nor control. Although a detective may solve the story's motivating crime, he entertains no illusions that this small victory makes the world a better place. One narrative model that *film noir* draws from such fiction implicates the detective when the crime he attempts to solve unexpectedly draws him into its consequences. He often becomes ensnared by a *femme fatale* or gets set up as the "fall guy" for a larger crime. Nearly everyone with whom he deals is duplicitous. Hard-boiled fiction was not limited to detective fiction; Cornell Woolrich's (1903–1968) *Phantom Lady* and James M. Cain's (1892–1977) *Double Indemnity* and *The Postman Always Rings Twice* share this perspective on life and provided sources for important *films noirs*.

Hard-boiled fiction—particularly the first-person narration of Chandler's novels—introduced a cynical, doomed, and grimly poetic tone. Its verbal style is apparent in both the wisecracks of the detective and in the moody, voice-over narration dominating many of the films.

German expressionist cinema gave *film noir* a mood, a visual style, and some themes. A cinema obsessed with madness, loneliness, and the perils of a barely coherent world, it emerged after Germany's devastating defeat in World War I and reflected the despair of the times. Its first major film was *Das Kabinett des Doktor Caligari* (*The Cabinet of Dr. Caligari*, 1920). Nearly everything in it is highly stylized, particularly the set design, which appears to be part of a demented dream, not unlike the despairing mood of many *noirs*.

By the mid-1920s, expressionism had become a widely respected style, imitated by Hollywood directors like John Ford (1894–1973), and by the 1930s, many expressionist directors and technicians had emigrated to Hollywood, influencing its emergent horror genre directly. A decade later, *film noir* applied these same tropes of madness, despair, and disorientation to the world of "normal," middle-class experience.

A sophisticated use of the sound track was a defining innovation of *film noir,* drawing upon techniques developed in American network radio. Network radio and sound film both began in the late 1920s, and by the 1940s, they enjoyed great success. It was not until then that Hollywood learned to use soundtracks in genuinely complex ways, rather than simply as adjuncts to image tracks. By then, network radio had developed writers, technicians, and actors skilled at presenting stories using sound alone; its popularity had accustomed listening audiences to understand complex layerings of sound.

Radio narration went beyond linear, retrospective storytelling and employed dynamic interactions between narrating voices ("It all began last Tuesday when …") and dramatic ones ("Who's there?"). Sometimes the same voice narrated and participated in the dramatic action—a common trope in *films noirs*, which used sound to present two versions of a single character simultaneously. The narrator's voice-over in *Double Indemnity*, for example, appears throughout the film, telling us his story at a time when he already knows he is doomed; he also speaks throughout the flashback scenes. We hear both his depressed narrating voice and his optimistic younger self, which has not yet learned what both narrator and viewer already know—that his scheme will fail. The aural and visual contrast between his optimistic self and the somber, despairing tone of his narrating self create complex layers of character.

Postwar disillusionment gave *film noir* a mood and a social context. Victory in World War II did not bring the peacetime happiness that many had anticipated. Films like *The Blue Dahlia* (1946) show wartime veterans feeling isolated after they return. This disillusionment is also evident in non-*noir* films of the era, such as that Christmas perennial, *It's a Wonderful Life* (1947), in which the ugly side of small town America drives a decent businessman to near-suicide. Its miraculously happy ending does not entirely erase the sinister darkness that its portrait of small town life creates.

Disillusionment came from many directions. Women, who had been encouraged to join the work force during the war, now felt pressured to leave it to make room for returning veterans. Labor unions, many of which had been forbidden to strike during the war, now demanded long-awaited benefits. The defeat of the Axis powers did not bring about international security, because the Cold War emerged, generating anxiety about Communist infiltration.

Technological advances made during the war allowed postwar filmmakers greater freedom from the confines of studios. Film stocks were improved, enabling cinematographers to capture a wider range of light than previously possible and, at the same time, to need less in the way of bulky lights; sound recording equipment, particularly improvements in the wire recorder, became more portable; lighter cameras with better lenses became available. Although traditionally composed films had always used location shooting, it had been cumbersome and expensive. Now these technological developments dovetailed with a public taste for "realism" in films and with critical respect for Italian neorealism, a new style from Italy that explored the unvarnished realities of contemporary life. In the United States, Louis de Rochemont (1899–1978), who had produced the *March of Time* newsreels, produced films such as *The House on 92nd Street* (1945), *Boomerang* (1947), and *Walk East on Beacon* (1952), which used a newsreel aesthetic. These films, and others like them, deal with a world of crime and betrayal, subversion, and people on the edge. Many have been called *films noirs*, but they look and feel differently from *films noirs* like *Double Indemnity* or *Scarlet Street*. They have a strong narrating presence, but instead of the tormented voice-overs of films like *Double Indemnity* or *Out of the Past* (1947), they often employ an authoritative "Voice of God" narrator associated with a governmental institution, such as the FBI or the Treasury Department. They have a very different look from the expressionistic films mentioned earlier, although some of their scenes do have a dark look. They often advertised themselves as "real" or "true," or "pulled from the headlines." *The House on 92nd Street* prides itself on including "actual FBI" surveillance footage. These films mark the first major reinvention of *film noir*.

Clearly, the term *film noir* casts a wide net and has meant different things at different times. Certain images, narrative structures, character types, and themes are widely perceived as typifying it, however. Standard perceptions of *film noir* include atmospheric black-and-white films from the 1940s and 1950s with specific character types, such as a hard-boiled detective, a *femme fatale*, a middle-class man in a doomed affair, a rootless drifter, a slick underworld night-club owner; narrative patterns, such as an adulterous couple whose murderous plot leads to their doom, a prosperous, middle-class life unraveling into death or madness, a detective investigating a mystery that turns on him, a drifter or criminal seeking a quick score and then drawn into murder and catastrophe, a couple on the run; iconic images and settings (desolate, nocturnal, urban streets; brightly lit, art-deco nightclubs; mysterious, darkened rooms lit through Venetian blinds); shadowy shots of someone watching from a hidden place; iconic performers (wise-cracking, trench-coated Humphrey Bogart; desperate, embittered Dick Powell; terrified, or arrogant, Barbara Stanwyck; sultry Lauren Bacall; Veronica Lake peering through her eye-shrouding hair; arrogant, smug Clifton Webb or George Macready; Robert Mitchum looking grimly resigned or dreamily indifferent; Dana Andrews methodically puzzling out a mystery). The overall atmosphere is one in which something—everything—has gone terribly wrong, a world heavy with doom, paranoia justified and closing in.

APPEAL

Given its doom-laden world, *film noir* offers the voyeuristic pleasure of watching transgression play itself out. Audiences saw morally compromised people doing immoral things; stories involved the forbidden, the sin-

ful. The films pushed the boundaries of contemporary censorship: their ads promised the titillations of easy women, violent men, and doomed enterprises—cheap thrills with dire consequences. In soliciting viewers' identification with doomed people, the films court masochistic pleasure.

A cliché about classical Hollywood films is that they required happy endings. *Film noir* challenges this generalization. Many *films noirs* develop virtually no expectation of happy endings; to the contrary, they quickly establish a foreboding of disaster. Characters in many films describe themselves as walking dead men. Part of the appeal of *film noir* lies in the expectation that things will turn out very badly.

Often, the retrospective, voice-over narrative structure of many such films removes the traditional pleasure—found particularly in mysteries—of wondering how the plot will turn out. The narrator often reveals the outcome at the beginning. The narrator of *Double Indemnity*, for example, confesses as the film begins that he committed murder for money and a woman and then tells us that he didn't get the money and he didn't get the woman. For the rest of the film, then, the audience knows that his plans will fail. The central character in *D.O.A.* (1950) announces at the beginning of the film that he has been murdered by poison and has only hours to live. The audience does not have to wonder what will happen to him; they already know. What, then, is the appeal?

Much of *noir*'s appeal is voyeuristic—the pleasure of watching the specifics of how it all came to this. Tabloid journalism provides a useful narrative analogue. A headline may announce "Man murders lover and her husband for insurance money: Gets nothing." The reader knows the outcome from the beginning but reads on to savor the crime's gory details. Virtually all *films noirs* from the 1940s and 1950s were set in the present. Characters looked and generally behaved like people that audience members might see when they left the theater. *Noirs* dealt with the kinds of tragedies, scandals, and duplicities that bordered on their audience's everyday experiences and that appeared regularly in tabloids.

HISTORY

A rough overview of *film noir* begins in the early 1940s with films like *The Maltese Falcon*, which presented a new, darker perspective on the characters and themes of hard-boiled fiction. Two earlier films, the 1931 *The Maltese Falcon* and the 1936 *Satan Met a Lady*, had been based upon Hammett's novel of the same name. Both handled crime in the lighthearted manner typifying detective films in the 1930s. John Huston's (1906–1987) 1941 film brought a new, grim tone to the

ROBERT MITCHUM
b. Bridgeport, Connecticut, 6 August 1917, d. 1 July 1997

Robert Mitchum's extraordinarily long and fertile Hollywood career developed chiefly around his association with *film noir*. As an actor, the tension between his half-asleep, dreamily indifferent expression and a powerful, broad-shouldered physical presence enabled him to dominate scenes while also seeming abstracted from them. He appeared to confront either success or doom as if he didn't really care, which made him ideal for *film noir*.

After his Academy Award® nomination for portraying the heroic, doomed lieutenant in *The Story of G.I. Joe* (1945), he was signed by RKO Studios, where he starred in important *films noirs* such as *Out of the Past* and *Crossfire* (both 1947). Even the westerns he made at this time, such as *Pursued* (1947) and *Blood on the Moon* (1948), were noted for their *noir*-ish tone.

Out of the Past is possibly the most iconic *film noir*, with its voice-over narration, atmosphere of doom, chiaroscuro lighting, emasculated men and *femme fatale,* and strong influence of Freudian concepts upon character construction and narrative organization. Mitchum plays a man whose hidden past catches up with him. A former private detective hired to find a *femme fatale,* Mitchum's character falls for her, an act that sends his life spiraling into murder, betrayal, and death. Having failed in his attempt to build a new life, he orchestrates his own death. Mitchum's haunting portrayal of a man losing everything important to him is one of his most eloquent.

Mitchum's rebellious off-screen reputation, culminating in his arrest for possession of marijuana in 1948, seemed to blend with his darker roles. This image was enhanced by his skill at playing unregenerate, psychotic villains in films like *Night of the Hunter* (1955), *Cape Fear* (1962), and in the television series *A Killer in the Family* (1983). A less-discussed counterpoint to this

aspect of his image was his career-long effectiveness at playing socially responsible authority figures in films like *Crossfire*, *The Enemy Below* (1957), *The Longest Day* (1962), and in the popular television miniseries *The Winds of War* (1983).

Long after the era of *film noir* ended, he contributed to the neo-*noir* revival of the 1970s, starring as Philip Marlowe in *Farewell, My Lovely* (1975) and *The Big Sleep* (1978). These films were remakes of classical *films noirs* (*Murder, My Sweet* [1944] and *The Big Sleep*, 1946), films in which Mitchum could have credibly starred thirty years earlier. By the 1970s, his very presence in a film carried with it evocations of *film noir*. While hosting a 1987 *Saturday Night Live* show, he even parodied his *film noir* image. Although he was at times mocked for sleepwalking through roles, he developed a singularly diverse and often nuanced repertory of performances.

RECOMMENDED VIEWING
The Story of G.I. Joe (1945), *Pursued* (1947), *Out of the Past* (1947), *Crossfire* (1947), *The Night of the Hunter* (1955), *Thunder Road* (1958), *Home From the Hill* (1960), *Cape Fear* (1962), *El Dorado* (1966), *Farewell, My Lovely* (1975), *A Killer in the Family* (TV series, 1983)

FURTHER READING
Belton, John. *Robert Mitchum*. New York: Pyramid, 1976.

Eells, George. *Robert Mitchum: A Biography*. New York: Franklin Watts, 1984.

Mitchum, Robert. *Mitchum: In His Own Words*, edited by Jerry Roberts. New York: Limelight, 2000.

Roberts, J. W. *Robert Mitchum: A Bio-bibliography*. Westport, CT: Greenwood, 1992.

Server, Lee. *Robert Mitchum: "Baby, I Don't Care."* New York: St. Martin's, 2001.

William Luhr

material. RKO used Chandler's novel, *Farewell, My Lovely* (1940), as the source for *The Falcon Takes Over*, a 1942 film in the earlier detective mode. Only two years later, the same studio used *Farewell, My Lovely* as the source for *Murder, My Sweet* but that film's *noir* style gave it an entirely different atmosphere. The flowering of *film noir* came with mid-1940s films like *Double*

Indemnity, Scarlet Street, Mildred Pierce, The Blue Dahlia, The Killers (1946), *Out of the Past, Detour, The Postman Always Rings Twice* (1946), and *The Big Sleep* (1946). At times, as in *The Stranger* (1946) and *Crossfire* (1947), *films noirs* moved beyond tormented, interpersonal issues and explicitly engaged contemporary social problems, such as fugitive Nazis and anti-Semitism. In the late

Robert Mitchum in* Out of the Past *(Jacques Tourneur, 1947). EVERETT COLLECTION. REPRODUCED BY PERMISSION.

1940s, documentary style entered *film noir* with films like *T-Men* (1947) and *Naked City* (1948). In the 1950s, *film noir* incorporated anti-communist (*Pickup on South Street*, 1953), anti-nuclear (*Kiss Me, Deadly*, 1955), and socio-medical (*Panic in the Streets*, 1950) concerns.

By the early 1960s, with the decline of black-and-white cinematography and the collapse of the studio system, *film noir* was dying out. Various films have been cited as marking its last gasp, including Orson Welles's (1915–1985) *Touch of Evil* (1958), Alfred Hitchcock's (1899–1980) *The Wrong Man* (1956), Samuel Fuller's (1912–1997) *Underworld U.S.A.* (1961), and Blake Edwards's (b. 1922) *Experiment in Terror* (1962). Although the commercial viability of *film noir* was declining in Hollywood, its international influence was growing. This is particularly evident in films of the French *Nouvelle Vague*, such as *À bout de souffle* (*Breathless*, 1960), *Alphaville* (1965), *Tirez sur le pianiste* (*Shoot the Piano Player*, 1960), and *La mariée était en noir* (*The Bride Wore Black*, 1968). That influence later appeared in the New German Cinema, the Hong Kong Cinema, and various Latin American cinemas, among others.

By the 1970s, neo-*noir* films acknowledged *film noir* as a past form, either by setting themselves during the 1930s–1950s era or, for those set in the present, making clear references to earlier films, as for example, *Chinatown* (1974), *Body Heat* (1981), *Blood Simple* (1984), *The Long Goodbye* (1973), and *Mulholland Falls* (1996). Neo-*noir* also includes remakes of earlier *films noirs*, like *Farewell, My Lovely* (1975), *The Postman Always Rings Twice* (1981), *D.O.A.* (1988), and *Kiss of Death* (1995). Just as *film noir* was parodied during its canonical era in films like *My Favorite Brunette* (1947), so it was later parodied during the neo-*noir* era in films like *Dead Men Don't Wear Plaid* (1982).

Beginning in the 1980s, neo-*noir* began linking *noir* with dystopian science fiction in films like *Blade Runner* (1982), *Radioactive Dreams* (1985), the *Terminator* series of films, and *Minority Report* (2002). *Film noir* presents a world gone sour and presumes the failure of utopian Modernism; similarly, an enduring strain of science fiction evident since George Orwell's 1948 novel, *1984*, has depicted the future as a failed past. The central character of the futuristic *Blade Runner* speaks with a world-weary cynicism that evokes that of 1940s hard-boiled detectives.

Extensive crossover influences have appeared in other media. While *film noir* was thriving, numerous radio series drew upon its *noir* conventions, including the *Philip Marlowe*, *Sam Spade*, and *Richard Diamond*, *Private Detective* series. Television series, from *Peter Gunn* to *Dark Angel*, have done the same thing. Novels, such as those by James Ellroy (b. 1948) (*The Black Dahlia*, 1987), have been called *film noir* fiction, and graphic novels by writers like Frank Miller (b. 1957) (*Sin City*) also draw extensively upon *noir* stylistics. Similar patterns exist in other media.

CRITICAL PERSPECTIVES

The critical and theoretical commentary upon *film noir* has been extensive. The history of *film noir* begins with international criticism— essays written in postwar France assessing new developments in American film. The context and historical moment is important. New Hollywood films had not been available in France since the time of the German occupation in 1940. When those films at last appeared in postwar Paris, critics like Nino Frank saw evidence of a new sensibility in them, which he termed *film noir*. Frank contrasted this sensibility with the work of Hollywood's older generation—directors like John Ford. Frank's use of the term *film noir* carried with it associations of "black" French films of the 1930s, such as Marcel Carne's (1909–1996) *Hotel du Nord* (1938) and *Le Jour se Leve* (1939), as well as with Marcel Duhamel's *Serie Noire* books. The first book-length study of *film noir*, Raymond Borde and Etienne Chaumeton's

***Jack Nicholson in Roman Polanski's* Chinatown *(1974), which began a wave of neo-noirs.* EVERETT COLLECTION. REPRODUCED BY PERMISSION.**

Panorama du Film Noir Americain, appeared in 1955. By the time the term caught on in English more than a decade later, *film noir* had come to mean a historically superseded film movement. These three critical perspectives—that of the mid-1940s, describing a vibrant, emerging sensibility; that of the 1950s, categorizing an established cycle; and that of the 1960s, describing a historical, archival category—should not be conflated. They come with different vantage points and different assumptions. They often presume a different body of films (with the post-1960s perspective expanding the canon exponentially). The first two draw upon primarily Modernist presumptions; the last often includes a postmodern sensibility.

The expansion and academicization of film discourse in the 1960s gave *film noir* its first widespread attention in English. Important articles by Raymond Durgnat in 1970, Paul Schrader in 1972, and Janey Place and Lowell Peterson in 1974 laid groundwork for exploring *film*

noir, posing major questions such as whether it is a genre or a visual style to the growing academic and journalistic film culture in Europe and the United States.

In 1981, Foster Hirsch's *The Dark Side of the Screen: Film Noir* detailed historical contexts and proposed major tropes of the form. Three years later, Spencer Selby took a virtually opposite approach in *Dark City: The Film Noir*. Lamenting what he considered to be the contemporary tendency to fit the films into grand categories, Selby provided detailed (primarily narrative) analyses of twenty-five individual films, along with appendices of historical and bibliographical data, to illustrate his premise that the films must be evaluated individually.

Since the late 1970s, psychoanalysis, particularly Lacanian psychoanalysis, has become the *lingua franca* of much discourse on *film noir*; it inflects many approaches. One such approach, as evidenced in collections of essays by E. Ann Kaplan and Joan Copjec, draws

ANTHONY MANN
b. San Diego, California, 30 June 1906, d. 29 April 1967

Although Anthony Mann's reputation as a director rests primarily upon his turbulent, complex 1950s westerns starring James Stewart, his style coalesced in the 1940s with a series of important *films noirs*. These films, with their disorienting, often baroque cinematography, malevolent environment, and violent, tortured characters, presage his later work. His Technicolor westerns of the 1950s and historical epics of the 1960s were shot with a broader palate and a resonant sense of landscape, and retreated farther into history, but they share with the *noirs* an entrapping environment populated by embattled, anguished men.

Mann began his directorial career in the 1940s making B films whose minimal budgets allowed him considerable creative freedom. Particularly in his 1940s work with cinematographer John Alton, Mann developed a distinctive visual style that made extensive use of oppressive darkness, intermittent light, and off-center, disorienting camera angles in complexly textured images. Such images are often as potent a component of the films as their characters and stories. Mann's films often erupt with shots of excruciating agony that make viewers gasp. An abrupt, low-angle shot in *Winchester 73* (1950), for example, shows Stewart brutally clawing a villain's face. The murderous savagery evident in Stewart's contorted face indicates that little difference exists between this "hero" and the villain.

T-Men (1947), perhaps the most distinctive of Mann's *films noirs,* deals with undercover US Treasury agents investigating a counterfeiting syndicate. Two scenes reveal much about Mann's compressed techniques. In one, a gangster locks an informer in a steam room to roast him to death. In a single shot, we see the trapped, terrified victim clawing at the room's window while his sadistic killer quietly watches from the other side of the window, only inches away. In the second scene, one treasury agent watches in impotent agony while another undercover agent, a close friend, is murdered. Both scenes painfully foreground the physical proximity, repressed terror,

impotent psychic agony, and sadism pervading Mann's enclosed, masculine world of embittered rivalries.

T-Men is framed as a documentary-style film about an actual Treasury Department case. Its unseen narrator, unlike the tormented narrators of many *films noirs*, speaks in a declamatory, newsreel-type tone, touting the glories of the Treasury Department. Shots of the department seem to belong in a different film—brightly lit, frontal, with monumental exteriors of its Washington, D.C., headquarters. These differ radically from shots of the criminal world—the nightmare-like, dark, cramped, sweaty images classically associated with *film noir*. These two styles provide contrast within the film and also presage the open landscapes of the westerns and epics to come. Although the palate of later films is broader, their oppressive universe breeding endless, useless masculine conflict and torment remains similar to that of Mann's *films noirs*.

RECOMMENDED VIEWING

Desperate (1947), *Railroaded* (1947), *T-Men* (1947), *Raw Deal* (1948), *He Walked by Night* (uncredited, 1948), *Border Incident* (1949), *Winchester 73* (1950), *The Naked Spur* (1953), *Man of the West* (1958), *El Cid* (1961), *The Fall of the Roman Empire* (1964)

FURTHER READING

Basinger, Jeanine. *Anthony Mann.* Boston: Twayne, 1979.

Kitses, Jim. *Horizons West: Directing the Western from John Ford to Clint Eastwood.* London: British Film Institute, 2004.

Smith, Robert. "Mann in the Dark." *The Film Noir Reader*, edited by Alain Silver and James Ursini, 167–173. New York: Limelight Editions, 1996.

White, Susan. "t(he)-men's room." *Masculinity: Bodies, Movies, Culture*, edited by Peter Lehman, 95–114. New York and London: Routledge, 2001.

Wood, Robin. "Man(n) of the West(ern)." *CineAction*, no. 46 (June 1998): 26–33.

William Luhr

Anthony Mann. EVERETT COLLECTION. REPRODUCED BY PERMISSION.

upon post-structuralist, feminist film discourse to examine gender constructions within the films. Another psychoanalytically inflected approach is Frank Krutnik's *In a Lonely Street: Film Noir, Genre, Masculinity* (1991), which relies on some of the tools of Structuralist genre study to focus upon issues of masculinity. Another approach is offered by Tony Williams (1988), who applies Gaylyn Studlar's work on masochism to films related to Woolrich's fiction and attempts to shift discussion of *film noir* from tropes of content to tropes of affect. This approach is also evident in recent work on trauma and anxiety done by E. Ann Kaplan and others.

In addition to gender-based approaches, recent articles dealing with racial representation in *film noir* have opened up an important new area of exploration, examining, for example, the erasure of peoples of color in many *films noirs* and the use in those films of highly coded racial imagery. As with so many other topics, this functions differently in films made during the classical *noir* period from the way it functions during the neo-*noir* era. Films made during the classical era are Anglo-centric

and seldom directly engage issues of race. However, significant patterns exist in ways in which many of those films not only erase or marginalize peoples of color but also symbolically associate them with the exotic and the dangerous. Neo-*noir* films, to the contrary, often explicitly address issues of race, commonly from a perspective sympathetic (while patronizing at times) to peoples of color. A number of such films have been based upon fiction by African American authors such as Walter Mosley (b. 1952), Chester Himes (1909–1984), and Donald Goines (1937–1974).

SEE ALSO *Crime Films; Expressionism; Genre*

FURTHER READING

Borde, Raymond, and Etienne Chaumeton. *Panorama du film noir americain, 1941–1953.* Paris: Editions de Minuit, 1955. Published in English as Borde, Raymond, and Etienne Chaumeton. *A Panorama of American Film Noir, 1941–1953.* San Francisco: City Lights Books, 2002.

Copjec, Joan, ed. *Shades of Noir: A Reader.* New York and London: Verso, 1993.

Gorman, Ed, Lee Server, and Martin H. Greenberg, eds. *The Big Book of Noir.* New York: Carroll and Graff, 1998.

Hirsch, Foster. *The Dark Side of the Screen: Film Noir.* San Diego: Barnes, and London: Tantivy Press, 1981.

———. *Detours and Lost Highways: A Map of Neo-Noir.* New York: Limelight, 1999.

Kaplan, E. Ann, ed. *Women in Film Noir,* 2nd ed. London: British Film Institute, 1998.

Krutnik, Frank. *In a Lonely Street: Film Noir, Genre, Masculinity.* New York: Routledge, 1991.

Luhr, William. *Raymond Chandler and Film,* 2nd ed. Tallahassee: Florida State University Press, 1991.

———, ed. *The Maltese Falcon: John Huston, Director.* New Brunswick, NJ: Rutgers University Press, 1995.

Naremore, James. *More Than Night: Film Noir in its Contexts.* Berkeley: University of California Press, 1998.

Palmer, R. Barton. *Hollywood's Dark Cinema: The American Film Noir.* Farmington Hills, MI: Twayne, 1994.

Silver, Alain, and James Ursini, eds. *Film Noir Reader.* New York: Limelight Editions, 1996.

Spencer, Selby. *Dark City: The Film Noir.* Jefferson, NC: McFarland, 1984.

Telotte, J. P. *Voices in the Dark: The Narrative Patterns of Film Noir.* Urbana: University of Illinois Press, 1989.

William Luhr

FILM STOCK

In 1889, Eastman Kodak introduced a flexible, transparent roll film made from a plastic substance called celluloid. Kodak chemists had perfected the celluloid film that had been invented and patented in 1887 by the Reverend Hannibal Goodwin. In 1891, working under Thomas Edison (1847–1931), W. K. L. Dickson (1860–1935) designed the first motion picture camera, the Kinetograph, which used Kodak celluloid film stock. By 1911, Kodak was manufacturing over 80 million feet of film stock annually for the film industry, and the company continued to be the major supplier of film stock internationally throughout the twentieth century. With the rise of the digital age in the twenty-first century, Kodak has evolved to produce and support digital filmmaking and projection equipment.

BASE AND EMULSION

Celluloid film is made up of a flexible, transparent base that is coated with a gelatin layer (the emulsion), which contains millions of tiny, light-sensitive grains. When the film is exposed by the shutter in the lens, the grains absorb light, creating a latent image that is not visible to the naked eye. The film is then treated with developing chemicals, which cause the exposed portions of the film to become visible in a negative image of the original scene: light and dark areas in a scene are reversed. The film is then "fixed," which removes the developing chemicals, and the undeveloped grains are washed away to prevent further exposure of the film. The negative film is then printed by allowing light to pass through it onto a second strip of film, creating a positive film for projection.

Early film stock was made of cellulose nitrate, an extremely flammable plastic. Nitrate film burns rapidly, even without a supply of air, and gives off poisonous and explosive gases. It has even been known to ignite spontaneously. Cameramen had to be extremely careful when using and storing nitrate film; one spark from a cigarette could cause an entire day's work to go up in flames. In 1897, a fire broke out in a French movie theater that was projecting a nitrate-based film, killing over 180 people. In 1914, a fire began in a California film-finishing house, destroying ten buildings. Kodak introduced a flame-resistant, cellulose triacetate film stock, also known as Safety Acetate, in 1909. But the film industry resisted Safety Acetate, which was less flexible, harder to splice, and wore out more quickly than nitrate film; studios continued to use the more flammable celluloid until Kodak introduced Improved Safety Base Motion Picture Film in 1948.

A few early film cameras used paper film stock. Evidence suggests that around 1883, French photography enthusiast Louis Le Prince (1842–1890) built and experimented with a single-lens camera that used a paper negative film. Prior to 1912, the Kinora Film Company offered an amateur camera and viewing device that utilized paper film stock in a flip-book format.

GAUGE AND SPEED

Film stock is available in a number of gauges, or widths. Wider gauges project a sharper image, while smaller gauges tend to be grainier. A number of experimental widths have been used in filmmaking throughout the history of cinema, but the most common gauges still in use today are 35 mm, 16 mm, 8 mm, Super 8 mm, and 70 mm.

Thirty-five mm, the gauge used in Edison's Kinetograph, quickly became the common width for filmmakers around the world. The Lumiére Brothers (Auguste [1862–1954] and Louis [1864–1948]) also used 35 mm film in their Cinématographe camera. In 1929, the American Academy of Motion Picture Arts and Sciences declared 35 mm the standard gauge of the film industry, and it remains the standard commercial gauge.

Because of its flammability and expensive two-step developing process, 35 mm was not a viable option for amateur filmmaking. In 1914, Kodak began experimenting with 16 mm acetate film that ran through the camera twice via a reversal method that produced a positive image film that did not need to be printed from a negative. The film was designed as 16 mm so that 35 mm nitrate film could not be split in half and slipped into the camera. Kodak didn't release the new gauge until after World War I, in July 1923. In 1928, Eastman Teaching Films, a subsidiary of Kodak, produced 16 mm films for use in the classroom on a range of academic subjects. In the late 1920s, studios began reprinting 35 mm commercial films on 16 mm and selling them for home viewing. But 16 mm didn't become commercially popular until World War II, when it was used for army training, education, and entertainment. Medical and industrial companies also began to use it for research purposes.

Since the 1920s, experimental, avant-garde, and independent filmmakers have used 16 mm for artistic or professional purposes. Some notable 16 mm films in this category include *Chelovek s kino-apparatom* (*The Man with a Movie Camera*, 1929) by Dziga Vertov, *Meshes of the Afternoon* (1943) by Maya Deren, *Wavelength* (1967) by Michael Snow, and *El Mariachi* (1992) by Robert Rodriguez.

In 1932, Kodak introduced 8 mm, a gauge that used the same processing equipment as 16 mm but cost about one third as much. Eight-mm cameras used 16 mm film that ran through the camera twice, each time exposing only half the film. The film was then slit in half and the two pieces spliced together. Eight mm (sometimes called "double eight") appealed greatly to the home movie market. The gauge was intended for moderate-income families, and Kodak devised marketing strategies that

Robert Rodriguez shot El Mariachi *(1993) on 16mm film stock.* © COLUMBIA PICTURES/COURTESY EVERETT COLLECTION. REPRODUCED BY PERMISSION.

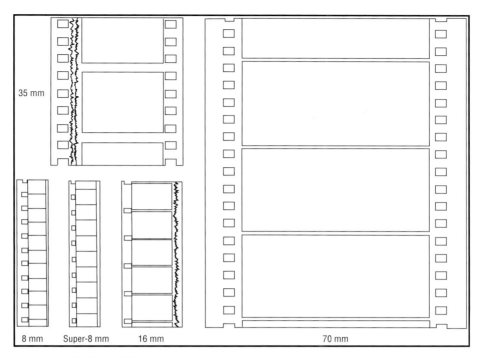

Diagram of relative film gauges. © THOMSON GALE. REPRODUCED BY PERMISSION.

stressed 8 mm's "family record" function. The famous Zapruder film, which recorded the assassination of John F. Kennedy in 1963, was shot using 8 mm film. In 1935, Kodachrome color film stock was introduced in both 8 mm and 16 mm gauges; by the 1950s, color amateur filmmaking had become very popular.

The next significant advance in amateur film stock came in 1965, with the release of Super 8 mm. The new gauge came pre-split and loaded in a drop-in cartridge, which eliminated 8 mm's tedious threading process. Super 8 mm could also project 50 percent more image area than regular 8 mm, because of a reduction in the size of the sprocket holes. By the end of the 1960s, most film stock manufacturers had halted production of regular 8 mm production altogether. Jim Jarmusch used Super 8 mm to film *The Year of the Horse* (1997), documenting Neil Young and Crazy Horse's concert tour.

Seventy-mm film, which projects an extremely high-resolution picture, became popular for commercial use in the mid 1950–1960s. When used in the camera, this film stock is actually 65 mm wide, but the negative is printed onto 70 mm film to allow for six tracks of surround sound. Seventy-mm's wide-screen format, sharp picture, and high-quality sound made it an ideal format for epics like *Ben-Hur* (1959), *Cleopatra* (1963), and *Lawrence of Arabia* (1962). The advent of low-grain 35 mm film stock and digital soundtrack systems led to a decline in 70 mm

use in the 1990s, and few 70 mm films are made today. A horizontal variant of 70 mm is now used for IMAX films.

The *speed* (sensitivity) of the film stock also affects the quality of the image in projection. Slow film stock is less sensitive to reflected light, so brighter light sources are necessary during shooting to produce sharp images. Slower stock also creates less contrast between light and dark areas within a composition; fast film stock is very sensitive to reflected light and produces distinct contrasts between light and dark within the frame. Fast stock is often used for documentaries, in settings where light options are limited, and in fiction films that try to capture a stark, documentary feel. *Film noir*, a genre popular in the 1940s, took advantage of faster film stock technology to capture striking shadows and slick, rainy, nighttime streets. Film stock is assigned a numeric value according to speed standards established by the ASA (American Standards Association), which became the basis for the ISO (International Organization for Standardization) speed system, now currently used worldwide. Doubling the value doubles the film speed, so a film stock rated 800 is twice as fast as one rated 400.

BLACK-AND-WHITE AND COLOR

Until 1925, Hollywood studios used orthochromatic Eastman Standard Negative stock. Orthochromatic film was only sensitive to the brightest natural light, so large ultraviolet lamps had to be used during shooting. It also registered only blue light, so anything colored red showed up on the film as black. This posed a problem for actors and actresses, whose flesh-toned faces appeared darker than normal on screen. Thus began the practice of using heavy white pancake makeup on the majority of screen personalities. In 1922, Robert Flaherty shot his documentary *Nanook of the North* on orthochromatic film stock, which beautifully accentuated the harsh, colorless landscape.

In 1922, panchromatic film, which was sensitive to all colors, became available for black-and-white filmmaking. The hard-edged blue orthochromatic gave way to the softer gradations of "pan," providing much more natural-looking visuals. But the film industry was hesitant to switch formats, believing orthochromatic was "good enough" to suit its purposes. In 1926, Flaherty shot *Moana*, a documentary containing lush, tropical scenery, using panchromatic film. It convinced Hollywood to make the change, and by 1930, orthochromatic film manufacturing had been discontinued.

Color was achieved in early cinema through methods of postproduction tinting and toning. Tinting is a technique that applies one or more colors to certain areas of the film stock by hand. The practice began as early as 1895, in an Edison-produced film, *Serpentine Dances*. In the film, a woman dances in circles as her dress and scarves change colors, as if by magic. Edison's crude tinting techniques proved difficult on the eyes, but by 1905, a stenciling process was perfected that created a bit more accuracy in color distribution on the celluloid. Georges Méliès (1861–1938) used tinting in *Le Rêve d'un astrome* (*An Astronomer's Dream*, 1898) and the first version of *Le Voyage dans la lune* (*A Trip to the Moon*, 1902); *The Great Train Robbery* (1903) contained tinted sequences, including the gunshot blast directed at the audience in the last scene.

Toning imparts a color to an entire black-and-white film. By 1920, over 80 percent of all Hollywood feature films used toning to represent particular settings or emotions: for example, amber for day or interior shots, blue for nighttime, red for battle scenes. In 1921, Kodak began manufacturing pre-toned film stock in nine different colors. After the arrival of sound technology in 1927, tinting and toning were temporarily halted because the processes interfered with the soundtrack, which ran alongside the image on the celluloid. By 1929, this problem had been corrected, and Hollywood continued to use tinted and toned stock copiously until more sophisticated color filming techniques were perfected—the preview trailer for *The Bride of Frankenstein* (1935), for example, was shot on green-toned film stock.

Dozens of experimental processes were tried in the early 1900s to capture realistic color on film, but most lacked quality and were quickly abandoned. Technicolor was invented in 1917 by Herbert Thomas Kalmus (1881–1963) and Daniel F. Comstock and eventually became the industry standard in Hollywood. The first version of Technicolor superimposed two colored images (one green, one red) onto the screen simultaneously. The process was too expensive to use for an entire feature film, but Technicolor sequences in black-and-white films quickly became fashionable in Hollywood—for example, in Cecil B. DeMille's *The Ten Commandments* (1923).

In 1932, Kodak introduced a Technicolor film stock capable of reproducing a reasonable range of hues, using a three-color process. With three strips of black-and-white film running together through the camera, the color image was recorded by separating its green, blue, and red properties onto each of the corresponding color-sensitive negatives. From these three negatives, three more strips of film (known as matrices) were printed; these were used to transfer corresponding dye images onto a single blank piece of film. Walt Disney was one of the first filmmakers to experiment with this process, creating *Flowers and Trees* (1932), the first animated short in full color.

During World War II, German manufacturers produced the first single-strip color negative, which is still in use. This process used three sensitive photographic emulsion layers, or *tripacks*, coated on a single base support. The eye perceives different wavelengths of light as particular colors in the spectrum. Special chemicals sensitive only to a specific group of light wavelengths allow for an image of a different color to be processed on each layer of film (blue, green, and red). This composite image is processed, much like black-and-white film, in negative, so colors are reversed until printed in positive. By 1953 this process was well established in the film industry; by 1955, the three-strip process had disappeared from use completely.

SEE ALSO *Cinematography; Color; Lighting; Technology*

FURTHER READING

Collins, Douglas. *The Story of Kodak*. New York: Abrams, 1990.

Happé, L. Bernard. *Basic Motion Picture Technology*. 2nd revised ed. New York: Hastings House, 1975.

Kattelle, Alan. *Home Movies: A History of the American Industry, 1897–1979*. Nashua, NH: Transition, 2000.

Limbacher, James L. *Four Aspects of the Film*. New York: Brussel & Brussel, 1969.

McKee, Gerald. *Film Collecting*. South Brunswick, NJ: Barnes, 1978.

Erin Foster

FILM STUDIES

From the outset, motion pictures have stimulated discussion and debate as a technology, a social phenomenon, a political tool, a moral danger, and an art. The earliest discussions and debates took place outside an academic context. From noted filmmakers such as Sergei Eisenstein (1898–1948), Vsevolod Pudovkin (1893–1953), and Maya Deren (1917–1961) to eclectic thinkers and social critics such as Siegfried Kracauer, John Grierson (1898–1972), and André Bazin, a body of knowledge began to develop that would provide a launching pad for the academic study of film in the years following World War II, especially the 1960s.

These pioneers also established a tradition of commentary about film that continues to operate independent of the university. Exemplified today primarily by the circulation of relatively formulaic film reviews, biographies, profiles, and box-office statistics, these popular forms of commentary work largely to support the dominant forms of feature filmmaking and to aid consumers of entertainment in their choice of films. The devoted amateur cinephile has given way to the professional film reviewer and the university scholar, although passionate engagement with the art and politics of film can still exist in both sectors.

FILM AS AN ART AND THE HUMANISTIC TRADITION

The rise of film studies within the university has typically sought to justify itself less on the grounds of film as a commodity to be consumed with the guidance of critics and reviewers and more on the grounds of film as an art form or cultural object to be understood for its formal qualities and social implications. Film studies took root in the academy in the wake of the enormous interest in European art cinema generated during the postwar period by filmmakers such as Roberto Rossellini (1906–1977), Ingmar Bergman (b. 1918), Akira Kurosawa (1910–1988), François Truffaut (1932–1984), Jean-Luc Godard (b. 1930), Claude Chabrol (b. 1930), Michelangelo Antonioni (b. 1912), Kenji Mizoguchi (1898–1956), and many others. Their work demonstrated that feature fiction films could address the same issues of alienation, spiritual hunger, historical memory, and formal experimentation that were evident in many works of literature and visual art. It was, in fact, in various humanities departments that film studies most frequently emerged as an academic subject. An older tradition of communication studies existed, and continues to exist, as a social science discipline, but the stress given in the social sciences to institutional factors, quantitative analysis of the industries and audiences for motion pictures, television and other media, and content analysis did not satisfy the same goals as humanistic approaches, which stressed interpretation of specific films and theorization about the cinema as both art form and cultural object. For the majority of film scholars, questions of industrial organization and measurable social effects took a subordinate place to questions of film structure, style, and meaning.

Treated as an art comparable to literature, painting, or sculpture, film called for study in terms of appreciation, differentiation, and interpretation. That is, an appreciation for film meant understanding what distinguished the medium from other arts and then differentiating among the myriad of actual films those that best exemplified the distinctive nature of the medium. The differentiation of films into clusters of various kinds also allowed for comparisons and contrasts to be made beyond the level of the individual film. Among the most significant of clusters were (1) the classic Hollywood film, from *Grand Hotel* (1932) to *Spartacus* (1960); (2) studio films—those made by MGM compared to those from Warner Brothers, for example; (3) genre film; (4) national cinemas (British, French, or Iranian cinema, for example, often with a focus on certain periods of notable achievement); and (5) the cinema of specific film directors or *auteurs*, such as John Ford (1894–1973), David Lynch (b. 1946), and Agnes Varda (b. 1926). Each choice of a cluster took support from methodological principles designed to facilitate understanding of that particular type of film, from the concept of continuity editing in classic Hollywood cinema to the concept of directorial style in *auteur* studies.

Initially, interpretation, or film criticism, revolved around an attention to details that showed how films conveyed meaning by cinematic means. Landscape, for example, was an important signifying element in westerns, whereas the jumpy editing style of Jean-Luc Godard's early films, such as *À bout de souffle* (*Breathless*, 1960), proved an essential part of his attempt to reinvent the classic style of Hollywood films. Similarly, Antonioni often conveyed alienation through his *mise-en-scène*—that is, through the way he arranged characters in space and moved them through it to suggest their isolation from each other (by looking off frame or in different directions, for example).

At a more abstract level, the art of cinema came to be identified either with editing as a quintessential element, since it allowed two different shots to produce a new impression or idea not contained in either shot by itself, or with the long take and the cinema's capacity to register the uninterrupted occurrence of an event through time. Through debates about the merits of different strategies by specific directors, critics sought to understand not only the complexity of individual films and clusters of films but of cinema itself. The broad question "What is cinema?" provoked answers that shaped what came to be known as film theory.

Efforts to develop a systematic understanding of film are almost as old as cinema itself. When these efforts took root within the university in the 1960s and early 1970s, they shared at least three characteristics with other forms of humanistic inquiry: (1) film is a medium of aesthetic importance; the most important dimension to cinema is its capacity to take form as art, just as the most important dimension of writing is its capacity to take form as literature; (2) film art, like literature, affects viewers in a similar, aesthetic manner that is removed from the contingencies of time and place; it transcends the local to attain a more timeless significance; and (3) the history of the cinema is the history of its emergence as an art form.

These characteristics set up a series of priorities that carried with them a set of consequences. The greatest emphasis went to studying fiction films, which drew upon a realistic narrative tradition to tell stories revolving around individual characters, their situation or environment, and their actions. The appreciation, differentiation, and interpretation of such stories were already a familiar part of literary analysis, and many of the tools that furthered understanding of literary form proved valuable to film study, such as the close formal analysis of specific texts by literary New Criticism.

New Criticism, represented by figures such as T. S. Eliot, John Crowe Ransom, Cleanth Brooks, and Alan Tate, was an American phenomenon that flourished from the 1930s to the 1950s. It sought to counter a sense of the evisceration of the emotional, affective dimension of life that science and technology threatened to impose by turning to literature, particularly poetry, as a social restorative. More crucially, as an influence, it took up the efforts by British critics such as F. R. Leavis and I. A. Richards to celebrate the internal coherence and experiential pleasure of the text itself. Biographical studies of the artist or author, examinations of a work's historical or social context, topical concerns, and social issues all took a back seat to close readings of the text in and of itself. The text became a virtual fetish, valued as the timeless triumph of the creative spirit.

New Criticism inspired many studies in film that aimed at appreciating the full impact of aesthetic choices made within specific films. Robin Wood has been among the best practitioners of such an approach, enriching it with a keen eye for the sexual politics of a wide range of films and a broad appreciation of fiction films from the high art of Mizoguchi and Marcel Ophuls (b. 1927) to "trash" genres such as horror films. During this period, or up until the 1980s, avant-garde cinema, which often explored cinematic form in ways that gave scant attention to narrative, and documentary, which often stressed social issues in ways that diminished the viewer's attention to cinematic technique, received less consideration.

Auteur theory, with its stress on the style or vision of the filmmaker as it emerged more from an analysis of his or her films than from biographical anecdotes or personal statements of intention, proved an extremely important aspect of film study. *Auteur* criticism was among the first of the critical methodologies to gain widespread currency in the 1950s and 1960s. The practice retains a high degree of currency some fifty years later, although its focus on close reading, the director as the sole creative force, and thematic preoccupations that seem to be segregated from their larger social, historical context have all come in for considerable correction. *Auteur* criticism initially spread from France, most notably from critics soon to become directors writing in *Cahiers du Cinema* such as François Truffaut, Jean-Luc Godard, Claude Chabrol, Jacques Rivette (b. 1928), and others. In English-speaking countries its appearance coincided with the rise of film studies as a discipline. It dovetailed handily with literary and art historical approaches to art via the Great Man theory, which consistently gave priority to men (seldom women) whose creative genius looms above those of lesser ability.

It also coincided, in France, with a rebellion, led by François Truffaut, against the institutionalized "tradition of quality," characterized by masterful but largely literary rather than truly cinematic achievements. Such work dominated the French cinema of the postwar years. Truffaut called for a cinema that explored cinematic means of expression with verve and imagination rather than one that subordinated technique to a careful but more theatrical development of characters and their conflicts. This stress led to a distinction between "metteurs en scene," directors who simply converted a script into a film as a builder might convert a blueprint into a building, and the "*auteur,*" a director whose vision and style transformed a script into something truly cinematic that could not be envisioned on the basis of the script alone.

It fell to an American newspaper critic, Andrew Sarris, to convert the French "*politiques des auteurs*" into an international phenomenon. Sarris chose to label it the "*auteur* theory," a term that lost the original emphasis of the French phrase on a policy or politics of the author and suggested something of a far more systematic nature. His own book, *The American Cinema*, proposed to trace the history of American cinema by classifying over 150 directors in categories ranging from the "Pantheon," for Charles Chaplin, Howard Hawks, Alfred Hitchcock, Orson Welles, and others, to "Oddities, One-Shots, and Newcomers," for John Cassavetes, Francis Ford Coppola, Ida Lupino, and others, or "Subjects for Further Research," for Tod Browning, James Cruze, Henry King, and others. *Movie*, in the UK, and *Film Comment*, in the US, followed the lead of *Cahiers du Cinema* in devoting large portions of their issues to studies of individual directors, often discovering stylistic and thematic consistencies in the work of directors who had seemed to be merely the hired-hands of the Hollywood studios.

Auteur criticism provided a conceptual framework not only for the analysis of the work of directors who clearly possessed a distinct visual style, such as Robert Bresson (1901–1909), Yasujiro Ozu (1903–1963), Bernardo Bertolucci (b. 1941), or Peter Greenaway (b. 1942). Even more valuably, it prompted the discovery of filmmakers of vision who might have otherwise been buried within the Hollywood system on routine assignments or as specialists in various genres. Once compared with the work of others working in the same genres, the films of Howard Hawks (1896–1977), Preston Sturges (1898–1959), Vincente Minnelli, Anthony Mann (1907–1967), and Robert Aldrich (1918–1983), for example, gained coherence for their thematic and stylistic continuity. Hawks, whose style was extremely conventional, nonetheless used westerns and action films to focus on rituals of male bonding that involve getting the job done with stoic determination, whereas his comedies explore the hilarious results of men falling under the sway of women who isolate and feminize them.

The emphasis on film as a transcendental art with an autonomous history took shape within a strongly national context, in keeping with the almost universal role of the humanities in cultivating a sense of national identity. American, British, French, Senegalese, Iranian, Japanese, Brazilian, Argentine, and many other national cinemas qualified as transcendental art with distinctive history but did so within a national context. The greatness of a German film in the 1920s might be tied to its distinct use of the Expressionist techniques common in German art at the time—a quality, for example, that distinguished German film from the montage principles of 1920s Soviet cinema. Similarly, American films were often said to exemplify the pursuit of individual happiness or the obstacles to its attainment, a consistent theme in American art and literature.

HUMANISTIC INQUIRY AND POLITICAL SIGNIFICATION

These types of film studies held sway during the transitional period during which film became accepted as a disciplinary focus and a departmental entity within the university. Even at this time, during the 1960s and 1970s, the field was not as homogenous as this account so far implies. The question of "What is cinema?" also took a turn toward the political, asking how film mattered within the larger social arena. At the same time, a wave of European critical theory exerted considerable influence throughout Europe and North America. This work tended to shift emphasis away from content analysis per se, as it was practiced in the social sciences, where form or style was of little importance, and instead stressed the mechanisms by which content arises in relation to specific institutional practices and linguistic or semiotic forms. Artistic expressiveness, or style, came to be considered less a matter of individual creativity and more a matter of institutional systems, which establish a context and set limits within which specific forms of expressivity can occur. Stress on the psychology of individual characters, for example, might be seen as a function of a realist tradition that tends to give priority to the individual as the primary social and historical force. Such a tradition, in turn, could be considered an ideology—a particular way of seeing the world that can be subjected to the same close scrutiny as the style of individual films.

Initially associated with structuralism and then with poststructuralism, continental theory posed numerous challenges to the humanistic tradition. Language itself, including the language of cinema—its narrative codes, formal structures, and expressive techniques—became regarded less as a vehicle for expressing already conceived ideas and more as a mechanism that actually generated the impressions that they only appear to represent. Realism, for example, serves to make its view of the world transparent, as if the world obviously and naturally exists in a certain way. Continuity editing, which tends to go unnoticed, reinforces such a view. Modernist techniques, on the other hand, question this naturalness and stress the disjointed, subjective, incommensurate view of the world that different individuals might have. Jump cuts and strange juxtapositions between people and places reinforce this view. In this regard, *The Best Years of Our Lives* (1946) exemplifies the realist film as *L'Année dernière à Marienbad* (*Last Year at Marienbad*, 1961) exemplifies the modernist film.

The idea that meaning is always tightly related to a specific context and to a specific form of expression was carried beyond the film itself and applied to the artist and viewer. In this case, artistic vision or individual identity was seen as always tightly related to the specific institutional mechanisms that generate a sense of self-expression and identity. Traditional literary and film criticism held that the creative artist possessed special powers that led to artistic excellence. Structural and post-structural theory instead proposed that all subjects—artists and filmmakers, critics and viewers—were constituted as subjects within specific cultural and institutional frameworks that set goals and limits for creativity. These frameworks served the specific needs or interests of an existing social system—that is, they were ideological. For the French political theorist Louis Althusser, this idea led to the influential argument that the very idea of an independent subject was itself the product of an ideological operation: individuals think of themselves as free, subject to no one, within a social field that makes this notion the cornerstone of a free-market economy in which shared awareness and collective action represent a limitation or diminution of a subject's individuality.

Althusser's most forceful statement of the idea of the individual subject as a product of ideology was his essay "Ideology and the Ideological State Apparatus" in *Lenin and Philosophy*. His line of thought was extended to the cinematic apparatus as an ideological device for the reinforcement of the status quo by French theorists at *Cahiers du Cinema* such as Jean Louis Baudry. Althussser stressed how the individual internalized assumptions about his status as a subject that inevitably placed an emphasis on how this internalization occurred. In film study, this led to a large quantity of work in the 1970s that attempted to make use of psychoanalytic theory to account for the effects of cinema on the viewer. *Screen* magazine, from the UK, became the leading proponent of this effort. One of the most influential articles on ideology and the subject was Laura Mulvey's essay, "Visual Pleasure and Narrative Cinema," first published in *Screen* in 1975 and anthologized many times since. The essay is discussed further in the next section.

The dominant narrative cinema came to be seen as serving an ideological function that confirmed the individual as a subject. The nature of the star system, the system of continuity editing, and narrative realism worked to make stories of individual characters and their fate appear to simply tell themselves as a natural expression of an obvious fact: individuals are the key creators of social structure and historical change. The mechanism that actually animates these individuals, narrative storytelling or, as it came to be known, the cinematic apparatus, remains basically unacknowledged, off-screen. Like a puppet master, it creates the illusion of an imaginary world and fictitious characters that have independent lives of their own.

Film theory thus identified the cinema as a system whose formal elements contribute to the ideology of the individual. Feminist film theory carried the analysis one step further. Laura Mulvey, in her pioneering essay, "Visual Pleasure and Narrative Cinema," noted that the individual subject who takes action in films—embarking on quests, courting a partner, solving a mystery, and so on—is almost invariably male, and the individual who awaits the outcome of such actions is almost invariably female. Paralleling this distinction, the camera encourages identification with the male hero; his look becomes the camera's look. We see the world from his point of view or from a point of view that places him front and center. Simultaneously, among the things the male hero sees when he looked out at the world around him is the female lead. She is there to be seen; she represents, in the words of Laura Mulvey, "to-be-looked-at-ness," a passive position that can be understood as a symptom of a social hierarchy between the sexes.

Whereas structuralism gave emphasis to the text itself and the principles that structured it, poststructuralism emphasized the context within which a film is

D. W. Griffith's **The Birth of a Nation** *(1915) is formally inventive but racist in its representation.* EVERETT COLLECTION. REPRODUCED BY PERMISSION.

received. A given structure to a text was no longer seen as fully determining meaning. Interpretation and meaning vary; formal qualities of the text set limits but do not predetermine meaning. The primary context is the actual viewing situation and the relation of the spectator to the screen. The differentiation between male and female spectators is one example of the way in which poststructural and feminist analysis have given added specificity to ideas about an ideological effect to cinema in general. The camera's gaze no longer affected all viewers equally, regardless of sexual identity. In many ways this represented the first of many cracks in the three basic assumptions that had underpinned much of the initial effort to introduce film studies into the university.

THE STUDY OF FILM AND POSTSTRUCTURALISM

By the 1980s poststructural theory and criticism had begun to adopt a new set of guiding assumptions. The new characteristics ascribed to cinema were three: (1) the social impact of films on specific viewers matters more than the general qualities of film as art; (2) art is not essentially transcendent but always tied to a social and historical context within which different responses and interpretations occur; and (3) the history of film is the story both of its rise as an art and of its social impact and political significance as a mass medium.

Rather than appreciating the art of cinema outside of any particular context, the new emphasis called for situating the art of any film in a specific context. The importance of *The Birth of a Nation* (1915) for the art of cinema because of its inventive use of cross cutting between simultaneous events to create suspense must now be situated in relation to the actual suspense created: would members of the Klu Klux Klan rescue the endangered white women from the clutches of an evil black man? This racist theme itself belonged within the historical context of race relations in the early twentieth century, when prejudice and stereotypes took different shape and had different status than they do today. Situating film within a specific context has also added new impetus to the study of documentary film. Extraordinarily popular compared to its more marginal status up until the early 1980s, documentary film study now consistently addresses aesthetic issues in relation to socially specific goals and effects.

The differentiation of films into various groupings continued as before but with an added emphasis on the historical context to which genres, movements, waves, the work of specific directors, and historical phases of national cinemas belonged. The attempt to understand "What is cinema?" became a question posed less in relation to traditional arts and more in relation to newer media like television, installation and video art, digital, interactive media, and the Web. Forms of overlap and convergence among these various forms made the isolation of cinema as a distinct medium a less compelling question than the continuities and discontinuities among a wide array of moving image media.

"Identity politics," which places great stress on defining the qualities that characterize a given group, often with a stress on the issue of stereotypes, the need for "positive images," and the search for alternative forms of narrative more commensurate with the group's shared values, gave rise to a flowering of film theory, criticism, and history from the perspective of African American, Native American, ethnic, and queer (a combination of gay and lesbian) perspectives.

This shift in emphasis from the close reading of texts isolated from their context began in the 1970s as an aspect of a cultural studies approach to film and other media. It gained strength in the 1980s as identity politics—in this case, the examination of cinema from the distinct perspective of a specific group—became an important aspect of political debate in the larger society. Anthologies such as *Unspeakable Images: Ethnicity and the American Cinema* and *Screening Asian Americans* provide a wealth of critical analysis devoted to issues that had gone largely unexplored by either *auteur* study or by ideological study that focused on the subject rather than the larger social system to which the subject belonged. Attention to a more socially and historically situated perspective challenged qualities previously taken for granted, such as heterosexual marriage as a marker of the happy ending, stereotypic representation of groups from Latinos and Latinas to Jews, and identification with male heroes but desire for female stars: the reversal of these conventions by gay and lesbian viewers, who desire differently, has undercut the universalizing claims of traditional film theory.

Also beginning in the 1980s, a call for a return to the history of film cast doubt on the received wisdom of existing film histories. Studies such as Miriam Hansen's *Babel and Babylon: Spectatorship in American Silent Film*, David E. James's *Allegories of Cinema: American Film in the Sixties*, and Jane M. Gaines's *Fire and Desire: Mixed-Race Movies in the Silent Era* all depart radically from the earlier tradition of tracing the rise of film as an art within various national contexts. Revisionist histories such as these set out to apply a more finely tuned analysis of the larger context in which films arose. They took into account the social, historical, economic, and ideological factors that both a more traditional emphasis on the rise of film as an art and *auteur* theory with its stress on the centrality of the author as understood solely from films themselves failed to do.

The new assumptions listed above that sought to contextualize the understanding of films also called for interpretations that differentiated among the responses of specific audiences and compared the responses of different audiences. African American women, for example, were far more receptive than white males to Julie Dash's *Daughters of the Dust* (1991), which tells the story of an African American family poised to embark upon profound changes at the start of the twentieth century. Even popular, mainstream films could no longer be understood from a single perspective. Different groups were shown to often read against the grain of the preferred meaning assigned by critics and marketers and to instead discover alternative meanings: slasher films, for example, which make violence against women grizzly "fun," often lead to male adolescents identifying, across the gender divide, with the "Final Girl," who vanquishes the male villain and restores order. The critic's own alignment in relation to the particulars of ethnicity, class, and gender has also become a more openly acknowledged aspect of film study since the universalizing voice of traditional criticism has become increasingly associated with a white, heterosexual male perspective that treats its own social viewpoint as normative.

Film studies scholars today continue to formulate theories about the broad patterns that characterize the cinema, but they do so in a form that gives heightened attention to the specificities of time and place. "Thick" interpretations, which attempt to grasp the multiple perspectives and divergent meanings that a given work conveys and prompts, have gained a stronger foothold than theorizations that view the cinema as a medium that functions in predetermined ways and produces consistent responses. Rather than serving as a form of social glue for the construction of a unified nation-state, the cinema has come to be seen as part of a highly contested cultural zone that no longer coincides with a single understanding of national or any other identity. The stakes of specific, often underrepresented groups seeking to claim a space within the cultural arena generally and film studies specifically have taken on great importance. Combined with mostly European theories of poststructuralism, these forces have altered the shape of film studies, proposing new ways to answer the perennial question, "What is cinema?"

SEE ALSO *Auteur Theory and Authorship; Criticism; Semiotics; Structuralism and Poststructuralism*

FURTHER READING

Bazin, André. *What Is Cinema?*, 2 vols. Translated and edited by Hugh Gray. Berkeley: University of California Press, 2005.

Bobo, Jacqueline. *Black Women as Cultural Readers*. New York: Columbia University Press, 1995.

Eisenstein, Sergei. *Film Form*. Translated by Jay Leyda. San Diego: Harcourt, Brace, Jovanovich, 1977.

Feng, Peter X. *Screening Asian Americans*. New Brunswick, NJ and London: Rutgers University Press, 2002.

Friedman, Lester D. *Unspeakable Images: Ethnicity and the American Cinema*. Urbana and Chicago: University of Illinois Press, 1991.

Gaines, Jane M. *Fire and Desire: Mixed-Race Movies in the Silent Era*. Chicago, IL: University of Chicago Press, 2001.

Gledhill, Christine, and Linda Williams, eds. *Reinventing Film Studies*. London: Arnold, and New York: Oxford University Press, 2000.

Hansen, Miriam. *Bable & Babylon: Spectatorship in American Silent Film*. Cambridge, MA: Harvard University Press, 1991.

James, David E. *Allegories of Cinema: American Film in the Sixties*. Princeton, NJ: Princeton University Press, 1989.

Kracauer, Siegfried. *From Caligari to Hitler: A Psychological History of the German Film*. Princeton, NJ: Princeton University Press, 2004.

Mulvey, Laura. "Visual Pleasure and Narrative Cinema." *Movies and Methods*, edited by Bill Nichols, vol. 2, 303–315. Berkeley: University of California Press, 1985.

Nichols, Bill. *Introduction to Documentary*. Bloomington: Indiana University Press, 2001.

Sarris, Andrew. *The American Cinema: Directors and Directions, 1929–1968*. New York: E. P. Dutton and Co, 1968.

Shohat, Ella, and Robert Stam, eds. *Unthinking Eurocentrism*. New York and London: Routledge, 1994.

Wood, Robin. *Personal Views: Explorations in Film*. London: Gordon Fraser, 1976. Revised edition; Detroit, MI: Wayne State University Press, 2006.

Bill Nichols

FINE ART

———■———

The cinema has engaged in a dialogue with the traditional fine arts—visual art, literature, music, theater, and architecture—from its inception to the present. The relationships between cinema, the "seventh art," to the other arts is indeed vast and complex. Film's ability to build convincing worlds with spatial depth recalls the functions of architecture, while music lends film its power to arouse abstract emotions that neither words nor images can fully express. The movies' emphasis on the body and human emotions connects it with the theater and poetry. Film's narrative emphasis has obvious affinities with prose fiction, and of course the medium's visual aspect aligns it with painting. Further, the ways in which cinema references art informs a variety of cultural discourses.

Born out of the circus, vaudeville, and the Grand Guignol, the cinema engaged in a dialogue with the arts and high culture during its early or primitive period, when one shot with movement inside the image was enough to capture the viewer's attention. The pioneers of filmmaking were well aware of the arts: Georges Méliès (1861–1938) was educated as an academic painter, and the Lumière brothers (Auguste Lumière [1862–1954] and Louis Lumière [1864–1948]), although trained as engineers and photographers, restaged the commonplaces of French Impressionist painting in their depiction of leisure time and daily life. The films of Méliès and the Lumières are marked by jokes, puns, parodies, puzzles, anagrams, riddles, and charades about the clichés of painting. Louis Lumière's short *Partie d'écarte* (*Card Game*, 1895), for example, recalls a trope familiar from Flemish genre painting to Cézanne's *The Card Players* (1890–1892). *D'écarte*, from the verb *écarter* (to separate), is a pun for *des cartes* (referring to cards).

The card game in this particular party represents the unpredictable nature of life, with its promises and surprises.

NATIONAL CINEMAS

Through the traditions of national cinemas, cultures represent themselves to audiences both at home and abroad. Hence the function played by the arts in the development of national cinemas is most significant. Before and after World War I, the various national film industries in Europe distinguished themselves through allusions to domestic aesthetic traditions. In Italy, for example, Giovanni Pastrone's epic *Cabiria* (1914) draws on the grand tradition of Italian opera, complete with monumental sets and masses of extras. In Germany, Robert Wiene's *Das Cabinet des Dr. Caligari* (1920) and F. W. Murnau's *Nosferatu* (1922) tap German romanticism's interest in origins and subjectivity while also drawing on the visual style of German expressionism. Both films cast the upheavals of the self in the jagged angles and skewed shapes familiar from German expressionist painting; the sets make visible a sense of spiritual anguish, and their natural locations suggest peaceful surfaces concealing mysterious evils. One of the most famous German expressionist films, Fritz Lang's *Metropolis* (1927), is an architectural film built on psychoanalytic allusions and images of industrial regimentation. In his direction of the actors and his handling of crowds, Lang was influenced by the theater of Max Reinhardt, who used sculptural groupings of automaton-like actors. By designing and streamlining the scenes featuring crowds—a feat of directorial control and vision—Lang evokes a sense of dehumanization.

In comparison to the expressionist taste for the supernatural, the so-called French impressionist avant-garde of the 1920s preferred a more psychological understanding of interiority. Germaine Dulac's *La Souriante Madame Beudet* (*The Smiling Madame Beudet*, 1922) uses musical allusions and visual effects to suggest the psychological complexities at the core of an unhappily married woman, thus depicting a feminine self torn by erotic repression and a desire for domestic rebellion. In the 1920s and 1930s, French surrealism thrived on unexpected analogies and unsettling disruptions of objects. The development of the surrealist director Jean Cocteau's esoteric shifts between word and image, tactile and visual references in *Le Sang d'un poète* (*Blood of a Poet*, 1930), anticipate many of Jean-Luc Godard's collages in *Pierrot le Fou* (1965). More generally, surrealism's taste for disruption anticipates the French New Wave's playful orchestration of literary, pictorial, musical, and popular sources in film. Before and after the revolutionary upheavals of May 1968, the French New Wave directors, especially Godard, wove together the legacies of different periods of film history, ranging from surrealist word–image games to the montage ensembles developed out of Soviet Constructivist art.

With film impressionism, surrealism, and expressionism, the national cinemas of France and Germany embraced the agendas of modernist avant-garde movements. Furthermore, around 1914 the Italian futurists published a manifesto about the cinema (they also made a few films, most of them lost). However, the silent Italian film industry steered away from avant-garde experimentation in favor of a more popular, operatic cinema based on great books and paintings of high culture. This edifying approach from Italy became a model for the development of the cinema in Hollywood as well. The Italian compromise between mass spectacle and famous works, populist entertainment and an attention to pictorial values, reappears in the work of the American director D. W. Griffith, notably *The Birth of a Nation* (1915), *Intolerance* (1916), and *Broken Blossoms or The Yellow Man and the Girl* (1919). Set in Victorian England and replete with opium dens and Buddhist references, *Broken Blossoms* is a melodrama whose artistic aspirations are confirmed by its tragic ending in which all three protagonists die. The film deals with alcoholism, family abuse, and racial miscegenation, deploying the style of Pre-Raphaelite painting in its representation of the self-effacing but sensuous character of the girl Lucy (Lillian Gish).

GENRE

By upgrading the melodrama with art-historical references, Griffith's *Broken Blossoms* paved the way for the stretching of genre films from formulaic narrative to more aesthetically complex works. Whether the narrative deals with the biography of a famous artist (the biopic) or with a famous battle (the historical film), it is possible to elevate genre to the "art" film. As the scholar Charles Tashiro has pointed out, some historical films depend on pictorial citations as period sources, including William Dieterle's *Juarez* (1939), with its literal restaging of Goya's 1814 painting *Executions of the Third of May 1808*, and Stanley Kubrick's *Barry Lyndon* (1975), which is informed by eighteenth-century portraiture and genre paintings ranging from Joshua Reynolds to John Constable. Bo Widerberg's *Elvira Madigan* (1967), though it does not recall any specific picture, is steeped in the colors, landscapes, fabrics, and atmospheres of impressionist painting.

American biopics devoted to the life of an artist, such as John Huston's *Moulin Rouge* (1952), about Henri de Toulouse-Lautrec, and Vincente Minnelli's *Lust for Life* (1956), about Vincent van Gogh, can be considered art films in a very loose sense. These films tend to recycle society's cliches about artists—notions of genius, madness, recklessness, inner torment, exile, and romance. Films as different as *Legal Eagles* (1986) and *Modigliani* (2004) suggest that making art goes hand in hand with living intensely, talent with struggle. As is apparent from the character of Waldo Lydecker (Clifton Webb) in *Laura* (Otto Preminger, 1944), Hollywood traditionally represents artistic figures and environments in a self-destructive or corrupting light; painting specifically is the equivalent of excess, color, femininity, vice, and solipsism. The French director Maurice Pialat takes a more sociological and existential approach to his subject in *Van Gogh* (1991), where art-making is still all-consuming and self-destructive yet leaves room for friends, family, and colleagues. As conceived by Pialat, Van Gogh is subjected to the value judgments of his period about the artist—entailing notions of femininity, creativity, and individuality—but he is not the embodiment of corruption and decadence.

The Hollywood musical, with its emphasis on costume, color, and set design along with music and dance, is a genre that evokes the relation of art and film through visual style. In *An American in Paris* (1951), for example, the set designs evoke the style of French impressionism. In another genre, film noir, chiaroscuro lighting and Gothic architecture show the influence of German expressionism, a sensibility that migrated from Europe to Hollywood. Another notable instance of generic reference to visual art is in the thrillers of Alfred Hitchcock, which from *Psycho* (1960) onward includes references to the paintings of Edward Hopper (1882–1967), an American artist famous for his deserted diners at night, lonely motels, uninhabited vistas, and isolated individuals.

The look of **Barry Lyndon** *(Stanley Kubrick, 1975) is informed by the painting styles of the eighteenth century.* EVERETT COLLECTION. REPRODUCED BY PERMISSION.

And in a science-fiction film with noirish underpinnings like Ridley Scott's *Blade Runner* (1982), the eclectic mix of architectural citations from various periods and styles endows the film with a strange nostalgia for a more authentic historical past in such a way as to calibrate the loss of memory and a jaded sensibility.

CINEMA AND ART

The marriage of art and cinema through genre in American cinema often resulted in the identification of art with elitism and deception. In European film history, the post–World War II art film developed in the film industries of France, Germany, and Italy. The film theorist and historian David Bordwell has argued that the "European art film" is more of a mode than a genre because its stylistic conventions stem from a general opposition to the rules of Hollywood cinema. Bordwell argues that films such as Michelangelo Antonioni's *L'Avventura* (1960) and Ingmar Bergman's *Persona* (1966) were born out of the rejection by Italian neorealism of Hollywood's causal storytelling, goal-oriented protagonists, and emphasis on narrative closure. By choosing ambiguity, unresolved narratives, directorial expressivity, location shooting, and existential malaise with a social consciousness, the European art film was an alternative to Hollywood in the 1950s.

Andre Bazin's influential role as a critic enabled the rise of Italian neorealism and the French New Wave. François Truffaut relied on artistic citations from French impressionism and early modernist painting in such films as *Jules et Jim* (1962) and *Les Deux anglaises et le continent* (*Two English Girls*, 1972); by contrast, Roberto Rossellini's neorealism has traditionally been praised for its newsreel look and rejection of art-historical sources. However, the argument that Italian neorealism exists outside of art history is naïve. In the Naples episode of *Paisà* (*Paisan*, 1946), for example, the relationship between figure and ground, with the big soldier and the small child sitting among the ruins, invokes the end of Renaissance painting's anthropocentric model. The urban landscape is an image of destruction and rubble, yet the two characters occupy the center of the frame so that the ruins amid which they sit acknowledge in reverse the humanist function of architecture in the Italian pictorial tradition.

Michelangelo Antonioni's L'Avventura *(1960) is an example of the European art film.* EVERETT COLLECTION. REPRODUCED BY PERMISSION.

Bordwell's model of the European art film applies to the self-reflexive, modernist films of the sixties but does not include the pastiche-like postmodernist films that began to appear in the 1970s and 1980s. *Back to the Future* (Robert Zemeckis, 1985) contains many references to Duane Hanson's hyperrealist sculptures, while Bernardo Bertolucci's *Il Conformista* (*The Conformist*, 1970) uses René Magritte's sleek irony and art-deco interiors. Lina Wertmüller's use of spaces suspended in time for *Film d'amore e d'anarchia* (*Love and Anarchy*, 1973) echoes the metaphysical atmosphere found in the paintings of Giorgio de Chirico. It is also important to remember that there are many other art films that, on the one hand, do not entirely follow Bordwell's model and, on the other, may have little to do with postmodern nostalgia. Thanks to their understanding of art-historical categories, these films are neither simply citational texts nor superficial and seductive pastiches compensating for an increasing sense of loss of memory and authenticity. And, finally, they are not always structured as travelogues of human alienation, a penchant triggered by neorealism's use of vignettes or sketches rather than coherent, causal narratives.

Filmmakers such as F. W. Murnau, Eric Rohmer, Alain Cavalier, and Andrei Tarkovsky are aware of the history of art to the extent that they move beyond it, treating it as a convenient storehouse of images. Their films can be called "visual form" films because these filmmakers incorporate the insights of pictorial genres into their own work. By taking seriously the links between landscape painting and subjectivity in, for example, *Nosferatu*, Murnau models his images on Caspar David Friedrich's vistas with precipices and fogs, eerie peaks and huge rocks. Murnau frames from behind small and lonely human figures, which he juxtaposes against vast natural spaces filled with a sense of the sublime; the director's insertion of an internal viewer matches Friedrich's use of the so-called *ruckenfigur*, a lone figure in a landscape, to underline how that landscape can be a figment of someone's mind yearning for the divine or sensing the possibility of horror. *Nosferatu* is therefore an example of the crossover between film and art in the context of silent German expressionism as a national cinema. Visual form is relevant to the tension between neoclassical and French romantic painting in Eric

Rohmer's *Die Marquise von O . . .* (*The Marquise of O*, 1976), an adaptation of Heinrich von Kleist's novella. By juxtaposing the sensuality of the word to the introspective qualities of the image, Rohmer questions the opposition of Enlightenment rationality and romantic impetuousness. Tarkovsky in *Andrei Rublev* (1969) uses fluid camera movements and shots of doors and windows to explore the hypnotic power of religious icon painting. Likewise, by using many close-ups on objects and an austere color scheme, Alain Cavalier in *Thérèse* (1986) links the genre of still-life painting to the humility of servants and the subordination of femininity.

Films that are part of a national cinema tradition (with or without a link to an avant-garde movement), modernist art films and postmodern pastiches, and visual-form films overlap the flexibility of these categories and bears witness to the richness of the encounter between art and film. Although the heyday of the European art film is over, cinema from Asia, the Middle East, Latin America, and Africa deserves much closer examination in the light of the relation between film and art. For example, the Iranian filmmaker Abbas Kiarostami's use of detailed images and vast landscapes relies heavily on the style of Persian miniature painting in his films *Ta'm e guilass* (*A Taste of Cherry*, 1997) and *Bad ma ra khahad bord* (*The Wind Will Carry Us*, 1999). Sergei Parajanov's *Sayat Nova* (*Color of Pomegranates*, 1968) combines Russian folk culture with performance art, while some of his compositions could easily be called installations and move from the screen to the art gallery. Although most of the critical work on film and art has relied on European case studies, it has become especially urgent to tackle Islamic and African visual traditions in order to achieve a better understanding of the art films that these areas of the world have produced. Japanese and Chinese cinema has drawn heavily from national traditions of woodblock printing and scroll painting.

American avant-garde filmmaking of the 1960s and 1960s was heavily influenced by minimalism in the visual arts. The films of Andy Warhol, Michael Snow, Hollis Frampton, and Paul Sharits are related to the work of artists such as Carl Andre, Robert Morris, Donald Judd, and Robert Smithson, all of whom worked in a variety of media. In the light of this awareness that what goes on in the art gallery relates to what happens on the screen, the American artist Eleanor Antin (b. 1935) coined the expression "black box, white cube"—the first term referring to cinema, the second to the art gallery. This phrase has been increasingly used by artists working in film and video, perhaps because so many mixed-media installations have blurred the boundaries between sculpture, film, architecture, video art, and painting.

SEE ALSO *Art Cinema; Expressionism; Surrealism*

FURTHER READING

Andrew, Dudley. *Film in the Aura of Art*. Princeton, NJ: Princeton University Press, 1984.

Bordwell, David. *Narration in the Fiction Film*. Madison: University of Wisconsin Press, 1985.

Dalle Vacche, Angela. *Cinema and Painting: How Art Is Used in Film*. Austin: University of Texas Press, 1996.

———, ed. *The Visual Turn: Classical Film Theory and Art History*. New Brunswick, NJ: Rutgers University Press, 2002.

Deleuze, Gilles. *Cinema*. Vol. 1: *The Movement-Image*. Vol. 2: *The Time-Image*. Translated by Hugh Tomlinson and Barbara Habberjam. Minneapolis: University of Minnesota Press, 1986–1989.

Desser, David, and Linda Ehrlich, eds. *Cinematic Landscapes: Observations on the Visual Arts and Cinema of China and Japan*. Austin: University of Texas Press, 1996.

Eisner, Lotte. *The Haunted Screen: German Expressionism and the Influence of Max Reinhardt*. Translated by Roger Graves. Berkeley: University of California Press, 1977.

Hollander, Anne. *Moving Pictures*. New York: Knopf: 1989.

Schrader, Paul. *Transcendental Style in Film: Ozu, Bresson, Dreyer*. New York: Da Capo Press, 1998.

Tashiro, Charles. *Pretty Pictures: Production Design and the History Film*. Austin: University of Texas Press, 1998.

Angela Dalle Vacche

FINLAND

During its heyday between 1930s and 1950s, domestic film production in Finland developed into a miniature image of the Hollywood film industry, yet with certain national characteristics based on the country's historical and political situation. Thus, for instance, due to Russian repression while Finland still was a Grand Duchy under the rule of Czarist Russia, film production was initially regarded as a national project aimed at reinforcing the identity of the Finnish people on the one hand, and at presentation of the country and its people to foreign nations on the other hand. Therefore, the first films made in Finland were short documentaries about the country's natural and industrial sites.

BEGINNINGS

Finland was an autonomous but oppressed part of the Russian Empire from the early nineteenth century until it became an independent republic in 1917. The first feature made in Finland, *Lönnbrännarna* (*Bootleggers*), premiered in 1907. The film, of which there remain only a few stills, was a result of a script contest aimed at creating a national cinema. However, Russian oppression and in its aftermath, the civil war—fought between Russian-inspired Bolsheviks and right-wing nationalists in 1917–1918—discouraged other serious efforts. The struggles for the new independent republic of Finland, ruled by the nationalists, delayed the advance of the film industry for another decade. From this period there also exists one of the world's oldest film censorship authorities (Suomen Elokuvatarkastamo), a state office that came to influence the development of the objectives and quality of Finnish film. It had the authority to decide specifically not only which films could be exhibited, but which were

"valuable" enough to be freed from the amusement tax. Throughout the early decades, a strong public notion in the country regarded cinema as "amusement"—as in opposition to art—dispensable, and hence, taxable.

One of the central figures in the early history of Finnish filmmaking was Erkki Karu (1887–1935), who founded the production company Suomi-Filmi in 1919 and directed a handful of successful rural melodramas. The decade of the 1930s was a consolidating period for the domestic film industry, during which Suomi-Filmi—together with Suomen Filmiteollisuus, also established by Karu—became fully integrated production companies, dominant in the field until the period of decline in the 1960s. Other important producers of features were Adams Filmi and Fennada-Filmi, while companies such as Aho & Soldan specialized in high-quality documentaries.

Toward the end of the silent era a handful of films were produced, many of which were Finnish plays and dramatic novels transformed into films. Apart from rural melodramas such as *Koskenlaskijan morsian* (1923) or classics like *Kihlaus* (1922), contemporary comedies in urban milieus, such as *Kaikki rakastavat* (1931), starring Finland's leading romantic leads Tauno Palo (1908–1982) and Ansa Ikonen (1913–1989), became fashionable.

Many were hesitant about investing in sound equipment in the early 1930s but what looked like a risk turned into a gold mine soon enough, for the Finnish people loved to hear their language spoken on the silver screen. The first sound film, *Aatamin puvussa ja vähän Eevankin* (*Dressed Like Adam and a Bit Like Eve, Too*) was released in January 1931. Successful foreign films, often Swedish, were adapted into Finnish milieux, and popular novels were transformed into film scripts. For the first time, domestic films could compete with foreign productions. However, few countries imported Finnish films. One of the most well-known films from the pre–World War II period, *Varastettu kuolema* (*Stolen Death*, 1938), was to represent Finnish cinema in retrospectives and festivals, but it was exported to Sweden only. Its director, Nyrki Tapiovaara (1911–1940), directed but four features, and his heroic death during the last days of the Winter War of 1939–1940 has contributed to the myth of him as the lost genius of Finnish cinema. *Varastettu kuolema* was photographed by Erik Blomberg (1913–1996), who would direct *Valkoinen Peura* (*The White Reindeer*, 1952), one of the country's internationally acknowledged productions, which won the International Prize at the Cannes Film Festival in 1953 and the Golden Globe in the United States in 1957.

The production pace was hectic during the war years (1939–1944) in spite of the impossible conditions, with a lack of film stock, the constant bombing of Helsinki, and many photographers and other male technicians called to the front. Due to obstacles such as commercial embargos, the influx of foreign films diminished, and distributors begged for new films. A number of costume melodramas such as *Kulkurin valssi* (*The Vagabond Waltz*, 1941) and *Katariina ja Munkkinimen kreivi* (*Catherine and the Count of Munkkinimen*, 1943) were made in response, as were popular military farces. Toward the end of the war, these farces pointedly ridiculed the hostile Soviet army, as in a series featuring two friends in arms called *Ryhmy and Romppainen* (1941, 1943, 1952). After the peace treaty between Finland and the Soviet Union in 1944, the authorities withdrew the two first films from the market in order not to offend the Eastern neighbor, now an important trading partner.

POSTWAR CINEMA

Apart from the control executed through the much-resented amusement tax, another means of state interference in the film industry was the grants and awards that were introduced during the latter half of the 1940s. After the establishment of the Finnish Film Foundation in 1969, the state also became a significant part in the production process—indeed, a prerequisite for the existence of a film industry in the country. But far from gaining control as in "totalitarian state propaganda," the establishment of the Foundation was foremost a protectionist move reflecting nationalist sentiments. By the 1960s, the attitudes toward cinema had changed in Nordic countries and to an increasing degree it was perceived as art in its own right. According to common

understanding, therefore, the government is responsible for providing support for the artistic development of film as well as for literature and the fine arts.

The Finnish authorities produced newsreels reporting on the current political situation during World War II, and the documentary stock produced by the Finnish Army and now stored in their archives is quite extensive. The government-financed *Suomi maksaa* (Leistelä, 1951), a report of the nation's efforts to pay the heavy national debts caused by the war against the Soviet Union, was a typical documentary during the late 1940s and 1950s. Finnish people were extremely proud of being the only nation in the post–World War II world that repaid the restoration loans guaranteed by the US government. The film breathes pride and self-confidence, not unlike the documentaries made during the early period of independence.

The disillusionment that followed World War II affected the topics of feature films: light comedies and romantic stories gave way to social dramas depicting the problems of people living in the shadows of urban backyards. Edvin Laine (1905–1989), one of the most significant of the postwar generation of film directors, produced *Ristikon varjossa* (*Hunting Shadows*) in 1945, and *Laitakaupungin laulu* in 1948. Laine also directed the most popular Finnish film ever, *Tuntematon sotilas* (*The Unknown Soldier*, 1955), the first realistic account of the war. The commercial success of the film unintentionally contributed to the crisis that ultimately brought about the bankruptcy of Suomen Filmiteollisuus: to avoid paying tax on the millions in profit the film generated, the company invested in too many hastily made new films of lesser quality.

On top of the insecure situation during the 1960s, with increasing production costs and declining film attendance that necessitated closing down movie theaters, the film industry was hit by a strike initiated by the Actors' Union, which was displeased with actors' salaries. The strike did not stop film production, however, but instead, introduced a whole new generation of actors, most notably in *Käpy selän alla* (1966), directed by Mikko Niskanen (1929–1990) with a script written by Marjaana Mikkola. Women screenwriters are not uncommon in the history of Finnish film: already in the 1920s, plays by dramatists such as Minna Canth (1844–1897) and Maria Jotuni (1880–1943) were adapted into films, and Valentin Vaala's (1909–1976) popular comedies in the 1930s to 1940s were the results of his cooperation with his leading lady, Lea Joutseno (1910–1977), and the writer Kersti Bergroth (1886–1975).

Yet it is hard not to see the history of Finnish cinema as a cavalcade of a handful of men: Risto Orko (1899–2001), the CEO of Suomi-Filmi, and Toivo Särkkä

Aki Kaurismäki's **Leningrad Cowboys Go America** *(1989) was an international hit.* © ORION FILMS/COURTESY EVERETT COLLECTION. REPRODUCED BY PERMISSION.

(1890–1975), the head of Suomen Filmiteollisuus, dominated the country's screens as directors for over thirty years. The first women directors appeared in the early 1960s. Ritva Arvelo (b. 1921) won the state award (an unnamed monetary award) with *Kultainen vasikka* (1961). Yet another twenty years would pass before women were able to establish themselves in the industry: Tuija-Maija Niskanen (b. 1943), the director of *Suuri illusioni* (*Grand Illusion*, 1985), and Kaisa Rastimo (b. 1961) with her *Säädyllinen murhenäytelmä* (*A Respectable Tragedy*, 1998) are among the most important. One of the most successful women in Finnish cinema since the early 1980s has been Pirjo Honkasalo (b. 1947), whose documentaries *Atman* (1996) and *Melancholian 3 Huonetta* (*The 3 Rooms of Meloncholia*, 2004) have received awards at numerous film festivals around the world.

The establishment of the Finnish Film Foundation contributed to structural changes within the industry during the 1970s. The old companies with their complex administration systems disappeared and smaller companies, often managed by the filmmakers themselves, emerged. This was in line with the contemporary view of the film director as *auteur* with full control over production, including right to the final cut. Such a view brought about a generation of independent film directors writing their own scripts and, like Jörn Donner (b. 1933), establishing their own production companies, Donner, also a well-known author, directed films such as *Sixtynine* (1969) and *Perkele! Kuvia Suomesta* (1971), examples of the soft porn wave of the period, whereas Risto Jarva's (1935–1977) productions reflected the era's social criticism with films such as *Bensaa suonissa* (*Gas in the Veins*, 1970) and *Jäniksen vuosi* (*The Year of the Hare*, 1977).

By the end of the millennium yet another significant change had taken place. It was clear that no Nordic country alone could generate the funds needed for the production of a feature film; cooperation was needed between the countries and their respective film institutes and television companies. The result was lengthy fund-raising and decision-making processes whereby only prestigious "heritage"-style productions became possible to realize, such as *Talvisota* (*The Winter War*, Pekka Parikka, 1989) with its painstaking and elaborated mass scenes depicting the battles of the Winter War.

From the 1980s on, the Finnish solution to the situation was provided by another generation of film directors with Aki (b. 1957) and Mika Kaurismäki (b. 1955) in the lead, making low-budget films with small, mobile units. While Mika Kaurismäki has invested in an international career, Aki has stayed in Finland faithful to his austere, stylized, and self-reflexive style in films such as *Tulitikkutehtaan tyttö* (*The Match Factory Girl*, 1990) and *Mies vailla menneisyyttä* (*The Man Without a Past*, 2002). In his films Aki Kaurismäki has tended to scrutinize nostalgic sentiments addressing the popular collective memory of the postwar Finnish generations. Other directors of his generation utilize heightened realism with postmodern tendencies such as split narrative and pastiched characters. Timo Koivusalo's (b. 1963) biopic *Rentun ruusu* (2001), about the life of popular 1970s protest singer Irwin Goodman, or Pekka Lehto's *Tango*

Kabaree (*Tango Cabaret*, 2001), featuring the dancer and celebrity Aira Samulin, are but two examples. Such forms of remembrance have not always ended up as box-office hits, whereas films depicting the wars of independent Finland always seem to manage to cover their costs.

SEE ALSO *National Cinema; World War II*

FURTHER READING

Cowie, Peter. *Finnish Cinema*. Helsinki: Suomen elokuvasäätiö, 1990.

Hillier, Jim, ed. *Cinema in Finland*. London: British Film Institute, 1975.

Nestingen, Andrew, and Trevor G. Elkington, eds. *Transnational Cinema in a Global North: Nordic Cinema in Transition*. Detroit, MI: Wayne State University Press, 2005.

Soila, Tytti, ed. *The Cinema of Scandinavia*. London: Wallflower Press, 2005.

Soila, Tytti, Astrid Söderbergh Widding, and Gunnar Iversen. *Nordic National Cinemas*. London and New York: Routledge, 1998.

Tytti Soila

FRANCE

Since World War I, French cinema has defined itself through its ambivalent relations with Hollywood cinema. Although French cinema was the dominant force in the international market until World War I, its influence extending as far as Australia, in the decades that followed the industry struggled to maintain its hold on French audiences. French stars, valued for their independence and their ability to represent "Frenchness" globally, have played an important role in this crusade. Though many would argue that this has been a losing battle, French product continues to dominate French screens, though, as often as not, it is the television screen that viewers watch today. Yet, initially, it was the French who discovered cinema as we know it.

SILENT CINEMA: 1895–1929

The invention of the cinema was credited to Auguste (1862–1954) and Louis Lumière (1864–1948), two brothers, who organized what is widely believed to be the first film screening on 28 December 1895, at the Grand Café in Paris, using the Lumière brothers' *Cinématograph*, which was both camera and projector. Though the American inventor Thomas Edison (1847–1931) had created film stock itself as early as 1889, it was the Lumière brothers who invented cinema as a mass entertainment event in which spectators were seated in front of a projected image, showing films such as *L'Arrivée d'un train à la Ciotat* (*Arrival of a Train at La Ciotat*, 1895), *La Sortie des usines Lumière* (*Employees Leaving the Lumière Factory*, 1895) and *Demolition d'un mur* (*Demolition of a Wall*, 1896). Their cinematographers, who traveled throughout the world shooting notable events, assembled a catalog of over one thousand

films during the next two years. In France, their major competitor was Georges Méliès (1861–1938), with his *Kinétograph*. His production company Star Film, founded in 1896, specialized in fantastic, magical tales, in contrast with the Lumière brothers, who concentrated on *actualités*. After making between six hundred and eight hundred films, Star Film went bankrupt in 1914, and Méliès ceased producing films in 1919.

A third significant figure in the development of French cinema was Charles Pathé (1863–1957) with his *Eknétographe*. Pathé founded Pathé Frères with his brother Émile in September 1896, and from 1902 his emblem, the red rooster, was synonymous with cinema around the world. Charles Pathé left France for the United States in 1914 because several of the most important branches of his company were located in territory occupied by the Germans. One of Pathé's major contributions to the development of cinema was to inaugurate in 1907 the tripartite system of production, distribution, and exhibition that characterizes the modern film industry. Under this system, exhibitors rent films through distribution companies. The number of film production companies quickly multiplied to include that of Léon Gaumont, who boasted the *Chronophotographe* and the first film director, Alice Guy (1873–1968).

The period of 1908 to 1914 is generally considered the golden age of comedy. During this era such stars as Max Linder (1882–1925), a brilliant comic actor who exerted a strong influence on comedians such as Charlie Chaplin and Harold Lloyd, and such directors as Jean Durand (1882–1946), as well as the animator Émile Cohl (1857–1938), came to the fore. Adaptations of novels were common, and feature-length films began to appear in 1911, as well as detective serials, associated with director Louis Feuillade (1873–1925). This period also saw the advent of Le Film d'Art, a company founded in February 1908, partly funded by Pathé. Le Film d'Art was noted for its production of quality filmed historical drama, such as *L'Assassinat du Duc de Guise* (*The Assassination of the duc de Guise*, 1908), directed by André Calmettes (1861–1942) and Charles Le Bargy (1858–1936) (who also took a leading role), with music by Camille Saint-Saëns.

Competition from American and Scandinavian producers had already weakened French international hegemony by 1912. Beginning in August 1914 with the onset of World War I, French film production dropped virtually to zero. After six months of inactivity, film production began again slowly with films like Feuillade's serial *The Vampires* (1915), which introduced one of the silent cinema's greatest stars, Musidora (1889–1957), who achieved great popularity in her role as the vamp Irma Vep.

POST–WORLD WAR I

The most salient feature of post–World War I France for future film scholars was the coalescence of the film culture around France's first cinéphiles and first avant-garde. Inspired by the influx of Hollywood films, a generation of young intellectuals took an interest in the cinema. An avant-garde sensibility emerged, championed by the journalist turned director, Louis Delluc (1890–1924), that had a profound influence on the development of cinema as a national art form, most notably on the New Wave in the post–World War II era. Although Delluc died in 1924, he gave his name to a prestigious prize for best film, and his writing influences French thought and film scholarship to this day.

For Delluc, cinema must be "cinematic" and "French." It must express the specificity of the cinematic medium as an art form while countering the tendencies of film as entertainment. Impressionism, associated with Delluc, was a loose and often inconsistent body of thought. The Impressionists reacted against the pictorial-realist tradition of French cinema by seeking inspiration in the editing and camera styles of new Hollywood directors, who had evolved away from a strictly documentary or theatrical presentation of story. Though often dismissed as melodramatic by contemporary audiences, films such as *La Roue* (*The Wheel*, Abel Gance, 1923) and *L'Inhumaine* (*The New Enchantment*, Marcel L'Herbier, 1923) exploited rhythmic editing, point-of-view shots, soft focus, and optical devices such as superimpositions to convey subjective experience. Writer-filmmakers associated with the movement such as Germaine Dulac (1882–1942) pursued the idea that film functioned like a language; however, the conviction that film was an art form rather than merely a vehicle for entertainment was Impressionism's most important legacy. Following his death, Delluc's influence was evident in the work of such directors as Dulac, Jean Epstein (1897–1953), Abel Gance (1889–1981), and Marcel L'Herbier (1888–1979), who remained affected by Impressionism goals while often moving in different directions. Dadaism and surrealism inspired a second avant-garde in 1923 and 1924. The American photographer Man Ray (Emanuel Rabinovich; 1890–1976) and the painter Fernand Léger (1881–1955) created experimental films that resembled the essay films of Dulac and the fantasies of the Brazilian expatriate director, Alberto Cavalcanti (1897–1982). Two directors who would leave their mark on French cinema as part of this movement were René Clair (1898–1981) and Luis Buñuel (1900–1983).

Though largely ignored by intellectuals, French cinema as a popular narrative form thrived during this period. Rarely exported, French popular film continued to appeal to French audiences, with serials such as *L'Enfant roi* (The Child King, Jean Kemm, 1923), or *Fanfan-la-Tulipe* (*Fanfan the Tulip*, René Leprince, 1925). Successful directors of the period included Julien Duvivier (1896–1967), Raymond Bernard (1891–1977), and Jacques Feyder (1885–1948). Facing increasing production costs, studios during this time inaugurated the European co-production, often working with German production companies.

Two of the most influential production companies, Ermolieff Films and Alexander Kamenka's L'Albatros, were founded by Russian émigrés, and produced films destined for the émigré audience as well as French works. This group of émigré Russians, known as *les Russes de Montreuil* (the Russians of Montreuil), included such directors as Yakov Protozanov (1881–1945), Victor (Vyatcheslav) Tourjansky (1891–1976), and Alexander Volkov (1885–1942), as well as technicians and actors and actresses. Kamenka produced notable works of French cinema, such as Clair's *Un Chapeau de paille d'Italie* (*An Italian Straw Hat*, 1928), and *Les Deux timides* (*Two Timid Souls*, 1928). Later Kamenka produced *Les Bas-fonds* (*The Lower Depths*, Jean Renoir, 1936), which won the Louis Delluc Prize.

During this period, many stars were recruited from the stage or cabarets, including Maurice Chevalier (1888–1972), already a star of the Parisian music halls, who attained prominence in a series of movies foreshadowing the great success he would achieve in America in the 1930s. Other stars from theater included Michel Simon (1895–1975), Gaby Morlay (1893–1964), and Albert Préjean (1893–1979). Simon, in particular, represented the French tradition of the "monstre sacré," or "eccentric," the flamboyant character actor with a singularly striking physiognomy, used to great effect in, for example, Renoir's *Boudu sauvé des eaux* (*Boudu Saved from Drowning*, 1932).

By the end of the 1920s, French cinema had recovered from the effects of World War I. Though the battle with Hollywood at the international box office had been lost, French cinema had acquired the position of a national art form that was distinct from the entertainments produced for the masses. Paradoxically, Hollywood films, because of their impact on the avant-garde during the war years, were a primary influence in creating a French cinema that was cinematic and French, in the terms defined by Delluc. It is in Hollywood film that the Impressionists found their inspiration—in the camera work and editing of D.W. Griffith (1875–1948), the lighting of Cecil B. DeMille (1881–1959), and the dreamlike scenarios of Charlie Chaplin (1889–1977). And it is Hollywood that left its imprint on the foundational avant-garde films of the dadaists and the surrealists—films such as Dulac's *La Coquille et Le Clergyman* (*The Seashell and the Clergyman*, 1928), and Buñuel's *Un Chien andalou* (*An Andalusian Dog*, 1929)—setting French cinema apart as the international forerunner of the "film-as-art" movement, a place that France arguably retained throughout the remainder of the twentieth century.

Although Hollywood was the object of polemical discussion, other national cinemas such as Russian cinema, particularly through émigré producers, and German cinema, in terms of financial backing, also influenced the directions of French cinema. French popular cinema—in the form of comedies and serials, as well as the popular *policier* (later known as the *polar*) or police film—continued to be effective in French theaters, constituting a parallel strand to the higher profile films praised by the intellectual elite. With the advent of sound, French cinema as art would encounter its biggest challenge.

SOUND FILM AND THE CLASSICAL ERA: 1929–1940

The first sound studios opened in France in the autumn of 1929, inaugurating the golden age of filmed theater, and also precipitating an aesthetic crisis manifested in heated debate about the nature of cinematic art. While adherents to the legacy of Impressionism, such as Gance and L'Herbier, clung to the primacy of the image as the fundamental element of film language, directors like Duvivier and Renoir embraced sound as integral to the film medium. The film industry was also subject to financial crisis and over the decade was reorganized around companies like La Société Nouvelle des Établissements Gaumont (the SNEG) and the Société Nouvelle Pathé-

Cinéma (SNPC). Nonetheless, some of the great films of the French cinema were produced between 1934 and World War II, in part as the result of an influx of directors and technicians fleeing the Nazis from other countries. One such figure was the German director Max Ophüls (1902–1957), creator of the film *La Tendre ennemie* (*The Tender Enemy*, 1936), who became a French citizen in 1938. The production of feature films stabilized at about 100 to 120 films per year, a level of production that remained more or less the norm for the rest of the century.

Two directors who forged their own style within the confines of the filmed theater genre were Marcel Pagnol (1895–1974) and Sacha Guitry (1885–1957). Pagnol, a successful director, writer, and producer, established his own studios in the South of France and produced a body of work associated with that region. Films for which he wrote the screenplay include the "Pagnol trilogy," made up of *Marius* (1931), *Fanny* (1932), and *César* (1936), dealing with the "little people" of Marseilles. The success of these films owed much to the superb performances of the actors, including (Jules) Raimu (1883–1946), Pierre Fresnay (1897–1975), Fernand Charpin (1887–1944), and Orane Demazis (1894–1991). Because of the subtlety and originality of his productions, and also because of the way that his work constituted an early exploration of regional identity, Pagnol's talent was recognized by critics such as André Bazin who, in principle, opposed the filmed theater style. Renoir's *Toni* (1935), a pivotal film in the development of the Italian neorealism, is one of the many films that demonstrated the importance of Pagnol's work for the future of French cinema. Both Pagnol's films and novels would influence the development of what is commonly called heritage cinema in the late 1980s and early 1990s. Guitry, less well known outside of France, was an actor and writer as well as a director. In his films of this period, he captured the essence of Parisian light comedy, a genre that disappeared during World War II. During this period French cinema also continued to borrow from the tradition of the music hall with films such as *Zouzou* (1934), starring the African American singer-dancer Josephine Baker (1906–1975).

In May 1936 the Popular Front, a historic alliance of leftist and radical interests, came to power, ruling until October 1938. This period, which saw the introduction of major social changes, such as paid holidays, trade union rights, and a public health service, unleashed a burst of creative intellectual and artistic energy, especially at the cooperative Ciné-Liberté, of which Renoir was a member. The rise and ascendancy of the Popular Front manifested itself in films that emphasized the worker. Renoir, for example, directed *Le Crime de Monsieur Lange* (*The Crime of Monsieur Lange*, 1936), the story of a worker's cooperative, the epic *La Marseillaise* (1938),

MARCEL CARNÉ
b. Albert Cranche, Paris, France, 18 August 1909, d. 31 October 1996

Marcel Carné is a controversial figure in French cinema, for while many see in his work an outmoded classicism that was transcended by the directors of the French New Wave, others find in it evidence of the vitality of studio filmmaking in the 1930s. Carné trained as a photographer and worked in journalism before hiring on as an assistant to René Clair and Jacques Feyder. Carné's first feature, *Jenny* (1936), starring Françoise Rosay, marked the beginning of his long and productive collaboration with the poet and scriptwriter Jacques Prévert.

Carné's genius lay in his ability to gather a team of creative artists: screenwriters (including Prévert), designers (including Alexander Trauner), composers (Maurice Jaubert, Joseph Kosma), and a bevy of French actors, including Jules Berry, Louis Jouvet, Michel Simon, and Arletty (Arlette-Léonie Bathiat). His most famous film is *Les Enfants de paradis* (*Children of Paradise*, 1945), which portrays the love affair between a *demi-mondain* (courtesan) and an actor.

From the mid-1930s until the late 1940s, Carné was one of the most respected and powerful directors in France. He initially influenced the direction of French cinema through his writing in *Cinémagazine*, inspiring poetic realism. Poetic realism, which Carné later called *le fantastique social* (social fantasy), espoused a pessimistic view of the human condition, which he conveyed through artful composition, careful *mise-en-scène*, polished acting,

high-key lighting, and tragic endings. His films in this style include *Hôtel du Nord* (1938), *Le Jour se lève* (*Daybreak*, 1939), and *Le Quai des brumes* (*Port of Shadows*, 1938), which sparked controversy for its morbid subject matter.

For better or for worse, Carné and his team communicated to a popular audience a pervasive atmosphere of melancholy that remains a milestone in French cinema. Following the end of his partnership with Prévert with *Les Portes de la nuit* (*The Gates of Night*, 1946) and *La Marie du port* (*Mary of the Port*, 1950), Carné lost his best collaborators, and his subsequent films were less accomplished.

RECOMMENDED VIEWING

Jenny (1936), *Drôle de drame, ou L'étrange aventure de Docteur Molyneux* (*Bizarre, Bizarre*, 1937), *Port of Shadows* (1938), *Hôtel du Nord* (1938), *Daybreak* (1939), *Les Visiteurs du soir* (*The Devil's Envoys*, 1942), *Children of Paradise* (1945), *Gates of Night* (1946)

FURTHER READING

Andrew, Dudley. *Mists of Regret: Culture and Sensibility in Classic French Film.* Princeton, NJ: University of Princeton Press, 1995.

Williams, Alan. *Republic of Images: A History of French Filmmaking.* Cambridge, MA: Harvard University Press, 1992.

Hilary Ann Radner

and was involved in the making of *La Vie est à nous* (*The People of France*, 1936), a communist propaganda film. Though light comedies and musicals were more popular with the public, these films were praised by critics and film historians. With the defeat of the Popular Front, the melancholic tendencies of poetic realism became more marked and were reflected in narratives dealing with doomed love affairs, betrayals, and murders, usually set in Paris in working-class settings. Such films are exemplified by *Le Quai des brumes* (*Port of Shadows*, 1938) and *Le Jour se lève* (*Daybreak*, 1939) by Marcel Carné (1909–1996). Both films starred Jean Gabin (1904–1976), who, with Arletty (Arlette-Léonie Bathiat; 1898–1992), came to incarnate French working-class values, especially in terms of their spoken delivery, which was marked by a

strong demotic accent. In addition to Carné, directors associated with this style were Renoir, Duvivier, and Jean Grémillon (1901–1959).

Renoir, who began his career with films like *La Fille de l'eau* (*Whirlpool of Fate*, 1925) and *Nana* (1926), both with the actress Catherine Hessling (1900–1979), is considered by many to be the most significant director of this period. His films ran the gamut of possible genres, from poetic realist films to avant-garde films, from comedies to popular melodramas, and from literary adaptation to Popular Front propaganda. Renoir's *La Grande illusion* (*The Grand Illusion*, 1937) and *La Bête humaine* (*The Human Beast*, 1938), both with Gabin, and his masterpiece, *La Règle du jeu* (*The Rules of the Game*, 1939), with Marcel Dalio (1900–1983), were box-office

Marcel Carné. EVERETT COLLECTION. REPRODUCED BY
PERMISSION.

triumphs. His career was interrupted by World War II, which he spent in Hollywood.

THE WAR YEARS: 1940 TO 1944

Though films were banned if deemed too demoralizing, the film industry was active during the nine months of French-German hostility in 1939 and 1940. Film production stopped completely during the summer of 1940; however, this hiatus inaugurated one of the most prosperous, if not the most creative, periods of French cinema.

Following the surrender of France to Germany, a new government was established at the small spa town of Vichy, in the unoccupied zone of central France, under the leadership of Maréchal Henri Philippe Pétain (1856–1951). Although autocratic and reactionary, the Vichy regime initiated an ambitious program to restore France to her former glory, including an effort to construct a quasi-mystical idealized vision of France grounded in a conservative social agenda and a focus on youth. The Vichy regime was quick to recognize the strategic importance of the film industry in advancing this agenda and almost immediately put in place structures that both supported and regulated the industry. In 1940, the Comité d'Organisation des Industries du Cinéma (Committee for the Organization of the Film Industry)

was established, as was the COIC, which would become the Centre National de la Cinématographie (National Center for Cinematography), the CNC, in 1946. The COIC immediately set up regulations for the film industry and also a system of state support. Notably, the COIC created what would become IDHEC, Institut des Hautes Études Cinématographiques (Institute for Film Studies) in 1944, under the direction of L'Herbier.

Financially, the COIC had a positive effect in terms of underwriting the French film industry, although it also served as a censorship arm of the Vichy government. In particular, it had an important function in terms of imposing restrictions on the activities of Jews in the film sector. A number of members of the film community fled to the United States, including such directors as Renoir, Clair, Duvivier, and Ophüls, as well as such actors as Gabin and Michèle Morgan (b. 1920). Others, like Pierre Chenal (1904–1990) and Louis Jouvet (1887–1951), took refuge in Latin America. In certain respects French cinema in 1941 was severely handicapped; nonetheless, the Vichy period proved to be a prosperous time for the industry overall. Cinemas were a popular haven from the cold and from the political and social pressures of the period. British and then American films were not available. For three years Hollywood was not a competitor in the French market, so audiences chose between German films, French films, and a few Italian films. A single national market encouraged big-budget productions, such as *Les Enfants du paradis* (*The Children of Paradise*, 1945), which was begun by Carné in 1943 as an Italian co-production.

The 220 feature-length films that constitute the Vichy cinema are not linked by any specific style or topic. The number of films that espoused right-wing views was no higher than during the prewar years (1934–1940); however, there was no counterbalancing progressive or leftist perspective. The settings lacked specificity—German uniforms and flags were rarely present within the frame—and the past, especially the nineteenth century, was preferred to the present. Popular genres included light comedies, thrillers, musicals, costume dramas, and a few fantasy films. A significant number of directors from the 1930s continued working through the 1940s, including Guitry, Pagnol, Grémillon, and Carné. New directors emerged from the ranks, including Jean Delannoy (b. 1908), Louis Daquin (1908–1980), André Cayatte (b. 1909), Claude Autant-Lara (1901–2000), Jacques Becker (1906–1960), Henri-Georges Clouzot (1907–1977), and Robert Bresson (1901–1999). Significant Vichy films include *La fille du puisatier* (*The Well-Digger's Daughter*, Pagnol, 1940), *Lumière d'été* (*Light of Summer*, Grémillon, 1943), *L'Assassin habite au 21* (*The Murderer Lives at Number 21*, Clouzot, 1942), and *Les Anges du péché* (*Angels of the Streets*,

Poetic realism in Marcel Carné's **Le Quai des Brumes *(Port of Shadows, 1938).*** EVERETT COLLECTION. REPRODUCED BY PERMISSION.

Bresson, 1943), based on a screenplay by Jean Giraudoux.

LEGACY AND REGENERATION: 1944 TO 1959

The end of the war and Liberation would present yet another challenge to the film industry. With Liberation came the creation of the Committee for the Liberation of Cinema and a journal, *L'Écran français* (French Screen), which appeared in July 1945. In the immediate postwar period, the French film industry was in crisis. Its equipment was outmoded or destroyed by the war and its personnel dispersed and demoralized. Most felt that the only solution was continuing the state regulation and support inaugurated by Vichy. In 1946 the CNC was created as an autonomous institution with the mandate of regulating and supporting the French film industry. It was funded through taxes levied on the industry itself. In the same year the Blum-Byrnes agreement was signed, which stipulated that during four weeks out of the year only French films could be shown in a given theater. In 1948, the period was extended to five weeks. In 1949, France signed an agreement with Italy that gave certain advantages to Franco-Italian co-productions. This agreement in turn supported the development of what came to be known as the Tradition of Quality.

The creation of the CNC, the regulations providing state-mandated support, the normalization of relations with the United States, and the creation of a film market enlarged initially by the addition of Italy laid down the basis for what has come to be known as the French mode of production—a compromise between state regulation and free trade under the guidance of the CNC. If, through its inception, this system was subject to controversy, in time it garnered strong popular support, particularly when other national cinemas in Europe suffered marked decline in the 1980s.

Though economically healthy, the industry was rigid, and from an artistic perspective it languished during the immediate post–World War II period. French cinema remained under the threat of censorship throughout the 1950s, when it touched on politically sensitive current events, such as the economic situation, the aftermath of World War II, the Cold War, the war in Indochina, and the Algerian War. This censorship program was effective particularly in terms of fostering a climate of self-censorship among directors and producers. By tacit agreement, there was little or no material produced that reflected on the war years or, more specifically, the problem of collaboration.

The French film industry was characterized by inflexibility, not only in terms of subject matter, but also in terms of personnel. Films were stylized, reflecting the domination of the industry by cinematographers and technicians who were protected and nurtured by the unionized structures of the big studios. Directors typically served long years of apprenticeship and were often forty years old before making a first film. One of the few directors to emerge in this period was Yves Allégret (1907–1986), who remained limited by his adherence to the traditions of the past. New, more notable actors and actresses included Simone Signoret (1921–1985), Gérard Philipe (1922–1959), and Madeleine Robinson (1916–2004).

This period was identified with the Tradition of Quality—dismissed by young critics of the period, such as François Truffaut (1932–1984), as "cinéma de papa" (daddy's movies). The Tradition of Quality emphasized craft over innovation, privileged established directors over new directors, and preferred the great works of the past to experimentation. Literary adaptation provided fertile ground for this decade, on the part of those who were anxious to prove the cultural superiority of French film in the face of a massive influx of Hollywood movies into the French market. Grémillon, Guitry, Pagnol, Renoir, Clair, and Duvivier continued to make films, as did the new generation that emerged during the Occupation. Autant-Lara, Clément, Georges Rouquier (1909–1989), Clouzot, Becker, Ophüls, Jean Cocteau (1889–1963), Bresson, and Jacques Tati (1908–1982) made significant films during this period. Characteristic Tradition of Quality films include *Douce* (*Love Story*, Autant-Lara, 1943), *La Symphonie pastorale* (Delannoy, 1946), and *Casque d'or* (*Golden Marie*, Becker, 1952). Actors associated with the Tradition of Quality are Philipe, Martine Carol (1922–1967), and Simone Signoret. Philipe's polished acting style and the sophisticated mature femininity of Carol and Signoret contrasted the youthful insouciance of the actors who would be used by the directors of the later New Wave.

The ciné-club movement, inaugurated by Delluc in the 1920s, became a significant force in French culture and in the development of French cinema. The ciné-phile—the amateur fanatic of film and film history—appeared as a distinct character on the French cultural scene and was defined as specifically French, as the word itself suggests. The ciné-club produced a new type of film spectator, film critic, and eventually director, preparing the way for the French New Wave. Such film critics as André Bazin, Alexandre Astruc, Truffaut, and Ado Kyrou (Adonis Kyrou) revived the debates of the Impressionists in the context of post–World War II France. *Cahiers du Cinéma* (1951) and *Positif* (1952) replaced *L'Écran français* (1943–1953) and remained important venues for discussion about film throughout the twentieth century. This lively intellectual climate was a major force in the dramatic changes in film aesthetics and the film industry that subsequently took place.

The government also played a role in fostering a new generation and a new type of director. A regulation eliminating the double-bill (two feature-length films) created a renaissance of short films, as did the new system of supporting film projects based on quality that had been inaugurated by the CNC during this period. Such directors as Alain Resnais (b. 1922), Georges Franju (1912–1987), and Pierre Kast (1920–1984), later known as part of *le groupe de trente* (the group of thirty), were already making short films that fell outside the Tradition of Quality. These short films were distributed via the ciné-clubs and the *art et essai* theaters, that is, small theaters that were the equivalent of the art house theater in Great Britain and the United States. By the end of the 1950s, the old guard had been successfully challenged in the popular arena by young filmmakers, such as Roger Vadim (1928–2000) with *Et Dieu...créa la femme* (*And...God created Woman*, 1955). Critical reception of the outsider filmmakers was equally positive, as in the case of Jean-Pierre Melville's (1917–1973) *Le Silence de la mer* (Silence of the Sea, 1949), Astruc's *Le Rideau cramoisi* (*The Crimson Curtain*, 1953) and *Les Mauvaises rencontres* (*Bad Liaisons*, 1955), *La Pointe-courte* (Agnès Varda, 1956), *Ascenseur pour l'échafaud* (*Elevator to the Gallows*, Louis Malle, 1958), *Un Amour de poche* (*Girl in His Pocket*, Kast, 1958), and *Goha* (Jacques Baratier, 1958). Some of these films, such as *La Pointe-courte*, starring Philippe Noiret (b. 1930), encountered legal problems that forced them to be shown clandestinely in the first instance and prevented widespread distribution until many years later. On the whole, however, most members of the CNC were sympathetic to the ideals of the young filmmakers and were instrumental in supporting the changes to the cinema that characterized the late 1950s and early 1960s.

FRANÇOIS TRUFFAUT
b. François Roland Truffaut, Paris, France, 6 February 1932, d. 21 October 1984

As a director, François Truffaut incarnates the virtues and weaknesses of the French New Wave. Much of his work reflects the troubled circumstances of his early life—illegitimacy, abandonment, and foster care. At age sixteen, Truffaut came under the influence of André Bazin, who served as a father figure and introduced him to the film society Objectif 49, a group that would become a forum for New Criticism. A noted critic from 1950, Truffaut wrote many periodical articles, including "Une Certaine tendance du cinéma française" (1954), in which he attacked the Tradition of Quality and set the agenda to revitalize French cinema.

Truffaut's work as a director is uneven. His first film, *Les Quatre cents coups* (*The 400 Blows*, 1959), starring Jean-Pierre Léaud as Antoine Doinel, was considered a triumph for a new generation of filmmakers because in it Truffaut introduced a more personal, spontaneous style that thumbed its nose at the stilted academic work of the studio directors who had dominated French film production during the postwar years. This film was financed by Truffaut's first wife, Madeleine Morgenstern, whose father owned one of the most powerful French distribution companies of the time, Cocinor. Despite his obsessive love of other women, she supported him throughout his career and was at his bedside when he died of a brain tumor at age fifty-two.

In a number of subsequent films, Truffaut used the Doinel character (played by Léaud) as an alter ego to mirror his own life, from the misunderstood child and troubled delinquent of *The 400 Blows* to the tormented lover and failed husband approaching middle age in *L'Amour en fuite* (*Love on the Run*, 1978). Truffaut is at his best when immersed in the study of character, as in *Jules et Jim* (*Jules and Jim*, 1962), in which the innocence, generosity, and tenderness of the three main characters is very sensitively captured, and at his worst when he attempts to imitate Hollywood directors such as Alfred Hitchcock, for whom he professed a strong admiration. An example of an unsuccessful effort to imitate a Hitchcock thriller is *La Mariée était en noir* (*The Bride Wore Black*, 1968), which even Truffaut declared he did not like much.

Truffaut's influence on cinema was international in scope. He conveyed in his films and in his writing an apparently inexhaustible and infectious enthusiasm for the possibility of authentic personal expression in the cinema. Perhaps his most moving film after *The 400 Blows*, *L'Enfant Sauvage* (*The Wild Child*, 1970) stars Truffaut as a scientist who attempts to communicate with an abandoned autistic child. Throughout his life, Truffaut believed that human communication could transcend language and culture. No doubt, his influence on young filmmakers derives from this faith.

RECOMMENDED VIEWING

Les Quatre cents coups (*The 400 Blows,* 1959), *Tirez sur le pianiste* (*Shoot the Piano Player,* 1960), *Jules et Jim* (*Jules and Jim,* 1962), *La Mariée était en noir* (*The Bride Wore Black,* 1968), *Basiers volés* (*Stolen Kisses,* 1968), *La Sirène du Mississipi* (*Mississippi Mermaid,* 1969), *Le' Enfant Sauvage* (*The Wild Child,* 1970), *Domicile conjugal* (*Bed & Board,* 1970), *Deux anglaises et le continent* (*Two English Girls,* 1971), *La Nuit américaine* (*Day for Night,* 1973), *L'Histoire d'Adèle H.* (*The Story of Adele H,* 1975), *L'Argent de poche* (*Small Change,* 1976), *L'Homme qui aimait les femmes* (*The Man Who Loved Women,* 1977)

FURTHER READING

Crisp, C. G. *François Truffaut.* London and New York: Praeger, 1972.

De Baecque, Antoine, and Serge Toubiana. *Truffaut: A Biography.* Translated by Catherine Temerson. New York: Knopf, 1999.

Petrie, Graham. *The Cinema of François Truffaut.* New York: A. S. Barnes and London: Zwemmer, 1970.

Truffaut, François. *The Films in My Life.* Translated by Leonard Mayhew. New York: Da Capo, 1994. Translation of *Les Films de ma vie* (1975).

———. *Letters of François Truffaut.* Edited by Gilles Jacob and Claude de Givray. Translated and edited by Gilbert Adair. Foreword by Jean-Luc Godard. Boston and London: Faber, 1989.

Hilary Ann Radner

By the end of the 1950s, French cinema had undergone a major transformation from a free-market economy to an economy largely submitted to state control. Stagnation had set in, provoking harsh criticism from a generation of film critics who had grown up with film as a major cultural force. The ciné-clubs had developed a

François Truffaut. © WILLIAM KAREL/SYGMA/CORBIS.

highly literate audience for film, sophisticated in their tastes, and informed about the historical issues governing the development of film. In the post–World War II years, debates about the status of film as art were reanimated by a new generation of critics writing for journals, such as *Cahiers du Cinéma,* and concerns about quality had become a paramount issue at the CNC. Polemical debates about the rigidity of the old guard created an environment receptive to a new kind of filmmaking, one that once again would define itself against Hollywood while looking to a number of Hollywood directors who had gained the status of *auteur* for inspiration.

THE FRENCH NEW WAVE AND ITS AFTERMATH: 1959 TO 1969

The term "New Wave" (Nouvelle Vague) was coined by the journalist Françoise Giroud in a series of articles published in *L'Express* during 1957, based on surveys conducted by the magazine. The term was taken up again by *L'Express* in 1959 to describe a new group of directors who showed films at the Cannes Film Festival that year. The epithet "New Wave" was exploited by Unifrance-

film, an official arm of the CNC, to popularize and distinguish these new French directors abroad and eventually became permanently associated with a group of young directors who emerged roughly at the end of the 1950s through the beginning of the 1960s. Also known as la Bande des Cahiers, these filmmakers were loosely united around a number of critics turned directors, such as Truffaut and Jean-Luc Godard (b. 1930), who published in *Cahiers du Cinéma.*

Though a few directors associated with the French New Wave made films before 1959, such as Roger Leenhardt (1903–1985) and Melville, the first films of 97 of the 192 new French filmmakers cited by *Cahiers du Cinéma* in the New Wave special issue (1962) appeared between 1958 and 1962. Truffaut's *Les Quatre cents coups* (*The 400 Blows*, 1959), often considered the benchmark film of the New Wave, was in fact preceded by films such as *Le Beau Serge* (*Handsome Serge*, 1958) and *Les Cousins* (*The Cousins*, 1959) by Claude Chabrol (b. 1930). The years 1958 and 1959 saw the deaths of a series of great directors who had produced significant work during the previous two decades—Ophüls, Grémillon, and Becker,

Jean-Pierre Leaud in François Truffaut's landmark New Wave film, **Les Quatre cents coup** *(The 400 Blows, 1959).* EVERETT COLLECTION. REPRODUCED BY PERMISSION.

leaving a number of studio-trained successors in the wings: Edouard Molinaro (b. 1928), Claude Sautet (1924–2000), and Michel Deville (b. 1931) had solid careers and often migrated to features destined for television in the late 1960s and 1970s. However, the hegemony of the old studio system was drawing to a close.

Popular cinema, *le cinéma du sam'di soir* (Saturday night movies), remained a significant box-office force, often in the form of star vehicles for actors such as Fernandel (1903–1971) and Gabin. The growing impact of television resulted in lower numbers of ticket sales, but cinema still overshadowed television as the single most popular form of mass entertainment. The big-budget Tradition of Quality films suffered the most, though the genre was kept alive through Italian co-productions and was revived as the heritage film in the 1980s.

The productions, values, and techniques of the French cinema industry changed radically in the years that followed, opening up a new mode of production grounded in the small-budget film that made way for a new generation of directors with a different artistic conception of film. New lightweight equipment and more sensitive film stock permitted young filmmakers who saw themselves as

auteurs to begin making films. These new technologies freed filmmakers from the constraints of the large studio-based, heavily unionized film crews that were integral to the film style associated with the Tradition of Quality.

The New Wave filmmakers might be said to share a certain sensibility—one that stood in stark contrast with the controlled *mise-en-scène,* trained performances, and studio lighting of the Tradition of Quality. By and large, New Wave directors favored improvisation and the use of available light, location shooting, direct sound, and vernacular language. Perhaps more importantly, this sensibility was associated with a mode of production, the small-budget film that gave the director complete artistic control, establishing him or her as the author or *auteur* of the work. The notion that the director functioned as the artistic creator of the film, with the film serving primarily as a vehicle for his or her vision, had a significant influence not only on film production but also on the way in which films were evaluated—in particular, in the context of a developing academic discourse on film.

New character types emerged with the New Wave, along with a more spontaneous acting style. Although the New Wave directors turned their backs on the established stars, the New Wave developed stars of its own, such as Jean-Paul Belmondo (b. 1933) and Jeanne Moreau (b. 1928), both of whom would go on to have international careers and have a significant impact on French cinema by sponsoring projects and taking a role in decisions about policy. Male stars such as Jean-Pierre Léaud (b. 1944) and Belmondo specialized in playing antiheroes, and together they formed the masculine face of the New Wave. Women stars such as Moreau, Bernadette Lafont (b. 1938), Anna Karina (b. 1940), and Brigitte Bardot (b. 1934) played either gamine embodiments of youthful sensuality, or dark, neurotic intellectuals.

Strategies used by the French New Wave, such as direct sound and location shooting, were also part of the *cinéma vérité* movement that developed during the same period, associated with figures such as the anthropologist-filmmaker Jean Rouch (1917–2004). Again, the relatively low budgets associated with this genre of filmmaking made it attractive to intellectuals interested in interrogating social norms and circulating anti-establishment political statements. Not since the early days of cinema had it been possible for so many people to make so many films. A new pattern was established: directors no longer necessarily spent years working in the industry and perfecting their craft before embarking on a solo project. A director might make one or two more or less successful films before moving to some other activity. Though in fact New Wave directors worked with small, well-established crews maintained from one film to the next, they were the significant driving force behind the look, structure, and feel of the films.

JEANNE MOREAU
b. Jeanne Moreau, Paris, France, 23 January 1928

As a star, a woman, and a national figure, Jeanne Moreau exemplifies the ideal of the French film actress in the post–New Wave era. Though overshadowed in the popular press by such stars as Brigitte Bardot and Catherine Deneuve, both of whom served as the model for Marianne, the official statue that represents France, Moreau, through her image as well as her position in the French film industry, embodied French femininity for a generation of film lovers. She personified the intelligent actress whose dark, mature, and potentially dangerous sensuality stood in stark contrast to the blonde sex kitten that dominated Hollywood screens. Moreau was considered un-photogenic, a *jolie laide*, whose personal magnetism and speaking voice overshadowed her features.

Her early background in theater lent credibility to her career in cinema, which began in 1948 and which includes over one hundred films. Her roles in films associated with the New Wave, such as *Ascenseur pour l'échafaud* (*Elevator to the Gallows*, 1958) and *Les Amants* (*The Lovers*, 1958), both directed by Louis Malle, gave her international prominence. Her portrayal of Catherine in *Jules et Jim* (*Jules and Jim*, 1962), directed by François Truffaut, New Wave director par excellence, solidified her star image. International films, including Michelangelo Antonioni's *La Notte* (*The Night*, 1961), Orson Welles's *Une Histoire immortelle* (*The Immortal Story*, 1968), Anthony Asquith's *The Yellow Rolls-Royce* (1964), and Carlo Diegues's *Joanna Francesa* (1973), also have featured prominently in her career.

Moreau took a substantial risk in choosing to work with young, relatively unknown directors in the late 1950s and the 1960s. Throughout her career, she made choices that reflected her sense of cinema as an art and, as a result,

she is universally respected for her professionalism and commitment. In addition to awards for specific roles (Cannes, 1960; Académie du cinéma, 1962; Célsar, 1990), she has received lifetime tributes from the Cannes Film Festival (1992), the Venice Film Festival (Golden Lion, 1992), and the American Academy of Motion Pictures Arts and Sciences (1998).

Moreau has been involved in all aspects of French cinema. She was twice Présidente of the Jury at the Cannes Festival, and in 1993, she was appointed Présidente of the Commission d'Avances sur Recettes, a body of experts that advises the Centre National de la Cinématographie. She has also supported Equinox, an organization she created in 1993 that holds annual workshops for new scriptwriters. Moreau has directed two films herself, *Lumière* (1976), a portrait of four film actresses, and *L'Adolescente* (*The Adolescent*, 1979), the evocation of a visit by a girl to her grandparents in Avignon on the eve of World War II. Moreau was elected a member of the Academy of Beaux Arts in 2001.

RECOMMENDED VIEWING

Ascenseur pour l'échafaud (Elevator to the Gallows, 1958), *Les Amants (The Lovers*, 1958), *Les Liaisons dangereuses (Dangerous Liaisons*, 1959), *La Notte (The Night*, 1961), *Jules et Jim (Jules and Jim*, 1962), *Le Journal d'une femme de chambre (Diary of a Chambermaid*, 1964), *La Mariée était en noir (The Bride Wore Black*, 1968), *Querelle* (1982), *La Femme Nikita (Nikita*, 1990), *L'Absence (The Absence*, 1993)

FURTHER READING

Vincendeau, Ginette. *Stars and Stardom in French Cinema*. London: Continuum, 2000.

Hilary Ann Radner

The New Wave philosophy did not mean that big-budget filmmaking was over in France or elsewhere, but it did introduce a parallel tradition that would make filmmaking more accessible to a wide range of individuals who declined to see cinema as mass entertainment, preferring to use film primarily as a form of personal or aesthetic expression. Within the New Wave, two equally important groups contributed to the rise of this new style in filmmaking: the very vocal group emerging out of *Cahiers du*

Cinéma, including Chabrol, Truffaut, Godard, Jacques Rivette (b. 1928), Eric Rohmer (b. 1920), and Jacques Doniol-Valcroze (1920–1989); and the equally productive, if less polemical, filmmakers who espoused a more personal vision, including Franju, Jean-Pierre Mocky (b. 1929), and Claude Lelouch (B. 1937). *Un homme et une femme* (*A Man and a Woman*, Lelouch, 1966) was arguably the most influential French film of the 1960s. Directors whose work was closely aligned with the new directions of current

Jeanne Moreau in* Secrets d'alcove (*The Bed, 1954).
EVERETT COLLECTION. REPRODUCED BY PERMISSION.

literature, such as Renais and Buñuel, were sympathetic to the New Wave if not technically among its members and contributed to the aesthetic fecundity of the period. Resnais, though often associated with the New Wave, is distinguished from the typical New Wave directors by his willingness to efface himself through the adaptation of works by other writers, and by his highly intellectualized approach. His major films from the late 1950s and 1960s include *Hiroshima mon amour* (*Hiroshima, My Love,* 1959), with a script by Marguerite Duras (1914–1996), and *L'Année dernière à Marienbad* (*Last Year at Marienbad,* 1961), produced in collaboration with Alain Robbe-Grillet (b. 1922), starring the cult actress Delphine Seyrig (1932–1990), and with costumes by Coco Chanel.

While the new breed of filmmakers was lionized at festivals, the career directors of established French cinema turned to television. The Buttes-Chaumont Studios, in particular, continued the Tradition of Quality in its productions for television. Directors emerged from the studio tradition, often the same age as the adherents of the New Wave, continued their careers—such as Delannoy, Gilles Grangier (1911–1996), and Denys de La Patellière (b. 1921). At Buttes-Chaumont these directors produced work that maintained the technical standards of the previous decades. Paradoxically, given France's reputation for intellectual fare, the biggest French box-office hit of all time was a popular comedy,

La Grande Vadrouille (*Don't Look Now We're Being Shot At,* 1966), directed by Gérard Oury (b. 1919) and starring Bourvil (1917–1970) and Louis de Funès (1914–1983).

The strikes and upheavals of May 1968 had an immediate if not necessarily lasting effect on French cinema, when demonstrators disrupted the Cannes Film Festival. Plans to reform the processes of production and distribution were put forward but eventually discarded. Individual reactions were varied: Malle gave up fiction film for two years in order to make documentaries; Godard threw himself into collective productions that were never commercially distributed.

CINEMA IN FLUX: 1970 TO 1989

By the early 1970s, the effects of the New Wave and of May 1968 had dissipated. Certain directors, such as Truffaut, were reintegrated into the French mainstream and directed films that clearly continued the tradition of French cinema associated with figures like Guitry and Renoir. Conversely, Godard and Rivette experimented with form and content, while others, like Bresson—never part of the New Wave—steadfastly pursued a personal itinerary. Directors like Louis Malle pushed the boundaries of film content with productions like *Le Souffle au coeur* (*Murmur of the Heart,* 1971), about incest, and *Lacombe Lucien* (1974), about a young peasant who collaborates with the Germans. In the aftermath of the New Wave, a new generation of young filmmakers emerged that included Maurice Pialat (1925–2003), Jacques Doillon (b. 1944), and Jean Eustache (1938–1981), who continued the auteurist tradition inaugurated by the *Cahiers* group. More importantly, the role of cinema in French culture changed irrevocably, as it was no longer the primary medium of mass entertainment. By the end of the 1970s, more people watched films on television than in theaters.

By the mid-1970s, French culture had freed itself from the rigid hierarchies and social behaviors that previously characterized everyday life; however, the utopian environment anticipated by the activists in the 1960s did not become a reality. Censorship policies were abandoned (though the category *X* was created for taxation purposes). The result was a flourishing tradition of soft-core pornography, exemplified by *Emmanuelle* (1974), directed by Just Jaeckin (b. 1940). Global consumerism appeared as if it would successfully colonize French culture, which seemed in danger of losing its specificity.

An exception to this trend was the growing tradition of women's cinema, which gravitated to the Festival international de films de femmes (French International Women's Film Festival), established in Sceaux in 1979 and moved to Créteil in 1985. A number of significant women filmmakers emerged from the woman's movement during the 1970s and went on to make important contributions to French cinema, including Yannick Bellon (b. 1924), Diane Kurys (b. 1949), and Coline Serreau (b. 1947). The influx of women filmmakers such as Christine Pascal (1953–1996) and Brigitte Roüan (b. 1946) who emerged through festivals and as graduates of French film schools, continued to grow over the next two decades. Significant women directors who appeared in the 1980s and 1990s include Josiane Balasko (b. 1950), Claire Denis (b. 1948), and Catherine Breillat (b. 1950).

During these years Hollywood film gained new ground, further diminishing an audience already depleted by television. Nevertheless, French cinema remained a force in French culture. Popular comedies such as *Les Aventures de Rabbi Jacob* (*The Adventures of Rabbi Jacob*, 1973), starring Louis de Funès, continued to have strong box-office appeal. But by the late 1980s, Hollywood films systematically outperformed French films at the French box office. The growing prominence of the Césars, the French "Oscar" (first awarded in 1976 and initially dismissed by the international film industry), testified to the continuing importance of film within French culture, despite diminishing box-office returns. By the 1990s, half of the French population would watch *la nuit des Césars* (the night of the Cesars) on television.

The government's sustained support for the film industry in France reflected this centrality. Under the socialist government (1981–1995), support was stronger than ever before, ensuring the survival of the industry during a period in which the European cinema as a whole suffered a serious decline. Initiatives inaugurated by Minister of Culture Jack Lang (b. 1939), including the creation of eight *maisons de la culture* (regional cinema centers), encouraged regional filmmakers. However, on the whole, Paris remained at the heart of French feature-length production through the 1970s and 1980s. A significant diversification of perspective resulted from the number of foreign directors who exploited the favorable conditions offered to the film industry by the French government. Directors such as Joseph Losey, Ettore Scola, Otar Iosseliani, Hugo Santiago, Edgardo Cozarinsky, Raoul Ruiz, Andrzej Zulawski, Andrzej Wajda, Krzysztof Kiéslowski, and Emir Kusturica all made films in France, financed, at least partially, by French money.

During the 1980s, encouraged by the Socialist government, the liberalization of French culture and society continued, manifested in cultural pluralism and cultural sensitivity. For example, under the leadership of French comedian and film actor Coluche (Michel Colucci; 1944–1986), the artistic community created Les Restos du Coeur, which provided free meals for the homeless. In general, the 1980s were marked by disillusionment with social reform and economic change, leading to the rise of

individualism of the 1990s and the gradual disappearance of the political film in France.

Until the mid-1980s, the success of popular cinema in France depended in large part upon film series co-produced by stars such as Belmondo, Alain Delon (b. 1935), and Funès. By the mid-1980s, this generation of stars had died or aged, and French cinema moved away from formula-driven production. Films such as *Trois hommes et un couffin* (*Three Men and a Baby*, 1985) and *La Vie est un long fleuve tranquil* (*Life Is a Long Quiet River*, 1987), box-office successes, were exceptions rather than the rule and did not fit any well-defined template. The number of box-office entries continued to fall, and by 1993 box-office receipts for French films were significantly less than for their Hollywood counterparts. The strategies and financial incentives promoted by Lang during this period insured that French filmmaking remained financially healthy; however, the industry's hold on French minds and culture waned. In particular, the youth segment that dominated audiences was more interested in foreign productions than in French material, an attitude that was reflected in the rise of international co-productions.

DISTRIBUTION AND THE EFFECTS OF TELEVISION: THE 1980s

By the end of the 1980s, it could no longer be said that cinema dominated the French cultural landscape. It had become merely one medium among many that appealed to French audiences. Beginning in the late 1970s, French cinema became part of *le paysage audiovisuel français* (the French audiovisual landscape). Though certain established film stars retained their impact, the new generation of French film stars failed to achieve the cult status of their predecessors. The national film star was eclipsed by international celebrities from a variety of media, including music and television. Certain French stars, such as Juliette Binoche (b. 1964) and Gerard Depardieu (b. 1948), achieved world standing through participation in international co-productions; however, it was the rare French star who migrated to Hollywood, where male stars such as Charles Boyer (1899–1978), Chevalier, and Louis Jourdan (b. 1920) had achieved success during the classical era. Other French stars, for instance Isabelle Huppert (b. 1955), extended their audience by appearing in theater productions. In general, French stars continued to cross between a variety of media, including film, television, café-theater, and advertising. New French stars, however, failed to achieve the kind of international notoriety conferred by the paparazzi on the likes of Bardot, Catherine Deneuve (b. 1943), Belmondo, and Delon in previous decades.

In the late 1970s and 1980s, television became a significant distribution network for film through the development of privately owned television stations, pay-

TV, and cable networks. Indeed, television became a repertory theater devoted to screening the entire archive of French cinema from the silent era onward. Theaters were unable to compete, and even *art et essai* theaters, with their niche audiences, were threatened with extinction.

Television channels were extremely competitive and quickly began producing films as well as distributing them, especially in order to offer new material during highly desirable time slots. The first attempts of this type date to 1959, but it was not until 1976 that television co-productions became popular, and by the beginning of the 1980s few films were produced without some sort of support from Canal Plus, a subscription-based, encrypted television distribution network and subsidiary of Vivendi, a multinational media company. Beginning in 1984, the television industry was taxed, and these new revenues offset the decline of ticket-entry based levies, which had been one of the primary sources of support for French cinema since the inauguration of the CNC and its policies.

The film industry received a further boost in 1985 when Lang created the Société de Financement des Industries Cinématographiques et Audiovisuelles program (SOFICA), which offered tax shelters to companies investing in the film industry. Despite a steady decline in cinema attendance throughout the 1980s that reached its nadir in the early 1990s, these efforts succeeded in providing a sound financial basis for the French film industry. Yet the rise of international co-productions threatened the distinctiveness of French films while contributing to the industry's health and stability. Television had a paradoxical effect on cinema in France: on the one hand, it successfully challenged film as the primary form of mass entertainment; on the other, it was a source of financial support that enabled the film industry to continue to produce French films for a French public while encouraging the development of financially advantageous international co-productions.

With the rise of television, the distributor became a major force in the French film industry. Family-owned theaters disappeared and were replaced by multiplexes. In 1970, Pathé and Gaumont jointly created a network of over four hundred theaters under an umbrella organization, G.I.E. In 1971, the theaters grouped under UGC, l'Union générale des cinémas (the General Union of Film Theaters), which had been requisitioned by the state after World War II, privatized and became the heart of a network of several hundred cinemas. Another network, Parafrance, developed with the support of the CNC. But this system was unstable. In 1983 the CNC, empowered by a decree issued by Lang, dissolved G.I.E. Pathé-Gaumont. By 1984, Parafrance was no more; however, Pathé and Gaumont reorganized, partitioned, and consolidated their shares of the market. The multiplex system became—the CNC's efforts notwithstanding—one of the formative influences on the further development of French cinema.

The major distributors were averse to taking risks. They evolved a system that maximized profit by saturating the national market with promotional materials and supporting multiple premieres in the most commercially viable locations. After 1989, it was not unusual to make eight hundred prints of a single film, which would then be shown simultaneously at ten percent of all theaters. The rising production costs made the financial risks greater, but the multiplex system also enabled producers to enjoy enormous financial rewards if they did have a box-office success. The incentive to produce blockbusters grew while the possibility of enjoying a modest success in a niche market diminished. Either a film made it big during the first week of its release or disappeared from the screen. Under this system, French cinema became even more vulnerable to the threat posed by Hollywood movies, particularly in the form of the blockbusters.

DEFEAT AND RENEWAL: SINCE 1990

Supported by Lang, heritage cinema, which favored literary adaptation, historical topics, costume dramas, and high production values, initially appeared as though it might revitalize the theatrical release. *Cyrano de Bergerac* (1990), by Jean-Paul Rappeneau (b. 1932), was a financial, critical, and popular success and was preceded by the successes of *Jean de Florette* (1986) and *Manon des sources* (*Manon of the Spring*, 1986) by Claude Berri (b. 1934). But this apparent trend immediately reversed itself. Big productions, such as *Jean Galmot, aventurier* (*Jean Galmot, Adventurer*, Alain Maline, 1990), bombed, while low-budget films, such as *La Discrète* (*The Discreet*, Christian Vincent, 1990), were box-office successes. The most obvious trend in this period was the grouping of individual filmmakers in terms of generations, beginning with an established group of still-active directors dating from the French New Wave period that included Bresson, Chabrol, Godard, Resnais, Rohmer, Rivette, and Varda. Other groups of younger filmmakers comprised those who positioned themselves as continuing the New Wave (André Téchiné [b. 1943], Benoît Jacquot [b. 1947], and Claude Miller [b. 1942]), those who saw themselves as reviving the cinema of quality (Michel Deville, Claude Sautet, Bertrand Tavernier [b. 1941]), and, finally, those who conceived of themselves as pursuing an individualist vision (Doillon, Maurice Pialat [1925–2003], Philippe Garrel [b. 1948], and Alain Cavalier [b. 1931]). Another group of very heterogeneous filmmakers is made up of directors united by their interest in social issues. Often referred to as *le jeune cinéma français* (young French cinema), this group includes

Anne Parillaud in Luc Besson's stylish **La Femme Nikita** *(*Nikita, *1990).* © SAMUEL GOLDWYN/COURTESY EVERETT COLLECTION. REPRODUCED BY PERMISSION.

women directors such as Breillat, as well as directors associated with *cinéma beur*, also known as cinema of the Mahgreb (such as Mehdi Charef [b. 1952] and Malik Chibane [b. 1964]), the *cinéma de banlieu* or neighborhood (such as Mathieu Kassovitz [b. 1964]), and regional cinema (Bruno Dumont [b. 1958]). This group also incorporated directors like Varda and Tavernier, whose more recent work, such as Varda's *Jane B. par Agnès V.* (*Jane B. for Agnes V.*, 1987) and Tavernier's *L. 627* (1992), were influenced by this new sensibility. This mulidirectional development suggests the ways in which as the millenium approached and passed, the ideal of French culture as homogeneous and grounded in French language and French heritage no longer reflected the lived experience of the younger generations of French citizens.

Perhaps the most obvious testimony to the transformation of the French cultural landscape is found in the *cinéma du look* (cinema of the look), a film genre influenced by cartoons, advertising, and music videos. This genre is sometimes associated with the Forum des Halles, referring to the designer chic, ultra-modern shopping complex in central Paris that became a focal point for youth culture after its opening in 1979. The obsession of the cinéma du look with style, inaugurated by *Diva* by Jean-Jacques Beineix (b. 1964) in 1981, repeatedly threatened to run out of steam, but it nevertheless maintained its impetus through the mid-1990s and beyond—often in the form of Hollywood productions, as in the case of Luc Besson (b. 1959). Besson, who emerged as one of the Forum des Halles directors alongside Beineix and Leos Carax (b. 1960), remained through the turn of the twenty-first century one of France's most bankable directors, even though his later films were often made abroad. In addition to slick, stylized framing, composition, lighting, and editing imported from the world of advertising, the films had in common a rejection of society and its values, emphasizing instead the individual's pursuit of happiness. Although routinely rejected by established French critics, these films and their directors proved so successful, especially in an international context, that eventually scholars of French culture were forced to take them seriously. Both heritage films—which tended toward costume super-productions, such as *La Reine Margot* (*Queen Marguerite*, 1994) or *Le*

Hussard sur le toit (*The Horseman on the Roof*, 1995) and the *cinéma du look*—fall into a category often referred to as "the new spectacular cinema," which depended on big budgets, heavy marketing, and concept promotion for its success. Attempts to mobilize these strategies pepper the French cinema of the 1990s and early 2000s, achieving variable success. In fact, the big successes of the early 2000s were by and large, relatively low-budget productions by Hollywood standards, such as *Le Fabuleux destin d'Amélie Poulain* (*Amélie*, 2001) by Jean-Pierre Jeunet (b. 1955), when French film outsold Hollywood film at the French box office for the first time in over a decade.

Equally significant were the number of French directors earlier in the decade, such as Jeunet and Jean-Jacques Annaud (b. 1943), who alternated between making Hollywood films for a global audience and French films for a French audience. Although heavily attacked for selling their "art," these directors maintained a profile as *auteurs* that can be identified as French. The consistency of their work depended upon an informal group of actors and actresses as well as crewmembers and even composers whose contributions were critical to reproducing a distinctive look and feel attributed to a given director.

While individual directors systematically represented French cinema abroad, typically the highest grossing French films at the French box office have been social comedies, such as *Marriages* (Catherine Martin, 2001). Comedies and romantic comedies, usually revolving around social mores and often featuring well-known actors and actresses, remained popular with French audiences; however, they were not formula-driven. These films were rarely attractive to foreign audiences, yet the increasing number of Hollywood remakes of French films since the early 1980s, usually comedies, such as Edouard Molinaro's *La Cage aux folles* (1978), remade by Mike Nichols as *The Birdcage* (1996), and Serreau's *Trois hommes et un couffin* (1985), remade by Leonard Nimoy as *Three Men and a Baby* (1987), indicate the sustained global interest in French cinema.

At the end of the twentieth century, French cinema appears to have revived. Its existence, though precarious, has been assured through vigorous state sponsorship. Films such as François Ozon's (b. 1967) *Sous le sable* (*Under the Sand*, 2000) and *The Swimming Pool* (2003) have pursued the *intimiste* subjects that characterized French cinema of the late twentieth century; however, the critical and intellectual hegemony spawned by the New Wave was displaced in the late 1990s and early 2000s by a more popular, less angst-ridden cinema with such films as *Amélie* (2001), Christophe Barratier's (b. 1963) *Les Choristes* (*The Chorus*, 2004), and Jeunet's *Un long dimanche de fiançailles* (*A Very Long Engagement*, 2004). This movement produced box-office successes that

brought French cinema out of the slump that it had experienced in the early 1990s. The major challenge that faced the French cinema at the turn of the millenium was maintaining its position in a global market while preserving its identity as a French cinema for French audiences.

France successfully upheld the status of audiovisual productions as "cultural exceptions" in General Agreement of Trade and Tariffs (GATT through 1993) and subsequent World Trade Organization (WTO) negotiations. The results were favorable conditions for French film in France and in Europe through the imposition of protective tariffs as well as quotas. Because of these and other measures on the part of the State, such as cross-subsidization from the television industry, the French share of the French box office has stabilized at about one third, after a few difficult years at the beginning of the 1990s. In spite of this success within the French market, France's share of the foreign market has continued to decline, particularly in terms of television rights. French producers have countered by co-producing more English-language films, such as Roman Polanski's *The Pianist* (2002).

The privileged status that French film has retained in the WTO negotiations might seem to be a victory for cultural purists. The French government, nonetheless, required the industry to be fiscally responsible and has directed its policies with a view to financial as well as cultural soundness. In the late 1990s, French film became more sensitive to box-office demand, producing, for example, a greater number of comedies geared toward a popular audience. Unfortunately, these films rarely did well abroad. Another strategy, more successful in terms of exportability, was the move toward higher-budget, more sophisticated films geared toward a younger audience, such as Kassovitz's *Les Rivières pourpres* (*Crimson Rivers*, 2000) and *Les Rivières pourpres: Les anges de l'apocalypes* (*Crimson Rivers 2: Angels of the Apocalypse*, 2004).

The *auteur* directors traditionally associated with French films were forced to produce films on ever-diminishing budgets and often resorted to film shorts. Aesthetic and formal experimentation moved out of the cinema into the museum, often crossing over into video and other media, as in the case of Godard's series *Histoire(s) du cinéma* (1989–1998). Some critics feared that this more personal and intellectual filmmaking might permanently disappear, to be replaced by films the likes of the "Crimson Rivers" series, that is, sensationalist star vehicles. Similarly, these same critics expressed concerns about whether this commercially viable cinema was really French. *The Pianist*, for example, does not feature a French director, a French star, or the French language. The question remained: would a popular French cinema be able to retain its hold on the French imagination as the cultural exception, as a cinema that challenged the global dominance of Hollywood, not simply within an economic arena but as the arbitrator of taste and culture? This question was first raised in the aftermath of World War I, and it has continued to be the crucial question facing French cinema at the turn of the millenium.

SEE ALSO *National Cinema; New Wave*

FURTHER READING

Abel, Richard. *French Cinema: The First Wave, 1915–1929.* Princeton, NJ: Princeton University Press, 1984.

Austin, Guy. *Contemporary French Cinema: An Introduction.* Manchester, UK: Manchester University Press, 1996.

Buchsbaum, Jonathan. *Cinema engagé: Film in the Popular Front.* Urbana: University of Illinois Press, 1988.

Crisp, Colin. *The Classic French Cinema, 1930–1960.* Bloomington: Indiana University Press, 1993.

Flitterman-Lewis, Sandy. *To Desire Differently: Feminism and the French Cinema,* expanded ed. New York: Columbia University Press, 1996.

Hillier, Jim, ed. *Cahiers du Cinéma, Volume 1: The 1950s—Neo-Realism, Hollywood, New Wave.* London: Routledge and Cambridge, MA: Harvard University Press, 1985.

———, ed. *Cahiers du Cinéma, Volume 2: The 1960s—New Wave, New Cinema, Re-evaluating Hollywood.* London: Routledge and Cambridge, MA: Harvard University Press, 1986.

Hughes, Alex, and James S. Williams, eds. *Gender and French Cinema.* Oxford and New York: Berg, 2001.

Lanzoni, Rémi Fournier. *French Cinema: From Its Beginnings to the Present.* New York: Continuum, 2002.

Marie, Michel. *The French New Wave: An Artistic School.* Translated by Richard Neupert. Oxford: Blackwell, 2003. Translation of *La Nouvelle Vague: Une École Artistique* (1997).

Powrie, Phil, and Keith Reader. *French Cinema: A Student's Guide.* London: Arnold, 2002.

Vincendeau, Ginette. *The Companion to French Cinema.* London: The British Film Institute, 1996.

———. *Stars and Stardom in French Cinema.* London: Continuum, 2000.

Hilary Ann Radner

GANGSTER FILMS

———————■———————

Gangster films are films about gangsters, professional criminals who have banded together to commit crimes. This much is simple, and indeed a great deal of the genre's enduring appeal lies in its bold simplicity. As Robert Warshow noted fifty years ago, gangsters act out movie audiences' most violently untrammeled fantasies of unlimited upward mobility by following the golden rule of prototypical gangster hero Tony Camonte in *Scarface* (1932): "Do it first, do it yourself, and keep on doing it." Commentators from Carlos Clarens to Eugene Rosow have observed how movie gangsters plot, steal, and kill their way to economic and social supremacy until, like Cody Jarrett in *White Heat* (1949), they are alone at the "top of the world," though their meteoric rise is unfailingly followed by an even swifter fall. Yet the very name of the gangster film indicates three decisive complications at the heart of the genre: the gangster's status as both villain and hero; the chicken-and-egg relationship between gangsters and their gangs; and the variously reflective relationship between gangs and the societies against which they wage their criminal wars.

These problems are illustrated by the work of two acknowledged masters of the genre, Raoul Walsh (1887–1980) and Howard Hawks (1896–1977). Despite, or because of, the best efforts of the FBI, which rose to prominence by publicizing its pursuit of real-life gangsters in the 1930s, gangsters are perversely heroic figures, larger-than-life lawbreakers who triumph, at least for a time, over the laws of a community less vibrant than they are. Yet they are defined first and foremost as members of a gang more powerful than any one member. Whether Walsh and Hawks are directing westerns, war films, or gangster films (Walsh's *High Sierra*, 1941, and *White*

Heat; Hawks's *Scarface*), they repeatedly explore the resulting tension between the heroic individual, almost always a male, and the community from which he derives his potency. In the case of the gangster film, a further complication, as Fran Mason has noted, emerges from the fact that criminal gangs, formed for the express purpose of providing a lawless alternative to the law-abiding social order, invariably cast themselves as imitations of the larger society in all its weaknesses. The resulting contradictions between heroism and heroic villainy, individual and communal identity, and lawless gangs and the laws necessary to their operation are the engine that drives the gangster film.

FROM NOBLE SAVAGE TO SOCIAL PROBLEM

Film gangsters are as old as film narrative. *The Great Train Robbery* (1903), with its twelve-minute story of a railroad heist marked by meticulous planning, unexpected violence, and condign punishment, would be acknowledged as the first gangster film if its gangster credentials were not overshadowed, as in similar films to come (*Jesse James*, 1939; *Rancho Notorious*, 1952; *Man of the West*, 1958), by its western *mise-en-scène*. Silent gangster films, however, were less likely to follow *The Great Train Robbery* than *The Musketeers of Pig Alley* (1912), in which the Snapper Kid, a tough, violent, personable criminal denizen of a New York ghetto, forms a momentary but touching alliance of convenience with the film's law-abiding heroine before returning to his life of crime. The leading gangsters of the American silent screen were noble savages, from the eponymous hero of *Alias Jimmy Valentine* (1915) to the economically successful but romantically doomed Bull Weed in

James Cagney at the "top of the world" in **White Heat** *(Raoul Walsh, 1949).* EVERETT COLLECTION. REPRODUCED BY PERMISSION.

Underworld (1927), a film whose influence on countless poetic French gangster tragedies of the 1930s (*Pépé le Moko*, 1936; *Le Jour se Lève* [*Daybreak*, 1939]) was almost as pervasive as on its American successor, the virtual remake *Thunderbolt* (1929), with Josef von Sternberg (1894–1969) again directing George Bancroft as the gangster star.

It is hardly surprising that these early films so inveterately romanticize the gangster. Urban lawbreakers living on the edge of polite society had a great deal in common with the working-class, largely immigrant audiences who followed their adventures in movie theaters. This subversive identification with the gangster hero was fostered throughout the 1920s by the Volstead Act, which made the sale of alcoholic beverages illegal from 1920 to 1933. So long as Prohibition was the law of the land in America, law-abiding citizens could get liquor only from underworld contacts. Hollywood's response was to paint the gangster as the disavowed Other of American society, the outsider without whom the social machinery lubricated by alcohol would have ground to a halt.

In the early 1930s, however, the image of the Hollywood gangster was dramatically transformed. The Great Depression, ushered in by the stock market crash of 1929, upended previously stable stratifications in American culture, ruining dozens of paper millionaires and throwing millions of Americans out of work. The Hollywood gangster, often based closely on the career of such real-life criminals as Al Capone (1899–1947) and John Dillinger (1903–1934), emerged as the logical hero for such a desperate moment, a rags-to-riches success story fueled by the dreams of audiences across the country. At the same time, a new complication emerged with the industry's widespread adoption of synchronized sound. Sound, as Jonathan Munby has pointed out, gave gangsters a voice, and that voice in such gangster classics as *Little Caesar* (1930), *Public Enemy* (1931), and *Scarface* was not only laconic and brutal but identifiably ethnic. No longer an urban Everyman, the gangster became the object of sociological study, a promethean overachiever whose ambition and greed doomed his aspirations to ethnic assimilation. Although James Cagney (1899–1986) as Tom Powers, the definitive Irish gangster in *Public Enemy*, and Paul Muni (1895–1967) as Tony Camonte were both given hand-wringing mothers as moral counterweights, their cautionary tales, along with that of Edward G. Robinson (1893–1973) as Rico Bandello in *Little Caesar*, strongly implied that ethnicity was fate.

Since 1930, Hollywood studios had subscribed to a Production Code designed to prevent government censorship. It was not until 1934, however, that the Code was widely enforced under public pressure organized in large part by the Catholic Legion of Decency. The effect on gangster films was immediate. The Code forbade many of the visual trappings on which gangster films had relied: drug use, automatic weapons, protracted scenes of violent death. More fundamentally, the Code ruled that crime was always to be punished, never presented as appealing. Overnight, gangster films like *The Story of Temple Drake* (1933) were pulled from release; post-Code gangsters like Duke Mantee in *The Petrified Forest* (1936) were less sympathetic and more vicious than their predecessors of a year or two earlier; and much of the energy that had once gone into gangster films was poured into police films like *"G" Men* (1935), whose fast-talking hero, Brick Davis (James Cagney), is given all the trappings of a gangster: fast cars, lethal firepower, and suspicious ties to organized crime. By the end of the decade, films like *Dead End* (1937) and *Angels with Dirty Faces* (1938) were treating the gangster as a deviant social problem to be explained rather than a mirror image of official American culture.

A METAPHOR FOR ALL SEASONS

The repeal of Prohibition in 1933 made the bootlegging gangster an instant anachronism, and the FBI's assault on organized crime throughout the decade drove the gangster underground. But he remained as a powerfully metaphoric figure that could be adapted to many uses. *High Sierra* squeezed weary but honorable ex-con Roy Earle (Humphrey Bogart) between the faithless gang that has sprung him from jail for one last job and the all-American girl who rebuffs his fatherly romantic advances. *The Phenix City Story* (1955) buried a plea for good government in the semi-documentary story of an

Alabama town run by a criminal syndicate. *The Killers* (1946), taking its cue from Ernest Hemingway's short story about a man who refuses to run from the two hit men looking for him, supplied a backstory for the doomed hero that used the expressionistic techniques of film noir to intensify its tale of an innocent hero caught in the toils of a gangster and his sultry girlfriend. Don Siegel's (1912–1991) 1964 remake of the film reimagined the hit men themselves as detectives defying their anonymous criminal client to figure out why their target failed to run. Most influentially of all, *The Asphalt Jungle* (1950) charted an urban landscape whose most respectable citizens were double-dealing hypocrites dependent on the honor of the petty criminals they used as pawns. *The Asphalt Jungle* inaugurated a new kind of gangster film: the heist or caper film in which the gang is assembled only for the purpose of pulling off a single job—an organization far more unstable than the gangs dominated by Tom Powers and Tony Camonte. Across the Atlantic, such pickup gangs became the subject of comedies in England (*The Lavender Hill Mob*, 1951; *The Ladykillers*, 1955) and Italy (*I Soliti ignoti* [*Big Deal on Madonna Street*, 1958]) as well as the existential melodrama *Rififi* (France, 1955).

The gangster might have continued indefinitely as an all-purpose metaphor for social deviance if not for three developments in the movie industry. First, the gradual decline of the studios after the Paramount decrees of 1948, requiring them to disband their vertically integrated monopolies, left movie stars, once treated as chattel, with ever more power over their projects. Second, the emerging medium of broadcast television pushed film studios to provide experiences television could not match. And third, a series of challenges to the Production Code during the 1950s and 1960s led to a new ratings system in 1969 that broke with the long-standing Hollywood practice of releasing only films every possible audience could watch to mark different films as appropriate for different audiences. The result throughout the industry was a series of star-driven vehicles with rapidly escalating budgets and increasingly liberal doses of sex, violence, and harsh language. It was a climate ripe for the reemergence of the gangster as a major figure.

Bonnie and Clyde (1967) and *The Godfather* (1972), the two films that most decisively marked the return of the gangster, both treated their heroes frankly as anachronisms in order to reveal the mythopoetic power beneath the genre's realism. For all the seedy glamour of their 1930s outfits and stolen cars, Bonnie and Clyde are children of the 1960s, counterculture heroes for a generation that no longer trusted the social institutions of the democratic state; the capitalistic economy; and their servants, the police. Michael Corleone, the dark hero of *The Godfather* and its two sequels (1974, 1990), was

JAMES CAGNEY
b. James Francis Cagney, Yonkers, New York, 17 July 1899, d. 30 March 1986

The toughest, most likable, and most endlessly imitated of all American film gangsters, Cagney was a paradoxical figure. His screen persona was a diamond in the rough, but he was also gifted at farce (*Boy Meets Girl*, 1938), physical comedy (*A Midsummer Night's Dream*, 1935), and song and dance, winning an Academy Award® for his role as George M. Cohan in *Yankee Doodle Dandy* (1942). Cagney's ruthless gangsters—Tom Powers in *The Public Enemy* (1931), Eddie Bartlett in *The Roaring Twenties* (1939), and Ralph Cotter in *Kiss Tomorrow Goodbye* (1950), among others—seem driven at once by their harsh environment and by a psychopathology that was purely amoral, a force truly beyond their power to control. Yet from the beginning, audiences found Cagney's insouciance irresistible. Even when he led the Dead End Kids astray in *Angels with Dirty Faces* (1938) or shoved half a grapefruit into Mae Clarke's face in *The Public Enemy*, he came across as somehow fundamentally decent.

Cagney's best movies show him driven by uncontrollable forces. In *White Heat* (1949), Cody Jarrett's snarling violence is consistently linked to both headaches that periodically incapacitate him and catastrophic disturbances in the physical world, like the climactic explosion at a gas refinery that finally sends Cody to a memorably suicidal apotheosis at the "top of the world."

Cagney was the most energetic, unreflective, and physically straightforward of all the great Hollywood studio stars. His proletarian heroes seem impatient with any thought that cannot immediately be translated into physical action. Unlike his contemporary Edward G. Robinson, another bantamweight who could play a hero

of almost any ethnic background, Cagney was invincibly Irish. Indeed, many of Cagney's fans were convinced that he was always playing himself, an unpolished mick from New York who had been in plenty of scrapes on the way to the top. Yet interviewers invariably found Cagney courteous, withdrawn, and essentially private. Like Cody Jarrett, who weeps on his mother's lap and then goes into the next room to resume the role of psychotic gang leader, Cagney perfected a style of acting that concealed artifice under the guise of self-expression. Although he never parodied his screen image as actors from Robinson to Marlon Brando did, his signature gangster persona brought a hard edge to heroes as different as FBI agent Brick Davis in *"G" Men* (1935) and C. R. MacNamara in *One, Two, Three* (1961), where he ran the Berlin operation of Coca-Cola exactly as if it were a gang and he were the last gangster in the world.

RECOMMENDED VIEWING
The Public Enemy (1931), *"G" Men* (1935), *A Midsummer Night's Dream* (1935), *Boy Meets Girl* (1938), *Angels with Dirty Faces* (1938), *The Roaring Twenties* (1939), *Each Dawn I Die* (1939), *Yankee Doodle Dandy* (1942), *Blood on the Sun* (1945), *13 Rue Madeleine* (1947), *White Heat* (1949), *Kiss Tomorrow Goodbye (1950)*, *A Lion Is in the Streets (1953)*, *Love Me or Leave Me (1955)*, *One, Two, Three* (1961), *Ragtime* (1981)

FURTHER READING
McCabe, John. *Cagney*. New York: Knopf, 1997.

Schickel, Richard. *James Cagney: A Celebration*. New York: Applause, 1999.

Warren, Doug. *James Cagney, The Authorized Biography*. New York: St. Martin's, 1983.

Thomas Leitch

presented even more forthrightly as a microcosm of the American dream, its promise to newly arrived immigrants, and its betrayal by the drive to assimilation and respectability. Both films weigh the gangster against the gang, a family ultimately destroyed by the very loyalties the gangster struggles to honor.

The cycle of nostalgic gangster films, including the French films *Borsalino* (1970) and *Stavisky* (1974) and

culminating in Sergio Leone's epic *C'era una volta in America* (*Once Upon a Time in America*, 1984), yielded in turn to a return of realism fueled by widespread public fear of urban crime in a civic culture apparently as intent on eradicating drug use as an earlier generation had been on criminalizing alcohol. Martin Scorsese (b. 1942), who had already anatomized criminal life in New York's Little Italy in *Mean Streets* (1973), attacked Francis Ford "volumes" of *Kill Bill* (2003, 2004) as just one more group of people going about a difficult job. The release of gangster films from all over the map, from recycled capers like *Heist* (2001) and *The Score* (2001) to Scorsese's opulently violent period piece *Gangs of New York* (2002) to the searing portrait of bored, overachieving Asian American high-school criminals in *Better Luck Tomorrow* (2002), show the gangster film flourishing in the new century even as American paranoia turned outward from domestic crime to international terrorism.

ORGANIZATION MEN

Gangster films have been categorized and theorized in many ways. Perhaps the most illuminating categories concern the different relations between gangster heroes and their organizations and between gangs and the larger society.

The earliest films to emphasize the fearsome power of gangsters came from abroad. In *Fantômas* and its four sequels (France, 1913–1914), Louis Feuillade (1873–1925) presented the gangster as a master of disguise capable of thwarting the police at every turn, a pattern expanded to epic length and complexity in Fritz Lang's (1890–1976) German film, *Dr. Mabuse, der Spieler: Ein Bild der Zeit* (*Dr. Mabuse, the Gambler*, 1922). These films present the gangster as an octopus and his organization as a vast, omnipotent conspiracy seen as if from a great distance. This paranoid pattern, common in American political thrillers, is rarely found in American gangster films; the closest American analogue is *The Phenix City Story*.

Far more common is the view of the gangster as a once-normal citizen corrupted by greed, lust, or a masculine drive to power. Films that begin their stories before the gangster's rise usually offer sociological explanations for the hero's moral deviance. *The Public Enemy* sets the pattern for gangster films that root organized crime in economic deprivation among urban immigrants. Despite its gangster trappings, most of the seven murders in *The Big Sleep* (1946) are committed to protect or avenge a lover or a spurned offer of love. The four heroines of *Set It Off* (1996) are driven to bank robbery by racism and the oppression of the white men who control their financial destiny. Criminal gangs in these films, as in *Once Upon a Time in America* and *Gangs of New York*, are often fatal extensions of generational rivalries or childhood friendships—a particularly prevalent motif in gangsta films like *Boyz N the Hood* and *Menace II Society*.

Against this view of criminal gangs as a deformed version of childhood gangs may be set the strictly professional view of gangsters in *The Asphalt Jungle*, in which each member of the gang is recruited for a particular skill

James Cagney. EVERETT COLLECTION. REPRODUCED BY PERMISSION.

Coppola's (b. 1939) idealized portrayal of a mob family in the *Godfather* films in his sharply revisionist *GoodFellas* (1990), which ended with its coked-up hero ratting out the friends who planned to kill him. Both films, along with *The Godfather, Part II*, helped establish Robert De Niro (b. 1943) as successor to Humphrey Bogart (1899–1957), the definitive gangster hero of his time: moody, barely controlled, and often psychotic.

But De Niro's Italian American gangster found a highly influential African American counterpart in the gangstas of *New Jack City* (1991), *Boyz N the Hood* (1991), *Menace II Society* (1993), *Sugar Hill* (1994), *Clockers* (1995), and *Dead Presidents* (1995). Still another international influence was supplied by the Hong Kong action films of John Woo (b. 1946), beginning with *Ying hung boon sik* (*A Better Tomorrow*, 1986), whose geometric opposition of cops to killers suggested a supercharged remake of such genre classics as *"G" Men*. Quentin Tarantino (b. 1963) combined the Hong Kong aesthetic of Woo and Johnny To (b. 1953) (*Dung fong saam hap* [*The Heroic Trio*, 1993] and other films) with an interracial gang and his own fashionable nihilism, choreographing Raoul Walsh to a laugh track in presenting the criminal heroes of *Reservoir Dogs* (1992), *Pulp Fiction* (1994), *Jackie Brown* (1997), and the two and paid a set wage, "like plumbers." American heist films, less brutal and romantic than French prototypes like *Rififi*, adopt a view of society at once technologically advanced and socially atavistic and ultimately ascribe the gang's failure to the unstable nature of the capitalistic ties that hold its members together. Frankly comic capers like *Ocean's Eleven* (1960, 2001), *The Hot Rock* (1972), *Bank Shot* (1974), and *Ocean's Twelve* (2004) get laughs by emphasizing the impossibility of the gang's task and the ingenuity of means taken to succeed. When the job looks easy, Hollywood caper films allow the gang to disintegrate under its own pressure, as in the obligatory double crosses of *The Killing* (1956), *Heist*, and *The Score*.

More broadly, criminal gangs can be framed explicitly as images of the societies they oppose. In comic versions like *The Ladykillers* (1955, 2004) and *A Fish Called Wanda* (1988), the gang's organization reflects the social order as it might be distorted by a funhouse mirror. But parody also informs less obviously comic versions like *The League of Gentlemen* (England, 1960), *Fargo* (1996), and Brian De Palma's (b. 1940) *Scarface* (1983), whose criminals, like the childlike, simian Tony Camonte in Hawks's *Scarface*, provoke laughter by their ill-informed attempts to mimic the behavior of the society whose most basic rules they are flouting. Still less comic versions like *The Godfather* films and *GoodFellas* exemplify John Baxter's premise that criminals are created by the society against which they think they are rebelling. Eugene Rosow has traced the closeness with which pre-Code gangsters reflected their audiences' fears and desires. More recently, the iconic gangster played by *Godfather* alumnus Al Pacino (b. 1940) in *Donnie Brasco* (1997) is destroyed by the undercover cop he adopts as his protégé as surely as the iconic gangster played by Robert De Niro in *Heat* (1995) faces off against the iconic cop played by Pacino as fully his equal, a potentially tragic figure destroyed by his mirror image. Like *"G" Men*, *Heat* reminds viewers that Hollywood cops are created in the image of Hollywood gangsters, not the other way around. The gangs and gangsters in these films, like Tom Hanks's doomed hit man in *Road to Perdition* (2002), are marked by the incompatible drives toward loyalty, equality, assimilation, and unlimited upward mobility characteristic of all American culture. Indeed Jack Shadoian, taking his cue from Robert Warshow, has called the gangster the archetypal American dreamer whose doomed trajectory reveals the futility of the American Dream.

Finally, gangsters can be portrayed as frankly heroic rebels against a corrupt or bankrupt society, more sympathetic, like Frankenstein's monster, than the society that has spawned and rejected them. The doomed robbers in *The Asphalt Jungle*, *Bonnie and Clyde*, *They Live by Night* (1949), and its remake, *Thieves Like Us* (1974), approach the frontier of the gangster film, a frontier crossed by outlaw films like *The Adventures of Robin Hood* (1938) and *Thelma and Louise* (1991). Tarantino's ironic spin on this pattern is to create a world in *Pulp Fiction* and *Kill Bill* from which the law and its representatives have vanished, leaving criminal culture, for better or worse, as the only game in town. Whether these films can truly be called gangster films is open to question. A world whose criminals provide the last best hope for the social order is a world in which gangsters like Robin Hood no longer seem like gangsters, no matter how many laws they break.

SEE ALSO *Crime Films; Genre*

FURTHER READING

Baxter, John. *The Gangster Film.* New York: Barnes and London: Zwemmer, 1970.

Brode, Douglas. *Money, Women, and Guns: Crime Movies from Bonnie and Clyde to the Present.* Secaucus, NJ: Carol, 1995.

Clarens, Carlos. *Crime Movies: From Griffith to the Godfather and Beyond.* Revised ed. New York: Da Capo, 1997.

Langman, Larry, and Daniel Finn. *A Guide to American Crime Films of the Thirties.* Westport, CT: Greenwood, 1995.

Leff, Leonard J., and Jerold L. Simmons. *The Dame in the Kimono: Hollywood, Censorship, and the Production Code from the 1920s to the 1960s.* New York: Grove Weidenfeld, 1990.

Leitch, Thomas M. *Crime Films.* Cambridge, UK and New York: Cambridge University Press, 2002.

Mason, Fran. *American Gangster Cinema: From Little Caesar to Pulp Fiction.* New York: Palgrave Macmillan, 2002.

McArthur, Colin. *Underworld U.S.A.* London: Secker and Warburg, 1972.

McCarty, John. *Bullets over Hollywood: The American Gangster Picture from the Silents to The Sopranos.* Cambridge, MA: Da Capo, 2004.

Munby, Jonathan. *Public Enemies, Public Heroes: Screening the Gangster Film from Little Caesar to Touch of Evil.* Chicago: University of Chicago Press, 1999.

Rosow, Eugene. *Born to Lose: The Gangster Film in America.* New York: Oxford University Press, 1978.

Shadoian, Jack. *Dreams and Dead Ends: The American Gangster/ Crime Film.* Cambridge: MIT Press, 1977.

Warshow, Robert. "The Gangster as Tragic Hero." In *The Immediate Experience: Movies, Comics, Theatre, and Other Aspects of Popular Culture.* Garden City, NY: Doubleday, 1962.

Yaquinto, Marilyn. *Pump 'Em Full of Lead: A Look at Gangsters on Film.* New York: Twayne, 1998.

Thomas Leitch

GAY, LESBIAN, AND QUEER CINEMA

The study of gay and lesbian cinema became a growing concern in the wake of 1970s feminist film theory and the discipline's increasing attention to issues of representation—of women, of racial and ethnic minorities, and eventually of gay and lesbian people. While there had been a few attempts to discuss onscreen homosexuality prior to that period (such as Parker Tyler's *Screening the Sexes: Homosexuality in the Movies* [1972]), the seminal text on the subject was Vito Russo's *The Celluloid Closet: Homosexuality in the Movies* (first published in 1981, revised and updated in 1987). In it, Russo examined over eighty years of film history, exploring the ways and means in which gay and lesbian people had been portrayed at the movies. Those images carried considerable cultural weight; for many people, these images were all they ever "saw" or "knew" about homosexuality before the sexual revolution of the 1960s.

The so-called Stonewall Riots that occurred in New York City in June 1969 are sometimes said to be the start of the modern gay and lesbian civil rights movement—the fight for civil rights and an end to discrimination. Before that time, gay and lesbian people were routinely fired from their jobs, denied housing, harassed, or arrested simply for being homosexual. They were classified as mentally ill by the psychiatric and military communities, and during the Red Scare of the 1950s they were considered national security risks. Like the struggle for racial or gender equality, the fight for gay and lesbian equality continues to this day, and the images that popular film and television create of homosexual people continue to influence both public perception and governmental policy.

In the last twenty years, the study of gay and lesbian cinema has expanded greatly beyond simplistic image analysis. Within academia, the development of third wave feminism and queer theory across many disciplines in the humanities has sought to rethink basic concepts about human sexuality, demonstrating the complexity of a subject that encompasses not only personal orientation and behavior but also the social, cultural, and historical factors that define and create the conditions of such orientations and behaviors. The term "queer," once a pejorative epithet used to humiliate gay men and women, is now used to describe that broad expanse of sexualities. Queer should thus be understood to describe any sexuality not defined as heterosexual procreative monogamy (once the presumed goal of any Hollywood coupling); queers are people (including heterosexuals) who do not organize their sexuality according to that rubric.

Recently, many of the theoretical issues raised by queer theory have found their way into gay and lesbian independent filmmaking, within a movement known as New Queer Cinema. Queer theory also helps us interrogate and complicate the category "gay and lesbian cinema." For example, the very meaning of the words "gay" and "lesbian"—how they are used and understood—has changed greatly over the decades, as have the conditions of their cinematic representation. There are great cultural and historical differences between films made by queer directors in 1930s Hollywood and those made by early twenty-first-century independent queer filmmakers. The characteristics that mass culture has used to signify homosexuality have also changed. While present-day films can be relatively forthright about sexuality, older films could only hint at it in various ways. Thus, many classical Hollywood performances, directors, and genres might be considered queer rather than gay, in that they do not explicitly acknowledge homosexuality, but nonetheless allow for spaces in which normative heterosexuality is threatened, critiqued, camped up, or shown to be an unstable performative identity.

THE CLASSICAL HOLLYWOOD BASELINE

Classical (and pre-classical) Hollywood films (those produced between the 1910s and the 1950s) had little interest in dramatizing homosexual lives or homosexual issues. The very structure of Hollywood narrative form was and is heterosexist: it almost always contains a male–female romance, regardless of story line or genre. If and when homosexual characters appeared in Hollywood films prior to the sexual revolution, they were almost always relegated to walk-on parts or small supporting roles. One notable early exception was *A Florida Enchantment* (1914), a comedy wherein female characters eat magical sex-changing seeds that turn them into women-chasing lotharios. Much more common was the stereotype of the "pansy," an effeminate male supporting character—often a butler, designer, or choreographer. When the Hollywood Production Code (which specifically forbade the depiction of what it called "sex perversion") was put into effect in 1934, these characterizations were forced further into the realm of connotation. Hollywood cinema under the Code continued to suggest queerness via the presence of effeminate men and mannish women, but these characters were never explicitly acknowledged as homosexual. Actors such as Edward Everett Horton (1886–1970), Eric Blore (1887–1959), and Franklin Pangborn (1888–1958) made careers for themselves by playing such roles.

Female characters in pre-Code cinema were stronger and more sexually forthright than in post-Code cinema, and occasionally they too gave off a queer aura. For example, Greta Garbo's (1905–1990) *Queen Christina* (1933) wears pants, runs a country, and kisses her chambermaid rather passionately on the lips—before she falls in love with a man. Similarly, in *Morocco* (1930), Marlene Dietrich's (1901–1992) character wears a tuxedo and vamps both men and women. Both actresses—Garbo and Dietrich—had large queer fan bases and many rumors surrounded their "real life" sexualities. Obviously, many queer actors and actresses worked (and continue to work) in Hollywood. Leading silent film stars Ramon Novarro (1899–1968) and Billy Haines (1900–1973) were gay, but as the Production Code was enforced and Hollywood grew more homophobic, their careers faded. Haines was fired from Metro-Goldwyn-Mayer because he refused to go along with studio publicity designed to hide his homosexuality. Such arranged publicity stunts included dates and even weddings—the so-called "marriage of convenience." For example, Rock Hudson (1925–1985) was briefly married in the 1950s to persuade his fans that he was indeed heterosexual.

Queer people also worked behind the camera in Hollywood, many in costume design (Orry-Kelly [1897–1964], Adrian [1903–1959]), set decoration (Jack Moore [1906–1998], Henry Grace [1907–1983]), and choreography (Charles Walters [1903–1982], Jack Cole [1911–1974]). There were also successful producers and directors who led quiet homosexual lives, including David Lewis (1903–1987), Ross Hunter (1920–1996), Mitchell Leisen (1898–1972), Edmund Goulding (1891–1959), Irving Rapper (1898–1999), Arthur Lubin (1898–1995), James Whale (1889–1957), George Cukor (1899–1983), and Dorothy Arzner (1897–1979). The last three of these are the best known, perhaps because their film work does show more obvious touches of a homosexual sensibility. Whale directed four of Universal's classic horror films (*Frankenstein*, 1931; *The Old Dark House*, 1932; *The Invisible Man*, 1933; and *Bride of Frankenstein*, 1935) with gay wit and innuendo. Arzner, one of the few women to direct in Hollywood during the classical era, made films such as *Christopher Strong* (1933) and *Dance, Girl, Dance* (1940) that showcased strong women and celebrated the bonds between them. Cukor, one of the classical era's most prolific directors, became known chiefly for his women's films and musicals, including *Camille* (1936), *A Star Is Born* (1954), and *My Fair Lady* (1964). Cukor's *Sylvia Scarlett* (1935) managed to skirt the Code's injunctions against "sex perversion" even as it featured a cross-dressing heroine (Katherine Hepburn as a young woman impersonating a boy) and all sorts of same-sex infatuations.

Queer filmmakers and fans were often drawn to the musical and the horror film, two genres that often acknowledged queer characters and seem to be steeped in queer sensibilities. The musical, although almost always containing a (highly contrived) heterosexual romance, creates a bright carnivalesque world in which fantasy and reality shift and blur. Real-life hatreds and biases are banished, and people are free to be expressively emotional and physical in nonviolent ways. *The Wizard of Oz* (1939), starring gay favorite Judy Garland (1922–1969) and a cast of misfit effeminate men, has become an iconic film in gay culture. The horror film often uses queer traits to characterize its monsters and mad scientists. For example, in *Mad Love* (1935) Peter Lorre's effeminate madman quotes Oscar Wilde, and vampires (like *Dracula's Daughter*, 1936) are almost always queerly sexual, seducing both men and women with their unnatural kisses. In fact, the lesbian vampire was the most common image of lesbians on American film screens before the 1980s. The need for queer spectators to rewrite such distorted images and reappropriate others

BARBARA HAMMER
b. Hollywood, California, 15 May 1939

Barbara Hammer is by far the most prolific lesbian filmmaker, having made over sixty films and videos since the late 1960s. Hammer's films are excellent examples of New Queer Cinema practice. They cross borders (between documentary, fiction, and experimental filmmaking), and focus on the complexities of human sexuality—especially the ways in which those sexualities have been socially constructed across time and place. Hammer's films explore love, sex, identity, humor, community, relationships, nature, and spirituality. Almost all are deeply personal, drawing on autobiographical elements and centering on the filmmaker as well as her friends and lovers.

Hammer's earliest films are set in and around San Francisco and reflect the mythic femininity that many lesbian-feminists of the 1970s were trying to reclaim. For example, *Menses* (1974) makes use of bold symbolism (blood, eggs), optical printing, and sound loops in order to exalt the essentially feminine process of menstruation. *Superdyke* (1975), in which a group of self-identified "Amazon" women wearing "Superdyke" T-shirts joyously overrun San Francisco, is even more playful in tone and form. In *Women I Love* (1979), Hammer experiments with pixilation (the animation of objects) as dancing fruits and vegetables unveil their inner selves to the camera, just as do the women in her life.

By the 1980s, Hammer was exploring and experimenting with digital technology. In *No No Nooky TV* (1987), she used computer-generated sounds and images to investigate technology's male biases, as well as to suggest how those forms might be reclaimed for lesbian feminist goals. She tackled the AIDS crisis directly in *Snow Job: The Media Hysteria of AIDS* (1986) and more indirectly in *Endangered* (1988), an abstract aural and visual collage that draws a connection between endangered species and the precarious nature of her own experimental film work wherein media technologies threaten to eradicate their living subjects altogether.

In the 1990s, Hammer made a series of longer, more theoretically informed films that investigate lesbian representability. The first of these, *Nitrate Kisses* (1992), begins with a consideration of how the American novelist Willa Cather's sexuality has been erased from history. The film explores queer sexualities hitherto hidden, including lesbian relationships during the Holocaust and gay male iconography of the 1930s. Hammer counters those historical musings with contemporary treatment of sexualities still considered taboo (even by many queers), including footage of two older women lovers and a sadomasochistic duo. As an interracial male couple has sex, Hammer overlays the written text of the Hollywood Production Code, in effect forcing that document to confront what it had censored for so long. Funny, complex, thoughtful, and challenging, the work of Barbara Hammer expands our notions of both film form and human sexuality.

RECOMMENDED VIEWING

Dyketactics (1974), *Menses* (1974), *Superdyke* (1975), *Women I Love* (1979), *Our Trip* (1980), *Sync Touch* (1981), *Snow Job* (1986), *No No Nooky TV* (1987), *Endangered* (1988), *Nitrate Kisses* (1992), *Tender Fictions* (1995), *History Lessons* (2000)

FURTHER READING

Dyer, Richard. "Lesbian/Woman: Lesbian Cultural Feminist Film." In *Now You See It: Studies on Lesbian and Gay Film*, 2nd ed., 169–200. London and New York: Routledge, 1990.

Foster, Gwendolyn Audrey. "Barbara Hammer, an Interview: Re/Constructing Lesbian Auto/Biographies in *Tender Fictions* and *Nitrate Kisses*." *Post Script* 16, no. 3 (Summer 1997): 3–16. Reprinted in *Experimental Cinema: The Film Reader*, edited by Wheeler Winston Dixon and Gwendolyn Audrey Foster, 283–297. London and New York: Routledge, 2002.

Haug, Kate. "An Interview with Barbara Hammer." *Wide Angle* 20, no. 1 (January 1998): 64–105. Also includes a critical essay, filmography, and bibliography.

Weiss, Andrea. "Transgressive Cinema: Lesbian Independent Film." In *Vampires 161*. New York: Penguin, 1993.

Harry M. Benshoff

Barbara Hammer. EVERETT COLLECTION. REPRODUCED BY
PERMISSION.

gave rise to the camp sensibility, the practice of ironically
decoding and making fun of heterocentrist culture. As
such, many gay men of the pre-Stonewall generation
simultaneously mocked and venerated Hollywood stars
such as Maria Montez (1917–1951), Bette Davis (1908–
1989), Joan Crawford (1904–1977), and Lana Turner
(1921–1995), actresses who always seemed to be performing—even in their real lives.

HOLLYWOOD AND THE SEXUAL REVOLUTION

Hollywood responded to the nation's changing sexual
mores throughout the 1950s and 1960s by slowly
amending and then eventually replacing the Hollywood
Production Code with the Motion Picture Association of
America (MPAA) Ratings System. In 1961 the Code
Administration agreed to allow onscreen homosexuality,
as long as it was treated with "care, discretion, and
restraint." What that really meant was that homosexuality could be represented, but that it should also be condemned. For example, the British import *Victim* (1961),
which centered on a gay blackmail case and argued that
social prejudice against homosexuals was wrong, was
denied a Seal of Approval. The first few American films

dealing with homosexuality that were approved by the
Code suggested that homosexuality would only lead to
tragedy. For example, in *Advise and Consent* (1962), a
past gay relationship is shown to be cause for suicide, and
in *The Children's Hour* (1962), a young woman hangs
herself after admitting that she is a lesbian.

Throughout the 1960s, homosexual innuendo
became a staple of smarmy sex comedies (*That Touch of
Mink*, 1962; *Staircase*, 1969; *The Gay Deceivers*, 1969),
and functioned as a signifier of ultimate villainy in action
and adventure films (*Lawrence of Arabia*, 1962; *From
Russia with Love*, 1963; *Caprice*, 1967). A few films
attempted to deal with sexuality in more complex ways:
Reflections in a Golden Eye (1967) and *The Sergeant*
(1968) centered on (repressed) homosexuality in the
military, even as their queer characters still met death
and destruction. Two of the most famous (and least
offensive) Hollywood films dealing with homosexuality
during this era were *The Killing of Sister George* (1968,
about lesbians in the British television industry) and *The
Boys in the Band* (1970, about a group of gay friends in
New York City). Both of these films had been based on
successful stage plays and explored issues of romance, the
closet, the possibility of blackmail and job loss, internalized homophobia, and the burgeoning (but still mostly
underground) gay and lesbian culture of many cities.
While these films may seem overly melodramatic or
stereotypical by today's standards, they did capture a
certain slice of reality for many urban homosexuals of
their era. Perhaps most importantly, no one died at the
end of them.

Throughout the 1970s, as homosexuals were becoming more visible in the real world, they once again
retreated from American movie screens. Queers were
occasionally seen as minor supporting figures, when they
were seen at all. Then, in the early 1980s, another small
cycle of gay-themed films appeared. Several of these
reworked the old queer psycho-killer stereotype: in
Dressed to Kill (1980), *Cruising* (1980), and *The Fan*
(1981), queers slashed their way onto multiplex movie
screens. Perhaps to atone for such images, Hollywood
also released a handful of films that featured sympathetic
queer characters. *The World According to Garp* (1982)
featured a male-to-female transsexual, while *Personal Best*
(1982) dramatized a lesbian relationship and issues of
bisexuality. Twentieth Century Fox released *Making
Love* (1982), a melodrama about a married couple coming to terms with the husband's latent homosexuality. By
far the most popular of these films was the old-fashioned
musical sex farce *Victor/Victoria* (1982), a film that featured Julie Andrews as a cross-dressing nightclub performer and Robert Preston as her flamboyantly gay best
friend.

Frances Lorraine and Sally Binford in Barbara Hammer's **Nitrate Kisses** *(1992).* © STRAND RELEASING/COURTESY EVERETT COLLECTION. REPRODUCED BY PERMISSION.

ALTERNATIVES TO HOLLYWOOD

Gay and lesbian concerns and characters often found more varied (and less pejorative) representations outside the Hollywood industry, in foreign, experimental, and documentary filmmaking. One of the first films ever to feature homosexual love as its theme was the Swedish film *Vingarne* (*Wings*, 1916), directed by Mauritz Stiller (1823–1928; who was himself homosexual). Carl Theodor Dreyer's *Mikaël* (1924), filmed in Germany a few years later, was drawn from the same source novel. In fact, Weimar Germany was home to gay directors like F. W. Murnau (1888–1931) (*Nosferatu*, 1922) and produced the first film to make a plea for homosexual rights and freedoms. *Anders als die Anderen* (*Different from the Others*, 1919) was made in conjunction with early sexologist and gay rights pioneer Magnus Hirschfeld (1868–1934). A few years later G. W. Pabst's famous film *Pandora's Box* (1929) featured a lesbian subplot. Perhaps the most well-known German film of this era

to deal with homosexuality was *Madchen in Uniform* (1931), a film about a schoolgirl's crush on her teacher. It should be noted that if and when these films played in America, they were often censored in ways that elided their homosexual content.

French avant-garde filmmaking also offered an alternative to Hollywood form and content. Poet and playwright Jean Cocteau's (1889–1963) film *Le sang d'un poète* (*Blood of a Poet*, 1930) explored homoerotic themes, and Jean Genet's (1910–1986) *Un chant d'amour* (*Song of Love*, 1950) centered on the homoerotic bonds between men in prison. One of the first American avant-garde films to deal with homosexuality was James Watson (1894–1982) and Melville Webber's (1871–1947) *Lot in Sodom* (1933). In the postwar era, Kenneth Anger's (b. 1927) *Fireworks* (1947), a surreal psychodrama about a young man's homosexual desires, both scandalized and inspired a new generation of filmmakers. Although Anger lived abroad for most of the

1950s, he returned to America to make his most famous film, *Scorpio Rising* (1964), a film that combines found footage, contemporary pop songs, and a host of other cultural artifacts to examine the homoerotic cult of the motorcyclist. Also making queer avant-garde films in the 1960s were Jack Smith (1932–1989) and Andy Warhol (1928–1987), two artists who were associated with the New York underground film scene. Jack Smith's *Flaming Creatures* (1963) featured characters (slave girls, vampires, Roman guards, etc.) and overly dramatic music drawn from exotic Hollywood melodramas. Andy Warhol's films (including *Haircut*, 1963; *Couch*, 1964; and *Lonesome Cowboys*, 1967) also parodied Hollywood style and conventions; his actors (many of whom were drag queens) called themselves "superstars" and behaved as if they were Hollywood royalty.

In the 1970s, prolific lesbian feminist filmmaker Barbara Hammer (b. 1930) began to make short experimental films. Her early work, made in and around San Francisco, captures the feel and spirit of the 1970s lesbian feminist community as it was then defining itself. Other lesbian feminists of the 1970s, including Greta Schiller (b. 1954) (*Greta's Girls*, 1978) and Jan Oxenberg (*Home Movie*, 1973), made films that documented the movement, and more recent experimental work by Su Friedrich (b. 1954), Michelle Citron, Michelle Parkerson (b. 1953), and Sadie Benning (b. 1973) forge important links to the New Queer Cinema movement of the 1990s.

The burgeoning gay and lesbian civil rights movement of the 1970s and 1980s was not confined to America: many western European nations and Canada also began to produce films that acknowledged or reflected the movement. In Germany, Rainer Werner Fassbinder (1946–1982) directed over forty films about race, class, and (homo)sexuality, while Rosa von Praunheim (b. 1942) and Ulrike Ottinger (b. 1942) made even more surreal excursions into the politics and pleasures of homosexuality. In England, Derek Jarman (1942–1994) made a series of highly stylized films (*Sebastiane*, 1976; *Jubilee*, 1977) that critiqued sexual repression and the British Empire. In Spain, Pedro Almodóvar (b. 1949) became one of the world's best known queer filmmakers, repeatedly winning international film prizes for his films. In Canada, John Greyson (b. 1960) made a series of short films and then features (*Moscow Does Not Believe in Queers*, 1986; *Pissoir* [*Urinal*, 1988]) that dealt with homophobia and the AIDS crisis. While a few foreign films dealing with homosexuality (including *La cage aux folles* [*Birds of a Feather*], 1978; and *Kiss of the Spider Woman*, 1985) became art-house hits in America during this era, many of the more queerly provocative works made abroad remained very difficult to see.

Starting in the 1970s, documentaries made by and about gay and lesbian people began to be produced. One of the first and most important of these, *Word Is Out* (1978), was made by a collective of gay and lesbian filmmakers, and told the stories of a cross-section of queer Americans. (The film remains a fascinating time capsule of 1970s culture and the nascent gay liberation movement.) Since then, gay and lesbian documentaries have brought to light stories and issues that mainstream media routinely ignores. Some of these films, such as *Before Stonewall* (1985) and *Silent Pioneers* (1985), documented forgotten aspects of gay and lesbian history. The Oscar®-winning documentary *The Times of Harvey Milk* (1984) chronicled the rise to power of the first openly gay city supervisor, as well as his eventual assassination by an unhinged right-wing politician. Other documentaries, such as *Common Threads: Stories from the Quilt* (1989) and *Silverlake Life* (1993), explored the AIDS crisis, and activist video collectives made pieces that helped spur education and organization. Marlon Riggs's (1957–1994) personal video documentary *Tongues Untied* (1989) remains the definitive statement on what it was like to be a black gay man in the 1980s. Countless other documentaries, such as *One Nation under God* (1993), *Ballot Measure 9* (1995), and *It's Elementary* (1996) continue to explore gay and lesbian lives and issues.

NEW QUEER CINEMA

The production of foreign, experimental, and documentary films that centered on queer issues eventually helped spark the production of gay and lesbian independent feature film production in America. The first batch of these films, including *Buddies* (1985), *Parting Glances* (1986), and *Desert Hearts* (1985), used realistic storytelling conventions to explore coming out, romance, and AIDS. Then, in 1991, a new crop of gay and lesbian films made waves at several international festivals. These films (including *Poison*, *Swoon*, *Paris Is Burning*, *The Living End*, *Edward II*, and *My Own Private Idaho*, all released in 1991) were made by more activist and theoretical filmmakers: Todd Haynes (b. 1961), Tom Kalin, Jennie Livingston (b. 1960), Gregg Araki (b. 1959), Derek Jarman, and Gus Van Sant (b. 1952). The films, many fueled by 1980s AIDS activism, engaged with concepts being formulated within queer theory, and collectively they became known as the New Queer Cinema. Christine Vachon (b. 1962), who has been dubbed the "Godmother of New Queer Cinema," produced several of these first films and has since then produced many more, including *Go Fish* (1994), *Postcards from the Edge* (1994), *Stonewall* (1995), *Boys Don't Cry* (2000), *Hedwig and the Angry Inch* (2001), and *Far from Heaven* (2002). Other important New Queer films include John

TODD HAYNES
b. Los Angeles, California, 2 January 1961

One of the most successful writer-directors of the New Queer Cinema, Todd Haynes was raised in California and studied semiotics and other aspects of cultural theory at Brown University, where he began to make short films. Haynes's work, like most New Queer Cinema, explores the cinematic representation of queer desires by foregrounding both history and film form.

The first Haynes film to garner widespread attention was *Superstar: The Karen Carpenter Story* (1987), a 45-minute biopic that explored the life and death (from anorexia nervosa) of 1970s singer Karen Carpenter. Audaciously, Karen Carpenter's life is enacted in the film by Barbie dolls, and is intercut with documentary-like inserts that describe and explore the medical and social implications of anorexia. While the very premise of *Superstar* creates a campy tone, the film is far from facile or condescending. Instead, the film asks its viewers to consider the connections between the ideals of feminine beauty, celebrity, mental illness, and middle-class repression. Its unlicensed use of the Carpenters' music (and perhaps its unflattering portrait of Karen's family) led to a lawsuit, and the film remains very difficult to see.

Haynes's first feature-length film, *Poison* (1991), was one of the defining films of the New Queer Cinema movement. It recalls the audacity of *Superstar*, and was itself the center of considerable controversy. *Poison* interweaves three separate but related stories, each shot in a different cinematic style. The first, "Homo," is based on the writings of gay writer Jean Genet, and explores the violent sexuality of men in prison. The second, "Horror," is about a scientist who accidentally ingests a sex-hormone serum, and is filmed as a pastiche of 1950s monster movies. The third story, "Hero," is a pseudodocumentary about a young boy who shoots his father and miraculously flies away from the scene. *Poison* was publicly denounced by some members of Congress (it had received some funding from the National

Endowment for the Arts) even as it won the Grand Jury Prize at Sundance.

Haynes's next feature, *Safe* (1995), starred Julianne Moore as a woman suffering from a viral-like illness that may or may not be psychosomatic. Exploring issues of contamination, isolation, and the toxic atmosphere of everyday life, the film was both an AIDS allegory and a critique of American self-obsession. *Velvet Goldmine* (1998), another queer art-house hit, examined the 1970s "glam rock" phenomenon in relation to sexuality, celebrity, and style. In 2002, Haynes's *Far from Heaven* (2002) was nominated for several Oscars®, including Best Original Screenplay. The film invokes the visual style of a lush 1950s melodrama, but explores issues that were taboo for films of that era: interracial romance and repressed homosexuality. As with the best of his work, *Far from Heaven* explores the intersection of film form and film content, showing how the discourse of cinematic style can create, contain, or otherwise influence the representation of queer desire.

RECOMMENDED VIEWING
Superstar: The Karen Carpenter Story (1987), *Poison* (1991), *Dottie Gets Spanked* (1993), *Safe* (1995), *Velvet Goldmine* (1998), *Far from Heaven* (2002)

FURTHER READING

Haynes, Todd. *Far from Heaven, Safe, and Superstar: Three Screenplays*. New York: Grove Press, 2003.

Naismith, Gaye. "Tales from the Crypt: Contamination and Quarantine in Todd Haynes's *Safe*." In *The Visible Woman: Imaging Technologies, Gender, and Science*, edited by Paula A. Treichler, Lisa Cartwright, and Constance Penley, 360–388. New York: New York University Press, 1998.

Saunders, Michael William. *Imps of the Perverse: Gay Monsters in Film*, 75–134. Westport, CT: Praeger, 1998. Also includes an interview with Todd Haynes.

Wyatt, Justin. *Poison*. London: Flicks Books, 1998.

Harry M. Benshoff

Greyson's *Zero Patience* (1993) and Cheryl Dunye's *Watermelon Woman* (1996).

New Queer Cinema has been called "Homo Pomo," because the movement's films make use of postmodern styles and ideas (as does queer theory itself). In most of these films there is a focus on permeable formal boundaries—the crossing of styles and genres. New Queer Cinema often questions essentialist models of identity, and shows how the terms "gay" and "lesbian" are inadequate when trying to define actual human experience. New Queer Cinema simultaneously draws on minimalism and excess, appropriation and pastiche, the mixing of Hollywood and avant-garde, and even the mix of fictional and documentary style. For example, *The Living End* reappropriates the Hollywood buddy/road movie for HIV-positive queers, while *Zero Patience* is a ghost story musical about AIDS. *Watermelon Woman* is a mock documentary about an African American lesbian actress who played "Mammy" roles in 1930s Hollywood; the film is a witty interracial lesbian romance as well as a thoughtful meditation on queer visibility and historical erasure.

New Queer Cinema is not without its detractors. Some have accused the movement of recirculating negative stereotypes such as the queer psycho-killer. Although films like *Swoon* and *The Living End* attempt to show how social forces and sexual repression can and do cause violence, some filmgoers still saw them as reconfirming harmful stereotypes. New Queer Cinema has also been charged with elitism, since it is frequently engaged with issues of queer and postmodern theory. As such, New Queer Cinema can be rigorous and difficult both thematically and formally, and many queer spectators, like straight spectators, prefer "feel good" Hollywood-style movies with happy endings.

Todd Haynes on the set of **Far From Heaven** *(2002).* © FOCUS FEATURES/COURTESY EVERETT COLLECTION. REPRODUCED BY PERMISSION.

Jonathan Rhys-Myers in Todd Haynes's **Velvet Goldmine** *(1998).* EVERETT COLLECTION. REPRODUCED BY PERMISSION.

Those "feel good" movies are also now being made by gay and lesbian independent filmmakers. For example, *The Incredibly True Adventure of Two Girls in Love* (1995), *Beautiful Thing* (1996), *Edge of Seventeen* (1998), and *Billy's Hollywood Screen Kiss* (1998) draw upon the conventions of Hollywood narrative form and the genre of the romantic comedy, placing lesbian and gay lovers into previously heterosexual roles. Films such as *Love! Valour! Compassion!* (1997) and *The Broken Hearts Club* (2000) mix humor with a few tear-jerking moments, and represent predominantly upper-middle-class white male characters. Independent lesbian films remain fewer in number, although films like *Better Than Chocolate* (1999) and *But I'm a Cheerleader* (1999) have been hits on the film festival and art house circuits. Queers of color and transgendered people have also been the subjects of recent American independent features, in films such as *Latin Boys Go to Hell* (1997), *Punks* (2001), and the Oscar®-nominated films *Before Night Falls* (2000) and *Boys Don't Cry.*

HOLLYWOOD TODAY

The rise of New Queer Cinema did not go unnoticed by Hollywood, and they briefly tried (unsuccessfully) to market a few films that explored more open parameters of sexuality, such as *Three of Hearts* (1993) and *Threesome* (1994). For the most part, when dealing with queer characters (which it still rarely does), Hollywood still prefers its previously succesful formulas and comfortable stereotypes. Queer gender-bending traits are still used to signify villainy—even in Disney films like *The Lion King* (1994) and *Pocahontas* (1995). The social problem film *Philadelphia* (1993), while a major critical and box office hit, was still a variation on the "tragic-homosexual-who-dies-at-the-end-of-the-film" stereotype. And drag queens are center stage in occasional comedies like *To Wong Foo, Thanks for Everything, Julie Newmar* (1995) and *The Birdcage* (1996). But in an era of nostalgic Hollywood blockbusters based on fantasy novels and comic books, Hollywood films that deal with actual gay and lesbian lives and issues are relatively rare.

A few new trends dealing with queer issues in Hollywood briefly surfaced in the late 1990s. The first was the reworking of the Hollywood buddy film formula so that it now comprised a straight female lead and her gay male best friend (allegedly bringing both women and gay men to the box office). Films such as *My Best Friend's Wedding* (1997), *The Object of My Affection* (1998), and *The Next Best Thing* (2000) explored the close bonds of friendship that often exist between gay men and straight women. (This is also the formula of the popular and award-winning TV situation comedy *Will and Grace* [NBC, 1998–2006]) While no one dies tragically in these new-age buddy films, and some of them have been moderate box office successes, they still tend to chafe at Hollywood films' need for happy heterosexual closure. Another recent trend in Hollywood's treatment of homosexuality is represented by a handful of films that explore the destructive dynamics of internalized homophobia. *American Beauty* (which won many Oscars® in 1999 including Best Picture) dramatized how repressed homosexuality can lead to vicious homophobia, violence, and murder—a theme also found in *The Talented Mr. Ripley* (1999), several recent documentaries, and even the Comedy Central TV show *South Park* (premiered in 1997—). Most recently, the highly acclaimed film *Brokeback Mountain* (2005) poignantly dramatized how homophobia and heterosexism can destroy human lives.

In Hollywood today, being openly gay or lesbian remains difficult for most actors. Many actors (and their agents and advisors) still fear that the public will not accept an openly gay or lesbian actor in a heterosexual role. However, in the late 1990s, a few Hollywood stars, including Ellen Degeneres (b. 1958), Nathan Lane (b. 1956), Rupert Everett (b. 1959), Rosie O'Donnell (b. 1962), and Sir Ian McKellen (b. 1939) led the way in being openly queer media personalities. Still, the vast majority of queer Hollywood actors remain in the closet, a fact that reinforces the notion that there is something wrong or shameful about being gay or lesbian. Behind the camera, more and more Hollywood queers are finding the space and acceptance to be who they are, making films and especially television shows in unprecedented numbers. The popular situation comedy *Ellen* (ABC, 1994–1998) broke down many barriers and has made television more gay-friendly than Hollywood film. Furthermore, subscription TV channels such as HBO and Showtime, because they do not have to sell their projects to America one film at a time, have also been able to produce more queer-themed work in recent years, including *More Tales of the City* (1998), *Common Ground* (2000), *Queer as Folk* (begun in 2000), *If These Walls Could Talk 2* (2000), and *Soldier's Girl* (2003). Mainstream Hollywood film, so often behind the rest of the media industries in relation to these issues, still continues to marginalize gay and lesbian lives and issues.

SEE ALSO *Camp; Gender; Queer Theory; Sexuality*

FURTHER READING

Aaron, Michele, ed. *New Queer Cinema: A Critical Reader.* Edinburgh: Edinburgh University Press, 2003.

Bad Object-Choices, eds. *How Do I Look?: Queer Film and Video.* Seattle: Bay Press, 1991.

Benshoff, Harry M., and Sean Griffin, eds. *Queer Cinema: The Film Reader.* London and New York: Routledge, 2004.

Creekmur, Corey K., and Alexander Doty, eds. *Out in Culture: Gay, Lesbian, and Queer Essays on Popular Culture.* Durham, NC: Duke University Press, 1995.

Dyer, Richard. *The Culture of Queers.* London and New York: Routledge, 2002.

———. *Now You See It: Studies on Lesbian and Gay Film.* 2nd ed. London and New York: Routledge, 2003 [1990].

Ehrenstein, David. *Open Secret: Gay Hollywood 1928–1998.* New York: William Morrow, 1998.

Fuss, Diana, ed. *inside/out: Lesbian Theories, Gay Theories.* London and New York: Routledge: 1991.

Gever, Martha, John Greyson, and Pratibha Parmar, eds. *Queer Looks: Perspectives on Lesbian and Gay Film and Video.* London and New York: Routledge, 1993.

Hanson, Ellis, ed. *Out Takes: Essays on Queer Theory and Film.* Durham, NC: Duke University Press, 1999.

Mann, William J. *Behind the Screen: How Gays and Lesbians Shaped Hollywood, 1910–1969.* New York: Penguin Books, 2001.

Russo, Vito. *The Celluloid Closet: Homosexuality in the Movies.* Revised ed. New York: Harper & Row, 1987.

Suarez, Juan A. *Bike Boys, Drag Queens, and Superstars: Avant-Garde, Mass Culture, and Gay Identities in the 1960s Underground Cinema.* Bloomington and Indianapolis: Indiana University Press, 1996.

Tyler, Parker. *Screening the Sexes: Homosexuality in the Movies.* New York: Da Capo Press, 1993 [1972].

White, Patricia. *Uninvited: Classical Hollywood Cinema and Lesbian Representability.* Bloomington and Indianapolis: Indiana University Press, 1999.

Harry M. Benshoff

GENDER

Traditionally, the term "gender" refers to the grammatical categories of masculine, feminine, and neuter, but in recent usage it refers more widely to sex-based social categories. Social scientists and anthropologists commonly distinguish gender, which is applied to social and cultural categories, from sex, which is reserved for biological categories. The distinction between sex and gender is underpinned by theories in the life and social sciences about the respective roles of nature and culture in the creation of human identity. Debates around sex and gender have tended to be controversial, and in recent years these have been intensified by medical and scientific research that has provided grounds both for and against the mapping of biological sex onto gender. Some of the most interesting perspectives on sex and gender have come from researchers studying intersexuality. In an influential paper published in 1993, biologist Anne Fausto-Sterling posits the existence of not two but five sexes—male, female, and three degrees of hermaphroditism. In the ensuing debate, which has practical bearings on gender assignment for hermaphrodite children as well as on a whole array of gender-rights issues, it has become clear that the variety of possible sexes and genders is greater than traditionally thought. Within most cultures, however, binary gender division is a persistent norm.

GENDER AND FILM

Feminist arguments against the concept of biologically determined gender identity began with the assertion by Simone de Beauvoir (1908–1986) that women are not born but made. The sex-gender paradigm was taken up widely in the 1970s and 1980s in feminist arguments for rights denied to women and girls on spurious biological grounds. The emphasis of feminist analysis was thus skewed toward deconstructions of gender, while sex itself remained relatively unexamined. Some feminist positions took advantage of the notion of a "real" or "natural" femininity that existed prior to the impositions of capitalist patriarchy, although ultimately all arguments for women's equality were undermined by such essentialism, to a greater or lesser extent.

In a groundbreaking essay published in 1975, Gayle Rubin coined the term "sex-gender system" to describe the ways in which societies transform biological sex into cultural gender and align the processes of human reproduction with those of economic production. Rubin's analysis places marriage, kinship systems, and heterosexuality at the heart of the sex-gender system. Her hypothesis exposed certain contradictions and differences that were particularly marked within American feminism at the time. One of these concerns the legacy of African Americans, whose slave ancestors were denied marriage and kinship and therefore a place in the sex-gender system as Rubin describes it, and for whom gender consequently has different meanings. The situation of African Americans draws attention to the need to conceptualize gender and its relationship with other social systems within historically specific frameworks. Lesbians also fall outside the gambit of Rubin's sex-gender system: by opting out of heterosexuality and its attendant kinship structures, they become radically other to the system. Although this outsider status legitimated lesbianism as a logical and effective expression of feminist dissent, it also contributed to the creation, in the 1980s, of an idealized image of lesbian sexuality that was widely rejected by queer culturalists in the 1990s. The "sex-gender system" failed as a universal paradigm but succeeded in establishing the importance of mapping convergences between particular social and economic systems in the production of gender.

The recognition that differences among women are at least as important to feminism as differences between women and men has enriched feminist thinking massively, but it has also placed the fundamental assumption of feminism—the commonality of women—under great pressure. Postmodern critical theorists see this as a good thing, potentially enabling the emergence of multiple and mutable sexual identities. In *Gender Trouble* (1990), the most widely influential deconstruction of gender identity published in the 1990s, Judith Butler argues that feminist assertions of the commonality of women as a group unwittingly contribute to the regulation of gender relations. Membership of the class of women, according to Butler, is not the inescapable consequence of biological femininity. Gender identities are not expressions of an essential core but performances built from citations and imitations specific to a given context. The hegemony of patriarchal heterosexuality is therefore neither natural nor inevitable. Butler argues that performances that subvert, confuse, or ironize gender norms have the power to unsettle or even unseat those norms. However, this reformulation of gender is not without drawbacks. Its dissolution of the concept of women as a class or category could be premature. Feminism is the struggle for women as a class and for the disappearance of that class, but it is possible that women as a class might disappear from postmodern feminist discourse while continuing to exist in all their diversity within other discursive and social formations. Further, the notion of gender identity as "free-floating" and flexible needs to be circumscribed by a recognition of the effects that normative social forces and their uneven application have on people of different cultures and conditions. Individualistic subversions of gender norms are not equally possible for all and do not necessarily benefit those who are left behind in the ghetto of women.

GENDER ON THE SCREEN

The absence of the physical body of the actor, and indeed, the relative unimportance of the spectator's own body, in the experience of film viewing should make cinema the perfect medium for the performance of diverse and free-floating gender identities, but the converse is more generally the case: the extent to which images of men and women are conventionalized in the cinema demonstrates the power of gender norms. Nevertheless, the history of cinematic representations of gender is characterized by tensions, contradictions, and change.

Between its invention in 1895 and the imposition of the Production Code in the early 1930s, American cinema was torn between the modern idea of the New Woman and the antimodern Cult of True Womanhood—a Victorian ideology that prescribed for women the four cardinal virtues of purity, piety, domesticity, and submission. In early cinema, before the stabilization of industry standards and norms and while cinema still lacked respectability, women on the screen were often active, sexual, and even feminist. Three types of movies were especially popular with women in the 1910s: serials such as *The Perils of Pauline* (1914), white slave films, and suffragist films. The possibility that these genres encouraged active, curious, militant female spectatorship was the cause of some social concern at the time, especially in the case of the white slave films. There was also concern that the movie theaters were drawing women into new and unsafe public spaces. Early cinema formed part of a modern urban cultural scene in which women's increased mobility was both cause and effect of changes in their social roles.

In later silent cinema, the dialectical tension between old and new model femininities can be most clearly seen in the contrasting stereotypes of the virgin, personified by stars like Mary Pickford (1893–1979) and Lillian Gish (1893–1993), and the vamp, most notoriously embodied by Theda Bara (1885–1955) and Clara Bow (1905–1965). D. W. Griffith (1875–1948), the director most prominently associated with the development of longer narrative films and with the effort to establish the cultural respectability of cinema, consciously drew on the theatrical and literary melodrama of the nineteenth century, in which heroines were virtuous, passive, and long-suffering. However, flapper films of the 1920s, such as *The Dancing Mothers* (1926) and *It* (1927), depicted and addressed the modern, active, independent women of the decade that began with their enfranchisement. The Hollywood libertarianism that made stars of Greta Garbo (1905–1990), Marlene Dietrich (1901–1992), and Mae West (1893–1980) and that created the new and violent masculinity of the gangster film seemed to have carried the day when, in the early 1930s, under pressure from the Legion of Decency, the Production Code came into force, installing sublimation and double standards at the heart of the Hollywood aesthetic.

The impact of historical events on gender roles often appears in indirect and mediated ways in Hollywood cinema. The Depression and the New Deal generated an ethos of selflessness that arguably informed maternal melodramas such as *Stella Dallas* (1937), although the film makes no explicit reference to the economics or ideology of the times. Many critics have noted the influence of World War II on gender roles in the woman's film and film noir, genres that have been said to participate

RUDOLPH VALENTINO
b. Rodolpho Alfonzo Raffaelo Pierre Filibert Gugliemi di Valentina d'Antonguola, Castellaneta, Italy, May 6, 1895, d. New York, New York, August 23, 1926

In his short career as a leading man, Rudolph Valentino was one of the great idols of the silent era and also one of its most controversial, splitting the audience along gender lines between women who adored him and men who loathed him.

After stints of begging, dishwashing, and taxi dancing, Valentino went to Hollywood, where he got his big break in 1921 when he was cast as the lead in Rex Ingram's *Four Horsemen of the Apocalypse*, the box-office hit that made him a star. At screenings of *The Sheik* (1921), women fainted in the aisles, inflamed by its heady cocktail of slavery, capture, peril, and romance. Valentino's star image was established by *The Sheik* in the form of a split personality: the hard-eyed wild man who, once wounded, could be tamed by the love of a good woman.

Valentino acquired a scandalous reputation as a result of bigamy charges brought by his first wife, Jean Acker, gossip about his sexual proclivities and competence, and a second marriage to the domineering Natacha Rambova, whose gift to him of a slave bracelet and whose friendship with lesbian actress Alla Nazimova undermined the star's protestations of "caveman" virility. On the release of *The Son of the Sheik* (1926), an editorial in the *Chicago Tribune* famously called him a "pink powder puff" and a "painted pansy." Women felt otherwise: after his death from peritonitis at the age of thirty-one, thousands of women took to the streets for his funeral, grieving hysterically. For a number of years, he remained the object of a posthumous cult with intimations of necrophilia.

Valentino's star image is a fascinating condensation of desires and anxieties popularized in the 1920s. His ethnic "otherness" was sublated into an erotic glamor that mobilized both desire for the exotic and fear of the alien.

His sleek and muscular body was adorned and displayed in ways that triggered expressions of anxiety about the nature of manliness. His sexual persona combined aggressiveness and passivity, sadism and suffering, active seduction and objectification in such a way as to make his films polymorphously perverse fantasies for female spectators frustrated by the conditions of their lives and their usual exclusion from active, desiring spectatorship in the cinema. If manliness in the cinema depends on the conventional deployment of a fetishistic gaze and stardom always invites a degree of fetishization, perhaps contradictions are inevitable in the notion of a manly film star. In Valentino's star image, with its visual emphasis on smooth, hard physicality and glamorous costuming, these contradictions coalesce, so that instead of exercising a fetishistic gaze, he became a fetish himself.

RECOMMENDED VIEWING
The Four Horsemen of the Apocalypse (1921), *The Sheik* (1921), *Blood and Sand* (1922), *Monsieur Beaucaire* (1924), *The Eagle* (1925), *The Son of the Sheik* (1926)

FURTHER READING
Anger, Kenneth. *Hollywood Babylon*. London: Arrow Books, 1986.

Hansen, Miriam. *Babel and Babylon: Spectatorship in American Silent Film*. Cambridge, MA, and London: Harvard University Press, 1991.

Rambova, Natacha. *Rudolph Valentino: Recollections*. New York: Jacobson Hodgkinson, 1927.

Studlar, Gaylyn. *This Mad Masquerade: Stardom and Masculinity in the Jazz Age*. New York: Columbia University Press, 1996.

Walker, Alexander. *Rudolph Valentino*. New York: Stein and Day, 1976.

Alison Butler

in the complex postwar readjustments of social roles for both men and women. The twin figures of the war veteran misfit and the woman whose contribution to the workforce is no longer required have been said to inform the maladjusted femininities and masculinities of many films of the late 1940s that otherwise lack explicit sociological

content, including *Leave Her to Heaven* (1945), *Mildred Pierce* (1945), and *Out of the Past* (1947).

Genre (which shares its etymological root with the word "gender") plays a crucial role in constructions of gender in classical Hollywood films. In the musical and the romantic comedy, the genders are represented as

Rudolph Valentino in **Son of the Sheik** *(George Fitzmaurice, 1926).* EVERETT COLLECTION. REPRODUCED BY PERMISSION.

ultimately complementary to each other, whatever initial incompatibilities might exist. In the western, gender divisions tend to be mapped onto archetypal oppositions between civilization and wilderness, posing a dilemma for the male hero, while the female characters are one-dimensional embodiments of the virtues and shortcomings of civilized society, above all in the stereotypes of the good-hearted saloon girl and the frontier wife and mother. The woman's film is defined by its female protagonist and the "feminine" concerns to which it gives pride of place; men are both extremely important in determining the fate of the heroine and somewhat peripheral to the dramatic interest of the film. Femininity is defined paradoxically in the woman's film, which conveys its undoubtedly conservative morality through cautionary tales of women who break its self-same rules. Thus Bette Davis (1908–1989) in *Jezebel* (1938), Joan Crawford (1904–1977) in *Mildred Pierce*, and Lana Turner (1921–1995) in *Imitation of Life* (1959) offer female spectators a vicarious escape from ordinary, dutiful lives as wives and mothers, while the punitively moralistic endings of the films reinforce the ideological correctness of conventional lives.

The end of the Production Code in the 1960s allowed for more sexualized renditions of established gender roles but did not necessarily give rise to more flexible and varied constructions of gender. The desublimation of Hollywood cinema resulted not only in more complex and adult female characters, like the neurotic prostitute (Jane Fonda) in *Klute* (1971), but also in the notorious sexual violence of *Straw Dogs* (1972). The most extreme transgressions of orthodox gender roles in this period occurred not in the films with liberal social values and realist aesthetics, but in those that engaged most profoundly with fantasy and desire. In *Psycho* (1960), for example, the Hitchcockian motif of the double operates across the gender divide, not only in Norman Bates's identification with his mother but also in the parallels that are established between Norman and Marion Crane. Although for Hitchcock the merging of male and female personalities signifies psychosis and death, *Psycho* nevertheless articulates the mutability of identity and the artificiality of the gendered self. More recently, the *Alien* films (1979, 1986, 1992, 1997) have developed this tradition, giving forceful expression to a wide range of (progressive and regressive) fantasies and anxieties about gender through the figure of Ripley (Sigourney Weaver), the female hero, and her alter ego, the shape-shifting, alien brood mother.

Hollywood constructions of gender have worldwide significance because of the global reach of the US film industry, but they are also part of American national culture. Ideologies such as "Momism" inflect femininity and masculinity in ways unique to US culture. Outside of Hollywood, configurations of gender are shaped by other cultural histories. In Polish cinema, for instance, representations of men and women are influenced by the iconography of the historic struggle for nationhood, in which the purity and selflessness of the mother serves and motivates the heroism of the son. In French cinema, conversely, it has been suggested that one of the most common Oedipal narrative tropes is the father–daughter relationship, in which female subjectivity is centered but also framed by paternal control. The distinctiveness of configurations of gender in national cinemas confirms the importance of conceptualizing gender in film studies within concrete historical and specific cultural terms.

THE GENDERED GAZE

The study of gendered representations in the cinema began in the early 1970s with Molly Haskell's *From Reverence to Rape: the Treatment of Women in the Movies* (1974). Haskell looks at images of women in movies made from the 1920s to the 1970s (the 1980s are included in the second edition), mainly—but not exclusively—in Hollywood. The book's scope is ambitious,

Representations of the feminine (Jennifer Jones and Lillian Gish) in **Duel in the Sun** *(King Vidor, 1946).* EVERETT COLLECTION. REPRODUCED BY PERMISSION.

identifying major themes in American cinema such as "The flight from women and the fight against them in their role as entrappers and civilizers" (p. 61). Haskell's critical method, which maps genres and stars historically, has been questioned subsequently by academic film theorists, although some of her ideas, such as the notion of star images as "two-way mirrors linking the immediate past with the immediate future" (p. 12), are more sophisticated than her detractors might suggest.

The study of images of women was crucial to the development of feminist film culture in the early 1970s but was superseded in the feminist film theory that emerged in the middle of that decade by textual approaches concerned less with the manifest content of films than with the ideological predispositions embedded in their syntax and in the apparatus itself. Drawing on post-structuralism, semiotics, and psychoanalysis, Claire Johnston developed a theory of cinematic representation based on an understanding of film narrative as a mythic system that naturalizes conventional gender relations. Within this system, the figure of woman functions not as a representation of female subjectivity but as the object of male desire. Thus Johnston's remark that "despite the enormous emphasis placed on woman as spectacle in the cinema, woman as woman is largely absent" (p. 26). However, rather than calling for the production of realistic or positive images of women, she argues that the more stylized and unrealistic a film's iconography, the more it de-naturalizes both itself and the ideology it serves. Unlike many feminists in the 1970s, Johnston does not reject popular cinema as a "dream machine" but embraces its contradictory possibilities. In her comments on the films of Dorothy Arzner (1900–1979), one of a very few female directors in the studio system, Johnston lays claim to a reflexive and critical strain within Hollywood cinema.

Working within the same feminist framework, in 1975 Laura Mulvey wrote what is perhaps the most celebrated and contentious essay in the history of film studies, "Visual Pleasure and Narrative Cinema." Mulvey's essay is also concerned with Hollywood but concentrates on looking at relations as they are systematized by mainstream conventions. In mainstream cinema, Mulvey contends, a gendered division of labor allies the male hero with the movement of the narrative and the female figure with its spectacle. The cinematic apparatus aligns the gaze of the spectator with that of the camera, and editing conventions subsume the look of the camera into that of the protagonist. This system of looks assumes narcissistic identification with the male protagonist of the narrative and voyeuristic enjoyment of the female object of the gaze. This enjoyment is, however, ambivalent, because of the castration anxiety engendered by the sight of the woman. The two forms of pleasure associated with the female image are also defenses against this threat: sadism, which acknowledges sexual difference and takes pleasure in investigating woman's guilt, and fetishism, which disavows sexual difference and worships woman (or a particular body part or item of clothing) as phallic substitute. Mulvey concludes her essay with a radical attack on the pleasures of mainstream cinema and calls for a cinema of "passionate detachment" in terms that strongly evoke the materialist avant-garde and the political counter-cinema of the 1970s. This analysis has been revisited and modified by many theorists and historians, including, on several occasions, Mulvey herself, and from this debate film studies has developed a complex understanding of cinema as a social technology of gender.

The initial emphasis on femininity in the study of gender in cinema clearly resulted from the political impulse to identify and work against gender inequalities. However, as Steve Neale and a number of other critics have argued, it is also important to analyze cinematic masculinities in order to better understand not only how these function to reinforce normative gender relations but also how they may transgress or destabilize them and in what ways they may be subject to transformation. Neale finds numerous instances in mainstream cinema of the male body functioning as visually pleasurable spectacle, but he argues that these images are encoded so as to disavow their eroticism—for instance, in shoot-outs in westerns or in fight sequences in epics. Rather than disputing Mulvey's account of gendered looking relations in mainstream cinema, Neale confirms it but points out the high degree of contradiction within an apparently normative system. Peter Lehman argues more trenchantly that in the proliferation of critical discourse on sexual representations of the female body and the relative paucity (until the 1990s) of critical discourse on sexual representations of the male body, film studies actually replicated the sexual ideology it aimed to deconstruct.

Scholarship on masculinity in films has clustered around a number of themes, including the idea of a crisis in masculinity during the postwar period and after, the fine line between homosociality and homosexuality, and the effects on male subjectivity of psychopathologies, such as hysteria and masochism. The notion of masquerade, initially introduced into feminist film theory by Claire Johnston and Mary Ann Doane, and developed in relation to Judith Butler's theorization of gender performativity, has been applied to cinematic masculinities by film theorists. Male masquerade is a notion with interesting implications, destabilizing hegemonic masculinity and effectively rendering all gender identities and relationships relational and contingent. The notion of male masquerade has been taken up most productively in historical work, such as Gaylyn Studlar's study of male stars of the silent era, which relates their performances of masculinity to specific cultural manifestations of the gender ideology of the times, ranging from the idealized masculinity of Douglas Fairbanks (1883–1939), contextualized in the movement to reform "boy culture" and resist the perceived threat of feminization, to the transgressive appeal of Lon Chaney (1883–1930), whose association with the grotesque and the liminal grounded his popularity with male fans.

Unlike the feminist criticism of the 1970s and 1980s, scholarship on masculinity in cinema has tended to focus on highly specific, often historical, examples rather than on developing a general theory, partly because of the prevailing fashion for historical rather than theoretical inquiry in film studies since the early 1990s, but also because it lacks the political impetus that feminist theory derived from the women's movement. Against the backdrop of declining feminism and resurgent, retro-styled masculinity in postmodern popular culture, there is a risk that critical discourses on masculinity in the cinema will lapse, unintentionally or otherwise, into conservatism and nostalgia. This risk is confronted directly and effectively by Sharon Willis's work on race and gender in contemporary Hollywood film, especially her essay on Quentin Tarantino (b. 1963), which uses a psychoanalytic framework to argue that his admiring imitation of African American masculinity is inflected by the conflict played out in his films between Oedipal structures (borrowed style, aging male stars) and ferocious preoedipal impulses (relentless bathroom references, anal rape). Tarantino's postmodern recycling of popular cultural masculinity, Willis notes, is self-consciously multicultural but inflected by regressive fantasies: his sense of the past from which he takes his reference points is nostalgic and private rather than historical and shared. Tarantino's films stand as a salutary reminder that irony, pastiche, and sexual transgression are not in themselves guarantees of a progressive or transformative critique of gender identities and relations.

TRANSGENDER IDENTIFICATIONS AND LOOKS

Until the late 1980s, theories of gendered spectatorship were characterized by a strong demarcation between the genders; transgender identification, when it was mentioned as a possibility, was understood as an imposition of patriarchal ideology or, at best, a tactic by which the female spectator might accommodate herself within the binary system of gendered looking without disturbing the hierarchical relationship between its basic terms. However, studies of stars and genres that seem to appeal to spectators across gender lines have enabled critics to develop complex models of cinematic identification that are more complex, fractured, and mutable.

Miriam Hansen's study of the massive popularity of Rudolph Valentino (1895–1926) among women concludes that the sexual ambiguity that became central to his image offered a space of resistance and rebellion to a particular group of female spectators caught up in the social and ideological contradictions of New Womanhood and the particular contradictions of Hollywood in an era in which female audiences were being recruited to the cinema as passive witnesses to their own subordination. In his films and in the star discourse around him, Valentino functioned as the focal point of a remarkably fluid field of sexual possibilities—a public fantasy figure whose constant shifts between sadism and masochism, potency and impotence, heterosexuality and homosexuality, femininity and masculinity, subjectivity and objectification allowed for complex and multiple permutations of desire and identification. The "Valentino syndrome," according to Hansen, is an example of a female subculture that, although distorted by consumerism, gave temporary expression to female desire and even a kind of female fetishism.

Transgender identification is even more central to the hypothesis offered by Carol J. Clover in her study of horror films made since the late 1970s. Overturning the common-sense view that horror films in which female characters are terrorized by male killers encourages male spectators to take sadistic pleasure in violence against women, Clover argues that the predominantly adolescent male audience of slasher films actually identifies with the female victim-hero, or "Final Girl," as Clover calls her, who after a terrifying ordeal, eventually overcomes the villain. Clover observes that both of the principal characters in the genre may be ambiguously gendered—the killer taking on aspects of a monstrous phallic femininity, for example, while the Final Girl is often a tomboy. Clover distinguishes between the actual gender of the characters and their figurative gender—that is, the ways

their significant attributes can be correlated to gendered subject positions. On this basis, she argues that the Final Girl is figuratively a boy whose suffering allows the majority audience to explore castration anxiety within the relative safety of vicariousness. Clover is reluctant to make any claims for the progressiveness of horror films on the basis of these insights, but her approach does highlight the mobility of cinematic identification and the permeability of the boundary between genders.

Yvonne Tasker argues that in the 1980s masculinity became more visible, a marked category in American action cinema signified by the "built" body created by the performer rather than by nature. The knowing performance of masculinity by the built male star enacts but also questions and parodies a previously naturalized gender stereotype. Moreover, the performance of masculinity is not the automatic prerogative of biological males. Tasker coins the term "musculinity" to describe the body type associated with the action hero, regardless of actual gender, and discusses the ways in which female bodies take on masculine functions in recent action cinema, as well as the ways in which male characters are sometimes reinscribed as feminine. Tasker concludes her study with a discussion of the films of Kathryn Bigelow (b. 1951), including *Blue Steel* (1990), a psychological thriller that consciously and critically explores the role of women in action cinema. *Blue Steel* uses cross-dressing rather than muscles to indicate the female hero's assumption of certain masculine functions while problematizing her relationship to these functions: Megan Turner (Jamie Lee Curtis) joins the police department in order to share in its patriarchal authority, but when the phallic power of her gun attracts a psychotic soul mate, she finds herself alone and under suspicion. Through this exploration of the antagonistic relationship between the female hero and patriarchal law, Bigelow constructs an allegory of the dilemma with which action cinema confronts both the female spectator and the feminist director. A noticeable difference between *Blue Steel* and the alternative feminist cinema of the 1970s is that rather than rejecting the idea of a woman acting like a man, the film simply points out that this is not institutionally sanctioned behavior.

Cross-dressing is a recurrent trope in both the women's films and the feminist theory of the 1990s, making the composite figure of the transsexual or the woman who passes for a man an emblem of social and sexual change for feminism as well as for queer cultural politics. In a short contribution to a debate about *Boys Don't Cry* (Kimberly Pierce, 1999) in the British journal *Screen*, Judith Halberstam suggests that the film is significant because, in a brief sequence, it requires the spectator to adopt a transgender gaze. The film is a fictionalized account of the life and death of Brandon Teena (Hilary Swank), a girl who passed for a boy and was raped and

KATHRYN BIGELOW
b. San Carlos, California, 27 November 1951

Among women directors, Kathryn Bigelow is exceptional for her acceptance by critics and audiences as an *auteur* and for the sustained and intelligent way she has engaged with traditionally "male" action genres. She trained as a painter at the San Francisco Art Institute and through the Whitney Museum's Independent Study Program before going on to study film at Columbia University, where she encountered critics Andrew Sarris and Peter Wollen. Her work has often been described as "painterly" for its stylish and controlled visual composition, but this is misleading praise insofar as it overlooks the equally controlled complexity of her well-crafted stories. Her first film, the experimental short *The Set-Up* (1978), deconstructs screen violence and established concerns she has pursued in her feature films. Like a number of female directors, Bigelow began her career in independent film in the 1980s, crossing over to Hollywood in the 1990s.

Bigelow's first feature, *The Loveless* (1982), co-written and co-directed by Monty Montgomery, is a revisionist biker movie that pays homage to the iconography of *The Wild One* (1954). The film's slow pace and formal style, characterized by long takes with a static camera, introduce a meditative distance on the subject matter. Its treatment of female characters suggests a nascent interest in exploring the place of women in a "male" genre. *Near Dark* (1987) is a generic hybrid—a vampire western in which the sympathetic outlaws are again subcultural outsiders, with the main female character a point of articulation for a complex clashing and blending of the generic codes of the western and the vampire film. *Blue Steel* (1990) is Bigelow's most explicitly feminist film, a psychological thriller that explores the position of the female hero in the action film. The ambivalence of Bigelow's engagement with action cinema is less pronounced in *Point Break* (1991), perhaps because of the film's emphasis on its male characters, although it does foreground the genre's submerged homoeroticism. A critical attitude to screen violence re-emerges in the neo-noir *Strange Days* (1995),

in which the invention of a virtual reality device for recording and replaying sense impressions gives rise to an underground economy dealing in extreme experiences, which are inevitably violent, sexual, or both. The central male character is made to experience sexual violence from the perspective of both perpetrator and victim, undergoing a transgender identification in the process, but as an allegory of voyeurism, *Strange Days* is ultimately unclear.

After a five-year break from directing for the cinema, Bigelow returned with *The Weight of Water* (2000), a surprising feminine thriller that was neither a critical nor a box-office success, and *K-19: The Widowmaker* (2002), a return to action, spectacle, and masculinity. Although the career difficulties that Bigelow has encountered since *Strange Days* are by no means entirely due to her situation as a woman director, the material with which she has worked most successfully emerged from a particular convergence of art, feminism, and cinema, and these may not adapt well to changed times.

RECOMMENDED VIEWING
Near Dark (1987), *Blue Steel* (1990), *Point Break* (1991), *Strange Days* (1995)

FURTHER READING
Grant, Barry Keith. " 'Man's Favorite Sport'?: The Action Films of Kathryn Bigelow." In *Action and Adventure Cinema*, edited by Yvonne Tasker, New York and London: Routledge, 2004: 371–384.

Islam, Needeya. " 'I Wanted to Shoot People'—Genre, Gender and Action in the Films of Kathryn Bigelow." In *Kiss Me Deadly: Feminism and Cinema for the Moment*, edited by Laleen Jayamanne, Sydney, AU: Power Institute of the Arts, 1995: 91–125.

Lane, Christina. *Feminist Hollywood from* Born in Flames *to* Point Break. Detroit, MI: Wayne State University Press, 2000: 99–123.

Redmond, Sean, and Deborah Jermyn, eds. *The Cinema of Kathryn Bigelow: Hollywood Transgressor*. London: Wallflower Press, 2003.

Alison Butler

Kathryn Bigelow at the time of **Point Break** *(1991).*
EVERETT COLLECTION. REPRODUCED BY PERMISSION.

murdered when his/her biological sex was discovered. The film presents Brandon's gender in an interesting way, showing the spectator right at the beginning how Brandon constructs his masculinity through costume and performance. Most spectators nevertheless suspend disbelief in Brandon's masculinity and, like his girlfriend Lana (Chloe Sevigny), accept him at face value for much of the film's duration. Knowledge and belief are thus made issues within the film's diegesis and for the audience, coming to a crisis in the sequence in which Brandon's attackers strip him naked in front of his friends. Lana refuses to look at Brandon's genitals, while Brandon escapes into fantasy in what Halberstam takes to be a representation of an "out of body" experience: he sees himself, fully clothed, amongst the onlookers, gazing at his naked body. The transgender gaze, Halberstam suggests, is a divided look, split between a self that is castrated and a self that is not. The deployment of a transgender gaze in conjunction with an empowered female gaze, according to Halberstam, establishes the authenticity of Brandon's masculinity, at least until the film's conclusion, when, Halberstam argues, Lana's acceptance of Brandon as a woman reestablishes normative gender conventions within a humanist perspective.

Transgender identification in the cinema is not a new phenomenon, but its occurrence in the context of the overt and positive representation of a transgender subject is, indicating that significant changes in the social organization and cinematic representation of gender have taken place. These changes, however, have not affected all aspects of society equally, as a glance at current statistics on the employment of women in the film industry shows.

In early cinema, before the production of film became a vertically integrated industry, women directors were common. Almost all of their careers ended with the transition to sound, which required massive financial backing and resulted in a reorganization of the film industry that closed down many of the small companies in which women directors worked. Between the late 1920s and the late 1970s, only a handful of women directors worked in Hollywood. With the impact of the women's movement, a number of female directors emerged through avant-garde and independent filmmaking, but most of them have had difficult careers, and their presence has not greatly altered the gender balance or macho character of the film industry (although it is interesting to note that in the last two decades, women have been comparatively successful as producers). In 2004, women comprised only 5 percent of all directors working on the top-grossing 250 Hollywood films (the figure rises to a still low 16 percent if executive producers, producers, writers, cinematographers, and editors are taken into account). Internationally, film is a male-dominated industry, although there are two countries with larger numbers of women directors: France and Iran. It is perhaps significant that both of these nations treat cinema as an art as well as a business, offering state support to filmmaking that is culturally distinctive in style and concerns. The slowness of change in gendered employment patterns in the film industry, compared to the relative speed with which the impact of feminism has been assimilated at the level of the cinematic image, shows how complex and uneven social and ideological changes can be.

SEE ALSO *Feminism; Gay, Lesbian, and Queer Cinema; Sexuality*

FURTHER READING

Butler, Judith. *Gender Trouble.* New York: Routledge, 1990.

Clover, Carol J. *Men, Women and Chainsaws.* Princeton, NJ: Princeton University Press, 1993.

De Beauvoir, Simone. *The Second Sex.* London: Jonathan Cape, 1953.

Fausto-Sterling, Anne. "The Five Sexes: Why Male and Female are not Enough." *The Sciences* 33, no. 2 (1993): 20–24.

Kathryn Bigelow's* Strange Days *(1995) with Angela Bassett and Ralph Fiennes questions assumptions about gender.
EVERETT COLLECTION. REPRODUCED BY PERMISSION.

Halberstam, Judith. "The Transgender Gaze in *Boys Don't Cry*." *Screen* 42, no. 3 (2001): 294–298.

Hansen, Miriam. *Babel and Babylon: Spectatorship in American Silent Film*. Cambridge, MA, and London: Harvard University Press, 1991.

Haskell, Molly. *From Reverence to Rape: The Treatment of Women in the Movies*. 2nd ed. Chicago: University of Chicago Press, 1987 [1974].

Johnston, Claire. "Women's Cinema as Counter Cinema." In *Notes on Women's Cinema*, edited by Claire Johnston, London: Society for Education in Film and Television, 1973.

Lehman, Peter. *Running Scared: Masculinity and the Representation of the Male Body*. Philadelphia, PA: Temple University Press, 1993.

Mulvey, Laura. *Visual and Other Pleasures*. Bloomington and Indianapolis: Indiana University Press, 1989.

Neale, Steve. "Masculinity as Spectacle." *Screen* 24, no. 6 (1983): 2–16.

Rubin, Gayle. "The Traffic in Women: Notes on the Political Economy of Sex." In *Toward an Anthropology of Women*, edited by Rayna Rapp Reiter. New York: Monthly Review, 1975.

Studlar, Gaylyn. *This Mad Masquerade: Stardom and Masculinity in the Jazz Age*. New York: Columbia University Press, 1996.

Tasker, Yvonne. *Spectacular Bodies: Gender, Genre and the Action Cinema*. London and New York: Routledge, 1993.

Willis, Sharon. *High Contrast: Race and Gender in Contemporary Hollywood Film*. Durham, NC, and London: Duke University Press, 1997.

Alison Butler

GENRE

———————————————

Genres are categories of kinds or types of artistic or cultural artifacts with certain elements in common. In film, common generic elements include subject matter, theme, narrative and stylistic conventions, character types, plots, and iconography. In film studies, the term serves simultaneously as: (1) An industrial approach, in which production, especially during the Hollywood studio era (1920s–1950s), is standardized, and marketing is geared toward concept labeling and packaging; (2) A consumer index, providing audiences with a sense of the kind of pleasures to be expected from a given film; and (3) A critical concept, a tool for theorizing relations between films and groups of films and for understanding the complex relationship between popular cinema and popular culture, and for mapping out a taxonomy of popular film.

Genres preceded cinema but were fundamental to it. The western, for example, was already established in literature before the invention of film, while the musical took much from preexisting theatrical forms. Classical literary theory distinguished differences between literature and popular writing and assumed judgments based on underlying assumptions of aesthetic value. Popular art, including film, is formulaic, and it has often been similarly criticized for lacking originality. However, genre theorist John Cawelti suggests that all art be thought of as existing on a continuum between invention and convention—a perspective that allows for a greater appreciation and understanding of genre texts and how they work.

Because genre movies are collaborative efforts that require the work of many individuals, they have been commonly understood as particularly good barometers of cultural attitudes, values, and trends. This is true not only

of individual genre movies, but also of the changing patterns and popularity of different genres and of the shifting relationships between them. For whether they are set in the past or in the future, on the mean streets of contemporary New York City or long ago in a galaxy far away, genre movies always are about the time and place in which they are made.

ELEMENTS OF GENRE

Fundamental to defining any genre is the question of corpus, of what films in fact constitute its history. In *Theories of Film* (1974), Andrew Tudor identifies a major problem of genre definition, which he terms "the empiricist dilemma," whereby a group of films are preselected for generic analysis to determine their common elements, although their common elements should be identified only after they have been analyzed. Tudor's pragmatic solution to this problem of definition is to rely on what he calls a "common cultural consensus," that is, to analyze works that almost everyone would agree belong to a particular genre and generalize out from there. This method is acceptable, he concludes, because "Genre is what we collectively believe it to be" (p. 139).

Nevertheless, while various genres have been established by common cultural consensus, a further problem is that different genres are designated according to different criteria. Such genres as the crime film, science fiction, and the western are defined by setting and narrative content. However, horror, pornography, and comedy are defined or conceived around the intended emotional affect of the film upon the viewer. Linda Williams has referred to horror, melodrama, and pornography as "body genres" because of the strong physical response—fear, tears, and sexual arousal, respectively—elicited by each. The extent to which films of these genres produce the intended response in viewers is commonly used as a determining factor in judging how good they are. Ultimately, whatever criteria one uses to establish a genre should allow for a productive discussion of the stylistic and thematic similarities among a group of films, and definitions should be flexible enough to allow for change.

In any art form or medium, conventions are frequently used stylistic techniques or narrative devices typical of (but not necessarily unique to) particular generic traditions. Bits of dialogue, musical figures, or styles and patterns of *mise-en-scène* are all aspects of movies that, repeated from film to film within a genre, become established as conventions. Conventions function as an implied agreement between makers and consumers to accept certain artificialities in specific contexts. In musicals the narrative halts for the production numbers, wherein characters break into song and dance; often the characters perform for the camera (rather than for an audience within the film) and are accompanied by off-screen music that seems suddenly to materialize from nowhere. Conventions also include aspects of style associated with particular genres. For example, melodrama is characterized by an excessively stylized *mise-en-scène*, while film noir commonly employs low-key lighting. Mainstream cinema also features numerous aural conventions on the soundtrack involving dialogue, music, and sound effects. Film scoring in all genres typically features Wagnerian leitmotifs associated with particular characters or places and is commonly used to enhance a desired emotional effect in support of the story. Different types of musical accompaniment are conventional in particular genres: sweeping strings are often used in romantic melodramas, for example, while electronic music or the theremin is used in science fiction for its futuristic connotations.

The familiarity of conventions allows both for parody and subversive potential. Parody is possible only when conventions are known to audiences. Much of the humor of Mel Brooks's (b. 1926) parodies depends upon viewers being familiar with specific genre films. In *Young Frankenstein* (1974), for example, when the monster and the little girl he meets have tossed all their flowers in the lake and she innocently asks what to throw in now, the monster looks at the camera, as if to ask the viewer to remember that in the original *Frankenstein* (1931) he stupidly drowned the girl, thinking she too would float. As well, conventions also can be used by filmmakers for disturbing purposes precisely because viewers expect them. George Romero (b. 1940) undermines numerous conventions of the classic horror film in *Night of the Living Dead* (1968), which is one of the main reasons

the film had such a powerful effect on audiences when first released.

The setting, the space and time when and where a film's story takes place, is more a defining quality of some genres than of others. Musicals, for instance, can take place anywhere, from the actual docks and streets of New York City in *On the Town* (1949) and *West Side Story* (1961) to the supernatural village in *Brigadoon* (1954). Romantic comedies and dramas, like some science fiction, may span different eras, as in *Somewhere in Time* (1980) and *Kate and Leopold* (2001). Horror movies often use isolated and rural settings and old dark houses with mysterious basements for psychological effect, but films such as *Rosemary's Baby* (1968) and *Dark Water* (2005) work by violating convention and setting their stories in contemporary and familiar locales rather than in exoticized foreign spaces like Transylvania. By contrast, the western by definition is temporally restricted to the period of the Wild West (approximately from 1865 to 1890) and geographically to the American frontier (broadly, between the Mississippi River and the west coast). Movies that change this setting to the present, such as *Lonely are the Brave* (1962) and *Hud* (1963) or "easterns" like *Drums along the Mohawk* (1939) and *The Last of the Mohicans* (1936, 1992), are considered exceptions to the norm; they are westerns for some viewers but not for others. Yet movies such as *Coogan's Bluff* (1968) and *Crocodile Dundee II* (1988), which import elements of the western into the contemporary urban East, are generally not thought of as westerns.

Character types are also important to genre films. Discussing characters in literature, novelist E. M. Forster distinguished two kinds of fictional characters: flat and round. Flat characters, which also may be "types" or "caricatures," are built around one idea or quality; it is only as other attributes (that is, "depth") are added that characters begin "to curve toward the round" (*Aspects of the Novel*, p. 67). In genre movies, characters are more often recognizable types rather than psychologically complex characters, as with black hats and white hats in the western, although they can be rounded as well. The femme fatale is a conventional character in film noir, like the comic sidekick, the schoolmarm, and the gunfighter in the western. Ethnic characters are often stereotyped as flat characters in genre movies: the Italian mobster, the black drug dealer, the Arab terrorist, the cross-section of soldiers in the war film's platoon. Flat characters are usually considered a failure in works that aspire to originality, but in genre works, flat characters are not necessarily a flaw because of their shorthand efficiency. In genre movies, character types often provide similar kinds of actions and purposes within the story.

EDWARD G. ROBINSON
b. Emmanuel Goldenberg, Bucharest, Romania, 12 December 1893, d. 26 January 1973

Of short stature and lacking the conventional handsome look of leading men, Edward G. Robinson nevertheless was one of the great male stars of the studio era. Along with James Cagney and Humphrey Bogart, he defined Hollywood's image of the tough guy for Depression-era audiences. Beginning his acting career in the theater, Robinson made his film debut in 1923 at age thirty in *The Bright Shawl* (1923). He became famous in 1931 in the archetypal gangster film *Little Caesar*, portraying the criminal Enrico Caesar Bandello, a hoodlum who rises to the top and then makes his inevitable fall.

With the success of *Little Caesar*, Robinson went on to play a string of criminal characters in a series of Warner Bros. films through the 1930s. Robinson sought to escape genre typecasting and expand his range, playing such roles as the title character in the biopic *Dr. Erlich's Magic Bullet* (1940), about the nineteenth-century scientist who developed a cure for syphilis, and the steadfast and paternal insurance agent Barton Keyes in the classic film noir, *Double Indemnity* (1944). However, a number of these subsequent roles clearly depended on Robinson's established gangster persona, such as the gruff ship's captain Larson in the adventure film *The Sea Wolf* (1941) and the cruel Dathan in *The Ten Commandments* (1956).

In John Ford's *The Whole Town's Talking* (1935), Robinson played a dual role as a gangster boss and a meek, law-abiding citizen, at once providing the pleasure of his established image as a criminal and exploiting his star appeal by making him a sympathetic protagonist with whom the audience could comfortably identify. Similarly, in Fritz Lang's masterful film noir *Scarlet Street* (1945), Robinson plays a mild-mannered clerk and henpecked husband who is driven to robbery, adultery, and finally murder. The film periodically references Robinson's gangster persona, as in the opening dinner party scene, which initially looks like a similar scene in *Little Caesar*;

but it then reveals his character, Christopher Cross, as a shy and repressed cashier who handles other people's money. Only later does he become a criminal, ironically making the initial mistaken impression, based on genre expectations, in fact true.

In the 1950s Robinson experienced a difficult divorce that forced him to sell much of his prized art collection. He was also called to testify before the House Un-American Activities Committee but was ultimately exonerated of Communist Party affiliation. Despite these troubles, he continued to make credible crime dramas throughout the decade. His subsequent career was irregular, but his final appearance in the science-fiction film *Soylent Green* (1973) allowed him to die onscreen in a fitting finale to one of Hollywood's most distinguished careers.

RECOMMENDED VIEWING

Little Caesar (1931), *The Whole Town's Talking* (1935), *Bullets or Ballots* (1936), *Confessions of a Nazi Spy* (1939), *Brother Orchid* (1940), *The Sea Wolf* (1941), *Double Indemnity* (1944), *The Woman in the Window* (1945), *Scarlet Street* (1945), *Key Largo* (1948), *The Cincinnati Kid* (1965), *Soylent Green* (1973)

FURTHER READING

Beck, Robert S. *The Edward G. Robinson Encyclopedia.* Jefferson, NC: McFarland, 2002.

Gansberg, Alan L. *Little Caesar: An Autobiography of Edward G. Robinson.* London: New English Library, 1983.

Hirsch, Foster. *Edward G. Robinson.* New York: Pyramid Books, 1975.

Parish, James Robert, and Alvin H. Marill. *The Cinema of Edward G. Robinson.* South Brunswick, NJ: A. S. Barnes, 1972.

Robinson, Edward G. *All My Yesterdays: An Autobiography.* New York: Hawthorn Books, 1973.

Barry Keith Grant

Of course, characters are embodied by actors, all of whom have distinct physical characteristics. The hard-boiled detective, Philip Marlowe, is different as played by Dick Powell (*Murder, My Sweet*, 1944), Humphrey Bogart (*The Big Sleep*, 1946), or Elliott Gould (*The*

Long Goodbye, 1973). Some actors (for example, Paul Muni [1895–1967], Gary Oldman [b. 1958], and Johnny Depp [b. 1963]) are known for chameleon-like performances, but many, whether they are featured stars or supporting actors, often play variations of a type. For

Edward G. Robinson in the mid-1930s. EVERETT COLLECTION. REPRODUCED BY PERMISSION.

this reason, they are often cast in similar films within the same genre and become associated with it. Fred Astaire (1899–1987) is always thought of in relation to the musical, Cary Grant (1904–1986) with screwball comedy, and of course John Wayne (1907–1979) with the western, even though all these actors also appeared in other kinds of films. Clint Eastwood's (b. 1930) strong association with the western lent such subsequent non-western roles as the tough detective Harry Callahan in *Dirty Harry* (1971) and its sequels added mythic depth.

Character actors contribute to the look of particular genres, populating the worlds of genre movies and becoming part of their iconography. Often they are known to viewers as vaguely familiar faces rather than by name. Richard Jaeckel (1926–1997), Jack Elam (1918–2003), Chill Wills (1903–1978), Paul Fix (1901–1983), and Slim Pickens (1919–1983) all appeared in countless westerns, so when they are in the same cast and many of them die in *Pat Garrett and Billy the Kid* (Sam Peckinpah, 1973), the film may be read as being as much about the death of the genre as it is a story about particular characters. Stars and genres reinforce each other, some actors offering definitive performances that forever associate them with a particular role and

genre, as was the case with Bela Lugosi's (1882–1956) portrayal of Dracula. Actors who succeed at playing a certain generic type are often trapped by such roles, fated to be typecast as similar characters. On the other hand, while Dick Powell (1904–1963) began as a romantic (juvenile) lead in several Warner Bros. musicals in the early 1930s, he managed to reshape his image entirely in the following decade, playing a tough guy in such noirs as *Murder, My Sweet, Cornered* (1945) and *Pitfall* (1948).

Because actors may become typecast, they can be cast in genre movies against type, as in the case of William Holden (1918–1981) playing the leader of *The Wild Bunch* (1969) or Tom Cruise (b. 1962) as a hit man in *Collateral* (2004). In the famous opening of *C'era una volta il West* (*Once Upon a Time in the West*, Sergio Leone, 1968), a Mexican family enjoying a pleasant picnic meal in front of its hacienda is suddenly and brutally gunned down by unseen assailants. In a long take, the killers ride in from the distance, and eventually we are able to discern that the leader is a grim-faced, blue-eyed Henry Fonda (1905–1982)—the same soft-spoken face that was Abraham Lincoln in *Young Mr. Lincoln* (1939) and Tom Joad in *The Grapes of Wrath* (1940). The moment has a greater emotional impact than it would if the actor had been a familiar Hollywood heavy.

Conventions, settings, and characters are part of a genre's iconography. Icons are second-order symbols, in that their symbolic meaning is not necessarily a connection established within the individual text, but is already symbolic because of their use across a number of similar previous texts. Ed Buscombe concentrates on the iconography of the western in drawing a distinction between a film's inner and outer forms. For Buscombe, inner form refers to a film's themes, while outer form refers to the various objects that are to be found repeatedly in genre movies—in the western, for example, horses, wagons, buildings, clothes, and weapons. The cowboy who dresses all in black and wears two guns, holster tied to either thigh, is invariably a villainous gunfighter. Just as religious icons are always already infused with symbolic meaning, so is the iconography of genre films. In a horror film, when the hero wards off the vampire with a crucifix, religious iconography works in support of film iconography: symbolically, such scenes suggest that the traditional values embodied in Christianity (and, by extension, western culture generally) are stronger than and will defeat whatever threatening values are assigned to the monster in any given vampire film.

Of course, while the icons of genre films may have culturally determined meanings, the interpretation or value attached to them is hardly fixed. Rather, the particulars of their representation in each genre film marks the relation of outer form to inner form and are indicators of the film's attitude and theme. Although a crucifix in a horror film is an icon of Christianity and dominant ideology, the film itself may either critique or endorse that ideology. In the western, the town always represents civilization, but every film will have a different view of that civilization. The town in, say, *The Gunfighter* (1950) has children and domestic spaces, representing the familial stability that the aging gunman can only long for, while in *McCabe and Mrs. Miller* (1971), the town springs up around a muddy, makeshift brothel, suggesting that base desire is at the core of civilization.

Finally, spectators are a crucial element of genre movies, for they address viewers in a particular way. Almost from the beginning, movies have been promoted in the media primarily through their generic affiliations. They signal to prospective viewers the type of story as well as the kind of pleasure they are likely to offer and assist them in choosing which movies or which kind of movie to see. Fans of particular genres comprise communities of readers: fans of horror films, for example, form a distinct subculture, with their own fanzines, memorabilia, websites, and discussion lists. Genre films work by engaging viewers through an implicit contract, encouraging certain expectations on the part of spectators, which are in turn based on viewer familiarity with the conventions. As Robert Warshow observes, the familiarity of viewers with generic convention creates "its own field of reference." In other words, familiarity with a generic field of reference allows spectators to enjoy variations, however slight, in a given film. The act of reading genre films implies active readers who bring their generic knowledge to bear in watching movies. A postmodern horror pastiche like *Scream* (1996) depends upon its viewers being generically literate.

THE CLASSIC STUDIO SYSTEM

For decades Hollywood produced appealing fantasies in an industrial context. Regularized film exhibition developed as a result of the popularity and rapid growth of nickelodeons, the first venues devoted exclusively to cinema exhibition. The steady demand for new films made year-round production schedules necessary and provided the impetus for the development of a factory-based (Fordist) mode of production. In the studio era, all members of cast and crew were workers under contract to the studio, and the different kinds of work—editing, music, script, and so on—were divided into departments.

Within this industrial context, genre movies are dependable products, assembly line products with interchangeable parts. The James Bond series has continued because of the formula—lots of action, fancy gadgets, beautiful women, and colorful villains—despite the changes in directors, writers, and even the actors playing Bond himself. Individual genre films may lift elements from one genre and put them into another, as *The Band Wagon* (1953) incorporates film noir and the detective film into the climactic ballet, "The Girl Hunt." Hybrid genre movies like *Abbott and Costello Meet Frankenstein* (1948) and *Billy the Kid versus Dracula* (1966) mix elements from seemingly disparate genres. More recently, movies like *Freddy vs. Jason* (2003) and *Alien vs. Predator* (2004), both of which are simultaneously hybrids and sequels, show the same process at work despite the end of the studio era. But hybridity has always been characteristic of genre films. *Stagecoach* (1939), one of the most famous and important westerns ever made, was described as a "*Grand Hotel* on wheels" on its release, and it also contains elements of the road movie and disaster film as well. Movies such as *The Thing* (1951), *Alien* (1979), and the movie on which it was in part based, *It, The Terror from Beyond Space* (1958), all combine elements of science fiction and horror, visually turning spaceships and laboratories into the equivalent of haunted houses.

Genre filmmaking thus developed quickly, with producers seeking maximum acceptance at the box office through the repetition and variation of commercially successful formulas. The formulaic qualities of genre films meant that studios could turn them out quickly, and audiences could understand them just as quickly. Genre movies allow for an economy of expression through conventions and iconography. This system of signification, developed over time and with repetition, served well the fast pace of classic narration in films intended to be shown as part of a double feature.

In the studio era, directors were employees, like the other members of a film's cast and crew. Even those few directors who wielded some degree of clout in Hollywood, like Frank Capra (1897–1991) and Alfred Hitchcock (1899–1980), had to work within the parameters of the producing studio's dominant style or genre. Directors, like actors and electricians, rarely had the right to final cut. Yet while some directors floundered against the pressures of the studio system, many in fact flourished, using the rules of genre as convenience rather than constraint, as guidelines from which to deviate or deepen rather than as blueprints to follow. By providing the received framework of genre, Hollywood gave filmmakers a flexible tradition within which to work. Some directors developed their vision within particular genres, such as Sam Fuller (1912–1997) with the war film, John Ford (1894–1973) with the western, and Douglas Sirk (1897–1987) with the melodrama. The auteur approach provided a way of looking at directors' style foregrounded against the background of genre.

Kurt Russell in John Carpenter's **Escape from New York** *(1981), an action film with elements of the western and science-fiction film genres.* EVERETT COLLECTION. REPRODUCED BY PERMISSION.

Despite its constraints, the studio system provided a stable context for filmmakers to work with consistency and to be expressive. As Robin Wood notes in *Howard Hawks* (1968), Hollywood is one of the few historical instances of a true communal art, "a great creative workshop, comparable to Elizabethan London or the Vienna of Mozart, where hundreds of talents have come together to evolve a common language" (p. 9). The justly famous opening scene of *Rio Bravo* (Howard Hawks, 1959) tells us almost everything we need to know about the heroes played by John Wayne and Dean Martin (1917–1995) well before the first word of dialogue is spoken. Director Hawks (1896–1977) uses the conventions of the western to express his sense of professionalism, heroism, and self-respect, which would not have been possible without the established conventions of the genre as his raw material.

MYTH AND HISTORY

Traditionally, the word "myth" refers to a society's shared stories, usually involving Gods and mythic heroes, that explain the nature of the universe and the relation of the individual to it. Such mythic narratives embody and express a society's rituals, institutions, and values. In the twentieth century, genre films, with their repetitions and variations of a few basic plots, were our mass-mediated mythic tales. Comparable to myths, genre movies may be understood as secular stories that seek to address and sometimes seemingly resolve our problems and dilemmas, some specifically historical and others more deeply rooted in our collective psyches. Structural anthropologist Claude Lévi-Strauss (b. 1908) claimed that all cultural myths are structured according to binary pairs of opposite terms. This approach is inviting for the analysis of genre films, which tend to work by reducing complex conflicts to the equivalent of black hats versus white hats. In his influential 1970 study of the western, *Horizons West*, Jim Kitses maps out a series of clear binary oppositions that are all variations of the conflict between wilderness and civilization.

Genre movies are always about the time in which they are made, not set, for entertainment inevitably contains, reflects, and promulgates ideology. It is in this sense of entertainment as ideology that Roland Barthes (1915–1980) conceives of myth. For Barthes, cultural myths endorse the dominant values of the society that produces them as right and natural, while marginalizing and delegitimizing others. In genre movies, as Barthes says of cultural myth generally, the Other becomes monstrous, as in horror films, or exoticized, as in adventure films. In westerns, for example, Indians are either demonized as heathen savages or romanticized as noble savages, but they are rarely treated as rounded characters with their own culture.

From this perspective, genre movies tend to be read as ritualized endorsements of dominant ideology. So the western is not really about a specific period in American history, but the story of Manifest Destiny and the "winning" of the West. The genre thus offers a series of mythic endorsements of American individualism, colonialism, and racism, as well as a justification of westward expansion. The civilization that is advancing into the "wilderness" (itself a mythic term suggesting that no culture existed there until Anglo-American society) is always bourgeois white American society. Similarly, the monstrous Other in horror films tends to be anything that threatens the status quo, while the musical and romantic comedy celebrate heteronormative values through their valorization of the romantic couple.

Still, the complex relation of genre movies to ideology is a matter of debate. On the one hand, genre films are mass-produced fantasies of a culture industry that manipulate us into a false consciousness. From this perspective, their reliance on convention and simplistic plots distract us from awareness of the actual social problems in the real world. Yet it is also true that the existence of highly conventional forms allows for the subtle play of irony, parody, and appropriation. Popular culture does tend to adhere to dominant ideology, although this is not always the case. Many horror films, melodramas, and film noirs, among others, have been shown to question if not subvert accepted values. Pam Cook takes a similar view of B movies and exploitation films, arguing that their production values, less sophisticated than those of mainstream Hollywood movies, are more readily perceived by viewers as representations.

Walter Brennan, John Wayne, and Dean Martin in Howard Hawks's **Rio Bravo** *(1959).* EVERETT COLLECTION. REPRODUCED BY PERMISSION.

Genre movies take such social debates and tensions and cast them into formulaic narratives, condensing them into dramatic conflicts between individual characters and society or heroes and villains. Thomas Schatz observes that "All film genres treat some form of threat—violent or otherwise—to the social order" (Schatz, p. 26). The gangster, the monster, the heroine of screwball comedy all threaten normative society in different ways. Some genre theorists argue that the overriding theme of genre films is some version of the individual in conflict with society, and that this tension represents the ongoing negotiation we all make between desire and restraint (what Freud called "civilization and its discontents"). The extent to which a genre film achieves narrative closure is an important factor in reading its political implications. Closure, usually in the form of an upbeat or happy ending, is—like all conventions—artificial, since life, unlike such stories, continues. For this reason, a lack of closure, suggesting that the lives of the characters carry on after the film ends, is associated more with realist films like *La Grande illusion* (*Grand Illusion*, 1937) and *Ladri di biciclette* (*Bicycle Thieves*, 1948) than with genre movies. Because films with closure leave the viewer with no unanswered questions about the fate of the major characters or the consequences of their actions, they are viewed as providing tidy but unrealistic solutions to real problems. Yet while closure may be provided by a film, it can be ironic, thus undercutting its own pretense at resolution, as some have argued about the psychiatrist's explanation for Norman as an aberrant "case" at the end of *Psycho* (1960).

Genres are neither static nor fixed; they undergo change over time, each new film and cycle adding to the tradition and modifying it. Some critics describe these changes as evolution, others as development, but both terms carry evaluative connotations. Some genre critics accept a general pattern of change that moves from some early formative stage through a classical period of archetypal expression to a more intellectual phase in which conventions are examined and questioned rather than merely presented, and finally to an ironic, self-conscious mode typically expressed by parody. However, generic phases do not fall into convenient chronological and progressive periods, but often overlap significantly. For some, the western evolved from the supposed classicism of *Stagecoach* to the end of the intellectual trail with *The Wild Bunch* just thirty years later and then to Brooks's *Blazing Saddles* (1974), marking the end of the classic western and the beginning of the parody or baroque phase. But the western was already parodied even before this intellectual period in such films as Buster Keaton's *Go West* (1925), *Destry Rides Again* (1932, 1939), and the Marx Brothers's *Go West* (1940). Tag Gallagher argues that there is no evidence that film genres evolve toward greater embellishment and elaboration; he cites, for example, the scene in *Rio Bravo* where a wounded villain's hiding place on the upper floor of the saloon is revealed by blood dripping down, but he points out that the same device was used by John Ford in *The Scarlet Drop* (1918) decades earlier and even then dismissed by critics as "old hat." Gallagher insists instead that even "a superficial glance at film history suggests cyclicism rather than evolution" (Gallagher in Grant, *Film Genre Reader III*, pp. 266–268).

In the 1970s, as Cawelti notes, there were particularly profound changes in American genre movies. Aware of themselves as myth, genre movies of the period responded in four ways: humorous burlesque, nostalgia, demythologization, and reaffirmation. This development was the result in part of the demise of the Hays Office in 1967 and the continuing breakup of the traditional studio system, allowing directors greater freedom in a more disillusioned and cynical era. Films like Francis Ford Coppola's (b. 1939) *The Godfather* (1972) and *Apocalypse Now* (1979); Martin Scorsese's (b. 1942) *Mean Streets* (1973) and *New York, New York* (1977); Robert Altman's (b. 1925) *McCabe and Mrs. Miller*, *The Long Goodbye* (1973), and *Nashville* (1975); and Brian de Palma's (b. 1940) *Sisters* (1973), *Phantom of the Paradise* (1974), and *Obsession* (1976) were genre movies by directors who had grown up watching genre movies on television and studying them in academic film programs. With a more contemporary sensibility, these filmmakers inevitably made genre films that were burdened by an awareness of generic myth. For Cawelti, the changes in the period's genre films were so profound that he wondered whether the traditional film genres had exhausted themselves and hypothesized that "the cultural myths they once embodied are no longer fully adequate to the imaginative needs of our time" (Cawelti in Grant, *Film Genre Reader III*, p. 260).

GENDER AND RACE

Among their conventions, genre movies feature standard ways of representing gender, class, race, and ethnicity. Into the 1980s, genres and genre movies remained almost exclusively the cultural property of a white male consciousness, the center from which any difference regarding race, gender, and sexuality was defined and marginalized. In all the action genres, it was white men who performed heroic deeds and drove the narrative. In every type of action film, women and visible minorities assumed subsidiary and stereotyped roles, serving such narrative functions as helper or comic sidekick for the heroic white male. The hypothetical viewer of Hollywood genre movies traditionally was, like almost all of the filmmakers who made the movies, white, male,

JOHN CARPENTER
b. Carthage, New York, 16 January 1948

John Carpenter is known primarily for his slick action sequences, which have established him as one of Hollywood's most skillful directors of violence and suspense. Working mostly in the horror and science fiction genres, Carpenter also works on the scripts, special effects photography, and electronic music scores for his films.

While a graduate student in film at the University of Southern California, Carpenter made several short films, including *The Resurrection of Bronco Billy*, which won an Academy Award® for Best Short Film in 1970, and, with classmate Dan O'Bannon, *Dark Star*, which he expanded into his first feature in 1974. Shot on a minuscule budget, *Dark Star* offers a blackly comic view of men in space overwhelmed by technology. Carpenter's follow-up, *Assault on Precinct 13* (1976), an audacious blend of Howard Hawks's western *Rio Bravo* (1959) and George Romero's cult horror classic *Night of the Living Dead* (1968), established the director as a promising young auteur. Carpenter's commercial breakthrough came with *Halloween* (1980), which launched a series of sequels (by other directors) and a cycle of similar slasher films. *Halloween* makes deft use of such techniques as the handheld camera and tension between foreground and background in the *mise-en-scène* to generate suspense and fear.

Carpenter works comfortably within genres, as with *Halloween*; but he also sometimes mixes conventions and iconography, as with *Escape from New York* (1981), a science fiction action film; *Big Trouble in Little China* (1986), a comic martial arts fantasy; and *Ghosts of Mars* (2001), a science-fiction horror film. At times Carpenter's action sequences seem to transcend their narrative constraints to become pure cinema. Sequences such as the famous lengthy point-of-view shot that opens *Halloween* and the astronaut's chase of a mischievous alien creature through the ship's elevator shaft in *Dark Star* show Carpenter's undeniable command of action and suspense through rhythm, editing, and use of music.

Thematically, Carpenter's films are concerned with issues of communication and isolation. In *Dark Star*, as the ship's crewmen grow apart through boredom and indifference, outer space becomes a metaphor for the psychological isolation of the crew. The final images of Carpenter's remake of *The Thing* (1982) show the last two surviving men warily sitting opposite each other, separated by the wide-screen composition, their mutual distrust graphically rendered in the image. *They Live* (1988), a science-fiction action film, cleverly offers a critique of mass culture in its story of a blue-collar worker who discovers a pair of sunglasses that allows him to see the subliminal messages, secretly delivered by aliens busily stripping the Earth of natural resources, encouraging political passivity and consumerism in all forms and media of popular culture.

RECOMMENDED VIEWING

Dark Star (1974), *Assault on Precinct 13* (1976), *Halloween* (1978), *The Fog* (1980), *Escape from New York* (1981), *The Thing* (1982), *Christine* (1983), *Starman* (1984), *Big Trouble in Little China* (1986), *Prince of Darkness* (1987), *They Live* (1988)

FURTHER READING

Billson, Anne. *The Thing*. London: British Film Institute, 1997.

Boulenger, Gilles. *John Carpenter: The Prince of Darkness*. Los Angeles: Silman-James Press, 2003.

Conrich, Ian, and David Woods, eds. *The Cinema of John Carpenter: The Technique of Terror*. London and New York: Wallflower Press, 2004.

Cumbow, Robert C. *Order in the Universe: The Films of John Carpenter*. Metuchen, NJ, and London: Scarecrow Press, 1990.

Muir, John Kenneth. *The Films of John Carpenter*. Jefferson, NC: McFarland, 2005.

Barry Keith Grant

and heterosexual. This white masculine perspective was an inextricable part of the genre system, which was built on certain gendered assumptions. Generally, the action genres—adventure, war, gangster, detective, horror, science fiction, and of course, the western—were addressed to a male audience, while musicals and romantic melodramas (also known as "weepies") were marketed as "woman's films." This distinction bespeaks wider patriarchal assumptions about gender difference in the real world.

John Carpenter on the set of **Starman** *(1984).* EVERETT
COLLECTION. REPRODUCED BY PERMISSION.

By the 1990s many genre movies were attempting to
open up genres to more progressive representations of
race and gender, often deliberately acknowledging and
giving voice to groups previously marginalized by mainstream cinema. The film that provided the impetus for
this new generic transformation was *Thelma and Louise*
(1991), about two women who, finding themselves on
the wrong side of the law, lead the police on a chase
through the Southwest. A big hit at the box office,
Thelma and Louise is a generic hybrid of the western,
the buddy film, and the road movie—three genres traditionally regarded as male. After *Thelma and Louise*,
many genre films seemed content merely to borrow its
gender gimmick, simply plugging others into roles traditionally reserved for white men. But in reversing
conventional representations, these films were prone to
fall into the trap of repeating the same objectionable
values. The question of whether female action heroes
such as Sigourney Weaver's Ripley in *Alien* (1979) and
its sequels, Linda Hamilton's Sarah Connor in
Terminator 2: Judgment Day (1991), or the assassins
played by Geena Davis in *The Long Kiss Goodnight*
(1996), Uma Thurman in the *Kill Bill* films (2003,

2004), and the trio of actresses in the *Charlie's Angels*
films (2000, 2003) are progressive, empowering representations of women or merely contain them within a
masculine sensibility has been a matter of considerable
debate.

Race, ethnicity, and nationality are commonly stereotyped in genre films, sometimes together. African
Americans have traditionally been cast in supporting
roles as clearly recognizable types. Except for such subsidiary and subordinate roles as maids, black faces also
were largely absent from Hollywood movies. Issues of
race appeared, safely coded within generic conventions,
particularly in the western, which on the surface relegates
the topic more safely to the nation's past rather than the
present. Asian Americans have been largely absent from
genre movies, as were Latinos until *West Side Story*. Since
the 1990s, generic Arabs have been depicted in action
movies as terrorists, as in *True Lies* (1994), *Executive
Decision* (1996), and *The Siege* (1998). By contrast,
Russians are friendlier in Hollywood movies following
the collapse of the Soviet Union and the end of the cold
war, as in *The Hunt for Red October* (1990) and *Enemy at
the Gates* (2001).

Outside Hollywood, there were separate but parallel
Yiddish and black or "race" cinemas. The height of
Yiddish film came in the 1920s and 1930s, and black
cinema peaked in the 1930s and 1940s. Both were institutionalized forms of cinema, with their own stars, directors, exhibition circuit, and audiences, and both were
organized along generic lines similar to Hollywood. There
were, for example, black melodramas, musicals, and westerns featuring African American stars. Hollywood, too,
tried all-black musicals such as *Hallelujah* (1929), *Cabin
in the Sky* (1943), and *Carmen Jones* (1954) as well as
dramatic films such as *The Green Pastures* (1936). The
practice of segregating casts by race was a reflection of the
segregationist and discriminatory practices of the era in
which they were made.

Encouraged by the success of *Cotton Comes to
Harlem* (1970), a cop film featuring two black detectives
(Godfrey Cambridge and Raymond St. Jacques), a cycle
of blaxploitation films followed. The term blaxploitation
was coined by the trade paper *Variety* to describe these
films, which appeared from the late 1960s through the
mid-1970s. As the civil rights movement gained momentum and became more militant, many black viewers
rejected the more accommodating images of established
black stars like Sidney Poitier (b. 1927) and Harry
Belafonte (b. 1927) and welcomed the newer action
movies with more macho black stars, such as ex-football
Hall of Famer Jim Brown (b. 1936) in films like *Black
Gunn* (1972) and *Slaughter* (1972). Richard Roundtree
(b. 1942) became famous as the suave black detective

John Shaft in *Shaft* (1971), billed as "the new James Bond," as did Ron O'Neal (1937–2004) as *Superfly* (1972). Pam Grier (b. 1949) in *Coffy* (1973) and *Foxy Brown* (1974) and Tamara Dobson (b. 1947) in *Cleopatra Jones* (1973) applied the same formula to female characters. The question of the extent to which blaxploitation was politically progressive has been a matter of debate, but the films did pave the way for a cycle of "salt-and-pepper" buddy movies beginning with *48 Hrs.* (1982) and the wider acceptance of black action stars such as Wesley Snipes (b. 1962) and Denzel Washington (b. 1954).

Although black cowboys existed on the frontier, their history has been suppressed by the predominately white iconography of the western. One of the most popular genres of race films was the western, with the first possibly being *The Trooper of Troop K* (1917), with black star Noble Johnson (1881–1978). In the late 1930s Herb Jeffries (b. 1911) appeared in a series of independently produced all-black musical westerns including *The Bronze Buckaroo* (1939) and *Harlem Rides the Range* (1939). In 1960, Ford's *Sergeant Rutledge* starred Woody Strode (1914–1994) as a cavalry soldier being court-martialed because of his race. During the blaxploitation era several westerns were made, the most notable being *Buck and the Preacher* (1972), directed by Sidney Poitier, about white bounty hunters looking to return former slaves to work on southern plantations after the defeat of the South in the Civil War. Starring Harry Belafonte along with Poitier, *Buck and the Preacher* employed many conventions of the genre while foregrounding issues of race relations. But for the most part, blacks had been absent from the Hollywood western—an absence so complete that it can serve as one of the major jokes in *Blazing Saddles*, which stars African American actor Cleavon Little (1939–1992) as a black Bart with his Gucchi saddlebags. *Posse* (Mario Van Peebles, 1993) overtly challenged this mythic erasure. It opens with a black man speaking directly to the camera, presenting the entire story in flashback, a framing device borrowed from *Little Big Man* (1970), an earlier revisionist western, here featuring Strode, an iconic actor who had appeared in several of Ford's westerns, including *Sergeant Rutledge*.

NATIONAL CINEMA AND GENRE

Although a good deal of contemporary theoretical work has questioned hegemonic concepts of the nation, and hence of the idea of national cinema, the genre approach is useful for approaching the idea of national cinema generally as well as for conceptualizing the contours of specific national cinemas. As Ella Shohat and Robert Stam point out, the movie audience is a "provisional 'nation' forged by spectatorship" (p. 155), and genre audiences form what Altman describes as "constellated" communities—groups of individuals who "cohere only through repeated acts of imagination"—in the context of cinema, an imagined connection among geographically dispersed viewers who share similar spectatorial pleasures and generic knowledge (*Altman*, pp. 161–162).

In developing a distinctive and vital national cinema, most countries have been forced to confront the global cultural domination of American film in some way. Hollywood, especially since the end of World War II, has successfully dominated numerous foreign film markets on every continent. Inevitably, then, national cinemas must find space in the market, both at the local and international level, in the context of Hollywood. Because Hollywood cinema is overwhelmingly a cinema of genre films, this means, in effect, working within the genre system. The frame of genre allows filmmakers the multiple benefits of working in forms familiar to audiences both at home and abroad, and thus it offers more lucrative potential to producers for foreign distribution. Distribution in other countries is particularly important in nations where the population is insufficient to sustain an indigenous film industry, for it provides the only hope for films to return a profit. At the same time, however, accepting generic forms from Hollywood also suggests the loss of any distinctive national features that might be expressed in cinema. This dilemma has informed the discourse of national cinema in many countries, especially Australia, Canada, Great Britain, and New Zealand, all of which share the English language with Hollywood.

Filmmakers from around the world have responded to the domination of American film by adopting Hollywood genres and "indigenizing" or reworking them according to their own cultural sensibility. Examples are the Italian "spaghetti western" or Hong Kong martial arts films. Other national cinemas have created their own genres. For example, German cinema in the 1920s and 1930s developed a distinctive genre of the mountain film, involving a character or group of characters striving to climb or conquer a mountain. The Heimatfilm, or Homeland film, is another genre of sentimental, romanticized movies about rural Germany and its inhabitants. In Indian cinema, *masala* (or mixed spice) films combine a variety of heterogenous generic elements, as by inserting musical sequences in a dramatic film in a way uncharacteristic of Hollywood.

In turn, Hollywood genre filmmaking has been influenced by some of these non-American genres. For example, Japanese samurai films gained popularity in Japan after World War II and became known in the West primarily through the films of Akira Kurosawa (1910–1998) starring Toshiro Mifune (1920–1997), including *Rashomon* (1950), *Shichinin no samurai* (*The Seven Samurai*, 1954), *Yojimbo* (*Yojimbo the Bodyguard*, 1961), and *Tsubaki Sanjûrô* (*Sanjuro*, 1961). *Red Sun* (1971) paired Charles Bronson (1921–2003) and Mifune in a buddy film in the American West, and several American genre movies have been remakes of these samurai films: *The Magnificent Seven* (1960) was based (as was the science fiction film *Battle Beyond the Stars*, 1980) on *The Seven Samurai*; *The Outrage* (1964) was based on *Rashomon*; and both the spaghetti western, *Per un pugno di dollari* (*A Fistful of Dollars*, 1964), and the action film, *Last Man Standing* (1996), with Bruce Willis, were based on *Yojimbo*. Although many international genre movies remain largely unknown to western audiences, as the film industry and popular culture generally become increasingly globalized and populations become more multicultural, inevitably genres will interact more intensively across national boundaries.

SEE ALSO *Studio System*

FURTHER READING

Altman, Rick. *Film/Genre*. London: British Film Institute, 1999.

Barthes, Roland. *Mythologies*. Edited and translated by Annette Lavers. New York: Hill and Wang, 1972.

Cawelti, John. *The Six-Gun Mystique*. 2nd ed. Bowling Green, OH: Bowling Green State University Popular Press, 1984.

Cook, Pam. "Exploitation Films and Feminism." *Screen* 17, no. 2 (Summer 1976): 122–27.

Forster, E. M. *Aspects of the Novel*. New York: Harcourt, Brace, 1927.

Grant, Barry Keith. *Film Genre: From Iconography to Ideology*. London and New York: Wallflower Press, 2006.

————, ed. *Film Genre Reader III*. Austin: University of Texas Press, 2003.

Kitses, Jim. *Horizons West: Anthony Mann, Budd Boetticher, Sam Peckinpah; Studies of Authorship within the Western*. London: British Film Institute, 1970; Bloomington: Indiana University Press, 1970.

Neale, Steve. *Genre and Hollywood*. London and New York: Routledge, 1999.

————, ed. *Genre and Contemporary Hollywood*. London: British Film Institute, 2002.

Schatz, Tom. *Hollywood Genres: Formulas, Filmmaking, and the Studio System*. New York: Random House, 1981; Philadelphia: Temple University Press, 1981.

Shohat, Ella, and Robert Stam. "From the Imperial Family to the Transnational Imaginary: Media Spectatorship in the Age of Globalization." In *Global/Local: Cultural Production and the Transnational Imaginary*, ed. Robin Wilson and Wimal Dissanayake, 145-170. Durham: Duke University Press, 1996.

Tudor, Andrew. *Theories of Film*. New York: Viking Press, 1974; London: British Film Institute, 1974.

Warshow, Robert. *The Immediate Experience*. New York: Atheneum, 1971.

Wood, Robin. *Howard Hawks*. London: British Film Institute, 1968; Garden City, NY: Doubleday, 1968.

Barry Keith Grant

GERMANY

German cinema, in its widest sense what the Germans call *Filmkultur* (film culture), illustrates many aspects of Germany's history, culture, commerce, and politics over more than a hundred years. Any account of world film-making must acknowledge the range of the German cinema's technical and aesthetic innovation, its difficult yet fascinating evolution, and the influence of its leading figures and works. Today it operates in a mediascape extending to European and global perspectives, and integrates into a converging network of production and consumption.

One index of German cinema's identity is public funding. At the national level, support is channeled by Filmförderungsanstalt (FFA, Federal Film Subsidy Institute) in Berlin; from Munich, the capital of the state of Bavaria, the Export Union promotes its image and sales abroad. Cinema as a cultural export is one of the functions of the Goethe-Institut München, combined with the Inter Nationes Bonn, in the state of Northrhine-Westphalia. All sixteen federal states, and many regional authorities, support film and media exhibition, education, training, and production by maintaining museums, archives, and municipal theaters, like the Stiftung Deutscher Kinemathek in Berlin or the Deutsches Filmmuseum in Frankfurt/Main, or by offering prizes, grants, and loans to filmmakers. Such complex networks of support and subsidy are also key elements in economic planning aimed at replacing failing industries, like steelmaking and mining, with expertise in media technology and production. For German *Filmkultur*, Berlin and Munich still dominate, but centers in the Rhineland cities of Düsseldorf, Cologne, and Karlruhe and in the North German port of Hamburg have arisen to challenge them.

EARLY YEARS: 1895–1918

In early 1895 Ottomar Anschütz (1846–1907) had paying audiences for his Tachyscope, an optical device capable of producing movement in single pictures, and on 1 November that year the Skladanowsky brothers projected what was arguably the first film show as public entertainment. The Skladanowskys' "Bioskop" projector was not, however, technically equal to that of the French Lumière brothers (Auguste [1862–1954] and Louis [1864–1948]), who are generally credited with the first authentic film show on 28 December 1895. Cinema originated as part of variety performances, and the first generation of exhibitors traveled around existing entertainment venues showing, between live acts, a mixture of short items featuring acrobatics, nature scenes, local events, and so on. Many of these items were realist documentation, but filmmakers were already developing film's capacity for the fantastical.

The most significant pioneers of German cinema were Oskar Messter (1866–1943) and Guido Seeber (1879–1940) in Berlin. Messter refined the technology, inventing the Maltese cross to synchronize film frames behind the projector's lens, and also a sound system using gramophones. He shot his own material, including regular newsreels, and initially used it to sell his equipment. Messter moved into exhibition and distribution and by 1913 was producing full-length features. As a director and cinematographer, Seeber developed German cinema's potential in lighting and effects photography, but perhaps his major contribution was to supervise the building in 1912 of the first major German studio at Babelsberg, a suburb of the city of Potsdam, just southwest of Berlin.

Up to 1906 German exhibitors made or bought their material, but by 1910 a second stage of development was under way with longer, multi-reel narratives, together with a change in ownership rights toward distributors, who now began renting prints. Cinema was moving out of its initial novelty phase and into premises built specifically to show films, some of which, like the Marmorhaus (Marble House) in Berlin, copied the opulence of established theater in an attempt to share its cultural recognition. Filmmakers strove to increase cinema's cultural capital by attracting bourgeois audiences, which would in turn serve to moderate censorship restrictions and entertainment taxes and to counter the efforts at controlling them by reform movements like those established in 1907 and again in 1917. Such movements promoted preventive censorship, requiring that films justify their right to be shown, and sought to co-opt the new medium for their own educational, reformist, or nationalist purposes. Filmmakers responded by producing what have come to be known as "authors' films." These might be adaptations from literature, with screenplays written by recognized authors—such as Hanns Heinz Ewers's scenario for Stellan Rye's (1880–1914) *Der Student von Prag* (*The Student of Prague*, 1913), a fantasy on the motif of the alter ego, and Paul Lindau's (1839–1919) version of his play *Der Andere* (*The Other*, 1913)—or films with rights to plays by renowned dramatists like Gerhart Hauptmann (1862–1946) or Arthur Schnitzler (1862–1931). Recognized names from the theater also came to act and direct, like the actor Albert Bassermann and the stage-director Max Reinhardt.

Most films functioned as popular entertainment, which demanded the recognizable patterns of genres with known stars and directors. Established popular traditions, such as fairy tales, operettas, and serial novels, made film dramas, melodramas, and comedies easily accessible, and fantastic narratives appeared alongside historical epic and costume extravaganzas. *Der Steckbrief* (The wanted poster, Franz Hofer, 1913) combined the fashion for detective stories with stylized settings. Hollywood provided models for slapstick comedy and even for a group of imitation westerns, some adapting the Wild West tales of the German nineteenth-century writer Karl May (1842–1912). Stars of the period included Paul Wegener (1874–1948), Bassermann, Henny Porten (1890–1960), and, above all, Asta Nielsen (1881–1972).

With the outbreak of World War I in 1914, the German industry moved into its final founding stage, consolidation. Nationalism had always marked German filmmaking, with groups like the Deutsche Flottenverein (Society for a German Fleet) and colonial societies producing films to promote their policies. And the German emperor, Wilhelm II, figured so frequently in newsreels that he was nicknamed the nation's first film star. As foreign competition declined, domestic production and exhibition expanded and came under increasing state influence aimed at harnessing the established entertainment function as both a distraction from the war's realities and as a vehicle for nationalist propaganda. Newsreel and documentary film adopted narratives supporting the war effort rather than depicting the realities of the Front. The military formed its own Bild-und Filmamt (Office for Photography and Film) in 1917, seeking to control all German filmmaking. Defeat nullified such ambition, but not before it generated the most famous studio in German cinema history. The Universum Film Aktiengesellschaft (Ufa) brought together private and state investment to buy up large parts of the industry, like Messter's studios and the German division of the Scandinavian Nordisk company, and dominated German *Filmkultur*, even through the Third Reich.

THE GOLDEN AGE: 1919–1933

Defeat brought two to three years of social and political turmoil until the Weimar Republic (named after the provincial town to which the postwar government fled to escape the upheavals in Berlin) stabilized Germany. Then the Great Depression of 1929 undermined the fragile economy and democracy, paving the way for Nazism. Yet this short period is known as the Golden Age of German cinema.

Initially, the German economy spiraled into inflation, which was not controlled until the US Dawes Plan guaranteed the currency in 1923. Yet the film industry remained active, with hundreds of production companies and distributors, and it expanded with the Emelka studios in Munich, later the Bavaria AG, the second traditional site of German filmmaking. The other major studio, Ufa, prospered initially, establishing prestige cinemas in Berlin and Hamburg and later building the leading soundstage at Babelsberg. The new republic rapidly established direct control over production with film assessment offices in Berlin and Munich, freeing individual films from the preventive censorship applied by law. However, the same body could also promote its educational criteria via tax breaks for "particularly valuable" films.

Yet German filmmakers' greatest advantage was international, as exported German films gained acclaim abroad. With foreign films also coming in, international opportunity meant negotiating with what was already the dominant global film industry, Hollywood. In 1921 a

European Film Alliance came about between the Hollywood company Famous Players and a group of ex-Ufa filmmakers, such as the entrepreneur Paul Davidson (1867–1927) and the directors Ernst Lubitsch (1892–1947) and Joe May (1880–1954). However, its management could not cope with the pressures of inflation and quickly declared bankruptcy. A few years later, Ufa, led by the most successful producer of the day, Erich Pommer (1889–1966), made the Parufamet agreement with the Paramount and Metro-Goldwyn studios. Ufa contracted for twenty US films each season and guaranteed the American studios 75 percent of its cinema's programs, and the Americans agreed to take ten Ufa films each. The German side needed the deal, as it also came with a loan of $4 million to pay off Ufa's debts. Unfortunately, it was not enough.

Already in 1919 Ufa had launched the first German international success for over five years with Lubitsch's costume drama, *Madame Du Barry*. Under the title *Passion*, this became a huge hit in the United States the next year, so that the director left for Hollywood in 1923 and never worked in Germany again. In early 1920 Robert Wiene's (1881–1938) *Das Kabinett des Doktor Caligari* (*The Cabinet of Dr. Caligari*), the film that came to characterize German expressionism, the dominant avant-garde art movement of the times, premiered in Berlin. It abandoned any attempt at realism, depicting the machinations of an evil doctor and showman with his exhibit, a sleepwalker, through bizarre, painted sets and exaggerated costume and acting styles, not least from the young Conrad Veidt (1893–1943), who also later left for Hollywood and is perhaps best known for his role as the Nazi commander in *Casablanca* (1941). *Caligari*'s theme of the corruption lurking behind respectability was so potentially controversial that the producers forced the addition of a conciliatory ending before release. Unlike Lubitsch's film, Wiene's made an international impression as innovative filmmaking, even if it did not enjoy the same popular success. Other examples are Fritz Lang's (1890–1976) *Dr. Mabuse, der Spieler* (*Dr. Mabuse: The Gambler*, 1922), centered on a mad criminal mastermind, and above all his *Der Müde Tod* (*The Weary Death*, also known as *Destiny* and *Between Two Worlds*, 1921), a film exploring the mysteries of life and death and displaying Lang's ability to visualize transcendent scenes architecturally. F. W. Murnau (1888–1931) made twenty-two films from 1919 to 1931, when he died in the United States. *Nosferatu, ein Symphonie des Grauens* (*Nosferatu the Vampire*, also known as *Nosferatu, a Symphony of Horrors*, 1922) is one of the most well-known expressionist films, while *Der Letzte Mann* (*The Last Laugh*, 1924) displayed a masterful use of the moving camera that did away entirely with the need for subtitles to tell its tale of a once-proud hotel

doorman who finds himself unemployed. Murnau came to the United States on the strength of these films, but with the exception of the exquisite *Sunrise* (1927), he was unable to find success within the Hollywood studio system. Expressionism was nearing its end in *Das Wachsfigurenkabinett* (*Waxworks*, Paul Leni, 1924), which told three fantastical tales with magnificent sets and featured three of the era's great stars: Veidt, Emil Jannings (1884–1950), and Werner Krauss (1884–1959).

In 1924 Fritz Lang adapted the expressionist style for the historical epic *Die Nibelungen*, which depicts the greatest German folk-myth. With his penchant for monumental effect combined with expressionistic devices, Lang made another of the milestone films of the Weimar Republic, *Metropolis*, in 1927. With two of German cinema's leading stars, Heinrich George (1893–1946) and Brigitte Helm (1906–1996), supported by an army of extras, the story shows an apocalypse averted in a supercity of the future and an idealistic conclusion uniting management and workers. Although it confirmed Ufa's technical prowess, the film also came close to bankrupting the company, precipitating eventual takeover by conservative, nationalist interests. However, *Metropolis* had impressed Dr. Josef Goebbels (1897–1945), who, as the Nazi propaganda minister after 1933, offered Lang a leading position in the industry. Lang left for Hollywood, where he managed a reasonably successful transition, producing films like *Fury* (1936), the anti-Nazi story *Hangmen Also Die* (1943), *Rancho Notorious* (1952), and *The Big Heat* (1953). He never reintegrated into the German industry after the war, although he accepted invitations to return to Germany to direct *Der Tiger von Eschnapur* (*The Tiger of Bengal*, 1959), *Das indische Grabmal* (*The Indian Tomb*, 1959), and *Die Tausend Augen des Dr. Mabuse* (*The Thousand Eyes of Dr. Mabuse*, 1960), reprising a motif from his early career.

In the late 1920s expressionism gave way to the technically and ideologically more sober style of the New Objectivity, which found cinematic expression in such films as Kurt (1902–2000) and Robert (1900–1973) Siodmak's *Menschen am Sonntag* (*People on Sunday*, 1930) and G. W. Pabst's (1885–1967) *Die freudlose Gasse* (*The Joyless Street*, 1925). The latter, a social drama set in a proletarian district of Vienna, combined social commentary with moralistic melodrama to show the corruption of speculators and the rescue of the heroine by an American Red Cross officer. It was also the film debut of Greta Garbo (1905–1990), who shortly afterward left for Hollywood and became a screen goddess. In the same genre, but ideologically uncompromising, is *Mutter Krausens Fahrt ins Glück* (*Mother Krause's Journey to Happiness*, 1929), made by director Piel Jutzi

---

F. W. MURNAU

b. Friedrich Wilhelm Plumpe, Bielefeld, Germany, 29 December 1888, d. 11 March 1931

Murnau took his professional name from a town in southern Bavaria favored by noted artists in the early part of the twentieth century. He earned a reputation as a creative genius who contributed to the German film industry's international ascendancy, but also as a director unable to manage the shift to Hollywood and all that such a move entailed.

After World War I, he became an apprentice to the theater director Max Reinhardt in Berlin. He directed his first film, *Der Knabe in Blau* (*The Boy in Blue*), in 1919 and had his first success with the romantic melodrama *Der Gang in die Nacht* (*The Dark Road*) in 1921. With the screenwriter Henrik Galeen, he made one of the signal films of German expressionism, *Nosferatu, eine Symphonie des Grauens* (*Nosferatu the Vampire*, 1922), the forerunner of the vampire genre and a cult film today. Murnau worked in a variety of styles but is best known for his expressionist films: *Herr Tartüff* (*Tartuffe*, 1926), from the seventeenth-century French comedy by Molière, and *Faust* (1926), from the celebrated play by Johann Wolfgang von Goethe.

Murnau's *Der letzte Mann* (*The Last Laugh*, 1924), one of the most significant films of the period, combined elements of expressionism and the subsequent New Objectivity. Murnau had Karl Freund, a leading cameraman of the day, shift his camera around and through the scenes, even going so far as to have Freund strap the unwieldy equipment onto his body. The film's groundbreaking visual effects support a story told from the perspective of the protagonist, a hotel doorman powerfully portrayed by Emil Jannings. *The Last Laugh* displays technical prowess, eschewing any title cards to support its narrative.

Murnau received official recognition at the premiere of *Faust* in 1926, but he left for the United States and a contract with Fox studios. There he made *Sunrise: A Song of Two Humans* (1927), an expressionist story of infidelity and murder with a visionary, dreamlike style, often ranked as one of the greatest silent films. It was a critical but not a commercial success. After *Four Devils* (1928) and *City Girl* (1930), Murnau quit the mainstream industry and took a loyal team to the South Pacific to produce *Tabu* (1931), a tale of love and death in paradise. He was killed in a car accident a week before its Hollywood premiere.

RECOMMENDED VIEWING

Nosferatu, eine Symphonie des Grauens (*Nosferatu the Vampire*, 1922), *Der letzte Mann* (*The Last Laugh*, 1924), *Faust* (1926), *Herr Tartüff* (*Tartuffe*, 1926), *Sunrise: A Song of Two Humans* (1927), *Tabu* (1931)

FURTHER READING

Eisner, Lotte H. *Murnau*. Berkeley: University of California Press, 1973; London: Secker and Warburg, 1973.

Fischer, Lucy. *Sunrise: A Song of Two Humans*. London: British Film Institute, 1998.

Fu, Winnie, ed. *The Psychic Labyrinth of F. W. Murnau*. Hong Kong: Hong Kong University Press, 2003.

Huff, Theodore. *An Index to the Films of F. W. Murnau*. New York: Gordon Press Publishers, 1998.

Petrie, Graham. *Hollywood Destinies: European Directors in America, 1922–1931*, revised ed. Detroit, MI: Wayne State University Press, 2002.

Stan Jones

(1896–1946) with the Marxist film collective, Prometheus. The film depicts a mother's suicide after her family is destroyed by unemployment and poverty and advocates working-class solidarity.

Lang also depicted the same milieu for his first sound film, *M—Eine Stadt sucht einen Mörder* (*M*, 1931), but used it for a crime thriller based on an actual case of a serial killer of children. *M* launched another significant star, Peter Lorre (1904–1964), who soon went on to prosper in Hollywood. In *M*, and in much of the earlier expressionist filmmaking from *Caligari* onward, the critic Siegfried Kracauer identified in the German culture and nation a significant reflection of individual and social psychoses, which would find an overt form in Nazism.

The introduction of sound in 1927 radically changed the longer-term prospects for German films internationally, as possibly the only rival industry to Hollywood now operated through a minority language. The first German sound film exhibited was Walter Ruttmann's (1887–1941) *Melodie der Welt* (*Melody of the World*, 1929), a travelogue dominated by music.

F.W. Murnau on location for* Tabu *(1931). EVERETT COLLECTION. REPRODUCED BY PERMISSION.

The shift to full use of sound's potential came with Josef von Sternberg's (1894–1969) *Der Blaue Engel* (*The Blue Angel*, 1930), starring Emil Jannings as a bourgeois schoolmaster seduced by a cabaret performer and Marlene Dietrich (1901–1992) as the seductive singer, Lola Lola. To counter the inevitable restriction to the natural territory of the German language, films like *The Blue Angel* and Ewald Dupont's (1891–1956) *Atlantic* (1929) were shot in several language versions simultaneously. By the end of 1930, sound films were the norm in production and exhibition.

The only declared Communist film produced in the whole period, *Kuhle Wampe oder: Wem gehört die Welt?* (*To Whom Does the World Belong?*, 1932), directed by Slatan Dudow (1903–1963) and written by the renowned playwright Bertolt Brecht (1898–1956), just managed to get a premiere in Berlin in 1932 after being refused three times by the censors. It depicts an encampment of the unemployed in the forests south of Berlin and is highly critical of state and religious authorities. Also typical of the times is the film version of Brecht's play, *Die Dreigroschenoper* (*The Threepenny Opera*, 1931); Brecht sued the director, G. W. Pabst, and his producers, claiming they had falsified the political message he sought from a story of the collaboration of crooks, police,

and banks. Brecht himself left Germany early in 1933, exemplifying the devastating impact of political developments on the nation's entire creative intelligentsia.

FASCISM: 1933–1945

On taking power in 1933, the Nazis brought all aspects of production together under the Reichsministerium für Volksaufklärung und Propaganda (Reich Ministry for Popular Enlightenment and Propaganda), led by propaganda minister Goebbels. Filmmakers, together with all writers, artists, musicians, and so on, had to belong to the Reichskulturkammer (Reich Chamber for Cultural Affairs). Consolidation of production companies meant that the studios Ufa, Tobis, Bavaria, and Terra soon came to produce more than 80 percent of all features. Prominent names, like so many anonymous individuals, had to leave or were threatened with literal destruction. Billy Wilder (1906–2002), Max Ophüls (1902–1957), Robert Siodmak, Erich Pommer, Detlef Sierck (Douglas Sirk; 1897–1987), Alexander Korda (1893–1956), and Arnold Pressburger (1885–1951) joined those who had earlier emigrated to other European countries or to Hollywood; but now they were in exile, with no guarantee of ever returning home. Those who stayed, like the actors Emil Jannings, Hans Albers (1925–1999), Kristina Söderbaum (1912–2001), Brigitte Horney (1911–1988), and Heinz Rühmann (1902–1994), or the directors Veit Harlan (1899–1964), Wolfgang Liebeneiner (1905–1987), and Leni Riefenstahl (1902–2003), could have successful careers if they obeyed the rules.

The onset of Nazi rule, like its downfall in 1945, marks a crucial shift in German history. But it did not happen overnight; rather, it was a transition to circumstances long foreseeable and thus meant a degree of continuity, at least initially. Possibly the world's most sophisticated industry lost much of that indeterminate factor vital in all filmmaking—talent—but it could still produce impressive films for its popular market, propagandistic tracts as features or as pseudo-newsreels, and some of the most vicious imagery ever screened. The Reich also carried on the Weimar Republic's assessment policy, granting films conducive to its ideology tax breaks, although these could not compensate for the loss of export markets, especially in the United States, which immediately declined. There were, however, some advantages, as foreign film imports declined, although never disappeared completely, with the major competitor, Hollywood, banned only in 1939. And, of course, from the later 1930s the expanding Reich brought captive audiences. By 1937 major parts of the industry were nationalized, and any independent filmmaking was banned in 1941, when the final consolidation created

Marlene Dietrich became a star in Josef von Sternberg's **Der Blaue Engel** *(***The Blue Angel***, 1930).* EVERETT COLLECTION. REPRODUCED BY PERMISSION.

an Ufa monopoly and meant direct rule by Goebbels from his ministry.

Popular entertainment continued with dependable genre films, comedies, musicals, and exotic adventures, all keeping to the classic conventions and styles of Hollywood while incorporating specifically German folklore, popular literature, and music. A satirical comedy such as *Amphitryon* (Reinhold Schünzel, 1935) could even imply social criticism, but was protected by its origin in a play by Heinrich von Kleist (1777–1811), a literary icon. *Heimat* (*Homeland*, Carl Froelich, 1938) starred Heinrich George in a melodrama of family relations. The film musical found an extreme form in *Wir tanzen um die Welt* (We Are Dancing Around the World, Karl Anton, 1939), combining revue, "backstage" musical, and love story with mass choreography reminiscent of Busby Berkeley spectaculars. The most successful popular entertainment was Veit Harlan's *Die goldene Stadt* (The Golden City, 1942), set in occupied Prague, a melodrama of betrayal and suicide with a strong message of local patriotism. Yet perhaps the high point came with Josef von Báky's (1902–1966) *Münchhausen* (*The Adventures of Baron Munchhausen*, 1943), an opulent fantasy adventure based on the "Baron of Lies" from popular German literature and intended to celebrate Ufa's twenty-fifth anniversary while displaying to the embattled Germans, and the world at large, the German industry's prowess, not least in color photography.

Epic filmmaking had already come in for nationalist exploitation in the "Prussia Films." It continued into the Third Reich, as Harlan produced *Der grosse König* (*The Great King*, 1942), in which a Germany at war in the seventeenth century parallels contemporary circumstances. The epic genre expanded to encompass various sorts of "great men" and "leaders" like the playwright

MARLENE DIETRICH
b. Maria Magdalene von Losch, Berlin, Germany, 27 December 1901, d. 6 May 1992

Appearing in over a dozen films by such renowned directors of the day as Maurice Tourneur, Curtis Bernhardt, and Alexander Korda, Marlene Dietrich achieved international stardom when, as the dance-hall girl Lola Lola, she stole *Der Blaue Engel* (*The Blue Angel*, 1930) from star Emil Jannings. In the film's final scene she scans the cabaret audience with a knowing smile and a provocative stance that established the outline of the iconic star she was to play all her life.

In 1930 she followed Josef von Sternberg, the director of *The Blue Angel*, to Hollywood. For five years at Paramount, von Sternberg and Dietrich collaborated on six films, from *Morocco* (1930) to *The Devil Is a Woman* (1935), establishing her as a screen goddess. The films experiment with expressionist lighting and texture even as they explore the nature of femininity. Dietrich learned a great deal from von Sternberg about constructing her own image, and although she could devise her own lighting arrangements for the most suitable effects, she could mock it too, as in Fritz Lang's *Rancho Notorious* (1952) and, memorably, in Orson Welles's noir masterpiece, *Touch of Evil* (1958).

Dietrich was approached by the Nazis but did not return to German filmmaking, becoming instead an American citizen and taking a public stance against fascism as a celebrated entertainer of Allied troops. She returned to Germany in 1945 for her mother's funeral but was unpopular because of her wartime allegiances. She appeared in a key role in Stanley Kramer's *Judgment at Nuremberg* (1961), for which she worked again briefly in Germany. However, she did not attend the Berlin premiere, which was a disaster, with the film opening and closing that same night. It was her last major film role, although she maintained a career in cabaret until an accident in 1973. Her last appearance on film was as a madame managing gigolos in post-1918 Berlin in *Schöner Gigolo, armer Gigolo* (*Just a Gigolo*, 1979). Not long before the end of her life, France awarded her its most prestigious decoration, the Légion d'Honneur, and the city paid for the Paris apartment where she lived for over twenty years. In Joseph Vilsmaier's *Marlene* (2000), a biopic with elements of pure invention, Katja Flint vainly tries to capture something of Dietrich's aura. Dietrich and her legend are remembered not only in her films but in Dietrich Square, off Potsdamer Platz in Berlin, and an archive devoted to her in the nearby Stiftung deutscher Kinemathek.

RECOMMENDED VIEWING
Der Blaue Engel (*The Blue Angel*, 1930), *Morocco* (1930), *Blonde Venus* (1932), *Shanghai Express* (1932), *The Scarlet Empress* (1934), *Desire* (1936), *Destry Rides Again* (1939), *Rancho Notorious* (1952), *Witness for the Prosecution* (1957), *Touch of Evil* (1958), *Judgment at Nuremberg* (1961)

FURTHER READING
Bach, Steven. *Marlene Dietrich: Life and Legend*. Cambridge, MA: Da Capo Press, 2000.

Riva, Maria, ed. *Marlene Dietrich: Photographs and Memories: From the Marlene Dietrich Collection of the Film Museum, Berlin*. London: Thames and Hudson, 2001.

Spoto, David. *Blue Angel: The Life of Marlene Dietrich*. New York: Cooper Square Publishers, 2000.

Stan Jones

Friedrich Schiller (1940), the inventor Rudolf Diesel (1942), and the physician Robert Koch (1939). However, the climax of this propagandistic adaptation of history came with Harlan's *Kolberg* (1945), a retelling of the defense of a Baltic port city against the French in the early nineteenth century. As the advancing Red Army took the actual town in 1944, Goebbels diverted resources of money, men, and materials—even interfering in the scriptwriting—to a spectacular war film designed to bolster the Germans' will to resist. The film itself, with its message of endless sacrifice and its production history, provides many insights into the self-destructive megalomania at the heart of Nazism.

Although far from *Kolberg* in style, Leni Riefenstahl's work, which is certainly better known today, is equally revealing of the Third Reich. Her pseudodocumentary, *Triumph des Willens* (*Triumph of the Will*, 1935) can still exert a dubious fascination with its narrative montage of the Nazis' annual rally in Nuremberg, for which Riefenstahl commanded significant resources to create an

Marlene Dietrich, 1936. EVERETT COLLECTION.
REPRODUCED BY PERMISSION.

eerily operatic celebration of the mystical union of Führer and *Volk* (people) as if it were staged precisely for her cameras. Nazi filmic propaganda reached its malevolent depths with depictions of the Jews. *Die Rothschilds* (The Rothschilds, Erich Waschneck, 1940) on the history of the famous financiers in England, was not a commercial success, but Harlan's *Jud Süss* (*Jew Süss*) of the same year brought the racist message very close to home by recounting the history of the eighteenth-century German financier Oppenheim via a bourgeois melodrama. *Der ewige Jude* (*The Eternal Jew*, 1940) shifts to pseudodocumentary to compile at the behest of the ministry a horrendous montage of allusions, false allegories, and arguments to convince viewers of a Jewish conspiracy for world domination. These films are straight propaganda, as the Nazis had by that time decided on the Final Solution to exterminate the Jews and all other undesirable groups and individuals. The propaganda pitch continued when the German-Jewish director Kurt Gerron (1897–1944), having been arrested by the Nazi SS and sent to the Theresienstadt concentration camp, was ordered to shoot a pseudodocumentary on the camp. *Der Führer schenkt den Juden eine Stadt* (*The Führer Gives a City to the Jews*, also known as *Theresienstadt*, 1944) presents the camp as a model community as a smokescreen for international

opinion. Having delivered the product, Gerron and his team were duly murdered.

SINCE 1945

The year 1945, unlike 1918, brought total defeat and occupation zones, permanent loss of territory and resources, floods of refugees, and a burden of historical guilt that still shapes German society today. The French, British, and Russian allies governed the country in increasingly uneasy cooperation until 1949, when two German states emerged, the Federal Republic of Germany (FRG) in the Western zones and the German Democratic Republic (GDR) in the Eastern, Soviet zone. With the building of the infamous Berlin Wall in 1961 and the sealing of the internal border, two Germanies were locked in stasis and integrated into their respective power blocs, NATO and the Warsaw Pact. In November 1989 the East German state finally collapsed and was rapidly absorbed into the Federal Republic.

Filmmaking carried on amid the ruins, not least because the occupying powers wanted it to, although they were themselves distracted by dismantling and profiting from the remains of Ufa. As early as May 1946, the Deutsche Film Aktiengesellschaft (DEFA, the German Film Company Limited) received a license from the Soviets for the Babelsberg studios. DEFA became the East German state's film company and thus the monopoly producer. Its first film, *Die Mörder sind unter uns* (*Murderers Among Us*, 1946) by Wolfgang Staudte (1906–1984) premiered as the first postwar German film. Dealing with the heritage of Nazism, it came to be known as a *Trümmerfilm* (rubble film), after its setting in ruined Berlin. Shot in film noir style with Hildegard Knef (1925–2002), one of the postwar cinema's major stars, it established antifascist filmmaking at DEFA. At the same time, private companies were appearing in the Western zones, such as Central Cinema Company-Film (CCC) and Berolina-Film in West Berlin, Filmaufbau in the provincial university town of Göttingen, and Real-Film in Hamburg. In Munich the Bavaria studios remained in public ownership until 1956.

Distribution companies in West Germany also acquired licenses from the Western allies and could import large quantities of foreign material that was new to Germany. This meant, above all, B pictures from Hollywood, thus reestablishing the abiding presence of the American industry. Audiences' preference for dubbing into German dates from this time. Some filmmakers, like Staudte, were able to work in both Germanies for a while, and until the Wall went up, West Berliners could work in Babelsberg. However, there was little cooperation between the two industries. The deterioration of relations between the former allies soon turned into the Cold War and meant that the Federal Republic at first banned all DEFA films, shifting to a more selective approach in the 1960s. Filmmaking came to reflect the *Wirtschaftswunder*, the rapid economic recovery of West German manufacturing and trade. Scarcely any films dealt with the division of Germany, and most tackled the problem of Nazism under the broad attitude of a liberal humanism, presenting ordinary Germans as victims of anonymous historical forces. This stance also enabled condemnation of Communism as a nonpolitical evil rather than acknowledging East Germany as any sort of comparator. Ufa style merged with that of Hollywood genres to offer "great men" films, *Heimatfilme*, popular depictions of idyllic local cultures, nostalgic historical costume dramas depicting "the good old days," and melodramas focusing on questions of personal identity and relations within families. These latter might ostensibly deal with social, even political, problems of the day but tended to deflect them into questions of emotional attachments and moralizing. Something of an exception were films dealing with young people, as they referred to the significant impact of US culture on the *Wirtschaftswunder* society, such as Georg Tressler's *Die Halbstarken* (*The Hooligans*, 1956), a depiction of young criminals notable for its realist style and for introducing new actors like Horst Buchholz (1933–2003), who went on to achieve stardom. Popular music featured in *Schlagerfilme* (pop films) catered to a youth audience alongside the remakes of musicals, revues, and operettas for more conservative tastes.

West German films from the 1950s did not export well, had few successes at international festivals, and always had to cope with competition from Hollywood. Filmmakers concentrated on what suited the domestic market. The state supported them by introducing the first of the permanent subsidy programs, levying tickets sold and offering production guarantees with the money, thus propping up a declining industry for reasons of cultural politics. As German consumers became increasingly affluent, chief among the new offers was television, with the first channel being established in 1954. By the early 1960s German film attracted less than a third of its home market, and its inadequacy was confirmed when the 1961 Berlinale (the Berlin Film Festival) refused to award the annual German film prize at all.

THE NEW WAVE

In the 1960s a young generation of West Germans began to reject the filmmaking of their parents (and even grandparents), as they were beginning to reject many of the premises on which their parents had reestablished their version of Germany. In 1962 a group of young film-makers published the *Oberhausen Manifesto* at the festival in the town of that name. They wanted a radical shift in *Filmkultur* to recognize cinema as an art equivalent to other arts and thus equally deserving of public support. The Young German Film sought new forms of expression while looking back to prewar cinematic traditions. It embraced American popular culture while criticizing much of American politics, particularly internationally. It turned to German literature for inspiration while rejecting notions of high and low culture and consciously stressing an auteur cinema.

The German state responded by expanding support agencies, subsidies, and training institutions. The Kuratorium Junger Deutscher Film (Board for Young German Film) offered, from 1964 on, interest-free loans to screenplays found worthy of support, yet first-time filmmakers still found it difficult to find distribution and exhibition. Established industry circles countered by securing loans from the Filmförderungsanstalt for companies demonstrating box-office success, which led to a flurry of cheap, often sensationalist productions. The new generation's films began to appear in 1966 with *Abschied von gestern* (*Yesterday Girl*) by Alexander Kluge (b. 1932), a film-essay challenging genre cinema with a fragmented narrative and a critique of social norms. Volker Schlöndorff (b. 1939) began his literary adaptations with his *Der junge Törless* (*Young Torless*, 1966) based on the famous novella by Robert Musil (1880–1942). Social realist, even documentary style went together with experimental and avant-garde developments and a wide-ranging critical stance toward modern mass culture and media. Jean-Marie Straub (b. 1933) and Danièle Huillet (b. 1936) influenced their contemporaries, although they never found a large audience, with films like *Chronik der Anna Magdalena Bach* (*The Chronicle of Anna Magdalena Bach*, 1968), which refused narrative authority and examined the relationship of time and space in film.

Parallel to these developments, mainline popular cinema carried on by producing pop music films, low-level porn under the guise of social comment on sexuality, detective stories, and even remakes of the Karl May westerns. However, by the early 1970s, with new film-makers gaining recognition overseas, cinema rapidly became one of Germany's cultural export flagships under the title New German Cinema, and was then validated by foreign opinion. German public identification with the new wave—some even proudly hailed it as a new "Golden Age"—was mixed with unease at the film-makers' potential excesses. The generation of the early 1960s stressed the *Autorenfilm* (author's film) as programmatic, as it privileged individual creativity against commercial and industrial expertise. This meant that filmmakers were not only their own directors but scriptwriters, producers, and editors as well. In 1971 these filmmakers launched a short-lived attempt to secure their own distribution by founding the Filmverlag der Autoren, but it was never able to compete with mainline companies.

Rainer Werner Fassbinder (1946–1982) was by far the most prolific and controversial filmmaker of this generation, with a formidable productivity from the late 1960s to his early death in 1982. He was also an important figure in radical German theater. His *Angst essen Seele auf* (*Ali: Fear Eats the Soul,* 1974) is still provocative in its depiction of love between a middle-aged German woman and an immigrant worker from North Africa. His *Chinesisches Roulette* (*Chinese Roulette,* 1976) offers remarkable shot compositions to support its melodrama, and his *Lili Marleen* (1981) takes up the theme of Nazism through an examination of the way Nazi media promoted a star cult. Probably his best-known film is *Die Ehe der Maria Braun* (*The Marriage of Maria Braun,* 1979), where his own "star" actress, Hanna Schygulla (b. 1943), portrays the career of a woman during the German "economic miracle," displaying the sexual politics that paralleled socioeconomic developments. With *Lola* (1981) and *Die Sehnsucht der Veronika Voss* (*Veronika Voss,* 1982), *The Marriage of Maria Braun* forms the "Trilogy of the Federal Republic," a tableau of the history, politics, culture, and style of Fassbinder's homeland.

Wim Wenders (b. 1945) is internationally celebrated and engages in the politics of *Filmkultur.* His *Im Laufe der Zeit* (*Kings of the Road,* 1976) set many of his thematic and stylistic trademarks, like his fascination with American culture and the figure of the lone male wanderer as hero, which resurfaced in his *Paris, Texas* (1984), made in the United States with French financing. After several years in the United States (including a notable but flawed cooperation with Francis Ford Coppola on *Hammett,* 1982), Wenders returned home and shot his masterpiece, *Der Himmel über Berlin* (*Wings of Desire*) in 1987, combining remarkable images from Berlin just before the Wall collapsed with a mythical love story of an angel and the woman for whom he forsakes immortality. Wenders returned to the United States to shoot *The Million Dollar Hotel* (2000), a bizarre detective story set in a rundown residential hotel in Los Angeles. Applying his trademarks to an American cast in an American setting, Wenders continues German cinema's tradition of interaction with the United States and its filmmaking. *In a Land of Plenty* (2004) has its title borrowed from poet/songwriter Leonard Cohen, and results from cooperation with US writers, producers, and cast on a US theme: the continuing legacy of Vietnam. Technologically, Wenders also broke new ground by shooting mainly digitally. *Don't Come Knocking* (2005) meant working with Sam Shepard again

and with a US cast, including Shepard himself, Tim Roth, and Jessica Lange. Its narrative resembles *Paris, Texas* in tracing the wanderings of a loner-male and his attempt to salvage his disastrous family relations. Wenders has also cooperated with Ry Cooder, on the documentary *Buena Vista Social Club* (1999), and with Martin Scorsese to contribute *The Soul of a Man* (2003) to Scorsese's TV series on the blues.

Werner Herzog (b. 1942) is regarded as one of the most eccentric figures of *das neue kino.* His films feature inspiring landscapes and controversial actors (the flamboyant Klaus Kinski [1926–1991], the strange Bruno S. [b. 1932]) at odds with their world. Herzog is also well known for the making of his films, whether hypnotizing the entire cast in *Herz aus Glas* (*Heart of Glass,* 1976), dragging a boat through the Amazon jungle for *Aguirre, der Zorn Gottes* (*Aguirre, the Wrath of God,* 1972), or feuding with actor Kinski. Other significant figures from this generation are Volker Schlöndorff, whose Oscar®-winning adaptation of Günter Grass's novel *Die Blechtrommel* (*The Tin Drum,* 1979) is a remarkable treatment of a powerful exploration of German identity, and Hans-Jürgen Syberberg (b. 1935), whose *Ludwig, Requiem für einen jungfräulichen König* (*Ludwig, Requiem for a Virgin King,* 1972) and *Hitler—ein Film aus Deutschland* (*Hitler: A Film from Germany,* 1978) present richly textured visions exploring the legacies of German Romanticism and nationalism, controversially depicting a particular German identity through irrational and nihilistic imagery.

Paralleling the New German Cinema, in the 1970s *Frauenfilm* (women's filmmaking) arose. Directors like Helke Sander (b. 1937), Helma Sanders-Brahms (b. 1940), Margarethe von Trotta (b. 1942), Ulrike Ottinger (b. 1942), and Jutta Brückner (b. 1941) have sought to redefine the practice and politics of filmmaking while criticizing the oppression and discrimination directed against women in the Federal Republic. The combination of national and family history in *Deutschland bleiche Mutter* (*Germany Pale Mother,* 1980), by Sanders-Brahms, sparked controversy. Von Trotta's *Die bleierne Zeit* (*Marianne and Juliane,* also known as *The German Sisters,* 1981) took up the story of the Ensslin sisters for a subtle examination of the effect of terrorism on daily life by combining radical politics with personal history.

The German New Wave petered out in the early 1980s, around the time of Fassbinder's death. The political climate had changed from the idealism of the 1960s to the violence of the "extraparliamentary opposition" of the 1970s, with countermeasures by the state, together with public opposition to projects like nuclear power and the presence of US nuclear weaponry on West German

WERNER HERZOG
b. Werner Stipetic, Munich, Germany, 5 September 1942

Werner Herzog, one of the leading figures of the New German Cinema, has remained a radical individualist and a cinematic visionary for over forty years. His films disturb by their questioning of the bases of human civilization and its values. He first attracted notice with *Lebenszeichen* (*Signs of Life*, 1968), a war story set on a Greek island, which depicts an individual soldier's futile revolt against his situation. Herzog won the Berlin International Film Festival prize that year for a first work, as well as a German Film Award for outstanding feature film.

In *Jeder für sich und Gott gegen Alle* (*The Enigma of Kaspar Hauser*, 1974) he commented on fundamental social values via the historical account of a strange foundling child in nineteenth-century Germany. Herzog also tackled a difficult play by Georg Büchner, from the mainstream of German theater, in *Woyzeck* (1979). Herzog's favorite actor, Klaus Kinski, draws on his characteristic intensity to portray the destruction of a simple little man caught in an absurd, authoritarian society. In *Nosferatu, Phantom der Nacht* (*Nosferatu*, 1978), an homage to the director F. W. Murnau, Kinski gives a remarkably nuanced portrayal of the Dracula figure as a lonely and driven predator envious of his victims for their human relations. With Kinski, Herzog also explored megalomania in *Aguirre, der Zorn Gottes* (*Aguirre, The Wrath of God*, 1972) and again in *Fitzcarraldo* (1982) and *Cobra Verde* (1987). *Fitzcarraldo* is an allegory of colonialism in its treatment of the actual historical events surrounding the hero's obsession with building an opera house a thousand miles up the Amazon River in the Peruvian jungle. During the shooting of this film, Herzog became involved with dangerous local politics, and one of his crew was killed while filming a wild ride down river rapids. *Cobra Verde* deals with the eighteenth-century slave trade between South America and Africa, with Kinski reprising his role of the obsessive adventurer who perishes through his overreaching ambition. After this film, Herzog and Kinski parted ways, as it was becoming increasingly difficult for the director to work with the erratic star.

Herzog also has produced several highly personal documentaries in Germany and elsewhere, and has done mainstream work for German TV. Among his impressive documentaries are *Mein Liebster Feind—Klaus Kinski* (*My Best Fiend*, 1999), about the director's tumultuous working relationship with Kinski; *Wheel of Time* (2003), about the Dalai Lama and Tibetan Buddhist rituals; *The White Diamond* (2004), about exploring the rainforest in a unique airship; and *Grizzly Man* (2005), about an actor who filmed himself living among grizzly bears and who, along with his girlfriend, was killed by one.

RECOMMENDED VIEWING

Aguirre, der Zorn Gottes (*Aguirre: The Wrath of God*, 1972), *Jeder für sich und Gott gegen Alle* (*The Enigma of Kaspar Hauser*, 1974), *Stroszek* (1977), *Woyzeck* (1979), *Nosferatu, Phantom der Nacht* (*Nosferatu*, 1978), *Fitzcarraldo* (1982), *Cobra Verde* (1987), *Mein Liebster Feind—Klaus Kinski* (*My Best Fiend*, 1999), *Wheel of Time* (2003), *The White Diamond* (2004), *Grizzly Man* (2005)

FURTHER READING

Corrigan, Timothy. *The Films of Werner Herzog*. London: Routledge, 1986.

Doll, Suzi, and Gene Walsh, eds. *Images at the Horizon: A Workshop with Werner Herzog*. Chicago: Facets Multimedia, 2002.

Stan Jones

---

soil. Many of these issues are reflected in *Deutschland im Herbst* (*Germany in Autumn*, 1978), a collaborative project between several directors to depict the impact on German society of terrorism and the state's response to it.

When a more conservative government was elected in 1982, the subsidy system ceased to favor art cinema, even as the new technologies shaping video and TV continued to reduce cinema audiences. Mainline filmmaking enjoyed a boost with Wolfgang Petersen's (b. 1941) film *Das Boot* (*The Boat*, 1981), a melancholy antiwar story of a doomed U-boat toward the end of World War II. The film's international success and the director's subsequent hit *Die unendliche Geschichte* (*The Never-Ending Story*, 1984) launched Petersen on the well-trodden trail to Hollywood. In the 1990s Roland Emmerich (b. 1955) followed him, becoming a top US director, with *Universal Soldier* (1992) and *Independence Day* (1996). Other filmmakers found support through

Werner Herzog. EVERETT COLLECTION. REPRODUCED BY
PERMISSION.

closer collaboration with TV and, revisiting staple genres,
the music industry.

Renewed public interpretation of the Third Reich
was also reflected in filmmaking, as in *Die weisse Rose*
(*The White Rose*, 1982) by Michael Verhoeven (b. 1938),
which depicted the courage of an actual student resistance group in Munich. He revisited the Third Reich in
1990 with a controversial film, *Das schreckliche Mädchen*
(*The Nasty Girl*, 1990), which used a mixture of techniques to focus on the difficulties experienced by a schoolgirl investigating her hometown under the Nazis.
Sansibar oder der letzte Grund (Sansibar, or the True
Reason, 1987) by Bernhard Wicki (1919–2000) explores
difficult questions of guilt and responsibility through the
allegory of an artwork rescued from the Nazis by a
Communist and a Jewish woman. The most celebrated
historical revision was Edgar Reitz's (b. 1932) *Heimat—
Eine deutsche Chronik* (*Homeland: A German Chronicle*,
1984), an epic depiction of a village in central Germany
from the 1920s to the 1950s that was made for both TV
and cinema release. Reitz's sequel, *Die Zweite Heimat—
Chronik einer Jugend* (*The Second Homeland: Chronicle
of a Youth*), thirteen episodes shot from 1988 to 1992,
continued the story into the 1960s. Both gained attention abroad and caused much debate in Germany as to
the cinematic depiction of memory and its relevance for
German identity. (*Heimat 3* was aired on German TV in

2004.) The particular parochialism of the state of Bavaria
appears in the work of Herbert Achternbusch (b. 1938),
such as *Servus Bayern* (*Bye-bye, Bavaria!*, 1977). In the
United States Percy Adlon (b. 1935) adapted this story in
Out of Rosenheim (*Bagdad Café*, 1987), which teamed the
Bavarian actress Marianne Sägebrecht (b. 1945) with the
American actor Jack Palance and achieved enormous
international success. However, the most successful
West German filmmaker of the 1980s was a newcomer,
Doris Dörrie (b. 1955), whose comedy *Männer...*
(*Men...*, 1985) combined a feminist viewpoint with
borrowings from Hollywood genres in an international
hit that set the stage for the more entertainment-oriented
filmmaking of the 1990s.

DEFA

From 1945 to 1990, when the company, along with the
state that owned it, disappeared, DEFA produced over
seven hundred films. When DEFA acquired the Ufa
premises in Babelsberg it took on a large number of staff
from the Third Reich. In 1953 the Soviets relinquished
any ownership, and under the Ministry of Culture DEFA
came to control all East German filmmaking. Alongside
those allowed to continue working, exiles like Slatan
Dudow (1903–1963) and Wilhelm Dieterle (1893–
1972) were encouraged to return. Thus the GDR's film
establishment was at odds with the official doctrine of
representing that German tradition and identity, which
had always abjured fascism. Whereas the West German
industry avoided political references in its films, the East
German industry had to include them in all films, but
only in forms dictated by the ruling Socialist Unity Party.

Already in 1951, with the continuity afforded by
folding Ufa into DEFA, Staudte was able to put out an
accomplished account of German imperial history, *Der
Untertan* (*The Kaiser's Lackey*), adapted from the novel by
Heinrich Mann. Slatan Dudow was one of the few filmmakers to examine the brutality of the Third Reich, as he
depicted the price paid by resistance circles in his *Stärker
als die Nacht* (Stronger Than the Night, 1954). Paralleling
the antifascist tradition, filmmakers were also required to
depict the reconstruction of the state on socialist lines in
a "socialist realist" style. When the cultural climate
thawed after Soviet dictator Joseph Stalin's death in
1953, genre filmmaking became easier (even allowing
the development of a subgenre of westerns told from
the viewpoint of the American Indians). In 1958 the
climate changed again as the Socialist Unity Party
attacked many DEFA filmmakers for undermining
socialism with critical viewpoints. Even well-established
directors like Kurt Maetzig (b. 1911), Konrad Wolf
(1925–1982), Jürgen Böttcher (b. 1931), and Heiner
Carow (1929–1997) had to negotiate with the ideological

Klaus Kinski in **Aguirre: der Zorn Gottes** *(Aguirre, The Wrath of God, 1970), one of several collaborations with director Werner Herzog.* EVERETT COLLECTION. REPRODUCED BY PERMISSION.

demands of their political masters; like many technicians, writers, and musicians, they were functionaries of the state on permanent contracts, and so faced changing demands for films that could educate, inform, and persuade, yet also entertain. However, filmmakers were not isolated from developments in other countries. Thus Frank Beyer (b. 1932) made his debut with *Fünf Patronenhülsen* (*Five Cartridges*, 1960), which showed influences from Russian filmmaking in its story of the International Brigade in the Spanish Civil War. The film featured Manfred Krug (b. 1937), the biggest star in the East German industry until his departure for the West in 1977 after a conflict with the party.

In 1965 the party intervened drastically by banning twelve completed films and dismissing some management at DEFA. Maetzig's *Das Kaninchen bin ich* (*I Am the Rabbit*, 1965) had passed all the censors, but, together with Frank Vogel's *Denk bloss nicht ich heule* (Just Don't Think I'm Crying, 1965), it was publicly criticized for being too skeptical and failing to contribute to a positive

identity for the state and banned anyway. Required conformity with established ideology and systems pushed formal and thematic innovation further toward what the authorities considered an elitism. At the same time mass audiences sought genre products, even those coming from Hollywood, as entertainment, or turned to TV (which itself could be risky if one's aerial pointed west). In this climate a group of films came to be known as *Regalfilme* (shelved films), of which *Spur der Steine* (*The Trace of Stones*, 1966), by rising star Frank Beyer, is the most celebrated. The film, which depicts an anarchic but effective band of carpenters at work on a major construction site, and their involvement with the site management and the party, implies that there might be a range of personal contributions possible under socialism. Although allowed a limited release, the film raised too much popular interest for the party to tolerate and thus was shelved. On its reappearance, in perfect condition twenty-five years later, it immediately became a German cinema classic.

The party became somewhat more confident of itself in the 1970s, particularly under Erich Honecker, who presided over increased international recognition and responded to Willy Brandt, the Chancellor of the Federal Republic, by allowing more contact with the West. Another thaw followed, on the basis of the GDR's having become a fully developed socialist society. In 1975 Frank Beyer's *Jakob, der Lügner* (*Jacob the Liar*) appeared and in 1977 became the only DEFA film ever nominated for an Oscar®. Adapted from a novel by Jurek Becker, it tells of resistance in the Warsaw Ghetto that was based on invented radio reports of imminent liberation by the Red Army.

By the end of the 1970s it was growing ever clearer that the state and the party had little support among the populace. Citizens were withdrawing into private spheres, or becoming outright dissidents, or simply leaving the country. In filmmaking the discontent was reflected in an alternative film culture centered in Berlin, Leipzig, and Dresden. DEFA had to accept increasing marginalization in public life, with very few films, like *Solo Sunny* (1980), co-directed by Konrad Wolf (1925–1982) and Wolfgang Kohlhaase (b. 1931), attracting any significant box office, particularly against mainstream Hollywood films. Films like *Das Fahrrad* (The Bicycle, 1982), directed by Evelyn Schmidt (b. 1949), one of the few women filmmakers in the East, or *Grüne Hochzeit* (Green Wedding, Herrmann Zschoche, 1989) were marked by disillusionment about any improvement in individual lives. DEFA's one success was in films for children, such as *Das Schulgespenst* (The School Ghost, Rolf Losansky, 1986), which deals with a young girl's identity problems through the motif of changing places with a ghost.

DEFA celebrated its fortieth anniversary in 1986, which artificially stimulated productivity, some of it already in anticipation of the GDR's own fortieth anniversary in 1989. In 1988 a group of young filmmakers put out a manifesto demanding an independent studio. It was suppressed, but the dissidents were allowed to form their own working group; their discontent thus was focused, but they had no time to make anything of it. Among the last products of DEFA's filmmaking were Heiner Carow's *Coming Out* (1989), the only East German film ever to deal with the official discrimination against homosexuals; *Letztes aus der DaDaeR* (The Last of the Gee-Dee-Arr, Jörg Foth, 1990); and *Das Land hinter dem Regenbogen* (The Country Beyond the Rainbow, Herwig Kipping, 1992), committing the studio's last resources to reckonings with the GDR. The direction for any remaining *Filmkultur* became apparent in *Der Bruch* (The Break, 1989), written by Kohlhaase and directed by Beyer, a straight crime-comedy genre product with no ideological trappings, based on a case from 1951 and featuring a range of noted West German actors.

SINCE 1990

In July 1990 the West's currency replaced the East's, and by early October performances in downtown Berlin of Beethoven's Ninth Symphony and a massive fireworks display signaled the end to two Germanies. The shift back to Berlin as the sole capital heralded a shift in the political landscape, as the conservative government in power since 1982 gave way in 1998 to a center-left coalition of the Social Democrats and the Green Party, the most durable product of the dissenting generation of the 1960s. The Federal Republic subsequently joined the European common currency zone, and thus has continued its role as the pivotal state in an expanded European Union.

Established filmmakers—Beyer; Herzog; Wenders, going back and forth between Berlin and the United States; Schlöndorff; Kluge, with his social commentaries through private TV; and von Trotta—continue to make films. They have been joined by another generation: Tom Tykwer (b. 1965), Doris Dörrie, Christoph Schlingensief, Carolina Link, Romuald Karmakar, Andreas Dresen, Fatih Akin, Angela Schanelec, Jürgen Vogel, and Oskar Roehler. Some, like Tykwer, have had remarkable success in the mainstream, even internationally, whereas others operate domestically, not translating out of the natural German territories.

All depend in various ways on German cultural politics and government subsidy and financing measures. In 1997 several German films did well, managing over three million viewers, through sheer box office appeal: *Rossini* (1997), Helmut Dietl's satire on the vanity of Munich's film establishment; *Knockin' on Heaven's Door* (1997), by Thomas Jahn; and *Kleines Arschloch* (*The Little Bastard*, 1997), by Michael Schaack and Veit Vollmer. The industry remained dependent on TV productions, with the attendant influence of producers on content and on exhibition rights. To address this issue, Michael Naumann, on becoming Minister for Culture and the Media, called a meeting of interested parties in an attempt to reform the subsidy system away from its commercial emphasis, a move not favored by TV interests. At the same time, large amounts of investment were actually leaving Germany to buy rights in foreign productions. As many deals would simply never see a return, this phenomenon became known in the United States as "stupid German money," and the bubble subsequently burst.

Four categories of subject matter have most closely reflected Germany's circumstances at the turn of the century: reworkings of late-twentieth-century history, especially that of East Germany; comedies of social manners and gender relationships among young West German urban professionals; depictions of immigrant and foreigner populations; and depictions of Berlin after the Wall. The wider historical past continues to circulate, more or less in the mainstream, and detective thrillers and road movies retain their appeal. Among the "reworkers," Andreas Kleinert (b. 1962) finished his training at DEFA just as it ceased to exist; yet he managed, in *Neben der Zeit* (Outside Time, 1995), to present an image of East Germany left behind by events and clinging to outdated habits. In 1999 he intensified that motif in a bleak picture of psychosis, *Wege in die Nacht* (*Paths in the Night*), which shows a former manager for the GDR leading an increasingly violent vigilante campaign against what he sees as the moral decay of the new Germany, until he himself becomes criminal and commits suicide. *Stilles Land* (*Silent Country*, 1992) by Andreas Dresen (b. 1963) takes a very "art house" form to show a provincial theater-group in the East overtaken in the midst of their rehearsals by the opening of the border, which confronts them with the existential question about their function in an indeterminate future. Tackling East Germany from a Western viewpoint, Detlev Buck's (b. 1962) *Wir können auch anders* (*No More Mr. Niceguy*, 1993) is a road movie about two country brothers who set off from the West to find their inheritance in the East; after hilarious adventures avoiding the law, they simply keep on heading east until they find an idyllic life in a Russian peasant community. *Goodbye Lenin!* (2003) by Wolfgang Becker (b. 1954) is an ironic tale of a young man who must pretend that East Germany still exists so as not to shock his fragile mother, who has just awakened from a coma that began before the fall of the Berlin Wall.

The mainstream of German production in the first half of the 1990s was characterized by lightweight comedies such as *Der bewegte Mann* (*Maybe, Maybe Not*, Sönke Wortmann, 1994), dealing with male gender identities and launching Til Schweiger (b. 1963) as the star of the time. Rainer Kaufmann's (b. 1959) *Stadtgespräch* (*Talk of the Town*, 1995) starred his partner, Katja Riemann (b. 1963), in a comedy of marital complications. Detlev Buck's *Männerpension* (*Jailbirds*, 1996), Sherry Horman's (b. 1960) *Frauen sind was Wunderbares* (Women Are Something Wonderful, 1994,) and Wortmann's *Das Superweib* (*The Superwife*, 1996) are all examples of a highly successful subgenre that presented German society as a sort of well-heeled sitcom driven by neurotic wisecracking. In the same general category of social comedy, Doris Dörrie has maintained her position, but her films, such as the episodic *Bin ich Schön?* (*Am I Beautiful?*, 1998), have a harder satirical and critical edge, depicting a society—as well as personal relations—given to meaningless consumerism.

Helmut Dietl's (b. 1944) satire *Schtonk!* (1992) is a darker film that returns to one of postwar filmmaking's regular motifs, Nazism. The film mocked the gullibility of editors of the popular magazine *Stern*, who were duped by forgers purporting to have Hitler's wartime diaries for sale. In it Götz George (b. 1938), a TV and film tough-guy star since the late 1960s, makes an outrageous appearance in a monstrous corset and dressing gown purported to be that of Hitler's henchman Hermann Goering. In 2004 *Der Untergang* (*The Downfall: Hitler and the End of the Third Reich*) by Oliver Hirschbiegel (b. 1957), which presents the last days of Hitler and his inner circle in the bunker under central Berlin, became an international success. The film was also the subject of much public debate for what some see as its relatively sympathetic treatment of Hitler as a human rather than as a monster. The director Joseph Vilsmaier (b. 1939)—whose films include *Stalingrad* (1993), *Comedian Harmonists* (1997), and *Marlene* (2000), the last two ostensibly biopics on a famous singing group and on Marlene Dietrich—produces for the mainstream, with significant production values; his work filters historical perspectives through personalities.

With the onset of the "Berlin Republic"—a concept arising from the post–Cold War relocation of the German government to that city—Berlin itself has become the focus of many films. Andreas Dresen's *Nachtgestalten* (*Night Shapes*, 1999) reveals the city's ugliness, its patient narrative the counterpart of the frenetic comedies of the early 1990s. By far the most widely acknowledged Berlin film has been Tom Tykwer's *Lola rennt* (*Run Lola Run*, 1998). Using parallel narratives and other devices from computer games, Tykwer's story of lovers threatened with extinction by their existence on the fringes of the underworld cemented his reputation internationally as one of German cinema's representative directors and propelled the film's female lead, Franka Potente (b. 1974), toward Hollywood.

In the mainstream genres, the thriller continues to appear and is especially prevalent on German TV. Examples include *Solo für Klarinette* (*Solo for Clarinet*, 1998), *Schattenboxer* (Shadow Boxer, 1992), *Kurz und schmerzlos* (*Short Sharp Shock*, 1998), and *Die Mutter des Killers* (The Mother of the Killer, 1996), and parodies like *Die Musterknaben* (The Favorite Sons, 1997) and *Zugvögel— . . . einmal nach Inari* (*Train Birds*, also known as *Trains'n'Roses*, 1998). Psychological thrillers include *Der Totmacher* (*Deathmaker*, 1995) and *Die Unberührbare* (*No Place to Go*, 2000), both German film prizewinners. *Die innere Sicherheit* (*The State I Am In*, 2000), also a prizewinner, investigates the 1960s generation, whose revolutionary visions are reduced to the shiftless existence of a couple still sought for alleged terrorism, together with their daughter, who knows no other existence than the one "underground." In 2004 *Die Fetten Jahre sind vorbei* (*over the Edukators*), the first

Franka Potente (right) in Tom Tykwer's kinetic Lola rennt *(*Run Lola Run, 1998*).* EVERETT COLLECTION. REPRODUCED BY PERMISSION.

German film for eleven years in competition at the Cannes Film Festival, took up the topic of activism and opposition in present-day Germany. In a satisfyingly ambiguous conclusion, the possibility of partnership across the generations is left open.

The industry maintains its own Spitzenorganisation (SPIO) in Wiesbaden as an umbrella for the major professional organizations. SPIO also supervises patents and copyrights and the TV rights to films, and decides on the German industry's entries for local and international festivals. It can also enforce the rulings of the Freiwillige Selbstkontrolle, the industry's voluntary self-censorship organization, established in 1949 after the model of the American Motion Pictures Producers and Distributors of America. In 1951 a film evaluation office, the Filmbewertungsstelle Wiesbaden, was established, the assessments of which can promote a film's chances of subsidy or block any hope of distribution. Germany's constitution guarantees freedom of expression, forbids censorship, and declares the federal states' rights to administer local exhibition; given the system of self-censorship, coupled with the subsidy system, government at various levels has great, if indirect, influence on what can be made and shown.

The Spitzenorganisation also produces a yearly compilation of statistics on the industry. In 2004 figures for premiered films for 1993 to 2003 show a gradual increase to around eighty per year, with a relatively constant proportion of foreign co-productions. The fragmented nature of the industry is evident in the fact that scarcely any production company managed more than one premiere; and the crucial importance of support from the film industry's rival, TV, is evident in the almost 50 percent of co-productions with companies in this sector. Showings of film on TV have burgeoned since the mid-1980s and, together with video production, sales, and rentals, show the biggest returns. This contrasts with the film industry's employment structure, where the overwhelming numbers, about 25,000 out of 37,000 members, are in film and video production. Regarding average production budgets, the German film industry is a global second-rank industry. Internationally, the chief market for German films is, not surprisingly, Europe, with over three times the turnover of exports compared with the next biggest market, the United States. The cinema audience is overwhelmingly young: ages fourteen to twenty-nine, with a sharp decline from about thirty up. For cinema visits, Germany ranks under the EU average, with scarcely two per head in 2003, and far behind the United States, at 5.4. However, the bottom line for the German industry is the dominance of the US product over the German home market: over 40 percent of films exhibited in 2003, and almost 80 percent of the total turnover, were from the United States.

For the foreseeable future *Filmkultur* is likely to remain a secondary, "foreign-language" cinema, dominated at home and abroad by the English-speaking industry led by Hollywood. In 2003 the introduction of film study in the German school system added to the ongoing debate on what constitutes the German artistic canon. Thus questions about the role of German cinema—in terms of national identity, high versus low culture, social relevance, commercial status, and international significance—have achieved an unprecedented public prominence.

SEE ALSO *Expressionism; National Cinema; Propaganda; Ufa (Universum Film Aktiengesellschaft)*

FURTHER READING

Bergfelder, Tim. *International Adventures: Popular German Cinema in the 1960s.* Oxford and New York: Berghahn Books, 2004.

Bergfelder, Tim, Erica Carter, and Deniz Göktürk, eds. *The German Cinema Book*. London: British Film Institute, 2002.

Elsaesser, Thomas. *New German Cinema: A History*. Basingstoke, UK: Palgrave Macmillan, 1989.

———. *Weimar Germany and After: Germany's Historical Imaginary*. London and New York: Routledge, 2000.

Elsaesser, Thomas, and Michael Wedel, eds. *The BFI Companion to German Cinema*. London: British Film Institute, 1999.

Ginsberg, Terri, and Kirsten Moana Thompson, eds. *Perspectives on German Cinema*. Boston: G. K. Hall, 1996.

Hake, Sabine. *German National Cinema*. London and New York: Routledge, 2002.

Halle, Randell, and Margarete McCarthy, eds. *Light Motives: Popular German Film in Perspective*. Detroit, MI: Wayne State University Press, 2003.

Kaes, Anton. *German Film Theory*. Princeton, NJ: Princeton University Press, 2004.

Knight, Julia. *New German Cinema: Images of a Generation*. London: Wallflower Press, 2003.

Kracauer, Siegfried. *From Caligari to Hitler: A Psychological History of the German Film*. Princeton, NJ: Princeton University Press, 1947; revised edition, 2004.

Kreimeier, Klaus. *The Ufa Story: The History of Germany's Greatest Film Company, 1918–1945*. Berkeley: University of California Press, 1999.

Schroeter, Katrin. *Border Crossings: National Identity and Nation Formation in German Films 1980–2000*. Stonington, ME: Pine Hill Press, 2003.

Sean, Allan, and James Sandford, eds. *Defa Film: East German Cinema, 1946–1992*. Oxford and New York: Berghahn Books, 1999.

Stan Jones

GREAT BRITAIN

Any consideration of the cinema of Great Britain raises two key problems. First is the dominance of Hollywood cinema. English is the primary language of British cinema and, of course, of Hollywood. Britain's decline in the twentieth century has been matched by the rise of the United States as an economic power. As a key American export, Hollywood film served as a considerable influence on and a hindrance to the development of cinema in Great Britain. The absence of any language barrier made the British market an attractive one for Hollywood. Throughout most of its history, British cinema has struggled to compete against the Hollywood monolith.

The second problem is the very notion of Great Britain itself, which is hardly a unified whole, but rather is composed of other nations, prominently England but also Scotland and Wales. Additionally, Northern Ireland—which together with Great Britain constitutes the United Kingdom (UK)—must compete with other UK films as well as with the burgeoning film industry in the Republic of Ireland. In both a critical and popular sense, it is England that has been equated with Britain, and it is the English film industry, with its economic base in London, that has dominated British cinema. A further complication is the United Kingdom's ties to the European Union, which has led to an increase in co-productions where aspects of national identity tend to become subsumed.

Presently, the United Kingdom averages about one hundred feature films per year, but this number includes co-productions in which British interests may comprise only a minority stake. In the 1980s the average number of features produced was only forty-three, so current numbers represent a substantial rise. Changes in funding practices, as well as increased emphasis on co-productions, are leading causes of this apparent production boom. Funding was previously much more closely tied to exhibition, or at least to the possibilities of exhibition, either theatrically or on television. Current funding is primarily through the National Lottery, the monies from which are doled out by various regional film bodies, which are able to encourage production but rarely provide exhibition outlets. Anxiety over the state of the British film industry has been a recurring issue throughout the industry's history. In reality, Great Britain shares fears of Hollywood dominance with numerous other nations and yet, despite an ongoing inferiority complex, has a cinema history that is rich, varied, and reasonably successful.

EARLY CINEMA PIONEERS

Great Britain was a key early adopter of emerging cinema technology. In fact, it could be argued that British cinema history predates even the arrival of the Lumière Brothers in 1895. Augustin Le Prince (1842–1890), who disappeared in 1890 while returning from a visit to his brother in his native France, was reputed to have successfully experimented with motion pictures. Patents for which Le Prince applied, as well as remnants of his work, suggest that his experiments were successful, yet his work seems to have had no real influence, and he remains a curious cinematic footnote. Instead, it is the first Lumière show, in London in February 1896, that may be said to have inaugurated cinema exhibition in Great Britain.

It was not long after this that homegrown British films began to emerge. There were three main centers of production for these early films: London, Yorkshire, and Brighton and Hove. The period between 1895 and 1905 can be seen as one of great productivity and influence, with the early British films being as innovative and prolific as their counterparts in France and the United States. Perhaps it was the influence of music hall traditions that enabled British film to emerge quickly as a world leader. Certainly, a great deal of the content of the films was derived from existing music hall acts, and undoubtedly the two popular forms shared audiences, particularly in more provincial towns and cities. Robert W. Paul (1869–1943) constructed a makeshift studio on the rooftop of the Alhambra theater in Leicester Square, making frequent use of music hall performers within his films. Another London-based company, the British Mutoscope and Biograph Company, constructed its film studio at the rear of the Tivoli Music Hall. In addition to the music hall, magic lanternists and other late-nineteenth-century showmen quickly adopted film as a new form of entertainment.

One of Great Britain's most significant film pioneers was Cecil Hepworth (1874–1953), the son of a renowned magic lantern showman. Hepworth began his film career assisting another key pioneer, the inventor and sometime filmmaker Birt Acres (1854–1918), who had collaborated with R. W. Paul (before the two bitterly fell out). After working for transplanted American producer Charles Urban at Maguire and Baucus, Hepworth founded his own company, along with his cousin, Monty Wicks, in 1899, under the name Hepworth and Company, building a studio in the back garden of a house in Walton-on-Thames, a suburb of London. In 1904 the company became the Hepworth Manufacturing Company, and Hepworth turned his attention away from directing and worked exclusively as a producer. His company was responsible for a number of key early films, the most notable of which was *Rescued by Rover* (1905), directed by Lewis Fitzhamon (1869–1961). This film, with its narrative of a "gypsy" kidnapping of a baby followed by its rescue, seems to have been the inspiration for D.W. Griffith's first film, *The Adventures of Dollie* (1908). In technical terms, *Rescued by Rover* was a major innovation, and it was also a tremendous audience pleaser. Despite its groundbreaking elements, the film arrived near the end of the early period of British innovation; so rather than heralding a move forward, it seems more the peak of a primitive mode of filmmaking that would soon be eclipsed by technological and economic developments in other countries.

Other early British filmmakers also influenced developments elsewhere. A key figure in Brighton and Hove was James Williamson (1855–1933), a pharmacist and photographer who began making films in 1897 under the Williamson Kinematograph Company name.

Williamson's *Fire!* (1901) was a tableaux film that employed the local Hove fire service in constructing a rescue narrative that included shots from both outside and within a burning building. The film was an obvious influence on Edwin S. Porter's later American film, *Life of an American Fireman* (1903). Williamson enjoyed success with his comedies as well as increasingly complex dramas until 1910, when changes in the economic models of international cinema led him to place his focus on the manufacture of camera equipment. George Albert Smith (1864–1959) of Brighton had enjoyed earlier success as an innovative operator of magic lantern shows, and he brought this same flair for innovation to the cinema. His films seem to have been less influential than those of some of his counterparts; rather, it is his technical developments that had the most lasting effect. Smith made innovative use of close-ups in such early films as the rather self-explanatory *As Seen through a Telescope* (1900) and *Grandma's Reading Glass* (1900); he also successfully incorporated trick elements such as reverse motion in *The House That Jack Built* (1900). His later career was devoted to the development of color in film through a two-color additive process known as Kinemacolor that he promoted along with Charles Urban.

This first decade of British film saw other noteworthy pioneers emerge, including the aforementioned R. W. Paul, whose Paul's Animatograph Works produced films by a number of other key figures. These included the magician W. R. Booth (1869–1938), whose films, including *The "?" Motorist* (1906), employed trick photography in the mode of Georges Méliès. Additionally, Frank Mottershaw's *A Daring Daylight Burglary* (1903), made for his Sheffield photo company, is a fast-paced action film that is said to have influenced Porter's *The Great Train Robbery* later that same year.

Still, despite its early influence, British cinema seemed to wane as other cinemas became more progressive and technically innovative. A reliance on adaptations of noted British novels and stage plays, while appeasing nationalist sentiments, left the British cinema stagy and wooden, with proscenium arch framing and side-to-side, stage-style movement dominating the structures of films. As the market for cinema changed, British companies were either reluctant or ill-prepared to meet the needs of the industry. Even before World War I, American companies were establishing offices in Britain, and exhibitors soon had an abundance of well-made titles at their disposal. Most of the early British pioneers had ceased making films, while those who continued, such as Hepworth, struggled. His one-hour version of *Hamlet* in 1913 was indicative of the reliance on stage adaptations. In 1923 he adapted Helen Mathers's 1875 novel, *Comin' Thro the Rye*, his second adaptation of the novel, and his company, renamed Hepworth Picture Plays, was unable to survive its critical and commercial failure. While it was an intrinsically British film in terms of subject matter, *Comin' Thro' the Rye* was made in a style that was outmoded, and it was no competition for the much slicker products arriving from Hollywood and elsewhere.

QUOTAS, QUOTA QUICKIES, AND SOUND

Responding to growing concerns over the increasing American dominance of the domestic market for films in Britain, Parliament in 1927 passed the Cinematograph Films Act, the first government intervention aimed at protecting the British film industry. The passage of this legislation was linked to the development of a growing cinema culture in Great Britain, which was also expressed through the founding of The Film Society in London in 1925 and the growing critical attention paid to film in the print media, including the specialist film magazine *Close Up*, which first appeared in 1927. The Act introduced a quota mandating a minimum allotment of screen time to British films that began at 5 percent in 1927 and was to rise to 20 percent by 1936.

The immediate effect of the legislation was a sharp rise in the number of British production companies, including British International Pictures, founded by John Maxwell as part of the vertically integrated Associated British Picture Corporation (ABPC) and the Gaumont-British Picture Corporation (GBPC), which merged a number of distribution, production, and exhibition companies under the auspices of Isidore Ostrer. The majority of the new companies floundered because their output was largely of inferior quality. The arrival of sound further hastened their demise. British International succeeded, as its Elstree studio was an early adopter of sound recording equipment. The larger company (ABPC) also controlled ABC Cinemas, a major British chain, guaranteeing itself an exhibition outlet for its productions. Gaumont-British survived because it too held extensive exhibition interests, and also because of a deal that Ostrer had struck with American producer William Fox, although the company remained under British control. This retention of control was not always the case in the industry. Significantly, the quota applied to films that were produced by a company constituted in the British Empire rather than specifically British-controlled companies. This led to the development of "quota quickies," films that satisfied the basic requirements of the quota system but that did not require large investment; these were frequently made by subsidiaries of the existing American majors, either within Britain or in some cases in Canada. While many critics have dismissed the bulk of these quota quickies, there is no doubt that

they resulted in a boom in British cinema production. In fact, exhibitors regularly exceeded the quota requirements that had been established.

The era saw the development of a viable and sustainable film culture in Britain. Numerous key figures emerged at this time, figures who would continue to be influential in British cinema in the ensuing decades. Gaumont-British had joined forces with Gainsborough Studios in 1927 and Gainsborough co-founder Michael Balcon (1896–1977) became head of production for both companies. Gaumont-British focused on the "quality" films, while Gainsborough was to create works with more popular appeal. Among the directors who had worked under Balcon at Gainsborough was Alfred Hitchcock (1899–1980). Hitchcock had his start in the film industry working on design and creating titles for the London office of the American firm Famous Players-Lasky (later Paramount). When the firm left London, Hitchcock moved to Gainsborough, where he was exposed to its German-based productions through the company's ties to Ufa. As part of his work for Gainsborough, Hitchcock was on the set of F. W. Murnau's *The Last Laugh* (1924), and the influence of German expressionism is evident in his early British work, including *The Lodger* (1927).

Hitchcock directed Britain's first feature-length sound film, *Blackmail* (1929). He actually shot two simultaneous versions of the film—one with sound, the other silent, as many theaters were not yet equipped with sound technology. The film was made for British International Pictures, which had lured Hitchcock away from Gainsborough with a large contract, expecting that Hitchcock would shoot only a portion in sound, but the director instead shot most of the film in sound. The film was a huge critical and commercial success, with even *Close Up*, whose critics were so often harshly critical of British film, willing to offer praise. Following his association with British International Pictures, Hitchcock returned to his working relationship with Balcon, making, among other films, *The Man Who Knew Too Much* (1934) and *The 39 Steps* (1935) for Gaumont-British. After Balcon left to become head of production at MGM-British, Hitchcock made *The Lady Vanishes* (1938) for Gainsborough, though the film was commissioned by MGM. The latter film was the third screenplay written by Frank Launder (1906–1997) and Sidney Gilliat (1908–1994), who would continue to be significant contributors to British cinema in writing, directing, and producing well into the 1970s.

Gaumont-British and Gainsborough aided the careers of other significant figures within British cinema. Among these were the directors Anthony Asquith (1902–1968) and Victor Saville (1895–1979). As a founding

---

ALEXANDER KORDA

b. Sándor Lászlo Kellner, Pusztatúrpásztó, Austria-Hungary (now Hungary),
16 September 1893, d. 23 January 1956

Hungarian-born, Korda became a naturalized British subject in 1936 and was the first film industry figure to be knighted, in 1942. Yet the issue of nationality and his relationship to the British film industry has always been a thorny one. Undoubtedly Korda played a central role in the development of the industry in Great Britain. His *The Private Life of Henry VIII* (1933) represented a major breakthrough for British cinema, paving the way for successes in the American market. At the same time, Korda's devotion to "prestige" pictures, ambitious costume films that most frequently chronicled key historical figures and that made use of theatrical traditions, encouraged the industry to strive for production standards it could not sustain, contributing to the industry's economic collapse in 1937.

By the time Korda came to Britain he had already established his filmmaking credentials in Hungary. After World War I, the unstable political situation and the rise of anti-Semitism in Hungary led Korda first to Vienna and then to Berlin, where his films enjoyed success. Then, after three dismal years in Hollywood, Korda moved to Britain in 1931.

His first British film was the quota quickie *Service for Ladies* (1932), soon followed by his first film for his own company, London Pictures, *Wedding Rehearsal* (1933), a film that established Korda's use of cherished national symbols in its opening shots of the Houses of Parliament and Westminster Abbey, as well as his use of familiar national sterotypes amongst his characters. Following the success of *The Private Life of Henry VIII*, Korda continued to make lavishly produced biopics, such as *The Private Life of Don Juan* (1934) and *Rembrandt* (1936). Neither film came close to matching the commercial success of *Henry VIII*, although *Rembrandt*, featuring another memorable performance from Charles Laughton, who had won an Acdemy Award for his portrayal of Henry VIII, is considered by many critics to be Korda's finest directorial effort.

After the commercial failure of the latter two biopics, Korda turned his attentions to producing, running London Films as well as the large studio he had built at Denham. At the outbreak of World War II, Korda was back in the United States (some commentators have suggested he was there covertly on behalf of the British government). He returned to directing with *That Hamilton Woman* (also known as *Lady Hamilton*, 1941), a period piece about the affair between Admiral Nelson and Lady Emma Hamilton that actually served as a propaganda film, with Napoleon established as an obvious parallel to Hitler. Korda's final two directorial efforts came after the war, with *Perfect Strangers* (1945) and the Oscar Wilde adaptation *An Ideal Husband* (1947). He died of a heart attack in London.

RECOMMENDED VIEWING

As Director and Producer: *Wedding Rehearsal* (1933), *The Private Life of Henry VIII* (1933), *Rembrandt* (1936), *The Lion Has Wings* (1939), *That Hamilton Woman* (1941), *An Ideal Husband* (1947); As Producer: *The Ghost Goes West* (1935), *The Drum* (1938), *The Four Feathers* (1939)

FURTHER READING

Drazin, Charles. *Korda: Britain's Only Movie Mogul.* London: Sidgwick and Jackson, 2002.

Korda, Michael. *Charmed Lives: A Family Romance.* New York: Random House, 1979.

Kulik, Karol. *Alexander Korda: The Man Who Could Work Miracles.* London: W. H. Allen, 1975.

Stockham, Martin. *Alexander Korda Film Classics.* London: Boxtree, 2002.

Scott Henderson

---

member of The Film Society, Asquith was able to incorporate his firsthand knowledge of Hollywood with his knowledge of European cinema. Asquith's early career indicated promise but was not met with much critical acclaim. In 1932 he joined Gainsborough, where he was involved in a range of projects and duties. Later in the decade he co-directed *Pygmalion* (1938), an adaptation of the George Bernard Shaw play, with the film's star, Leslie Howard. With this film Asquith finally received the break that would help propel him to greater recognition

Alexander Korda. EVERETT COLLECTION. REPRODUCED BY
PERMISSION.

through films such as *Fanny By Gaslight* (1944), made for
Gainsborough, and *The Importance of Being Earnest*
(1952), which starred Michael Redgrave (1908–1985),
as well as a number of collaborations with playwright
Terence Rattigan, including *The Winslow Boy* (1948) and
The Browning Version (1951).

Gainsborough and Gaumont-British were more
significantly involved in the early career of Victor
Saville. Saville had first entered film as a producer,
along with Michael Balcon, in 1923 with *Woman to
Woman* (directed by Graham Cutts). When Balcon
became head of production at Gaumont-British,
Saville became the studio's most prolific director with
films such as *Hindle Wakes* (1931) and *Evergreen*
(1934). After a brief time as an independent producer,
Saville found himself producing films for MGM,
including *The Citadel* (1938), a very successful adaptation directed by the American, King Vidor, followed by
an even more successful *Goodbye Mr. Chips* (1939),
directed by Sam Wood. The start of World War II
found Saville in Hollywood, where he remained producing and then directing films for MGM—except for
a brief stay as a director at Columbia—until his return

to Britain, briefly, to shoot films in 1949 and 1952,
and then permanently in 1960.

The success enjoyed by the likes of Saville, and by
studios such as Gaumont-British and British International,
was overshadowed by the breakthrough success of a film
made by an independent company affiliated with United
Artists. Alexander Korda's *The Private Life of Henry VIII*
(1933) was produced by Korda's own London Films.
United Artists was willing to take a chance on a British
film being acceptable for the American market and had a
true success on its hands when the film became the biggest
international British hit to that point. Despite the fact that
Korda was Hungarian and had previously failed in his
attempt to make it in Hollywood, the film's subject matter
was resolutely British. The success of the film led to
renewed enthusiasm within the British film industry and
indicated that it was possible for British film to compete
with Hollywood. Korda's film has the distinction of being
the first British film to win an Academy Award®, with
Charles Laughton taking the Oscar® for Best Actor.
Unfortunately, Korda's subsequent films could not match
the success of *The Private Life of Henry VIII*, and the
industry's optimism quickly waned as the creation of
lavish "prestige" pictures could not be sustained and further success in the American market did not seem to be
forthcoming. Ironically, it was more frequently in the
quota quickies where the next generation of British film
talent cut its teeth. Directors such as Michael Powell
(1905–1990) as well as actors including Laurence Olivier
(1907–1989), Vivien Leigh (1913–1967), John Mills
(1908–2005), and James Mason (1909–1984) all found
opportunity in the low-budget sector.

While American-affiliated companies continued to
churn out the low-budget quickies, the British companies invested more heavily in expensive films aimed at
cracking the American market. Asquith moved to
London Films to shoot *Moscow Nights* (1935), while
Saville's Victor Saville Productions was among those
who made films for Korda in this era. In 1937 the
bubble burst, and by 1938 the boom was definitely
over. Denham Studios, which Korda had constructed
for the production of "prestige" pictures, was losing
money and eventually was merged with J. Arthur
Rank's Pinewood Studios. The second Cinematograph
Films Act was passed in July 1938, and among its
regulations was an attempt to end the practice of quota
quickies by instituting a minimum cost of £7,500 and
permitting films that cost three times the minimum to
count for double quota assessment. The onset of World
War II, following a severe decline in production after
the bust of 1937, meant that the effects of the 1938 act
were never really felt.

***Charles Laughton with Binnie Barnes in* The Private Life of Henry VIII *(Alexander Korda, 1933).* EVERETT COLLECTION. REPRODUCED BY PERMISSION.**

JOHN GRIERSON AND THE DOCUMENTARY MOVEMENT

Parallel to the developments in feature filmmaking, another influential response to American dominance of British cinema emerged. The British documentary movement, led by the Scot, John Grierson (1898–1972), offered a distinctive riposte to Hollywood by focusing on fact and public information. While studying in the United States under a Rockefeller fellowship from 1923 to 1927, Grierson developed his interest in mass communication, in which he perceived the potential to educate the public and influence opinion. By making films that were not dependent upon box-office receipts, Grierson saw an opportunity to address social and political issues that were unlikely to be covered by the commercial film industry. At the same time, however, his reliance on government and industrial sponsors created restrictions on subject matter, and most of the films made under Grierson's auspices seem like public-

relations exercises rather than cinema providing any sustained social or political analysis. Nonetheless, many critics see Grierson's influence as crucial in the development of British cinema. His approach to documentary filmmaking has positioned a "realist" orientation as one of the fundamental tenets of what is often identified as British cinema. This is in sharp contrast to some of the more escapist tendencies seen in many of the "prestige" productions of commercial cinema in Britain during the 1930s.

Grierson was the director of only one film, *Drifters* (1929), a documentary about herring fishing in the North Sea. In 1929 he helped set up the documentary film unit of the Empire Marketing Board under the direction of the board's secretary, Stephen Tallents. The development of such official and public-sector film units is a key component of Great Britain's cinema history and has served as a model for subsequent developments in both the public and private spheres. In 1933 the Empire

Marketing Board was dismantled and the film unit was moved to the General Post Office. Following the outbreak of World War II, the unit was taken over by the Ministry of Information and became the Crown Film Unit. By 1940 Grierson was in Canada, where he helped found the National Film Board.

Despite its ties to the "real," the documentary film movement in Great Britain was in many ways an innovative form, concerned with aesthetics and a vital contributor to the development of an identifiable national cinema. With films such as *Industrial Britain* (1933), Grierson introduced a top-down, voice-of-god narration style whose purpose seemed to be public education. *Industrial Britain* was initially directed by Robert Flaherty, and Grierson had persuaded Gaumont-British to distribute the film. Unsatisfied with Flaherty's methods, however, particularly the American's tendencies toward lyrical images, Grierson took control of the film, shot additional material, and added the authoritative voice-over that is characteristic of his work. Two GPO films, *Coal Face* (1935), directed by Alberto Cavalcanti (1897–1982), and *Night Mail* (1936), directed by Harry Watt (1906–1987) and Basil Wright (1907–1987), make use of the poetry of W. H. Auden and the music of Benjamin Britten in an attempt to combine more formal aesthetic concerns in addition to addressing a sense of "Britishness." Two of the figures to emerge within the movement were Cavalcanti, who succeeded Grierson as director of the GPO unit in 1937, and Humphrey Jennings (1907–1950), whose early collaborations with Cavalcanti at the GPO were often criticized as too experimental. The Brazilian-born Cavalcanti had been involved with the French avant-garde cinema of the 1920s, while Jennings was a leading modernist and surrealist with concurrent interests in painting, poetry, and theater, among other pursuits.

It was in his wartime documentaries that Jennings truly shone. His contributions to the Crown Film Unit's efforts are among the most memorable and critically discussed of the era. These include *Listen to Britain* (1942, with co-director Stewart McAllister), a film without commentary that instead relies upon associative montage to connect varied images through sounds, helping to create a sense of social cohesion through mass observation. *Fires Were Started* (1943) stretches the definition of documentary by presenting a fictional narrative shot in a documentary style so that it seems to capture the reality of London during the blitz. *A Diary for Timothy* (1945) comes after the end of the war but is without doubt a wartime documentary. The film uses the fictional diary of a baby, Timothy, who was born in 1944 and whose first year of life has been connected to the end of the war, to "observe" the nation while also addressing the future and reinforcing sense of community, the heart of all of Jennings's films.

WARTIME FEATURE FILM PRODUCTION

In 1940 Cavalcanti left the Crown Film Unit to become an associate producer and director at Ealing Studios. That such a key figure of the British documentary movement could operate within one of the country's emerging commercial production companies reinforces the influence that documentary realism was to have on the future of British cinema. After taking over as head of Ealing in 1938, Balcon had brought in a number of documentary filmmakers as part of his attempt to have the studio make films that would more accurately reflect the national character than had been the case before. Ealing was one of only three pre-war British studios to continue operating during the war, along with Korda's London Studios and Gainsborough. All three studios made films supporting the war effort and reinforcing a sense of community, largely through representing the lives of ordinary Britons in wartime. The film that perhaps best embodied this approach is the aptly titled Gainsborough production *Millions Like Us* (1943), scripted and directed by Launder and Gilliat. The film focuses primarily on a group of ordinary women who take wartime work in an airplane factory. The film employs numerous conventions drawn from documentary traditions and points to the increasing significance of social realism as a hallmark of British film. The importance of community and the everyday is also evident in Cavalcanti's Ealing film, *Went the Day Well?* (1942), in which a small Oxfordshire village is infiltrated by Nazis before the villagers realize it and strike back. The film's incorporation of idealized aspects of everyday village life, alongside moments of action and violence, reinforces the manner in which national character was being reflected.

While the turn toward realism is a significant aspect of British cinema in this period, it was not the only option pursued by producers or favored by audiences. It has been argued that critics championed realism, and hence it was films that corresponded to realist ideals that received the most critical acclaim, particularly in discussions related to a national cinema, both at the time and among the subsequent generation of scholars and critics. For filmgoers, though, the consensus was not so clear: Gainsborough made numerous popular escapist melodramas in this period. The theatricality favored by Korda in the 1930s had not entirely disappeared following the slump of the late 1930s. While the Gainsborough melodramas were frequently derided as too far-fetched, with settings either in exotic locales or a "fantasy" past, they did have a particular appeal for audiences, especially the female audience for which the war had brought a new

Roger Livesey and Wendy Hillier in **I Know Where I'm Going** *(Michael Powell, 1945).* EVERETT COLLECTION. REPRODUCED BY PERMISSION.

economic and sexual independence. Stars such as James Mason (1909–1984) and Margaret Lockwood (1916–1990) came to embody aspects of sexual desire that were not being found elsewhere on British screens. The escapist, melodramatic nature of the wartime Gainsborough films was perhaps most evident in *Madonna of the Seven Moons* (Arthur Crabtree, 1945), which is set in what is meant to be 1930s Florence but seems more an exotic admixture of southern European stereotypes and English mannerisms and accents. Despite its many contrivances, *Madonna of the Seven Moons* was a commercial success, indicating that British audiences were more than happy to indulge in artifice and escapism.

Key purveyors of such artifice were Michael Powell (1905–1990) and his collaborator Emeric Pressburger (1902–1988). Powell had already directed a number of quota quickies and low-budget features before first collaborating with Pressburger in 1939. While their early wartime propaganda features, such as *49th Parallel*

(1941), set in Canada and starring Laurence Olivier, helped establish their reputation, it was the more lavish spectacles they created for their own production company, The Archers, that truly made the pair vital figures in British cinema. The mysterious and spiritual *A Canterbury Tale* (1944), in which a group of modern-day pilgrims makes its way to Canterbury cathedral against the backdrop of World War II, demonstrated the pair's willingness to push boundaries both narratively and visually. In *Black Narcissus* (1947) and *The Red Shoes* (1948), Powell and Pressburger operated even more concretely within an expressionist mode of cinema; the former film was a sensual melodrama set in the Himalayas, while the latter was set in the world of ballet, where an ambitious young ballerina is torn between love and ambition.

Other "quality" films of the era reflected this dynamic between realist and expressionist modes of cinema. For example, a film that seems, at first glance, to be

334

a "heritage" costume drama is Laurence Olivier's *Henry V* (1944), which uses the Shakespearean play to create a propaganda film. Henry's leadership of an English army defeating a European foe after crossing the English Channel had obvious parallels to events of the day, particularly the Normandy campaign. The film itself is dedicated "To the Commandos and Airborne Troops of Great Britain," making the ties even more explicit. Yet this Technicolor extravaganza also works well as a form of popular entertainment and taps quite effectively into the aspects of heritage Britain mined by Korda a decade earlier.

Henry V was produced by Two Cities films, a company that had come into being in 1937 and was guided by an Italian, Filippo Del Giudice. Not unlike the Hungarian-born Korda, Del Giudice was a non-Briton spearheading a company that primarily focused on making quintessentially British films. In order to secure adequate financing for the ambitious *Henry V*, Del Giudice allowed the Rank Organisation to obtain a controlling interest in Two Cities. It was one of numerous acquisitions made by the ever-expanding Rank company. The Rank Organisation, under the leadership of its founder J. Arthur Rank, was the dominant British film company throughout much of the 1930s, 1940s, 1950s, and into the 1960s. By 1946 Rank's holdings included five studios, a number of production companies, a distribution arm, and more than 650 cinemas. Rank's vertical integration gave it a position of prominence in Britain comparable to the Hollywood majors in the US. Among the production companies that Rank acquired was Gainsborough in 1936. For the first decade Gainsborough was run relatively autonomously, but starting in 1946 Rank intervened more directly in the operations at the studio, and it slowly lost its autonomy as the Rank Organisation's consolidation began to point to an era where making films with wide appeal, rather than innovative films, would become an increasingly dominant trend.

POSTWAR FILM

The successes of the wartime cinema suggested that the cinema of Great Britain had reached a new level of maturity and was poised to flourish and possibly escape from the shadow of Hollywood. There were some notable successes, including two films adapted from Graham Greene (1904–1991) novellas. One, *Brighton Rock* (John Boulting, 1947), starred a young Richard Attenborough (b. 1923) as Pinky Brown, the teenaged leader of a gang of Brighton thugs. The second, *The Third Man* (1949), directed by Carol Reed (1906–1976), was a thriller set in divided postwar Vienna and starred Joseph Cotton and Orson Welles; some have claimed it as the greatest British

film of all time. Yet while the immediate postwar years held a great deal of promise, the cinema of that era did not necessarily live up to the expectations for it. By the 1950s the British market was effectively controlled by two firms, Rank and Associated British Picture Corporation (ABPC). Additionally, cinema attendance declined from the peak of the war years. As indicated by Rank's increased intervention in Gainsborough, consolidation meant that costs could be reined in, so that while money was still lavished on quality films being made by bigger-name directors, the bulk of the company's output was material that would fill out programs in Rank-owned theaters. Rank also hoped to make greater inroads into the American market and saw the bigger-budgeted epics as a means of achieving this. A number of Britain's key directors in effect became independent contractors to Rank, and producing such films as Powell and Pressburger's *Black Narcissus* and *The Red Shoes* and David Lean's (1908–1991) *Brief Encounter* along with his subsequent success, *Great Expectations* (1946).

Most key personnel left Gainsborough after Rank began his interference in 1946. Rank named Sydney Box the new head of Gainsborough, hoping that Box could continue the studio's commercially successful tradition of melodrama. Box, however, was more interested in social realism, and the period of Box's leadership, in which he was hampered by a myriad of organizational problems, saw a dramatic decline in the studio's box-office appeal until Rank closed Gainsborough in 1950. One key personnel move made by Box during his short tenure was the appointment of his sister, Betty Box (1915–1999), to head of production at Gainsborough's Islington studio. While she struggled under difficult conditions, Box established herself as a significant producer, and once Gainsborough closed, she continued to work for Rank at Pinewood Studios. Her biggest success was with *Doctor in the House* (1954), the first film in a long-running series. *Doctor in the House* starred Dirk Bogarde (1921–1999), whose success in the title role helped establish him as the "Idol of the Odeons." Bogarde dominated the British box office and popularity polls through much of the 1950s, reprising his Doctor role in three sequels as well as starring in another Betty Box–produced film, *A Tale of Two Cities* (1958), an adaptation of Dickens's novel. Bogarde's later career was marked by more serious roles, beginning with *Victim* (1961), the first British film to deal explicitly with homosexuality, and including Joseph Losey's (1909–1984) *The Servant* (1963) and *Accident* (1967).

Bogarde's popularity in the 1950s was tied to his involvement in genre films, which had become a commercial staple of the British market. Ealing Studios under Michael Balcon had emerged from the war with a

MICHAEL POWELL and EMERIC PRESSBURGER
Michael Powell, b. Bekesbourne, Kent, England, 30 September 1905, d. 19 February 1990
Emeric Pressburger, b. Miskolc, Austria-Hungary, 5 December 1902, d. 5 February 1988

As Britain's most famous producing-directing team, Powell and Pressburger divided critical opinion between those who demanded social realism within cinema and those who supported an auteurist vision. With the rise of auteur theory in journals such as the UK-based *Movie*, the work of Powell and Pressburger received a more positive critical reevaluation. At the box office, the duo's fantastical, mystical tales enjoyed great success.

A pair of propaganda films, *49th Parallel* (1941) and *One of Our Aircraft Is Missing* (1942), early in World War II won them admiration. In 1943 they established their own production company called the Archers, for which they made a succession of popular and significant films. The first was another propaganda film, *The Life and Death of Colonel Blimp* (1943), but as it was critical of the British military leadership, it was frowned upon by the War Office as well as by Winston Churchill.

A tale of modern-day pilgrims, *A Canterbury Tale* (1944) opens with a shot that suggests a Chaucerian past but then pans up to an airplane flying overhead. The film combines the duo's trademark stylistic flair with mysticism. That mysticism returned in *"I Know Where I'm Going!"* (1945), a romance shot in the Scottish islands with the war kept in the distant background. After the war the team continued to explore the exotic and fantastic with two classic melodramas, *Black Narcissus* (1947), about nuns establishing a religious community in the Himalayas, and *The Red Shoes* (1948), based on a Hans Christian Andersen fairytale about a ballerina torn between the composer she falls in love with and her tyrannical balletmaster. Both films enjoyed international success and were a key part of the brief postwar boom in British cinema. After 1949 the pair began making films for Alexander Korda, and the Archers name disappeared.

Although they had some moderate successes as they tried to help Korda crack the international market, their success was nowhere near that of the previous decade. The pair went their separate ways after *Ill Met by Moonlight* flopped in 1957.

Before teaming with Pressburger, Powell had directed the thriller *Two Crowded Hours* (1931), followed by numerous quota quickies. The producer Joe Rock then allowed Powell to make a film of his own choosing, *The Edge of the World* (1937), shot in the Scottish Hebrides, the locale to which he would return for *"I Know Where I'm Going!"*. Following the end of his collaboration with Pressburger, Powell made the notorious *Peeping Tom* (1960). The negative reaction to his somewhat sympathetic portrayal of a sadistic killer all but ended Powell's career, though some critics later hailed the film as a masterpiece.

RECOMMENDED VIEWING
Powell: *The Edge of the World* (1937), *Peeping Tom* (1960); Powell and Pressburger: *49th Parallel* (1941), *One of Our Aircraft Is Missing* (1942), *The Life and Death of Colonel Blimp* (1943), *A Canterbury Tale* (1944), *"I Know Where I'm Going!"* (1945), *Black Narcissus* (1947), *The Red Shoes* (1948), *The Tales of Hoffman* (1951)

FURTHER READING
Christie, Ian. *Arrows of Desire: The Films of Michael Powell and Emeric Pressburger*. London: Waterstone, 1985.

———, ed. *Powell, Pressburger and Others*. London: British Film Institute, 1978.

Gough-Yates, Kevin, ed. *Michael Powell in Collaboration with Emeric Pressburger*. London: British Film Institute, 1971.

Powell, Michael. *A Life in Movies*. London: Heinemann, 1986.

Scott Henderson

continued focus on representing national character. The studio had a highly favorable financing and distribution deal with the Rank Organisation that afforded it a great deal of autonomy, so it was Balcon's personal vision that largely drove the studio. It was in the genre of comedy, and specifically the emergence of what came to be known as the "Ealing Comedy," where the studio truly flourished.

When Ealing Studios was sold to the BBC in 1955, Balcon unveiled a plaque that read: "Here during a quarter of a century were made many films projecting Britain and the British character." This sensibility is what

Michael Powell (right) and Emeric Pressburger. EVERETT COLLECTION. REPRODUCED BY PERMISSION.

drove the Ealing Comedies and made them unique. They captured an almost quaint sense of Britishness, employing national stereotypes and placing realistic characters in unexpected situations, usually representing everyman's struggle against authority. Ealing had produced earlier comedies, but it was in 1949, with the successive release of *Passport to Pimlico* (directed by Henry Cornelius), *Whisky Galore!* (directed by Alexander Mackendrick), and *Kind Hearts and Coronets* (directed by Robert Hamer), that the Ealing Comedy tradition became firmly established. A number of successes followed, including Mackendrick's *The Man in the White Suit* (1951), *The Maggie* (1954), and *The Ladykillers* (1955) and Charles Crichton's *The Lavender Hill Mob* (1951). While the Ealing Comedies enjoyed success in both the American and Continental European markets, Balcon had hoped to produce films that would help to export his particular vision of British character. Charles Frend's biopic, *Scott of the Antarctic* (1948), and Basil Dearden's *The Blue Lamp* (1950), a crime thriller that had been a British success, failed to have the impact for which Balcon had hoped. As the British market declined in the 1950s, overseas markets became more important for the economic health of British studios. Balcon's inability to adequately gauge those markets is what inevitably led to the closing of Ealing Studios in 1955.

Another particularly British comic success has been the Carry On films, created by the team of producer Peter Rogers and director Gerald Thomas, which began with *Carry On Sergeant* (1958). This first film introduced the series's tendencies to poke fun at familiar British institutions, in this case National Service (which is somewhat akin to the American National Guard). As the series progressed, the humor became bawdier and the targets for satire extended beyond institutions and into other facets of British life, including familiar film and television genres in films such as *Carry on Screaming!* (1966) and *Carry on Spying* (1964). In many ways, once one gets beyond the sexual double entendres and other outlandish humor, the Carry On films seem to further Balcon's notions of "projecting Britain and the British character."

Carry on Screaming! and *Carry on Spying* spoof two other key genres to emerge in the 1950s and into the 1960s, the Hammer horror film and the James Bond spy thrillers, respectively. Hammer Films was established in 1948 when a company called Exclusive Films wound down. The managing director of Hammer was James Carreras (1909–1990), the son of one of Exclusive's co-founders. Carreras's attitude was that films were commercial products and thus needed to be profitable. He sought ways to cut costs while retaining quality, and the genre film was the answer. Horror was not the initial focus; rather, the company concentrated on producing films with characters already known to the audience, presuming that there would be a ready-made market. Characters were drawn from familiar radio shows and from well-known myths and legends, including figures such as Robin Hood and Dick Turpin. Later, using the familiar characters of Count Dracula and Baron Frankenstein, the studio established the genre for which it is best known. Following the success of a science-fiction-horror film, *The Quatermass Xperiment* (1955, directed by Val Guest), Carreras decided that Hammer should focus on another horror subject, leading to *The Curse of Frankenstein* (1957), directed by Terence Fisher. This was soon followed by another Fisher film, *Dracula* (1958), starring Christopher Lee. The company's continued willingness to adapt to the changing whims of the horror market, exploiting each subsequent trend, has kept it in business up to the present day, although it suffered through some lean times.

Another enduring British genre has been the cycle of James Bond films. While changing key actors over the years, including the lead on a number of occasions, and making changes that reflect shifting social and cultural norms, the series has remained relatively stable in terms of structure. James Bond, secret agent 007, represents a sophisticated, cynical, sexy, and stylish British masculine ideal. Starting with *Dr. No* (1962), directed by Terence Young, the series—based on the novels of Ian Fleming

(1908–1964)—has seen twenty official Bond films made as of 2002. The first actor to play Bond was a Scot, Sean Connery (b. 1930), who has remained a fan favorite. The ongoing significance of the Bond character, not only within Britain but also worldwide, was evident in popular debate in 2005 over the choice to play the next Bond; there was much dismay when producers opted for the Englishman Daniel Craig (b. 1968) for the role. The franchise started by producers Albert "Cubby" Broccoli (1909–1996) and Canadian Harry Saltzman (1915–1994) has created an enduring legacy within British cinema and around the world.

Saltzman came to the Bond franchise after having been a significant player in the emergence of a British New Wave in the 1950s. He had been a co-founder of Woodfall Films along with theater and television director Tony Richardson (1928–1991) and playwright John Osborne (1929–1994). The initial aim of Woodfall was to adapt the stage plays of Richardson and Osborne. Richardson's association with cinema involved friendships with some of the young writers from the influential critical journal *Sequence*, including the journal's co-founder, Lindsay Anderson (1923–1994), and Karel Reisz (1926–2002). It was with Reisz that Richardson co-directed his first film, *Momma Don't Allow* (1956), a Free Cinema documentary capturing the youthful energy of the Wood Green Jazz Club in North London. Free Cinema gained its name because it operated outside of the constraints of the commercial cinema. The name was originally appended to a showing of short films programmed by Anderson, Reisz, and Richardson, including their own work. The name soon came to apply to the work itself of Anderson and his cohorts. Significant to the success of Free Cinema was the funding the films received from the British Film Institute's (BFI) Experimental Film Fund. The BFI was involved in film production in Great Britain from 1952 until the closing of its Production Board in 1999. The fund was initially aimed at promoting technological development in film and supporting new filmmakers for whom other support would be hard to come by. By the end of the 1950s it was this latter initiative that became the primary focus of the Fund. The key figures of the Free Cinema movement were among the first to benefit from this initiative, which helped launch the careers of many notable British directors, including Ridley Scott (b. 1937), his brother Tony (b. 1944), Peter Watkins (b. 1935), Ken Russell (b. 1927), and numerous other figures who would make their mark on British and world cinema in the ensuing decades.

The approaches to drama of Osborne and Richardson closely matched the concerns of the Free Cinema filmmakers, and Richardson's films became a key part of the social realism movement. He adapted two of Osborne's plays, *Look Back in Anger* (1958) (a play that contributed to the coining of the term "angry young men" to describe the key players of the era) and *The Entertainer* (1960), before turning more resolutely to a realist aesthetic in *A Taste of Honey* (1961) and *The Loneliness of the Long Distance Runner* (1962). These latter two films were part of the New Wave cinema referred to as "kitchen sink films," in reference to the frequency in which drab locations such as working-class kitchens appeared in the films as markers of class and place. These films tended to focus on the plight of working-class males as they came to terms with a shifting economy, moving away from heavy industry and toward consumerism. This was certainly the focus of Reisz's *Saturday Night and Sunday Morning* (1960), set (and shot) in Nottingham, whose main character, Albert Finney's Arthur Seaton, came to embody the epitome of the genre's Northern working-class male.

A key issue here was voice. While earlier films had represented the working class, the workers were—much as in Griersonian documentaries—spoken for or represented on screen by others, who spoke with theatrical pronunciations (often called Received Pronunciation [RP] English, or more colloquially, BBC English). In the British New Wave, real working-class lives and concerns were placed on screen. The relaxation of censorship toward the end of the 1950s, and the fact that these initial films were not as constrained as others by commercial interests, meant that authentic issues could be brought to the screen and authentic voices and dialects could be heard. This was a key era for the development of social realism in British cinema, helping to cement the importance of social realism as part of a national cinema in Britain.

THE 1960s AND 1970s

The year 1960 saw the release of Michael Powell's *Peeping Tom*, a film in which serial killer Mark Lewis (Carl Boehm) films his female victims, hoping to capture the expression of fear at the moment of their deaths. The film's addressing of issues such as voyeurism and sexuality, and its somewhat sympathetic portrayal of the killer, led to a harsh critical backlash against it; quite abruptly, the film all but ended Powell's career. Revisionist critics have hailed *Peeping Tom* as a disturbing masterpiece that cleverly addresses the voyeuristic impulses that drive cinema itself. Critical response aside, the film indicates that British cinema was not devoted solely to social realism. Boehm's Mark Lewis was one of a number of cinematic anti-heroes found in 1960s British cinema. Michael Caine's title character in *Alfie* (1966), a carefree womanizer, was another, earning him an Academy Award® nomination.

The more positive response to *Alfie* may also have been part of a more open discussion of sexuality that was part of the dramatic social upheaval of the 1960s and points to the "swinging London" image that appeared in the latter half of the decade. A crucial musical influence on this era were The Beatles, and the overt adoration of them by their female fans has been considered by some commentators as one of the aspects of the sexual revolution. The Beatles were the focus of two films, *A Hard Day's Night* (1964) and *Help!* (1965), both directed by Richard Lester (b. 1932), and an animated feature, *Yellow Submarine* (1968), directed by George Dunning. The Lester films became a cultural phenomenon, particularly *A Hard Day's Night*, which combined the kinetic filming style and rapid-fire humor of the Carry On films with location shooting and other aspects of social realism.

While British popular cinema incorporated a range of styles throughout the 1960s, social realism was still significant during the entire decade as some of the young filmmakers to emerge in the late 1950s continued to mature in their work. Lindsay Anderson followed up on his 1950s Free Cinema documentaries with two key 1960s features. *This Sporting Life* (1963) starred Richard Harris (1930–2002) as a troubled rugby player. The film was shot in the area around Wakefield, Yorkshire, and Anderson's use of location and the authenticity in his evocation of working-class life makes this one of the most significant of the New Wave films. With *If . . . .* (1968), Anderson seemed to capture the zeitgeist. The figure of Malcolm McDowell (b. 1943) as a well-armed schoolboy atop the roof of the Cheltenham school (Anderson's own alma mater) offered a memorable image in a year rocked by student uprisings in the Western world. The impact of social realism was also evident in Ken Loach's (b. 1936) critically and commercially successful *Kes* (1969), the story of a working-class boy whose grim future prospects are alleviated as he gains personal satisfaction in learning to train and fly a kestrel. This was only Loach's second feature film, the first being *Poor Cow* (1967), but he had honed his skills working in television, making a number of films for BBC's *The Wednesday Play*. Loach's television success indicated the important role television was to have in nurturing British filmmakers. Numerous British films that were made for television saw theatrical release in other countries, even when they received no, or very limited, theatrical release in Britain. This has remained the case even with more recent Loach films such as *The Navigators* (2001), a drama focused on the plight of laborers within Britain's privatized railway system.

The 1970s have been viewed critically as yet another period of crisis within British cinema. Attendances continued to drop, Hollywood influence was significant, and the innovation and promise of the New Wave was becoming an increasingly distant memory. Yet there was still innovation and controversy too as censorship restrictions were further relaxed, opening up debates around the influence of cinema on society. One director who was clearly caught in this crossfire was Stanley Kubrick (1928–1999). Although American-born, Kubrick had taken up residence in the UK in order to make his films far from the reach of meddling studio heads. *A Clockwork Orange* (1971), Kubrick's adaptation of Anthony Burgess's novel, became a controversial touchstone for debates over cinema censorship and regulation. When a number of local authorities opted to ban the film after alleged "copycat attacks" mimicking the film's ultraviolent youth, Kubrick withdrew it from the British market. A unique quirk in the British regulatory system allows films that have approval from the British Board of Film Classification to be rejected by local authorities, as was the case with *A Clockwork Orange* and more recently, Canadian David Cronenberg's *Crash* (1996). An earlier controversy had erupted around *The Devils* (1971), directed by Ken Russell. Russell had already made cuts to appease the censorship board, but the film was still banned by a number of local authorities. Russell's tendency toward graphic cinematic displays made him one of the most notorious and interesting figures of the era. The reputation he had garnered for films such as *Women in Love* (1969), his adaptation of D. H. Lawrence's novel, and *The Music Lovers* (1970), which focused on the sex life of the composer Pyotr Ilich Tchaikovsky and his wife, was cemented with the release of *The Devils*. This seemed to inspire Russell to pursue extravagance, such that his later films like *Lisztomania* (1975) and *Valentino* (1977) seem almost to be parodies of his earlier works, courting further controversy.

Another controversial figure was Nicolas Roeg (b. 1928), whose work was notably graphic at times but also, in structure, decidedly anticommercial and confrontational. Roeg first made a splash with *Performance* (1970), co-directed with Donald Cammell. The film follows a gangster on the run from the mob who takes refuge in the home of a reclusive rock star, played by Mick Jagger. Increasingly, the identities of the two men become blurred, both narratively and visually, as the film works constantly to disorient the spectator. Roeg's first solo film as director was *Walkabout* (1971), which follows three children lost in the Australian outback. This was followed by the taut psychological horror, *Don't Look Now* (1973), perhaps best remembered for its graphic conclusion. Roeg's later films have been somewhat uneven, and as is the case with Russell, he has had difficulty recapturing the level of critical acclaim he had enjoyed earlier in his career.

The ensemble crew of Monty Python also courted trouble with censorship bodies, particularly for parodying

GLENDA JACKSON
b. Birkenhead, England, 9 May 1936

Glenda Jackson received her training at the Royal Academy for Dramatic Art and commenced a stage career in 1957. Her first major stage success was her performance as Charlotte Corday in *Marat/Sade*, a 1964 production by Peter Brook's Theatre of Cruelty; she recreated the role in the 1967 film version of the play. Jackson's intensity in her roles in the films of Ken Russell, which at the time pushed boundaries in popular cinema, brought her attention and admiration. She won her first Academy Award® for Best Actress for her portrayal of Gudrun Brangwen in Russell's controversial adaptation of the D. H. Lawrence novel *Women in Love* (1969). She later portrayed Brangwen's mother, Anna, in Russell's adaptation of Lawrence's *The Rainbow* (1989).

Jackson gave a memorable performance, displaying intense physicality and sexuality, as Tchaikovsky's nymphomaniac wife in Russell's *The Music Lovers* (1970), yet she was also adept at comedy, winning her second Oscar® for her performance in Melvin Frank's *A Touch of Class* (1973) alongside George Segal. In a memorable television role, Jackson cut a stunning figure by shaving her head to play Queen Elizabeth I in the BBC television miniseries *Elizabeth R* (1971), for which she won two Emmy Awards.

It is Jackson's repeated portrayals of strong women that helped make her stand out from among her contemporaries. Her theatrical training is evident in her willingness to devote herself wholly to each role she plays. In addition to her Emmy and Academy Award® honors, Jackson has been nominated for Broadway's Tony Awards on four separate occasions. Other honors include being named a Commander of the Order of the British Empire in 1978 and having a theatre named in her honor in Birkenhead. Jackson's film career was preempted by her move into politics in 1992, when she became a member of Parliament for Hampstead and Highgate in London. She ran unsuccessfully for the position of mayor of London in 2000 but remains active in Labour Party politics. In May 2005 she was reelected MP for the fourth time.

RECOMMENDED VIEWING
Marat/Sade (1967), *Women in Love* (1969), *The Music Lovers* (1970), *A Bequest to the Nation* (also known as *The Nelson Affair*, 1973), *Hedda* (1975), *Turtle Diary* (1985), *The Rainbow* (1989)

FURTHER READING
Woodward, Ian. *Glenda Jackson: A Study in Fire and Ice.* London: St. Martin's Press, 1985.

Scott Henderson

the story of Christ in *Life of Brian* (1979). The film used the story of Brian, whose life parallels that of Christ, to provide typical "Monty Python" humor as it had been developed in their sketch television show, *Monty Python's Flying Circus* (1969–1974). The troupe's first cinematic effort, *And Now for Something Completely Different* (1971), directed by Ian McNaughton, is a compilation of their television work. With Terry Jones as director, the troupe became more ambitious and cinematic by tying its unique brand of comedy to narrative, first in *Monty Python and the Holy Grail* (1974), which was co-directed by Terry Gilliam; then *Life of Brian*; and finally *Monty Python's The Meaning of Life* (1983). The troupe employed absurdist humor, which at times could be quite graphic, as part of a broader satire of contemporary British society and mass culture more generally.

The 1970s also witnessed a rise in art cinema with directors such as Derek Jarman (1942–1994) and Sally Potter (b. 1949) emerging. Jarman had been a set designer on Russell's *The Devils*. His first series of features were all low-budget affairs shot on Super 8mm. *Sebastiane* (1976), co-directed with Paul Humfress, was notable for its portrayal of homosexual desire as it traced the martyrdom of St. Sebastian. Jarman's work was known for its anachronistic flourishes, evident in *Jubilee* (1977), which captures the punk ethos in its exploration of Queen Elizabeth II's jubilee year as seen through the eyes of Queen Elizabeth I and her astrologer magician, John Dee. Jarman followed this with *The Tempest* (1979), adapted from Shakespeare, although Jarman's most noted work is likely the beautifully shot *Caravaggio* (1986). Jarman's eye for the beautiful is also evident in *The Last of England* (1988), which saw him return to the Super 8mm format in an effort to visually depict the rot he perceived to be at the core of Thatcher's England.

Glenda Jackson in **The Romantic Englishwoman** *(Joseph Losey, 1975).* EVERETT COLLECTION. REPRODUCED BY PERMISSION.

Potter's *Thriller* (1979) was a short film written, directed, edited, and produced by Potter herself with funding from the Arts Council of Great Britain. Potter consistently challenges viewers and has been a particular favorite of feminist critics for her willingness to deconstruct the masculine values of cinema. The success of *Thriller* permitted Potter the opportunity to make her first feature, *The Gold Diggers* (1983). She did work for television through much of the 1980s before returning to the screen with the ambitious *Orlando* (1992), starring Tilda Swinton (b. 1960). *Orlando* adapts the Virginia Woolf novel and updates it to the 1990s as it follows its lead character through four hundred years of history (including a sex change) in its episodic exploration of social and gender roles. Potter has continued to work within mainstream art cinema with *The Tango Lesson* (1997); *The Man Who Cried* (2000), which featured Johnny Depp; and *Yes* (2004).

FROM THE 1980s TO THE PRESENT

If the 1970s saw the critical estimation of British cinema at a low ebb, then the tide rose very quickly at the beginning of the 1980s. The breakthrough commercial success for British cinema was Hugh Hudson's *Chariots of Fire* (1981), which follows the stories of two British athletes, Harold Abrahams (Ben Cross) and Eric Liddell

(Ian Charleson), at the Paris Olympics in 1924. The film's Academy Award® for Best Picture, followed by a win for Richard Attenborough's *Gandhi* (1982), suggested a resurgence for British cinema on the international stage. These two award-winning films were both epic period pieces that recalled the Korda era. Their success helped revitalize the industry, but the significant changes were occurring on a much smaller scale.

The most significant development was a shift in funding. It was the funding provided by Channel Four that seemed to bring new vitality to British cinema. It also brought an increased regional sensibility as funding was no longer concentrated in the hands of London-based producers. It was not only different regions but different underrepresented groups whose voices were finally becoming part of British cinema. As its name implies, Channel Four was the fourth terrestrial television channel launched in Britain, first appearing in 1982. In an effort to maintain its arts-focused mandate and to provide quality material for the channel, a separate films arm, Film on Four, was established. During the years of Margaret Thatcher's Conservative governments, which were not at all kind toward the arts, the money, support, and exhibition provided by Channel Four were vital to the British film community.

A number of key films, and key figures, in British cinema of the 1980s and 1990s emerged as a result of the Films on Four funding. Among the first successes of the program were Peter Greenaway's *The Draughtsman's Contract* (1982); Neil Jordan's *Angel* (1982); and Stephen Frears's *My Beautiful Laundrette* (1985), written by Hanif Kureishi. *My Beautiful Laundrette* suggested the potential of the Channel Four films to uncover new voices within British cinema. Kureishi's script, which explores the burgeoning gay relationship between two men, one white and one Pakistani, opens up many questions around identity in Britain and highlighted some of the difficulties that second-generation immigrants had in negotiating between cultural traditions and a British way of life. A number of key films emerged in the following two decades that explored the South Asian diasporic experience. Among these were Gurinder Chadha's *Bhaji on the Beach* (1993), which uses an outing to a typical British seaside resort to focus on the experiences of Asian women of different generations; the comedic, yet touching *East Is East* (1999), directed by Damien O'Donnell and based on the semiautobiographical play by Ayub Khan-Din; and *Bend it Like Beckham* (2002), which continues Chadha's exploration of gender issues in its focus on an Asian girl who would rather play soccer than learn traditional Indian cooking methods.

Other cultural groups in Britain have also found filmic means of making their voices heard. In 1983 a

Sally Potter and Pablo Veron in Potter's **The Tango Lesson** *(1997).* EVERETT COLLECTION. REPRODUCED BY PERMISSION.

group of black independent filmmakers established the production collective Sankofa. With funding from the Greater London Council (a progressive political body disbanded by Margaret Thatcher in 1986) and Channel Four, the members of Sankofa sought ways of telling stories employing their own cultural voices. The most notable member of the collective has been Isaac Julien (b. 1960), whose early films for the group included *Who Killed Colin Roach?* (1983); *Territories* (1985); and his meditation on the gay, black American poet Langston Hughes, *Looking for Langston* (1988). With funding from the BFI, Julien was able to make his debut feature, *Young Soul Rebels* (1991), a thriller that offers a rather idealistic portrait of racial togetherness among London's various music subcultures in the late 1970s.

Funding through bodies such as Channel Four and the BFI kept British filmmakers independent of Thatcherism and more recently of the New Labour ideals of Tony Blair. The filmmakers' response was films that were largely critical of the dominant vision of Britain. These films began to break the hegemonic representation of Britishness that had dominated the national cinema by

opening up issues of gender, sexuality, race, and class. This is not to say that there have not been investments made in more commercial cinema. FilmFour, as Film on Four came to be called in the 1990s, invested in international hits such as *Four Weddings and a Funeral* (1994, directed by Mike Newell). The "heritage" film also became a major staple of British popular cinema and a successful international export. A number of Ismail Merchant (1936–2005) and James Ivory (b. 1928) co-productions were staple fare for this genre. The Ivory-directed *A Room with a View* (1985) followed on the heels of *Chariots of Fire* and *Gandhi* and helped to establish the key stylistic parameters for the genre. Later successful heritage films such as Shekhar Kapur's *Elizabeth* (1998) and John Madden's *Shakespeare in Love* (1998), another Oscar® winner for Best Picture, helped to cement the reputation of this area of British cinema.

In contrast to these versions of heritage Britain, the trend toward social realism has remained strong in many of the smaller British films that have been made in recent decades. Among the filmmakers who have consistently employed this strategy has been Mike Leigh (b. 1943). Leigh's first feature was *Bleak Moments* (1971), but subsequently he turned to television, where his improvisational methods were more readily funded. He worked there until making his second feature, *High Hopes*, in 1988. Yet another film supported by Channel Four, as well as British Screen, the film is a family drama that is used as a poignant rejoinder to the consumerism spawned by Thatcherism. Leigh's focus on the working class continued in a series of social realist films, including *Life is Sweet* (1990), *Naked* (1993), *Secrets and Lies* (1996), and *Career Girls* (1997). All of these films focused on contemporary Britain, but Leigh demonstrated his ability to explore similar themes around class and British society employing historical subjects, as in *Topsy-Turvy* (1999), which examines the world of Gilbert and Sullivan, and *Vera Drake* (2004), which examines abortionist Drake's clash with British society in the 1950s.

While the films of the 1960s New Wave had focused on Britain's working class, more recent films have traced the lives of the underclass, former members of the working class who have been left behind in the new, technological economy during the reigns of Thatcher and Blair. Films such as Peter Cattaneo's *The Full Monty* (1997), Mark Herman's *Brassed Off* (1996) and *Little Voice* (1998), and Carine Adler's *Under the Skin* (1997), along with the continued work of Ken Loach, explore the desperate attempts at survival for those who have been cut off from Britain's economic boom. While such films offer positive moments, their use of location shooting and devout attention to detail do much to reveal the dark underbelly of Britain's current success.

Since the winding down of Channel Four's funding of films in 2002, the funding model in Great Britain has continued to evolve. The UK Film Council was set up in 2000 by the Labour government. The role of the council is to dispense money raised via the National Lottery to nine different regional screen agencies in England as well as the Welsh Development Agency, Scottish Enterprise, and the Department for Enterprise, Trade and Investment in Northern Ireland, each of which administers its own film-funding initiatives. The result is an increased regional diversification within British cinema.

SCOTLAND AND WALES

While earlier efforts such as those of the New Wave in the 1960s had moved their focus beyond London and the Home Counties, the regionalism on offer extended north to cities such as Nottingham but still remained predominantly English in nature. With the emergence of alternative funding bodies such as Channel Four, and more recently the National Lottery, a greater awareness of regionalism has become necessary for any understanding

of British cinema. It is nearly impossible today to conceive of one single cinema of Great Britain.

Scotland as a setting has been employed in numerous British films, notably Ealing films such as *The Maggie* and *Whisky Galore!*. It has of course also featured in the telling of Scottish legends, such as those of Shakespeare's Macbeth or Rob Roy. Additionally, Scotland provided a number of key figures to the British industry, among them John Grierson. An indigenous Scottish film industry, however, took far longer to develop. While much of the UK and Ireland prospered from the shifting economy of the 1980s and 1990s, former industrialized areas in Britain's north—particularly in Scotland—and in parts of Wales, where heavy industry and mining had been dominant industries, struggled immensely. Using cinema to voice the concerns of underrepresented contemporary Scots was a significant breakthrough. One director who managed to do so successfully was Bill Forsyth (b. 1946). After having made short documentaries, Forsyth directed his first feature, *That Sinking Feeling* (1980), about a group of unemployed Glasgow youth involved in a robbery of stainless steel sinks. This was followed by *Gregory's Girl* (1981), which used a social realist aesthetic and a tale of adolescent love to explore life in Scotland's postwar "new towns." Perhaps Forsyth's most successful film was the low-key comedy, *Local Hero* (1983), produced by David Puttnam. The film evoked the humor of the Ealing comedies as it explored the clash between contemporary consumerism, represented by an American oil company, and traditional Scottish values, represented by a local fishing village. Forsyth later spent time working in the United States before returning to Scotland to make *Gregory's Two Girls* (1999), a sequel to *Gregory's Girl*.

Restless Natives (1985), produced by Channel Four and directed by an American, Michael Hoffman, is a film that essentially modernizes the myth of Rob Roy. It follows two Edinburgh youth who, cut off from the new economy, turn to robbing the tour buses that seem now to dominate their landscape, only to find that their exploits become a bigger tourist draw than any scenery the Highlands has to offer. The main characters of *Restless Natives* are possibly the comedic predecessors of the youth of Danny Boyle's *Trainspotting* (1996), a film adapted from a stage play that itself was adapted from a novel by Irvine Welsh. The film's dry wit, its harrowing portrayal of heroin abuse among the disenfranchised youth of Edinburgh, its contemporary soundtrack, and Boyle's slick shooting style resulted in *Trainspotting* becoming one of the main exports of mid-1990s "Cool Brittania"—this despite the fact that its extensive use of working-class Scottish slang and authentic dialect meant that it had to be offered with subtitles in many other English-speaking markets (particularly the United

States). Another film that required subtitles was *Ratcatcher* (1999), directed by the photographer-turned-filmmaker Lynne Ramsay (b. 1969). Set during a garbage strike in Glasgow of the 1970s, the film's use of local dialect, along with its attempts to make use of costume and other authentic historic elements, make the film an ironic sort of heritage film, uncovering a heritage that official Britain may prefer be left forgotten.

Perhaps Wales's biggest claim to film culture has been in the figures that it has exported to Hollywood, including the likes of Richard Burton (1925–1984), Anthony Hopkins, and Catherine Zeta-Jones. The Welsh industry has been small and itself is split between English-language films made in Wales and Welsh-language films that have, understandably, a very limited audience. Likely the most popular Welsh-language film of all time is *Hedd Wyn* (1992), directed by Paul Turner, which was nominated for an Academy Award® for Best Foreign Language film. Endaf Emlyn (b. 1944) directed the Welsh-language feature *Gadael Lenin* (*Leaving Lenin*, 1993), a film that explored relationships among a group of Welsh youth on a school trip to Russia. Justin Kerrigan's *Human Traffic* (1999) captures the youthful vibrancy of contemporary Cardiff. Only one of the film's main characters possesses a Welsh accent; the rest are from various other parts of the UK. In this way, Kerrigan is able to address the changing nature of the Welsh capital as it has become a key center of technological development and has undergone a boom that has transformed it from a Welsh city to a UK city. Other films have focused on the Welsh underclass. *Twin Town* (1997), directed by Kevin Allen, is in the British underclass film tradition in its representation of a dysfunctional working-class family in Swansea.

Given an increased focus on regional filmmaking, a migratory and multicultural population, the ever-increasing economic significance of the European Union, and the growth of co-productions as part of the global cinema market, any secure definitions of what constitutes a British cinema can no longer exist. Instead, Great Britain can now be seen as a significant cinema center where a multitude of voices can be found.

SEE ALSO *Class; Documentary; Early Cinema; Heritage Films; National Cinema; New Wave; Realism*

FURTHER READING

Ashby, Justine, and Andrew Higson, eds. *British Cinema, Past and Present*. London and New York: Routledge, 2000.

Barr, Charles, ed. *All Our Yesterdays: 90 Years of British Cinema*. London: British Film Institute, 1986.

Curran, James, and Vincent Porter, eds. *British Cinema History*. London: Weidenfeld and Nicholson, 1983.

Dickinson, Margaret, and Sarah Street. *Cinema and State: The Film Industry and the British Government, 1927–84*. London: British Film Institute, 1985.

Friedman, Lester, ed. *Fires We Started: British Cinema and Thatcherism*. Minneapolis: University of Minnesota Press, 1993. Revised ed., London: Wallflower Press, 2006.

Higson, Andrew. *Waving the Flag: Constructing a National Cinema in Britain*. Oxford and New York: Clarendon Press, 1995.

———, ed. *Dissolving Views: Key Writings on British Cinema*. London and New York: Cassell, 1996.

———, ed. *Young and Innocent?: The Cinema in Britain, 1896–1930*. Exeter, UK: University of Exeter Press, 2002.

Hill, John. *British Cinema in the 1980s: Issues and Themes*. Oxford and New York: Oxford University Press.

Leach, Jim. *British Film*. Cambridge, UK and New York: Cambridge University Press, 2004.

Murphy, Robert, ed. *The British Cinema Book*. London: British Film Institute, 1997.

———, ed. *British Cinema of the 90s*. London: British Film Institute, 2000.

Petrie, Duncan. *Screening Scotland*. London: British Film Institute, 2000.

Street, Sarah. *British National Cinema*. London and New York: Routledge, 1997.

Scott Henderson

GREAT DEPRESSION

The Great Depression refers to that period of American history between the stock market crash of October 1929 and the US entry into World War II following the Japanese bombing of Pearl Harbor on 7 December 1941. Although the United States had experienced other significant depressions before—the periods between 1839 and 1843, 1873 and 1879, and 1893 and 1896 offer three examples—the Great Depression was particularly sustained and persistent. The only major depression to take place after the movies were firmly established as an industry and popular art form in the United States, it generated considerable economic strain on the industry—especially in the early 1930s—eroding the audience and encouraging the industry to win back its audience in a variety of ways, some of which led to tensions between the industry and certain segments of American society. The film industry responded to its critics, and as the decade wore on, a resurgent national confidence in the system coincided with some shifts in the films produced by the industry.

THE DEPRESSION AND INDUSTRY FINANCES

The economic downturn of the Depression was precipitated by a rapid decline in values of stock at the New York Stock Exchange in the fall of 1929. Black Thursday (24 October) and Black Tuesday (29 October) were key moments in the collapse. Overall, the Dow Jones Industrial Average dropped from a high of 381 on 3 September to a low of 198 before the end of the year. The economy continued to decline through 1932, when the Dow Jones industrial average bottomed out at 41. Between 1929 and 1933, when Franklin Delano Roosevelt (1882–1945) assumed the presidency, consumption had

plummeted 18 percent, construction by 78 percent, and investment by 98 percent. National income had been cut in half, five thousand banks had collapsed, and over nine million savings accounts evaporated. Nonfarm unemployment reached 25 percent in the United States, and most farmers were struggling to survive because of severely depressed prices for the crops they grew and livestock they raised.

Inevitably, such an economic climate hit Hollywood hard. The industry had enjoyed a period of prosperity in the 1920s, building luxurious movie palaces and, from 1927 on, cashing in on the novelty of the newly developed technology of talking films. Between 1930 and 1933, however, movie attendance dropped from around ninety million admissions per week to sixty million admissions, and average ticket prices dropped from 30 cents to around 20 cents over the same span. Industry revenues dropped from $720 million in 1929 to $480 million in 1933, while total company profits of $54.5 million in 1929 gave way to total company losses of $55.7 million in 1932.

At the time of the stock market crash the film industry was organized by a studio system, and most of the important films produced in Hollywood in the 1930s were made by five studios that owned theater chains and three smaller studios that did not. The "Big Five" that owned theaters faced particularly pronounced strains following the crash because of the investments they had made in building theaters in the 1920s. Of that group, RKO, Fox, and Paramount all went into bankruptcy or receivership in the early 1930s, Warner Bros. managed to stay afloat only by selling off nearly one-quarter of its assets, and only MGM—which had much smaller theater holdings than Paramount—continued to make a profit, although its profits dropped from $15 million in 1930 to $4.3 million in 1931. (Fox returned to stability by merging with the independent production company Twentieth-Century in 1935.)

The "Little Three" managed a bit better. Both Columbia and Universal, production companies that owned no theaters, survived in part by making low-budget "B movies" that were often shown as double features. Columbia did better from 1934, when Frank Capra's (1896–1991) *It Happened One Night* became a hit. Universal was in constant financial difficulty, recording small losses each year between 1932 and 1938, although the popularity of their horror films early in the decade and Deanna Durbin (b. 1921) musicals later on kept the losses from growing even higher. United Artists, essentially a distribution company for its owners, such as Charlie Chaplin (1889–1977), and talented independent producers such as Samuel Goldwyn (1882–1974) and Walter Wanger (1894–1968), lost money only in 1932, although its profits in the later 1930s were very modest.

Movie exhibition was also affected by the economic downturn. One major effect was the decline of construction of new theaters following the boom of movie-palace building in the 1920s. As movie attendance began to decline significantly in the early 1930s some theater owners also began to offer giveaway programs (like "dish night") or games of chance (SCREENO, a variety of bingo, was the most popular), particularly on the traditionally slow nights of Monday and Tuesday, to get more people back into the theaters. Theater owners also sought to reduce costs by cutting staff—hiring fewer ushers, for example—or, in the bigger urban theaters, by eliminating live shows that supplemented the movie program. Some theaters turned to double features, thus boosting the demand for B movies by companies such as Monogram and Republic. The only major new expense made by many theater owners in the Depression, especially in the South and West, was the installation of air conditioning, which because of technological advances became more affordable than it had been in the 1920s. By the end of the decade attendance inched back to 1929 levels. In this improved financial environment, the giveaway programs and the games of chance began to disappear.

Indeed, the industry began to rebound after the dark years of 1932 and 1933, in part because of New Deal legislation. President Roosevelt's National Industrial Recovery Act (NIRA) went into effect in June 1933, and its strategy for recovery was in part to permit certain monopolistic practices by major industries, including the film industry. Even though the Supreme Court eventually struck it down in 1935, the NIRA also authorized the organization of labor unions and collective bargaining, a tendency strengthened with the passage of the Wagner Act in 1935. From 1933 on various groups of Hollywood workers sought and eventually succeeded in establishing unions recognized by the studios, including the Screen Actors Guild (recognized in 1937), the Screen Directors Guild (1939), and the Screen Writers Guild (1941). By the time the United States entered World War II, the industry was largely unionized.

The evolution of the industry through the Depression can be grasped in part through numbers. Box-office receipts bottomed out in 1933 at $480 million, gradually growing to $810 million in 1941, which slightly exceeded the $720 million receipts of 1929. Total company losses of $55.7 million in 1932 were reduced to losses of $4.9 million in 1933, after which the bottom line improved to profits of $9 million in 1934, up to $34 million in 1941. Only in 1943, however, with profits of $60.6 million, did Hollywood exceed the $54.5 million of profits in 1929. In the most general terms, after spiraling downward from 1929/1930 to 1932/1933, the economic condition of the industry reversed itself and gradually improved for the rest of the decade, even though attendance and profits did not return to 1929 levels until after World War II was well underway. The economic conditions of the Depression surely tested the movie industry.

THE MOVIES OF "PRE-CODE HOLLYWOOD"

The period from the 1929 stock market crash until the establishment of the Production Code Administration in June 1934 has been called "pre-code Hollywood." Although film historians have argued about how different pre-code films were from films made later in the decade, a solid argument can be made that there was a distinctive difference. Andrew Bergman suggests in *We're in the Money* that the popular cycles of pre-code Hollywood—such as gangster films, fallen-women films, backstage musicals, social-problem films, and "anarchic" comedies—were distinctly connected to the economic distress of the early 1930s and the social-psychological anxieties it produced. Robert Sklar extends this argument in *Movie-Made America*, labeling the early 1930s the "golden age of turbulence" and the post-code Depression films the "golden age of order." Although Richard Maltby has usefully suggested that the majority of films in pre-code Hollywood were tamer and more conventional than the films Bergman and Sklar highlight, it does seem that during the early 1930s, more so than just before and just after that period, filmmakers were more likely to make, and audiences were more likely to respond to, films that called into question dominant attitudes toward sexuality, upper-class respectability, and the institutions of law and order.

PARE LORENTZ
b. Leonard MacTaggart Lorentz, Clarksburg, West Virginia, 11 December 1905, d. 4 March 1992

Pare Lorentz was the most influential maker of and advocate for government-sponsored documentary films in the United States during the Great Depression. After studying journalism at West Virginia Wesleyan College and the University of West Virginia, Lorentz left for New York in 1925 and adopted his father's first name, Pare. From 1927 to 1932 he reviewed films for the magazine *Judge*. After that, he continued to write movie reviews and essays for a variety of publications for the rest of the decade. Some of this work was collected in *Lorentz on Film* (1975).

In 1934 Lorentz published *The Roosevelt Year: 1933*, a book of photographs with accompanying text that sought to dramatize the Depression and the emergence of the New Deal. Lorentz originally had hoped to make a film, but had been unable to arrange financing. However, in June 1935 Rexford Tugwell, head of the US Resettlement Administration, hired him to make films about the plight of farmers in the Depression. The first film project focused on the Dust Bowl. Made for less than $20,000, *The Plow That Broke the Plains* (1936) demonstrated how the drought, dust storms, and market collapse forced Great Plains farmers to leave the land, then concluded with the government's plan of resettlement and soil conservation. Although the film garnered generally positive reviews, Hollywood caused difficulties for Lorentz, making it hard for him to obtain stock footage and discouraging theaters from showing a government-sponsored film that would compete with its newsreels. Lorentz's next film, *The River* (1938), featured footage of the devastating floods in early 1937 to depict the problems of flooding, soil erosion, and poverty in the Tennessee and Mississippi Valleys and to suggest how the

establishment of the Tennessee Valley Authority confronted those problems through flood control, electrification, and conservation measures. More positively reviewed and widely distributed than *Plow*, *The River* received the best documentary award at the Venice Film Festival in 1938, winning over Leni Riefenstahl's *Olympia*.

That year President Roosevelt named Lorentz director of the US Film Service. In that capacity he oversaw the making of Joris Iven's *The Power and the Land* (1940) and Robert Flaherty's *The Land* (1940) and made one film himself, *The Fight for Life* (1940), an account of infant mortality, malnutrition, and child poverty in the United States that won the National Board of Review's best documentary award. Its controversial topic and critical subject matter angered many congressmen, however, and the US Film Service was eliminated when Congress refused to fund it in the spring of 1940. Lorentz's next project, a documentary on unemployment called *Ecco Homo*, was never made.

RECOMMENDED VIEWING
The Plow That Broke the Plains (1936), *The River* (1938), *The Fight for Life* (1940)

FURTHER READING
Lorentz, Pare. *FDR's Moviemaker: Memoirs and Scripts*. Reno: University of Nevada Press, 1992.

————. *Lorentz on Film: Movies 1927–1941*. New York: Hopkinson and Blake, 1975.

Snyder, Robert L. *Pare Lorentz and the Documentary Film*. 2nd ed. Reno: University of Nevada Press, 1993. The original edition was published in 1968.

Charles J. Maland

The classic gangster films, whose plots were drawn to a greater or lesser extent from headlines about real gangsters such as Chicago's Al Capone, offer a good example. In them an ethnic American, usually of Italian descent, such as Rico in *Little Caesar* (1931) or Tony Camonte in *Scarface* (1932), or Irish extraction, such as Tommy Powers in *Public Enemy* (1931), rises from rags to riches by consolidating power in the prohibited liquor trade,

only to be killed in the film's climax, a victim of his ambition, ruthlessness, and notoriety. James Cagney (1899–1986) and Edward G. Robinson (1893–1973) became closely associated with this genre. In the fallen-women films a woman is driven by economic circumstances to become a prostitute or kept woman. Greta Garbo (1905–1990) (*Susan Lenox, Her Fall and Rise*, 1931), Joan Crawford (1904–1977) (*Possessed*, 1931, and

Rain, 1932), Marlene Dietrich (*Blonde Venus*, 1932), Jean Harlow (1911–1937) (*Red Dust* and *Red-Headed Woman*, both 1932), and Barbara Stanwyck (1907–1990) (*Baby Face*, 1932) were among the best-known actresses who appeared in films of this cycle. The backstage musicals, most notably *The Gold Diggers of 1933* and *42nd Street* (both 1933), achieved popularity by combining Busby Berkeley's production numbers with a plot about a producer and cast working together to put on a show despite the depression economy. The story type from pre-code Hollywood that embraced the era most directly was the social-problem film, a type common in the 1910s but much less so in the 1920s. *I Am a Fugitive from a Chain Gang* (1932) was one of the most acclaimed at the time, but also noteworthy were *Wild Boys of the Road* (1933) and the independently financed *Our Daily Bread* (1934). Finally, the irreverence of the anarchic comedies such as the Marx Brothers's *Duck Soup* (1933) satirized political authority and respectability, while Mae West's (1893–1980) comedies such as *She Done Him Wrong* (1933) and *I'm No Angel* (1934)—which she both wrote and starred in—featured a self-confident, voluptuous woman who openly uses her charm and physical allure to wrap men around her finger, refusing to accept the culture's prescribed role for female respectability.

THE BATTLE OVER CONTROL AND "POST-PCA" DEPRESSION MOVIES

The popularity and pervasiveness of the gangster films, the fallen-women films, and West's brazen comedies played a significant role in the protests by a variety of pressure groups against the movie industry between 1932 and early 1934. Among the most prominent of the protesters was the Legion of Decency, a Catholic organization that sought to pressure the movie industry to follow the guidelines of the Hollywood Production Code of 1930. The Studio Relations Committee, an industry self-regulation body, was ostensibly charged with seeing that the studios followed that code, but it did not possess adequate power to compel the studios to adhere to it. Desperately seeking to find ways to reverse the decline in attendance, the studios regularly ignored the code in many of their productions. When the Legion of Decency began to threaten a widespread national boycott of the movies early in 1934, however, the studios decided that it would be in their best interests to set up a body that would enforce the code more strictly. They did so in June 1934 by establishing the Production Code Administration (PCA) and appointing as its director Joseph Breen. From that point on, the PCA more strictly enforced the code by reviewing and making suggestions on all studio scripts before they went into production, then doing the same with all completed films before issuing a PCA certificate. Member studios agreed not to release any film before the PCA granted it a certificate.

Regular monitoring of studio films by the PCA, as well as a gradual restoration of national confidence engendered by Roosevelt's New Deal programs between 1933 and 1935, contributed to some shifts in movie cycles after 1934. For example, Warner Bros. revised the gangster formula by making the protagonist not a gangster but a law-enforcement official in *G-Men* (1935), starring James Cagney. It was one of the top ten highest-grossing films of 1935 and paved the way for similar films, such as *Bullets or Ballots* (1936), starring Edward G. Robinson as a police detective, and *Marked Woman* (1937), starring Humphrey Bogart (1899–1957) as a crusading district attorney. The fallen-woman and Mae West films, which were either forbidden or seriously constrained by the PCA, made way for one of the most popular and accomplished genres in the late 1930s, the screwball comedy. The surprise success of Capra's *It Happened One Night* (1934), which was made before the PCA was established, helped establish the cycle. An unlikely comic romance about a spoiled heiress (Claudette Colbert) and a gruff and pragmatic newspaper reporter (Clark Gable), the film became the first movie to win the five major Oscars®—for film, director, actress, actor, and screenplay (Robert Riskin)—and set the stage for a variety of successful screwball comedies. Noting the code's prohibitions against overt portrayals of sexuality, Andrew Sarris has called the genre the "sex comedy without sex," suggesting that instead of turning the female protagonists into sex objects, the screwball comedy endowed them with spontaneity, wit, vitality, and often professional achievements in the working world (p. 8). Capra's *Mr. Deeds Goes to Town* (1936), Gregory La Cava's (1892–1952) *My Man Godfrey* (1936), Leo McCarey's (1898–1969) *The Awful Truth* (1937), George Cukor's *Holiday* (1938), and two films by Howard Hawks (1896–1977), *Bringing Up Baby* (1938) and *His Girl Friday* (1940), are among the many accomplished films of the genre. In their focus on a rocky but ultimately successful romance, these screwball comedies resembled the Fred Astaire–Ginger Rogers musicals of the middle and late 1930s—including *Top Hat* (1935), *Swing Time* (1936), and *Shall We Dance* (1937)—which replaced the backstage musicals popular in the early 1930s. Each of these emerging cycles—law-official crime films, screwball comedies, and romantic musicals—exhibited more confidence in the prevailing order than had many of the popular cycles of the early 1930s.

Another shift following the establishment of the PCA (and the gradual improvement of economic conditions) was the move toward more expensive, "prestige films." These films were expensive to make, but they also were most likely to appear on *Variety*'s list of the top ten

The Joad family in The Grapes of Wrath *(John Ford, 1940), adapted from John Steinbeck's novel.* ® ™ AND COPYRIGHT © 20TH CENTURY FOX FILM CORP./COURTESY EVERETT COLLECTION. REPRODUCED BY PERMISSION.

highest-grossing films in the last half of the decade. The prestige films encompass a variety of different story types, but they included adaptations of literary classics and best-selling novels, swashbuckling adventure stories, and "biopics"—biographical films about famous people. The first group included cinematic versions of Shakespeare's plays, such as *A Midsummer Night's Dream* (1935) and *Romeo and Juliet* (1936), adaptations of nineteenth-century novels, such as *David Copperfield, A Tale of Two Cities,* and *Anna Karenina* (all 1935), and adaptations of twentieth-century novels such as *The Informer* and *Mutiny on the Bounty* (both 1935),

Anthony Adverse (1936), *Lost Horizon* and *The Good Earth* (both 1937), the monumentally successful *Gone With the Wind* (1939), and the critically acclaimed *Grapes of Wrath* (1940). Successful costume/adventure films appeared with *Captain Blood* (1935) and *Anthony Adverse* (1936), and crested with *The Adventures of Robin Hood* (1938). The biopics portrayed the lives of people as different as Jesse James, Alexander Graham Bell, and Thomas Edison, but one particularly effective set were three films starring Paul Muni (1895–1967): *The Story of Louis Pasteur* (1936), *The Life of Emile Zola* (1937), and *Juarez* (1939).

The popularity of two child stars in the middle and latter part of the decade suggests that American movies were playing a role in the reconsolidation of American culture—in restoring confidence in the system—as the country began to pull out of the Depression. From 1935 to 1938 Shirley Temple (b. 1928), thanks to the success of such films as *Curly Top* (1935) and *The Littlest Rebel* (1936), topped the Quigley Publications poll of top box-office stars in the United States. From 1939 to 1941, Mickey Rooney (b. 1920)—MGM star of the Andy Hardy series, *Boys Town* (1938), and "let's put on a show" musicals such as *Babes in Arms* (1939)—topped the list. In both cases the child actors showed vitality, resilience, and good cheer in overcoming whatever obstacles they confronted.

As the United States moved into the latter part of the decade, Hollywood, like American culture as a whole, began to exhibit a reawakened interest in defining national traditions and values. This trend emerged in part as a response to the growing international threat of fascism in Germany and Italy. The Los Angeles area, which became home to many prominent refugees from Germany, became a center of antifascist activity in the United States, led by groups such as the Hollywood Anti-Nazi League. The movies participated in this exploration of national traditions and critique of fascism both domestic and, eventually, foreign. *Fury* (1937), directed by refugee Fritz Lang (1890–1976), explored the psychology of a mob action that led to lynching. Capra's *Mr. Smith Goes to Washington* (1939) and *Meet John Doe* (1941) confronted a prototypically American hero with a sinister antagonist whose wealth, power, and ambition threatened to disrupt the democratic system. The historical settings of films such as *Young Mr. Lincoln*, *Drums Along the Mohawk*, and *Gone With the Wind* (all 1939) were central to their narrative concerns. The reappearance of the "A" western in late-1930s movies such as *Dodge City*, *Union Pacific*, and *Stagecoach* (all 1939) also contributed to the interest in American national traditions. Other important films from the end of this period include *The Grapes of Wrath* (1940), which shows how the Joad family are victimized by the dust bowl and a harsh economic system, and Orson Welles's (1915–1985) audacious, probing critique of an American tycoon, *Citizen Kane* (1941). Although the PCA discouraged filmmakers from making films that criticized other nations—in part because it hurt foreign rentals—overtly anti-Nazi films gradually began to appear even before the United States declared war in December 1941, most notably in *Confessions of a Nazi Spy* (1939) and Chaplin's satiric attack on fascism, *The Great Dictator* (1940).

If one surveys American movies during the Depression in an extreme long shot, two impulses come into clear focus. One impulse, an aesthetic of movies as entertainment, which had established itself firmly during the 1920s, held that movies should enable viewers to escape from their problems for two hours. However, a counter impulse, which emerged from the distressing social and economic conditions following the stock market crash, pressured filmmakers to acknowledge and grapple with the social realities of the day. Although the latter impulse never became dominant, in part because of the industry's constant attention to the box-office potential of projects, it did lead to some of the most disturbing and powerful films of pre-code Hollywood and to the most critically acclaimed and widely discussed films later in the decade. With the American entry to World War II in December 1941, the industry officially moved out of the Depression and into a new era.

SEE ALSO *Gangster Films; Populism; Screwball Comedy*

FURTHER READING

Balio, Tino. *Grand Design: Hollywood as a Modern Business Enterprise, 1930–1939*. History of the American Cinema. New York: Scribner, 1993.

Bergman, Andrew. *We're in the Money: Depression America and Its Films*. New York: Harper and Row, 1971.

Doherty, Thomas Patrick. *Pre-Code Hollywood: Sex, Immorality, and Insurrection in American Cinema, 1930–1934*. New York: Columbia University Press, 1999.

Giovacchini, Saverio. *Hollywood Modernism: Film and Politics in the Age of the New Deal*. Philadelphia: Temple University Press, 2001.

Gomery, Douglas. *Shared Pleasures: A History of Movie Presentation in the United States*. Madison: University of Wisconsin Press, 1992.

Jacobs, Lea. *The Wages of Sin: Censorship and the Fallen Woman Film, 1928–1942*. Wisconsin Studies in Film. Madison: University of Wisconsin Press, 1991.

Maltby, Richard. "The Production Code and the Hays Office." In *The Grand Design: Hollywood as a Modern Business Enterprise, 1930–1939*, edited by Tino Balio, 37–72. Berkeley: University of California Press, 1993.

Sarris, Andrew. "The Sex Comedy Without Sex." *American Film 3* (March 1978): 8–15.

Schatz, Thomas. *The Genius of the System: Hollywood Filmmaking in the Studio Era*. New York: Pantheon, 1988.

Sklar, Robert. *Movie-Made America: A Social History of American Movies*. New York: Random House, 1975.

Charles J. Maland

GREECE

———■———

The history of the Greek cinema is inextricably bound to the complex political history of Greece in the twentieth century. What constituted the legitimate Greek state was still at issue in the early part of that century. Millions of culturally Greek individuals lived under the rule of the Ottoman Empire, Italy, Britain, and other nations that controlled regions of mainland Greece and numerous Greek islands. The problematics of who and what is Greek remain a perennial challenge for Greek cinema.

THE EARLY YEARS

When "moving pictures" arrived in Greece in 1897, one- or two-reel films were usually presented as acts in variety shows or as carnival attractions. These foreign imports included the pioneering work of filmmakers such as Georges Méliès (1861–1938) and the Lumière brothers (Auguste [1862–1954] and Louis [1864–1948]). The first known Greek film, *Gyanikes pou klotoun* (*Women Weaving* or *The Weavers*, 1905), was made by the Manakia brothers (Yannakis [1879–1954] and Miltos [1881–1964]), whose identity and importance would be the subject of Theo Angelopoulos's (b. 1935) *To Vlemma tou Odyssea* (*Ulysses' Gaze*, 1995). One year after *Women Weaving [The Weavers]*, the tradition of the Greek "journal" film—a fusion of genuine newsreel footage with more formal documentary elements—took form with a short celebrating that year's Olympic games. In 1907, a second journal film and the first with a title, *Eorti tou Vasileos Georgiou I* (The Festival of King George I), celebrated the virtues of the Greek king. The first movie theaters opened in Smyrna and Athens at this time. Actor Spiros Dimitrakopoulos founded Athini Films in 1910 and began to produce comedic shorts and documentaries celebrating archeological sites.

Golfo, the first Greek feature, was released in 1915. Based on a pastoral play, it is a kind of Romeo-and-Juliet story in a Greek mountain setting. Three more features appeared shortly after *Golfo*, but the public was far more taken by journal films that dealt with the Balkan Wars of 1912 and 1913 and then World War I. These Greek films contain most of the only surviving footage of events such as the burning of Smyrna in 1922. The immediate impact of *Golfo* had been negligible, but the mountain romance was destined to be a popular genre. In 1932, *Golfo* was remade as the first Greek talking picture. In 1955, there would be three more remakes, one enjoying a huge box office success; and in 1975, Angelopoulos would feature the play as a central theme in *O Thiassos* (*The Traveling Players*).

Greek cinema began to find a more regular audience with a series of comedies made in the early 1920s. The Greek comedians usually offered characters resembling those associated with American film personalities such as Charlie Chaplin and Roscoe "Fatty" Arbuckle. The industry's first feature to become a box-office hit was *Fate's Disowned Child* (1925), an urban melodrama, and the foundations of a viable industry began to take shape shortly thereafter with the establishment of Dag Film in 1927. Thirty silent features were produced between 1925 and 1935 by production companies located in Athens, Patras, and Thessaloniki. Some films drew as many as forty thousand viewers, and the concept of a movie star began to take hold. *Daphne and Chloe* (1931), a lyrical romance in which the pubescent heroine appears nude during a bathing scene, may constitute a first in cinema, since it precedes the better known ten-minute nude sequence in *Ecstasy* (1933) that featured Hedy Lamarr.

Despite its limited successes, Greek film production and exhibition through the 1920s and 1930s remained hostage to political events. From 1924 to 1928, there were eleven coups and three general elections that produced no less than ten prime ministers. A relatively stable period during the regime of Eleuthérios Venizelos (1928–1932) was then followed by constant military intrigues that were capped by the dictatorship of General Ioannis Metaxas (1936–1941). Further social disruption was caused by the absorption of 1.5 million refugees from Asia Minor into a population of less than 10 million. In this climate, film production remained chancy, and post-production often had to be done abroad.

During the occupation of Greece in World War II, Greeks generally boycotted German and Italian films, but when Filopoimin Finos (1908–1977), who had produced and directed *The Song of Parting* (1939), was able to produce the Greek-language *The Voice of the Heart* (1943), it drew a stunning 102,237 admissions. Attending a screening of this film was seen as an assertion of Hellenic identity during an occupation that caused the death of 10 percent of the population. Five other films were made during the occupation, but production was curtailed when Finos and others were arrested by the Germans for participating in the resistance. Finos survived and became the leading producer of Greek films for nearly two decades.

From the end of the occupation until the late 1960s, a Greek film industry modeled on the Hollywood studio system produced well over one thousand films. Although directly serving a small language group, Greek cinema of the studio era produced filmmakers and actors such as Melina Mercouri (1920–1994), Michael Cacoyannis (b. 1922), and Irene Papas (b. 1926) who gained international fame and won a world audience for bouzouki musicians such as Manos Hadjidakis and Mikis Theodorakis. It also produced national stars such as George Foundas (b. 1924) (melodrama), Aliki Vougouhlaki (1934–1996) (musicals), and Thanassis Vengos (b. 1927) (comedy).

During the postwar era, the Greek government used a variety of means to discourage political dissidence in the arts. While most of the film industry was content to churn out musicals, comedies, and melodramas that caught the popular pulse without raising any political critiques, a number of filmmakers on the edge of the industry used indirect discourse to challenge the political status quo. *Magic City* (1954), for example, used a crime

film format to deal with the issues of the 1922 refugees and the poor of Athens. *Stella* (1955) championed working-class music and feminist ideals. *O Drakos* (*The Ogre of Athens*, 1956) used a theme of mistaken identity to critique society. *To Koritsi me ta Mavra* (*The Girl in Black*, 1956) addressed the tensions between rural and urban Greek values with gripping portraits of artists, fishermen, and village women.

THE NEW GREEK CINEMA

The advent of television in the mid-1960s coincided with a coup d'etat by Greek colonels on 21 April 1967. The increasingly mediocre fare being churned out by the studio system was not attractive enough to compete with the new medium, and the strict censorship of the junta kept any socially engaging films off Greek screens. The studio system imploded, and the only group left making films in Greece consisted of a handful of young writer-directors who desired to take Greek cinema in an entirely new direction. They loudly and even rudely rejected the populist art of the studio system with visions of an ultramodernist cinema driven by auteurs. Although this group began making films during the junta years, their movement blossomed in the ten years following the summer 1974 fall of the junta.

What became known as the New Greek Cinema was largely committed to a modernist aesthetic that disdained the star system, montage, the three-act narrative, and other Hollywood norms associated with popular cinema. Many of the new writer-directors also had a leftist political orientation and greatly admired Italian neorealism. A persistent problem for them was that their political positions impelled them to seek a mass audience while their aesthetics often drove that audience away. By far the most successful in resolving this contradiction of content and form were Pantelis Voulgaris (b. 1940) and Theo Angelopoulos. Voulgaris stayed closer to the neorealistic standard in what proved to be his most successful films, *To Proxenio tis Annas* (*The Engagement of Anna*, 1972), *Petronia Chronia* (*Stone Years*, 1985), and *Ola Ina Dromos* (*It's A Long Road*, 1995). Angelopoulos, on the other hand, undertook one aesthetic experiment after another. He achieved both a massive popular audience in Greece and international critical acclaim with his *The Traveling Players*, a film that rewrote Greek political history from a leftist perspective.

Greek social problems received an engaging expressionistic treatment in Nikos Papatakis's (b. 1918) *I Voski* (*Thanos and Despina*, 1968). Similar concerns were given surrealistic treatment in Nikos Panayotopoulos's *I Tembelides tis Eforis Kiladas* (*The Slothful Ones of the*

THEO ANGELOPOULOS
b. Theodoros Angelopoulos, Athens, Greece, 27 April 1935

Theo Angelopoulos is the most important filmmaker in the history of Greek cinema. In contrast to both avant-gardists who disdain politics and leftists who appropriate popular genres, Angelopoulos has insisted that to have a revolutionary impact, both the form and content of a film must challenge convention. His signature trademarks are slow pacing and continuous shots that can last for many minutes. His four-hour long *O Thiassos* (*The Traveling Players* 1975), which appears on most lists of the greatest films of the twentieth century, uses less than one hundred shots to explore the history of mid-century Greece. Angelopoulos is also fond of manipulating time, sometimes going chronologically backward and forward within a single shot. His films often include dead spots that invite the viewer to think about what has just transpired on the screen. Motionless tableaus and direct address to the camera by actors shedding their film identities are other favored techniques.

Angelopoulos received his film training in Paris, where he worked with Jean Rouch. Upon returning to Greece, he was a film critic for left-wing journals. His first feature film, *Anaparastassi* (*Reconstruction*, 1968), examined a murder through multiple tellings in the manner of Akira Kurosawa's *Rashomon* (1950). In *Meres tou 36* (*Days of 36*, 1972), *Oi Kynighoi* (*The Hunters*, 1977), and *Megaleksandros* (*Alexander the Great*, 1980), he offered a history of Greece from an anti-authoritarian leftist perspective. In *Taxidi sta Kithira* (*Voyage to Cythera*, 1984), *O Melissokomos* (*The Beekeeper*, 1986), and *Topio stin Omichli* (*Landscape in the Mist*, 1988), Angelopoulos weighed traditional Greek values against those of the emerging new Europe. *To Meteoro Vima tou Pelargou* (*The Suspended Step of the Stork*, 1991), *To Vlemma tou Odyssea* (*Ulysses' Gaze*, 1996) and *Mia Aioniotita kai mia Mera* (*Eternity and a Day*, 1998)

examined the problems of national borders and ethnic identity. Almost all of these films won prestigious international prizes, a pattern crowned by the Palme d'Or for *Eternity and a Day*.

With the onset of a new century, Angelopoulos announced the most ambitious project of his career—a trilogy that would comment on the history of Europe in the twentieth century through the prism of the experience of the Greek nation. He told reporters, "I breathe in epic terms. This is my fate." The first of the trilogy, *To Livadi pou Dakryzei* (*The Weeping Meadow*, 2004), done in a manner that reflected the sweep of *The Traveling Players* but with more of the character development in films such as *Eternity and a Day*, deals with refugees from Asia Minor in Greece through the end of the Greek civil war in 1949. Part two of the trilogy will carry the story to the Soviet Union.

RECOMMENDED VIEWING

Anaparastassi (*Reconstruction*, 1968), *O Thiassos* (*The Traveling Players*, 1975), *Megaleksandros* (*Alexander the Great*, 1980), *Mia Aioniotita kai mia Mera* (*Eternity and a Day*, 1998), *To Livadi pou Dakryzei* (*The Weeping Meadow*, 2004)

FURTHER READING

Fainaru, Dan, ed. *Theo Angelopoulos: Interviews*. Jackson: University Press of Mississippi, 2001.

Georgakas, Dan. "A Reconsideration of Theodoros Angelopoulos's *Alexander the Great*." *Journal of Modern Greek Studies* 18, no. 1 (May 2000): 171–182.

Horton, Andrew. *The Films of Theo Angelopoulos: A Cinema of Contemplation*. Princeton, NJ: Princeton University Press, 1997.

———, ed. *The Last Modernist: The Films of Theo Angelopoulos*. Westport, CT: Greenwood Press, 1997.

Dan Georgakas

Fertile Valley, 1978). Yorgos (George) Katakouzinos's *Angelos* (*Angel*, 1982) created a sensation with its explicit homosexual themes, and *Timi tis Agapis* (*The Price of Love*, 1984) by Tonia Marketaki (b. 1942) set a new cinematic standard for Greek feminism with a historical romance set at the turn of the twentieth century.

Generally speaking, however, as a group the filmmakers of the New Greek Cinema failed to achieve the consistent quality of Voulgaris and Angelopoulos.

An important new force in Greek filmmaking appeared in 1981 when the government offered significant financial assistance with the establishment of the Greek

***Theo Angelopoulos at the time of* Topio stin omichli
(Landscape in the Mist, *1990).* EVERETT COLLECTION.
REPRODUCED BY PERMISSION.**

Film Centre in order to fund and promote Greek
cinema. Ten years later, the annual national film festival
held in Thessaloniki since 1960 became the Thessaloniki
International Film Festival. While national production
remained a major element in the festival, broader Greek
film culture was nourished by the annual presentation of
hundreds of foreign films and dozens of foreign filmmakers. The festival saw its mission as the promotion of
artistic rather than commercial cinema. Among its priorities was providing considerable space to Balkan filmmakers, first-time directors, and various regional
cinemas.

Although coproductions with other nations became
common by the 1990s, the New Greek Cinema lost
momentum. Directorial idiosyncrasies, eccentricities,
and excesses were often passed off as style and individual
vision. The national audience began to avoid Greek-
language films. While American films usually drew more
than 500,000 admissions and 85 percent of all screens,
the majority of Greek films drew less than 10,000, and
any Greek film that drew more than 100,000 was considered a success.

An unexpected development was that the old studio
films being shown regularly on television proved very
appealing to a generation that had not even been born
when they were made. As the twentieth century came
to an end, a new generation of filmmakers began to
challenge the political economy of the Greek film world
by aiming for popular audiences with independent productions that often employed new low-cost technology.
No Budget Story (Renos Haralambidis, 1998) and *O
Orgasmos tis Ageladas* (*The Cow's Orgasm*, Olga Malea,
1996), films dealing with the problems of the contemporary generation, captured the popular imagination
with formats akin to the American independent cinema
of the 1950s. *I epitesi tou yiyantiaou mousaka* (*The
Attack of the Giant Moussaka*, 2000), a send-up of
science fiction films that combined criticism of Greek
mass media with a hilarious gay subtext, reached beyond
Greece to find an international cult audience. Even
Angelopoulos became slightly more conventional by
casting international stars and shortening the length of
his films to more traditional running times. *I Earini
Synaxis ton Agrofylakon* (*The Four Seasons of the Law*,
Dimos Avdeliodis, 1999) successfully revived some of
the elements of studio comedies. The surprise pop hit of
the 1990s, however, was *Safe Sex* (1999), a soft-core
porn film that leaped to the top of the Greek charts
with over one million admissions. Its drawing card was
that it used actors from Greek television sitcoms in
dicey sexual situations. While critics rightly denounced
its vulgarity, *Safe Sex* brought mass audiences back to
Greek-language films. Subsequently, an increasing
number of Greek-language films began to pass the
100,000 admissions mark.

During the first years of the twenty-first century,
Greek cinema often dealt with the cultural identity problems associated with the new Europe, especially the
unprecedented influx of refugees fleeing collapsing states
in the region. A hit of 2003 was *Politiki Kouzina*
(*A Touch of Spice*, Tassos Boulmetis, [b. 1957]), which
dealt with the expulsion of Greeks from Istanbul in the
1950s. The following year Voulgaris released *Nyfes*
(*Brides*, 2004), a film about a group of picture brides
who emigrated to America in 1922. Both films were box
office sensations with more than one million admissions.
Angelopoulos took up a related theme in a trilogy that
sought to reflect the history of Europe throughout the
twentieth century by focusing on the history of the
Greeks. The first film of the trilogy, *To Livadi pou
Dakryzei* (*The Weeping Meadows*, 2004), begins with
Greeks from the Black Sea fleeing the Bolshevik
Revolution and continues through the end of Greek civil
war in 1949.

One new element in twenty-first-century Greek film
is a group of women who have raised feminist concerns

within an art form long dominated almost exclusively by male directors. Award-winning works include *Alexandria* (Mario Illioú, 2001), *Tha to Metaniossis* (*Think It Over*, Katerina Evangelakou, 2002), *Diskoli Apocheretismi: O Babas Mou* (*Hard Goodbyes: My Father*, Penny Panayotopoulou, 2002), and *Close, So Close* (Stella Theodoraki, 2002). Other women have reached the forefront of the avant-garde scene and the documentary genre. Lucia Rikaki (b. 1961) offered a rare look at the deaf community in Greece with her *Ta logia tis siopis* (*Words of Silence*, 2002) and Lydia Carras addressed ecological themes in *Foni Aegeou* (*The Voice of the Aegean*, 2004).

Amid these dynamic trends, the old auteurist ideal has remained in place, maintaining considerable resistance to any thinking about film as a collaborative enterprise and to conventional narrative formats. Nevertheless, both established and emerging filmmakers continue to pursue and reach popular audiences at home and abroad, seeking formats that fuse the integrity and artistry of the auteurist ideal with the populist verve of the best studio-era productions.

SEE ALSO *Art Cinema; National Cinema*

FURTHER READING

Bacoyannopoulos, Yannis, and Andreas Tyros, eds. *Cinemythology: A Retrospective of Greek Film.* Athens: Greek Film Centre, 1993.

Constantinidiis, Stratos E., ed. *Journal of Modern Greek Studies: Greek Film—A Special Issue* 18, no. 1 (May 2000).

Georgakas, Dan, and Andrew Horton, eds. *Film Criticism* 27, no. 2 (Winter 2002–2003). (Special issue on Greek cinema.)

Koliodimos, Dimitris. *The Greek Filmography: 1914 through 1946.* Jefferson, NC: McFarland, 1999.

Dan Georgakas

GUILDS AND UNIONS

———————■———————

Labor unions and guilds have been organized in film industries in many countries. Typically, these organizations have focused on specific types of workers, such as actors, directors, and technical workers—for example, the Alliance of Canadian Cinema, TV and Radio Artists (ACTRA), the Directors Guild of Great Britain (DGGB), and the Australian Theatrical & Amusement Employees' Association (ATAEA).

In the early history of film, workers often were organized by trade unions from related industries, such as the theater and the electrical industry. Eventually unions and guilds were formed specifically to organize film workers, and most of these labor groups are still active in film and television industries. Like other labor unions, film labor organizations represent their members in negotiations for wages, benefits, and working conditions, in addition to providing a variety of other services. Some guilds also become involved in negotiating royalty payments, conditions for screen credit, and other issues. Unions and guilds also engage in political activities through lobbying or election campaigning.

Also like other labor organizations, film unions and guilds continue to be challenged by political and economic developments in society in general and film industries in particular. For instance, the global expansion of the film industry during the last few decades of the twentieth century had an impact on film workers in various ways. While film labor organizations around the world have developed and are organized similarly, the focus of this article is on US unions and guilds both as an exemplar and because of the current global prominence of Hollywood films and companies.

While unions and guilds were active in the US film industry early in the twentieth century, the more specialized labor organizations, such as the Screen Actors Guild (SAG) and the Directors Guild of America (DGA), emerged in the 1930s during an especially intense period of labor organizing. Although film labor groups in the US were challenged in various ways by the anticommunism of the late 1940s and early 1950s, the groups survived and expanded to include television workers in the 1950s and 1960s. Trade unions and guilds continue to play major roles in the current US entertainment industry.

Film workers in the US represent a highly skilled and specialized labor force, but unemployment is high. For instance, it has been estimated that 85 percent of actors are out of work most of the time. There are some unusual or unique characteristics of film work, as well. Some workers, such as writers, directors and actors, share in the profits of films through profit participation deals. Others may become employers themselves through their own independent production companies or in projects where they serve as producer or director. For example, Billy Crystal worked as an actor in *City Slickers II: The Legend of Curly's Gold* (1994), but also was the film's producer. There also are keen differences between above-the-line and below-the-line workers, with consequent differences between the labor organizations that represent these different types of labor. Above-the-line labor organizations involve "creative" workers (writer, director, actors), while below-the-line labor refers more to "technical" laborers (camera operators, editors, gaffers, etc.). The organization of entertainment unions along craft lines rather than as a vertical, industrial structure has tended to inhibit labor unity within the industry.

Generally, motion picture production is labor-intensive, meaning the largest part of the budget is spent on labor. The cost of key talent (especially actors and actresses) is a significant part of the budget for a typical Hollywood film. Above-the-line talent can often represent 50 percent of a production budget, and has been identified as one of the key reasons why the costs of Hollywood films have skyrocketed.

ABOVE-THE-LINE GUILDS

The Writers Guild of America (WGA) is the collective bargaining representative for writers in the motion picture, broadcast, cable, interactive, and new media industries. The guild's history can be traced back to 1912 when the Authors Guild was first organized as a protective association for writers. Subsequently, drama writers formed a Dramatists Guild and joined forces with the Authors Guild, which then became the Authors League. In 1921, the Screen Writers Guild was formed as a branch of the Authors League, although the organization operated more as a club than a guild.

Finally, in 1937, the Screen Writers Guild became the collective bargaining agent of all writers in the motion picture industry. Collective bargaining actually started in 1939, with the first contract negotiated with film producers in 1942. A revised organizational structure was initiated in 1954, separating the Writers Guild of America, west (WGAw), with offices in Los Angeles, from the Writers Guild East (WGAE), in New York.

While it may be difficult to determine how many people claim to be Hollywood screenwriters, it is even more difficult to assess how many writers in the industry actually make a living from their writing efforts. According to the WGAw, 4,525 members reported earnings from writing in 2001, while 8,841 members paid dues in at least one quarter of that year. Based on these figures, the guild reported a 51.2 percent employment rate. However, only 1,870 of those reporting earnings were designated as "screen" writers, and that group received a total of $387.8 million in 2001. The Guild also points out that there is a 20 percent turnover among their members each year.

While the minimum that a writer must be paid for an original screenplay was around $29,500 in 2001, much higher amounts are often negotiated. Writers also receive fees for story treatments, first drafts, rewrites, polishing existing scripts, and so on. Other important earnings come from residuals and royalties.

Another area of crucial importance to writers (and others involved in film production) is the issue of screen credits, or the sequence, position, and size of credits on the screen, at the front and end of a film, and in movie advertisements. Credits are a vital issue for many Hollywood writers not only because of their impact on their reputations, but because bonuses and residuals are based on which writers receive final credit. Credits or billing issues may be significant negotiating points in employment agreements and the guilds have developed detailed and often complex rules. The WGA rules generally require a 33 percent contribution to the screenplay from the first writer for credit, while subsequent writers must contribute 50 percent. However, when an executive on a project also becomes a subsequent writer, that executive must contribute "more than 50 percent" to receive credit or, if part of a team, "substantially more than 60 percent" for credit.

The Directors Guild of America (DGA) represents directors, unit production managers, assistant directors, and technical coordinators in television and film. The Guild was formed in 1960 from the merger of the Screen Directors Guild and the Radio and Television Directors Guild. The organization's membership was about 13,100 in 2005.

While the producer manages the overall film project, the director is in charge of production and is usually considered the "primary creative force" in a film's manufacture. The director controls the action and dialogue in front of the camera and is therefore responsible for interpreting and expressing in a film the intentions of the screenwriter and producer as set out in the screenplay. The director is usually hired by the producer, although some directors also become involved as some kind of producer in some films. Interestingly, most directors make only one movie, while only a handful make ten or more.

The DGA negotiates a basic agreement for its members, who then arrange individual contracts with the producer or producing company with terms and conditions applicable to a specific film. Director's agreements include employment terms (salary, and so forth), but also issues relating to creative control such as details regarding the director's cut and final cut of a film. Prompted especially by the introduction of colorized films, the DGA has lobbied strongly for a moral rights law for creative personnel to prevent changes in their work.

The Screen Actors Guild (SAG) was organized in 1933, after several other organizations had attempted to organize film performers, including the Academy of Motion Picture Arts and Sciences (Clark and Prindle). The history of SAG was at first dominated by the attempt to establish a guild shop (a system under which all actors employed on a film must join the guild), and then by gaining compensation for actors in the constantly expanding forms of distribution (television, video cassettes, etc.). SAG's concern with such compensation is not an insignificant issue considering that its members gained more than $1 billion in 1987 merely from residual payments for TV reruns of old films. Much more revenue has been earned from home video and other new distribution outlets.

Like the DGA, SAG negotiates a basic agreement for its members; however, individual actors and actresses also contract for individual films, sometimes using agents or managers to represent them.

In 1992 the 3,600 members of the Screen Extras Guild (SEG) became a part of SAG's union coverage, primarily because SEG lacked the clout to deal with producers and most extras were working nonunion. Serious discussions of a merger have also taken place between SAG and the American Federation of Television and Radio Artists (AFTRA). AFTRA was formed in 1937 to represent radio and then television performers. The organization's primary jurisdiction is in live television, but AFTRA shares jurisdiction with SAG for taped television productions. As of 2005 AFTRA represents over 70,000 performers in radio, television, and sometimes, film.

The American Federation of Musicians (AFM) represents musicians across many industries, including film. The trade group, which was formed in the 1890s, has negotiated contracts with the film industry since 1944, and has been especially concerned with new technological developments in sound recording.

BELOW-THE-LINE UNIONS

The International Association of Theatrical and Stage Employees (IATSE or IA) has been the most powerful union in the US film industry. Formed at the end of the nineteenth century, IATSE organized stage employees in the United States and Canada. As the entertainment industry expanded, IATSE grew to include motion picture projectionists and technical workers at the Hollywood studios and film exchanges throughout North America. When television was introduced, IATSE organized technical workers in the new medium. IATSE's history includes some dismal chapters from the 1930s when racketeers and criminals extorted funds from union members, as well as assisting in the ugly blacklisting activities that tainted Hollywood in the 1940s.

IATSE represents technicians, artisans and craftspersons in the entertainment industry, including live theater, film and television production, and trade shows. More than 500 local unions in the US and Canada are affiliated with IA. IATSE has a tradition of local autonomy, with a variety of craft-based locals involved in collective bargaining agreements. However, nationwide agreements for film production personnel are negotiated,

as well. Moreover, Local 600, the International Cinematographers Guild—which was formed in 1996 through a merger of regional groups—is national rather than local in its membership.

IA covers a wide range of employees in film production distribution and exhibition. Among the classifications of workers represented are art directors, story analysts, animators, set designers and set decorators, scenic artists, graphic artists, set painters, grips, electricians, property persons, set builders, teachers, costumers, make-up artists, hair stylists, motion picture and still camerapersons, sound technicians, editors, script supervisors, laboratory technicians, projectionists, utility workers, first aid employees, inspection, shipping, booking, and other distribution employees. IA's bargaining strength comes from this "complete coverage" of all the crafts involved in the production of theatrical, motion picture, or television products, with workers involved in every phase of a production, from its conception through every aspect of its execution.

The National Association for Broadcast Employees and Technicians (NABET) grew first out of radio, and then television broadcasting. The union was organized at the National Broadcasting Corporation (NBC) as a company union (an industrial organization rather than craft oriented) as an alternative to the larger and more powerful International Brotherhood of Electrical Workers (IBEW) (Koenig, *Broadcasting and Bargaining*). NABET's relatively militant history is replete with skirmishes with IBEW and IATSE, as well as continuous rumors of a merger with the larger IATSE.

In 1990, NABET's Local 15, which organized 1,500 freelance film and tape technicians in New York, merged with IATSE. Then, in 1992, most of the other NABET locals joined the Communication Workers of America (CWA), effective January 1994. About 9,300 NABET members became a part of the much larger CWA, which by 2005 represented over 700,000 workers in telecommunications, printing, broadcasting, health care, and other fields, in both the private and public sectors. While most of NABET's members were to be moved to an independent broadcasting arm within CWA, NABET's West Coast Local 531 agreed to merge with IATSE because of its 500 members' closer affiliation with the film industry. Thus, IATSE became the only union in the United States to represent behind-the-camera film workers.

The International Brotherhood of Teamsters is the largest and strongest union in the US and also is active in the motion picture industry, organizing studio transportation workers on the West Coast and various other workers. In 2005 the Teamsters claimed a general membership of over 1.4 million in the United States and Canada; its Hollywood Local 399 had over 4,000 members working as drivers, location scouts, and other personnel in the film industry. Casting directors also joined the Teamsters in that year.

PRESSING ISSUES FOR HOLLYWOOD UNIONS AND GUILDS

Some of the biggest headaches facing Hollywood unions and guilds are the proliferation of nonunion production, the relocation of production sites all over the country and the world (runaway production), and the growing strength of the entertainment conglomerates that own the Hollywood majors.

The issue of nonunion production begins in the film capital itself. While film and television production around Los Angeles seems to ebb and flow depending upon a number of different factors, there has been an increase in the amount of nonunion production in Hollywood. For instance, only 40 percent of the permits issued by the City of Los Angeles for film work in January 1989 were for unionized productions. However, more recently, IATSE claimed that less than one-third of the films released in the United States are made with union labor. Not only is nonunion labor typically considered less costly, but the established entertainment unions often are perceived as uncooperative and too demanding. It might be noted that independent productions sometimes try to avoid union labor, however, most of the larger and more successful independent companies still work with the unions due to their continuing role in the overall industrial process of Hollywood.

Runaway production has been an ongoing problem for Hollywood labor unions and guilds. The lure of lower budgets with nonunion workers has attracted producers to right-to-work states, such as Florida, as well as other states that have recognized film and television production as a boost to local economies. Meanwhile, foreign locations, such as Eastern Europe and parts of the Third World, offer low budgets and exotic locations. Most recently, Canada has lured film and television production away from Hollywood with offers of trained workers, tax breaks, and a favorable exchange rate. Pressure from the availability of a nonunion option and runaway production has forced the unions to make concessions during contract negotiations, as well as to push for government remedies.

Both of these situations can be explained by film companies' attempt to lower labor cost, in addition to the ready supply of nonunion workers, both in Hollywood and other locations. The abundance of available labor also may be related to the popularity of media in general. The growth of media education at universities and colleges, as well as the increased visibility of film and television production in the popular press, means that there is a glut of eager workers for Hollywood companies to employ, very often without union affiliation. Hollywood also seems to have a fantasy quality, as even "regular" work in the film industry seems glamorous.

While studios try to blame unreasonable union demands for the increase of nonunion production and the flight to nonunion locations, labor leaders (especially from below-the-line unions) claim that they are not the problem. Rather, they point to the skyrocketing costs of above-the-line talent, with especially high salaries going to high-profile actors and actresses. Some union officials point out that film costs will not come down unless studios control above-the-line costs, especially the huge salaries of some stars. The lack of unity among entertainment unions also has been blamed for the growth of nonunion filming. Some of the mergers mentioned previously may help to alleviate this problem, yet the organization of labor along craft lines still exacerbates the situation.

While Hollywood companies have become more diversified, union representation also has followed. The different types of businesses incorporated by Hollywood companies have involved further differentiation of labor, making it difficult for workers to form a united front against one corporation. For instance, workers employed by Disney include animators at the Disney Studio, hockey players on Disney's hockey team, the Anaheim Mighty Ducks, and Jungle Cruise operators at Disney's various theme parks. The differentiation of labor is especially apparent at the theme parks owned by many Hollywood companies, in particular Disney, Universal, Paramount, and Time Warner. Workers at these sites are represented by a wide array of labor organizations, many of which are unrelated to those unions active in the film industry.

Generally, then, the trend toward diversification has contributed to a weakening of trade unions' power as well as a further lack of unity among workers. More than one observer has noted that in the twenty-first century films are produced and distributed by conglomerates that own businesses outside of entertainment. Thus, if film production is halted because of labor problems, the conglomerate's income may slow a bit, but it can still survive with money from other sources.

So the pressures are mounting on labor organizations in the entertainment field. Hollywood unions and guilds have faced difficult struggles in the past, combating a range of problems from difficulty of gaining union recognition in the 1930s to ideological assaults such as the blacklisting period of the 1940s and 1950s. They continue to face further challenges from antiunion sentiments, nonunion workers, and runaway production, as well as power struggles with diversified corporations actively involved in international markets.

SEE ALSO *Credits; Crew; Direction; Production Process; Screenwriting; Studio System*

FURTHER READING

Clark, Danae. *Negotiating Hollywood: The Cultural Politics of Actors' Labor.* Minneapolis: University of Minnesota Press, 1995.

Hartsough, Denise. "Crime Pays: The Studios' Labor Deals in the 1930s." In *The Studio System,* edited by Janet Staiger. New Brunswick, NJ: Rutgers University Press, 1989.

Koenig, Allen E., ed. *Broadcasting and Bargaining: Labor Relations in Radio and Television.* Madison: University of Wisconsin Press, 1970.

Prindle, David F. *The Politics of Glamour: Ideology and Democracy in the Screen Actors Guild.* Madison: University of Wisconsin Press, 1988.

Miller, Toby, Nitin Govil, John McMurria, and Richard Maxwell. *Global Hollywood.* London: British Film Institute, 2001.

Wasko, Janet. "Challenges to Hollywood's Labor Force in the 1990s." In *Global Productions: Labor in the Making of the "Information Society",* edited by Gerald Sussman and John A. Lent, 173–189. Cresskill, NJ: Hampton Press, 1998.

———. *How Hollywood Works.* London and Thousand Oaks, CA: Sage, 2004.

Janet Wasko

HERITAGE FILMS

———■———

L. P. Hartley's *The Go-Between* (1953), the novel that inspired what may have been the first contemporary heritage film, offers the perfect epigram for the form: "The past is a foreign country. They do things differently there." Significantly, many of the hallmarks of the heritage film are present in this early example: directed in 1970 by Joseph Losey (1909–1984), a transplanted American (many heritage films emanate from national "outsiders"), *The Go-Between* is a stately, handsome adaptation of a respected novel set in a pre-war English country house and involving the sexual maturation of its young protagonist. Moreover, many of the questions arising from attempts to define the heritage film are also present in this example. Is it a form that has served to bolster the British film industry? or Does it represent a kind of filmic colonization of British stories and screens by Britain's former possessions? Does the form manifest geographical limitations that mean that it might be better denominated the English heritage film?

Film scholars cannot even agree on whether heritage films constitute a genre, partly because such films share only loosely associated tropes or iconographical elements and partly because they so readily appear to collapse into neighboring genres, such as the costume film, the historical film, the war film, and the prestige literary adaptation. In practice, the heritage film ranges widely over source material (from E. M. Forster and Henry James to working-class autobiographies from World War II), era, and nation: there are French heritage films, including *La Reine Margot* (*Queen Margot*, Patrice Chéreau, 1994) and *Manon des sources* (*Manon of the Spring*, Claude Berri, 1986), and now German heritage films dealing with the Holocaust, such as *Aimée & Jaguar* (Max

Färberböck, 1999). The locus classicus of the heritage film nonetheless remains the narrative of pre–World War I or interwar England; it is often an adaptation of an esteemed literary property and typically invokes what might be termed heritage landmarks, such as Oxbridge colleges and National Trust properties.

GENRE?

It is in part through their treatment of landscape that heritage films as a group begin to display what might be viewed as generic characteristics. John Hill suggests that the heritage film typically focuses on the relationships among a group of characters rather than on the destiny of a single character; and has a slow pace, a preference for dialogue over action, and an approach to *mise-en-scène* that exceeds motivations found in the narrative or that does not necessarily express characters' emotions (1999, p. 80). Places and objects are displayed rather than dramatized, leading to what Andrew Higson calls "heritage space"—the film serves as a jewel box for the arrangement and contemplation of heritage properties (Higson in Friedman, p. 117). This approach to technique often emphasizes *mise-en-scène* over other cinematic elements, such as editing, and is a large part of the pleasure in spectacle to be found in such films.

Critical response to this stylistic aspect has been divided, with conservative critics arguing that British film should explore and valorize a glorious past, and left-leaning critics expressing concern over the often limited heritage on display, particularly in terms of the exclusion of working-class experience. Working-class characters may function merely as observers or chorus members in dramas often consumed with the problems of those

"Heritage space" in The Remains of the Day *(James Ivory, 1993), with Anthony Hopkins.* © COLUMBIA PICTURES/COURTESY EVERETT COLLECTION. REPRODUCED BY PERMISSION.

possessing or seeking an independent income. The Thatcher government's investment in the projection of heritage culture as a manifestation of a revived Britain (witnessed by the National Heritage Acts of 1980 and 1983) added to the ideologically suspect nature of heritage films in the eyes of some critics (Higson, pp. 51–54). Lutz Koepnick has argued that the heritage film produces "usable and consumable pasts . . . history as a site of comfort and orientation" (p. 51)—hence the occasional dismissal of heritage films as the "Laura Ashley school of filmmaking." A number of critics have noticed that the heritage film's desire for authenticity and its close attention to the look of objects create a kind of break between images and narrative, with objects constituting a conservative commentary on what might have originally been a work of social satire (such as the 1988 adaptation of Evelyn Waugh's *A Handful of Dust* by Charles Sturridge [b. 1951]).

Heritage films' characteristic contest between the consequences of using period objects and the critical projects of their source texts may further intensify the critical uncertainty about whether such films genuinely or reliably constitute a genre. One way of addressing that uncertainty has been to consider what kinds of audiences consume these films, a question considerably complicated by the international flavor of the production and consumption of heritage films. While at first blush the project of the heritage film would appear to be to bring Britain's glorious past to the screen, viewers may be struck by British heritage films' exceptional reliance upon American audiences not only for their ultimate global box-office success but also for access to *British* audiences. The average Briton attends one film in a theater annually; most film consumption in Britain takes place via the television and VCR—Britons have one of the world's highest rates of VCR use. Consequently, any "British" cinema is necessarily mediated by television and probably influenced by the tastes of other Anglophone audiences. In a pattern that heritage films pioneered but that now transcends genre, theme, and film style, British films are often given only limited or no release at all domestically until an American run has established their marketability, at which point they are re-exported to their country of manufacture.

THE HERITAGE FILM AND THE UNITED STATES

If British television pioneered the production of handsome adaptations of popular pre-war narratives, American public television trained American audiences to consume them. American series such as *Masterpiece Theatre* and *Mystery!* showcased quality British television programming from the 1970s; film and television production reinforced each other (and established a pattern of crossover labor), with, for example, Sturridge's lush Granada Television adaptation of *Brideshead Revisited* appearing in the same year (1981) that *Chariots of Fire* took American movie theaters by storm. Less obvious is that success on the small screen should translate to success on the large screen. Nonetheless, the heritage film spoke to the institutional needs of both British and American filmmakers and distributors in the 1980s. The modest budgets by American standards made heritage films attractive to US distributors, who found that the films could be gratifyingly profitable in extended runs at a limited number of well-chosen theaters, such as the Paris in New York City, before going on to stepped releases elsewhere in the nation. In the British context, heritage films operated as a heaven-sent solution to the financing problems created by the introduction of the Films Bill in 1984–1985, which removed earlier government supports to the film industry (Quart in Friedman, p. 23). Because of its connection to a small but reliable niche audience in the United States and in Britain, the heritage film could expect to recuperate its costs outside the UK, which most British films must hope to do to become profitable.

The heritage film in fact operated internationally as a kind of highly accessible art film. It was frequently distributed through small art cinemas, promising a kind of reliable upper-middlebrow visual pleasure without necessarily demanding the kinds of interpretive effort typical of films such as *L'Année dernier 'a Marienbad* (Alain Resnais, 1961). Rapturous acclaim via the Oscars®, such as was received by *Chariots of Fire* (four Academy Awards®, seven nominations) and for James Ivory's *A Room with a View* (1985) (three Academy Awards®, seven nominations), coupled with good box office, did not merely add to the films' prestige: on some level, American involvement and reception helped constitute the constellation of characteristics that typified the heritage film. For example, James Ivory (b. 1928), an American director—his collaborators, producer Ismail Merchant (1936–2005) and screenwriter Ruth Prawer Jhabvala (b. 1927), are respectively Pakistani and German by birth—is responsible for seven of the iconic heritage films of the 1980s and early 1990s.

NEW UNDERSTANDINGS OF THE HERITAGE FILM

So is the heritage film merely light entertainment for export—a kind of film tourism that reflects American expectations about a Britain ossified in a long Edwardian summer? Does it undermine any hope of representing Britain in all its complexity and change? Claire Monk argues that critics who dismiss the heritage film as ideologically suspect, boringly predictable, or merely a creature of American taste approach it too reductively. Part of the problem is indeed the capaciousness of the term "heritage film," coupled with the assumption that it describes a stable, unchanging genre (2002, p. 7). Monk has attempted to periodize heritage films, separating those of the 1980s and early 1990s from later entrants, which she characterizes as "post-heritage" by virtue of their self-conscious foregrounding of strategies designed to subvert the supposed conservatism of the heritage film or to undercut the primacy of the potentially too-dominant *mise-en-scène* (Monk in Vincendeau, p. 7). She argues that critics too readily assume that heritage films operate in ways entirely analogous to, say, National Trust landmarks—that a heritage film has a unitary, conservative meaning derived exclusively from its setting. As Monk observes, this approach hardly allows for the complexity of the interactions among a film's characterization, narrative, and dialogue, all of which may undercut the potential conservatism of reviving the past by filming its surviving material manifestations (2002, p. 188). Monk thus sees important distinctions among heritage films—for example, *A Room with a View* is considerably less conservative than *Chariots of Fire*, because the former permits its female protagonist to come to an important understanding about her agency and the nature of her sexual desires while the latter offers a less complex story line concerned with the creation and training of the British Olympic team in 1924.

Critics such as Monk and Richard Dyer see an exploration of sexuality, including homosexuality, as key to many heritage films. At the very least, it is fair to say that one of the major plot engines of the heritage film is the *Bildungsroman*, the coming to maturity of the young protagonist, typically dramatized at a moment of difficult self-discovery, as in *Maurice* (Ivory, 1987), *The Wings of the Dove* (Iain Softley, 1997), or *Elizabeth* (Shekhar Kapur, 1998), all of whose protagonists possess desires that are difficult, if not impossible, to reconcile with social expectations. Stories of homosexual desire and illicit female pursuit of agency or control fit very naturally into the framework of the *bildungsroman*.

Characteristically, even the earliest cycle of heritage films offers the spectacle of desire often frustrated but sometimes achieved, causing critics to debate the question of the heritage film's progressivism or lack thereof. Are the films progressive because they offer the spectacle of gay men or women longing for things they ought not to have (but sometimes get)? Are they conservative

MERCHANT-IVORY
James Ivory, b. Berkeley, California, 7 June 1928
Ismail Merchant, b. Ismail Noormohamed Abdul Rehman, Bombay,
India, 25 December 1936, d. London, England, 25 May 2005
Ruth Prawer Jhabvala, b. Cologne, Germany, 7 May 1927

As a production team, Merchant-Ivory was responsible for more than thirty films over 42 years, making the partnership of director James Ivory, producer Ismail Merchant, and novelist/screenwriter Ruth Prawer Jhabvala among the most productive and durable of independent filmmakers. While the team remained active through 2005, Merchant also increasingly directed his own projects, including three features since *Cotton Mary* (1999).

The team's first feature, *The Householder* (1963), was the first to involve Jhabvala's services as screenwriter; showing the influence of Indian director Satyajit Ray, it led to further projects exploring Indian life and celebrating the sensibility and richness of its cinema. *Shakespeare Wallah* (1965) narrates the fortunes of a troupe of traveling players, both English and Indian, in the post-Independence, movie-mad 1960s, while *Bombay Talkie* (1970) analyzes the disastrous association between an English novelist played by Jennifer Kendal and an Indian film star played by her real-life husband, Shashi Kapoor. This sequence of films set in India showcased a number of persistent production strategies, namely the foregrounding of ensemble playing, an ability to enlist the help of more established filmmakers (such as Ray, who wrote the music for *Shakespeare Wallah*), a feel for identifying up-and-coming talent (when he worked with Merchant-Ivory, Kapoor had not yet become a major star), and an anthropological sense of place and social fabric reflecting not only the team's interests but also Ivory's beginnings in documentary.

Possibly as a result of their own disparate national and social backgrounds, Merchant-Ivory consistently pursue the question of what a character experiences when he or she attempts to penetrate a closed social milieu, ranging from the desire to master the mores of a foreign culture to the aspiration to control the hierarchies of theater stage or film screen. The indispensable closed social milieu is the sexual couple or close friendship that becomes a sexual triangle with the arrival of an outsider, permitting the intense exploration of patterns of domination within friendship and amorous coupling. Merchant-Ivory films often concern the failure to read social codes, be they those of privileged pre-war Anglophones (*Heat and Dust*, 1983; *Howards End*, 1992; *The Remains of the Day*, 1993; *Savages*, 1972), or of modern New York City (*Jane Austen in Manhattan*, 1980). Refreshingly, Merchant-Ivory films can imagine that defying social codes does not invariably result in happiness; sometimes their films examine the costs of desire for both the desiring character and society at large.

RECOMMENDED VIEWING
Shakespeare Wallah (1965), *Bombay Talkie* (1970), *Roseland* (1977), *Jane Austen in Manhattan* (1980), *Heat and Dust* (1983), *A Room with a View* (1985), *Maurice* (1987), *Howards End* (1992), *The Remains of the Day* (1993), *The Golden Bowl* (2000), *Le Divorce* (2003)

FURTHER READING
Long, Robert Emmet. *The Films of Merchant Ivory*. (Revised). New York: Harry N. Abrams, 1997 [1991].

Pym, John. *The Wandering Company: Twenty-One Years of Merchant Ivory Films*. London and New York: British Film Institute and Museum of Modern Art, 1983.

Anne Morey

because they appear to admire the past in which these things were often denied to these people?

Recent heritage films are striking for the large number that foreground activities such as painting (as in *Carrington* [Christopher Hampton, 1995]) or theater (for instance, *Topsy-Turvy* [Mike Leigh, 1999] and *Finding Neverland* [Marc Forster, 2004]) in order to dramatize creative work or activities that might be described as play. In these examples, the heritage film offers the best possible motivations for the minute inspection of *mise-en-scène*: either it proves to be the very fabric of the narrative, as when Dora Carrington gradually paints every square inch of her cottage in a kind of autobiography of her attachment to Lytton Strachey, or it

Producer Ismail Merchant (left) and director James Ivory in the 1970s. EVERETT COLLECTION. REPRODUCED BY PERMISSION.

presents the details of late nineteenth-century theatrical production as part of the exploration of grown men (W. S. Gilbert and J. M. Barrie) sojourning in extended, profitable fantasy. The heritage film here signals one of its major attractions—that the denial of desire can be perversely sexy, even progressive, particularly when coupled with the satisfactions of carefully wrought spectacle and performance. In short, one of the great appeals of the heritage film is that it bridges the fabled divide in English cinema between fantasy and realism.

SEE ALSO *Great Britain; Historical Films*

FURTHER READING

Friedman, Lester, ed. *Fires Were Started: British Cinema and Thatcherism.* Minneapolis: University of Minnesota Press, 1993; Revised ed., London: Wallflower Press, 2006.

Higson, Andrew. *English Heritage, English Cinema: Costume Drama Since 1980.* Oxford: Oxford University Press, 2003.

Hill, John. *British Cinema in the 1980s: Issues and Themes.* Oxford: Clarendon Press, 1999.

Koepnick, Lutz. "Reframing the Past: Heritage Cinema and Holocaust in the 1990s." *New German Critique* 87 (2002): 47–82.

Monk, Claire, and Amy Sargeant, eds. *British Historical Cinema: The History, Heritage and Costume Film.* London and New York: Routledge, 2002.

Vincendeau, Ginette, ed. *Film/Literature/Heritage: A Sight and Sound Reader.* London: British Film Institute, 2001.

Anne Morey

HISTORICAL FILMS

———■———

Beginning in 1915 with *The Birth of a Nation*, directed by D. W. Griffith (1875–1948), the historical film has been one of the most celebrated forms of cinematic expression as well as one of the most controversial. As a genre, it has maintained a high degree of cultural prominence for nearly a century, and it has established itself as a major form in nearly every nation that produces films. But it has also consistently provoked controversy and widespread public debate about the meaning of the past, about the limits of dramatic interpretation, and about the power of film to influence popular understanding and to promote particular national myths.

The historical film has often served as a vehicle of studio prestige and artistic ambition, and many distinguished directors have made major contributions to the genre. Steven Spielberg (b. 1946), Martin Scorsese (b. 1942), Oliver Stone (b. 1946), John Sayles (b. 1950), Edward Zwick (b. 1952), Bernardo Bertolucci (b. 1941), and Roman Polanski (b. 1933) have made important and powerful historical films that have reawakened interest in aspects of the past that were not previously well-represented or understood. For many societies, the historical film now serves as the dominant source of popular knowledge about the historical past, a fact that has made some professional historians anxious. Other historians, however, see these films as valuable for the discussions and debate they generate. Films such as Spielberg's *Schindler's List* (1993), and Stone's *JFK* (1991), for example, have fostered a widespread and substantial public discussion that has contributed to historical appreciation and understanding.

Although several types of film can be grouped under the heading of the historical, Natalie Zemon Davis usefully defines the historical genre as being composed of dramatic feature films in which the primary plot is based on actual historical events, or in which an imagined plot unfolds in such a way that actual historical events are central and intrinsic to the story. This broad, plot-based characterization of the genre captures the specific and unique character of the historical film, which depends for its meaning and significance on an order of events—historical events—that exist outside the imaginative world of the film itself. Within this somewhat narrowed framework, however, there are still large variations in the types of films that can be considered historical films. Because the genre overlaps with other well-established genres, it is useful to consider the historical film in terms of several subtypes. These include the epic, the war film, the biographical film, the period or topical film, and what might be called the metahistorical film—films such as *JFK* or *Courage Under Fire* (Zwick, 1996) that present the past from multiple, conflicting viewpoints in an attempt to illustrate the complexity of representing the historical past.

THE BEGINNINGS OF THE HISTORICAL FILM

Epic films made in Italy between 1910 and 1914 were the first to capture the spectacular power of the cinema to recreate the past, and the first to extend the screening time of films to two and three hours or more. Films such as *Quo Vadis?* (1912), *Cabiria* (1914), and *Spartaco* (1913) were vast, sweeping depictions of the ancient world that united spectacle, lavish set design, and narrative in a way that had an enormous influence on film style, and that brought an extraordinary amount of publicity to the

Oliver Stone's JFK *(1991) is a metahistorical film.* EVERETT COLLECTION. REPRODUCED BY PERMISSION.

films even prior to their release. The Italian epics of the early silent period were a particular incentive to D. W. Griffith, who after seeing *Quo Vadis?* in 1913 decided to make a two-reel biblical film, *Judith of Bethulia* (1914). The grandest of the Italian epics, *Cabiria*, by Giovanni Pastrone (1883–1959), commanded such public attention for its length, epic form, and massive sets that just hearing about it prompted Griffith to begin planning his own epic, *The Birth of a Nation* (1915). And after seeing *Cabiria*, Griffith began planning an even larger-scale narrative that would interweave four historical periods, resulting in the ambitious *Intolerance* (1916).

The Birth of a Nation is generally credited with inaugurating the genre of the historical film in the United States. Although films that used historical settings and included historical characters were fairly common by 1915, they could not be considered serious attempts to understand or explain the past; rather, they consisted of romances, costume dramas, tales of adventure, or small historical vignettes set within larger dramatic narratives, such as the scene in *Uncle Tom's Cabin* (1903) with Little Eva looking down from heaven on the divisive events of American history. *The Birth of a Nation*, on the other

hand, attempts to offer an explanation and interpretation of the most troubled and divisive period in US history; despite its offensive stereotypes and obvious racism, it poses serious questions and makes serious interpretations about the meaning of the past.

In its ambitiousness, notoriety, and insistence on presenting a serious, if deeply flawed, interpretation of the meaning of the past, *The Birth of a Nation* brings into relief the distinctive characteristics of the genre and provides a blueprint for the future development of the historical film. It melds an elaborate family romance with a story of national trauma and national reconciliation; it employs a visual vocabulary consisting of wide panoramic shots, elaborate cross-cutting, and the use of close-ups as a form of historical commentary and analysis; and it insists on the authenticity of its representations by closely imitating battlefield daguerreotypes, by asserting the fidelity of its depiction of Lincoln's assassination, and by dwelling on the lived spaces of the historical past, the porches, picket fences, and dirt roads of the South. Although it was challenged at the time, its depiction reflected the beliefs of the most powerful school of American historians of that era, including President Woodrow Wilson (1856–1924), who after a private screening purportedly commented: "It's like writing history with lightning. And my only regret is that it is all so terribly true."

The negative publicity generated by *The Birth of a Nation* intensified Griffith's ambition to make a great historical film. *Intolerance*, over three hours long, combines four stories set in different time periods and interweaves the stories in a complex arrangement, like a musical fugue. The thematic link among these stories is the idea of intolerance through the ages and its overcoming through love. By cutting these four stories together through parallel editing—which up to that time had been used strictly for cutting between parallel actions in the same time frame—Griffith tried to articulate a universal historical patterning, one that linked the story of Christ's crucifixion with a modern story of injustice, together with the fall of ancient Babylon, and the story of the St. Bartholomew Day Massacre in sixteenth-century France. This innovative use of parallel editing to link and harmonize four separate historical narratives was a dazzling conceptual breakthrough, but the film was not well received by the public and became a massive commercial failure.

Griffith's influence on the development of a cinematic style of historical narration is perhaps best seen in the Soviet cinema of the 1920s. Sergei Eisenstein (1898–1948) expanded on Griffith's formal innovations in editing to create an even more advanced visual aesthetic known as montage editing, a style characterized by rapid, dynamic combinations of shots of very short length. Eisenstein used this style to create a history or, better, a foundational mythology for the fledgling Soviet Union. In *Bronenosets Potyomkin* (*Battleship Potemkin*, assistant-directed by Grigori Aleksandrov, 1925), Eisenstein takes a small-scale historical incident—the mutiny by a small group of sailors on board the battleship *Potemkin* during the czarist period—and turns it into a stirring dramatization of the power of the proletariat to overcome oppression and create a revolution. In *Oktyabr* (*Ten Days that Shook the World* and *October*, assistant-directed by Grigori Aleksandrov, 1927), also known as *Ten Days That Shook the World*, Eisenstein presents the turbulent events of the ten days of the Bolshevik Revolution. The film combines close attention to the actual events with an elaborate set of visual ideas including the use of visual metaphors, repetition, humor, and a highly charged sense of movement and dynamism.

The Soviet filmmakers were experimental in their treatment of the historical past, exploring ways of creating a revolutionary historiography for a revolutionary time. The style of historical narration that they pioneered

had an impact on the Latin American cinema of the 1960s and, later, on Stone's *JFK* and *Nixon* (1995).

THE EVOLUTION OF THE HISTORICAL FILM: THE WAR FILM

The war film is one of the great modes of cinematic expression. Many war films have been lauded for their realism and their focus on the cruelties of war, as well as for their portraits of heroism. Outstanding examples of the subgenre include formidable Hollywood productions such as *The Charge of the Light Brigade* (1936), *The Longest Day* (1962), *Tora! Tora! Tora!* (1970), *Glory* (1989), and *Saving Private Ryan* (1998), but also more subdued treatments of war and resistance such as Roberto Rossellini's (1906–1977) *Roma, città aperta* (*Rome, Open City*, also known as *Open City*, 1945) and *Paisà* (*Paisan*, 1946).

The Big Parade (1925) and *All Quiet on the Western Front* (1930) were extraordinarily successful works that established the war film in the United States as an important subgenre of historical filmmaking. *The Big Parade*, directed by King Vidor (1894–1982), contains memorable World War I battle sequences, especially a night battle scene that captures the nightmarish aspect of war on the western front, and became the model for many subsequent films. Lewis Milestone's (1895–1980) *All Quiet on the Western Front* won international and popular acclaim, as well as Oscars® for Best Picture and Best Director in 1930, for its portrait of the horrors of war as experienced by a young German soldier. The film marked the first time Germans were treated sympathetically in Hollywood films made after the war. In the most extensive use of moving camera in a sound film up to that time, Milestone used a mobile crane to create elaborate moving camera shots for the battle scenes. The film not only established the power and commercial viability of the war film, but it also established the Great War as an enduring emblem of human loss. Posing serious questions about ideals such as nationalism, patriotism, and the dehumanizing effects of war, *All Quiet on the Western Front* articulated the antiwar sentiment later taken up by war films such as *Paths of Glory* (1957), *Born on the Fourth of July* (1989), and *Apocalypse Now* (1979).

Darryl F. Zanuck's (1902–1979) *The Longest Day* initiated what has become a historical film staple of combat spectaculars. The combination of extraordinary realism in the battle scenes and exceptional attentiveness to the small dramas unfolding among the individual soldiers provided the model for many films to come, among them *Apocalypse Now* and *Saving Private Ryan*. The film also set a new standard for authenticity in the historical genre, in some scenes replicating the Normandy invasion so closely that stills taken from the shooting of the film

ROBERTO ROSSELLINI
b. Rome, Italy, 8 May 1906, d. 3 June 1977

One of the most influential filmmakers in the history of world cinema, Roberto Rossellini followed an idiosyncratic artistic path that brought him world attention. Over the course of his career, Rossellini continually defied expectations and consistently forged his own creative path, a quality that gives his work an unequaled variety and range. Following an apprenticeship making films for the fascist government of Italy in the early 1940s, Rossellini first achieved renown with his neorealist films *Roma, città aperta* (*Rome, Open City*, 1945) and *Paisà* (*Paisan*, 1946). In the 1950s he made a series of films with actress Ingrid Bergman, including *Viaggio in Italia* (*Journey to Italy*, 1953), which opened a new creative focus on the psychology of the couple. In the 1960s and 1970s he changed course again, making a series of didactic films on the history of western civilization for Italian and French television.

Rome, Open City, represents a fundamental breakthrough in film style and subject matter. Using the streets and apartments of Rome directly following the Nazi occupation, and employing a largely nonprofessional cast, *Rome, Open City* crystallized the emerging aesthetic of neorealism, which became one of the most celebrated film movements of the twentieth century, the emblematic filmic expression of the harsh social and psychological conditions of modern life. Rossellini followed with two additional films dealing with the devastation of World War II, *Paisan* and *Germania anno zero* (*Germany Year Zero*, 1948), that employed the look and feel of documentary and merged it with the dramatic plotting of the fiction film to create a powerful sense of social truth.

After seeing *Rome, Open City* and *Paisan* in New York, the actress Ingrid Bergman wrote to Rossellini expressing her admiration for his work. They married in 1950 and began a collaboration that would result in several important films, including *Stromboli* (1950), *Europa '51* (*The Greatest Love*, 1952), and *Journey to Italy*. At this point in his career, however, Rossellini's critical reputation was suffering from his supposed turning away from overtly social subjects to more psychological, "involuted" concerns. Critics in France, however, especially those associated with *Cahiers du cinéma*, argued that these films represented a fresh and liberating approach to filmmaking, one that was psychologically complex and daring.

In 1964, Rossellini again changed direction and began a series of "didactic" history projects for Italian and French television. These films, including *La Prise de pouvoir par Louis XIV* (*The Rise to Power of Louis XIV*, 1966), *L'Età di Cosimo de Medici* (*The Age of the Medici*, 1973), and *Agostino d'Ippona* (*Augustine of Hippo*, 1972), among others, were explorations of the historical past shorn of dramatic fictional plotting. Concentrating on the behavioral details of the period, Rossellini foregrounded his own "didactic" role as historian-narrator by using a zoom lens, called the Pancinor, to highlight certain elements of the scene.

RECOMMENDED VIEWING
Roma, città aperta (*Rome Open City*, 1945), *Paisà* (*Paisan*, 1946), *Germania anno zero* (*Germany Year Zero*, 1947), *Stromboli* (1950), *Viaggio in Italia* (*Journey to Italy*, 1953), *Il Générale della Rovere* (*General della Rovere*, 1959), *La Prise de pouvoir par Louis XIV* (*The Rise to Power of Louis XIV*, 1966)

FURTHER READING

Bondanella, Peter. *The Films of Roberto Rossellini*. Cambridge UK, and New York: Cambridge University Press, 1993.

Brunette, Peter. *Roberto Rossellini*. Oxford: Oxford University Press, 1987.

Forgacs, David. *Rome, Open City*. London: British Film Institute, 2000.

Forgacs, David, Sarah Lutton, and Geoffrey Nowell-Smith. *Roberto Rossellini: Magician of the Real*. London: British Film Institute, 2000.

Rossellini, Roberto. *My Method: Writings and Interviews*, edited by Adreano Apia. New York: Marsilio, 1995.

Robert Burgoyne

Roberto Rossellini at the time of Socrates *(1970).* EVERETT COLLECTION. REPRODUCED BY PERMISSION.

and stills taken from the actual invasion are nearly indistinguishable.

In the late 1970s the American cinema began to take on the subject of Vietnam. Francis Ford Coppola's *Apocalypse Now* and Michael Cimino's *The Deer Hunter* (1978) both portrayed the war as a pathological endeavor that foreboded the ruin of a generation of young Americans. It was not until 1986, however, with the release of Oliver Stone's *Platoon*, that the Vietnam subgenre began to flourish as a dominant mode of cinematic expression. Stone followed *Platoon* with *Born on the Fourth of July*, an antiwar film that dealt with the trauma of the returning Vietnam veteran. A sober and scathingly critical work, *Born on the Fourth of July* followed in the tradition of *The Best Years of Our Lives* (1946) in illustrating the profound alienation of returning veterans who have been traumatized by the experience of war.

The traditional war film experienced a resurgence at the turn of the century with films such as *Saving Private Ryan*, *Black Hawk Down* (2001), *Glory*, *Pearl Harbor* (2001), and *The Patriot* (2000), which together reestablished the power and appeal of films that crystallize the heroism and sacrifice that war entails. Noted for the authenticity of its battlefield sequences as well as for its evocation of nostalgia for the certainties of the "last good war," *Saving Private Ryan* resurrected the traditional war film, which had fallen into disrepute in the post-Vietnam period, and reestablished it as a dominant form in American cinema. *Saving Private Ryan* also broke new ground in its technological innovations, most evident in the Omaha Beach landing sequence, in which the film blends computer-generated imagery, live-action photography, reenactments of documentary photographs and

sequences, accelerated editing, slow-motion cinematography, and electronically enhanced sound design. The film combines the traditions of the war film—stressing the importance of the individual soldier and the success of the collective endeavor mounted on his behalf—with advanced visual and acoustic techniques that give it a powerful claim to battlefield authenticity and realism.

THE EPIC

Giovanni Pastrone's *Cabiria* was quickly followed in Italy by many films dealing with ancient Rome and Greece. In America, after *The Birth of a Nation* established the viability of longer, ambitious historical films, MGM in 1925 released *Ben-Hur*, directed by William Wyler (1902–1981), which became a commercial blockbuster. Cecil B. DeMille's (1881–1959) *The Ten Commandments* (1923) established Hollywood as the major producer of epic films in the 1920s.

In the 1930s and early 1940s, however, the epic form waned as audience tastes turned to contemporary subjects, exemplified in the sophisticated musicals and comedies of Hollywood and in the Italian "white telephone" comedy genre (films about the rich and idle). But the form returned full force in the early 1950s, with *Quo Vadis* (Mervyn LeRoy, 1951), and *The Robe* (Henry Koster, 1953), and the first film to be shot in CinemaScope. The epic, with its lavish sets and mass choreography of crowds and armies, lent itself to the widescreen format that was one of Hollywood's responses to the threat of television. For most critics *Ben-Hur* represents the high point of the style. *King of Kings* (Nicolas Ray, 1961), and *El Cid* (Anthony Mann, 1961), were also accomplished works, as was DeMille's *The Ten Commandments* (1956), which marked a return to the subject he had first treated in 1923.

The epic form in Hollywood reached its zenith in the early 1960s with three films: *Spartacus* (Stanley Kubrick, 1960), *Cleopatra* (Joseph L. Mankiewicz, 1963), and *The Fall of the Roman Empire* (Mann, 1964). (*Spartacus*, which gave screenwriter credit to Dalton Trumbo [1905–1976], a prominent leftist who had been blacklisted in Hollywood for refusing to cooperate with the House Un-American Activities Committee, became known as "the film that broke the blacklist.") However, *The Fall of the Roman Empire* did poorly at the box office, and from 1964 until the mid-1990s the epic was decidedly out of fashion. With *Braveheart* (Mel Gibson, 1995) and *Gladiator* (Ridley Scott, 2000), the epic renewed itself in a way that heralded a return to cultural prominence. *Gladiator*, in particular, provides a fascinating example of the use of new visual technologies to narrate the past. Its elaborate use of computer-generated imagery recreates

OLIVER STONE
b. New York, New York, 15 September 1946

One of the most accomplished filmmakers working in contemporary Hollywood, Oliver Stone is also one of the most controversial, creating vivid dramas of American history and politics that have provoked equal parts admiration and outrage. His film about the Kennedy assassination, *JFK* (1991), for example, created a searing controversy that led to denunciations by leading politicians, journalists, and historians. Ultimately, however, it resulted in legislation authorizing the Assassination Records Review Board, which assembled and made available millions of pages of documents on the assassination previously withheld from the public. In 1998 the Review Board specifically credited *JFK* with arousing public opinion to pressure Congress into passing the legislation. Arguably, no American work of art, with the possible exception of Harriet Beecher Stowe's *Uncle Tom's Cabin* (1852), has had as direct or consequential an impact on American history as *JFK*.

Asserting his political orientation with his first major films, Stone's early works combine an explicitly political viewpoint with dramatic plotting and sympathetic characters. *Salvador* (1986) and *Platoon* (1986) are emotionally wrenching depictions of the conflicts in El Salvador and Vietnam. Following *Platoon*, which won Academy Awards® for Best Picture and Best Director, Stone made two films dealing with domestic American life, *Wall Street* (1987) and *Talk Radio* (1988). *Born on the Fourth of July* (1989) took up the subject of Vietnam again and won for Stone his second Oscar® for Best Director. A powerful film about the loss of national ideals and purpose, rendered through the experiences of a wide-eyed, all-American hero who comes home a disillusioned paraplegic, the film reads as a culminating statement against the war and its pointless sacrifice of a generation of young people. Stone completed his

Vietnam trilogy with *Heaven and Earth* (1993), a beautiful and highly stylized portrait of a young Vietnamese woman and her experiences during the war and its aftermath.

With *The Doors* (1991), *Natural Born Killers* (1994), and *Nixon* (1995), Stone extended his stylistic range, which had largely been tied to realist modes of representation, to include an array of subjective, dreamlike devices including disorienting, rapid-fire montage, superimpositions, and elaborate layering of the sound track. In these films, Stone creates an expressionistic portrait of American reality, dramatizing the frenzied, driven, and ultimately self-destructive aspects of American culture. His more recent films, including *Any Given Sunday* (1999) and *Alexander* (2004), represent a departure from the political focus of his major works, which stand among the most provocative and powerful in cinema history.

RECOMMENDED VIEWING
Salvador (1986), *Platoon* (1986), *Born on the Fourth of July* (1989), *JFK* (1991), *Natural Born Killers* (1994), *Nixon* (1995), *World Trade Center* (2006)

FURTHER READING
Kagen, Norman. *The Cinema of Oliver Stone*. London: Continuum, 2000.

Kunz, Don. *The Films of Oliver Stone*. Lanham, MD: Scarecrow Press, 1997.

Silet, Charles L.P., ed. *Oliver Stone: Interviews*. Jackson: University Press of Mississippi, 2001.

Stone, Oliver, and Zachary Sklar. *JFK: The Book of the Film*. New York: Warner Bros., Inc. and Regency Enterprises V.O.F., 1992.

Toplin, Robert Brent, ed. *Oliver Stone's USA*. Lawrence: University Press of Kansas, 2000.

Robert Burgoyne

the Colosseum, the Roman Forum, and an exceptional sense of realism in its gladiator contests. With varying degrees of critical and box-office success, twenty-first-century directors have made more films in the epic genre, including *Troy* (Wolfgang Petersen, 2004), *Alexander* (Stone, 2004), and *The Passion of the Christ* (Gibson, 2004).

THE BIOGRAPHICAL FILM
The biographical film, or biopic, also has a long and distinguished history in world cinema, with several works attaining high status for their critical as well as their commercial success. For example, *The Private Life of Henry VIII* (Alexander Korda, 1933) was the British

Oliver Stone during production of **Alexander** ***(2004).*** © WARNER BROTHERS/COURTESY EVERETT COLLECTION. REPRODUCED BY PERMISSION.

cinema's first international success; Charles Laughton (1899–1962) won a Best Actor Oscar® for his portrayal of the monarch. The French film *Napoléon* (Abel Gance, 1927) brought a similar sense of national pride to a country whose film industry had been devastated by World War I. Still regarded as one of the most outstanding achievements in the history of the cinema, *Napoléon* was seen as the culmination of the French cinema's rise from near annihilation in 1914. *The Last Emperor* (Bernardo Bertolucci, 1987), which won nine Academy Awards®, was the first film to be shot on location in Beijing's Forbidden City, heralding a more open era in Chinese–Western cultural relations.

The biopic emerged as a recognizable subgenre in the 1930s. The first biopic is generally considered to be the George Arliss (1868–1946) vehicle *Disraeli* (1929), marketed as a Warner Bros. prestige production. Arliss also starred in *Alexander Hamilton* (1931) for Warner Bros. and in *Voltaire* (1933). The commercial and critical accomplishment of these works paved the way for several later Warner Bros. films directed by William Dieterle (1893–1972), including *The Story of Louis Pasteur*

(1935), for which Paul Muni (1895–1967) won the Oscar® for Best Actor; *The White Angel* (1936), the story of Florence Nightingale; and *The Life of Emile Zola* (1937) and *Juarez* (1939), both also starring Muni.

Biographical films are often driven by a national, myth-making impulse. *Young Mr. Lincoln* (1939), starring Henry Fonda (1905–1982) in his first film with John Ford (1894–1973), and *Abe Lincoln in Illinois* (1940), starring Raymond Massey (1896–1983), were not so much historical as mythological exercises, as neither film was particularly accurate with regard to the actual events of Lincoln's life nor to his character. Nevertheless, *Young Mr. Lincoln*, in particular, succeeded in elevating Lincoln's early years to the level of national myth.

Eisenstein's *Ivan Groznyy I* (*Ivan the Terrible, Part One*, 1944) focused on an individual protagonist, rather than the collective protagonist of his earlier films, in part to rally the Russian people during World War II by giving them a historical hero who had unified Russia, fought off treachery, and defeated external enemies in the sixteenth century. Unlike his earlier *Aleksandr Nevskiy*

La Prise de pouvoir par Louis XIV (**The Rise to Power of Louis XIV**, *1966) was one of several historical biographies Roberto Rossellini made for television.* EVERETT COLLECTION. REPRODUCED BY PERMISSION.

(*Alexander Nevsky*, co-directed by Dmitri Vasilyev, 1938), however, which focused on the story of a thirteenth-century prince who defeated an invading Teutonic army, *Ivan the Terrible, Part One* is less a symbol of the Russian people than a portrait of a fully rounded character, complex and beset by internal conflicts. Although *Ivan the Terrible, Part One* received the Stalin Prize, *Ivan Groznyy II* (*Ivan the Terrible, Part Two*, co-directed by M. Filimonova, 1958) was condemned by Stalin and suppressed. *Ivan the Terrible, Part One* has long been considered one of the most important and original films in world cinema in terms of its formal design; the two parts taken together may also be the first biographical film to explore the darker side of its main character.

As the biopic matured as a form, its subjects became more complex. *Lawrence of Arabia* (David Lean, 1962), starring Peter O'Toole, for example, paints an arresting portrait of its main character that shows him as both heroic and fatally flawed. *Patton* (Franklin Schaffner, 1970) took a similar approach, with George C. Scott

(1927–1999) depicting the main character as both a noble warrior and vainglorious egomaniac. The complex and subtle shadings of character that distinguish films such as *Lawrence of Arabia* and *Patton* are also found in later examples of the form. Works such as Bertolucci's *The Last Emperor* and Stone's *Nixon* are distinguished examples of films that take a complicated view of the link between the individual subject and the historical process, refusing to see the individual agent as simply the crystallized expression of historical forces. *Malcolm X* (Spike Lee, 1992) and *Gandhi* (Richard Attenborough, 1982) as well as *Schindler's List*, consider the question that is at the heart of the biographical film: the relationship between the currents and forces of history and the charismatic individual who strives to shape those forces.

THE TOPICAL FILM

Many important historical films center on a particular incident or focus on a specific period rather than on the grand narratives of war, heroic individual action, or the emergence of a race or nation in the form of the epic. The topical, or period, film is exemplified by such celebrated works as Rossellini's *Rome, Open City* and *Paisan, Senso* (Luchino Visconti, 1954), *La Marseillaise* (Jean Renoir, 1938), *Danton* (Andrzej Wajda, 1982), *Gallipoli* (Peter Weir, 1981), and *Titanic* (James Cameron, 1997). Two other notable examples, *Eight Men Out* (1988) and *Matewan* (1987), are the work of the independent film-maker John Sayles. Commenting on *Matewan*, Sayles explained that, rather than recreate an entire fifteen-year period in American labor history, he focused on the Matewan Massacre, an incident in the mining industry, as one episode that epitomized that period. Similarly, *Eight Men Out*, a film that focuses on the Black Sox scandal of 1919, in which several players conspired to throw the World Series, dug under the surface of the incident to show the period as a moment of cultural transition in which sports, advertising, public relations, gambling, leisure, and mass communications were beginning to transform the nation from an agrarian culture to an urban, commodity-based society.

Other historical films are important for their exactitude of period detail and for their deep understanding of the difference between the past and the present. Such films fully express a cultural order that, organized according to different allegiances and beliefs, has become remote. These include *Le Retour de Martin Guerre* (*The Return of Martin Guerre*, Daniel Vigne, 1982), *Black Robe* (Bruce Beresford, 1991), and *Daughters of the Dust* (Julie Dash, 1991). *Black Robe* centers on the challenges facing Jesuit missionaries in French Canada in the 1600s, in particular the attempt by one young priest to travel to a distressed mission in the Ottawa River Valley, a journey that becomes an ordeal. The film captures the strangeness and sense of otherness that the priest experiences while traveling among the Algonquins who serve as his trading partners and guides, but it also gives us the perspective of the Indians and effectively opens a window onto their cultural sensibility. Each culture is presented to the viewer in its unfiltered strangeness, as it was to the other in 1634.

THE METAHISTORICAL FILM

Certain films can be called metahistorical because they offer embedded or explicit critiques of the way history is conventionally represented. *Courage Under Fire*, for example, employs multiple flashbacks from different points of view to piece together a disputed account of a female air force officer's death. *Walker* (Alex Cox, 1987) brings present-day objects from consumer culture into its collage-like narrative of the nineteenth-century adventurer William Walker, who declared himself emperor of Nicaragua. What these films have in common is the

attempt to interrogate the process of historical representation, both written and filmed. *JFK* presents a provocative interpretation of the assassination of John F. Kennedy in a highly charged, polemical style that mixes idioms, splices together documentary and historical footage, and uses montage editing to disorient and "agitate" the viewer in a manner that calls into question accepted interpretations of the past. *Hitler—ein Film aus Deutschland* (*Hitler: A Film from Germany*, also known as *Our Hitler*, Hans-Jürgen Syberberg, 1978) attempts to confront the German amnesia concerning Hitler by rendering the phenomenon of Hitler's rise as a disorienting operatic production, calling to mind the German fascination with and investment in this form. The film's extreme length (seven hours and nine minutes), its use of dolls, dummies, and caricatures—Hitler is portrayed variously as a house painter, Chaplin's Great Dictator, a Frankenstein monster, and Parsifal—underscores the way historical events and characters take on meaning through their representations in the media.

In a very different way, a series of films that Rossellini made for French and Italian television late in his career can also be seen as metahistorical works. In these "history lessons," Rossellini explored the lives and times of various historical personages in a studiously nondramatic, nonpsychologized way. His films *La Prise de pouvoir par Louis XIV* (*The Rise of Louis XIV*, 1966), *Socrate* (*Socrates*, 1970), and *L'Età di Cosimo de Medici* (*The Age of the Medici*, 1973) were made with nonprofessional actors and avoid following the dramatic arc of most fictional historical films. Rossellini attempts to capture the dailiness of life in past historical times, bringing an almost documentary approach to the treatment of the past.

THE COSTUME DRAMA

The costume drama can be distinguished from other variants of the historical film by virtue of its fictional basis. Its plot is most often based on a fictional literary source, and it does not depend on actual historical events as its main focus or framing material. Nevertheless, the costume drama provides many pleasures for viewers, for it often features a sumptuous recreation of a historical period and setting, with the density of detail in the costumes and décor providing a source of sensual pleasure that equates history with emotion and passion. The Gainsborough Studio in the 1940s produced a number of notable costume dramas, including adaptations of literary works such as *The Man in Grey* (1943), *Fanny by Gaslight* (1944), and *The Wicked Lady* (1945).

Costume dramas such as *The Mask of Zorro* (1998) and *Dangerous Liaisons* (1988) employ historical settings for their aesthetic value, allowing the viewer to become a voyeur of the past. Historical films in general appeal to this emotional, voyeuristic interest on the part of the spectator, but the costume film allows its fullest expression, untrammeled by the sociopolitical conflicts that dominate the plots of films that deal with actual historical events.

THE DOCUDRAMA

The docudrama, another type of visual narrative dealing with the past, has gained a significant place in television broadcasting, with such well-known titles as *Brian's Song* (1971), *Roots* (1977), and *Everybody's Baby: The Rescue of Jessica McClure* (1989). The genre in its original form combined documentary and drama, categories usually conceived as separate. According to Janet Staiger, the docudrama derives from the early US television program *You Are There* (1953–1957), which featured staged interviews with actors representing the actual participants in historical events, such as the conquest of Mexico. The "you are there" form, however, has fallen into disuse, and most docudramas employ mainstream forms of dramatic representation and apply them to historical events. They combine fictional narrative techniques with an explicit claim to record or report "reality," a characteristic of television broadcasting in general. In blending narrative and documentary style, the docudrama sets forth a moral view of reality, an ethical response to the "real world," which is initially presented as disordered and irrational.

CONCLUSION

The historical film emerged as a strong genre form very early in cinema history and has renewed itself many times over the course of the twentieth century and into the twenty-first. Although the world of the past is its subject, the genre is often in the vanguard in terms of visual style and cinematic technique. The dramatic, compelling portraits of the past that are brought to life in the historical film have made it one of the most prestigious as well as one of the most controversial genres in film. It provides both a lens onto the past, which it frequently recreates with exquisite attention to detail and period style, while also reflecting the cultural sensibility of the period in which it was made. Above all, the historical film provides an emotional connection to history in a way that foregrounds the power and importance of the past in shaping the cultural imaginary in the present.

SEE ALSO *Biography; Epic Films; Genre; Melodrama; Vietnam War; War Films; World War I; World War II*

FURTHER READING

Burgoyne, Robert. *Film Nation: Hollywood Looks at U.S. History.* Minneapolis: University of Minnesota Press, 1997.

Carnes, Mark C., ed. *Past Imperfect: History According to the Movies.* New York: Henry Holt, 1995.

Custen, George. *Bio/Pics: How Hollywood Constructed Public History.* New Brunswick, NJ: Rutgers University Press, 1992.

Davis, Natalie Zemon. *Slaves on Screen: Film and Historical Vision.* Cambridge, MA: Harvard University Press, 2000.

Elley, Derek. *The Epic Film.* London: Routledge and Kegan Paul, 1984.

Harper, Sue. *Picturing the Past: The Rise and Fall of the British Costume Film.* London: British Film Institute, 1994.

Kaes, Anton. *From Hitler to Heimat: The Return of History as Film.* Cambridge, MA: Harvard University Press, 1989.

Rosenstone, Robert A. *Visions of the Past: The Challenge of Film to Our Idea of History.* Cambridge, MA: Harvard University Press, 1995.

Sobchack, Vivian, ed. *The Persistence of History: Cinema, Television, and the Modern Event.* New York: Routledge, 1996.

Sorlin, Pierre. *The Film in History: Restaging the Past.* Totowa, NJ: Barnes and Noble, 1980.

Suid, Lawrence H. *Guts & Glory: The Making of the American Military Image in Film.* Lexington: University Press of Kentucky, 2002.

Wyke, Maria. *Projecting the Past: Ancient Rome, Cinema, and History.* New York: Routledge, 1997.

Robert Burgoyne

HOLOCAUST

Holocaust films narrate or document the persecution and genocide of Jews and others under the Nazi Third Reich of Adolf Hitler (1933–1945). From the 1935 Nuremberg Laws that excluded Jews from citizenship of the Reich, to the 9 November 1938 *Kristellnacht* attacks on Jews, their synagogues, and their businesses, to the 1941 Wannsee meeting at which Nazis planned the final solution, to the rounding up of Jews not only in Germany but in all German occupied territory, to the operation of the Nazi death camps and other acts of mass murder, these most tragic and traumatic events in modern history constitute the Holocaust, or as it is also called, the Shoah.

REPRESENTATION AND THE HOLOCAUST

Ever since the appearance of Steven Spielberg's (b. 1946) *Schindler's List* (1993), only eight years after Claude Lanzmann's (b. 1925) *Shoah* (1985), these two films have come to represent the polarities in a debate on how cinema should tell stories about the Holocaust. Lanzmann's film gathers first-person reports that center on the process of systematic arrest, transport, internment, and annihilation of Europe's Jewish population; it eschews dramatization in favor of the setting of these interviews against the contemporary landscapes at the sites in which the tragic events took place. It strategically refuses to recreate past horrors except through verbal tellings, so that the visual in this film rests only on the speakers and on landscapes that are otherwise silent about the events that once occurred there.

These contemporary landscapes mark the terrain of a refusal to fill an absence, a refusal to take us back to a history that in its magnitude exceeds any examples that would partially serve to represent it. The Shoah must be unrepresentable, beyond figuration, beyond parable, or even symbolization. Yet *Shoah* is a documentary concerned with documents, and with oral history as a form of documentation. Its goal is to highlight the alibis that can distort historical memory, that can allow populations to deny the Shoah. Lanzmann's interviews cover some material already recorded in histories, such as Vrba's testimony. To hear such testimony directly, presented with all its emotional weight for the victims, is newly compelling. The secretly recorded interviews with former Nazis need to be heard in the context of the victims' interviews, to hear in contrast the emotional withdrawal and denial that occurred, especially vivid when the former Nazis report facts that coincide with the victims' accounts. The interviews with Polish peasants and workers reveal not only anti-Semitism and complicity in the past, but lingering anti-Semitism embedded within their narratives. Chillingly, the brunt of this anti-Semitism is steeped in Christian references; the cultural framework through which they view Jews has not changed.

Schindler's List, by contrast, fictionally amplifies a fragment of Holocaust history for emotional affect. In flamboyant *mise-en-scène* and camerawork often reminiscent of Orson Welles's *Citizen Kane* (1941), Spielberg employs the tropes of Hollywood filmmaking to frame an individual act of resistance on the part of one-time Nazi sympathizer Oskar Schindler (Liam Neeson) to save the Jewish slave laborers he employed at his armament factory. However late in the war and perhaps self-interested his acts might have been, the film highlights his conversion into hero. Enfolded within this story, images of deportation and a death camp give us the backdrop of the cataclysmic events that surrounded Schindler's Jews, yet even this aspect remains controversial for certain misleading representations. One such instance is a concentration camp shower sequence that the prisoners fear will be a gassing, but it turns out in this case to be only a shower. The sequence is disturbing for how it conforms, however temporarily, to Holocaust denials. *Schindler's List* met with some critical disdain not only for such narrative moments, but also for the melodramatic style used to connect to a mass audience.

These cornerstones of recent Holocaust representation follow many other documentaries and fiction films that have told various aspects of Holocaust history. The long history of both documentaries and fiction films has a cumulative resonance. The Holocaust as historical trauma that took place at so many different locales and created so many specific and individual tragedies, has not one story to tell, but many.

Alain Resnais's (b. 1922) *Nuit et brouillard* (*Night and Fog*, 1955), filmed at Auschwitz, features a voice-over essay by survivor Jean Cayrol in montage with black-and-white documentary images (both those the Germans took to document their atrocities and those liberators took as evidence) and Resnais's evocative color footage of the deserted remains of the camp. Some of the documentary footage was first shown at the Nuremburg trials and would later be featured in *Judgment at Nuremburg* (1961) by Stanley Kramer (1913–2001). In Resnais's film, it is presented with bitter irony as the film strives for both a poetic discourse and reflexively addresses the dynamic of witnessing itself. Controversially, it does not focus on Jewish annihilation (Cayrol was a Catholic victim), but it is haunting philosophical commentary on evil and responsibility.

Die Mörder sind unter uns (*Murderers Among Us*, 1946), a German film made in the Soviet-controlled sector of Berlin, may be the first fiction film about the Holocaust. A survivor of the camps, again a Catholic, returns to her apartment only to find that she must share it with the former Nazi soldier who now occupies it. The film's title accuses the guilty, but its narrative works to expiate guilt and offer redemption, strategies that fit a communist agenda for the construction of what would become the German Democratic Republic.

In contrast, it was not until *The Diary of Anne Frank* (1959), directed by George Stevens, that a US filmmaker produced a major feature about the Holocaust. Adapted from the Broadway hit, the film garnered three Academy Awards® and was nominated for five others, including Best Picture and Best Director. Capturing the tension of hiding from the Nazis in an Amsterdam attic, the film also works as a serious family drama about intergenerational

conflicts and coming of age, although this aspect, found in Anne Frank's original diary, led some to argue that American filmmakers could only approach the Holocaust in terms that were familiar to families of the 1950s.

East European Jewish survivors were able to write and to film Holocaust narratives for their State industries, with Poland and Czechoslovakia providing particularly stunning works. For example, *Obchod na korze* (*The Shop on Main Street*, Ján Kadár, 1965) employs a surrealist sensibility to present Slovak townspeople welcoming the Nazis. A microcosmic look at how economic gain can combine with prejudice to engender a Holocaust, the film is set in a dry goods store run by an aged Jewish widow, played by Yiddish theater star Ida Kaminska (1899–1980). *Pasazenka* (*The Passenger*, Andrzej Munk) is another superb film, completed in Poland in 1963, after the filmmaker's untimely death. When a Polish Auschwitz-Birkinau survivor recognizes a German woman on a passenger ship as her former captor, the film's main story enfolds in flashbacks to the camp. Through its calm, complicit witnessing, similar to that of *Shoah*, this film effectively portrays mass murder in the banal guise of a day's work.

Perhaps influenced by some of this fine European work, Sidney Lumet (b. 1924) made *The Pawnbroker* (1964) from a novel by Edward Lewis Wallant. This film takes a stunning look at the Holocaust trauma of survivor Sol Nazerman (Rod Steiger), once a professor of history in Germany (Poland in the novel), now a pawnbroker in New York, whose memories intersperse the narrative. He recalls an incident from the camp in which an escaped prisoner, Nazerman's friend, who has been tracked down by the German guards and their dogs, is tortured and killed in front of the other prisoners. Another flashback memory shows Nazerman's wife being forced to service Nazi soldiers, a memory evoked by a black prostitute's offering her services to him at his pawnshop. Such associative montages set up a metaphoric parallel between the concentration camp and urban poverty, as well as explore the nature of a survivor's guilt and trauma.

American television has played an important role in representing the Holocaust, notably with the mini-series *Holocaust* (1978) and *Playing for Time* (Daniel Mann, 1980). Melodramatic tropes structure *Holocaust*, as they do *Schindler's List*, but the earlier television serial tries to give a more extensive view of different localities of the Holocaust. By following various members of a Jewish family named Weiss and interweaving their stories with a German lawyer, Eric Dorf, who eventually joins the SS, throughout Hitler's reign in Germany, the serial interweaves victims' and perpetrators' perspectives. Only one of the Weiss's sons survives World War II, while the fate of the other family members allows the multi-part drama to portray the Warsaw ghetto and three different camps: Auschwitz, Buchenwald, and Terezienstadt. Such multiple-perspective mechanisms are repeated in another television serial, *The Winds of War* (1983), directed by Dan Curtis (1927–2006) and adapted by Herman Wouk from his novel, as well as by its sequel, *War and Remembrance* (1988), again by Curtis and Wouk. Across the two serial works (1,600 minutes in total), we follow Jewish characters who become Holocaust victims, Natalie Jastrow-Henry and her uncle Aaron Jastrow (both played by different actors in the second series—Ali McGraw then Jane Seymour, John Houseman then John Gielgud). Later films, such as *Sunshine* (István Szabó, 1999), used a family melodrama to narrate different perspectives on a sweep of history. Arthur Miller (1915–2005) adapted the autobiography of Fania Fénelon, a member of the Auschwitz prisoners' orchestra, for the TV movie *Playing for Time*. Scenes of an orchestra also appear in *The Passenger*; both films use the existence of the orchestra to underscore the horrendous cultural contradictions in Nazi ideology and practice. These films highlight the ways appreciation of classical music (the Nazis established five orchestras in Auschwitz alone, and each camp had its performing ensembles) coexisted with the ability to commit atrocities, thus underscoring that Western cultural values did not foreclose barbarism. They also highlight the dilemma of the cultural Kapo, the performers who, like the Jewish concentration camp workers, were allowed to live while others died. Against their will, the Kapo were forced to contribute to the running of the camp, to become complicit in genocide. *Playing for Time* dramatizes the anguish of this treacherous position.

Many documentaries, including numerous Academy award winners, have chronicled many aspects of the Holocaust. *Let My People Go* (John Krish, 1961) treats the liberation of the camps, as does *Ihr zent frei* (Dea Brokman and Ilene Landis, 1983). *Genocide* (Arnold Schwartzman, 1981) attempts a comprehensive overview by combining still images and clips with letters and memoirs read as voice-over. *The Long Way Home* (1997) by Mark Jonathan Harris (b. 1941) looks at postwar Jewish refugees. His *Into the Arms of Strangers: Stories of the Kindertransport* (2000) joins a more personal retelling in Melissa Hacker's *My Knees Were Jumping: Remembering the Kindertransports* (1996), about the Jewish children sent to Britain in order to survive.

RECENT HOLOCAUST FILMS

With all the controversy surrounding Holocaust dramas, it is no wonder that a Holocaust comedy whose second half is set in a concentration camp, Roberto Benigni's (b. 1952) *La Vita è bella* (*Life is Beautiful*, 1997), evoked bitter criticism. The film has been likened to the satire in Charlie Chaplin's *The Great Dictator* (1940), although the context through which Chaplin's deflation of Hitler earned its acclaim differs. A scene early in the film in which the hero, Guido (Benigni), comically disrupts a fascist classroom in particular merits the comparison. Like *Schindler's List*, *Life is Beautiful* tries to wrench from the Holocaust context an uplifting narrative of survival and redemption, here specifically by focusing on the extended conceit of a father shielding his son from the horrors of their exportation from Ferrara and internment in a concentration camp by spinning innocent fantasy explanations for horrible events. The film works best as a fantasy because such a shielding would never have been possible, and the truth of the Shoah is that even young children in the camps knew the pain of their existence all too well. To follow this film, one must grant it its moment-to-moment ironies, as each new atrocious aspect becomes a comic fantasy. Whether or not one finds such irony compelling, a fascinating image appears at the end of the film, after the liberation: father and son rejoin the wife on a hill, symbolically reclaiming the land.

In an Italian cultural context, the film can be seen as celebrating Italian Jewish survivors. For Italy, like France, offers a different setting for Holocaust films, one with questions specific to national cultural history. American audiences embraced, but sometimes misunderstood aspects of an earlier Italian film about the Holocaust, Vittorio De Sica's (1901–1974) *Il Giardino dei Finzi-Contini* (*The Garden of the Finzi Continis*, 1970), adapted for the screen by Giorgio Bassani from his important novel, set in his hometown, Ferrara, Italy. The film focuses on an upper-class family in Ferrara, who under the rise of Italian fascism retreat to their enclosed villa, yet where they entertain a few close friends with tennis and social gatherings. Many wondered about the depiction of Jews as upper-class blonds, ignoring the specificity that the film and the novel before it address Jewish assimilation in Northern Italy. The film traces the arrest and deportation of the family along with other Jews. The garden of the title represents the passivity of this family of means, living too long in denial.

Roman Polanski's (b. 1933) *The Pianist* (2002), adapted by Ronald Harwood from Wladyslaw Szpilman's autobiography, masterfully witnesses the Holocaust from hiding. It tells the story of an accomplished musician who becomes subject to the Nazi anti-Jewish laws. Szpilman (Adrien Brody) and his family are forced to move to the Jewish ghetto of Warsaw, and when his family is deported to a death camp, Szpilman is sent to a German forced labor compound. He witnesses the Warsaw ghetto uprising in 1943,

Adrien Brody in Roman Polanksi's* Le Pianiste *(The Pianist, 2002). © FOCUS FEATURES/COURTESY EVERETT COLLECTION. REPRODUCED BY PERMISSION.

followed by the revolt throughout the city begun in August 1944. In an encounter between Szpilman and a Nazi officer among the ruins of one of his hideouts shortly before the Nazi defeat in Poland, the officer begs him to play once more—and lets him live—a sign of the officer's own alienation.

The return of music at the end of *The Pianist* is an example of a trend in some recent Holocaust films to emphasize the return to decency after the depraved onslaught of barbarity. These recent endings contrast with those especially of earlier East European Holocaust films, such as Andrzej Wajda's (b. 1926) *Kanal* (1957), about Warsaw's resistance. This shift cannot just be assumed to come from the passage of time alone, for the pressure of commercial distribution to a contemporary world market weighed on Polanski in ways that were not a factor for his compatriot Wajda. It is striking that Polanski, himself a Holocaust survivor as a child, returned to Poland to tell this story, finally, at this late stage in his career, thus releasing his survivor pain.

SEE ALSO *World War II*

FURTHER READING

Baer, Elizabeth Roberts, and Myrna Goldenberg, eds. *Experience and Expression: Women, the Nazis, and the Holocaust.* Detroit, MI: Wayne State University Press, 2003.

Colombat, André. *The Holocaust in French Film.* Metuchen, NJ: Scarecrow Press, 1993.

Doneson, Judith E. *The Holocaust in American Film.* Philadelphia: Jewish Publication Society, 1987.

Eisenstein, Paul. *Traumatic Encounters: Holocaust Representation and the Hegelian Subject.* Albany: State University of New York Press, 2003.

Fensch, Thomas, and Herbert Steinhouse. *Oskar Schindler and His List: The Man, the Book, the Film, the Holocaust and Its Survivors.* Forest Dale, VT: Paul S. Eriksson, 1995.

Grobman, Alex, Daniel Landes, and Sybil Milton. *Genocide, Critical Issues of the Holocaust: A Companion to the Film, "Genocide."* Los Angeles: Simon Weisenthal Center, 1983.

Hoberman, J., and Jeffrey Shandler, eds. *Entertaining America: Jews, Movies, and Broadcasting.* New York and Princeton: Jewish Museum and Princeton University Press, 2003.

Insdorf, Annette. *Indelible Shadows: Film and the Holocaust,* 3rd ed. Cambridge, UK and New York: Cambridge University Press, 2003.

Lanzmann, Claude. *Shoah: An Oral History of the Holocaust: The Complete Text of the Film.* New York: Pantheon Books, 1985.

Lewis, Stephen, and Aron Appelfeld. *Art Out of Agony: The Holocaust Theme in Literature, Sculpture and Film.* Montreal and New York: CBC Enterprises/Les Enterprises Radio-Canada, 1984.

Loshitzky, Yosefa, ed. *Spielberg's Holocaust: Critical Perspectives on "Schindler's List."* Bloomington: Indiana University Press, 1997.

Mintz, Alan. *Popular Culture and the Shaping of Holocaust Memory in America.* Seattle: University of Washington Press, 2001.

Sobchack, Vivian, ed. *The Persistence of History: Cinema, Television, and the Modern Event.* New York: Routledge, 1996.

Turim, Maureen. *Flashbacks in Film: Memory and History.* New York: Routledge, 1989.

———. "The Trauma of History: Flashbacks upon Flashbacks." *Screen* 42, no. 2 (Summer 2001): 205–210.

Maureen Turim

HONG KONG

Hong Kong cinema is shaped by two major factors—geographical location and politics. As a major port and trading center, Hong Kong was the first Chinese city exposed to the invention of cinema. During the "Chinese war against Japanese aggression" (World War II), due to its geographical marginality from China, Hong Kong became the wartime filmmaking capital. Hong Kong's British colonial status also protected it from the subsequent Chinese civil war and the eventual takeover of mainland China by the Communist Party in 1949. The subsequent exodus of money and talents from the mainland provided the base for a permanent filmmaking capital. In the 1980s, after the Sino-British Joint Declaration affirmed the coming (1997) reunification of Hong Kong with China, anxiety permeated the political climate, and Hong Kong cinema, which had established its own subjectivity, found itself in crisis. The new challenge became the process of internationalization, which has required a commercial strategy for combating global competition and a political position to fend off interference from China.

EARLY CINEMA: 1896–1923

According to Hong Kong film historian Yu Mo Wan, among all Chinese societies (the China mainland, Taiwan, Hong Kong, and the diasporic communities overseas), Hong Kong was the first to encounter cinema. During early 1896 the Lumière brothers came to Hong Kong to shoot *actualités*—scenes of city life—thus marking the beginning of cinema in China. Later that year the Edison Company also came to shoot film in both Hong Kong and Shanghai, and it edited the footage to form two films, *Shanghai Police* and *Hong Kong Street Scenes*.

Their exhibitions were the first commercial screenings in Hong Kong and Shanghai.

Between 1896 and 1903 all film activities (production and exhibition) in Hong Kong were carried out by Westerners. Short films, which came mostly from the United States, were shown in open spaces beside crowded markets. But the rainy weather of Hong Kong proved too much of a challenge, and soon screenings were moved indoors to restaurants and Cantonese opera houses. In 1901 Hong Kong opened its first nickelodeon, He Lio Garden (Joy Garden), a few years ahead of the opening of a similar theater in Shanghai.

Most film scholars take 1909 as the real beginning of Hong Kong cinema. That year saw the first (Hong Kong) Chinese-directed narrative film, *Tou Shao Ya* (Stealing the Roasted Duck), a comedy about a poor man who steals a roasted duck from its plump owner and is eventually caught by the police. It was produced by the Asia Motion Picture Company (headquartered in Shanghai and owned by the American Benjamin Polaski), directed by Leung Sui Bor, and shot in Hong Kong. In 1913 Polaski met another Hong Kong Chinese, Li Man Wei (1893–1953), and together they formed the Wah-Mei (China-US) Production Company. Li would later become the "father" of Hong Kong Cinema.

In 1923 Li, along with his friend Leung Sui Bor, his cousin Li Hai Tsan, and his brother Li Pei Hai, formed the first Hong Kong Chinese-owned production company, Man Sun (Minxin) Motion Picture Production Company. A few years later, he built theaters and studios, thus setting up vertical integration, a complete (albeit unstable, because of the politics of China) infrastructure

Wong Kar Wei. © WARNER INDEPENDENT PICTURES/COURTESY EVERETT COLLECTION. REPRODUCED BY PERMISSION.

for film production. With Man Sun as a model, smaller film companies rapidly formed. Between 1930 and 1937, the eve of the Japanese invasion of China, some fifty small film companies were making Cantonese films and screening them in Hong Kong, Macau, southern China, Malaya, Singapore, the Philippines, and Chinatowns in Australia, the United States, and Canada. Most of these films were genre movies made with shoestring budgets: comedies, dramas, swordplay epics, and Cantonese operas. Many of these small companies survived for no more than one or two films.

WARTIME AND POSTWAR CINEMA

The Japanese bombed Shanghai in 1932, disrupting film production. By 1937 the film industry in China dispersed from Shanghai to Chungking (the wartime capital) and Hong Kong. Between 1933 and 1941 four hundred Cantonese films were made in Hong Kong, many with patriotic themes. When the Japanese occupied Hong Kong in 1941 production abruptly ceased, though the screening of films, mostly American, continued. By 1943 the occupying Japanese formed a coalition and

began to make pro-Japan films without the participation of Hong Kong film companies.

Immediately after World War II ended the Great China Film Company, which had existed before the war, resumed filmmaking in both Cantonese and Mandarin. One year later, a new company, Yung Wah (Yonghua), was formed by a rich, well-educated film enthusiast, Lee Tsu Wing from Shanghai. Yung Wah made Mandarin films that were lavishly supported by money, stars, and directors from Shanghai. Among them were the excellent actresses Li Li-Wah and Lin Dai, and directors Li Han Hsiang (Li Hanxiang; 1926–1996) and Chiang Nam. All of these talents stayed in Hong Kong after the collapse of the company in the early 1950s and became the core group of filmmakers for the later, dominant Shaw Brothers company. Yung Wah's first film, *Guo hun* (*Soul of China*, 1948), was a box-office success. It was directed by Shanghai's Po Man Chun, who later would become one of the most important directors in Chinese film history. In contrast, Cantonese films were made with much less money by smaller companies, and the quality was usually poor.

During this time, a number of left-wing filmmakers came from China to Hong Kong to make films, includ-

WONG KAR WEI
b. Shanghai, China, 1958

Among the Hong Kong New Wave filmmakers, Wong Kar Wei is perhaps the most celebrated by critics. He is a winner of many awards, including a best director award at the Cannes Film Festival for *Chun guang zha xie* (*Happy Together*, 1997). Wong's films are usually narrated by characters' internal monologues, which creates a seemingly haphazard, fragmented postmodern style. They reflect modern living, urban alienation, lost opportunities, transient love relationships, and acute melancholy.

At the age of five Wong and his parents moved to Hong Kong from Shanghai. Since he could not speak the local (Cantonese) dialect, his first few years were spent going to movie houses, which later became his obsession. Upon graduating from Hong Kong Polytechnic, where he studied graphic design, he joined TVB, the most popular local TV production and broadcasting channel at the time, becoming a scriptwriter for TV drama series. The popular TV soap opera series "Don't Look Now" ("Ge Dou Bou," 1982), of which Wong was one of the major writers, attracted quite a bit of attention at the time because of its unusual story. Wong started his film career as a scriptwriter, making his directorial debut with *Wang jiao ka men* (*As Tears Go By*, 1988), which was shown during the critics week at the Cannes Film Festival in 1989. It was unique in its untraditional narrative structure and visual style.

His second film, *A Fei zheng zhuan* (*Days of Being Wild*, 1991), marked the beginning of his long-term partnership with cinematographer Christopher Doyle. It is set in the 1960s, a period that continued to attract Wong in his later films. Although *Days* won five Hong Kong Film Awards, including for best film and best director, its unfamiliar style and story (or, for some, lack thereof) led to its box-office failure. Four years later, Wong tried his hand at a period martial-arts genre film, *Dong xie xi du* (*Ashes of Time*, 1994). During a break from the frustrating production of this film Wong made a quickie, *Chong qing sen lin* (*Chungking Express*, 1994), essentially a prank of

two consecutive love stories in which no one seems to get it right. The film, which was endorsed by Quentin Tarantino but was reluctantly distributed by Miramax, soon became a cult film in the United States and Europe, and it raised Wong to auteur status.

Wong works with the same crew and cast (mostly superstars such as Tony Leung, Maggie Cheung, and Andy Lau) for most of his films. His work is marked by mesmerizing visuals that draw attention to themselves and refuse any deep historical reading. His images almost always reside in the contemporary time period even when they are images of the past. Using the strengths of Doyle, whose hand-held camera effectively translates light and shadow into mood and style, Wong's films are about lost moments that sink deeply into one's emotional memory, a (lost) past filtered through the desire of the present. Thus, *Days of Being Wild* is a memory of the 1960s constructed through the experience of modern living in the 1980s, *Chungking Express* is about the 1970s imagined from the metropolitan view of the 1990s, and *Happy Together* is an old-style romance conducted through the culture of twenty-first-century global migration.

RECOMMENDED VIEWING

Wang jiao ka men (*As Tears Go By*, 1988), *A Fei zheng zhuan* (*Days of Being Wild*, 1991), *Chong qing sen lin* (*Chungking Express*, 1994), *Chun guang zha xie* (*Happy Together*, 1997), *Hua yang nain hua* (*In the Mood for Love*, 2000), *2046* (2004)

FURTHER READING

Abbas, Ackbar, et al. *Wong Kar-Wai*. Paris: Dis Voir, 1997.

Payne, Robert. "Ways of Seeing Wild." *Jump Cut*, no. 44 (Fall 2001).

Teo, Stephen. *Wong Kar Wai: Auteur of Time*. London: British Film Institute. 2005.

Jenny Kwok Wah Lau

ing the well-known directors Tsoi Chu San, Hsieh Tung San, Pai Yen, and Oa Lin. Among some of their works were *Wild Fire and Spring Wind* (*Ye Huo Chun Feng*, 1948) and *Floating Family* (*Fu Zhai*, 1949).

After 1949, the shipping tycoon Loke Wan To began to pay attention to Hong Kong. Loke's Cathay Organization (headquartered in Singapore), which already controlled the entertainment industries in

Malaya, Singapore, Sarawak, and Brunei, began to buy up theaters in Hong Kong. Later, Loke set up Cathay Film Production in Hong Kong, and was able to dominate the domestic industry between 1957 and 1961. After Loke was killed in a plane crash in 1964, his rival Run Run Shaw soon gained the upper hand.

THE SHAW (MANDARIN) EMPIRE

In 1934, largely due to the unstable political situation in China, the second son of the Shaw family, Runde, had been sent to Hong Kong to set up a branch of Tin Yat, Shaw's film company in Shanghai. From the late 1930s until the Japanese occupation of Hong Kong, a good number of Cantonese films were produced in Tin Yat's Nan Yang Studios, including such classics as *The Tearful Bauhinia* (*Qi Jing Hua*, 1934), *I Have Wronged My Loved One* (*Ge Ge Wo Fu Ni*, 1935), and *Poison Rose* (*Du Mei Gui*, 1935).

In 1954 Cathay (Wah Mou) and Yung Wah, the two biggest companies at the time, were busy building big studios, and preparing even bigger budgets and more lavish (Mandarin) films. (Yung Wah soon went bankrupt, having lost the China market due to ideological clashes with the Communists.) Meanwhile, Runde's company, now called Shaw and Sons, had only two Mandarin directors, Li Han Hsiang (1926–1996) and Ho Meng Wah. Furthermore, he sold the Nam Yang studios and did not do much with his new project, the Clear Water Bay studio construction. Seeing no promising plan from Runde, in 1958 younger brother Run Run Shaw (b. 1907) left Singapore for Hong Kong and became the managing director of the company. He immediately planned for twenty Mandarin films and twelve Cantonese films, and began the construction of the Clear Water Bay studio complex, clearly preparing for serious competition with Lee and Loke. But the swift action of Run Run was not appreciated by Runde, who took over the company again while Run Run started another company, Shaw Brothers (SB). The inaugural film of Shaw Brothers was *Jiang shan mei ren* (*Kingdom and the Beauty*, 1959), directed by Li Han Hsiang and starring Lin Dai (1934–1964), who later became the biggest female star in Hong Kong cinema history. This mega-budget (Mandarin) film was a colossal success, establishing the dominance of Shaw Brothers. By 1961 Run Run Shaw had completed Clear Water Bay (which was run by a staff of close to two thousand), bought up theater chains, built up his star system, established an acting school, and set up technician-training classes. In doing so, he became the first and only person to ever have full control of every aspect of filmmaking in Hong Kong.

During this time and until the 1970s Mandarin films were mainstream. The large population of Chinese refugees who fled the Communist rule in the mainland constituted the majority of the audience. They favored nostalgic stories of their homeland and did not mind—indeed, some preferred—the use of Mandarin in their films. Furthermore, many of the filmmakers themselves were from the mainland, so Mandarin was also their preferred dialect. With strong financial backing from both previously wealthy Shanghai families and the nationalist government in Taiwan, as well as strong talent, Mandarin cinema prevailed even in this Cantonese-speaking community. Some of the classics of the time included *Bu liao qing* (*Love Without End*, 1960), *Liang shan ba yu zhu ying tai* (*Love Eterne*, 1963), *Dubei dao* (*One-Armed Swordsman*, 1967), *Long men ke zhen* (*Dragon Gate Inn*, 1966), and *Hsia nu* (*A Touch of Zen*, 1969). The key directors of the time included Li Han Hsiang, Chang Cheh (1923–2002), and King Hu (1931–1997), with Li being the most versatile in making films in several genres.

Even though Run Run Shaw was a hardworking and insightful leader, his accomplishments owed much to his right-hand man of twenty years, Raymond Chow (b. 1929), who left Shaw in 1970 to form his own company, Golden Harvest. Chow, who was well educated, had a different management style: instead of tight personal control in the manner of Run Run Shaw, Chow adopted a more hands-off approach. Chow's new company became competitive with Shaw when it formed a distribution partnership with Cathay and later contracted Bruce Lee (1940–1973) as its major actor. Its first success was Bruce Lee's *Tang shan da xiong* (*The Big Boss*, 1971). With the sudden death of Lee in 1973, Golden Harvest declined until the arrival of a rising star, the social satirist Michael Hui (b. 1942). In 1974 Hui's wildly popular comedy *Gui ma shuang xing* (*Games Gamblers Play*) proved to be a forerunner of the Hong Kong New Wave. From then on, Golden Harvest was Hong Kong's dominant production house, forming partnerships with US studios and international distributors, including Columbia Tristar and New Line Cinema. Golden Harvest was also successful in its international productions, with box-office hits such as *Enter the Dragon* (1973), *Cannonball Run* (1980), and the *Teenage Mutant Ninja Turtles* television series (1990–1993). It also produced almost all of the films featuring Jackie Chan (b. 1954) during the 1980s and 1990s.

HONG KONG NEW WAVE: 1979–1984

The Hong Kong New Wave burst onto the international film scene in 1979. During the late 1970s the film industry in Hong Kong suffered a serious decline in audience numbers, largely due to the popularization of television. Most studios were desperate to find solutions

Maggie Cheung and Tony Leung in Wong Kar Wei's international hit, Hua yang nain hua *(*In the Mood for Love, *2000).*
EVERETT COLLECTION. REPRODUCED BY PERMISSION.

and therefore were willing to innovate. In addition, a new class of nouveau riche formed during the economic take-off of the 1970s were interested in investing in the film industry. Thus, between 1979 and 1980 about thirty to forty new directors made their debuts. All of their films used Cantonese, and many were technically superior to earlier films made by the established studios, and more contemporary in style and theme. Important examples include *Feng jie* (*The Secret*, Ann Hui, 1979), *Liang zhu* (*Butterfly Murders*, Tsui Hark, 1979), *Ming jian* (*The Sword*, Patrick Tam, 1980), and *Fu zi qing* (*Father and Son*, Allen Fong, 1981). Although these films are generically and stylistically heterogenous, one common characteristic of these New Wave films was that they shared a "Hong Kong–centered" sensibility, unlike the films of their refugee predecessors, who had taken Hong Kong as a temporary residence before their final return to China. This generation that grew up in Hong Kong fundamentally changed the look and the nature of its cinema.

Many New Wave productions were creative explorations of social issues and cinematic traditions, but not all were commercially successful. For instance, after several commercial failures Tsui Hark (b. 1950), one of the leading directors of the New Wave, found himself working for a newly formed commercial studio, Cinema City Company, which specialized in combining action with comedy. Its style combined glamorous visuals, fast editing, and modern urban settings. By using big budgets, big casts, and extensive packaging and publicity, it quickly rose to the top in the 1980s. Among its most successful hits were *Zuijia Paidang* (*Aces Go Places*, 1982) and its four sequels. New successful production houses such as Cinema City began to replace the old studio system of Shaw Brothers, which officially closed down production in 1986. Since then the financing of films usually have come from one of the three companies—Golden Harvest, Golden Princess (financier of Cinema City), and D&B Company—which control both production and distribution.

Because industry financing came from a small number of companies, it is not surprising that the New Wave's freedom from strict commercial demands would be short-lived. By the mid-1980s a "Second Wave" was taking shape, working more within the confines of the commercial system while continuing the technological advances and the social sensibility of the First Wave. The Second Wave was composed of some of the New Wave directors such as Tsui Hark, Yim Ho (b. 1952), and Ann Hui (b. 1947), as well as younger directors such as Mabel Cheung (b. 1950), Clara Law (b. 1957), and Wong Kar Wei (b. 1958). Second Wave films dealt with contemporary issues, particularly those related to the 1997 reunification of Hong Kong with China. Like their First Wave predecessors, many of the Second Wave's works were shown on the international festival circuit, at the Cannes Film Festival, New York Film Festival, and Tokyo International Film Festival. Some major works of this period include *Center Stage* (*Ruan Linguy*, 1992), by Stanley Kwan (b. 1957) and *Floating Life* (*Fu Sheung*, 1996), by Clara Law. Many of its popular productions, such as the *Aces Goes Places* series, beat Hollywood films at the domestic box office. During this time, Hong Kong films dominated the markets of Korea, Japan, Taiwan, and mainland China.

THE CHALLENGE OF GLOBALIZATION

Prompted by anxiety over the imminent 1997 reunification with China, a significant number of Hong Kong's film producers, directors, scriptwriters, actors, and actresses emigrated throughout the 1980s and early 1990s. Some were drained by Hollywood, but many simply gave up their careers. In addition to talent loss, Hong Kong suffered a serious economic downturn during the 1990s, and even the bigger studios such as Golden Harvest were affected. As well, pirated tapes, VCDs, and DVDs flooded the local market. By 1999 audience attendance had hit bottom; the only films that attracted a wide market were Hollywood blockbusters such as *The Lion King* (1994) and *Titanic* (1998).

At the same time, the commercial potential of Hong Kong cinema drew international attention. The success of *Ying xiong ben se* (*A Better Tomorrow*, 1986) by John Woo (b. 1946) in the United States had a lasting impact, popularizing Chinese kung fu in American action movies. Since then, many Hong Kong films have been shown in mainstream (versus art) cinemas in the United States. Directors such as John Woo and Tsui Hark, and actors such as Jackie Chan, Chow Yun-fat (b. 1955), and Jet Li (b. 1963) frequently work in Hollywood on films for

global distribution. Chan's *Ngo si sui* (*Who Am I?*, 1998), for example, attempts to connect Hong Kong with the international community in its action-packed story involving a transnational mafia, the CIA, and locations in Africa and Amsterdam. Like many other films made during the 1990s, it also considers the question of identity, but seeks to answer it through a superficial connection with global communities. Since then, Chan has continued to build his world cinema either through local producers, with Hollywood financing (*Rush Hour*, 1998), or by coproduction (*Bor lei jun* [*Gorgeous*], 1999, and *Shanghai Noon*, 2000). Since the late 1990s and early 2000s, coproduction became increasingly necessary, for financing and to facilitate world distribution.

Amidst the gangster fantasies, ghost stories, and absurd comedies (especially those by the popular comedian Stephen Chow [b. 1962]) of the 1990s and 2000s, there were a number of important realist films made by a little-known loner, Fruit Chan (b. 1959), the first and arguably the only independent feature filmmaker of the period. *Xianggang zhizao* (*Made in Hong Kong*, 1997), *Qu nian yan hua te bie duo* (*The Longest Summer*, 1998), and *Liulian piao piao* (*Durian Durian*, 2000) have neither big action nor big stars, but their observations of the lives of ordinary Hong Kong citizens is poignant. The significance of these films for independent filmmaking, which was previously almost absent in Hong Kong, is still unknown. Major companies such as Golden Harvest and other production houses founded in the 1980s are still trying to find ways to adapt to the challenges of the twenty-first century.

SEE ALSO *China; Martial Arts Films; National Cinema*

FURTHER READING

Jarvie, Ian C. *Window on Hong Kong: A Sociology Study of the Hong Kong Film Industry and Its Audience*. Hong Kong: University of Hong Kong Press, 1977.

Teo, Stephen. *Hong Kong Cinema: The Extra Dimension*. London: British Film Institute, 1997.

Yu, Mo Wan. *Stories of the Beginning of Hong Kong Cinema*. Hong Kong: Wide Angle Publishing, 1985.

Jenny Kwok Wah Lau

HORROR FILMS

Horror films take as their focus that which frightens us: the mysterious and unknown, death and bodily violation, and loss of identity. They aim to elicit responses of fear or revulsion from their audience, whether through suggestion and the creation of mood or by graphic representation. Horror paradoxically provides pleasure, providing a controlled response of fear that is presumably cathartic. Stories of fear and the unknown are timeless, no doubt beginning around the prehistoric campfire. It is around such a fire on the beach at night that John Houseman dramatically recounts the scary legend of Antonio Bay to the engrossed children in the opening of John Carpenter's *The Fog* (1980). With roots in such precinematic forms as medieval woodcuts, Grand Guignol theater, and the gothic novel, the genre has been popular since the beginning of cinema, as evidenced by the fantastic films of Georges Méliès from the first years of the twentieth century. Many of Méliès's short trick films dealt with monsters (a dervish in *Le Monstre*, 1903), ghosts (*Le Revenant, 1903*), magic (*La statue animée*, 1903), and the devil (*Les trésors de Satan*, 1902)—subjects that were to become central to the genre as it developed over time.

Horror films address both universal fears and cultural ones, exploiting timeless themes of violence, death, sexuality, and our own beastly inner nature, as well as more topical fears such as atomic radiation in the 1950s and environmental contamination in the 1970s and 1980s. As Stephen King observes, horror "is extremely limber, extremely adaptable, extremely *useful*" (p. 81). Horror addresses that which is universally taboo or abject but also responds to historically specific concerns. Both kinds of fears are addressed by the main categories of horror, as Roy Huss and T. J. Ross usefully group them: gothic horror, monster terror (overlapping here with science fiction), and psychological thriller. Because horror provides us with manageable experiences of fear, it is one of the most sustained of film genres, as popular today as it has ever been.

EARLY HISTORY

Unlike such genres as the musical and the gangster film, which had to wait for the development of sound, horror movies were an important genre in the silent era. Mary Shelley's *Frankenstein* (1818) was filmed as early as 1910, and in France, Louis Feuillade's serial *Les Vampires* (1915–1916) made use of earlier narratives with female vampires. Audiences were familiar enough with horror conventions that by 1927 they were being parodied in *The Cat and the Canary*.

The first significant cycle of horror films appeared in German expressionist cinema, a movement that began with the influential *Das Cabinet des Dr. Caligari* (*The Cabinet of Dr. Caligari*, 1920), directed by Robert Wiene. Its plot involves an evil mesmerist who forces a somnambulist to commit murder. Designed by expressionist artists Hermann Warm, Walter Reiman, and Walter Röhrig, the film contains almost no right angles in its distorted buildings and streets; shadows were painted directly on the walls and floors rather than created by lighting, and the make-up and acting are deliberately stylized. The film's design visualizes the madness of the inmate in the insane asylum who narrates the story. *Caligari* was a significant international hit and inspired the many films to follow.

A specific period or movement of German silent cinema in the 1920s, German expressionism eschewed realism in favor of projecting onto the exterior world abstract representations of intense inner emotion, whether of characters in the narrative or of the artists themselves. Characteristic techniques of German expressionist cinema include an emphasis on extreme angles, chiaroscuro lighting, distorting lenses or sets, and stylized acting and makeup. The films were shot mostly in the studio, many at Universum Film Aktiengesellschaft (Ufa, the largest studio in the country), with an artificial look that deliberately sought to exclude the natural world. Thus German expressionism was a style ideally suited to the horror film, and many of the films dealt with the popular horror themes of psychological breakdown and madness and the supernatural, including *Der Golem, wie er in die Welt kam* (*The Golem: How He Came into the World*, 1920); *Der Müde Tod* (*The Weary Death*, also known as *Between Two Worlds*, 1921); *Nosferatu, eine Symphonie des Grauens* (*Nosferatu, a Symphony of Terror*, also known as *Nosferatu the Vampire*, 1922), the first adaptation of Bram Stoker's *Dracula* (1898); *Der Student von Prag* (*The Student of Prague*, 1926); and *Faust* (1926). Production of expressionist films in Germany peaked in the mid-1920s, and the movement dissipated in the early 1930s with the coming of sound and the emigration of many German directors, cinematographers, actors, and other film workers to the United States as the Nazis rose to power. In Hollywood they worked their way into the studio system, where they contributed significantly to the development and look of the horror film, particularly those produced at Universal, and later in the 1940s to the distinctive style of film noir.

In contrast to German cinema, the comedies and westerns already characteristic of Hollywood in the silent period expressed upbeat and open moods that were unsuitable to the dark and claustrophobic worlds of traditional horror. It was not until much later that Hollywood would turn for inspiration to the strong vein of horror that ran through American literature, from the demonization of native Americans and the wilderness in the fiction of Charles Brockden Brown, James Fenimore Cooper, Nathaniel Hawthorne, and others to the more straightforward horror tales of Edgar Allan Poe and H. P. Lovecraft. But while horror was not a Hollywood priority in this period, Lon Chaney (1883–1930), known as "The Man of a Thousand Faces" for his mastery of makeup, emerged as the first American star of the genre in such roles as Quasimodo in *The Hunchback of Notre Dame* (1923) and *The Phantom of the Opera* (1925), and in eight collaborations with the director Tod Browning. Unique among silent film stars, Chaney was known for portraying monstrous, physically deformed, and psychologically tortured characters.

HORROR IN THE STUDIO ERA

Dr. Jekyll and Mr. Hyde (1920), starring the highly regarded stage actor John Barrymore, helped legitimize the genre in Hollywood, but the genre was not clearly established until shortly after the arrival of sound when Universal Studios produced a cycle of horror films, notably Browning's *Dracula*, with Bela Lugosi, and James Whale's *Frankenstein*, with Boris Karloff, both released in 1931. Lugosi and Karloff became the great horror stars of the 1930s, attaining iconic status in American popular culture. For three decades the studio produced a series of loose sequels and spinoffs, including *The Bride of Frankenstein* (1935), *Frankenstein Meets the Wolf Man* (1943), and *House of Frankenstein* (1944), ending in the 1950s with parodies featuring Abbott and Costello, another important Universal asset. The Universal films were heavily influenced by the *mise-en-scène* of German expressionism: for example, *The Mummy* (1932), another Karloff vehicle, was directed by German cinematographer Karl Freund, who had photographed *Der Golem* and Fritz Lang's *Metropolis* (1926), among others, before emigrating to Hollywood in 1929. Universal was run by Carl Laemmle, himself born in Germany. The popular mythology of Frankenstein's creature, the vampire, the werewolf, and the mummy (the latter invented by the movies) were established and reworked in the studio's horror films.

Although other studios produced the occasional big-budget horror film, such as Paramount's remake of *Dr. Jekyll and Mr. Hyde* (1932) with Fredric March and RKO's *King Kong* (1933), Universal dominated the genre during this period. The major exception was MGM's *Freaks* (1932), directed by Browning. The story involves a traveling circus sideshow and the cruel woman trapeze artist who exploits them. Browning used a group of people with actual physical oddities, and the climax, in which they pursue the trapeze artist in the rain and mud, is particularly chilling. Uniting in camaraderie, the "freaks" are depicted as more humane than the physically normal characters, anticipating the reinterpretation of the monsters that would characterize horror films from the 1960s onward. Evidently this was a radical reversal that was ahead of its time: the film was severely cut for its American release and banned for thirty years in Great Britain.

The war years saw the unwelcome intrusion of real horror on a global scale, and Hollywood movies accentuated the positive to boost morale on the home front. From 1942 to 1946 at RKO, the producer Val Lewton (1904–1951), a former script editor for David O. Selznick,

LON CHANEY
b. Leonidas Chaney, Colorado Springs, Colorado, 1 April 1883, d. 26 August 1930

Known as "the man of a thousand faces," Lon Chaney was the first major star of the horror genre. As the child of deaf-mute parents, Chaney learned the expressive possibilities of pantomime, a skill he brought to the silent screen in a series of bizarre characters, often featuring some variation of grotesque distortion.

After his beginnings as a comedian and dancer in the theater, Chaney went to Hollywood in 1912. He appeared in a steady stream of films from 1914 on, playing villains in formula Westerns as well as a variety of other strange characters, from a French Canadian in *Nomads of the North* (1920) to Fagin in *Oliver Twist* (1922) to a one-eyed hoodlum in *The Road to Mandalay* (1926). Chaney was famous for his skill with makeup, and publicly emphasized the extremes that he would undergo to create his monstrous, distorted outsiders. In *The Penalty* (1920), he plays a criminal kingpin whose legs had been mistakenly amputated, requiring him to wear a painful leg harness so that he could walk on his knees as if they were stumps; in *The Unknown* (1927) he played Alonzo the Armless, a circus knife-thrower, with his arms strapped tightly to his body. As Quasimodo in *The Hunchback of Notre Dame* (1923), he wore a hunch in a harness that had a combined weight of seventy pounds.

Chaney made eight films with director Tod Browning, beginning with *The Wicked Darling* in 1919, and including *The Unholy Three* (1925), *The Unknown*, and *West of Zanzibar* (1928), their last film together. Chaney's skill at physical metamorphosis combined with Browning's gift for macabre horror stories to create a series of films about masochistic men ridden with castration anxiety. This preoccupation reached a peak in *The Unknown*, where the viewer finally discovers that Alonzo really does have arms, which he keeps secret, but then amputates them in a doomed attempt to win the sympathy of the woman he loves.

Chaney's last role was as Echo, a criminal ventriloquist in the remake of *The Unholy Three* in 1930, his only talking film. He used five different voices in the movie, showing that he could make the transition to talkies. But shortly after the film's release, Chaney died from a hemorrhage in his throat. After Chaney's death, his son Creighton changed his name to Lon Chaney Jr. and followed in his father's footsteps by starring in a series of horror films, the most notable of which was his tragic Larry Talbot in *The Wolf Man* (1941).

RECOMMENDED VIEWING

The Hunchback of Notre Dame (1923), *He Who Gets Slapped* (1924), *The Phantom of the Opera* (1925), *The Unholy Three* (1925), *The Unknown* (1927), *West of Zanzibar* (1928), *The Unholy Three* (1930)

FURTHER READING

Anderson, Robert Gordon. *Faces, Forms, Films: The Artistry of Lon Chaney*. South Brunswick, NJ: A. S. Barnes, 1971.

Beck, Calvin Thomas. *Heroes of the Horrors*. New York: Collier Books, 1975.

Blake, Michael F. *The Films of Lon Chaney*. Lanham, MD: Vestal Press, 1998.

———. *Lon Chaney: The Man Behind the Thousand Faces*. Vestal, NY: Vestal Press, 1993.

Barry Keith Grant

made a series of nine horror films with several directors, including *I Walked with a Zombie* (1943), directed by Jacques Tourneur, and *The Body Snatcher* (1945), directed by Robert Wise, that exploited ambience and suggestion through economical means. Tourneur's *Cat People* (1942), for example, concerns a young woman, Irena (Simone Simon), who believes the superstition of her Old World village upbringing that she will turn into a dangerous leopard when emotionally or sexually aroused; but there is no transformation scene such as those in horror movies about werewolves and adaptations of *Dr. Jekyll and Mr. Hyde*, in which such scenes are not only a convention but a visual centerpiece. In one scene the woman Irena sees as her rival, swimming alone in an indoor pool at night, hears faint footsteps and sees an indistinct shadow cross the wall, and when the cold and frightened woman goes to retrieve her robe, she finds it shredded, as if it had been ripped by the claws of an animal. Similarly, in *The Leopard Man* (1943), also directed by Tourneur, we hear the violent death of a

Lon Chaney in London After Midnight *(Tod Browning, 1927)*. EVERETT COLLECTION. REPRODUCED BY PERMISSION.

teenage girl attacked by the title creature, but all we see is her blood oozing under the locked door of her house.

In the 1950s horror overlapped significantly with science fiction. Cold War and atomic age anxieties produced numerous monster movies with creatures that had mutated or reawakened from eons of slumber because of nuclear radiation and testing. Monsters such as the giant dinosaur of *The Beast from 20,000 Fathoms* (1953), the giant ants of *Them!* (1954), and the creature in *Behemoth, the Sea Monster* (also known as *The Giant Behemoth*, 1959) all are the results of nuclear testing, as is the radioactive cloud that causes *The Incredible Shrinking Man* (1957) to shrink and *The Amazing Colossal Man* (1957) to grow. *The Thing from Another World* (1951) set the tone for the decade's monster movies. Based on a novella by the science fiction writer John W. Campbell, the film sacrifices almost all the scientific reasoning featured in the story to emphasize instead the inarticulate howlings of a vegetable-like creature, who somehow possesses technological knowledge way beyond that of earthlings and is bent on killing humans for their blood.

By the mid-1950s the youth audience had emerged as a significant consumer group, particularly for moviegoing, and many horror films, from *I Was a Teenage Frankenstein* (1957) and *I Was a Teenage Werewolf*

(1957) to *The Horror of Party Beach* (1964), were produced with the aim of appealing to adolescent viewers. American International Pictures (AIP), an American film distribution and production company founded in 1954 by James H. Nicholson and Samuel Z. Arkoff, specialized in B movies—teen pics, exploitation films, and horror films such as *The She-Creature* (1956), *Terror from the Year 5000* (1958), and *Attack of the Puppet People* (1958). A few of these were directed by Roger Corman (b. 1926), including the campy *A Bucket of Blood* (1959). One of the independent companies that showed the way in the 1950s toward the strategy of targeting market segments, AIP moved from distribution into production and eventually began making movies with higher production values, beginning in 1960 with Corman's *House of Usher*, a loose adaptation of a Poe short story, which starred Vincent Price and was shot in color and Cinemascope. Corman made several other films for the company based on Poe themes with Price, including *The Masque of the Red Death* (1964), which features cinematography by the British cult director Nicolas Roeg. Also in the 1950s and early 1960s, the exploitation master William Castle (1914–1977) moved from thrillers and westerns into horror with a series of gimmicky horror films including *The Tingler* (1959), *Thirteen Ghosts* (1960), and *Mr. Sardonicus* (1961).

In England, Hammer Film Productions Ltd. released several classic science fiction films along with their other dramas, including *The Quatermass Xperiment* (1955) and *X the Unknown* (1956), but launched in earnest into the production of horror with *The Curse of Frankenstein* (1957), directed by Terence Fisher (1904–1980), a studio stalwart. Hammer went on to produce a substantial series of horror films that revisited the monsters of old, including Frankenstein's creature, Dracula, and the Mummy, through the 1970s, as well as inventing new ones (*The Gorgon*, 1964). The Hammer films revitalized the genre by revisiting but also updating its traditional gothic iconography with a bold use of color and a decidedly modern dose of sexual content. Many of these films starred Peter Cushing and Christopher Lee, who were the most familiar and consistently productive horror stars of the period.

BODY HORROR

The British film *Peeping Tom* (1960) and *Psycho* (1960) radically reconfigured the genre by focusing on psychologically disturbed characters in mundane contexts rather than supernatural situations in gothic settings. *Psycho*, directed by Alfred Hitchcock and adapted from Robert Bloch's 1959 novel, which in turn was based in part on the real-life exploits of multiple murderer Ed Gein, has proven to be perhaps the most influential horror film ever

Michael Redgrave as the ventriloquist attacked by his dummy in the omnibus British horror film **Dead of Night** *(Alberto Cavalcanti, Basil Dearden, Robert Hamer, Charles Crichton, 1945).* EVERETT COLLECTION. REPRODUCED BY PERMISSION.

made. Set in contemporary motel rooms, hardware stores, and used car lots, Hitchcock's film imagined the site of horror in the quotidian world of the viewer, showing that horrifying violence was an integral part of middle-class America, repressed beneath its seemingly placid exterior. Roman Polanski's *Rosemary's Baby* (1968) and William Friedkin's *The Exorcist* (1973) continued in the same direction, depicting satanism in contemporary New York and Washington, respectively. Both films were big-budget commercial blockbusters, and they helped bring horror more squarely into the mainstream.

In 1968 came the phenomenal box-office success of George A. Romero's independent *Night of the Living Dead*, one of the first midnight movies (which theaters scheduled for special midnight showings after the mainstream films had finished). Made in black-and-white on a small budget, the film became a huge cult success. Its low-budget aesthetic, combined with a new graphic representation of bodily violation—we are shown cannibalistic zombies eating steaming entrails—and its uncompromising violation of numerous horror conventions resulted in the film's powerful effect on viewers. Following in the style of

graphic bodily violation introduced by Herschell Gordon Lewis in such films as *Blood Feast* (1963) and *Two Thousand Maniacs!* (1964), Romero's sequel, *Dawn of the Dead* (1978), took graphic violence to a new level, and instituted a cycle of so-called splatter films that focused on bodily violation. A few years before *Dawn*, Tobe Hooper's *The Texas Chainsaw Massacre* (1974) devoted most of its running time to the sadistic torture of its female protagonist. The Canadian filmmaker David Cronenberg made several horror films concerned with bodily invasion, including *Shivers* (also known as *They Came from Within*, 1975), with its repulsive sluglike parasites that enter the body through the range of human orifices; *The Brood* (1979), featuring scenes of monstrous parturition; *Scanners* (1981), in which heads explode in a spray of gristle and blood; and his version of *The Fly* (1986), in which a scientist's body slowly falls away as he metamorphoses into an insect. Splatter was taken to comic extremes in Peter Jackson's *Braindead* (also known as *Dead Alive*, 1992) and Sam Raimi's *The Evil Dead* (1981). Clive Barker's *Hellraiser* (1987) focused intently on the pain of the flesh with scenes of flaying, bondage, and torture.

Following Romero, several young directors established their reputations by working primarily in horror, most notably Brian de Palma (*Sisters*, 1973; *Carrie*, 1976; *Dressed to Kill*, 1980), Wes Craven (*The Last House on the Left*, 1972; *The Hills Have Eyes*, 1977; *A Nightmare on Elm Street*, 1984), Larry Cohen (*It's Alive*, 1974; *God Told Me To* [also known as *Demon*], 1976), and John Carpenter (*Halloween*, 1978; *The Fog*, 1980; *Christine*, 1983, based on Stephen King's novel). Many of these horror movies, like *Psycho* and *Night of the Living Dead*, subverted the genre's traditional distinctions between good and evil, normal and monstrous, critiquing the horrors of mainstream society rather than projecting the monstrous onto the exotic "other." Horror films were thus a significant part of the overall reexamination of genre movies that took place in American cinema in the 1970s.

However, the huge commercial success of Carpenter's *Halloween* spawned a cycle of slasher films that bespoke a much more conservative vision. Most featured elaborate serial killings strung together by weak plots. Slashers typically feature psychotic males, frequently masked like Jason Voorhees in *Friday the 13th* (1980) and its sequels, who set about systematically to kill an isolated group of people, usually teenagers. Often the killer is motivated by a past sexual trauma activated by the sexual promiscuity of the victims he stalks, and the killings often seem to be a punishment for being sexual active or precocious, as is the case in the famous opening tracking shot of *Halloween*. Commonly a handheld camera is used to signify the killer's point of view, yet to what

GEORGE A. ROMERO
b. New York, New York, 4 February 1940

A key figure in the new wave of horror films in the 1960s and 1970s, George A. Romero brought an entirely new sensibility to the genre, drastically reinterpreting some of its classic monsters and infusing it with a political consciousness and ironic self-awareness, as well as a level of explicit gore that had been largely lacking before. His first film was *Night of the Living Dead* (1968), which established a new zombie mythology that has spawned an entire subgenre.

Romero made industrial and commercial films in Pittsburgh before directing *Night of the Living Dead*, which became a cult favorite and one of the first midnight movies. Often serving also as cinematographer, editor, or screenwriter for his films, Romero is clearly an auteur with an original approach to the horror genre. Romero's vision comes through in the offbeat *Knightriders* (1981), a non-horror film that he wrote, edited, and directed. Its far-fetched story about an itinerant band of motorcyclists who operate a fair like a medieval guild is silly as drama, but makes perfect sense as an auteurist expression of the theme of group solidarity against the threat of cultural homogenization—a theme that also runs through his four zombie films.

Romero's earlier horror films, made on minimal budgets, deconstruct many of the conventions of classic horror and examine their ideological assumptions from a more critical and distanced perspective. *Martin* (1977), for example, is a vampire film without a true vampire. The young man of the title has been warped by Old World superstition, his grandfather raising him to believe that he has been cursed to be a vampire. Forcing transfusion on his victims to fulfill what he believes to be his vampiric fate, Martin has been made monstrous by irrational fear. *Hungry Wives* (*Season of the Witch*, 1972), similarly, shows that the very concept of the witch is grounded in patriarchal oppression of women.

Romero's later films, for which he tended to have bigger budgets, have also been less adventurous thematically. *Creepshow* (1982), written by Stephen King, and *Monkey Shines: An Experiment in Fear* (1988) are more conventional and lack the daring of Romero's zombie films, a territory that he has mined for almost forty years. A decade after *Night*, *Dawn of the Dead* (1978) was an apocalyptic masterpiece that raised the bar for splatter effects. Romero also combined comedy and horror in a striking blend that introduced a generation of subsequent horror directors, most notable among them Peter Jackson. *Land of the Dead* (2005) brought the political satire in these films about the American populace as soulless cannibals to the fore.

RECOMMENDED VIEWING

Night of the Living Dead (1968), *Hungry Wives* (*Season of the Witch*, 1972), *The Crazies* (1973), *Martin* (1977), *Dawn of the Dead* (1978), *Knightriders* (1981), *Day of the Dead* (1985), *Night of the Living Dead* (screenplay, 1990), *Land of the Dead* (2005)

FURTHER READING

Gagne, Paul R. *The Zombies that Ate Pittsburgh: The Films of George A. Romero*. New York: Dodd, Mead, 1987.

Romero, George A., and Susanna Sparrow. *Dawn of the Dead*. New York: St. Martin's, 1978.

———, et al. *Martin*. New York: Stein and Day, 1977.

Waller, Gregory. *The Living and the Undead: From Stoker's Dracula to Romero's Dawn of the Dead*. Urbana: University of Illinois Press, 1986.

Williams, Tony. *The Cinema of George Romero: Knight of the Living Dead*. London and New York: Wallflower Press, 2003.

Barry Keith Grant

extent this use of the subjective camera encourages a seemingly amoral identification on the part of the viewer with the murderer rather than his victims has been a subject of much debate. It was slasher films that to a large extent spurred a censorship debate in Great Britain and prompted the passage of the Video Recordings Bill. By the mid-1980s the slasher film was in decline, but self-conscious postmodern slashers such as *Scream* (Craven, 1996) and its sequels, in which the characters are as familiar with the conventions of the genre as the audience, have proved popular.

Horror has been a Hollywood staple since the 1930s, but, in addition to Hammer horror in Great Britain, there are also other national cinemas with rich horror traditions. In Italy, for example, *giallo*, graphic thrillers and horror films, flourished in the 1950s and 1960s.

George Romero at the time of **Dawn of the Dead** ***(1978).*** ©
UNITED FILM/COURTESY EVERETT COLLECTION. REPRODUCED
BY PERMISSION.

Predating slasher films, the *giallo* ("yellow") takes its
name from the color of the covers of pulp detective
novels published in Italy in the 1940s and 1950s. The
genre includes both police films (*giallo-poliziesco*) and
horror films (*giallo-fantastico*), featuring an overtly
expressionist stylization. The Italian directors Mario
Bava (1914–1980), with films such as *La Maschera del
demonio* (*Black Sunday*, 1960) and *Terrore nello spazio*
(*Planet of the Vampires*, 1965) and Dario Argento, with
such films as *L'Ucella dalle piume di cristallo* (*The Bird
with the Crystal Plumage*, 1970), *Profondo rosso* (*Deep
Red*, 1975), and *Tenebre* (*Unsane*, 1982) have become
cult figures.

In Japanese cinema, both horror films, like *Kurutta
Ippeji* (*A Page of Madness*, 1926), *Onibaba* (*The Demon*,
1964), and ghost films, like *Kwaidan* (*Ghost Stories*, 1964),
and *Ugetsu monogatari* (*Tales of Ugetsu*, 1953), were prominent. A new wave of Japanese horror films includes Hideo
Nakata's *Ringu* (*Ring*, 1998) and *Honogurai mizu no soko
kara* (*Dark Water*, 2002), both of which were remade,
with mixed success, in Hollywood.

CRITICAL DEBATES

For the film scholar Siegfried Kracauer, German expressionist cinema was both a harbinger and a cause of the
rise of fascism in Germany. The films' avoidance of the
real world, both visually in the use of stylized studio sets,
and narratively in the frequent appearance of monstrous
figures like Caligari and Nosferatu who command the
will of others, was symptomatic of the German people's
turning away from political responsibility and an explanation of their embrace of Hitler. There has been more
critical commentary on horror than any other film genre,
with the possible exception of the western; and although
today Kracauer's interpretations seem rather reductive,
they share with all subsequent critical analyses of the
genre the fundamental assumption that horror films, like
most genre movies, reflect the values and ideology of the
culture that produced them. Don Siegel's *Invasion of the
Body Snatchers* (1956), for example, about an invasion of
alien seed-pods that replace people with emotional replicas, is typically discussed in relation to American contemporary culture in the 1950s. Unlike earlier horror
films, *Invasion of the Body Snatchers* imagines infection
on an apocalyptic rather than personal scale, as in the
vampire myth, a clear reflection of Cold War fears of
nuclear destruction. But even as Americans felt threatened
by possible nuclear war and Communist infiltration, the
film also expresses a fear of creeping conformism at home.
Invasion makes the commonplace seem creepy, and in the
climax a mob of plain-looking townsfolk pursue Miles
and Becky out of town in a horrific evocation of the kind
of witch-hunting mentality witnessed in the United
States just a few years before the film's release. The film's
ambiguous ending (how could the FBI or anyone possibly contain the pod invasion, which by now has spread
much wider than the town of Santa Mira?) initiated a
trend that would continue in the revisionist horror films
of the 1960s and 1970s, and is indicative of larger
cultural tensions.

In a number of essays published in the late 1970s,
Robin Wood set the critical agenda for much of the
theory and analysis of horror. He offered a structural
model of horror, informed by Freudian theory, built
around a fundamental binary opposition of normal and
monstrous. Wood was responding to the progressive
wave of horror films by such directors as Romero,
Hooper, Craven, and Cohen. For Wood, "the true subject of the horror genre is the struggle for recognition of
all that our civilization *re* presses or *op* presses" (as quoted
in Britton et al., p. 10). He argued that the manner in
which any given horror narrative resolves this conflict
reveals its ideological orientation, and further, that most
movies will be conservative, repressing desire within the
self and disavowing it by projecting it outward as a
monstrous Other. The monster thus is usually understood as the "return of the repressed." This interpretation
applies particularly well to horror stories featuring the
premise of the beast within, like *The Wolf Man* (1941) or

***Just plain folks turn into zombies in George Romero's apocalyptic* Night of the Living Dead *(1968).* EVERETT COLLECTION. REPRODUCED BY PERMISSION.**

the various versions of *Dr. Jekyll and Mr. Hyde.* According to such a reading, the monster (representing a challenge to the dominant values of heterosexual monogamy), must be defeated by the male hero in order for him to take his proper place in patriarchy by successfully pairing with the inevitable female love interest, typically represented as the attractive daughter of the scientist or lovely lab assistant. Horror films such as *Frankenstein, Dracula,* and *Creature from the Black Lagoon* (1954) follow this narrative pattern.

Wood provides a list of specific Others in the horror genre: women, the proletariat, other cultures, ethnic groups, alternative ideologies or political systems, children, and deviations from sexual norms. All of these have been taken up by critics of the genre over the last two decades, although the last category—deviations from sexual norms—has been the one most frequently explored. However, some feminist critics have shown how horror monsters may be read as projections of masculine desire

and anxiety over sexual difference. Following from Wood's perspective, many horror films are about anxieties over masculine performance, with women as the victims of male aggression. However, Carol Clover has argued that horror is potentially empowering for women. Her emphasis on the one female, or "final girl," who often survives the killer's rampage in slasher movies, transforming from terrified screamer to active heroine, killing the killer, has influenced numerous readings of horror films from *Halloween* to *Alien* (1979) and its sequels. Finally, some readings, such as that offered by Harry Benshoff, find in the genre a consistent monstrous representation of queerness and challenges to normative masculinity.

Perhaps because horror tends to raise questions about gender and its "natural" boundaries, women have been relatively important in the genre, first as consumers of gothic novels and later as makers of horror films. Significantly, although women have found it difficult throughout film history to become directors, they are noticeably prominent in horror film production, as evidenced by Stephanie Rothman's *The Velvet Vampire* (1971) and *Terminal Island* (1973); Amy Jones's take on the slasher film, *The Slumber Party Massacre* (written by Rita Mae Brown, 1982); Katt Shea Rubin's two *Stripped to Kill* movies (1987, 1989) and *Poison Ivy* (1992); Mary Lambert's two *Pet Sematary* movies (1989, 1992); Kristine Peterson's *Body Chemistry* (1990); Fran Rubel Kuzui's *Buffy the Vampire Slayer* (1992); Kathryn Bigelow's *Near Dark* (1987); and Mary Harron's *American Psycho* (2000).

Critics have also examined representations of class and race in horror films. Mark Jancovich has persuasively linked the development of horror to the rise of the bourgeoisie and the dialectic of class. A classic horror film like *King Kong* (1933) evokes the fear of racial miscegenation in the figure of the dark ape, the beast in love with the (white) beauty, while fundamental to Dracula's appeal is his suave aristocratic bearing. Some late-twentieth-century horror films, such as *The People Under the Stairs* (1991), *Candyman* (1992), and *Tales from the Hood* (1995), covering territory explored only occasionally in earlier films such as *I Walked with a Zombie* (1943) and *Blacula* (1972), have addressed issues of racial difference in horror. Questions of race in horror emerged with the casting of a black actor as the hero in *Night of the Living Dead*: killed by redneck vigilantes at the end of the film, his body is unceremoniously tossed onto a bonfire in freeze frames that evoke the contemporary racial violence then erupting across America.

Some critics have extended the psychoanalytic approach to horror beyond the texts themselves to account for the spectatorial pleasures of watching horror films, an act that on the surface might seem inexplicable given that the experience arouses fear rather than pleasure. Critics have also argued that horror films are particularly enjoyed by adolescents because in their awkwardness they can easily empathize with the monsters, who are social outcasts, and because they express in metaphoric form the physical changes—the hairiness of the werewolf, the sexual drive of the vampire—that occur with the onset of puberty. Certainly horror films do function as adolescent rites of passage and socialization, but such theories do not account for the appeal of all horror films. Whatever the particular fears exploited by horror films, they provide viewers with vicarious but controlled thrills, like the fright one gets from an amusement park ride. It is no accident that so many theme park rides are horror oriented. As Bruce Kawin says in

his essay "Children of the Light," "A good horror film takes you down into the depths and shows you something about the landscape." Like Charon, who in Greek mythology ferries the souls of the dead, the horror film takes you on "a visit to the land of the dead, with the difference that this Charon will eventually take you home, or at least drop you off at the borders of the underworld" (p. 325).

SEE ALSO *Cold War; Cult Films; Exploitation Films; Expressionism; Fantasy Films; Feminism; Genre; Germany; Great Britain; Makeup; Teen Films; Violence*

FURTHER READING

Benshoff, Harry. *Monsters in the Closet: Homosexuality and the Horror Film*. Manchester, UK, and New York: Manchester University Press, 1997.

Britton, Andrew, Richard Lippe, Tony Williams, and Robin Wood. *American Nightmare: Essays on the Horror Film*. Toronto: Festival of Festivals, 1979.

Clover, Carol J. *Men, Women, and Chain Saws: Gender in the Modern Horror Film*. Princeton, NJ: Princeton University Press, 1992.

Creed, Barbara. *The Monstrous-Feminine: Film, Feminism, Psychoanalysis*. London and New York: Routledge, 1993.

Grant, Barry Keith, ed. *The Dread of Difference: Gender and the Horror Film*. Austin: University of Texas Press, 1996.

Grant, Barry Keith, and Christopher Sharrett, eds. *Planks of Reason: Essays on the Horror Film*, revised ed. Lanham, MD: Scarecrow Press, 2004.

Huss, Roy, and T. J. Ross, eds. *Focus on the Horror Film*. Englewood Cliffs, NJ: Prentice-Hall, 1972.

Jancovich, Mark. *Horror*. London: Batsford, 1992.

Kawin, Bruce. "Children of the Light." In *Film Genre Reader III*, edited by Barry Keith Grant, 324–345. Austin: University of Texas Press, 2003.

King, Stephen. *Danse Macabre*. New York: Everett House, 1981.

Kracauer, Siegfried. *From Caligari to Hitler: A Psychological History of the German Film*. Princeton, NJ: Princeton University Press, 1947.

McCarty, John. *Splatter Movies: Breaking the Last Taboo of the Screen*. New York: St. Martin's, 1984.

Schneider, Steven Jay, and Tony Williams. *Horror International*. Detroit, MI: Wayne State University Press, 2005.

Waller, Gregory A. *American Horrors: Essays on the Modern American Horror Film*. Urbana and Chicago: University of Illinois Press, 1987.

Wells, Paul. *The Horror Genre: From Beelzebub to Blair Witch*. London: Wallflower Press, 2000.

Barry Keith Grant

HUNGARY

For a small country with a post–World War I population of around ten million, whose history is filled with wars, revolutions, political repression, and foreign domination, Hungary's achievement in filmmaking is extraordinarily impressive. This history itself has provided a major source of thematic material, as has Hungary's rich literary tradition. Almost from its beginnings, film has been taken seriously as an art in the country. Even in the decades from 1950 to 1990, when the film industry was completely under government control, this control was exerted more lightly and with a greater respect for artistic achievement than in any other country of the Soviet bloc. It might even be said that the market-driven policies that have dominated since 1990 have had a detrimental effect on the overall quality of the country's cinema.

In addition to fiction feature film, Hungary has a strong tradition of documentary filmmaking and also of animation, the latter primarily through the work of the Pannónia Studio and directors such as Sándor Reisenbüchler (1935–2004) and Marcell Jankovics (b. 1941). And, though Hungarian cinema is freely acknowledged to be a director's medium, much of the credit for the achievement of its best films must go to such fine actors as Zoltán Latinovits (1931–1976), Miklós Gábor (1919–1998), Mari Törőkcsik (b. 1935), and György Cserhalmi (b. 1948), and to such superb cinematographers as György Illés (b. 1914), János Kende (b. 1941), Elemér Ragályi (b. 1939), and Lajos Koltai (b. 1946).

THE SILENT ERA

An estimated 460 films were made in Hungary during the silent period, almost all considered lost. Recent rediscoveries and restorations, however, have brought a few representative works to light.

Hungarian film exhibition began with screenings of films by Louis Lumière and Georges Méliès in Budapest cafés. The Urania Scientific Society is credited with the first Hungarian-made film, *A Táncz* (*The Dance*), in 1901. The National Association of Hungarian Cinematographers had been formed by 1909, and some 270 permanent cinemas had been established throughout the country by 1912. The first Hungarian feature film, *Ma és holnap* (*Today and Tomorrow*), directed by Mihály Kertész (1886–1962) (who later gained Hollywood fame as Michael Curtiz), appeared in 1912. Production then expanded rapidly, as did serious intellectual interest in film as expressed in specialist film journals. There was also room for escapist melodramas such as those produced by the prolific Alfréd Deésy (1877–1961), which had little specifically Hungarian about them. His surviving films, *Aphrodite* and *The Young Wife* (both 1918), revel in an "international" style of languid eroticism among wealthy characters, but with a moralistic and even sentimentally religious conclusion. The surviving work of Jenö Janovics (1872–1945) also falls into the category of sexual/moralistic melodrama, with *Din Grozaviile lumii* (The Specter of the World, 1920) issuing dire warnings of the dangers of syphilis.

Sándor (later Alexander) Korda (1893–1956) was a major figure of the time, as critic, director, and producer, though only one of his twenty-four films from this period, *Az Aranyember* (*Man of Gold*, 1918), is known to survive in full. Based, like many other Hungarian films, on a book by the popular nineteenth-century novelist Mór Jókai, it achieves an epic scale through exciting camerawork, vigorous characterization, and atmospheric lighting, prefiguring Korda's films of the 1930s in Britain. Counterbalancing "entertainment" films were those that focused on social and political injustices. *A Megfagyott gyermek* (*The Frozen Child*, Béla Balogh, 1921) provides an unusual perspective on poverty-stricken, working-class life in Budapest through the sufferings endured by two abandoned children.

The year 1919 saw a major turning-point in the history of Hungarian film, with the nationalization of the film industry under the short-lived Communist government of the Republic of Councils. Thirty-one films were shot or completed in this four-month period, until the overthrow of this government and the White Terror that followed forced many of the most talented members of the film industry to flee abroad. Those who left, then or during a later period, included the directors Korda, Kertész, and Pál Fejös (later Paul Fejos; 1884–1960), the scriptwriter Lajos Bíró (1880–1948), and (using the names by which they became commonly known), the actors Peter Lorre (1904–1964), Bela Lugosi (1882–1956), Paul Lukas (1895–1971), and Vilma Banky (1898–1991). Another prominent exile at this time was the film theoretician and scriptwriter Béla Balázs (1884–1949), author of the classic *Theory of Film* (English translation, 1953). After 1991, under the repressive right-wing government, film production declined steadily until, by the end of the 1920s, it was almost nonexistent.

STAGNATION AND CENSORSHIP: 1930–1963

A partial recovery of the industry—in quantity though not in quality–took place throughout the 1930s, assisted by a government levy on the foreign films that now swamped the market. The emphasis was largely on glossy romantic comedies, erotic melodramas, and musicals, the most popular of which was *Meseauto* (*The Dream Car*), directed by Béla Gaál (1893–1944) in 1934. The film with the most lasting appeal was the comedy *Hyppolit, a lakáj* (*Hyppolit, the Lackey*, István Székely, 1931). In contrast to this trend are two fine films by Paul Fejos, who returned to Hungary after some years in Hollywood to make *Tavaszi zápor* (*Spring Shower*, also known as *Marie, a Hungarian Legend*) and *Ítél a Balaton* (*The Judgment of Lake Balaton*, both in 1932. Official disapproval of the films' explicit social criticism, however, drove Fejos to leave Hungary once more, this time for good. *Hortobágy* (*Life on the Hortobagy*, Georg Höllering, 1936), a mixture of fiction and documentary set on the Hungarian *pustza*, or great plain, is another major work of the period.

The outbreak of World War II, in which Hungary found itself allied with Germany until it made a disastrous attempt to change sides near the end, saw an unexpected increase in film production, combined with a ban on importing American films in 1942. Production increased to a total of some forty or fifty films annually by 1944, almost all of them thrillers, comedies, or sentimental dramas, often with a strongly nationalistic streak and subjected to strict, politically based censorship. Almost the only film of lasting quality to emerge from this period was *Emberek a havason* (People on the Alps, 1942), directed by István Szöts (1912–1998), with its magnificently photographed mountain scenery and a strong social theme based on the contrast between city and country values. The film was attacked by both left and right, and Szöts was unable to make another film until 1947, when his almost equally impressive *Ének a búzamezökröl* (*Song of the Cornfield*) was promptly banned by the Communist-controlled government. Szöts finally left Hungary for Austria in 1957.

In the immediate postwar period, a devastated and barely functioning film industry made only fourteen films between 1945 and 1948. Though private financing of film continued for a time, the feuding members of the postwar coalition government struggled for control of the industry, culminating in a second nationalization by the successful Communists in 1948. The only worthwhile film of this period (apart from the banned *Song of the Cornfield*) was another lasting classic, *Valahol Európában* (*It Happened in Europe*, Géza von Radványi, 1947), with a script by Béla Balázs, who had returned from exile to help reestablish the country's film industry. It is a moving and unsentimental account of how the moral influence of an elderly musician helps a group of boys, orphaned and made homeless by the war, go on to lead civilized and socially productive lives.

Nationalization brought, as for other film industries in the Soviet bloc, a demand for "socialist realism" in the style and content of the cinema: straightforward, uncomplicated narrative, with a clear distinction between "good" (Communist) and "evil" (reactionary and capitalist) characters, and subject matter inspired by "the new spirit of a new era," charting the inevitable victory of Communism over its internal and external enemies. For a few years overt propaganda of this type predominated, occasionally modified and given greater sophistication by the more talented directors. The first film of the new system, *Talpalatnyi föld* (*Treasured Earth*, Frigyes Bán, 1948), is actually one of the better examples, telling its standard story of class conflict in a restrained and powerful manner.

Film directors wishing to work in the industry now had first to graduate from the Academy for Theater and Film Art, established in 1948, and, until 1959, they could offer their services to only one studio, Hunnia (later called Mafilm). The training received in the

Academy was excellent and wide-ranging, and in 1963 four new studios were created, usually headed by a respected figure in the industry rather than a bureaucrat, offering more freedom of subject matter to directors. Nevertheless, throughout this whole period, until the collapse of the Communist system in the early 1990s, every script had to pass over a series of bureaucratic hurdles before acceptance, with the same process being repeated for the finished film.

Hungary's Stalinist years of the early 1950s, marked by political repression, show trials, and imprisonment or execution of "enemies of the people," produced few films of note before 1954–1955, when Felix Máriássy's (1919–1975) *Budapesti tavasz* (Springtime in Budapest, 1955), set during the Soviet "liberation" of the city in 1945; Zoltán Fábri's (1917–1994) *Hannibál tanár úr* (*Professor Hannibal*, 1956); and Zoltán Várkonyi (1912–1979) and Károly Makk's (b. 1925) *Simon Menyhért születése* (The Birth of Menyhért Simon, 1954) infused some freshness, intellectual integrity, and genuine humanity into some of the mandated themes. Várkonyi's *Keserû igazság* (*The Bitter Truth*, 1956), however, which dealt openly with official corruption and negligence, was immediately banned and not released until 1986. The 1956 revolution (officially termed the "Counterrevolution" for the next three decades) against Communist control, and savagely repressed by Soviet tanks, brought a relatively brief clampdown, during which filmmakers concentrated on safe literary adaptations or offered psychological studies on private, nonpolitical themes. Even in this atmosphere, however, *Bakaruhában* (*A Sunday Romance*, also known as *In Soldier's Uniform*, Imre Fehér, 1957), and Fábri's *Körhinta* (*Merry-Go-Round*, 1955), brought a genuine breath of fresh air into the inevitable theme of class conflict.

In 1959 the Béla Balázs Studio was created to allow young filmmakers to produce experimental short films with considerable freedom of style and content. This, together with the impact of neorealism, the French New Wave, and the films of Ingmar Bergman, Federico Fellini, and Michelangelo Antonioni, led to the appearance of a new generation of directors, ready to take advantage of the relaxation in cultural policy at the time, and with a sophisticated understanding of what was happening in the world of cinema outside their own country. It was these filmmakers who inaugurated the great period of Hungarian cinema.

INTERNATIONAL SUCCESS: 1963–1989

By 1963 an overall pattern had emerged under which directors were allowed considerable latitude in subject matter and style, provided they did not directly challenge the government's authority and steered clear of controversial treatment of the 1956 revolution. Although the finest films of this period were rarely box office successes within Hungary, the government promoted and supported them for the cultural prestige they earned abroad, especially at major film festivals, and also out of a genuine respect for their artistry. They were adequately funded, and comparatively few films were banned; the most notorious example, the satire on 1950s bureaucracy, *A Tanú* (*The Witness*, Péter Bácsó, 1969), was finally released ten years later.

The films of this period fall mainly into two groups: the so-called parables, which took some historical incident from Hungary's past and interpreted it so that it had clear affinities with the present day, and films set in the present, which offered cautious criticism of the gulf between official rhetoric and the often grim realities of Hungarian life. One way or another, almost all the major films had a political as well as a private dimension, as in the early, semiautobiographical films of István Szabó (b. 1938), such as *Álmodozások kora* (*The Age of Daydreaming*, also known as *Age of Illusions*, 1964) and *Apa* (*Father*, 1966), which the director himself described as "the autobiography of a generation."

The strongest international impact in the 1960s was made by Miklós Jancsó (b. 1921). Films like *Szegénylegények* (*The Round-Up*, 1965), *Csillagosok, katonák* (*The Red and the White*, 1967), and *Még kér a nép* (*Red Psalm*, 1971), while often dealing with obscure incidents from Hungarian history, fascinated audiences elsewhere with their direct presentation of political oppression and brutality, the stark black-and-white photography of the earlier films, and the sinuously balletic, lengthy camera movements of the later ones. István Gaál's (b. 1933) powerful *Magasiskola* (*The Falcons*, 1970) provided a more abstract, less historically specific allegory of the totalitarian mentality. The theme of collectivization—the forced transfer of individual peasant ownership of the land to collective farming—was handled with intelligence and objectivity by Sándor Sára (b. 1933) in *Feldobott kö* (*The Upthrown Stone*, 1969) and, in visually spectacular but more ambiguous fashion, by Ferenc Kósa (b. 1937) in *Tízezer nap* (*Ten Thousand Days*, 1967). Károly Makk's *Szerelem* (*Love*, 1971) dealt movingly with the return home of a political prisoner in the early 1950s, while *Hideg napok* (*Cold Days*, András Kovács, 1966) tackled head-on one of the most shameful Hungarian actions in World War II, the massacre of hundreds of Serb civilians by Hungarian soldiers in what is now Novi Sad.

A reorganization of production and loosened bureaucratic control in the 1970s brought new themes and approaches. The so-called Budapest School combined the revived interest in documentary with a fictional

MIKLÓS JANCSÓ
b. Vács, Hungary, 27 September 1921

Jancsó grew up in the Hungarian countryside and developed there an interest in folk art that exercised a strong influence on his films. He studied law and ethnography at the University of Kolozsvar and, after a period as a Soviet prisoner-of-war toward the end of World War II, he graduated from the Academy of Theater and Film Art in 1950.

His earliest films were documentaries that conformed to the official requirements of the period, and this was also largely true of his first two features. With *Szegénylegények* (*The Round-Up*) in 1965, however, he abandoned almost completely the dogmas of socialist realism both in theme and style. Set in the aftermath of the Hungarian War of Independence in 1848, it adopts the "Aesopian" tactics favored by directors of the time of using a period setting to comment obliquely on current political and social trends. This was followed by *Csillagosok, katonák* (*The Red and the White*, 1967), set in postrevolutionary Russia in 1918, as small groups of pro- and anti-Soviet soldiers skirmished continuously. *Csend és kiáltás* (*Silence and Cry*, 1967) is set in Hungary in 1919 following the suppression of the short-lived Communist government that seized power after the end of World War I. These films attracted international attention, despite their obscure (to non-Hungarians) subject matter, for their astonishing visual power and the universality of their themes. The cruelties, humiliations, and atrocities inflicted on their victims by those in power are presented in a cold, almost impersonal manner, controlled by rigorously formal framing and complex camerawork.

Over much of the next decade Jancsó divided his time between Hungary and Italy, producing a series of films that continued his investigations into the nature of repressive political power and how to resist it, while moving toward a style that is often purely symbolic and ritualistic, relying heavily on intricately choreographed and lengthy sequence shots. The finest film of this period is acknowledged to be *Még kér a nép* (*Red Psalm*, 1971), set during a period of peasant agitation for land reform at the end of the nineteenth century.

With *Szörnyek évadja* (*Season of Monsters*, 1987) Jancsó moved to a contemporary setting and to visual motifs based on ubiquitous television screens that record the action and also present different perspectives on it. The themes of such films as *Jézus Krisztus horoszkópja* (*Jesus Christ's Horoscope*, 1988) and *Kék Duna keringö* (*Blue Danube Waltz*, 1992) challenge the assumption that freedom from Soviet control in the "New Hungary" will automatically end corruption and the abuse of political power. After returning to documentaries for most of the 1990s, Jancsó resumed feature filmmaking in 1998 with a series of satirical and anarchic comedies. These have proved the most popular of his films to date within Hungary, and the director has been adopted as a guide and inspiration by a new generation of filmmakers.

RECOMMENDED VIEWING

Így jöttem (*My Way Home*, 1965), *Szegénylegények* (*The Round-Up*, 1965), *Csillagosok, katonák* (*The Red and the White*, 1967), *Csend és kiáltás* (*Silence and Cry*, 1967), *Fényes szelek* (*The Confrontation*, 1969), *Még kér a nép* (*Red Psalm*, 1971), *Szerelmem, Elektra* (*Electra, My Love*, 1974), *Zsarnok szíve, avagy Boccaccio Magyarországon* (*The Tyrant's Heart*, also known as *Il Cuore del tirrano*, 1981), *Jézus Krisztus horoszkópja* (*Jesus Christ's Horoscope*, 1988), *Kék Duna keringö* (*Blue Danube Waltz*, 1992), *Utolsó vacsora az Arabs Szürkénél* (*Last Supper at the Arabian Grey Horse*, 2001)

FURTHER READING

Bachman, Gideon. "Jancsó Plain." *Sight and Sound* 43 (Autumn 1974): 217–221.

Horton, Andrew James. "The Aura of History." *Kinoeye* 3, no. 3 (2003).

Houston, Penelope. "The Horizontal Man." *Sight and Sound* 38 (Summer 1969): 116–120.

Petrie, Graham. "Miklós Jancsó: Decline and Fall?" In *Politics, Art and Commitment in the East European Cinema*, edited by David W. Paul, 189–210. London: Macmillan, 1983.

———. *Red Psalm*. Trowbridge, Wiltshire, UK: Flicks Books (Cinetek series), 1998.

Graham Petrie

Miklós Jancsó. EVERETT COLLECTION. REPRODUCED BY PERMISSION.

approach to produce a series of "pseudodocumentaries" in which an actual incident was recreated using nonactors whose own lives resembled those of the original people involved. *Filmregény* (Film novel, István Dárday, 1977) is perhaps the best-known example of this style, which was also adopted in the early films of Béla Tarr (b. 1955), such as *Családi tüzfészek* (*Family Nest*, 1979). Other trends of the period involved a closer examination of the 1950s and 1956 in particular, with Pál Gábor's (1932–1987) *Angi Vera* (1978), *Szerencsés Dániel* (*Daniel Takes a Train*, Pál Sándor, 1983), Péter Gothár's (b. 1947) *Megáll az idö* (*Time Stands Still*, 1982), and the first of Márta Mészáros's (b. 1931) four "Diary" films, *Napló gyermekeimnek* (*Diary for My Children*, 1984) enjoying considerable international success. Meanwhile, *Szindbád* (*Sindbad*, Zoltán Huszárik, 1971), *Meztelen vagy* (*The Legend about the Death and Resurrection of Two Young Men*, Imre Gyöngyössy, 1971), and *Kutya éji dala* (The Dog's Night Song, Gábor Body, 1983), though not ignoring social issues, presented them in dreamlike, almost surrealistic fashion. And controversial topics such as lesbianism and incest were broached in Makk's *Egymásra nézve* (*Another Way*, 1982) and *Visszaesök* (*Forbidden Relations*, Zsolt Kézdi-Kovács, 1983), respectively.

Increasing financial stringency throughout the 1980s led several directors to make co-productions with other European countries. With the exception of István Szabó's Central European trilogy, beginning with the Oscar®-winning *Mephisto* (1981), few of these films were successful either financially or artistically.

POST-COMMUNIST BLUES: 1989 TO THE PRESENT

The end of Communist rule from 1989 onward also meant the end of government subsidy and control of the film industry. Directors could no longer rely on adequate financial support, entailing no pressure to be commercially successful as long as their work had artistic merit. Moreover, their "oppositional" subject matter, whether direct or oblique, no longer had much relevance in a newly democratic system. The move toward privatization of the film industry was confusing and erratic, complicated by a flood of Hollywood movies that dominated the newly constructed multiplexes, as well as by the challenge of video and television. Co-productions in one form or another became almost mandatory, with a consequent dilution of one of the main strengths of the country's cinema, its strongly nationalistic character.

The immediate result was a drastic drop in the number of feature films produced annually, rarely numbering more than fifteen to twenty, though there was a corresponding increase in documentaries and short films, which could be shot cheaply on 16mm or video. Many of the older generation of directors proved unable or unwilling to adapt to these new circumstances and fell silent. Younger directors tried to compete with Hollywood by choosing overtly commercial subjects filled with crime, violence, explicit sex, and car chases but lacked the technical resources and expertise to carry these through successfully. Yet a tradition of quality filmmaking has continued, helped to some extent by a recent levy on television profits aimed at supporting the film industry, and by the creation in 1991 of the Motion Picture Foundation of Hungary, which provides competitive and partial subsidies to projects considered to have artistic merit.

Some degree of international success in this period was achieved by such films as *Az én XX. századom* (*My Twentieth Century*, Ildikó Enyedi, 1989), *Gyerekgyilkosságok* (*Child Murders*, Ildikó Szabó, 1993), *Woyzeck* (János Szász, 1994), *Szenvedély* (*Passion*, György Fehér, 1998), *Bolse Vita* (Ibolya Fekete, 1996), and *Csinibaba* (*Dollybirds*, Péter Timár, 1997), but the overall bleak and pessimistic tone of many of these films gives them little popular appeal. István Szabó's Canadian co-production *Sunshine* (*A Napfény íze*, 1999), an English-language film, won and was nominated for several European and American

Miklós Jancsó's **The Red and the White** *(1967).* EVERETT COLLECTION. REPRODUCED BY PERMISSION.

film awards, and Miklós Jancsó attained unprecedented popularity at the age of eighty with a series of anarchic comedies. The most influential of contemporary directors, however, is Béla Tarr, whose films *Sátántangó* (*Satan's Tango*, 1994) and *Werckmeister harmóniák* (*Werckmeister Harmonies*, co-directed by Ágnes Hranitzky, 2000) have attained cult status abroad. Their often inordinate length, however (*Sátántangó* is almost seven hours long), their bleak and melancholy atmosphere, and the slow pace filled with lengthy camera movements have generally restricted their appeal to film festivals and showings at cinematheques and film museums. They prove, however, that the tradition of challenging and subversive Hungarian cinema is not yet dead.

SEE ALSO *National Cinema*

FURTHER READING

Burns, Bryan. *World Cinema: Hungary*. Trowbridge, UK: Flicks Books, and Cranbury, NJ: Associated University Press, 1996.

Cunningham, John. *Hungarian Cinema: From Coffee House to Multiplex*. London: Wallflower Press, 2004.

Liehm, Mira, and Antonin J. Liehm. *The Most Important Art: Eastern European Film after 1945*. Berkeley: University of California Press, 1977.

Nemeskürty, István. *Word and Image: History of the Hungarian Cinema*. 2nd ed. Budapest: Corvina Books, 1974.

Paul, David W., ed. *Politics, Art and Commitment in the East European Cinema*. London: Macmillan, 1983.

Petrie, Graham. *History Must Answer to Man: The Contemporary Hungarian Cinema*. Budapest: Corvina Books, 1978.

Portuges, Catherine. *Screen Memories: The Hungarian Cinema of Márta Mészáros*. Bloomington: Indiana University Press, 1993.

Stoil, Michael Jon. *Cinema Beyond the Danube: The Camera and Politics*. Metuchen, NJ: Scarecrow Press, 1974.

Graham Petrie

IDEOLOGY

The concept of ideology is often associated with the work of Friedrich Engels (1820–1895) and Karl Marx (1818–1883). In general, Marxists approach cultural forms as emerging from specific historical situations that serve particular socioeconomic interests and that carry out important social functions. For Marx and Engels, the cultural ideas of an epoch serve the interests of the ruling class by providing ideologies that legitimate class domination. "Ideology" is a critical term used in Marxist analysis that describes how the dominant ideas of a ruling class promote the interests of that class and help mask oppression and injustices. Marx and Engels argued that during the feudal period, piety, honor, valor, and military chivalry were the ruling ideas of the reigning aristocratic classes. During the capitalist era, values of individualism, profit, competition, and the market became the dominant ideology of the new bourgeois class, which was then consolidating its class power. Because ideologies appear natural and common-sensical, they often are invisible and elude criticism.

Marx and Engels began their critique of ideology by attempting to show how ruling ideas reproduce dominant societal interests and relations and serve to naturalize, idealize, and legitimate the existing society, its institutions, and its values. In a competitive and atomistic capitalist society, it appears natural to assert that human beings are primarily self-interested and competitive, just as in a communist society; it seems natural to assert that people are cooperative by nature. In fact, human beings and societies are extremely complex and contradictory. Ideology smoothes over contradictions, conflicts, and negative features, idealizing human or social traits like individuality and competition, which are then elevated into governing concepts and values.

MARXIST APPROACHES TO CULTURE AND IDEOLOGY

Many later Western Marxists developed these ideas, although they have tended to ascribe more autonomy and importance to culture than classical Marxism did. Within the Marxian tradition, a more positive concept of ideology, developed by Vladimir Lenin (1870–1924), sees socialist ideology as a positive force for developing revolutionary consciousness and promoting socialist development (Lenin, 1987). For the Italian Marxist theorist Antonio Gramsci (1891–1937), the ruling intellectual and cultural forces of an era constitute a form of *hegemony*, or domination by ideas and cultural forms that induce consent to the rule of the leading groups in a society. Gramsci argued that the unity of prevailing groups is usually created through the state—for instance, the American revolution or the unification of Italy in the nineteenth century. The institutions of "civil society" also play a role in establishing hegemony. Civil society, according to Gramsci, includes the church, school, media, and other forms of popular culture. Civil society mediates between the private sphere of personal economic interests and the family and the public authority of the state, serving as the locus of what Jurgen Habermas (b. 1929) described as "the public sphere."

Gramsci defined ideology as the ruling ideas that constitute the "social cement" unifying and holding together the established social order. While Marxist cultural critics like Gyögy Lukács (1885–1971) tended to see ideology as a manipulative force that helps ensure the rule of the dominant class, Ernst Bloch (1885–1977) instead stressed the utopian dimensions of Western culture and the ways in which cultural texts encode yearnings for a better world and a transformed society. Bloch's hermeneutic approach to Western culture in books like *The Principle of Hope* (1986) sought out visions of a better life in cultural artifacts ranging from the texts of Homer and the Bible to modern advertising and department store displays. Bloch's utopian impulse challenged film and cultural studies to articulate how culture provides alternatives to the existing world and how images, ideas, and narratives can promote individual emancipation and social transformation.

Bloch developed a type of cultural theory and ideology critique that is quite different from Marxist models that presents ideology critique as a tool for demolishing bourgeois culture and ideology—in effect, conflating bourgeois culture and ideology. This model—found in critiques by Lenin and most Marxist-Leninists—interprets dominant ideology primarily as a process created through mystification, error, and domination. This is contrasted to scientific or Marxist critical theory, in which ideology critique demonstrates the errors, mystifications, and ruling class interest within ideological artifacts, which are then smashed and discarded by the heavy hammer of the ideology critic.

Bloch, however, was more sophisticated than those who simply denounced all ideology as false consciousness or stressed the positive features of socialist ideology. Rather, Bloch sees emancipatory-utopian elements in all living ideologies, and deceptive and illusory qualities as well. For Bloch, ideology is "Janus-faced," or two-sided: it contains errors, mystifications, and techniques of manipulation and domination, but it also contains a utopian residue or surplus that can be used to critique society and to advance progressive politics. Bloch also perceived ideology at work in many phenomena usually neglected by Marxist and other ideology critiques: daydreams, popular literature, architecture, department store displays, sports, clothing, and other artifacts of everyday life. He believed that ideology critique should examine everyday life, as well as political texts and positions and the manifestly political ideologies of films, television, and other forms of mass-mediated culture.

Drawing on Bloch, Herbert Marcuse (1898–1979), and other neo-Marxist theorists, Fredric Jameson (b. 1934) has suggested that mass cultural texts often have utopian moments. He has proposed that radical cultural criticism should analyze both the social hopes and fantasies in film as well as the ideological ways in which fantasies are presented, conflicts are resolved, and potentially disruptive hopes and anxieties are managed (Jameson, 1979, 1981). In his reading of *Jaws* (1975), for instance, Jameson notes that the shark stands in for a variety of fears—uncontrolled organic nature threatening the artificial society; big business corrupting and endangering community; disruptive

sexuality threatening the disintegration of the family and traditional values—that the film tries to contain through the reassuring defeat of evil by representatives of the current class structure. Yet *Jaws* also contains utopian images of family, male bonding, and adventure, as well as socially critical visions of capitalism articulating fears that unrestrained big business would inexorably destroy the environment and community.

THE FRANKFURT SCHOOL

The term "Frankfurt School" refers to the work of members of the *Institut für Sozialforschung* (Institute for Social Research), which was established in Frankfurt, Germany, in 1923 as the first Marxist-oriented research center affiliated with a major German university (Kellner, 1989). The Frankfurt School coined the term "culture industry" in the 1930s to signify the industrialization of mass-produced culture and the commercial imperatives that constructs it (Adorno and Horkheimer, 1972). Its critical theorists analyzed mass-mediated cultural artifacts as products of industrial production, demonstrating that commodities of the culture industry exhibit the same features as other mass-produced objects: commodification, standardization, and massification. The culture industry has the specific function, however, of providing ideological legitimation of existing capitalist societies and of integrating individuals into its way of life.

The critiques of the culture industry developed in T. W. Adorno (1903–1969) and Max Horkheimer's (1895–1973) famous *Dialectic of Enlightenment* (1972) contain many, albeit unsystematic, references to Hollywood film. Film in the culture industries has been organized like industrial production and uses standardized formulas and conventional production techniques to mass-produce films for purely commercial, rather than cultural, purposes. Films reproduce reality as it is and thus encourages individuals to adjust and conform to the new conditions of industrial and mass society:

> They hammer into every brain the old lesson that continuous friction, the breaking down of all individual resistance, is the condition of life in this society. Donald Duck in the cartoons and the unfortunate in real life get their thrashing so that the audience can learn to take their own punishment. (Adorno and Horkheimer, 1972, p. 138)

The positions of Adorno, Horkheimer, and other members of the inner circle of the Institute for Social Research were contested by Walter Benjamin (1892–1940), an idiosyncratic theorist loosely affiliated with the Institute. Benjamin, writing in Paris during the 1930s, discerned progressive aspects in new technologies of cultural production such as photography, film, and radio. In "The Work of Art in the Age of Mechanical

Reproduction" (1934), Benjamin noted how new mass media were supplanting older forms of culture; mass reproduction of photography, film, recordings, and publications was replacing older emphasis on originality and "aura" in works of art. Benjamin believed that freed from the mystification of high culture, mass culture could create more critical individuals capable of judging and analyzing their culture, just as sports fans can dissect and evaluate athletic activities. In addition, Benjamin asserted that processing the rush of images of cinema helps viewers create subjectivities better able to parry the flux and turbulence of experience in industrialized, urbanized societies.

For Benjamin, the proliferation of mass art, especially through film, would bring images of the contemporary world to the masses and would help raise political consciousness by encouraging scrutiny of the world. Benjamin claimed that the mode of viewing film breaks with the reverential mode of aesthetic perception and awe encouraged by the bourgeois cultural elite, who promoted the religion of art. Montage and "shock effects" in film, mass spectatorship, discussion of issues that film viewing encourages, and other factors in the cinematic experience produce, in Benjamin's view, new social and political experiences of art that erode the private, solitary, and contemplative aesthetic experiences encouraged by high culture and its priests. Against the contemplation of high art, the "shock effects" of film produce a mode of "distraction" that Benjamin believed makes possible a "heightened presence of mind" and cultivation of "expert" audiences able to examine and criticize film and society (pp. 237–241).

Benjamin wished to promote a radical cultural and media politics able to create alternative oppositional cultures. Yet he recognized that media such as film could have conservative effects. While he believed that the loss of "aura," of magical force in mass-produced works is progressive and opens out cultural artifacts to increased critical and political discussion, Benjamin recognized that film could also create a new kind of ideological magic through the cult of celebrity and techniques like the close-up, which used film technologies to fetishize certain stars or images. Benjamin was thus one of the first radical cultural critics to look carefully at the form and technology of media culture while appraising its complex nature and effects.

POST-STRUCTURALISM AND THE POLITICS OF REPRESENTATION

Reacting against existential and Hegelian Marxism and the ultra-left political groups influenced by it, Louis Althusser (1918–1990) and a school of structural Marxists developed more "scientific forms" of Marxism and ideology

while maintaining their commitment to revolutionary politics. A member of the French Communist Party, Althusser argued in *For Marx* (1970) that Marxism provided scientific perspectives on capitalism that made possible a revolutionary transition to socialism. In *Reading Capital* (1997), he maintained that Marx's scientific critique of capitalist political economy provided the foundations for a theory of society. Althusser's "structuralist Marxism" analyzed relations between the structures of the economy, state, ideology, and social institutions and their grounding in capitalist relations of production—"in the last instance" the determining force of all social life.

Althusser helped shift the discussion of "ideology" to focus on the everyday practices and rituals organized by social institutions that he termed "ideological state apparatuses" (schools, religion, the family, the media, and others). Their material practices, he argued, are parts of a closed system in which individuals are constantly "interpellated" into a social order, becoming unconsciously constituted as subjects by dominant social institutions and discourses. His most widely read essay, "Ideology and Ideological State Apparatuses," outlines his basic assumption that experience, consciousness, and subjectivity are themselves effects of an imaginary relationship between an individual and his/her real conditions of existence—a relationship that is constructed by the ideological state apparatuses, which reify social hierarchies and induces people to consent to systems of oppression.

Structuralists, like members of the Frankfurt School, were soon criticized for being too deterministic, for having an impoverished concept of subjectivity, and for missing the complexities and vicissitudes of history. A post-structuralist turn therefore found theorists like Roland Barthes (1915–1980) and the *Tel Quel* group in France turning toward history, politics, and active and creative human subjects, as well as developing a more complex model of textuality. The post-structuralist turn moved away from the more ahistorical, scientific, and objectivist modes of thought in structuralism. The post-structuralist moment was a particularly fertile one, with important theorists like Barthes, François Lyotard, and Michel Foucault writing groundbreaking works on culture and ideology, and younger theorists like Jacques Derrida, Jean Baudrillard, and Paul Virilio entering into their productive periods.

In *Mythologies* (1972, 1957), Roland Barthes critically dissected a wide range of contemporary forms of culture, demonstrating his unique method of ideological interpretation and critique. According to Barthes, the mythology dissected in his essay "Operation Margarine," for example, embodies the fundamental rhetorical and ideological operations of French bourgeois culture. Margarine, in Barthes's account, is a highly artificial substance transfigured by advertising into a natural, beneficial, and acceptable substitution for butter. Analyzing ads that admit margarine's deficiencies and then trumpet its benefits, Barthes claims that such advertising techniques provide an "inoculation" against criticism of its imperfections. A similar operation, he claims, is typical in discourses on topics like the military, church, and capitalism, in which their limitations are mentioned in order to highlight their necessity and importance for the social order.

Likewise, mythologies obscure history, transforming contingent factors into natural essences, as if it were natural that an African soldier salute the French flag, in Barthes's famous example of a photograph that erases all of the evils of French colonization in an idealized image. Constructing an argument that anticipates postmodern emphasis on difference and otherness, Barthes points out how myths erase what is different and dissimilar, assimilating otherness to nature, as when the image of the French soldier folds the African into the French empire, or margarine ads assimilate an artificial substance into the order of culinary appropriateness. Barthes's method of analyzing rhetorical strategies of media culture and taking apart the mythologies that colonize social life help to produce a critical consciousness in his reader.

Sophisticated new theoretical approaches to the production of the works of film and its production of ideology began emerging in the 1960s, including those analyses published in *Cahiers du cinema* and the extremely influential British journal *Screen*, which translated many key *Cahiers* texts and other works of French film theory, including those of Roland Barthes and Christian Metz. These generated much more sophisticated formal approaches to film (Metz, 1974; Heath, 1981). The *Cahiers* group moved from seeing film as the product of creative *auteurs*, or authors (their *politique du auteurs* of the 1950s), to focusing on the ideological and political content of film and how film transcoded dominant ideologies. At the same time, French film theory and *Screen* focused on the specific cinematic mechanisms that helped produce meaning. These theorists and others analyzed how ideology permeated cinematic form and content, images and narrative, symbols and spectacle (Nichols, 1981; Kellner and Ryan, 1988).

Post-structuralism stressed the text's openness and heterogeneity, its embedded in history and desire, its political and ideological dimensions, and its excess of meaning. The conjunction of post-structuralism in the academic world and new social movements stressing the importance of race, gender, sexuality, and other markers of group identity led to expansion of the concept of ideology to many new dimensions and thematics. British cultural studies, for instance, adopted a feminist perspective, paid greater attention to race, ethnicity, and nationality, and sexuality in response to social struggles and movements (Kellner, 1995).

Earlier Marxist concepts of ideology presupposed a homogenous ruling class that unambiguously and without contradiction articulates its class interests through a monolithic ideology. Since its class interests were thought to be predominantly economic, ideology in this model referred primarily to ideas that legitimated the class rule of capitalists. Ideology was thus viewed as that set of ideas that promoted the capitalist class's economic interests. During the 1960s and 1970s, however, this model has been contested by theorists who have argued that an orthodox Marxist concept of ideology is reductionist because it equates ideology solely with those ideas that serve class or economic interests, leaving out such variable and significant factors as sex and race. Reducing ideology to class interests makes it appear that the only significant domination in society is one of class or economic domination, whereas many theorists argue that sex and race oppression are fundamentally important and indeed intertwined in fundamental ways with class and economic domination.

READING RAMBO IDEOLOGICALLY

Thus many critics have proposed that ideology be extended to cover theories, ideas, texts, narratives, and images that legitimate domination of women and people of color by white men and that thus serve the interests of ruling powers. Such ideology critique criticizes sexist and racist ideology as well as bourgeois-capitalist class ideology. To carry out an ideology critique of *Rambo: First Blood Part II* (1985), for instance, it wouldn't be enough simply to attack its militarist or imperialist ideology and the ways that the militarism and imperialism of the film serve capitalist interests by legitimating intervention in Southeast Asia (Kellner, 1995). To carry out a full ideology critique, one would also have to examine the film's sexism and racism, showing how representations of women, gender, the Vietnamese, the Russians, and so on are a fundamental part of the ideological text of *Rambo*.

In regard to gender, for instance, one might note that Rambo instantiates a masculinist image of gender that defines masculinity in terms of the male warrior with the features of great strength, effective use of force, and military heroism as the highest expression of life. Symptomatically, the woman characters in the film are either whores, or, in the case of a Vietnamese contra, a handmaiden to Rambo's exploits who functions primarily as a seductive force, seducing Vietnamese guards (a figure also central to the image of woman in *The Green Berets*, 1968), or a destructive one, when she becomes a woman warrior, a female version of Rambo. Significantly, the only moment of eroticism in *Rambo*

Sylvester Stallone as John Rambo in **First Blood** *(Ted Kotcheff, 1982).* © ORION/COURTESY EVERETT COLLECTION.
REPRODUCED BY PERMISSION.

(brief and chaste) comes when Rambo and his woman agent kiss after great warrior feats. Seconds after the kiss, the woman herself is shot and killed—the moral being that the male warrior must go it alone and must thus renounce women and sexuality. This theme obviously fits into the militarist and masculinist theme of the film as well as the representation of ascetic male heroes who must rise above sexual temptation in order to become maximally effective saviors or warriors.

The representations and thematics of race also contribute fundamentally to the militarist theme. The Vietnamese and Russians are presented as alien Others, as embodiments of Evil, in a typically Hollywood manichean scenario that presents the Other, the Enemy, "Them," as evil and "Us," the good guys, as virtuous, heroic, good, and innocent. *Rambo* appropriates stereotypes of the evil Japanese and Germans from World War II movies in its representations of the Vietnamese and the Russians, thus continuing the manichean Hollywood tradition of substituting past icons of evil for contemporary villains. The Vietnamese are portrayed as duplicitous

bandits, ineffectual dupes of the evil Soviets, and cannon fodder for Rambo's exploits, while the Soviets are presented as sadistic torturers and inhuman, mechanistic bureaucrats.

The stereotypes of race and gender in *Rambo* are so exaggerated, so crude, that they point to the artificial and socially constructed nature of all ideals of masculinity, femininity, race, and ethnicity. Thus, expanding the concept of ideology to include race and sex helps provide a multidimensional ideology critique, which expands radical cultural criticism while enriching the project of ideology critique.

Ideologies should be analyzed within the context of social struggle and political debate rather than simply as purveyors of false consciousness whose falsity is exposed and denounced by ideology critique. A diagnostic ideology critique looks behind the façade of ideology to see the social and historical forces and struggles that require it and to examine the cinematic apparatus and strategies that make ideologies attractive. Such a model of ideology criticism is not solely denunciatory; it also looks for socially critical and oppositional moments within all ideological texts, including conservative ones. As feminists and others have argued, one should learn to read texts "against the grain," yielding progressive insights even from reactionary texts.

SEE ALSO *Marxism; Propaganda*

FURTHER READING

Adorno, T. W., and Max Horkheimer. *Dialectic of Enlightenment*. New York: Seabury, 1972.

Althusser, Louis. *Lenin and Philosophy, and Other Essays*. London: New Left Books, 1971.

Barthes, Roland. *Mythologies*, edited and translated by Annette Levers. New York: Hill and Wang, 1972.

Benjamin, Walter. "The Work of Art in the Age of Mechanical Reproduction." *Illuminations*. Edited by Hannah Arendt. New York: Harcourt, Brace & World, 1968, 217–251. The original essay was published in 1934.

Bloch, Ernst. *The Principle of Hope*. Cambridge, MA: MIT Press, 1986.

Gramsci, Antonio. *Selections from the Prison Notebooks*. London: Lawrence & Wishart, 1971.

Habermas, Jurgen. *The Structural Transformation of the Public Sphere: An Inquiry into a Category of Bourgeois Society*. Boston and London: Blackwell, 1992.

Heath, Stephen, *Questions of Cinema*. Bloomington: Indiana University Press, 1981.

Jameson, Fredric. "Reification and Utopia in Mass Culture." *Social Text* 1 (Winter 1979): 130–148.

Lenin, Vladimir Ilyich. *The Essential Lenin*. New York: Dover, 1987.

Kellner, Douglas. *Critical Theory, Marxism, and Modernity*. Cambridge, UK, and Baltimore, MD: Polity Press and John Hopkins University Press, 1989.

———. *Media Culture: Cultural Studies, Identity, and Politics between the Modern and the Postmodern*. London and New York: Routledge, 1995.

———, and Michael Ryan. *Camera Politica: The Politics and Ideology of Contemporary Hollywood Film*. Bloomington: Indiana University Press, 1988.

Metz, Christian, *Language and Cinema*. The Hague: Mouton, 1974.

Nichols, Bill. *Ideology and the Image: Social Representations in the Cinema and Other Media*. Bloomington: Indiana University Press, 1981.

Douglas Kellner

Index

This is a cumulative index for volumes 1 through 4 of the encyclopedia. **Bold** *volume and page numbers (e.g.,* **3:437–439***) refer to the main entry of the subject. Page numbers in* italics *refer to illustrations, figures, and tables.*

References to contributors of articles in this encyclopedia may appear in the index but the best way to find a writer's article(s) is to look in the List of Articles; a person's name is listed under the article title.

A

À bout de souffle
- art cinema, 1:115, 118
- auteurism, 1:146
- camera movement, 1:191
- editing, 2:121
- film noir, 2:226
- film studies, 2:236
- music, 3:181
- New Wave launched by, 3:236, *236,* 237, 238
- performance elements, 1:21
- screenwriting, 4:36
- sexuality, 4:64

À nous la liberté, 3:193
Aag, 3:15
De Aanslag, 3:231
Aardman Animation Studio, 1:89
Aaron, Jane, 1:227
Aaron Loves Angela, 1:65
Aarseth, Espen, 4:309, 312
Aatamin puvussa ja vähän Eevankin, 2:249
Abaloos, Pierre, 1:195
Abashiri Bangaichi, 3:69
Abbott and Costello
- agents and agencies, 1:72
- choreography, 1:280
- genre, 2:301
- horror films, 2:392
- parodies, 3:263
- slapstick comedy, 4:90
- Universal, 4:296–298, *299*

Abbott and Costello Meet Frankenstein, 2:301
Abbott, Bud. *See* Abbott and Costello
Abbott, John, 1:106
ABC (American Broadcasting Company), 4:353–354
Abe, Kôbô, 1:40
Abe Lincoln in Illinois, 1:163; 2:375
Abel, 3:234
Abel, Richard, 1:27
Abel, Robert, 1:91, 92
Abi va Rabi, 3:29
Abismos de passion, 3:148
The Abominable Dr. Phibes, 3:4
Aboriginal Australians, 1:139
Abouna, 1:56
Abouseif, Salah, 1:98
About a Boy, 1:262
About Adam, 3:36
Above Suspicion, 2:182
Above the Law, 3:122
ABPC. *See* Associated British Picture Corporation (ABPC)
Abraham Lincoln, 1:163
Abrahams, Harold, 2:341
Abrahams, Jim, 2:74; 3:263
Abril despedaçado, 1:176
Abril, Victoria, 2:198
Abschied von gestern, 2:317; 3:244
Abu Seif, Salah, 2:130
Abu-Assad, Hany, 1:98, 102
Abuladze, Tengiz, 4:20
The Abyss
- Danish cinema, 2:43
- disaster film, 2:74
- fantasy, 2:191
- nature, 3:220
- social critique in, 4:30
- special effects, 4:123
- technology, 4:205

Academic journals, 3:77–78
Academy Award® Theater, 3:381
Academy Awards®, **1:1–9;** 3:307–308
- and the Academy of Motion Picture Arts and Sciences (AMPAS), 1:1–2
- categories, 1:3–5
- early history, 1:2
- educational activities, 1:5, 7
- nominations and voting, 1:3; 3:306–307
- notable winners of, 1:7–8, 63
- Oscar® statuette, 1:3–4
- protest and critque, 1:8–9
- Science and Technology Council, 1:7; 3:307
- special awards, 1:4–5

Academy of Motion Picture Arts and Science (AMPAS), 1:1–2
Accattone, 3:127

directors, 1:9
stereotypes of, 1:59; 3:205, 340
See also Race and ethnicity
African Hunt, 3:216
The African Lion, 3:218
African Mirror, 1:55
The African Queen, 1:6, 41, 234, 403;
 4:286
African Queen Productions, 1:53
Afrique 50, 1:56
Afrique, je te plumerai, 1:57
Afrique-sur-Seine, 1:49
After Hours, 1:407; 3:9
Afterimage, 3:77
Agadati, Baruch, 3:37
L'age d'or, 2:189; 3:124
The Age of Innocence, 1:42, 375,
 384, 407
Agee, James, 1:300; 2:1, 92; 4:89
Agents and agencies, **1:71–77**
 after MCA's divestiture, 1:75–76
 beginnings, 1:71–72
 postwar changes to, 1:73–74
 for radio and the movies, 1:72–73
 television, 1:74–75
Agnès, 2:195
Agoniya, 4:16
Agostino d'Ippona, 2:372
Las aguas bajan turbias, 1:111
Aguirre, der Zorn Gottes, 2:318,
 319, *321*
Ahen senso, 3:64
Ahlam el Madina, 1:99
Ahlberg, Mac, 3:285
Ahwesh, Peggy, 2:161
Ai, 2:157
Ai no Corrida, 3:69–70
Aïda, 3:48
Aileen: Life and Death of a Serial Killer,
 2:98
Aimée & Jaguar, 2:363
AIP. *See* American International
 Pictures (AIP)
Air Bud, 1:83
Air Force, 1:*145*
Airplane!, 1:358, 388; 2:74; 3:261, 265
Airplane Drone, 3:64
Airport, 1:74; 2:74; 4:300
Ajani-Ogun, 1:55
Akahige, 3:70
Akeley, Carl, 3:216
Akerman, Chantal, 2:65
Akibiyori, 3:62, 65
Akira, 1:226, 368; 2:191; 3:184; 4:26

Aktorzy Prowincjonalni, 3:274
Akutagawa, Ryonosuke, 1:40
Al Ard, 2:129, 130
Al Attrach, Farid, 2:129
Al di là delle nuvole, 1:116
Al futuwa, 2:130
Al Gharib al saghir, 1:99
Al Muhajir, 2:129
Al Mumiya, 2:130
Al Mutaham al bari, 1:98
Al Mutamarridun, 2:130
Al Rihani, Naguib, 2:129
Aladdin, 1:86, 227, 260
Alam Ara, 3:14
The Alamo, 2:133, 136; 3:317
Alaouié, Borhan, 1:99
Alarcón, Sebastián, 1:268, 269
Alba de América, 4:111
Al-Bashkateb, 2:128
Alberini, Filoteo, 3:41
L'Albero degli zoccoli, 3:49, 228
Albers, Hans, 2:313
Albertazzi, Giorgio, 1:*120*
Alcott, John, 1:289, 293
Alda, Alan, 4:178
Aldredge, Theoni V., 1:381
Aldrich, Robert, 1:317; 2:237; 3:334
Alea, Tomás Gutiérrez, 1:17; 2:11–16;
 3:130, 345
Aleandro, Norma, 1:112
Aleichem, Sholem, 4:397
Alekan, Henri, 1:293
Alekandrov, Grigori, 4:15
Aleksandr Nevskiy, 2:120, 121,
 375–376; 3:341
Aleksandrov, Grigori, 2:371
Alemán, Miguel, 3:148
Alexander, 2:138, 374, *375*
Alexander, Ben, 1:252
Alexander Hamilton, 2:375
Alexander Nevsky, 3:181, 182, *183;*
 4:15, 117
Alexander, Scott, 2:28
Alexandra...Why?, 2:129, 130
Alexandria, 2:355
Alexandria, Again and Forever, 2:129
Alexandria...New York, 2:129
Alexandrov, G. V., 4:101
Alexeieff, Alexander, 1:93, 213
Alfie, 2:338–339
Alfred Hitchcock Presents, 1:214
Algar, James, 3:218
Alger, Horatio, 1:304, 310

Algeria, 1:99; 2:58–59; 3:345
Algiers, 4:285
Ali, 1:9
Ali, Mustafa Abu, 1:99
Alias Jimmy Valentine, 2:271
Alice, 1:89, 90, 222
Alice Adams, 1:6
Alice Doesn't Live Here Anymore, 1:255,
 407; 2:55; 3:419
Alice in den Städten, 3:420
Alice in Wonderland (Disney), 1:336;
 3:414
Alice's Restaurant, 3:130; 4:324
Alicia en el Pueblo de Maravillas, 2:15
Alien, 4:57
 action heroines, 1:34
 animal actors, 1:79
 color in, 1:339
 credits, 1:384
 dialogue, 2:52
 gender, 2:290
 genres, 2:301, 306
 scholarly criticism of, 4:31
 social critique, 4:30
 use of conflict in, 1:27
Alien Resurrection, 1:92; 4:57
Alien 3, 4:57
Alien vs. Predator, 2:301
Alien Zone, 4:30
Aliens, 4:57
Aliens of the Deep, 3:220
Alison, Joan, 4:36
Alive from Off Center, 2:41
Al-Kompars, 1:102
All About Eve, 1:7; 2:53, 55
All About My Mother, 3:136
All About Oscar®, 1:2; 3:307
All for Old Ireland, 3:34
All My Life, 2:157
All Night Long, 3:286
All of Me, 4:46
All or Nothing, 1:306
All Quiet on the Western Front, 1:252,
 344; 2:371; 4:295, 337
All That Heaven Allows, 2:196; 3:125,
 134, 135, 136, *137*
All That Jazz, 1:281, 282, 375
All the King's Men, 1:343, 349, 350;
 3:280
All the President's Men, 2:212, *213;*
 4:355
All the Pretty Horses, 4:363
Allá en el Rancho Grande, 3:148
Al-Lail, 1:102

American Psycho, 2:399

American Releasing Corporation, 2:164

American Society of Cinematographers (ASC), 1:285–286

American Splendor, 1:366

American Telephone and Telegraph Corporation (AT&T), 3:379–380

An American Tragedy, 3:252

American Wedding, 1:81

An American Werewolf in London, 1:359; 3:115

The Americanization of Emily, 4:38

America's Sweethearts, 4:46

Amerikaner Shadkhn, 4:398

Der Amerikanishce Freund, 4:305

Ames, Preston, 1:341

AMIA. *See* Association of Moving Image Archivists (AMIA)

Amies, Hardy, 2:197

Amir, Aziza, 2:128

Amistad, 1:376

The Amityville Horror, 3:4

Amnesia, 1:269

Among the Cannibal Isles of the South Seas, 3:216

El Amor brujo, 2:37

L'Amore, 1:118; 3:45; 4:64

Amores perros, 3:150

Amos 'n' Andy, 3:377, 383

L'Amour à vingt ans, 3:182

Un Amour de poche, 2:259

L'Amour en fuite, 2:260

L'Amour fou, 3:241

AMPAS. *See* Academy of Motion Picture Arts and Science (AMPAS)

Amphityron, 2:314

Amsterdam Global Village, 3:233

O amuleto de Ogum, 1:175

Amy!, 2:206

An American in Paris, 1:287

Anamorphic lenses, 1:185

Anand, Dev, 3:17

Anaparastassi, 2:353

Anatomie de l'enfer, 4:62, 67

Anatomy of a Murder, 1:384, 402

Anchors Aweigh, 1:227; 2:36; 3:193

Ancillary markets distribution, 2:84

And Now for Something Completely Different, 2:340

And Then There Were None, 4:34

Andanggaman, 1:52

Andaz, 3:15

Der Andere, 2:310

Anders als die Anderen, 2:281; 4:60

Anderson, Benedict, 3:205

Anderson, Christopher, 1:159

Anderson, Eddie, 1:281

Anderson, Gilbert M. "Bronco Billy," 4:358

Anderson, Joseph L., 3:60

Anderson, Lindsay, 1:121, 146; 2:5, 95, 338, 339; 3:244

Anderson, Maxwell, 4:284

Anderson, Paul Thomas, 1:358; 4:46

The Anderson Platoon, 4:316

The Anderson Tapes, 1:401

Andersson, Bibi, 1:*119,* 232

Andersson, Harriet, 1:118, 232

Andersson, Liv, 2:64

Andrei Rublyov, 2:247; 3:405

Andreotti, Giulio, 3:44

Andrews, Dana, 2:224

Andrews, Julie, 2:280; 4:38

The Andromeda Strain, 2:188

The Andy Griffith Show, 1:75, 255

Andy Hardy, 4:54

Andy Hardy Gets Spring Fever, 3:156

Angel, 2:341

An Angel at My Table, 1:138, *140*

El Ángel exterminador, 3:149

Angel Eyes, 3:89

Angel Face, 1:405

Angel Heart, 1:405

The Angel Levine, 2:27

Angela Anaconda, 1:93

Angelopoulos, Theo, 1:121, 195; 2:351, 353, *354;* 4:40, 404

Angelos, 2:353

Angels from Hell, 4:316

Angels with Dirty Faces, 2:273, 274

Anger, Kenneth, 1:203; 2:21, 152–153, 155, 281–282; 4:63, 187

Anger Management, 1:80

Les Anges du péché, 2:257

Angi Vera, 2:405

Angst essen seele auf, 1:*308;* 2:318; 3:136, 367, 372

Animal actors, **1:79–84**
   examples of memorable, 1:79
   in production, 1:79–81
   star system, 1:82–84
   structuring, 1:81–82

Animal Crackers, 3:254

Animal Farm, 1:80, 225, 227

Animal House, 2:17

Animal Locomotion, 3:304

Animal Planet, 3:219

The Animal World, 2:75; 3:219

Animated Conversations, 1:89

Animation, **1:85–96**
   alternative methods, 1:93–95
   of animals, 1:81
   Canadian, 1:213
   cartoon, 1:85–86, **221–227**
   crews, 1:396
   digital, 1:89–93
   experimental, 2:153
   Japanese, 2:367; 3:71, 183–184
   music, 3:182–184
   3D stop-motion, 1:86–89
   Zagred school, 4:404

Anime, 1:367; 3:71, 183–184

Anka, Paul, 1:209

Ankur, 3:21

Anna Boleyn, 1:162; 2:172; 4:278

Anna Christie, 2:54; 3:155, 156

Anna en Bella, 3:233

Anna Karenina, 1:39; 2:349; 3:156, *156,* 380

Annabelle Butterfly Dance, 2:33

Annaud, Jean-Jacques, 2:268; 3:220

Anne of Green Gables, 1:252

L'Année dernière à Marienbad, 1:118, 371; 2:196, 238, 264, 365; 3:236, 242

Annie, 1:263

Annie Hall
   Academy Award®, 4:288
   animal actors, 1:80
   comedy, 1:360, *362*
   costumes, 1:381
   fashion, 2:195, 198
   romantic comedy, 4:6
   titles, 1:388

The Anniversary Party, 4:305

Another Country, 1:167

Another Dawn, 1:98

Anschütz, Ottomar, 2:309

Anstey, Edgar, 2:90

Antek Policmajster, 3:272

Anthapan Krong Muang, 3:104

Anthony Adverse, 2:349

Anthony, Joseph, 1:39

Anthrax, 2:73

Anticipation of the Night, 1:195; 2:159

Antigone/Rites of Passion, 2:40

Antin, Eleanor, 2:247

Anti-Semitic films, 2:316; 4:387, 389
   See also specific films

Antonia's Line, 3:234

animation, 1:85
children's film, 1:260
color, 1:336
a nature film, 3:218
production process, 3:338
RKO, 3:409
Bamboozled, 1:60
Ban ni gao fei, 1:276
Bananas, 4:288
Band of Brothers, 4:341
The Band Wagon
choreography, 1:279
cinematography, 1:294
color, 1:*340,* 341
dance, 2:36, 38
genre, 2:301
melodrama, 3:138
MGM, 3:160
music, 3:189
producer, 3:313
Bande à part, 3:238
O bandido da luz vermelha, 1:175
Bang Rajan, 3:106
Bangue-Bangue, 1:175
Bani-Etemad, Rakshan, 3:30
The Bank Dick, 4:296
Bank Shot, 2:276
Banks, Russell, 1:214
Banky, Vilma, 2:402
Bannerjee, Subir, 1:256
Banshun, 3:62
Banton, Travis, 1:376, 377, 381, 382
Banvard, John, 3:303–304
Bao gio cho den thang muoi, 3:106
Bao wei wo men de tu di, 1:272
Bara no soretsu, 3:69
Bara, Theda, 2:288; 4:60
Barabás, Stanislav, 2:27
Baranski, Andrzej, 3:276
Barb Wire, 1:366
Barbarella, 1:201, 367; 2:20
Barbash, Uri, 3:*39*
Barbershop, 1:70
Barbershop 2, 1:70
Barbin, Pierre, 1:107
Barclay, Barry, 3:248, 249
Bardem, Juan Antonio, 4:111
Bardot, Brigitte, 1:118; 2:83, 166, 262, 265; 4:157
Barefoot in the Park, 2:212
Barenholtz, Ben, 2:21
Barker, Clive, 2:395; 3:113
Barker, Cordell, 1:227
Barker, Lex, 1:155

Barker, Robert, 3:303
The Barkleys of Broadway, 2:38
Barn Rushes, 2:158
Barnes, Binnie, 2:*332*
Barnet, Boris, 4:13
Barnette, Neema, 1:69
Barnum, P. T., 3:356
Barr, Charles, 2:6
Barr, Tim, 1:88
Barra ya Isti Mar, 1:99
Barratier, Christophe, 2:268
Barravento, 1:173
Barré, Raoul, 1:221
Barreto, Bruno, 1:176
Barrett, Franklyn, 1:132, 139
Barrett, Kym, 1:381
The Barretts of Wimpole Street, 3:314
Barry, Iris, 1:106, 107
Barry, John, 3:172, 176
Barry Lyndon
adaptations, 1:40
cinematography, 1:289
collaboration, 1:322
costumes, 1:381
direction, 2:70, *71*
fine art, 2:244, *245*
Barrymore, Drew, 1:256
Barrymore, John
Columbia Pictures, 1:346
horror films, 2:392
MGM, 3:155, 156
Paramount, 3:253
radio programs, 3:382
romantic comedies, 4:3
screwball comedies, 4:44, 45
Barrymore, Lionel, 3:155, 156
Barsaat, 3:15
Bart the Bear, 1:84; 3:*220,* 220
Barthelmess, Richard, 1:125, 251, 259
Barthes, Roland
cinephilia, 1:300
criticism, 2:7–8
culture and ideology, 2:409–410
feminism, 2:201
genres, 2:303
influence by Brecht, 1:20
on realism, 3:201, 392
semiology and, 4:50
status of cinema, 1:106
Bartkowiak, Andrzej, 1:293
Bartlett, Scott, 2:149
Bartok, 1:166
Barton, Rebecca, 2:162
Base, film, 2:231
Les Bas-fonds, 1:404; 2:254

Bashan yeyu, 1:273
Basic Instinct, 1:241, 405
Basinger, Kim, 3:187
Bass Brothers Enterprise, 4:333
Bass, Jules, 1:89
Bass, Saul, 1:383, 384, *385,* 387, *387,* 389
Bassani, Giogio, 2:381
Bassermann, Albert, 2:310
Bassett, Angela, 3:376
Bassori, Timité, 1:52
Bastion Point Day 507, 3:249–250
Bata, Bata...Paano ka ginawa, 3:269
Bataan, 1:305; 4:323, 337, 341–342
Bataille de boules de neige, 1:19
Batalla de Chile, 1:266
Bates, Alan, 1:166
Bates, Kathy, 1:249
Bathiat, Arlette-Léonie, 2:256
Batista, Fulgencio, 3:344
Batman (comic books), 1:366
Batman (movie)
distribution, 2:82
fantasy films, 2:192
lighting, 3:93
merchandising, 3:141, 143
sequels and series, 4:37, 54
Batman (television show), 1:201, 204
Batman Forever, 3:23
Batman Returns, 3:295
Battaglia di Algeri, 3:47, 345
Battisti, Carlo, 3:*227*
Battle Beyond the Stars, 3:10
Battle Cry, 4:342
Battle Cry for Peace, 4:375–376
The Battle of Algiers, 1:99, *330,* 330; 2:99; 3:49
realism, 3:391
The Battle of Chile, 1:266, 268
Battle of Manila Bay, 4:345
The Battle of Midway, 2:93; 4:394
The Battle of San Pietro, 2:94; 4:395
Battle of the River Neretva, 4:404
The Battle of the Somme, 4:377–379
Battleground, 4:341
Battles without Honor and Humanity, 3:69
Battleship Potemkin
art cinema, 1:117
canon and canonicity, 1:218
censorship, 1:243
class in films, 1:305
collaboration, 1:323
documentary elements in, 2:91

Benigni, Roberto, 1:234; 2:381; 3:56, 57

Benjamin, Arthur, 3:175, 180

Benjamin, Robert S., 4:286

Benjamin, Walter, 1:12, 300; 2:408–409; 3:123

Benji, 1:260, 403

Benn, Gottfried, 2:172

Bennett, Bill, 3:421

Bennett, Constance, 4:46

Bennett, Joan, 1:377

Benning, James, 2:161

Benning, Sadie, 2:161, 282; 4:304

Benôit, Pierre, 1:38

Bensaa suonissa, 2:251

Benton, Brook, 1:388

Benvenuti, Leo, 4:36

Beppie, 3:232

Beresford, Bruce, 1:137, 1:136, 139; 3:420

Berg-Ejvind och hans hustru, 1:322

Bergen, Edgar, 1:4, 72

Berger, Ludwig, 3:232; 4:278

Berger, Warren, 3:284

Die Bergkatze, 2:176

Bergman, Ingmar, 1:*119;* 4:*193*
    art cinema, 1:115, 118
    auteurism, 3:235
    biography, 4:192
    casting, 1:231, 232–233
    censorship, 1:243
    child actors, 1:256
    cinematography, 1:285
    collaboration, 1:322–323
    criticism, 2:6
    direction, 2:64
    disaster films, 2:74
    distribution, 2:83
    exploitation films, 2:165
    fantasy films, 2:190
    film studies, 2:235
    fine art, 2:245
    Hungarian cinema, 2:403
    realism and, 3:200
    religion and, 3:403
    road movies, 3:421
    screenwriting, 4:40
    Swedish, 4:191–193

Bergman, Ingrid, 2:372; 3:46, 228, 350; 4:*37, 354*

Bergroth, Kersti, 2:250

Bergson, Henri, 1:361–362

Berkeley, Busby
    B movies, 3:159
    biographical films, 1:166
    biography, 3:191

camera movement, 1:192

cameras and camera movement, 3:*188, 192,* 193, 194

choreography, 1:280

dance, 2:34–35

and the decline of musicals, 3:189

the Depression, 2:348

Berlanga, Luis, 4:111

Berle, Milton, 1:74

Berlin Alexanderplatz, 3:182

Berlin: Die Sinofonie der Grofsstadt, 2:91

Berlin International Film Festival, 2:210

Berlin, Irving, 1:279, 381; 2:38; 3:186

Berman, Pandro S., 3:408

Bernal, Gael García, 1:339

Bernal, Ishmael, 3:268

Bernanos, Georges, 1:39

Bernard, Raymond, 2:254

Bernhardt, Curtis, 2:315

Bernhardt, Sarah, 2:214; 3:112

Berns, Mel, 3:112

Bernstein, Elmer, 1:383; 3:176, 177

Bernstein, Walter, 1:313; 4:39

Berri, Claude, 2:266

Berry, Chuck, 3:192

Berry, Halle, 1:*4,* 9, 34; 3:12

Berry, Jules, 1:246

Bertini, Francesca, 3:41

Bertolucci, Bernardo
    adaptations, 1:40
    co-productions, 1:371
    direction, 2:64
    film studies, 2:237
    fine art, 2:246
    historical films, 2:369
    Italian cinema, 3:47, 50–51, 55
    Loquasto, Santo and, 3:327
    Marxism and, 3:126
    neorealism, 3:228
    New Wave, 3:244
    sexuality in films of, 4:65
    use of color, 1:339

Bertrand, Ina, 1:131

Berwick, Ray, 1:80

Beshara, Khairy, 2:130–131

Bessie, Alvah, 1:312, 313; 3:128

Besson, Luc, 2:198, 267, *267;* 3:206
    religion and, 3:405

Best in Show, 3:265

The Best Little Whorehouse in Texas, 1:249; 3:415

The Best Man, 1:69, 70

The Best of Everything, 2:18–19

The Best of Youth, 3:57

The Best People, 4:3

The Best Year, 3:415

The Best Years of Our Lives
    acting, 1:12
    character actors, 1:245
    choreography, 1:288
    the Cold War, 1:315
    film studies, 2:238
    historical film, 2:373
    RKO, 3:407, 413
    screenwriting, 4:33

BET (Black Entertainment Television), 2:38, 40

La bête humaine, 1:404; 3:388

Better Living through Circuitry, 2:41

Better Luck Tomorrow, 1:128; 2:275

Better Than Chocolate, 2:285; 3:9

Between Friends, 1:211

Beuamarchais, Pierre-Augustin, 3:125

Beulah, 3:382

Beur cinema, 2:59–60

Bevan, Billy, 1:132

The Beverly Hillbillies, 3:265

Beverly Hills Cop, 3:8, 259, 318

Beverly Hills Cop 2, 3:318

Der Bewegte Mann, 2:323

Bewitched, 1:351

Beyer, Frank, 2:321, 322

Beyond the Poseidon Adventure, 2:75

Beyond the Valley of the Dolls, 1:204, 204

Beyond the Walls, 3:39, *39*

Beyrouth ya Beyrouth, 1:99

Beyroutou el lika, 1:99

Bezeten, 3:232

Bezhin lug, 4:14

Bezucelná procházka, 2:26

BFI. *See* British Film Institute (BFI)

Bhabha, Homi, 3:205

Bhaji on the Beach, 2:341; 3:208–209

Bhakta Dhruva, 1:262

Bhosle, Asha, 3:18, 182

Bian cheng san xia, 3:118

Biberman, Herbert, 1:313; 3:128, 129

Bielik, Palo, 2:27

Bielinsky, Fabién, 1:114

Bier, Susanne, 2:44, 47, 48

Big, 1:282; 2:188

The Big Bird Cage, 2:168

The Big Boss, 3:118, 119, *121*

The Big Broadcast of 1936, 3:383

The Big Bus, 2:74, 76

VOLUME 1: 1–410; VOLUME 2: 1–412; VOLUME 3: 1–422; VOLUME 4: 1–408

VOLUME 1: 1–410; VOLUME 2: 1–412; VOLUME 3: 1–422; VOLUME 4: 1–408

Breil, Joseph Carl, 3:174

Breillat, Catherine, 2:71, 265, 267; 3:289; 4:62, *63, 67*

Brenda Starr, 1:349

Brennan, Walter, 2:*303;* 4:178, 360

Brennan, William, 3:284

Brenon, Herbert, 3:34

Bresan, Vinko, 4:407

Bresson, Robert
adaptations, 1:39
art cinema, 1:118
auteurism, 1:144; 3:235
casting, 1:235
characterizations, 1:17
criticism, 2:6
film studies, 2:237
French cinema, 2:257, 259
performance elements, 1:12
realism, 3:391
religion and, 3:404

Breton, André, 3:125; 4:183

Breuer, Josef, 3:349

Breve cielo, 1:114

Brewster, David, 3:301

Brialy, Jean-Claude, 1:291; 3:244

Brian's Song, 2:377

Brice, Fanny, 1:72, 162

The Bride of Frankenstein, 1:203; 2:234, 392; 4:294, *297*

Bride of the Monster, 2:18

Brideshead Revisted, 2:365

The Bridge, 2:171

The Bridge on the River Kwai, 1:343, 351; 2:136; 4:39, 337

Bridges, Lloyd, 1:246, 313

Bridget Jones's Diary, 1:249; 4:45, 46

The Brig, 2:156

Brigadoon, 2:36, 188, 298

Briggs, Raymond, 1:227

Bright Eyes, 1:253, 254, 261

Bright Leaves, 2:94

Bright Road, 1:62

The Bright Shawl, 2:299

Brighton Rock, 1:32, 40; 2:335

Brignone, Guido, 3:42

Briley, John, 4:38

Brilliance, 1:92

Bringing Out the Dead, 1:407

Bringing Up Baby
animal actors, 1:83
auteurism, 1:143
awards, 1:6
comedy, 1:361

the Depression, 2:348
dialogue, 2:55
RKO, 3:407, 409
romantic comedy, 4:3, 5, 6
screenwriting, 4:33–34
screwball comedy, 4:43, 44, 46, *47*

Bringing Up Father, 1:365

Brisbin, David, 1:289

Briski, Norman, 1:112

Briskin, Sam, 1:344, 346

Britain Prepared, 4:377

British Academy Film Award, 1:9; 3:309

British Board of Film Censors (BBFC), 1:239–240; 2:339

British Film Institute (BFI), 1:108, 219; 2:338, 342

British Mobile Cinema Unit, 4:377

Britten, Benjamin, 2:90; 3:180; 4:102

Britton, Andrew, 2:2, 6

Broadbent, Jim, 1:233, 249; *309*

Broadcast News, 1:384

Broadway, 1:344; 4:295

Broadway Melody, 1:280; 3:155, 187

Broadway Revue of 1929, 3:189

Broccoli, Albert "Cubby," 2:338; 4:287–288

Brocka, Lino, 3:268

Brockett, Jim, 1:81

Brody, Adrien, 2:*382*

Brokeback Mountain, 1:128; 2:286; 4:363–364

Broken Arrow, 3:372; 4:64

Broken Barrier, 3:248

Broken Blossoms
acting, 1:17
Asian American, 1:125
child actors, 1:251
fine art, 2:244
music, 3:174
narrative, 3:199
parodies of, 3:263
sexuality in, 4:60
special effects, 4:122
United Artists, 4:283

The Broken Hearts Club, 2:285

Broken Lance, 1:314

Bromberg, J. Edward, 1:23

Bronenosets Potyomkin. See Battleship Potemkin

Bronfman, Edgar, Jr., 1:74

Bronson, Charles, 1:371; 2:308; 4:70

Brontë, Charlotte, 1:40

Brontë, Emily, 1:40

A Bronx Morning, 2:152

The Bronze Buckaroo, 2:307

Bronze Venus, 1:60

The Brood, 1:210; 2:395

Brooks, Cleanth, 2:236

Brooks, Louise, 3:112

Brooks, Mel
biography, 3:264
comedies, 1:358, 359
genre, 2:298, 304
parodies, 3:263, *265*
screenwriting, 4:36

Brooks, Peter, 3:139

Brooks, Philip, 1:56

Brooks, Richard, 3:99

Brooks, Sue, 1:139

Broomfield, Nick, 2:98

Brosnan, Pierce, 3:34

O Brother, 1:249; 3:419; 4:37

Brother From Another Planet, 3:8, 10; 4:29

Brotherhood of Man, 1:227

The Brothers Karamazov, 3:*100*

Broughton, James, 2:153

The Brown Bunny, 4:67

Brown, Charles Brockden, 2:392

Brown, Clarence, 1:42

Brown, Garrett, 1:4, 191, 293

Brown, Harry, 3:267

Brown, Jim, 1:66; 2:306

Brown, Johnny Mack, 1:156

Brown, Nacio Herb, 3:186

Brown, Treg, 1:223

Brown, Trisha, 2:40

Browning, Tod, 2:237, 392, 393; 3:113

The Browning Version, 1:46; 2:331

Bruce, Lenny, 1:282

Bruce, Nigel, 1:155

Der Bruch, 2:322

Bruckheimer, Jerry, 3:*317, 318, 319*

Brückner, Jutta, 2:318

De Brug, 3:231

Bruno S., 2:318

Brusati, Franco, 3:52

Brusse, Ytzen, 3:232

Brute Force, 1:406; 4:296–297

Brynner, Yul, 3:335

Bu jian bu san, 1:276

Bu liao qing, 2:388

Bu Wanchang, 1:271

Buache, Freddy, 1:106

Bubble, 3:27

Buchan, John, 4:142

Catholic Legion of Decency, 4:322, 324

Cathy Come Home, 3:390

Cats and Dogs, 1:92

Cat's Eye, 1:256

Cattaneo, Peter, 2:343

The Caucasian Chalk Circle, 1:20

Caught in the Draft, 4:394

Cavalcade of Stars, 3:356

Cavalcânti, Alberto, 1:170; 2:90, 254, 333; 4:101

Cavalier, Alain, 2:246, 247

Cavani, Liliana, 3:48, 51

Cave-In, 2:75

Cavell, Stanley, 1:361–362; 2:10; 3:391; 4:3

Cayatte, André, 2:257

Cayrol, Jean, 2:380; 3:241

La caza, 4:112

CBS radio, 3:380

Cech panen kutnohorských, 2:26

Ceddo, 1:50

Cedrick the Entertainer, 1:355

Ceiling Zero, 1:143

Cel animation process, 1:221–222

The Celebration, 2:48

Celebrity directors, 2:67–71

Céline at Julie vont en bateau, 3:241

The Cell, 1:81, 380

The Celluloid Closet, 2:277

The Cemetery Club, 1:70

Cenevski, Kiril, 4:407

Cengić, Bata, 4:406

Censorship, **1:237–244**
    African cinema, 1:56
    American, 1:237–239
    art cinema, 1:118
    British, 1:239–241
    Chinese, 1:277
    of crime films, 1:399
    early, 2:109
    Egyptian, 2:128
    exhibition and distribution, 1:242–243
    of gangster films, 2:273
    history, 2:219
    Hungarian, 2:402–403
    Indian, 3:20
    Japan cinema, 3:63–64
    Philippines, 3:268, 269
    pressure groups and media effect on, 1:241–242
    of sex, 1:243–244; 4:59–61
    Spanish, 4:110
    of violence, 4:321–322

See also Production Code, Motion Picture

The Center of World, 1:127

Center Stage, 2:390

Central do Brasil, 3:421

Centre Stage, 1:165

C'era una volta il West, 1:246, 385; 2:274, 300; 3:55; 4:70, 104

Cercle du Cinéma, 1:107

Le cerf-volant, 1:102

Cerný Petr, 2:27–28

Cerruti, Nino, 2:198

Un Certain Regard, 2:58

Cervantes, Behn, 3:268

César, 2:255

Cet obscur objet du désir, 3:125, 350

CGI. *See* Computer-generated imagery (CGI)

Chabrol, Claude
    art cinema, 1:118
    auteurism, 1:144, 148; 3:235
    cinephilia, 1:300
    co-productions, 1:371
    film studies, 2:235, 237
    French cinema, 2:261, 263
    French New Wave and, 3:237, 243
    music used by, 3:181

El Chacal del Nahueltoro, 1:266

Chacotero Sentimental, 1:269

Chadha, Gurinder, 1:129; 2:341; 3:22, 208, *208*

Chadwick, Paul, 1:368

Chahine, Youssef, 2:129, 130, *130*

Chaibancha, Mitr, 3:103

Chamberlain, Richard, 1:*137*

Chambers, John, 3:109

Chambers, Marilyn, 1:210; 3:286

Chameleon Street, 1:68

Chamoun, Jean, 1:99

The Champ, 1:8, 252, *252,* 256

Champion, Gower, 1:282

Chan Is Missing, 1:127

Chan, Jackie, 1:32, 208, 383; 2:388, 390; 3:121–122; 4:157–158

A Chance to Live, 1:8

Chanchada, Brazilian, 1:170

Chandler, Raymond, 1:44, 45, *46;* 2:222, 225

Chanel, 2:196

Chanel, Coco, 2:264

Chaney, Lon, 1:164, 245; 2:292, 392, 393, *394;* 3:110, *111,* 154

Chaney, Lon, Jr., 1:155, 246

Chang Cheh, 2:388; 3:118

Chang, Fruit, 2:390

Change of Habit, 3:192

Channel Four, 2:341–342, 343

Un chant d'amour, 4:63

The Chant of Jimmie Blacksmith, 1:139

Chapayev, 4:15, 17

Un chapeau de paille d'Italie, 2:254

Chaplin, Charlie
    acting skill, 1:12
    children's films, 1:262
    class in films, 1:304
    clown comedy, 1:353, 355
    collaboration, 1:322
    comedy, 1:*354,* 356, 357, 360
    Coogan, Jackie, 1:251
    criticism of, 4:285
    the Depression, 2:346, 350
    direction, 2:63
    early cinema, 2:114
    film artistry, 1:217
    film studies, 2:237
    French cinema influence, 2:253, 255
    Greek cinema, 2:351
    Holocaust, 2:381
    influence of, 3:57
    Italian, 3:48, 57
    Loren, Sophia, 3:48
    Marxism, 3:124
    music composed by, 3:175
    parodies, 3:262
    repeated takes by, 3:333
    screwball comedies, 4:43
    slapstick comedy, 4:87
    special award, 1:4
    star system, 4:78
    United Artists, 3:316; 4:283, 284, 286

Chapman, Michael, 1:293

Character, 3:234

Character actors, **1:245–250;** 2:298–300; 4:178–181

Character Generators, Inc., 2:41

Charbonneau, Pierre, 2:40

Charell, Erik, 4:280

The Charge of the Light Brigade, 1:29, 47; 2:371; 3:4

Chariots of Fire, 2:341, 342, 365; 4:136

Charisse, Cyd
    choreography, 1:279–280, 281
    cinematography, 1:294
    dance, 2:36, 38
    musicals, 3:194
    use of color, 1:339, *340,* 341

Charlie and the Chocolate Factory, 1:81

DC Comics, 1:366

De Alencar, José, 1:169, 170

De Andrade, Joaquim Pedro, 1:171, 174, 176

De Antonio, Emile, 2:99; 3:343, 345

De Balzac, Honoré, 1:39; 2:9; 3:386

De Barros, Luiz, 1:170

De Beauregard, Georges, 3:237

De Beauvoir, Simone, 2:287

De Bont, Jan, 1:285

De Broca, Philippe, 3:237

De Carlo, Yvonne, 1:208

De Cervantes, Miguel, 3:417

De Chomon, Segundo, 4:107

De Forest, Lee, 4:201

De Fuentes, Fernando, 3:148

De Funès, Louis, 2:264, 265

De Givenchy, Hubert, 2:196

De Haas, Max, 3:232

De Havilland, Olivia, 1:29, 30; 4:172, 173, 350–351

De Jong, Ate, 3:234

De la Iglesia, Eloy, 4:114

De la Loma, José Antonio, 3:287

De la Madrid, Miguel, 3:150

De la Parra, Pim, 3:232

De La Patellière, Denys, 2:264

De Laclos, Choderlos, 2:28

De lampedusa, Giuseppe, 1:40

De Lauretis, Teresa, 2:205; 3:365

De Leon, Mike, 3:268

De liguorio, Eugenio, 1:266

De Minder gelukkige terugkeer van Joszef Katus, 3:232

De Niro, Robert, 1:*406*
    casting, 1:233–234
    Creative Artists Agency, 1:76
    crime films, 1:405
    editing, 2:117
    gangster films, 2:275
    performances and fans, 1:15

De Noorderlingen, 3:234

De Orduña, Juan, 4:111

De Palma, Brian, 1:296; 2:123, 276, 304, 395; 3:7

De Robertis, Francesco, 3:43, 223

De Rochemont, Louis, 2:88, 223

De Santis, Giuseppe, 3:42, 44, 225

De Santis, Pasqualino, 1:293

De Sica, Vittorio
    casting, 1:235
    censorship, 1:243
    collaboration, 1:323
    co-productions, 1:371

    the Holocaust, 2:381
    Italian cinema, 3:42–43, 43–44, 47, 49, 53, 57
    Loren, Sophia, 3:48
    Marxism and, 3:125–126
    neorealism, 3:223, 224–226
    realism, 3:386, 387, 388–389, 391
    typage, 1:14

De Vaal, Jan, 1:106

De Wilde, Brandon, 1:253

The Dead, 1:41

Dead Birds, 2:97

Dead End, 2:273; 4:284

Dead Letter Office, 1:140

Dead Man, 1:11; 3:419

Dead Men Don't Wear Plaid, 1:359; 2:226; 3:261

Dead of Night, 2:*395*; 4:317

Dead Poets Society, 1:134

Dead Presidents, 2:275

Dead Ringers, 2:64

The Dead Zone, 1:208

Deadline U. S. A., 1:403

Deadly Is the Female, 3:418

Dean, James, 4:*211*
    adaptations, 1:42
    biography, 4:210
    cult films, 2:21
    merchandising, 3:142
    semiotics, 4:50
    Warner Bros., 4:353

DeAngelis, Michael, 3:368

Dear America: Letters Home from Vietnam, 4:320

Dear Diary, 3:57

Dear Wendy, 2:49

Death in Brunswick, 1:140

Death in Venice, 1:40, 381; 3:47, 126, 326

The Death of a Black President, 1:55

Death of a Bureaucrat, 2:12, 13, 15

Death of a Salesman, 1:350

The Death of Stalinism in Bohemia, 1:90

Death Race 2000, 3:418

Death Takes a Holiday, 2:191

Death Wish, 4:327

Deathdream, 4:317

Debord, Guy, 2:157

The Debussy Film, 1:166

The Debut, 1:128

Decaë, Henri, 1:290, 293; 3:240

The Decameron, 3:50, 127

Decca Records, 1:74

Deception, 4:278

Le Déclin de l'empire américain, 1:212

Deconstructing Harry, 4:6

DeCordova, Richard, 1:259; 4:155, 160

Dee, Ruby, 1:69

Deep Blue, 3:220–221

Deep Core, 2:73, 76

Deep Impact, 4:31, 327

Deep in My Heart, 1:281

Deep Red, 3:55

Deep Throat, 1:243; 2:17, 46; 3:284, *285*

Deeper into Movies, 3:76

Deep-focus cinematography, 1:12

The Deer Hunter, 1:35, 296; 2:373; 3:130, 140; 4:289–290, 319

Deer, James Young, 3:373

Deésy, Alfréd, 2:401

Deewar, 3:14, 16

Defending Your Life, 4:6

The Defiant Ones, 1:63, 64; 3:307; 4:286

The Defilers, 2:167; 3:5

Defoe, Daniel, 1:39, 40

The Degenerates, 2:167; 3:5

Degeneres, Ellen, 2:286

Degl, Karel, 2:25

Dehn, Mura, 2:40, 41

Le Déjeuner de bébé, 1:180

Dekalog, 3:402

Del Giudice, Filippo, 2:335

Del Mundo, Clodualdo, Jr., 3:268

Del Rio, Dolores, 3:86, 212, 374

Del Toro, Benicio, 3:89

Delannoy, Jean, 1:144; 2:6, 257

Délano, Jorge, 1:265

Delerue, Georges, 3:176, 181, 244

Deleuze, Gilles, 2:204

Delgado, Fernando, 4:108

Delgado, Marcel, 1:87

Deliberate camp, 1:201, *204*

Delirium, 3:74

Deliverance, 1:296

Delluc, Louis, 1:299; 2:254, 255; 4:83

Delon, Alain, 1:118, 371, 377; 2:265

Demarest, William, 2:56

Demazis, Orane, 2:255

Dementia 13, 3:4, 6

DeMille, Agnes, 1:279, 283; 2:36

DeMille, Cecil B.
    biographical films, 1:162
    casting, 1:229

Farrell, Glenda, 1:155, 405
Farrow, Mia, 4:178
Fascism, 3:42–43
Fashion, **2:195–199**
Fassbinder, Rainer Werner
  adaptations, 1:40
  art cinema, 1:121
  biography, 3:367
  class in films, 1:*308,* 309
  film studies, 3:135–136
  gay, lesbian, and queer cinema,
    2:282; 3:*366*
  German cinema, 2:318
  mise-en-scène, 3:167
  music used by, 3:182
  New Wave, 3:244
  queer theory, 3:*364*
  race and ethnicity addressed by,
    3:372
Fast and Loose, 4:3
The Fast and the Furious, 3:4
Faster, Pussycat!, 2:20
Fat City, 1:41
Fat Girl, 4:62
Fatal Attraction, 1:84, 405; 3:259;
  4:131
Fate's Disowned Child, 2:351
Father and Daughter, 3:233
Father and Master, 3:49
Father Knows Best, 3:382
Father of the Bride, 1:253; 4:56
Father's Little Dividend, 1:253; 4:56
Fatima's Coochee-Coochee Dance, 1:19
*Fatto di sangue fra due uomini per causa
  di una vedova,* 3:52
Faulkner, William, 1:39
Faust, 1:38, 90; 2:172, 312, 392
Faustman, Hampe, 4:193
Faustrecht der Freiheit, 3:136, 367
Favela dos meus amores, 1:170
Faye, Safi, 1:53
Fear, 3:74
Fear and Desire, 2:70
Fear Factor, 2:94
Fear in the Night, 1:158
Fear of a Black Hat, 3:9
Fearless, 1:134
Fearless Nadia, 3:16, 19
Federal Hill, 3:9
Fei Mu, 1:272
A Fei zheng zhuan, 2:387
Feiffer, Jules, 1:366, 368
Fejös, Pál, 2:402
Feldman, Charles K., 1:72; 4:353

Feldman, Marty, 1:359; 4:181
Feldman, Phil, 2:117
Feldobott kö, 2:403
Felicia's Journey, 1:214, 215
Felix, Seymour, 1:280
Felix the Cat, 1:222, 260
Fellini, Federico
  art cinema, 1:115, 118
  casting, 1:234
  choreography, 1:282
  class in films, 1:307
  co-productions, 1:371
  costumes, 1:377, *381*
  direction, 2:69, 71
  distribution, 2:83
  dubbing and subtitling, 2:104
  exploitation films, 2:165
  fantasy films, 2:190
  graphic novels, 1:368
  Hungarian cinema, 2:403
  Italian cinema, 3:44, 45–46, 47,
    51, 52, 53, 55
  Japanese cinema, 3:67
  neorealism, 3:224, 228
  realism and, 3:200
  road movies, 3:420
  screenwriting, 4:40
  sexuality in films of, 4:64
Fellini Satyricon, 3:47, 324
Fellini's Casanova, 3:55
Fellow Travelers, 3:39
De fem benspand, 2:48
Female Perversions, 3:9
The Feminine Mystique, 2:201
Feminism, **2:201–207**
  from archival research to cine-
    psychoanalysis, 2:202–204
  beyond cine-psychoanalysis,
    2:204–207
  pornography and, 3:288–289
  sex-gender system and, 2:287–288
  See also Gay, lesbian, and queer
    cinema; Woman's pictures
La femme au couteau, 1:52
Une femme douce, 1:39, 235; 3:238
La Femme Nikita, 2:267; 4:57
La Femme Piège, 1:368
Fenelon, Moacyr, 1:170
Feng jie, 2:389
Feng Xiaogang, 1:276
Feng yun er nü, 1:272
Ferguson, Perry, 1:322
Ferman, James, 1:244
Fernandel, 2:262
Fernández, Emilio, 3:148
Ferrell, Will, 1:354–355

Ferrer, Jose, 3:87
Ferreri, Marco, 4:111
Ferrez, Júlio, 1:169
Ferro, Pablo, 1:383
Festen, 1:191; 2:48
Festivals, **2:209–215**
  awards, 3:309
  future of, 2:214–215
  history of, 2:209–211
  independent films and, 3:11, 207
  leading, 2:211–214
  lesser-known, 2:214
Fetchit, Stepin, 3:374
Fétiche, 1:262
Die Fetten Jahre sind vorbei, 2:323
Feu Mattias Pascal, 1:38
Feuillade, Louis
  archives, 1:107
  French cinema, 2:254
  gangster films, 2:275
  horror films, 2:391
  series, serials and sequels, 4:*54,* 55,
    56
A Few Good Men, 1:406
Feyder, Jacques, 1:38; 2:254, 256
Les fiançailles de M. Hire, 1:39
Fiddler on the Roof, 1:208; 2:82; 3:191
Field of Dreams, 1:355; 3:281
Field, Patricia, 1:382
Field, Syd, 4:40
Fielding, Henry, 1:40
Fields, Freddie, 1:75, 76
Fields, W. C., 1:43; 2:53; 3:253, 254
The Fiend Without a Face, 3:23
15 Kham Duen 11, 3:106
The Fifth Element, 1:372; 2:198; 3:206
55 Days at Peking, 2:133, 136
Figgis, Mike, 3:338; 4:305
Fight Club, 1:391; 3:131, 167
The Fight for Life, 2:347
Fighting Film Collections, 4:392
The Fighting 69th, 4:338
Figueroa, Gabriel, 1:293
A Filipinola in America, 1:126
Filipinos Retreat from Trenches, 1:124
La Fille de l'eau, 2:256
La fille du puisatier, 2:257
Film About a Woman Who..., 2:160
Film Archives Advisory Committee/
  Television Archives Advisory
  Committee (FAAC/TAAC), 1:107
Film as Film, 1:150; 2:7
Film Comment, 2:162, 237
Film Culture, 2:155, 157–158; 3:75

France, *continued*
    1944-1959, 2:258–261
    1970-1989, 2:264–265
    1990 to present, 2:266–269
    adaptations, 1:38
    and Africa, 1:51–52
    art cinema, 1:117, 120
    cinephilia, 1:299–300
    development of motion picture
        cameras in, 1:180
    distribution and the effects of
        television in, 2:265–266
    film festivals, 1:6; 2:210, 211–214,
        250
    music, 3:180–182
    New Wave Cinema, 2:261–264;
        3:49, 126, 228, 237–245
    postwar criticism, 1:142–144
    post-World War I, 2:254–255
    realism, 3:388
    road movies, 3:420
    semiology and cultural theory of,
        4:50
    silent cinema, 2:253–254; 4:82–83
    Vietnam and, 3:106
    during World War I, 4:379–381
    during World War II, 4:389–392
Francesco, 3:405
Francesco guillare di deo, 1:165; 3:405
Francis, Ève, 1:299
Francis, Freddie, 1:293
Francis, Kay, 1:73, 156
Francis the Talking Mule series, 1:83;
    4:297, 299
Franco, Francisco, 1:112; 2:103;
    3:341; 4:111–112
Franju, Georges, 1:106, 107; 2:259;
    3:236
Frank, Melvin, 2:340
Frank, Nino, 2:226
Frank, Robert, 3:7
Franken, Al, 3:383
Frankenheimer, John
    action and adventure films, 1:31
    adaptation, 1:46
    Cold War, 1:318
    dialogue, 2:52
    Internet, 3:26
Frankenstein
    adaptations, 1:38
    camp, 1:203
    censorship, 1:239; 4:322
    disaster film, 2:73
    fans and fandom, 2:182
    fantasy film, 2:189
    genre, 2:298
    horror film, 2:391, 392, 398

    literary roots of, 3:24
    makeup, 3:113, *114,* 115
    mise-en-scène, 3:164
    Universal Studios, 4:294
Frankenstein Meets the Wolf Man,
    2:392; 3:330
Frankfurt School, 2:408–409
Frankfurt, Stephen, 1:383, 387; 3:357
Franklin, Ben, 1:355
Franklin, Carl, 3:9
Franklin, Harold B., 2:147
Franny's Feet, 1:93
Franz Kafka's It's A Wonderful Life, 1:8
Fraser, Brendan, 1:97
Frau im Mond, 1:323
Frauen sind was Wunderbares, 2:323
Fray, 1:368
Freaks, 2:21, 392; 3:314
Freaky Friday, 1:255
Frears, Stephen, 2:341; 3:372, 390
The Fred Allen Show, 3:382
Freda, Riccardo, 3:55
Freddy vs. Jason, 2:301
Frederics, John, 1:377
Free Cinema movement, 2:95
Free Fall, 1:213
Free Radicals, 2:153
A Free Ride, 3:284
Free Willy, 1:83, 256, 264
Free Willy 3, 3:249
Freed, Alan, 3:192
Freed, Arthur, 1:322; 3:159–160,
    189, 313
Freeman, Al, Jr., 1:66
Freeman, Morgan, 1:249
Freeway, 3:419
Freleng, Fritz, 1:223, 224, 387
Frémaux, Thierry, 2:211
The French Connection, 1:399, 406;
    4:327
French Dressing, 1:166
The French Lieutenant's Woman, 1:39
French literature adaptations, 1:39
Frend, Charles, 2:337
Fresa y chocolate, 2:12, 15, *15;* 3:345
Freshwater Assassins, 3:217
Fresnay, Pierre, 2:255
Freud, 3:349
Freud, Sigmund, 1:357; 2:205; 3:349,
    364–365; 4:132
Die Freudlose Gasse, 1:305; 2:176, 311
Freulich, Roman, 2:152

Freund, Karl, 1:293; 2:64, 392; 3:113;
    4:278
Fric, Martin, 2:26, 27
Fricker, Brenda, 3:36
Frida, 3:178
Friday Foster, 2:168
Friday Night Lights, 4:135
Friday the 13th, 2:188, 395; 3:115;
    4:54, 326
Friedan, Betty, 2:201
Friedhofer, Hugo, 3:176
Friedkin, William, 2:395
Friedman, David F., 2:167
Friedrich Schiller, 1:163
Friedrich, Su, 2:282
Friendly, Fred, 2:94
Friendly Persuasion, 4:39
Friese-Greene, William, 2:105
The Fringe Dwellers, 1:139
Fritz the Cat, 1:86, 227, 366
Fröken Julie, 1:47
From Caligari to Hitler, 2:176; 3:391
From Hell, 1:367, 402
From Here to Eternity, 1:234, 343, *350,*
    351, 358; 3:265; 4:337
From Reverence to Rape, 2:202,
    290–291
From Russia with Love, 1:318; 4:288
The Front, 1:313
Front credits, 1:383
The Front Page, 1:249; 4:33
The Frontier, 1:268, 269
Frontier Films, 2:93
Frontier Marshall, 4:360
Frosty the Blowman, 3:288
Frye, Brian, 2:162
Fu Manchu, 1:125; 3:112; 4:142
Fu Sheng, 3:118
Fu zi qing, 2:389
The Fugitive, 1:402, 406
*Der Führer schenkt ded Juden eine
    Stadt,* 2:316
Fukusaku, Kinji, 3:69
Fulci, Lucio, 3:55
Full Metal Jacket, 2:65, *70;* 4:319
The Full Monty, 2:343
Fuller, Dolores, 2:*20*
Fuller, Loie, 2:33
Fuller, Samuel
    auteurism, 1:144, 147; 3:235
    camera movement, 1:195, 197
    cinephilia, 1:300
    Cold War, 1:315

Gibson, Mel
  action hero, 1:32
  Australian cinema, 1:138–139
  casting, 1:231
  fashion, 2:197
  Gallipoli, 1:134
  Irish cinema, 3:36
  Miller, George, 1:137
  religion, 3:401, 403
  as a star, 4:155
Gibson, William, 1:131–132; 4:26
Gidal, Peter, 2:158
Gielgud, John, 2:381
Gierek, Edward, 3:274
The Gift Girl, 1:97
Gigi, 3:138, 160
Gigot, 3:193
Gilbert, Craig, 2:94
Gilbert, John, 3:155, 156, 380
Gilda, 1:348, 349, 376
Gilliam, Terry, 2:157; 3:335; 4:31
Gilliat, Sidney, 2:329
Gilligan's Island, 4:27
Gimme Shelter, 2:95
Ginger, 1:261
Ginger e Fred, 3:45
Ginger Mick, 1:132
Gion no shimai, 1:303; 3:61
Una Gionata particolare, 3:48
Giordano, Marco Tullio, 3:57
Giorno, John, 2:154
Giral, Sergio, 2:14
Girard, François, 1:212
Giraud, Jean, 1:367
Giraudoux, Jean, 2:258
The Girl and Her Trust, 2:119
The Girl Can't Help It, 3:192
Girl Crazy, 3:159
Girl Detective, 4:53
A Girl of the Bush, 1:132
The Girl of the Golden West, 1:280
Girl Spy, 4:53
Girlfriend, 4:66
Girls' Cinema, 3:75
Girls in Chains, 1:157
The Girls Who Had Everything, 1:112
Giroud, Françoise, 3:237
Gish, Lillian
  biography, 4:162
  children's films, 1:259
  in children's roles, 1:251
  cinematography, 1:290
  conceptions of character, 1:17
  gender, 2:288, *291*

MGM, 3:154
  parodies, 3:263
  representational acting style, 1:19
  The Scarlet Letter, 1:42
  sexuality, 4:60
Giulietta degli spiriti, 2:190
Give the Girl a Break, 1:282
Givenchy, Hubert de, 1:381
Gladiator, 3:140
  costumes, 1:381
  editing, 2:123
  epic film, 2:133, 138
  historical film, 2:373–374
  Nielsen, Connie, 2:49
Glamour and disillusionment in spy
  films, 4:141–142
Glanzelius, Anton, 1:256
Glas, 3:232
The Glass Key, 3:256
Glass, Philip, 3:178–179
Gleason, James, 1:321
Gledhill, Christine, 3:134, 136, 139
Glen or Glenda, 1:201; 2:19
Glengarry Glen Ross, 1:402
The Glenn Miller Story, 1:164; 4:297
Glenn, Pierre-William, 1:295
Glennon, Bert, 1:285; 3:95
Glens Falls Sequence, 2:152
Gli Ultimi giorni di Pompeii, 3:41
Glinski, Robert, 3:276
Globalization, 2:57–60, 390;
  3:244–245, 258–259
    See also Co-productions; Diasporic
      cinema; National cinema
Gloria, 3:7
Gloria Company, 4:278
Glory, 1:9; 2:371, 373
Glover, Savion, 2:35
Go Fish, 2:282; 3:9
Go! Go! Go!, 2:154
Go, Man, Go!, 1:124
Go Tell the Spartans, 4:319
Go West, 2:304; 3:262
The Go-Between, 2:363
Godard, Jean-Luc
  art cinema, 1:115, 118
  auteurism, 1:144, 146, 150; 3:235
  biography, 3:238
  cinephilia, 1:300, 301
  co-productions, 1:371
  criticism, 2:7
  direct cinema, 1:18
  direction, 2:65
  distribution, 2:83
  documentary, 2:92

  editing and frame composition,
    1:23
  experimental films, 2:160
  festivals, 2:212
  film studies, 2:235, 236, 237
  fine art, 2:244
  French cinema, 2:261, 263, 268
  French New Wave and, 3:237,
    241
  influence by Brecht, 1:20, 21
  influence of, 1:127
  Iranian, 3:30
  Italian, 3:49
  Kiarostami, Abbas, 3:30
  lighting used by, 3:100
  Marxism and, 3:125, 126
  music used by, 3:181
  narrative theory and, 3:201, 202
  on the New Wave, 3:240
  religion and, 3:405
  road movies, 3:420
  screenwriting, 4:36, 39
  sound, 4:104
  technology used by, 4:203
  use of color, 1:340
  video, 4:304
Godbout, Jacques, 1:211
Goddard, Paulette, 1:355, 356; 3:255
The Goddess, 1:272; 4:38
The Goddess of 1967, 1:140
The Godfather
  Academy Awards®, 1:8
  Brando, Marlon, 1:22
  censorship, 1:241
  cinematography, 1:293
  class in films, 1:309
  crime film, 1:401, 404, 405, 407
  gangster film, 2:273–274, 276
  genres, 2:304
  independent films, 3:7
  race and ethnicity and, 3:374
  screenwriting, 4:37
  sound, 4:105
  success of, 3:251
  violence in, 4:327
The Godfather: Part II, 1:405; 2:275;
  3:258; 4:37, 56, 327
The Godfather: Part III, 4:37
The Gods Must Be Crazy, 1:55
Godzilla King of Monsters, 1:318; 2:18,
  189; 3:65; 4:29
Godzilla vs. the Smog Monster, 4:29
Goebbels, Joseph, 2:27, 91, 311, 315;
  4:280, 385–387
Goering, Hermann, 2:323
Goetz, William, 1:*337;* 4:297–298
Goha, 2:259

Grant, Cary
    animal actors, 1:83
    auteurism, 1:143
    biography, 4:44, *45*
    Columbia Pictures, 1:347–348
    costumes, 1:378
    film narrative, 3:196
    genres, 2:300
    Italian cinema, 3:43, 48
    Loren, Sophia, 3:48
    musicals, 3:186
    RKO, 3:407, 409, 410
    romantic comedies, 4:4–5
    screwball comedies, 1:361;
       4:46, *47*
Grant, Dwinell, 2:152
Grant, Madison, 3:371
The Grapes of Wrath
    adaptations, 1:42
    casting, 1:233
    cinematography, 1:288
    class in films, 1:305
    the Depression, 2:349, *349,* 350
    genres, 2:300
    Marxism and, 3:128
    populism and, 3:280
    a road movie, 3:418
Grass: A Nation's Battle for Life, 3:370
Grass, Günter, 2:318
The Grass Is Greener, 2:197
Gratz, Joan, 1:89
Grauer, Rhoda, 2:41
Graves, Ralph, 1:344
Gray, David, 4:3
Grazer, Brian, 3:317
Grease, 1:282; 2:37; 3:143, 192, 258;
    4:56
Grease 2, 1:282; 4:56
Greased Lightning, 1:65
The Greaser's Revenge, 3:86
The Great Adventure, 3:217
Great Britain, **2:327–344**
    1960s and 1970s, 2:338–341
    1980s to the present, 2:341–343
    adaptations, 1:39, 40
    animation, 1:87
    art cinema, 1:117–118, 120
    authorship and film criticism,
       1:147–149
    Cold War themes, 1:318
    documentary, 2:95
    early cinema pioneers, 2:327–329
    early production in, 2:110–111
    New Wave cinema, 2:338; 3:244
    postwar film, 2:335–338
    quotas, quota quickies, and sound,
       2:329–331

Scotland and Wales, 2:343–344
    wartime feature film production,
       2:333–335
    during World War I, 4:377–379
    during World War II, 4:389–392
The Great Caruso, 1:164–165
The Great Depression, 2:90–94,
    345–350; 3:155–158
The Great Dictator, 1:356, 357; 2:350,
    381; 4:284, 285
The Great Escape, 3:261
Great Expectations, 1:43, 44; 2:198,
    335
The Great Gatsby, 1:42, 381; 2:198
Great Gildersleeve, 1:72
The Great Outdoors, 1:84
The Great Train Robbery
    animal actors, 1:84
    British cinema, 2:328
    camera movement, 1:189
    canon and canonicity, 1:218
    chase and pursuit in, 1:27, 37
    children's films, 1:259
    cinematography, 1:285
    collaboration, 1:324
    color in, 1:333, 335
    early cinema, 2:107, 108, *109,* 114
    editing, 2:119
    film stock, 2:234
    first western, 4:358
    gangster film, 2:271
    violence in, 4:321
The Great War, 3:53–54, 57
The Great White Way, 1:280
The Great Ziegfeld, 1:162; 3:186, 189
The Greatest Show on Earth, 1:84;
    2:135; 3:258
The Greatest Story Every Told, 2:137;
    3:401; 4:289
Greece, **2:351–355;** 3:128
Greed, 1:39; 3:314
    auteurism, 1:142
    direction, 2:66, *68*
    Hersholt, Jean, 2:49
    lighting, 3:98
    postproduction, 3:337
    Thalberg, Irving and, 3:315
    violence in, 4:322
Green, Adolph, 3:189
Green, Alfred, 1:349
The Green Arrow, 1:368
The Green Berets, 1:320; 2:410; 3:345;
    4:316
Green Card, 1:134
The Green Carnation, 1:165
Green Dragon, 1:128

Green Fields, 4:398–399
The Green Hat, 1:38–39
The Green Hornet, 3:118, 119, 382
Green, Jack, 3:95
Green, Joseph, 3:272; 4:401
The Green Pastures, 1:61; 2:306
The Green Slime, 2:73
Greenaway, Peter
    adaptations, 1:46
    art cinema, 1:121
    British cinema, 2:341
    costumes, 1:379
    direction, 2:64
    film studies, 2:237
    Italian cinema, 3:47
    music used by, 3:180
Greenberg, Richard, 1:383
Greene, Graham, 1:39, 40; 2:335;
    3:*213*
Greene, Lorne, 1:209
Greenfield, Amy, 2:40
Greenlee, Sam, 1:67
Greenstreet, Sidney, 1:246
Greenwich Village Follies, 1:381
Greenwood, Charlotte, 1:279
Greer, Howard, 1:376, 377, 381, 382
Greer, Jane, 1:402
Greer, Jo Ann, 1:395
Greetings, 4:317
Gregory's Girl, 2:343
Gregory's Two Girls, 2:343
Grémillon, Jean, 2:256, 259
Gremlins, 1:227; 3:8
Gremlins 2, 1:227
Grey Gardens, 2:97
Grey, Rudolph, 2:19
Grey, Virginia, 1:261
Grey, Zane, 1:133; 4:360
Greyfriars Bobby, 1:83
Greyson, John, 2:282, 283
Greystoke, 1:81
Il Grido, 2:103; 3:164
Grieg, Edvard, 3:174
Grier, Pam, 1:31, 68; 2:168, 307;
    3:293
Grierson, John
    art cinema, 1:117
    British cinema, 2:332–333, 343
    class in films, 1:305
    computer-generated imagery, 1:93
    documentary, 2:87, 88–90
    film studies, 2:235
    National Film Board of Canada,
       1:208, 209, 213

VOLUME 1: 1–410; VOLUME 2: 1–412; VOLUME 3: 1–422; VOLUME 4: 1–408

Joanna Francesa, 1:172; 2:263
Jobs, Steve, 1:91
Joe Macbeth, 1:37; 4:57
Joe's Apartment, 1:92
Joe's Bed-Stuy Barbershop, 1:69
Joffrey, Robert, 2:40
John, Elton, 1:227
Johnny Concho, 1:384
Johnny Got His Gun, 1:316
Johnny Guitar, 1:311; 2:17
Johnny Larsen, 2:46
Johnny Staccato, 1:18
Johnny Tremain, 1:260
Johnny Wadd, 3:286
Johnson, Emery, 1:97
Johnson, Louis, 2:37
Johnson, Martin E., 2:98; 3:216
Johnson, Milliard, 1:131–132
Johnson, Noble, 1:59, 60; 2:307; 3:3
Johnson, Osa, 2:98; 3:216
Johnson, Randal, 1:175
Johnston, Claire, 2:291, 292
Johnston, W. Ray, 1:155–156
Joie de Vivre, 1:223
Jókai, Mór, 2:401
Le Joli mai, 3:236
Jolie, Angelina, 1:34
Jolson, Al, 1:60; 3:174, 185–186, 374
Jolson Sings Again, 1:349
The Jolson Story, 1:349
Jones, Amy, 2:399
Jones, Bill T., 2:40
Jones, Buck, 1:156
Jones, Chuck
 cartoons, 1:85, 86, 223, 224, *225, 226*
 computer-generated imagery, 1:92
 festivals, 2:214
 Honorary Award Oscar® recipient, 1:5
Jones, Jennifer, 2:*291*
Jones, Quincy, 1:5
Jones, Shirley, 1:234
Jones, Terry, 2:340
Jones, Tommy Lee, 1:249
Jonson, Tor, 2:19
Jonze, Spike, 3:47
Jordan, Michael, 4:138
Jordan, Neil, 2:341; 3:35, *35, 36*
Jory, Victor, 1:133
José Rizal, 3:269
Josef Kilián, 2:29
Joseph, Erik, 4:40

Josephson, Erland, 1:232
Josie and the Pussycats, 1:366
Jost, Jon, 2:152
Jotuni, Maria, 2:250
Le Jour se lève, 1:118, 404; 2:226, 256; 3:388
Jourdan, Louis, 2:265
Journal d'un curé de campagne, 1:39
Journal inachevé, 1:268
Journal of British Cinema and Television, 3:77
Journal of Frankenstein, 3:73
Journal of Popular Film and Television, 3:77
Journals and magazines, **3:73–78**
Journée scandinave, 3:217
The Journey, 1:255
Journey for Margaret, 1:253, 261; 3:158
Journey to Italy, 2:372
Journey to the Center of the Earth, 4:121
Joutseno, Lea, 2:250
Jouvet, Louis, 2:257
Jovovich, Milla, 2:198; 4:*311*
The Joy Luck Club, 1:127, *129*
The Joy of Sex, 3:288
Joy Ride, 3:418
Joyce and Selznick Agency, 1:72
Ju Dou, 1:275
Juarez, 1:162; 2:244, 349, 375
Jubilee, 2:340
Jud Süss, 2:316; 4:387, 389
Jude, 1:40
Judell, Ben, 1:156
Judex, 4:55
Judge, 2:347
Judge Dredd, 1:366
Judge, Mike, 1:227
Judge Priest, 3:374
Judgment at Nuremberg, 2:49, 315, 380; 4:286
Judith of Berthulia, 2:370
Juice, 1:68
Juju, 1:53
Jules et Jim, 1:191; 2:245, 260, 263; 4:40
Julia, Raul, 3:89
Julien Donkey-Boy, 2:65
Julien, Isaac, 2:342
Julien, Max, 1:65
Juliet of the Spirits, 1:380, *381*
Julio comienza en Julio, 1:268

Julius Caesar, 1:22
Jump Cut, 3:77
Der junge Törless, 2:317
Jungle Adventures, 3:216
Jungle Book, 4:333
Jungle Cat, 3:218
Jungle Fever, 1:68, 375, 377, 387
Jungle Jim, 4:296
Jungle Princess, 1:380
Junior Prom, 1:253
Ju-on: The Grudge, 3:71
Jurácek, Pavel, 2:28, 29
Jurado, Katy, 1:246
Jurassic Park, 4:*301*
 action films, 1:32
 animation, 1:92
 costumes, 1:385
 disaster films, 2:75
 fantasy films, 2:191
 sound, 4:105
 special effects, 4:119
Just Another Girl on the I.R.T., 1:68–69; 3:9
Justin, John, 1:61
Justiniano, Gonzalo, 1:269
Jutra, Claude, 1:211, 212; 3:244
Jutrisa, Vladimir, 1:225–226
Jutzi, Piel, 2:311–312
Juvenile Passion, 3:239

K

K-19, 2:294
Kaagaz Ke Phool, 3:16
Das Kabinett des Doktor Caligari, 3:124
 art cinema, 1:117
 canon and canonicity, 1:218
 expressionism, 2:173; 4:81
 fans and fandom, 2:182
 fantasy film, 2:188
 film noir, 2:223
 fine art, 2:243
 German cinema, 2:311
 horror film, 2:391
 mise-en-scène and, 3:164
Kaboré, Gaston, 1:52
Kabuki stories, 3:60–61
Kachyna, Karel, 2:27, 29
Kadár, Ján, 2:380
Kaddu Beykat, 1:53
Kael, Pauline, 3:*77*
 auteurism, 1:147, 150
 biography, 3:76
 cinephilia, 1:301
 criticism, 2:7, 8; 3:75

Klee, Paul, 2:171
Klein, Calvin, 2:198
Klein, Cesar, 2:174
Kleine, George, 3:357
Kleinert, Andreas, 2:323
Kleines Arschloch, 2:322
The Kleptomaniac, 1:304, 310; 2:107
Klimov, Elem, 4:16, *17*
Kline, Herbert, 2:26
Kline, Kevin, 1:355
Klinger, Barbara, 2:180; 3:138–139
Klitzsch, Ludwig, 4:278–279
Klopčič, Matjaž, 4:408
Klos, Elmar, 2:27
Kluge, Alexander, 1:121; 2:317, 322; 3:244
Klute, 1:380; 2:290
En kluven värid, 3:217
Di Klyatshe, 4:398, 399
Der Knabe in Blau, 2:312
Knef, Hildegard, 2:316
Knick Knack, 1:92
Knife, 1:98
Knight, Charles, 1:87
Knightriders, 1:247; 2:396
Knock on Any Door, 1:403
Knockin' on Heaven's Door, 2:322
Knocknagow, 3:34
Knowles, Harry, 3:75–76
Knute Rockne-All American, 4:135
Kô kaku kidôtai, 2:191
Kobayashi, Akira, 3:65
Kobayashi, Masaki, 3:65
Kobieta Samotna, 3:274
Koch, Howard, 3:382; 4:36
Koch, Robert, 2:315
Kod fotografa, 4:404
Kodak. *See* Eastman Kodak
Koehler, William R., 1:83
Koenig, Wolf, 1:209; 2:95
Koepnick, Lutz, 2:364
Koerner, Charles, 3:412–413
Kohlberg, 2:315
Kohlhaase, Wolfgang, 2:322
Kohon, David José, 1:114
Koike, Kazuo, 1:368
Koivusalo, Timo, 2:252
Kojak, 4:300
Kojima, Goseki, 1:368
Kokoda Front Line, 1:134
Koldberg, 4:280–281
Kolejnosc Uczuc, 3:276

Kolski, Jan Jakub, 3:276
Koltai, Lajos, 2:401
Kolya, 2:31
Komorowska, Maja, 3:271
Kondriatuk, Andrzej, 3:276
Konets Sankt-Peterburga, 3:340
Kongi's Harvest, 1:53, 66
Konkurs, 2:28
Kono Vank?, 1:262
Koopman, Elias, 3:2
Kopple, Barbara, 3:313, 345
Korch, Morten, 2:44
Korda, Alexander, 3:216
   British cinema, 2:330, *331,* 336
   class in films, 1:305
   German cinema, 2:313, 315
   Hungarian cinema, 2:401–402
   United Artists, 4:284, 285
Korda, Zoltan, 1:329
Korea, 3:79–83
Korean War, 4:340
Koreeda, Hirokazu, 3:71
Körhinta, 2:403
Korine, Harmony, 2:65
Körkarlen, 1:38
Kornet er i Fare, 2:44
Korngold, Erich Wolfgang, 3:175, 176
Korol Lir, 1:46; 4:18
Koroshiya 1, 3:71
Korotkie vstrechi, 4:18
Kortner, Fritz, 2:176
Kosciuszko pod Raclawicami, 3:271
Koshikei, 3:69
Kosintsev, Grigori, 3:182
Koskenlaskijan morsian, 2:249
Kosleck, Martin, 1:155
Kosloff, Theodore, 1:280; 2:34
Kotcheff, Ted, 1:208
Kounavudhi, Vichit, 3:104
Kouyaté, Dani, 1:52
Kovács, László, 1:293; 3:244
Koyaanisqatsi, 3:179
Kozara, 4:404
Kozashvili, Dover, 3:39
Kozintsev, Grigori, 1:46; 4:18
Kozure Ôkami, 1:368; 3:69
Krabbé, Jeroen, 3:*233,* 234
Kracauer, Siegfried
   documentary, 2:87
   expressionism, 2:174, 175–176
   film studies, 2:235
   German cinema, 2:312
   horror films, 2:397

   realism and, 3:388, 391
   sound, 4:100–101
Kragh-Jacobsen, Søren, 2:46, 48
Krajinka, 2:31
Krajobraz po bitwie, 3:275
Kramer, Stanley, 1:232, 351; 2:315, 380; 3:48, *371*
   United Artists, 4:286
Kramer vs. Kramer, 1:291, 352
Kramp, Fritz, 2:128
Krasker, Robert, 1:293
Krauss, Rosalind, 3:164
Krauss, Werner, 2:176, 311; 4:278
Krazy Kat, 1:221
Kren, Kurt, 2:161
Kreutzerova sonáta, 2:26
Kricfalusi, John, 1:227
Krin, Arthur B., 4:286
Krishna, Srinivas, 3:22, 209
Krizenecký, Jan, 2:25
Kroitor, Roman, 1:209
Krug, Manfred, 2:321
Kruger, Otto, 1:246, 247
Krummerne, 2:47
Krumped, 2:41
Krush Groove, 1:68
Krutnik, Frank, 1:405; 2:229; 4:89
Krvavac, Hajrudin, 4:406
Kryl'ia, 4:18
Krzyz Walecznych, 3:273
Krzyzacy, 3:274
Ku nao ren de xiao, 1:273
Kuang liu, 1:272
Kubelka, Peter, 2:158; 4:102
Kubik, Gail, 3:183
Kubitschek, Juscelino, 1:171
Kubrick, Stanley
   adaptations, 1:37, 40
   British cinema, 2:339
   censorship, 1:243
   cinematography, 1:289
   Cold War, 1:314–315, 320
   collaboration, 1:322
   credits, 1:385–386
   direction, 2:64, *65,* 70, *71*
   fine art, 2:244
   independent films, 3:7
   MGM, 3:160
   mise-en-scène, 3:166
   music used by, 3:194
   performance elements, 1:24
   postmodernism, 3:294
   religion, 3:401

VOLUME 1: 1–410; VOLUME 2: 1–412; VOLUME 3: 1–422; VOLUME 4: 1–408

Louis, Jean, 1:376, 381; 2:196
Louisiana Story, 1:186, *187;* 2:89, 95; 3:176
Lourié, Eugène, 1:323
Love, 3:155, 380
Love & Basketball, 1:69
Love Actually, 4:6
Love Affair, 1:359; 4:45
Love Affair; or the Case of the Missing Switchboard Operator, 4:405
Love and Anarchy, 3:52, 53
Love and Death, 1:360; 3:261; 4:288
Love at First Bite, 3:4
The Love Boat, 4:27
Love Brewed in the African Pot, 1:53
The Love Bug, 1:260; 4:333
Love Camp 7, 2:167; 3:5
A Love Divided, 3:36
Love Me Forever, 1:346
Love Me or Leave Me, 1:234; 3:186
Love Me Tonight, 3:186
The Love Parade, 3:186; 4:4
Love Story, 3:251, 258
Love Streams, 3:8
Love! Valour! Compassion!, 2:285
Lovecraft, H. P., 2:392
Løvejagten, 2:43
Lovelace, Linda, 3:285–286
The Loveless, 2:294
Lovell, Alan, 2:7
Lovely, Louise, 1:132
The Lovers, 3:243
Lovett, Richard, 1:76
Loving You, 3:192
Low, Colin, 1:209
Lowder, Rose, 2:158–159
The Lower Depths, 1:22, 47
Loy, Myrna, 1:5; 3:156, 382
Lu Xiaoya, 1:273
Lu Xun, 1:272
Lubin, Arthur, 1:156; 2:278
Lubin, Siegmund, 1:333
Lubitsch, Ernest, 4:5
    auteurism, 1:142
    biography, 4:4
    choreography, 1:280
    clown comedy, 1:353
    expressionism, 2:172, 176; 4:82
    German cinema, 2:311
    musicals, 3:186, 194
    Paramount and, 3:253
    romantic comedies, 4:2, 3
    sound, 4:101
    Thalberg, Irving and, 3:314

Universum Film Aktiengesellschaft, 4:278
Lucas, George
    American Graffiti, 3:383
    computer-generated imagery, 1:91
    direction, 2:69
    editing, 2:123, 124–125
    family adventure films, 1:32
    fantasy films, 2:191
    independent films, 3:7–8
    merchandising, 3:144, *145*
    Paramount and, 3:259
    road movies, 3:419
    science fiction films, 3:25
    sound, 4:105
    special effects, 4:123
Lucas, Tim, 3:74
Lucas, Wilfred, 1:132
Lucasfilm, 3:25–26, 144, 259
Luce, Henry, 2:97
Luci del varietà, 3:48
Lucia, 2:14
Luck of the Irish, 3:34
Lucky Luciano, 3:49
Ludwig, Requiem für einen jungfräulichen König, 2:318
Ludzie Wisly, 3:272
Lugosi, Bela
    B movies, 1:156, 157, 158
    cinematography, 1:290
    genres, 2:300
    horror films, 2:392
    Hungarian cinema, 2:402
    studio system, 4:172
    Universal, 4:295
    Wood, Edward D. Jr., 2:19
Luhrmann, Baz, 1:46, 140; 2:37; 3:187, 194, 206
Lukács, Gyögy, 2:407; 3:123
Lukas, Paul, 2:402
Luke, Keye, 1:125
Lukeman, Noah, 4:40
Lumet, Sidney, 1:46, 319; 2:380; 4:219, *220*
Lumière, 2:263
Lumière brothers
    adaptations, 1:37
    animal actors, 1:79, 82
    Arab cinema, 1:104
    British cinema, 2:327
    cinematography, 1:285
    class in films, 1:304
    collaboration, 1:321
    colonialism and postcolonialism, 1:325
    Cuba, 2:11

    documentary, 2:88
    early cinema, 2:105
    expressionism, 2:176
    festivals, 2:210
    film narrative and, 3:195–196
    film stock, 2:232
    fine art, 2:243
    French cinema, 2:253
    Germany, 2:309
    Greek cinema, 2:351
    Hong Kong, 2:385
    Hungary, 2:401
    influence on Peter Elfelt, 2:43
    Japanese cinema, 3:59
    motion picture cameras, 1:180, 182, 185
    nature films, 3:215
    pre-, 3:303, 329
    propaganda films, 3:339
    psychoanalysis and, 3:349
    realism and, 3:386
Lumière d'été, 2:257
Luna, José Juan Bigas, 4:114
Lunacharsky, Anatoly Vasilyevich, 4:10
Lupino, Ida, 1:*146;* 2:202, 203, 237
Luruli, Ntshavheni Wa, 1:55
Lust for Life, 2:244
Lust in the Dust, 3:261
Lux Radio Theater, 3:356, 381
Luxo Jnr, 1:92
Lye, Len, 1:93; 2:153; 3:338
Lye, Reg, 1:135
Lyell, Lottie, 1:132
Lynch, David
    art cinema, 1:121
    auteurism, 1:151
    direction, 2:63
    film studies, 2:236
    independent films, 3:9
    midnight movies, 2:21
    psychoanalysis and, 3:350–351, 353
    road movies, 3:419
    sound, 4:105
Lynn, Carol, 2:41
Lynn, Jeffrey, 1:*400*
Lyotard, Jean-François, 3:291

M

M, 1:404; 2:175, 312; 3:175; 4:101
The "?" Motorist, 2:328
Ma and Pa Kettle series, 4:297, 299
Ma és holnap, 2:401
Ma l'amour mio non muore, 3:41
Ma Xiaoying, 1:276

Marty, 4:38

The Martyrdom of Nurse Cavell, 1:132

Marvin, Harry, 3:2

Marvin Josephson Associates, 1:76

Marvin, Lee, 1:249; 4:*343*

Marx brothers, 3:185; 4:46
    clown comedy, 1:353, 354, 355
    the Depression, 2:348
    disaster films, 2:75
    genres, 2:304
    Paramount, 3:253, 255, *256*
    radio programs, 3:382
    slapstick comedy, 4:87, 89

Marx, Karl, 2:407; 3:123

Marxism, 2:407–412; **3:123–131**
    1960s and after, 3:130–131
    early, 3:123–124
    Hollywood and the left,
      3:128–130
    and the Third World, 3:130

Mary Jane's Mishap, 2:111

Mary Poppins, 1:260, 282; 2:188;
    4:332, *334*

Masala, 1:215; 3:209

La Maschera del demonio, 2:397; 3:100

Masculin, féminin, 3:237

Masculinity. *See* Gender

M*A*S*H, 1:313, 387; 2:55; 3:7, 346,
    395; 4:103, 338

Masina, Giulietta, 1:118, *381;* 3:45

The Mask, 1:55, 339; 2:191

The Mask of Zorro, 2:377

Mason, Fran, 2:271

Mason, James, 1:196; 2:331, 334

Mason, Richard, 1:125

The Masque of the Red Death, 1:42;
    2:165, 394

Masri, Mai, 1:99

Mass for the Dakota Sioux, 2:157

Mass, William, 2:153

Massey, Raymond, 1:163, 208, 386;
    2:375

Massine, Leonide, 2:40

Massip, José, 2:14

Mast, Gerald, 1:353

Master and Commander, 1:134; 4:119,
    124, 125

The Master and Margaret, 4:16, 404

The Master of Ballantrae, 1:30

Masterpiece Theater, 2:365

Mastroianni, Marcello, 3:*54,* 225
    art cinema, 1:118
    Bemberg, María Luisa, 1:112
    casting, 1:234

Italian cinema, 3:45, 48, 51
    Ruiz, Raúl, 1:267

Mat, 1:117; 3:340; 4:11, 83

Mata Hari, 1:162; 3:156

Matadeira, 1:176

Os matadores, 1:176

The Match Maker, 3:33

Maté, Rudolph, 1:349

La Maternelle, 1:262; 3:388

Matewan, 2:377; 3:9, 10

Mather, Helen, 2:328

Matka Joanna od Aniolow, 3:273

Matou a familia e foi ao cinema, 1:175

Matrimonio all'italiana, 3:48

The Matrix
    Australian cinema, 1:138
    choreography, 1:283
    costumes, 1:381
    fantasy film, 2:188, 191
    fashion, 2:195
    fight choreography, 1:32
    internet promotion, 3:24, 25
    music, 3:176
    religion in, 3:399
    science fiction, 4:26
    special effects, 4:121
    Time Warner, 4:347, 355
    use of conflict in, 1:27

The Matrix Online, 3:25; 4:347

The Matrix Revolution, 1:397; 3:25;
    4:347

Matsumoto, Toshio, 3:69

Matsushita, 1:74, 76; 4:293, 302

A Matter of Life and Death, 1:388

Matthau, Walter, 1:229, 249

Maugham, W. Somerset, 1:41–42

Mauldin, Bill, 1:*43*

Maunder, Paul, 3:248

Mauri, 3:250

Maurice, 2:365

Mauro, Humberto, 1:170

Les Mauvaises recontres, 2:259

Max Havelaar, 3:232

Max Payne, 4:309

Maxim Company, 4:278

Maxwell, John, 2:329

The May Irwin Kiss, 1:19

May, Joe, 2:311; 4:278

May, Karl, 2:310, 317

Mayer, Carl, 2:173, 174

Mayer, Louis B., 1:2, 5, 378; 2:141;
    3:153–156, 158–160

Mayersberg, Paul, 1:147; 2:6

Mayfield, Curtis, 1:65

May-Film Company, 4:278

Maynard, Ken, 1:156

Maynila, 3:268

Maysles, Albert, 2:95, 97

Maysles, David, 2:95, 97

Mazzola, Mario, 1:340

MCA. *See* Music Corporation of
    America (MCA)

McArthur, Colin, 1:150; 2:7

McCabe and Mrs. Miller, 4:103
    casting, 1:233
    cinematography, 1:296
    dialogue, 2:55
    editing, 2:124
    genres, 2:301, 304
    populism and, 3:280

McCarey, Leo
    Columbia Pictures, 1:347
    criticism, 2:4, 6
    the Depression, 2:348
    direction, 2:67
    Goldwyn, Samuel, 4:284
    Paramount, 3:255, 256
    RKO, 3:413
    screenwriting, 4:34
    screwball comedies, 4:43

McCarthyism and Joseph McCarthy,
    1:311–314, 317; 2:94; 3:128–129,
    160, 343

McCarty, John, 1:402, 404

McCay, Winsor, 1:85, 221, *222,* 368;
    2:107

McClure's Ladies World, 4:55

McCormack, Patty, 1:253

McCoy, Tim, 1:156

McCracken, Joan, 1:282

McDaniel, Hattie, 3:*159,* 374, 382;
    4:179

McDonald, Bruce, 3:421

McDormand, Frances, 1:405; 4:181

McDowall, Roddy, 1:253

McDowell, Malcolm, 1:357; 2:339;
    3:194

McEllhatten, Mark, 2:162

McElwee, Ross, 1:194; 2:94

McGann, Brad, 3:250

McGrath, Doug, 1:*212*

McGrawy, Ali, 2:381

McGregor, Ewan, 3:187

McHale's Navy, 4:338

McIntyre, Hercules, 1:132

McKee, Robert, 4:40

McKellar, Don, 1:213

McKellen, Ian, 2:286

McKenna's Gold, 1:351

Minh-ha, Trinh T., 1:56; 2:98, 160–161

Ministry of Fear, 2:175

Minnelli, Liza, 1:282, 362, 382; 2:18; 4:46

Minnelli, Vincente
    Alton, John, 3:99
    auteurism, 1:145, 147
    camera movement, 1:195
    criticism, 2:6
    direction, 2:67
    film studies, 2:237
    fine art, 2:244
    lighting used by, 3:99
    melodramas, 3:134, 138, *139*
    musicals, 3:159, 194
    road movies, 3:418

Minnie and Moskowitz, 1:18

Minoes, 3:234

Minority Report, 1:31, 245, 297; 2:226; 4:28

Minter, Mary Miles, 1:124; 4:79

Minuit, Peter, 2:75

Une minute de soleil en moins, 1:103

Il mio corpo per un poker, 3:52

Il mio viaggio in Italia, 2:197

The Miracle, 1:118

Miracle in Milan, 3:53

The Miracle of Morgan's Creek, 3:256; 4:5

Miracle on 34th Street, 1:253, 261; 2:22

Miracle Woman, 1:344, 346

The Miracle Worker, 1:253, 262; 4:324

Miracolo a Milano, 3:224, 225, 226

Miramax, 1:241; 3:9, 11, 12, 207, 214, 319

Miranda, Carmen, 1:170, 381; 3:87

Mirbal, Al-Amin, 1:99

Mirish Company, 4:286

Mirish, Harold, 4:286

Mirish, Marvin, 4:286

Mirish, Walter, 4:286

Miró, Pilar, 4:114

Mirror stage and psychoanalysis, 3:351–352

Mirza, Saeed, 3:21

Miscasting, 1:234–235

Miscegenation and the Production Code, 3:370–372

Misdirection, 3:266

Mise-en-scène, 1:203; 2:379; **3:163–167**
    auteurism, 1:144–147

camera movement, 1:189; 3:165–167
    costumes, 1:379
    criticism, 2:8
    dance, 2:34
    direction, 2:65
    dubbing and subtitling, 2:104
    early cinema, 2:112
    elements of, 3:163–164
    experimental films, 2:158
    exploitation films, 2:167
    expressionism, 2:176, 180
    fantasy films, 2:193
    film studies, 2:236
    filmmakers and, 3:164
    French cinema, 2:256, 262
    genres, 2:298
    heritage films, 2:363, 365
    horror films, 2:392
    Italian cinema, 3:47
    journals, 3:77–78
    Korean film, 3:82
    lighting and, 3:93
    melodrama and, 3:134, *137*
    postmodernism and, 3:293

Les Miserables, 4:285

The Misfits, 2:21

Mishima, 1:380

Misora, Hibari, 3:65

Miss Annie Rooney, 1:254

Miss Frontier Mail, 3:16

Miss Sadie Thompson, 1:348

Missing, 3:128, 207

Missing in Action, 4:319

The Mission, 3:370, 405

Mission: Impossible (movie), 1:138; 3:259, 317

Mission Impossible (television), 3:258

Mission to Moscow, 1:312; 3:128

Mississippi, 3:372

Mississippi Masala, 1:127; 3:372

The Mississippi Mermaid, 1:44

Mr. and Mrs. Jones, 4:53

Mr. and Mrs. Smith, 3:409

Mr. Arkadin, 1:219

Mr.. Chedworth Steps Out, 1:133

Mr. Deeds Goes to Town, 1:344; 3:257
    class in film, 1:305
    comedy, 1:355
    the Depression, 2:348
    populism and, 3:279, 280
    screwball comedy, 4:45

Mister Ed, 3:113

Mr. Magoo, 1:223

Mr. Moto, 4:54

Mr. Peter's Pets, 2:167; 3:5

Mr. Sardonicus, 2:394

Mr. Smith Goes to Washington, 1:343, 344, 347; 3:128
    casting, 1:230
    class in films, 1:305
    the Depression, 2:350
    editing and frame composition, 1:23, 24
    Mitchell, Thomas in, 1:246, 248
    populism and, 3:279
    populist comedy, 1:355

Mr. Wrong, 3:249

El misterio de la Puerta del Sol, 4:108

Les Mistons, 3:237

Mrs. Doubtfire, 3:112

Mrs. Miniver, 1:245; 3:158

Mrs. Parkington, 3:158

Misumi, Kenji, 3:69

Mita, Merata, 3:249

Mitchell, Alice Miller, 4:80

Mitchell Brothers, 3:286

Mitchell, Eric, 2:161

Mitchell, George, 1:337

Mitchell, James, 1:281

Mitchell, Margaret, 3:315

Mitchell, Phil, 1:92

Mitchell, Thomas, 1:246, 247, *247,* 248

Mitchum, Robert, 1:229; 2:224, 225, *226;* 3:318

Mitrikeski, Antonio, 4:407

Mitrović, Žika, 4:407

Mitry, Jean, 2:219

Mitt hem är Copacabana, 3:217

Mitt liv som hund, 1:256

Mix, Tom, 3:3, 373

Miyake, Issey, 1:380

Miyazaki, Hayao, 1:86
    cartoons, 1:226, 227
    fantasy films, 2:191
    Japanese cinema, 3:71
    manga, 1:368

Mizoguchi, Kenji
    art cinema, 1:121
    camera movement, 1:190, *191*
    canon and canonicity, 1:219
    cinephilia, 1:300
    criticism, 2:6
    direction, 2:65
    fantasy films, 2:190
    film studies, 2:235
    Japanese cinema, 3:61, 63, 64, 65

Mizrahi, Moshe, 1:291

Mo' Better Blues, 3:177

VOLUME 1: 1–410; VOLUME 2: 1–412; VOLUME 3: 1–422; VOLUME 4: 1–408

VOLUME 1: 1–410; VOLUME 2: 1–412; VOLUME 3: 1–422; VOLUME 4: 1–408

Perkins, Marlin, 3:218

Perkins, V. F., 1:147, 150; 2:6–7

Perla w Koronie, 3:274

Perojo, Benito, 4:107

Péron, Juan Domingo, 1:111–112

Perri, 3:218

Perri, Dan, 1:383

Perry, Joseph, 1:131

Persona, 1:*119,* 233; 2:245

Personal Best, 2:280; 4:138

Perspective Canada, 1:213

Persuasion, 1:40

Perversidade, 1:170

Pesci, Joe, 1:233, *406*

Pescucci, Gabriella, 1:375

Pestonji, Rattana, 3:103

Pet Sematary, 2:399

Pétain, Maréchal Henri Philippe, 2:257

Peter and the Wolf, 3:181

Peter der Grosse, 2:172

Peter Ibbetson, 3:257

Peter Pan, 1:336; 2:188

Peters, Jon, 1:352

Petersen, 1:136

Petersen, Axel, 2:44

Petersen, Wolfgang, 2:55, 73, 319

Peterson, Kristine, 2:399

Peterson, Lowell, 2:227

Peterson, Oscar, 1:213

Peterson, Rex, 1:83

Peterson, Sidney, 2:153

Petit à petit ou les lettres Persanes, 1:53

Le Petit soldat, 1:330; 3:100, 237

Les Petites guerres, 1:99

Petri, Elio, 3:48, 51

Petria's Wreath, 4:404

The Petrified Forest, 1:403; 2:273

Petrijin Venac, 4:404

Petronia Chronia, 2:352

Petrović, Aleksander, 3:244; 4:404, 407

Le Peuple migrateur, 3:220

Pevnost, 2:31

Peyote Queen, 2:156

Pfahler, Kembra, 2:161

Pfeiffer, Michelle, 4:163

PGA (Producers Guild of America). *See* Producers Guild of America (PGA)

Phalke, Dhundiraj Govind, 3:13–14

Phantasmagoria, 1:221

The Phantom Carriage, 1:38

Phantom Lady, 1:44; 2:221, 223

The Phantom of the Opera, 2:392; 3:111, 311, 357; 4:295

Phantom of the Paradise, 2:304

The Phantom Stockman, 1:135

The Phantom Tollbooth, 1:260

Phase IV, 1:384

Phasmatropes, 1:221

Phenakistiscopes, 1:179, 221

The Phenix City Story, 2:273, 275

Phffft!, 1:351

Philadelphia, 2:285

The Philadelphia Story, 1:6, 230, 359, 380; 4:3, 5

Philipe, Gérard, 2:259

Philippines, **3:267–269**

Phoenix, River, 3:335

Photographie électrique à distance, 2:112

Photography

    beginnings of, 3:300–302

    director of, 1:394–395; 2:62, 64; 3:95

    principal, 3:333–335

Photoplay, 3:74–75

The Photoplay, 3:351

Physical special effects, 4:117–122

Pialat, Maurice, 1:39, 291; 2:244, 264, 266

The Pianist, 2:268, 381, *382*

The Piano, 1:243

    Academy Award®, 1:9, 138, 256

    censorship, 1:140

    colonialism, 1:330

    New Zealand and, 3:250

    screenwriting, 4:38

Piatka z Ulicy Barskiej, 3:272, 275

Picasso, Pablo, 2:171

Piccadilly, 1:124

Picchio, Ana María, 1:114

Piccioni, Giuseppe, 3:57

Pichul, Vasily, 4:20

Pickens, Slim, 2:300

Pickford, Mary, 4:*80*

    biography, 4:79

    Chaplin, Charlie, 1:356

    children's films, 1:259

    in children's roles, 1:251

    cinematography, 1:285

    collaboration, 1:322

    divorce of, 4:79

    early cinema, 1:208; 2:114

    feminism, 2:202

    gender, 2:288

    makeup, 3:112

    sexuality of, 4:60

    star system, 4:78

    United Artists and, 3:316; 4:283, 286

    Zukor, Adolf and, 3:252–253

Pickup on South Street, 1:147, 315; 4:143

Picnic, 1:350; 3:129

Picnic at Hanging Rock, 1:134, 136

Picon, Molly, 4:400, 401

Pictorial News, 4:377

The Picture of Dorian Gray, 1:202

Picture palace theaters, 4:241–245

Picture Personalities, 4:148

The Picture Show Man, 1:137

Picturegoer, 3:75

Pidgeon, Walter, 3:158

Pie, Pie Blackbird, 2:35

Pie, Tramp and the Bull Dog, 1:82

Pièces d'identités, 2:59

Pierce, Jack P., 3:113–115

Pierce, Kimberly, 3:9

Pierre Vallières, 2:157

Pierrot le Fou, 2:244; 3:237, 420

The Pigkeeper's Daughter, 2:167

The Pilgrim, 1:356

The Pillow Book, 1:379

Pillow Talk, 1:245; 4:300

Pillsbury, Sam, 3:248, 249

Un Pilota ritorna, 1:116; 3:43

Pilsuski, Józef, 3:272

Pincus, Edward, 1:186

Pinelli, Tullio, 3:51; 4:40

Ping yuan you ji dui, 1:272

Pink Flamingos, 1:201; 2:21

Pink Floyd: The Wall, 2:17; 3:192

Pink Panther, 4:54

The Pink Panther, 1:81, 387; 4:286

The Pink Panther Strikes Again, 4:288

Pinky, 1:61; 3:372; 4:64

Pinocchio

    "art" of animation, 1:85, 223

    children's films, 1:260; 4:331

    color in, 1:336

    fantasy film, 2:189

    RKO, 3:409

Pinochet, Augusto, 1:266

Pinter, Harold, 1:39; 4:231, *232*

Pippa Passes, 3:97

Pirandello, Luigi, 1:38; 3:42

Piranha, 3:10

The Pirate, 2:37, *173;* 3:138, 160, 189

Pirates of the Caribbean, 1:29; 3:318

The Pit and the Pendulum, 2:165; 3:4

VOLUME 1: 1–410; VOLUME 2: 1–412; VOLUME 3: 1–422; VOLUME 4: 1–408

VOLUME 1: 1–410; VOLUME 2: 1–412; VOLUME 3: 1–422; VOLUME 4: 1–408

VOLUME 1: 1–410; VOLUME 2: 1–412; VOLUME 3: 1–422; VOLUME 4: 1–408

Steele, Bob, 1:156

Steele, Lisa, 4:304

Steenbeck, 2:117–118

Steenburgen, Mary, 1:249

Steig, William, 4:35

Stein, Jules, 1:72, 73, 74

Steinbeck, John, 1:43, 305; 2:*349*; 3:417

Steiner, Max, 3:175, 176

Steiner, Ralph, 3:7

Steklý, Karel, 2:27

Stella, 4:368

Stella Dallas, 1:252; 2:205, 288; 3:134; 4:370–371

Stelling, Jos, 3:234

Stendhal, 1:39; 3:50

Stenka Razin, 4:9

The Stepford Wives, 4:29

Stephenson, James, 1:15

Stereoscopes, 3:300–301

Stereotypes
  African Americans, 1:59; 3:205, 340
  Arab and Muslim, 1:97–98; 3:205
  fans and fandom, 2:181–183
  film studies of, 2:240
  genre movies and, 2:304–307
  Hollywood whiteness and, 3:372–375
  Latino, 3:85–86
  makeup and, 3:112
  Native American, 3:205, 211–212

Sterling, Bruce, 4:26

Stern, 2:323

Stern, Howard, 3:383

Stern, Philip van Doren, 4:35

Stern, Tom, 3:95

Sternad, Rudolph, 1:349

Sterne, 3:236

Steven, Geoff, 3:248

Stevens, George
  adaptations, 1:44
  auteurism, 1:147
  collaboration, 1:322
  the Holocaust, 2:380
  Paramount, 3:258
  as producer-director, 3:316
  RKO, 3:407, 409
  United Artists and, 4:289

Stewart, Anita, 1:280

Stewart, James
  agents and agencies, 1:73
  casting, 1:230, 234
  cinematography, 1:295
  collaboration, 1:321; 4:360

Columbia Pictures, 1:346, 350
  editing, 2:123
  Italian cinema, 3:43
  Music Corporation of America, 1:73
  populism and, 3:281
  screwball comedy, 1:361; 4:46
  Universal and, 4:297

Štiglic, France, 4:408

Still of the Night, 1:291

Stiller, Maurice, 4:56, 189–190

Stiller, Mauritz, 1:38, 322; 2:281

Stilles Land, 2:323

Still/Here, 2:40

Stillman, Joe, 4:35

The Sting, 1:74, 249; 2:212; 4:300

Stock companies, 1:231–234, 321–322

Stock, film, 1:338; **2:231–234**

Stoker, Bram, 2:392

The Stolen Children, 3:57

Stoller, Shirley, 3:*56*

Stoloff, Morris, 1:349

Stone, Fred, 2:33

The Stone Killer, 4:317

Stone, Matt, 1:227

Stone, Oliver
  Asian American cinema, 1:127
  biographical films, 1:165, 166
  historical films, 2:369, *370, 373, 374, 375*
  Vietnam War films, 3:130

Stone, Sharon, 1:405

Stonewall, 2:282

Stonewall Riots, 2:227

Storaro, Vittorio, 1:297

Store Forventninger, 2:44

Stork, 1:136

Storm Boy, 1:136, 137

Storm, Esben, 1:136

Storm Over Bengal, 3:4

Stormy Weather, 2:35

The Story of a Love Affair, 1:116

The Story of a Three Day Pass, 1:63

The Story of Alexander Graham Bell, 1:230

The Story of Bob and Sally, 2:164

The Story of Dr. Wassell, 3:257

The Story of G. I. Joe, 2:225; 4:285

The Story of Louis Pasteur, 1:162; 2:349, 375

The Story of Mankind, 2:75

The Story of Temple Drake, 2:273

The Story of the Kelly Gang, 1:131

The Story of the Mosquito, 1:221

The Story of Vernon and the Irene Castle, 2:38; 3:409

Stouffer, Marty, 3:219

Stowe, Harriet Beecher, 2:374

Straayer, Chris, 3:365–366

Strachey, Lytton, 2:366

La Strada
  auteurism, 3:45, 46
  co-productions, 1:371
  dubbing and subtitling, 2:104
  neorealism, 3:228
  as a road movie, 3:421

Straight Out of Brooklyn, 1:68

Stramm, August, 2:172

Strand, Paul, 2:152; 3:7

Strand Theater, 2:*144,* 145

Strange Days, 1:297; 2:294

Strange Illusion, 1:157

Strange Invaders, 1:311

The Strange Ones, 1:293

The Stranger, 2:225

Stranger in a Strange Land, 4:26

Stranger on the Third Floor, 2:221

Stranger Than Paradise, 3:8, 319, 419

Strangers on a Train, 1:45, 79, 193, 234; 3:335

Strangers When We Meet, 3:129

Strasberg, Lee, 1:22, 23; 2:64

Strategia del rango, 1:40

Strategic Air Command, 1:314

Strathairn, David, 1:245; 3:8

Straub, Jean-Marie
  acting, 1:21
  experimental films, 2:160
  Marxism and, 3:126–127
  narrative theory and, 3:201
  New Wave, 2:317; 3:244

Strauss, Johann, 1:162

Strauss, Richard, 1:388

Straw Dogs, 2:123, 124, 290; 4:326

Strawberry and Chocolate, 2:12, 15, *15;* 3:345

Strawberry Fields, 1:128

S:TREAM:S:S:ECTION: S:ECTION:S:S:ECTIONED, 2:158

Streb, Elizabeth, 2:40

Streep, Meryl, 1:7, 15, 17; 4:178

The Street, 1:95, 213

Street Angel, 1:2

Street Corner, 2:164

Street of Crocodiles, 1:95

Street Scene, 4:284

VOLUME 1: 1–410; VOLUME 2: 1–412; VOLUME 3: 1–422; VOLUME 4: 1–408

Tavel, Ronald, 2:154

Tavernier, Bertrand, 1:372; 2:266, 267

Taves, Brian, 1:29, 154

Taviani, Paolo, 3:48, 49, 228

Taxi Driver
Academy Awards® and, 3:307
child actors, 1:255
children's films, 1:263
crime film, 1:405, 407
cult film, 2:20
editing, 2:117
Hollywood New Wave, 1:351
Indian, 3:17
mise-en-scène and, 3:164
music, 3:171
a road movie, 3:418
urban thrillers, 3:17
violence in, 4:317, 327

Taxidi sta Kithira, 2:353

Taylor, Elizabeth
Academy Awards®, 1:8
animal actors, 1:*83*
casting, 1:235
as child actor, 1:253; 3:158
costumes, 1:376, 377, 380
fashion, 2:195
The Jean Hersholt Humanitarian
Award, 1:5

Taylor, Frederick W., 1:391

Taylor, Grant, 1:135

Taylor, Greg, 2:180

Taylor, Helen, 4:372

Taylor, Richard, 1:380; 4:124, *125*

Taylor, William Desmond, 4:79

Taymor, Julie, 3:9

Tchelitchev, Pavel, 2:40

Tchelley, Hanny, 1:52–53

The Te Kooti Trail, 3:248

Tea and Sympathy, 3:138; 4:65

Teacher's Pet, 1:245

The Teahouse of the August Moon,
1:234

Team America, 1:98

The Tearful Bauhinia, 2:388

Tearing Down the Spanish Flag, 4:338

Tears of the Sun, 4:342

Teatro Amazonas, 2:159

Téchiné, André, 2:266

Technicolor, 1:333, *334,* 335–337;
4:200

Technology, **4:197–205**
color and sound, 4:199–201
digital age, 4:203–205, 224–226
early motion picture, 4:197–199
television, 4:201–203

Teddy at the Throttle, 1:358

Teen films, **4:207–215**
1980s resurgence, 4:211–213
early, 4:207–208
emergence of, 4:208–211
since the 1990s, 4:213–215

Teena, Brandon, 2:293, 295

Teenage Caveman, 2:74; 3:190

Teenage Monster, 3:190

Teenage Mutant Ninja Turtles, 1:260;
2:388

Tel al-Zaatar, 1:99

Telenovelas, 1:175

Telephoto shots, 4:71

Television, **4:217–227**
1960-1980 film on network,
4:221–223
biographies, 1:167
British, 2:341
cartoons, 1:225–227
Columbia Pictures, 1:350, 351
digital technology and the future
of film and, 4:224–226
effect on agents and agencies,
1:74–75
effect on B movies, 1:159
and film before 1960, 4:218–221
film exhibition after, 2:142–143
French, 2:265–266
Holocaust programs, 2:380–381
homosexuality on, 2:286
impact of cable and home video
on, 4:223–224
lighting, 3:99
movie distribution to, 2:84
nature films, 3:218–219
New Hollywood and, 2:85
Paramount and, 3:258–259
parodies, 3:263–265
pay, 2:84
radio after, 3:383–384
reality, 2:94; 3:219
relationship between film and,
4:217–218
studio system and, 4:174–176
technology, 4:201–203
Universal, 4:300
video, 4:303–307
Vietnam War, 4:315, 325
Warner Bros., 4:352–355
westerns, 4:362

Television and Video Preservation
Foundation (NTVPF), 1:109

Television and Video Preservation 1997,
1:109

Television Spy, 1:314

Tell Them Willie Boy Is Here, 1:313

The Tell-Tale Heart, 1:223

Telluride Film Festival, 2:214

Telotte, J. P., 4:30

The Tempest, 1:38, 46; 2:340

The Tempest of Life, 3:29

Temple, Shirley, 1:*255*
as child actor, 1:252, 253, 254
children's films, 1:261
choreography, 1:281
cultural conventions in
performances, 1:17
the Depression, 2:350
merchandising, 3:357
musicals, 3:194
race and ethnicity and, 3:374

Tempos difíceis, 1:44

10, 1:359

The Ten Commandments
color in, 1:335
epic film, 2:133–137, *137;* 3:401
film stock, 2:234
genres, 2:299
historical film, 2:373
international productions, 1:370
sexuality in, 4:61
success of, 3:253, 258

Ten Days, 2:120

Ten Days That Shook the World, 2:371

Ten Second Film, 2:149

Ten Tall Men, 1:97

Tenda dos milagros, 1:174

Tender Comrade, 1:313, 314, 316;
3:413

La Tendre ennemie, 2:255

Tenebre, 2:397

Teng Wenji, 1:273

Tengoku to jigoku, 1:399; 3:70

Tenku no Shiro Laputa, 1:227

Tenney, James, 2:157

Tennyson, Alfred Lord, 1:47

Teno, Jean-Marie, 1:57

Tenshi No Kokotsu, 3:69

Tent City, 3:38

Tent-pole pictures, 1:70

Teorema, 1:120; 3:127

Teplitzky, Jonathan, 1:140

Terminal Identity, 4:30

Terminal Island, 2:399

The Terminator, 1:27, 33; 2:52; 3:115;
4:31, 56, 328

Terminator 2: Judgment Day, 1:33
action heroines, 1:34
cinematography, 1:293
computer-generated imagery, 1:92
fantasy film, 2:191

VOLUME 1: 1–410; VOLUME 2: 1–412; VOLUME 3: 1–422; VOLUME 4: 1–408

SCHIRMER ENCYCLOPEDIA OF FILM